MIGRATION IN AFRICA

This book introduces readers to the age of intra-African migration, a period from the mid-19th century onward in which the center of gravity of African migration moved decisively inward. Most books tend to zoom in on Africa's external migration during the earlier intercontinental slave trades and the more recent outmigration to the Global North, but this book argues that migration within the continent has been far more central to the lives of Africans over the course of the last two centuries. The book demonstrates that only by taking a broad historical and continent-wide perspective can we understand the distinctions between the more immediate drivers of migration and deeper patterns of change over time.

During the 19th century Africa's external slave trades gradually declined, whilst Africa's expanding commodity export sectors drew in domestic labor. This led to an era of heightened mobility within the region, marked by rapidly rising and vanishing migratory flows, increasingly diversified landscapes of migration systems, and profound long-term shifts in the wider patterns of migration. This era of inward-focused mobility reduced with a resurgence of outmigration after 1960, when Africans became more deliberate in search of extra-continental destinations, with new diaspora communities emerging specifically in the Global North.

Broad ranging in its temporal, spatial, and thematic coverage, this book provides students and researchers with the perfect introduction to the age of intra-African migration.

Michiel de Haas is an assistant professor at the Rural and Environmental History Group at Wageningen University.

Ewout Frankema is Professor and Chair of Rural and Environmental History at Wageningen University. He is Editor-in-Chief of the *Journal of Global History* and a research fellow of the UK Centre for Economic Policy Research (CEPR).

MIGRATION IN AFRICA

Shifting Patterns of Mobility from the 19th to the 21st Century

Edited by
Michiel de Haas and Ewout Frankema

Cover image: TBC

First published 2022
by Routledge
4 Park Square, Milton Park, Abingdon, Oxon OX14 4RN

and by Routledge
605 Third Avenue, New York, NY 10158

Routledge is an imprint of the Taylor & Francis Group, an informa business

© 2022 selection and editorial matter, Michiel de Haas and Ewout Frankema;
individual chapters, the contributors

The right of Michiel de Haas and Ewout Frankema to be identified as the authors
of the editorial material, and of the authors for their individual chapters, has been
asserted in accordance with sections 77 and 78 of the Copyright, Designs and Patents
Act 1988.

The Open Access version of this book, available at www.taylorfrancis.com, has
been made available under a Creative Commons Attribution-Non Commercial-No
Derivatives 4.0 license.

Trademark notice: Product or corporate names may be trademarks or registered
trademarks, and are used only for identification and explanation without intent to
infringe.

British Library Cataloguing-in-Publication Data
A catalogue record for this book is available from the British Library

Library of Congress Cataloging-in-Publication Data
Names: Haas, Michiel de, editor. | Frankema, Ewout, editor.
Title: Migration in Africa : shifting patterns of mobility from the 19th to the
21st century / edited by Michiel de Haas and Ewout Frankema.
Description: New York, NY : Routledge, 2022. | Includes bibliographical
references and index.
Identifiers: LCCN 2021049486 (print) | LCCN 2021049487 (ebook) | ISBN
9781032125299 (hardback) | ISBN 9781032125244 (paperback) | ISBN
9781003225027 (ebook)
Subjects: LCSH: Africa—Emigration and immigration—History. | Migration,
Internal—Africa.
Classification: LCC HB2121.A3 M534 2022 (print) | LCC HB2121.A3
(ebook) | DDC 304.8096—dc23/eng/20211221
LC record available at https://lccn.loc.gov/2021049486
LC ebook record available at https://lccn.loc.gov/2021049487

ISBN: 978-1-032-12529-9 (hbk)
ISBN: 978-1-032-12524-4 (pbk)
ISBN: 978-1-003-22502-7 (ebk)

DOI: 10.4324/9781003225027

Typeset in Bembo
by codeMantra

CONTENTS

List of Figures	*ix*
List of Tables	*xi*
List of Maps	*xiii*
List of Contributors	*xv*
Preface	*xix*

Introduction | 1

1 The Age of Intra-African Migration: A Synthesis | 3
Michiel de Haas and Ewout Frankema

Part One
Slavery and Migration in the 19th Century | 35

2 Migration in the Contexts of Slaving and States in 19th-Century
West Africa | 37
Gareth Austin

3 Boom and Bust: The Trans-Saharan Slave Trade in the 19th Century | 56
Mohamed Saleh and Sarah Wahby

4 Slaves, Porters, and Plantation Workers: Shifting Patterns of
Migration in 19th- and Early 20th-Century East Africa | 75
Karin Pallaver

vi Contents

Part Two
Frontiers, Connections, and Confrontations in the 19th Century   93

5   Cattle, Climate, and Caravans: The Dynamics of Pastoralism, Trade, and Migration in 19th-Century East Africa   95
N. Thomas Håkansson

6   Migration and State Formation in Pre-colonial South Africa: Why the 19th Century Was Different   112
Lyndal Keeton and Stefan Schirmer

7   The Settlers of South Africa: Economic Forces of the Expanding Frontier   135
Johan Fourie

Part Three
Colonial Policies and Labor Mobility   155

8   Forced Labor and Migration in British East and West Africa: Shifting Discourses and Practices during the Colonial Era   157
Opolot Okia

9   Governing Free and Unfree Labor Migration in Portuguese Africa, 19th–20th Century   178
Filipa Ribeiro da Silva and Kleoniki Alexopoulou

10   Migration and Stabilization: Mining Labor in the Belgian Congo, Northern Rhodesia, and South Africa   203
Dácil Juif

Part Four
Shifting Patterns of Circulation and Settlement in the 20th Century   229

11   Cash-Crop Migration Systems in East and West Africa: Rise, Endurance, Decline   231
Michiel de Haas and Emiliano Travieso

12   From Temporary Urbanites to Permanent City Dwellers? Rural-Urban Labor Migration in Colonial Southern Rhodesia and the Belgian Congo   256
Katharine Frederick and Elise van Nederveen Meerkerk

Contents **vii**

13 Urban Migration in East and West Africa since 1950: Contrasts and
Transformations   281
Felix Meier zu Selhausen

Part Five
Conflict and Mobility in the 20th Century   **309**

14 African Military Migration in the First and Second World Wars   311
David Killingray

15 From Integration to Repatriation. Flight, Displacement, and
Expulsion in Post-colonial Africa   330
Ewout Frankema

Part Six
The End of the Age of Intra-African Migration   **353**

16 Counting and Categorizing African Migrants, 1980–2020: Global,
Continental, and National Perspectives   355
Patrick Manning

Epilogue   **377**

17 Migration and Development: Lessons from Africa's
Long-Run Experience   379
Michiel de Haas and Ewout Frankema

Index   *391*

FIGURES

1.1	Annual migration of Africans and Europeans to the Americas, 1500–1875	4
1.2	Share of international migrants from sub-Saharan Africa and Africa (including North Africa) that have moved outside the continent, 1960–2020	5
1.3	Value of slaves and commodities exported from West Africa, 1700–1910	17
3.1	Estimate of the total number of slaves crossing the Sahara per century	59
3.2	Slave imports by country in North Africa (1700–1895)	60
3.3	Slave population by country in North Africa (1835–91)	61
3.4	Prices of slaves in different markets of West Africa (1783–1900)	67
3.5	Slave prices in Cairo slave markets (1800–77)	70
4.1	Slaves retained on the East African coast and Zanzibar, 1810s–90s	80
4.2	Destinations of the East African slave trade in the 19th century	81
6.1	Changes in resource value and the cost of conflict	127
6.A1	Payoffs for hawk and dove strategies	133
9.1	Arrivals of workers (*Serviçais*) in São Tomé and Príncipe according to their place of origin, 1876–1965 (percentage)	184
9.2	Contracted and re-contracted workers (*Serviçais*) in São Tomé and Príncipe according to their place of origin, 1915–37 (percentage)	184
9.3	Skilled migrant workers in Angola according to their place of origin and "race," 1950	185
9.4	Skilled workers in Angola according to their place of origin and "race," 1950	185
9.5	Migrant workers in Mozambique per district and according to their place of origin, 1950	186
9.6	Structure of the *Curadorias* in Portuguese Africa and beyond (19th–20th century)	187
9.7	Recruitment process	189
9.8	Agencies for labor recruitment to São Tomé and Príncipe	190
9.9	Workers (*Serviçais*) repatriated from São Tomé and Príncipe to their place of origin, 1906–60 (percentage)	191

x Figures

10.1	South African gold output and inflation-adjusted average annual price	210
10.2	Congolese and Zambian copper output and inflation-adjusted average annual price	220
10.3	Number of workers, Katanga and Copperbelt, 1911–64	220
11.1	Per capita volumes of cash-crop exports, 1850–2017 (centered five-year moving averages, peak year=1)	234
11.2	Unskilled nominal wage ratio between sending and receiving regions, 1900–69	238
11.3	Rainfall seasonality in sending regions (solid lines) and receiving regions (dotted lines)	242
11.4	Wage ratios and cocoa exports in Ghana and Côte d'Ivoire (five-year-centered averages)	244
11.5	Migrants coming annually to the Gambia and Buganda relative to total receiving population, 1904–60	247
12.1	Background of laborers in Leopoldville, Elisabethville, and Stanleyville, 1951	260
12.2	Nominal monthly wage of unskilled male day labor in the Belgian Congo	262
12.3	Welfare ratios of unskilled wages (Leopoldville & rural regions) and mining wages (Katanga) in the Belgian Congo, 1920–58 (1 = subsistence level for a family of 4)	263
12.4	Average nominal wages for African labor, Southern Rhodesia, 1946–63	264
12.5	Average annual white European and black African nominal wages per worker, Southern Rhodesian manufacturing sector, 1938–66	274
13.1	Urban agglomerations (≥10,000) and urbanization in sub-Saharan Africa, 1950–2015	284
13.2	Urbanization rates and number of urban centers in East and West Africa, 1950–2015	285
13.3	Natural increase and residual migration in urban growth, c. 1960–70	288
13.4	Natural increase and residual migration in urban growth, 2000–10 average	289
13.5	Sex ratios in East and West Africa's major cities, 1948–2015	291
13.6	Age distribution of Lagos' population, 1931	295
13.7	Age at migration to Kampala, 1951	296
13.8	Age at migration to Mombasa and Nairobi (>14 years), 1999 and 2009	296
13.9	Educational attainment gap of rural residents and urban migrants, 2010	298
13.10	Slum population as percentage of urban population, 1990–2014	300
15.1	African refugees as a percentage share of the world total and relative to the African population as a share of the world total, 1960–2020	334
15.2	Number of countries involved in major armed conflicts in Africa, 1960–2018	335
15.3	Total number of refugees in Africa (bars, left-hand Y-axis) and as a % share of Africa's population (line, right-hand Y-axis), 1960–2018	336
15.4	Number of refugees from major African sending areas, 1960–2018	338
17.1	The relationship between development and migration aspirations and capabilities	380
17.2	African GDP per capita and emigrant stock, 1960–2020	382

TABLES

1.1	Intra- and extra-continental migration from sub-Saharan Africa and Africa, including North Africa, 1960–2019 (emigrant stocks, numbers per 10,000 residents in Africa)	25
3.1	Lovejoy's estimates of the percentage of slave exports by sector	56
7.1	Average ownership and production by district, 1790	138
8.1	Import of bicycles into Kenya Colony	163
8.2	Paid forced labor in Kenya Colony	168
9.1	Migration within the colonies	181
9.2	Migration between Portuguese colonies and to neighboring countries	182
9.3	Armed forces in Portuguese Africa (1910–30): total size and share per 1,000 inhabitants	186
9.4	Drivers of migration within Portuguese Africa and to neighboring colonies	192
9.A1	Arrivals of workers in São Tomé and Príncipe according to their place of origin, 1876–1965	200
9.A2	Contracted and re-contracted workers in São Tomé and Príncipe according to their place of origin, 1915–61	201
9.A3	Workers repatriated from São Tomé and Príncipe to their place of origin, 1906–60	202
10.1	Number of black mineworkers by mine in Kimberley in the 1880s	209
10.2	Black workers in the South African mines, totals and percentages	212
10.3	Origin of laborers at the UMHK in total numbers and percentages	216
10.4	Stabilization in Katanga	218
10.5	Percentage of workers married	222
10.6	Black–white mineworker ratio (black miners per white miner)	222
11.1	Enumerated migrant population of Uganda's cash-crop zone	246
11.2	Enumerated migrant population of Ghana's cash-crop zone	246
12.1	Urbanization rates in Southern Rhodesia and Congo, 1936–61	257
12.2	Africans in employment in Southern Rhodesian towns, 1956	259

xii Tables

12.3	Sex ratios in a number of cities, Congo, 1952, and Southern Rhodesia, 1962	261
12.4	Percentage of households in income brackets relative to the Poverty Datum Line (PDL), Salisbury, 1957	265
12.5	Population development Southern Rhodesia and the Belgian Congo, 1901–60	266
13.1	Number of major urban settlements (>300,000) by size in sub-Saharan Africa, 1950–2020	284
13.2	The largest 20 urban agglomerations by population (million) in East and West Africa	286
14.1	Carrier forces in military campaigns, 1914–18	318
14.2	African forces in the Second World War	321
15.1	Numbers and shares of IDPs and international refugees (RFGs) in major African wars, 1954–present	339
15.2	Selection of mass expulsions in Africa, 1950–2000	344
16.1	Population by continent, 1980–2020, in millions, with continental landmass	357
16.2	World population: average annual change by continent, within five-year periods, in millions of persons	357
16.3	World urban population in millions, by continent	358
16.4	World urban population: average annual change by continent, within five-year periods, in millions of persons	359
16.5	Estimated conflict and disaster migrants in Africa. Stocks, in thousands	361
16.6	African total population by region, in millions	362
16.7	African urban population by region, in millions	363
16.8	Urban population as a percentage of total population, by African region, 1980–2020	364
16.9	International migrant stocks in Africa by region of African origin, in thousands	364
16.10	International migrant stocks overseas by region of African origin, in thousands	365
16.11	Stocks of migrant groups by African region, 2005, in thousands	366
16.12	Average annual flow of migrants, in thousands, by nation	367
16.13	Annual remittances in millions of US dollars by nation, 1980–2018	369
16.14	Annual remittances in millions of US dollars by nation, 2010–2018	369
16.15	African migration stocks and average remittances, 2010–18	371
16.16	Overseas migration stocks and average remittances, 2010–18	371

MAPS

3.1	Trans–Saharan trade routes	62
3.2	Present Trans–Saharan migration routes	72
4.1	Legal slave trading zones in East Africa in the 19th century	77
4.2	Main caravan roads and urban centers in 19th-century East Africa	79
5.1	Pastoralism and intensive cultivation in East Africa	98
5.2	Trade routes for the dispersal of cattle from northern East Africa to central Kenya and northern Tanzania in the 19th century	103
6.1	Selected trade routes	116
6.2	Mfecane Equilibrium polities and migration	122
7.1	Cape settler farms in 1850 with the 37 Fourie farms in black	140
7.2	Cape settler farms in 1850 with Voortrekker routes and 1910 South African provinces	144
7.3	Change in white population density, 1911 to 1936	148
10.1	Origin and destination of migrants to the South African mines	207
10.2	Origin of migrants to the Congolese and Northern Rhodesian Copperbelt mines	217
11.1	Location of four cash-crop migration systems	233
13.1	African cities by size range, 1950	282
13.2	African cities by size range, 2015	283
14.1	African military migration: the First World War	315
14.2	African military migration: the Second World War	322

CONTRIBUTORS

Kleoniki Alexopoulou obtained her PhD in economic history from Wageningen University in the Netherlands (2018). She is currently a postdoc researcher in economic history at Nova University of Lisbon in Portugal and research fellow in modern and contemporary history at Panteion University of Social and Political Sciences in Athens, Greece.

Gareth Austin is Professor of Economic History at Cambridge University. He taught previously at the University of Ghana, the London School of Economics, and the Graduate Institute of Geneva. Publications include *Labour, Land and Capital in Ghana* (2005) and (editor) *Economic Development and Environmental History in the Anthropocene* (2017).

Michiel de Haas is an Assistant Professor at the Rural and Environmental History Group at Wageningen University, where he obtained his PhD in 2017. His research focuses on migration, inequality, and rural development in 19th–20th century Africa, Uganda in particular. He publishes in the fields of economic history, African studies, and development.

Johan Fourie is Professor of Economics at Stellenbosch University where he teaches graduate and undergraduate courses in economic history and quantitative history. He obtained his PhD from the University of Utrecht in 2012.

Ewout Frankema is the Chair of the Rural and Environmental History Group at Wageningen University, editor-in-chief of the *Journal of Global History*, and research fellow of the Centre for Economic Policy Research (CEPR). He obtained his PhD in economics from the University of Groningen in 2008.

Katharine Frederick obtained her PhD in economic history from Wageningen University in 2018, and is currently an Assistant Professor of Economic and Social History at Utrecht University in the Netherlands.

xvi Contributors

N. Thomas Håkansson is Emeritus Professor of Rural Development at the Swedish University of Agricultural Sciences and Adjunct Professor of Anthropology at the University of Kentucky. He specializes in economic anthropology and political ecology and has conducted research on the history of intensive agriculture and political economy in Tanzania and Kenya for the last 25 years.

Dácil Juif obtained her PhD in economic history from the University of Tübingen (2014) and is currently an Associate Professor in Economic History at Universidad Carlos III de Madrid, research fellow of the Figuerola Institute of History and Social Science, and an associate editor of the *Industrial History Review* (RHI-IHR).

Lyndal Keeton obtained her PhD from the University of the Witwatersrand (Wits) in 2016. She is currently a senior research fellow at the Institutions and Political Economy Group (IPEG) and a lecturer in the School of Economics and Finance (SEF) at her alma mater.

David Killingray, PhD (School of Oriental and African Studies), Professor Emeritus, Goldsmiths, and Senior Research Fellow, School of Advanced Study, University of London, in retirement continues to research and write on aspects of African, Caribbean, imperial, and local history.

Patrick Manning is Professor Emeritus of World History at the University of Pittsburgh. He is the author of works including *The African Diaspora* (2009), *A History of Humanity* (2020), and *Methods for Human History* (2020). He is completing a history of African population and migration over the long term.

Felix Meier zu Selhausen is a Postdoc researcher at the Rural and Environmental History Group at Wageningen University. He obtained his PhD from Utrecht University (2015). Previously, he was a British Academy postdoctoral fellow at the University of Sussex. He has published in the fields of economic history, economics, and development.

Elise van Nederveen Meerkerk is Professor of Economic and Social History at Utrecht University, the Netherlands. Her research focuses on labor history, gender history, colonial history, and the history of textile production. She currently leads the EU-funded ERC Project "Race to the Bottom" (CoG #771288).

Opolot Okia is Professor of African History at Wright State University in Dayton, Ohio, in the US. His research has focused on the issue of colonial-era forced labor in Africa. He was previously a Fulbright Scholar at Makerere University in Uganda and Moi University in Kenya.

Karin Pallaver is an Associate Professor at the University of Bologna, where she teaches African history and Indian Ocean history. Her research concentrates on the social and economic history of East Africa under colonial rule, with a special focus on currency and labor history.

Filipa Ribeiro da Silva obtained her PhD in history from Leiden University. She is currently a senior researcher at the International Institute of Social History and member of the Global Collaboratory on the History of Labour Relations. Her research interests are on slave trade, labor migration, and coerced work.

Mohamed Saleh is Professor of Economics at the Toulouse School of Economics, University of Toulouse Capitole, a research affiliate at the Centre for Economic Policy Research, and a member of the Institute for Advanced Study in Toulouse. His research is focused on economic history and political economy.

Stefan Schirmer taught courses in economics and economic history at Wits University for many years and published over 30 academic articles. He spent time at the London School of Economics and Oxford University. He is currently Senior Visiting Fellow of the School of Economics and Finance at Wits and a research director at the Centre for Development and Enterprise.

Emiliano Travieso studied economic history at Universidad de la República (Montevideo) before earning a PhD from the University of Cambridge (2020). He is currently an Assistant Professor of Economic History at Universidad Carlos III de Madrid and a research fellow of the Carlos III-Juan March Institute.

Sarah Wahby is a PhD student of public policy at the University of Minnesota. Her areas of interest are policy evaluation and political economy.

PREFACE

Migration experiences are central to the lives of millions of Africans. However, contrary to the extensive historical literature on Africa's external slaves trades and the burgeoning social science literature on the recent outmigration of Africans to Europe, studies of migration *within* the African continent have remained fragmentary and regionally focused. In this volume, we aim to address this gap by offering a survey and synthesis of migratory developments within Africa from the early 19th to early 21st century. By situating shifting patterns of mobility in Africa within a global perspective, we highlight how the period between 1850 and 1960 can be considered as an "Age of Intra-African Migration." With the gradual demise of Africa's external slave trades and growing local demand for (slave) labor by expanding commodity exports – a process that had started well before the colonial "scramble" – the gravity center of African migration moved decisively inward. What followed was an era of heightened mobility within the region, marked by rapidly rising and vanishing migratory flows, increasingly diversified migration systems, and profound shifts in continental migration patterns. This era of intra-African migration came to an end with the resurgence of outmigration in the 1960s. This time Africans were more deliberately in search of extra-continental destinations, with new diaspora communities emerging specifically in the Global North. In 17 chapters contributed by 20 authors, we analyze major patterns of intra-African migration over the past two centuries, and propose an analytical framework to study them. Central to this framework is the distinction between "contextual" drivers of migration, which are endogenous to the spatial opportunity gaps that incentivize human mobility in specific times and places, and exogenous "macro-historical" drivers of shifting migration patterns such as demographic growth, state formation, technological change, capitalism, and changing belief systems, forces that can only be revealed through a long historical view.

The idea to compose a volume on migration in Africa took shape during conversations with several colleagues from the *African Economic History Network* during the XVIIIth World Economic History Congress in Boston, 2018. These dialogues led to the organization of three workshops held at Wageningen University (December 2018), the University of Barcelona (October 2019), and online (May 2020), in the midst of what later proved to be

xx Preface

the first wave of Covid-19. We thank the Wageningen School of Social Sciences (WASS) for funding part of our endeavor. We gratefully acknowledge financial support from the Netherlands Organisation for Scientific Research to publish this book in Open Access. The funding pertains to the project "South–South Divergence: Comparative Histories of Regional Integration in Southeast Asia and Sub-Saharan Africa since 1850" (NWO VICI Grant no. VI.C.201.062) led by Ewout Frankema.

A special thanks goes to Dirk Hoerder, who planted the seed for this book, by pointing us to the lack of a work of synthesis on intra-African migration and to Patrick Manning for endorsing the idea and providing invaluable feedback on the outline of the project, and Elise van Nederveen Meerkerk for perceptive comments on the full manuscript. We also wish to thank Helena Hurd and Rosie Anderson, our partners at Routledge, who have steered the book through publication with impressive speed and diligence, and Kathrin Immanuel at CodeMantra, who coordinated the copy-editing. We cannot in person acknowledge the many colleagues, both authors and commenters, who have made distinct intellectual contributions to this book, other than saying that we tremendously enjoyed the journey. The volume is truly the result of a collective effort and commitment to the project, in which drafts were exchanged and deadlines met with impressive discipline. Our indebtedness is even larger to all historians who introduced us via their work into the dazzling world of long-run African mobility. Some of them, including Dennis Cordell and Patrick Harries, passed away recently. Others, such as Philip Geoffrey Powesland, Joel Gregory, and Francois Manchuelle, did so tragically, at the heights of their careers, as they were still advancing their own perspectives on intra-African migration. Perhaps this is one reason why a historical survey of the age of intra-African migration has been waiting for so long. We can only hope that the books sparks further dialogue and research on the topic, and those who inspired our efforts but were unable to engage with us critically would have been pleased with the result.

Michiel de Haas & Ewout Frankema
Wageningen, 21 October 2021

Introduction

1

THE AGE OF INTRA-AFRICAN MIGRATION

A Synthesis

Michiel de Haas and Ewout Frankema

1 The age of intra-African migration

Western public perceptions of African migration history tend to concentrate on two of its most dramatic and visible forms. First, the intercontinental slave trades, which involved the forced displacement of an estimated 18 million people across the Atlantic and Indian Oceans as well as the Sahara and Red Sea from the 16th century through to the late 19th century, of which about two-thirds ended up in the Americas (Manning 1990, 84; see also Eltis 2000; Campbell 2004, 2005; Klein 2010). Second, the more recent irregular waves of African migration to Europe, which are expected by many to further intensify considering Africa's ongoing demographic expansion and limited economic opportunities for its aspirational young generations (European Commission, Joint Research Centre 2018; United Nations Development Programme 2019).

Attention to both expressions of mobility, past and current, is certainly warranted. Slave migration had a distinctly violent and pernicious character and left deep legacies across the globe. Likewise, in the context of overwhelming global disparities in wealth and security, it is of eminent importance to address the plight of African migrants crossing the Mediterranean. Yet, when we view Africa's long-term migration experience solely as an "exodus" of its young and able across the oceans, we unduly understate the historical and contemporary importance of migration *within* Africa, and the many important connections between mobility within and beyond the continent. Surveying and synthesizing the diversity of migration patterns that have emerged, transformed, and disappeared *within* Africa from the 19th to the 21st century contributes to correcting this imbalance, which is the central aim of this book.

While mobility has always been integral to human societies, the long-distance movement of individuals and groups across oceans and between world regions has expanded to unprecedented rates in the past two centuries. In the context of accelerating globalization, industrialization, colonization, decolonization, and the increasing pace of demographic growth and technological change, global patterns of human mobility have transformed with dizzying speed. Notably, Africans were highly visible as intercontinental movers in the first half of the 19th century and the later part of the 20th century, but largely absent

DOI: 10.4324/9781003225027-2

from intercontinental migration in the long intervening century between 1850 and 1960. This book captures the ways in which African migration changed across the continent over this long century; how people moved over short and long distances, as laborers in mines and on farms, as temporary sojourners and permanent settlers, to rural and urban destinations, voluntarily or forced, spontaneously or assisted, and individually or in groups. We will argue that such mobility was entangled with the same processes of globalization, industrialization, and imperialism that spurred migrant flows between and within other world regions (McKeown 2004; Hatton and Williamson 2005). By placing African continental migration in a long-term global perspective, this volume seeks to fill an important gap in the study of global migration and African history.

Until the 1820s, for every European that migrated to the Americas, four to five Africans disembarked (Eltis 1983, 255). In contrast, while the trans-Atlantic slave trade dwindled, over 50 million European migrants converged upon the Americas in the period 1850–1940. Figure 1.1 visualizes this shift. Asian long-distance migration also surged as, from c. 1830 onward, Indian and Chinese migrants provided a source of cheap labor – both indentured and voluntary – after the abolition of slavery in the British, and, subsequently, French empires (Northrup 1995; Huff and Caggiano 2007). Some 50 million migrants, also mostly from India and China, converged upon the export-oriented colonial economies of

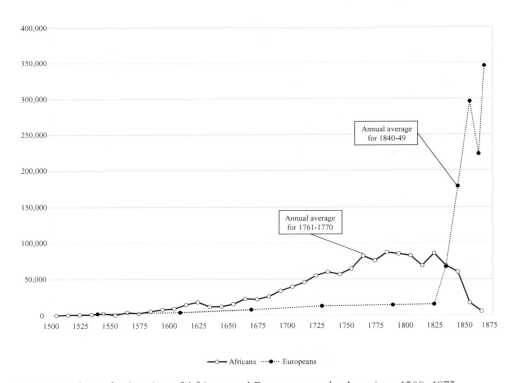

FIGURE 1.1 Annual migration of Africans and Europeans to the Americas, 1500–1875.
Sources: African migration from slavevoyages.org. European migration 1501–1820 from Horn and Morgan (2005, 21–22) and 1820, 1820–59 from Eltis (1983, 256), and 1861–80 from Ferenczi and Willcox (1929, 192). The dots represent mid-period annual averages; two examples of periods to which the annual averages apply are indicated in the graph.

Southeast Asia. Another 50 million migrants colonized the Russian and Chinese frontiers in Northeast Asia (McKeown 2004, 156). This surge in long-distance migration across the globe – sometimes spontaneous, at other times assisted, overwhelmingly voluntary, and facilitated by the revolutions in transportation and information technology – is widely referred to as the "age of mass migration" (Hatton and Williamson 1998).

Curtin (1997, 76) summarized the momentous shift in Africans' role in this age of mass migration: "the African slave trade was phased out of existence. In its place came new global patterns of migration. Africa was to play a part, but no longer the central part, in intercontinental migration." Africans first reappeared in large numbers outside the continent, and only transiently, when they were mobilized during the First, and especially the Second World War, to fight in the European and Asian theaters. Yet, as Figure 1.2 illustrates, the tide really turned from the 1960s onward, when North African migration to Europe led the way, but extra-continental migration from sub-Saharan Africa, be it for purposes of seeking prosperity, escaping violent conflict, or both, began to rise as well (Flahaux and De Haas 2016; Manning, Chapter 16, this volume).[1] Estimates on the number of residents living outside their country of birth, compiled by the World Bank (WB) and the United Nations (UN), show that only 13 out of every 10,000 African-born individuals lived outside the continent in 1960. In 2019, this figure had risen to 81, a six-fold per capita increase which,

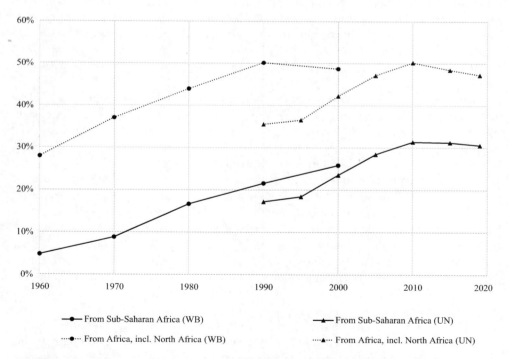

FIGURE 1.2 Share of international migrants from sub-Saharan Africa and Africa (including North Africa) that have moved outside the continent, 1960–2020.
Source: Migration data from the World Bank, Global Bilateral Migration Database (indicated as WB), and United Nations (indicated as UN). More analysis of the UN data in Manning, Chapter 15.

if we factor in population growth, corresponds with a 30-fold *absolute* increase (see Table 1.1 for sources).

Many African intercontinental movers were highly educated and moved via regular channels to diverse destinations across North America, Europe, and the Middle East (Lucas 2015). Still, most of the scholarly, political, and public attention goes out to irregular migration to Europe, involving dangerous and often fatal Saharan and Mediterranean crossings, generating anxieties and controversies in the receiving societies. Recent alarmist claims of an African "exodus" or "invasion" (Asserate 2018; Smith 2019) are overblown and hardly backed up by numbers (De Haas 2008). Nevertheless, these migratory flows should be expected to further intensify in the coming decades, considering the overwhelming global disparities in wealth, employment, and security (Hatton and Williamson 2003; Lucas 2015; Carling and Schewel 2018; European Commission, Joint Research Centre 2018; De Haas 2019; United Nations Development Programme 2019; Clemens 2020).

But what happened in the long century separating Africa's two global diasporas – the external slave trades and today's intensified extra-continental migration? In this book we refer to this era as the "age of intra-African migration," and view it as a constituent manifestation of the global "age of mass migration." As will become clear, we do not seek to argue that intra-African migration was unimportant before the decline of the slave trades.[2] We also do not propose that Africans entirely refrained from intercontinental mobility during the age of intra-African migration.[3] Nor do we posit that intra-African migration has lost its relevance as African intercontinental migration has become more important in recent decades, or that it is set to dwindle in the near future.[4] What we do argue, instead, is that the age of intra-African migration saw *an accelerated succession of overlapping migration patterns within the African continent which were driven, in large part, by the same forces that shaped the global age of mass migration.*

There are at least three reasons to view Africa's internal migration history as an *integral part* of the global historical migration dynamic. First, the growing volume of migrants in Africa was consistent with the growing global significance of migration, which involved intensified inter- as well as intra-regional moves. Second, African migration was responsive to the widening spatial opportunity disparities resulting from accelerated economic and political globalization after c. 1820, in ways broadly comparable to migration in other parts of the world. As we will see, European industrialization and improving terms of trade for tropical commodities during much of the 19th century intensified demand for labor – both coerced and free – in labor-scarce regions of commodity production. Spatially uneven opportunity structures that emerged in this period also fueled large-scale rural and urban migration. In addition, shifting patterns of African mobility were driven by changing ideologies concerning labor coercion, transformative declines in transportation costs, and imperial expansion and conflict, all of which are best understood in a global perspective. Third, changing patterns of African migration were directly connected with the intercontinental migration of Europeans and Asians, especially from India and the Middle East, into Africa. These latter groups of immigrants, although making up a very small proportion of the population in most regions of Africa, had a disproportionally large impact on the opportunities and constraints faced by migrants, imposing new territorial borders, labor relations, and spatial distributions of economic activity in the receiving societies.

The magnitude of intra-African migration in this era was remarkably large. For example, according to a widely circulated estimate, in the vast region west of Nigeria, the ratio of population in the labor-supplying interior savanna zones versus the coastal cash-crop zones shifted from roughly 1:1 to 1:2 between 1920 and 1970, largely as the result of labor migration (Amin 1995, 35–6; Curtin et al. 1995, 466). With a total estimated population of 45 million in 1970 (United Nations 2019), this implies a "net" shift of 7.5 million people, or 17% of the region's total population.[5] While we are certainly not the first to observe and explain such momentous shifts, the analytical framework we apply will move beyond oversimplified interpretations of a purported transition from "traditional" to "modern" migration, or from "forced" to "voluntary" mobility. Such dichotomies have long dominated our understanding of historical migration in Africa's 19th and 20th century. The new framework we propose is partly conceptual, distinguishing between migration *flows*, *systems,* and *patterns*, and classifying different types of migration and migrants. It is also partly explanatory, distinguishing "contextual" drivers, which include the forces that are *endogenous* to specific migration flows and systems, from "macro-historical" drivers, which encompass fundamental societal transitions that have initiated long-term shifts in overarching migration patterns across the continent and beyond. We view these drivers as operating simultaneously. Transcending earlier debates, we do not seek to argue that migration should be explained with reference to *either* local conditions *or* external forces but instead take a pluralist approach in which general macro-historical trends intertwine with the place- and time-specific unfolding of migratory activity.

We continue in Section 2 with a review of the African migration historiography. We elaborate our conceptual framework in Section 3. Section 4 offers our synthesis of the age of intra-African migration, which we argue consisted of five shifting patterns of migration that are explored in greater detail in this volume. Section 5 provides a brief reflection on the renewed global diaspora of Africans.

2 Historiographic foundations for a synthesis

Numerous scholars have recognized the centrality of migration in Africa's modern history. Historians, in particular, have produced rich long-run accounts of specific migrations systems, including Harries (1994) on Mozambican migrants to South Africa, Manchuelle (1997) on the Soninke diaspora, and Cordell, Gregory, and Piché (1996) and Piché and Cordell (2015) on the Burkinabe diaspora. However, attempts at historical synthesis and long-term, continent-wide comparisons of migration have remained limited to a few short essays, including a statement on Africa and global migration in the *longue durée* (Curtin 1997), a review of migration in Africa from 1900 to 1975 (Cordell 2013), and a brief survey on African migration history (Usman and Falola 2009). Specifically, the broader *patterns* and deeper *drivers* that characterize the age of intra-African migration have remained understudied and superficially theorized, and are yet to be interpreted in the context of the dramatic shifts in global mobility that occurred during the "age of mass migration" (c. 1850–1940). Moreover, migration *within* Africa is underrepresented in a growing body of macro-regional histories which explore migration as one of the core phenomena of globalization, regional integration, and transnational connections across Eurasia (Moch 1992; Lucassen and Lucassen 2009, 2014; McKeown 2010; Siegelbaum and Moch 2015) and the Indian and Atlantic oceans (Hatton and Williamson 1998; Eltis 2000; Campbell 2004,

8 Michiel de Haas and Ewout Frankema

2005). In this section we review the key strands in the historiography on migration in Africa, highlight gaps and prevailing misconceptions in the literature, and make our case for a new, pluralistic framework.[6]

The early roots of scholarship on African migration are found in the studies and reports written and commissioned by officials of and advisors to the European colonial bureaucracies. Such writings were typically motivated by the instrumental concern of how to pin down "drifting" African populations —nomadic pastoralists as well as shifting cultivators — in designated tribal areas and how to get sufficient African workers to offer their labor at the right place and at rates low enough to satisfy foreign employers, investors, and colonial governments (Orde-Browne 1933). Central were concerns of "detribalization" of laborers, the merits and dangers of oscillating versus permanent migration, and the position of women and children in migration systems (Read 1942; Cooper 1996). Reflecting preoccupations of governance and labor supply, biased and poorly informed conceptions of Africa's migration history emerged, for example, presuming that Africans tended to move collectively and in waves of settlers or invaders and that individuals were instead firmly embedded in tribal structures and inherently reluctant to move.

Many such preconceptions were challenged, but others were reinforced when, post-Second World War, the issue of labor migration began to attract sustained attention from anthropologists (Schapera 1947; Richards 1954), economists (Elkan 1959; Berg 1961), and sociologists (Mitchell 1959). These studies shared a common concern with the role of migration in processes of economic development and "modernization." Despite the richness of some of these accounts, they were often commissioned by colonial states and mostly refrained from fundamentally challenging the structures of colonialism. A particularly innovative contribution was made by anthropologist Hill (1963), who demonstrated that Ghana's cocoa revolution was realized not by immobile and tradition-minded peasants, but by mobile farmers with a capitalist mindset, who invested in land and accumulated large farms outside their home region.

Throughout the colonial era, dissenting observers and the incipient *International Labour Organization* had drawn attention to how colonial policies produced flight as well as exploitation and high mortality among recruited migrant laborers (Cadbury 1910; Ross 1925; Buell 1928). During the 1950s, with Africa still under colonial rule, the Saint Lucian economist and Nobel Prize winner Lewis (1954) and Burmese economist Myint (1958) began to address the role of colonial extraction in generating migration flows in Africa more systematically. After independence, and especially during the 1970s and 1980s, scholarly debates took a decisively critical turn, using Marxist and World Systems approaches to link migration explicitly to underdevelopment. Numerous studies emphasized the extractive conditions engineered by European capitalists and colonizers, ranging from the strategic introduction of direct (monetary) taxes and the formation of native reserves, to outright force (Arrighi 1970; Wolpe 1972; Amin 1974; Van Onselen 1976).

In his influential and encompassing iteration of this position, Samir Amin (1972, 1974, 1995) argued that cheap labor supply to core areas of commodity extraction, such as mines and cash-crop plantations, was crucial to the functioning of colonial capitalism. To generate such supply colonizers systematically disrupted livelihoods in migrant-sending regions, which were designated as "labor reserves." Migration further contributed to such peripheralization, as it drained their productive and reproductive labor. The shape that labor migrations took, Amin argued, depended on whether they emerged in areas dominated by

European settlers and mining in Southern and Eastern Africa, the "Africa of the labour reserves," or in the indigenous cash crop economies of West Africa, the "Africa of the colonial trade economy," where slave-based production systems were reshaped to fit the interests of European colonizers.

While Amin and others diametrically opposed the earlier view that migration was a "natural" or "functional" aspect of modernization and instead focused on the role of global power structures, they simultaneously reinforced the prevailing dichotomy between "traditional" and "modern" migration. Amin even posited that "before European colonization, Africa was the scene of mass movements of peoples" (Amin 1974, 66), and juxtaposed this "traditional" migration of peoples (note the plural!) to the "modern" migration of laborers, "[taking] their place in an organised and structured host society" (Amin 1995, 29). Either praising or lamenting it, modernization and underdevelopment scholars converged in their attribution of this purported transition from "traditional" to "modern" migration to the rapid diffusion of capitalist relations of production under European colonial rule.

Following broader trends in migration studies – and the social sciences in general – scholarship since the 1990s has shifted away from grand theoretical paradigms of modernization and underdevelopment, toward a more contextualized treatment of migrant experiences and aspirations, and the ways in which migrants carved out spaces to exert their agency within broader colonial and post-colonial structures. More attention has been paid to the role of culture, identity, and the lived experiences of migrants and people in the sending communities (Harries 1994; Dougnon 2007; Guthrie 2016). Historians have emphasized the importance of gender and family for migration across Africa (Stichter 1985; Walker 1990; Bozzoli and Nkotsoe 1991; Rodet 2009; Penvenne 2015). The work on the Soninke diaspora by Manchuelle (1997), and labor migration in South Africa and Mozambique by Harries (1994), in particular, has uncovered deep histories of mobility, with both continuities and complex shifts between the pre-colonial, colonial, and post-colonial eras. Moreover, complex linkages between slavery and migration have been revealed, as forced and voluntary mobility often complemented or even reinforced one another for much of the 19th and 20th centuries (Harries 1981, 2014; Rockel 2006; Rossi 2014). Scholars have also increasingly explored the links between mobility, territory, and state formation in pre-colonial and colonial times (Kopytoff 1987; Herbst 1990; Nugent and Asiwaju 1996; Geschiere 2009; Vigneswaran and Quirk 2015).

All the while, social scientists' burgeoning output on post-colonial African migration has become fragmented into vast parallel scholarships on urbanization, refugees, and international migration, typically taking little heed of developments in both historical scholarship and adjacent fields that study African mobility.[7] An extensive literature on African urbanization and internal migration emerged from the 1960s onward, as newly available spatial statistics enabled geographers and demographers to quantify such processes, and to lay an empirical foundation to inform independent African states with data and theoretical insights to govern demographic shifts (Kuper 1965; Prothero 1965; Mabogunje 1968; Hance 1970; Oucho and Gould 1993; Adepoju 2003). Recent studies on contemporary international migration have focused on the effect of economic development on emigration rates and the role of migration and remittances on development (Gupta, Pattillo and Wagh 2009; Lucas 2015; Flahaux and De Haas 2016; Dinkelman and Mariotti 2016), as well as migrant identities and networks and policy responses (De Bruijn, Van Dijk, and Foeken 2001; Berriane and de Haas 2012; Kane and Leedy 2013; Moyo, Laine, and Nshimbi 2021). Scholars have

10 Michiel de Haas and Ewout Frankema

also begun to harness historical data to explore the determinants, extent, and consequences of urban growth in Africa (Fay and Opal 2000; Fox 2012; Potts 2012; Jedwab and Moradi 2016). In the meanwhile, studies of the refugee crises in post-independence Africa have focused mainly on developments in (inter)national refugee regimes, in laws and policies, or have taken a decidedly critical sociological approach, but most of this work is ahistorical (Gatrell 2013, 11; Williams 2020, 560–1).

Social scientists widely hold that African migration, especially out of the continent, has been intensifying as a result of people's growing aspirations and abilities to move in a context of limited economic growth and fast demographic expansion (Hatton and Williamson 2003; Lucas 2015; Carling and Schewel 2018; European Commission, Joint Research Centre 2018; Hein De Haas 2019; United Nations Development Programme 2019; Clemens 2020). However, this conclusion is typically drawn with little consideration of deeper historical migration shifts *within* Africa and the possible connections these may have with the growth of extra-continental migration today, an issue that we take up further in our epilogue to this volume.

This concise review of key strands in the African migration historiography reveals an increasingly rich understanding of migration and mobility across the African continent. Nevertheless, and perhaps *because of* the contextual focus of historians and the disciplinary compartmentalization and lack of temporal depth of social scientists, attempts to synthesize long-run patterns of intra-African migration remain wanting. The starkly dichotomous "traditional-modern" framing remains notably influential in descriptions of African historical migration (Aina and Baker 1995; Cohen 1995; De Bruijn and Van Dijk 2003, 287; Usman and Falola 2009; Cordell 2013, 180–8; Fernandez 2013, 135; De Haas, Castles, and Miller 2020), despite recurrent critiques (Amselle 1976; Gerold-Scheepers and Van Binsbergen 1978; Manchuelle 1997; De Bruijn, Van Dijk, and Foeken 2001; Bakewell and De Haas 2007). Our contribution is a new pluralistic analytical framework that highlights five macro-historical drivers that interacted with a great variety of contextual drivers to produce numerous unique migration systems as well as five overarching shifting patterns of African migration. We will now introduce the conceptual building blocks of this framework.

3 A conceptual framework for the study of African migration history

3.1 Who is a migrant?

Precise definition of who is a migrant has proven to be a problematic and often politicized exercise. Definitions revolving around the crossing of international borders or migrants' specific objectives and characteristics are of practical use for policy makers working in contexts where definitions have direct legal and administrative repercussions (UNHCR 2016; IOM 2019; Migrant Observatory 2019). However, they are too restrictive to form the basis of a study of historical migration. It does not serve our purposes to impose a strict classification by migrants' objectives or characteristics, as we are interested precisely in the many ways in which forced/free, internal/international, and "economic"/"political" migration were related and made up shifting patterns of migration. We also want to avoid making our discussion of migration contingent on a specific definition of borders and nations. Borders have certainly been a relevant factor in African mobility, creating "barriers, conduits, and opportunities" (Nugent and Asiwaju 1996). However, during much of the age of intra-African migration, "international" borders with clearly defined implications for citizenship and sovereignty were mostly absent in Africa (Kopytoff 1987; Herbst 2000). Colonial and post-colonial borders often created artificial and arbitrary boundaries, but also changed the meaning of territoriality itself and interrupted wider circulatory flows of traders and pastoralists (Nugent and Asiwaju 1996; Mbembe 2000; Mathys 2021). Today, many African borders remain exceptionally porous (Lucas 2015: 1452–53).

To analyze the full breadth of migration manifestations in Africa over a two-century period, we adopt a migration typology proposed by world historian Patrick Manning. This typology takes the "community" with loosely defined cultural, linguistic, economic, and environmental characteristics as its starting point (Manning 2006; Lucassen and Lucassen 2017; Manning 2020). First, Manning distinguishes *home-community migration*, involving movement *within* a defined community. Prominent among home-community migrants have been women moving to their husbands' homesteads upon marriage. In Africa, as remarked by Cordell (2013, 187), "spanning the pre-colonial, colonial, and contemporary eras, these moves by women most certainly dwarfed male migration." However, because home-community migration is so distinct from other types of migration, it falls outside this volume's scope.[8]

Colonization is Manning's second migration type, involving the founding of a new community either by colonizing a previously uninhabited area or by expelling previous inhabitants. Colonization has long been viewed as the principal form of "traditional" African migration, described by Kopytoff (1987) as the "reproduction of African traditional societies" along "internal frontiers." However, while frontier migration certainly was a dominant pattern of African migration in the *longue durée*, several authors in this book show that the unclaimed and empty lands on which Kopytoff's analysis was predicated were no longer common in large parts of 19th-century Africa (Austin, Chapter 2). Notably, colonization was also not the most common type of migration associated with European settlement in Africa.[9] To be sure, European invaders (for this terminology, see below) in the Cape Colony did gradually dispel the Khoisan as they expanded the frontier of their farm and grazing lands. However, they (as well as most European farmers in Zimbabwe, Kenya, Algeria, and other places) required the nearby presence of an African workforce, and certainly after the abolition of slavery had few incentives to expel indigenous populations entirely (Fourie, Chapter 7). On a comparatively limited scale, colonization took place throughout the 20th century, in a context of colonial and post-colonial schemes, often coercive, aiming to mitigate localized population pressures, spur agricultural development, and resettle refugees and others in camps and newly created "villages" (Van Leeuwen 2001; Van Beusekom 2002; Machava 2019).

Whole-community migration, Manning's third type, involves the forced or voluntary displacement of an entire community. Forced whole-community migration has occurred especially in the pre-colonial and post-colonial eras in response to inter-community conflicts or excessive state violence. For example, entire communities were displaced in 19th-century Southern Africa, as a chain of white and black population movements resulting from African and colonial state formation reverberated deep into the continent (Fourie; Keeton and Schirmer, Chapters 6 and 7). In the post-colonial era, communities were displaced as a result of conflict and resultant famine, such as in the case of the Ethiopian refugee crisis in 1984–85 (Frankema, Chapter 15). During the colonial and, especially, post-colonial period, whole-community migration, often involuntary, also resulted from land reform, conservation, and development projects, most notably dam construction (De Wet 1994; Cernea 1997; Hoppe 2003; Schmidt-Soltau 2003). One could argue that nomadic pastoralist groups

12 Michiel de Haas and Ewout Frankema

such as the Fulani or Maasai engage in voluntary whole-community migration as well, but it should be noted that it is (increasingly) rare that pastoralists move into entirely uninhabited spaces and that pastoralist mobility has numerous cross-communal elements as well (De Bruijn and Van Dijk 2003; Håkansson, Chapter 5).

Finally, *cross-community migration* refers to the selective movement of individuals or subgroups between communities, either forced or voluntary. Our volume stresses the importance of this type of migration in 19th- and 20th-century Africa. There are four roles in which migrants cross between communities. *Sojourners* reside only temporarily in a receiving community, and their mobility often generates sustained patterns of "circulation" of people, ideas, and remittances between sending and receiving communities. The systems of voluntary rural-rural and rural-urban migration that emerged in East and West Africa over the 20th century involved large numbers of sojourners (De Haas and Travieso; Frederick and Van Nederveen Meerkerk; Meier zu Selhausen, Chapters 11–13). In contrast, *settlers* stay permanently in a new host community. In the 19th century, enslaved people who were either traded or taken as war booty made up a large body of (involuntary) settlers in places like the Sokoto Caliphate (Lovejoy 2005). Indeed, as Cordell (2013, 180) notes, slavery was almost by definition linked to resettlement, as enslaved women and men derived much of their controllability and market value from being "removed from their homelands, societies, and families." There are many instances where sojourning evolves into resettlement (De Haas and Travieso; Frederick and Van Nederveen Meerkerk, Chapters 11 and 12) or where settlers are expelled and forced to return or move on (Frankema, Chapter 15). *Invaders* are those who move to a different community, usually as a group, to seize and dominate the local population. If we implement this terminology consistently, European "settlers" or "colonists" are to be classified as invaders, considering their efforts to exploit local labor resources (one might argue that missionaries are more appropriately viewed as settlers). Finally, *itinerants* move from community to community without a clearly defined home, which mainly applies to particular groups of traders and pastoralists.

3.2 Agency and migration

The social science migration literature has long centered around the rather mechanistic and impersonal "push-pull" framework which views migration as an outcome of some structural disequilibrium between sending and receiving regions, usually linked to income (Lee 1966; Harris and Todaro 1970). Scholarship has since moved on to a more migrant-centered, agency-based approach, conceptualizing mobility as a strategy of people to fulfill their *aspirations* in a context of *spatial opportunity disparities* or *gaps*, which may be economic (e.g., wage differentials) but also related to other factors, such as freedom from home-community obligations or state repression (De Haas 2010; Carling and Schewel 2018; Van Hear, Bakewell, and Long 2018). Agency, then, resides, in people's *ability* to use mobility to navigate spatial opportunity disparities in pursuit of their aspirations. Such ability can be framed, following Amartya Sen, in terms of migrants' *capabilities*: access to the resources, such as money, network, family support, and legal status, required to make migration decisions (Hein de Haas 2019). One can use capabilities to pursue voluntarily mobility, but also (and more commonly) to be voluntarily immobile. Those who aspire to move but are unable to do so because they lack the capabilities are "trapped." Those who are compelled to move even though they would prefer to stay are "displaced" (cf. Lubkemann 2008; Schewel 2020).

When is migration *voluntary*? Conceptual clarity on the terms "forced" and "voluntary" or "coerced" and "free" migration is desirable, but the distinction is negotiable and indeed remains subject to controversy (Eltis 2002; Brown and Van der Linden 2010; Erdal and Oeppen 2018). To facilitate analytical clarity and conceptual distinction in a book that spans the full spectrum from slave kidnapping to free labor migration, we adopt a specific and narrow definition of the term "forced" migration based on two defining characteristics, of which at least one has to be fulfilled. First, *forced migration* occurs when someone's decision to move, including the when and where, is taken by another person, or organization. This definition excludes underaged children who move with their parents (migration of children in Africa is not specifically addressed in this volume, but see Razy and Rodet 2016). Second, forced migration occurs when people experience an *overwhelming pressure* (force majeure) to move due to conditions beyond their control (e.g., warfare, disaster, persecution), paired to an *urgency* to leave much more behind than one ideally would if there was no such pressure. This definition separates war refugees, expellees, exiles, as well as kidnapped slaves from those who choose to move for reasons that may be related both to *constraints* to pursue human aspirations in the sending regions (e.g., family obligations, unemployment or environmental degradation) and to *opportunities* to pursue aspirations or enhance capabilities in the receiving regions.[10] Although less frequently discussed in the book, we also encounter situations where people are forced into immobility. Here, we reserve the term "forced" for those whose ability to move is physically constrained by another person or organization (an owner, employer, or the state), such as slaves or people subjected to other forms of bonded labor relations or stringent exit restrictions (for examples from the colonial era, see Okia; Ribeiro da Silva and Alexopoulou, Chapters 8 and 9).

3.3 Flows, systems, drivers, and patterns

We now face a task to develop a framework that allows us to synthesize long-run, historical changes in *patterns of migration* in a way that goes beyond the oversimplified paradigm of a transition from "traditional" to "modern" migration with the imposition of colonial rule and the purportedly sudden introduction of capitalism as a single critical juncture. The "shifting patterns" framework we propose builds on identifying spatially demarcated *migration flows* and *systems* which collectively make up temporally demarcated but continent-wide *migration patterns*. Further, we distinguish between *contextual drivers* of migration flows, which are specific to individual migration systems, and *macro-historical drivers* of migration patterns, which affect multiple systems at once, and typically operate in the long run.

The term *migration flow* refers to the movement of people between a place of origin and a place of destination. Sustained flows of migration emerge when information costs decline after the first pioneering migrants have successfully navigated uneven opportunity structures between the sending and receiving region. In the context of cross-community migration it is also important to appreciate the role of migration networks that facilitate migrants' movement and settlement (De Haas 2010). Within such networks, we can distinguish *recruiters* who either persuade (voluntary) or seize (involuntary) migrants; *dispatchers* who make arrangements for sending migrants on their way; *facilitators* who provide facilities (food, shelter, security, information) on the way and upon arrival; and *connectors* who provide new arrivals with an entry into the labor market and other aspects of society (Manning 2020). Recruiters and facilitators played a central role in the trans-Saharan slave trades (Saleh and

Wahby, Chapter 3), the East African caravan trades (Pallaver, Chapter 4), and the Southern African mining migration systems (Juif, Chapter 10). Connectors were vital in a context of voluntary migration, such as the rural-rural and rural-urban migration systems discussed in this book (De Haas and Travieso; Frederick and Van Nederveen Meerkerk; Meier zu Selhausen, Chapters 11–13). Migrant flows, and counterflows in the case of circulating sojourners, always have some substance in numbers of migrants.[11] Flows are also characterized by certain compositional markers related to gender, age, ethnicity, race, class, skill, education, religion, or nationality and are spatially circumscribed in terms of the routes that migrants travel from sending to receiving areas. Flows can emerge and dry up in a matter of days or weeks, for instance, in the case of instant flight, but they can also be sustained for decades if not centuries, as in the case of the trans-Saharan slave trades.

Migration flows then constitute the backbone of a *migration system* which we define as *one or multiple flows of people that bridge distinct locations with uneven opportunity structures* (for more intricate definitions and discussion, see Mabogunje 1970; De Haas 2010; Bakewell 2014). A necessary condition for migration is the (perceived) existence of uneven opportunity structures. When uneven opportunity structures inform migration (affecting the decision-making of migrants directly, or through agents responsible for their mobility) we refer to them as "drivers." Such drivers include the prevalence of violence, political oppression and persecution, and opportunities for trade, work, and settlement, among many other factors. In many cases, drivers change over time, and can even result in a reversal of the direction of mobility. This was the case, for example, with the early colonial slave exodus in West Africa (Rossi 2014), and post-colonial expulsions (Frankema, Chapter 15). Past migration within the system often contributes to such reversals, for instance, when a swelling number of labor migrants drives down wages in the host region and raises wages in the sending region, thus erasing the opportunity disparities that had provoked migration in the first place (for theory, see De Haas 2010; for examples in African history, see De Haas 2019; De Haas and Travieso, Chapter 11). When similar migration systems emerge simultaneously, while remaining spatially disconnected, we refer to a *migration pattern*. A pattern arises from the deeper macro-historical forces that operate on a continental or even global scale.

4 Shifting patterns of intra-African migration

The age of intra-African migration was characterized by a rapid succession of overlapping shifts in migration patterns. What caused these shifts? We observe five categories of macro-historical drivers that embed the age of intra-African migration firmly within the global age of mass migration. That is to say, even though all of these macro-historical drivers were operating at a global scale, they produced distinctly "African" patterns of migration as they interacted with social, economic, and political orders that characterized (a large part of) the continent. These macro-historical drivers also interacted with more local, context-dependent dynamics to produce diverse but patterned migration outcomes across the continent.

The five categories of macro-historical drivers are (in random order): (1) accelerated *demographic growth*, which in 20th-century Africa has generated a fundamental shift away from labor scarcity to abundance, put increasing pressure on available land and water resources, and increased populations' share of young people (who are more prone to migrate);

(2) continent-wide processes of *state formation* induced by internal conflicts and forceful external intervention (colonial rule), intensifying the contestations over territory, resources, and citizenship; (3) uneven *market expansion* and integration into global capitalist systems, processes that were ongoing long before the onset of colonial rule but intensified markedly in the 20th century; (4) *technological change* which has dramatically altered the possibilities and costs of long-distance transportation and communication over land and water, human health and life expectancies, and the aspirations and capabilities of migrants, in Africa and elsewhere; (5) *changes in belief systems*, which have progressively undermined the perceived legitimacy of slavery, forced labor and colonial rule, and which have given rise to broadly shared notions of both human rights and exclusive citizenship of nation-states. The contextual drivers that have shaped individual migration systems are not discussed here, but surface in the individual chapters of this volume.

We have not singled out *environmental* change as a distinct macro-historical driver of shifting patterns of intra-African migration. This does not mean that we consider the environment irrelevant to migration shifts. Indeed, various chapters in this book reveal how human mobility in Africa has often been a response to spatially diverse ecological contexts and how specific environmental complementarities, shocks, and changes affected or even prompted migration (Håkansson, Chapter 5; De Haas and Travieso, Chapter 11). The environment was also an important driver in the southern migration of Fulbe herds into the humid savannas of West Africa in a context of climatic changes since the 1960s, which is covered elsewhere (De Bruijn and Van Dijk 2003; Bassett and Turner 2007). However, these environmental drivers were specific to regions, such as the Sahel, rather than spanning most of the continent. In other words, they shaped individual migration flows and systems, but not entire patterns. As such, we have chosen to view the environment as a contextual driver of migration.

However, the dividing line here is not sharp and the links between historical environmental change and shocks and migration remain to be studied in more depth, potentially revealing wider patterns. For example, prolonged droughts affected large parts of Africa in the early and late 19th century (Nicholson, Dezfuli, and Klotter 2012, 1227), plausibly affecting migration on a continental scale as well. Likewise, the Rinderpest that swept across sub-Saharan Africa between 1888 and 1897 and killed over 90% of African cattle (Sunseri 2018) likely shaped subsequent migration patterns. Certainly, prolonged droughts and the Rinderpest shock deeply affected patterns of mobility in 19th-century East Africa, as Håkansson (Chapter 5) shows. Today, in a context of global climate change, notions of "climate migrants" or "climate refugees" abound (Rigaud et al. 2018, vii). Still, the link between environmental change and migration remains contested, and it is far from evident that environmental pressures have a systematic – let alone uniform – impact on migration outcomes in Africa and beyond (Findley 1994; Mueller, Gray and Hopping 2020).

The remainder of this introduction distinguishes five shifting patterns of migration that characterized the era from the decline of the transoceanic slave trades to the resurgence of global migration of Africans. As a final preliminary, we note that while these shifts were important and likely unprecedented in terms of their volume and speed, they do not signify the beginning of a "dynamic modernization" in contrast to an earlier "static tradition." Several chapters in our volume show that frontier colonization and whole-community migration – often held up as key expressions of "traditional" migration – had already been subject to major transformation, diversification, and decline *at a much earlier date*, before the onset of the era of intra-African migration. Engaging with Kopytoff (1987), Austin (Chapter 2) argues that by the 19th century, voluntary frontier colonization in West Africa was severely constrained by intense slave trading and violent state formation. In the West African interior, the formation of Jihadi states induced large-scale flight, invasion, and settlement, most notably of Fulbe pastoralists (Hanson 1996). In Southern Africa, expansionist states and trekking Boers generated violent processes of displacement, which overturned earlier patterns of cross-community migration – which in turn also does not fit the "traditional" label (Austin; Keeton and Schirmer; Fourie, Chapters 2, 6, and 7). In 19th-century East Africa, voluntary pastoral mobility was still pervasive but likewise had many cross-community elements (Håkansson, Chapter 5). Understanding this complexity, temporal depth and spatial diversity of "pre-colonial" migration is poorly served by a "traditional versus modern migration" dichotomy. The age of intra-Africa migration did not originate in a uniform or traditional setting, and did not set the wheels of African migration history in motion. Our volume thus leaves substantial scope for a systematic analysis of earlier shifting migration patterns, before the 19th century.

4.1 The inward turn: slavery and the commercial transition

Two reinforcing processes were key to the inauguration of the age of intra-African migration. First, the demise of the transoceanic slave trades which halted the "drain" of young men and women from sub-Saharan Africa. This not only enhanced possibilities of long-term demographic growth *within* Africa (Manning 2010; Frankema and Jerven 2014), but also affected the distribution of power between and within communities. Second, a steep rise in global demand for African agricultural commodities in combination with a major decline in overseas transportation costs, which made the production of a wide range of (tropical) agricultural commodities in Africa increasingly lucrative, and resulted in a "commercial transition" that gained momentum in the first half of the 19th century (Law 1995). Progressive abolition and increasing domestic production of cash crops (as well as artisanal goods and transport services) led to a notable intensification of slave mobilization across Africa, producing a relative shift of forcibly displaced Africans from extra-continental to intra-continental destinations, a shift that began long before the export trade subsided entirely toward the end of the century.

Recent estimates suggest that one in every five Africans may have been enslaved at the high point of internal enslavement in the third quarter of the 19th century, and in some places this may have been as much as one in two (Coquery-Vidrovitch 2021; Manning 2021). This intensification of slavery in Africa ties in with concurrent intensification of slave-based commodity production in Cuba, the US South, and Brazil in the 19th century, which has been referred to as the "second slavery" (Tomich 2004). Figure 1.3 illustrates the "inward" transition from slave exports to domestic commodity production in West Africa at large. Commodity exports surged from the 1760s onward and began to exceed the total value of Atlantic slave exports in the 1830s, while, after a temporary low between 1808 and 1820 as a result of British abolition, the value of slave exports recovered and stabilized until c. 1850.

Austin (Chapter 2) explores the migratory repercussions of the commercial transition and the intensification of internal slave mobilization in the context of land abundance

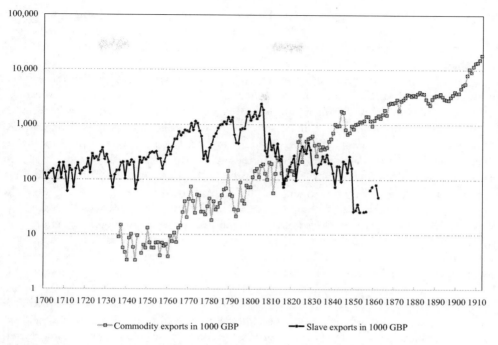

FIGURE 1.3 Value of slaves and commodities exported from West Africa, 1700–1910.
Source: Frankema, Williamson and Woltjer (2018, 234).

and labor scarcity in West Africa. In Eastern Africa, slave trading surged from the 1780s through to the 1870s, when Britain enforced prohibition of slave shipping to all overseas destinations, including Pemba and Zanzibar. Illicit trading continued into the early 1900s as French and Afro-Arab traders held on (Campbell 2004, 2005; Allen 2015). As Pallaver (Chapter 4) shows, the majority of slaves captured in the East and Central African interior during the 19th century were retained *within* Africa, at the Swahili coast, Zanzibar, and the Mascarenes, and thus co-constituted the 19th-century shift form extra-continental migration toward slave-based commodity production in the region. All the while, as Saleh and Wahby (Chapter 3) demonstrate, the long-standing trans-Saharan trade also received new impulses from rising labor demands in North Africa, and particularly from the Egyptian cotton plantations, which flourished due to the US civil war-induced cotton famine in the 1860s.

Certainly, trade of slaves between and ownership of (predominantly female) slaves by African societies long pre-dated the commercial transition and was at least partly a "by-product" of the transoceanic slave trades. What changed in the 19th century was that it became much more common to capture slaves for local production, or sell them to African final buyers (Lovejoy 2012). These practices were often coordinated by newly emerging or expanding polities, such as the powerful Sokoto Caliphate and other Jihadi states in the interior West African savanna (Austin, Chapter 2). In the Great Lakes region

18 Michiel de Haas and Ewout Frankema

the Kingdom of Buganda organized raids and offered local opportunities to put slaves to productive use (Pallaver, Chapter 4). Meanwhile, commercialization also stimulated various forms of non-slave mobility, to carry goods, engage in trade, or provide specialized artisanal skills.

As forced intercontinental migration of Africans was progressively suppressed over the 19th century and intra-African labor mobility intensified, Africa also moved toward becoming a net immigrant continent, a topic that is not explored in the chapters of this volume but deserves a mention as an important feature of the age of intra-African migration. Freed slaves and descendants of slave migrants came back to numerous regions in Africa. Most notably along the West African coast, these Afro-American settlers crucially shaped receiving communities (Harris 1993; Matory 1999; Akyeampong 2000). From the mid-19th century, the largest migratory inflows, however, came from Europe, the Middle East, and South Asia. New waves of invasion and settlement beyond a narrow set of coastal enclaves were enabled by the wider availability of quinine, the invention of the machine gun, and the diffusion of steam-powered transportation. Immigrants established themselves across the continent as free and indentured laborers, traders, farmers, industrial entrepreneurs, soldiers, missionaries, and colonial officials (Curtin 1997). Extra-continental immigrants have left deep imprints on the design of African states, their administrative systems, economic infrastructures, religious beliefs (e.g., spread of Christianity and new forms of Islam), cuisines, and sports (Akyeampong 2000). European invasion also provoked violent conflict, resistance, and flight. The territorial states imposed by colonial powers, moreover, reconfigured the political and legal framework migrants were confronted with during the colonial and post-colonial eras (Frankema, Chapter 15). Migrant flows into Africa largely receded with independence and even reversed in many cases, as expatriate settlers left the continent in waves of expulsion and voluntary departure. Recently, migrant flows into Africa have picked up again, most notably with the arrival of what one source estimates to be over a million Chinese migrants (French 2015), people who either are staying temporarily to work for a Chinese company, mostly in mining or construction, or have moved on personal title often with the aim to stay, marry, set up a business, or buy real estate.[12]

4.2 From forced to voluntary labor migration under colonial rule

The shift from export slavery to slave-produced commodities was followed by another shift, this time away from coerced labor toward the increasing use of voluntary labor in the expansion of export commodity production zones. In the long run, the transition from "forced" to "free" labor mobilization was unmistakable (Austin; Pallaver; Okia; De Haas and Travieso, Chapters 2, 4, 8 and 11). Until the final quarter of the 19th century, wage labor markets were rare in sub-Saharan Africa, but by the mid-20th century, these had become the dominant way in which the colonial state, expatriates, and African farmers contracted outside labor. However, the shift was neither smooth nor swift. In some cases, abolition triggered large-scale mobility, as previously displaced slaves returned home or moved on to different regions to seek work and new lives (Austin, Chapter 2; Rossi 2014). In other cases, colonial states failed to abolish slavery or emancipate slaves and often condoned the use of slave labor well into the 20th century (Lovejoy and Hogendorn 1993; Klein 1998; Deutsch 2006). In the context of northern Nigeria, the demise of slavery under colonial rule took almost 40 years, characterized as a "slow death" by Lovejoy and Hogendorn (1993).

In South Africa's Cape Colony slavery was already abolished in the 1830s, and this was one of the forces setting the north- and eastward trek by Cape settlers in motion (Fourie, Chapter 7). However, in South Africa as well as many other places, the transition to voluntary wage labor followed a winding path of alternative forms of labor coercion, many of which were backed up or even initiated by colonial governments (Okia, Chapter 8; also Allina 2012; Okia 2012; Harries 2014; Van Waijenburg 2018). Depending on where labor was demanded, forced recruitment could result in either forced mobility (e.g., to build a railroad or extract minerals) or forced immobility, as communities were pinned down in labor-scarce regions (typically to produce agricultural commodities). Labor was also mobilized by colonial states using more indirect forms of coercion, such as land alienation and restrictions on independent cultivation of valuable export crops by African farmers in sending regions, methods that were most widely applied in the context of European settler agriculture and mining industries in Southern, Central, and, to a lesser extent, Eastern Africa (Juif; Frederick and Van Nederveen Meerkerk, Chapters 10 and 12). In other cases colonial policies were designed explicitly to restrict Africans' mobility and tie laborers to local plantations or settler farms, and to criminalize migration or "flight" (Okia, Chapter 8). Direct forms of coerced labor mobilization were most visibly, unapologetically, and persistently pursued in Belgian and Portuguese Africa (Ribeiro da Silva and Alexopoulou, Chapter 9), but they were also widely present in British and French colonies (Van Waijenburg 2018; Okia; Killingray, Chapters 8 and 14). Especially after the 1920s, when the completion of rudimentary infrastructures began to reduce the need for forced labor mobilization, voluntary labor migration increased. At the same time, labor coercion became increasingly controversial in European metropoles, where scandals about the maltreatment of forced laborers tilted public opinion against the maintenance of forced labor schemes (Okia, Chapter 8).

In East and West Africa, however, much of the increasing labor mobility occurred on African initiative. It is important to note that such forms of voluntary labor migration existed in many African regions long before the imposition of European colonial rule. In some 19th-century instances, migrant laborers worked for wages, for example, the Nyamwezi porters in East Africa (Pallaver, Chapter 4) or the migrant farmers in the Senegambia (De Haas and Travieso, Chapter 11). In a pattern that had even deeper roots, sojourning migrants offered their labor outside their own communities, working to obtain some form of in-kind payment, such as a cow, before parting ways again. Such was the case, for example, with impoverished pastoralists in East and Southern Africa, seeking to rebuild their herds (Håkansson; Keeton and Schirmer, Chapters 5 and 6). Under colonial rule, rural labor migrants, many of whom were former slaves (Rossi 2014), swelled in numbers, and were increasingly working for wages or as sharecroppers. As most of Africa's commercialization occurred in relatively small areas with low population densities, migrants often covered large distances to participate in mining and cash-crop economies (Juif; De Haas and Travieso, Chapters 10 and 11). As Manchuelle (1997, 7) has noted, the "traditional-modern" dichotomy that has long shaped our understanding of Africa's migration history came with the assumption that African traditional economies "had to be disrupted in order for [voluntary] labor migration to take place." However, from the perspective of the rural migrants themselves, as well as their host communities, the rise of large-scale voluntary labor migration was certainly not that abrupt, and the logic behind their mobility not as novel. What stands out is the *scale*

20 Michiel de Haas and Ewout Frankema

of rural migration in the first half of the 20th century, driven by the growing opportunity gaps that emerged between rural hinterlands and enclaves of export commodity production.

While their mobility sustained colonial treasuries and spurred wealth accumulation by colonial or indigenous elites, voluntary migrants also pursued their own aspirations, and exerted a considerable degree of agency, thwarting colonial extraction strategies, crossing imperial borders, and supplying their labor in places where better wages and working conditions were on offer. In numerous cases, large-scale uncontrolled migration flows between empires emerged, especially from French, Belgian, and Portuguese to British territories. Modern infrastructures facilitated voluntary movement, but many labor migrants were willing to cross distances up to 1,000 kilometers on foot if traveling by rail or lorry was not an option. In East and West Africa, voluntary migrants moved and eventually settled in such large numbers in rural receiving communities that by the mid-20th century their presence contributed significantly to the closing of wage gaps between sending and host regions (De Haas and Travieso, Chapter 11). As such, voluntary labor migration crucially shaped the nature, extent, and spatial patterns of economic development in colonial Africa. In Southern Africa, circular migration patterns were sustained much longer, especially in South Africa where labor laws stipulated that migrant workers should leave their families at home and return after the expiration of their contract (Cordell 2013; Juif, Chapter 10).

4.3 Shifting destinations: from rural to urban

While urbanization has deep roots in many parts of Africa, until the 20th century only a small share of Africans lived in cities and towns, especially south of the Sahara (Coquery-Vidrovitch 2005; Freund 2007). Urban growth in the 19th century was largely a result of the same processes of commercialization and state consolidation that occasioned the intensification of slave mobilization and the flourishing of trading diasporas (discussed below). During the colonial era, urban agglomerations grew in number and size, and developed a range of functions, as sites of government, commerce, mining, and industry (Frederick and Van Nederveen Meerkerk, Chapter 12). Some of the largest cities in Africa today sprang up along newly built railroads, in areas that were previously economically marginal and barely inhabited (Jedwab and Moradi 2016). Until the mid-20th century, the majority of voluntary labor migrants was destined for rural areas, but by mid-century urban destinations quickly gained in relative and absolute importance (Juif; Frederick and Van Nederveen Meerkerk; Meier zu Selhausen, Chapters 10, 12 and 13). Many growing cities, such as Abidjan, Accra, Dakar, Kampala, and Lagos, were located close to areas that had previously attracted numerous rural migrants. As such, urban migration further compounded momentous spatial demographic shifts, often from interior to coastal areas.

Several factors contributed to the shift toward urban migration destinations. Initially, colonial authorities had discouraged Africans' access to urban areas, often with legal restrictions to permanent urban settlement. As the colonial era progressed, however, policies that sought to sustain circular migration and control urban spaces were loosened, especially from the 1940s onward (Juif; Frederick and Van Nederveen Meerkerk; Killingray, Chapters 10, 12, and 14) – in sharp contrast to the tightening of urban migration restrictions that occurred simultaneously in South Africa (Ogura 1996). Moreover, the deeper penetration of commercialization and capitalism into African economic life drove occupational diversification in both unskilled and skilled types of work, a process that was especially concentrated in (and fostered the development of new) urban areas which attracted a growing number of migrants. Colonial and post-colonial governments also actively attempted to spur development by taxing rural areas, and investing in urban economies, which further attracted migrants toward urban agglomerations. Urban migration rates, while still high, have shifted beyond their peak in many African countries. Especially since the 1980s the pace of urban migration has slowed down. Urban growth is now primarily fueled by increasing life expectancies and the growing presence of women of child-bearing age in urban areas (Meier zu Selhausen, Chapter 13).

The gender composition of rural-urban migration flows changed substantially in the course of time. Initially, migration to newly emerging mining, industrial, and trading centers was heavily dominated by male migrants, who would work for several months to years to earn cash and then return home. In later phases, women increasingly joined their husbands in cities, or migrated to cities independently, stimulated by expanding opportunities of service sector employment, urban healthcare, and schooling (Frederick and Van Nederveen Meerkerk; Meier zu Selhausen, Chapters 12 and 13). The timing of shifts in the gender balance of urban migration took place earlier in "older" West African cities, where women tended to be heavily involved in retail trading, than in the younger (colonial) cities in parts of East and Southern Africa, where male and female jobs tended to be more strictly separated and work outside the home remained a male prerogative for a much longer time (Meier zu Selhausen, Chapter 13). Here, the transition from a circular male migration system to one of family-oriented labor stabilization was strongly mediated by a set of colonial institutions that either discouraged or supported the settlement of labor migrants and families in cities (Juif; Frederick and Van Nederveen Meerkerk, Chapters 10 and 12).

4.4 The decline of specialized migrant diasporas: trade, religion and education

Migration systems always have some selective elements, for example, being biased toward men, educated, or high-status individuals, or specific ethnic or religious groups. Some migration systems, however, stand out for their narrower or more circumscribed markers of distinction. A key example of such specialized migration was the long-distance trading diasporas that flourished across Africa as a result of deepening integration with global markets during the 19th-century "commercial transition" (Austin; Pallaver, Chapters 2 and 4). Migrant trade networks fulfilled an important function in overcoming cultural and institutional barriers between numerous disparate and sometimes antagonistic communities (Curtin 1984; Lydon 2009). The diasporic Juula, Hausa, Nyamwezi, and Swahili who came to dominate long-distance trade networks formed moral communities, deriving their reputation and cohesion from specific characteristics such as ethnicity, faith, and literacy. Traders often resided in separate "stranger quarters" that underlined their status, and their ability to reap profits depended on their trusted status, their control over specific trade routes, and their ability to breach information asymmetries about supply, demand, quality, and price gaps. They operated across towns at important trading nodes and in turn fostered the growth of such towns (presaging much faster urbanization later on, see Section 4.3 above), as well as the spread of literacy and new religions. These cross-community trading networks also involved the mobility of large numbers of porters (carriers) who, in the case of the Nyamwezi, were free laborers, and became increasingly specialized itinerants, trading between the coast and interior of East Africa (Pallaver, Chapter 4).

Diasporas and caravans lost their central role in African long-distance trade relatively quickly after the onset of colonial rule, although they never disappeared entirely. Three factors contributed to this decline. First, new motorized transport technologies drastically lowered overland transportation costs and rerouted trade, while facilitating the mobility of workers and the inland diffusion of imported commodities (Gewald, Luning, and van Walraven 2009). The construction of long-distance railroads was particularly crucial in this respect. Second, circulating voluntary labor migrants took over the role of organized caravans of porters in carrying commodities from and to remote rural areas that were not, or marginally, integrated into motorized transportation networks (De Haas and Travieso, Chapter 11; Frederick 2020). This transition from porterage – free and enslaved – to labor migration was mostly gradual and often involved porters who started to spend more time at their destinations as laborers, or abandoning trade altogether in favor of labor migration (Michiel de Haas 2019, 391). By bringing back consumer goods upon their return, rural migrants continued to arbitrage prices for long and contributed to the integration of commodity as well as labor markets. Third, the role of trading diasporas in breaching cultural barriers was reduced by the progressive *internal integration* of colonial territories and post-colonial states (e.g., through the introduction of national languages, currencies, and trade taxes) – as well as their *mutual separation*. In turn, the decline of trading diasporas may have contributed to the weakening of cross-communal ties and a lower appreciation of "strangers," especially from beyond national boundaries (Frankema, Chapter 15). At the same time, the erection of new barriers has also generated opportunities for cross-border trade and smuggling of goods and people. In some regions, especially the Sahara, old as well as new long-distance networks continue to flourish until today (Scheele 2012; Walther 2015).

While this is a topic our volume's individual chapters do not address, it is important to note here that the arrival of missionaries in the late 19th and early 20th century, and the rising demand for modern education and specific occupations tied to colonial state formation, generated opportunities for new types of diaspora formation, which were often grafted onto preceding trade networks. Examples include the Baganda, who branched out in the Great Lakes region as Christian evangelists and colonial administrators (Roberts 1962), Yoruba kola traders in Asante who came to form the backbone of the colonial police force (Abaka 2009), and educated Dahomeyans who spread throughout Francophone West Africa as colonial intermediaries (Challenor 1979). Manchuelle's (1997) study of the Soninke provides an interesting case of how a diasporic network can transform and expand over decades or even centuries. Soninke elites dominated the most lucrative types of labor migration across West and Central Africa in the early 20th century and subsequently pioneered migration to France as well. In recent decades, diasporas have increasingly branched out of the African continent. Pentecostal Ghanaians, for example, have come to form a diasporic network stretching across the Americas, Europe, and Africa (Akyeampong 2000).

4.5 From absorption to expulsion: violence, state formation, and attitudes toward "strangers"

One of the most consequential long-term transitions in migration patterns is the shift from "absorption" to the "expulsion" of migrants, linked to changing attitudes of migrant-receiving communities and states in Africa toward the desirability of immigration and the integration of "strangers." The formation and transformation of polities in 19th- and 20th-century

Africa was often violent and disruptive, causing recurring waves of forced migration, including the mobilization of slaves for local armies, courts, or plantations, as well as flight and mass displacement (Austin; Keeton and Schirmer; Fourie, Chapters 2, 6, and 7). However, whereas slaves in pre-colonial times and forced labor migrants in the colonial era were taken toward centers of economic, social, military, and cultural activity, in the post-colonial era people were increasingly expelled, repatriated, or isolated (Frankema, Chapter 15). Where slaves had been captured to be, ultimately, integrated into their host societies, and colonial states had opened their borders to large flows of labor migrants, the post-colonial default was to get rid of people, if needed by force. Cohen has imaginatively labeled this distinction as one between "two forms of engagement with strangers – the anthropophagic, where outsiders are swallowed and digested, and the anthropoemic, where aliens are discarded, institutionalized, incarcerated or expelled" (Cohen 2019, 45; also see Frankema, Chapter 15).

The single most important long-term driver of this shift from "absorption" to "expulsion" was demographic growth. Whereas state institutions in the pre-colonial and colonial era were determined by local contexts of labor scarcity, seasonal or structural, the gradual but sustained transition in land-labor ratios turned unskilled labor into an abundant factor. Strangers were more often regarded as competitors for jobs, limited public provisions, and scarce natural resources. Another key factor was the changing role of territorial borders and associated notions of citizenship. Post-colonial African states adopted (much) stricter immigration acts than their colonial predecessors, and initiated numerous waves of expulsion of "illegal" (read non-national) residents, mostly labor migrants who had sometimes lived for decades in the receiving community, but without formal residence permits (Frankema, Chapter 15). These expulsions, which in some cases involved hundreds of thousands of people, often took place in the wake of economic contraction. The transition of colonial borders into national borders demarcating sovereign territories gave political leaders a clear mandate to expel people on the basis of their different national identity. Further, the ethnic dimension of land conflict between "sons of the soil" and immigrants in Africa is often stressed in the context of mounting population densities, but as pointed out by Boone (2017), post-colonial states also played a key role in (re)structuring access to land, and thus also shaped the nature and extent of land-related conflict and its repercussions for immigrant settlers.

The shift from absorption to expulsion can also be observed in the ways in which states amassed military power and exercised violence. During what Richard Reid (2012) has termed the violent "military revolution" of 19th-century Africa, pre-colonial states, such as expansionist Jihadist caliphates of the West African interior, amassed large armies, often made up of enslaved recruits (Laband 2017), a practice that survived into the First World War (Killingray, Chapter 14). In the colonial era, large numbers of soldiers were recruited into colonial armies, and were of crucial importance in the conquest and "pacification" of African – and sometimes Asian – colonies.[13] Soldiers and other workers were also mobilized in large numbers to serve during both world wars, on the continent as well as European and Asian theaters (Killingray, Chapter 14).[14] In contrast, decolonization and post-colonial conflicts more often involved large-scale displacement of unwanted residents. Close to a million French settlers and tens of thousands of Algerian soldiers who had served in the French army were pushed out of Algeria in the early 1960s (Eldridge, 2016). Between the early 1960s and mid-1990s violent conflict in the Great Lakes region, the Horn of Africa, and former Portuguese Africa (to mention the largest hotbeds) led to millions of forcibly displaced who sought refuge in neighboring countries (Frankema, Chapter 15).

As noted, flight from violent conflict and state repression had been prevalent in pre-colonial and colonial Africa too. However, while in the colonial era flight was often an unintended, or even undesired, consequence of repressive taxation and labor recruitment policies (Okia; Ribeiro da Silva and Alexopoulou, Chapters 8 and 9), in post-colonial Africa it resulted from deliberate attempts by states to push people out of the community and territory. In this regard, the great surge in refugees in the wake of wars of decolonization and contentious nation-state formation was unprecedented. National identity and sovereignty became key in the granting of formal refugee status to migrants who had left their homes in fear of violence, persecution, or because of war-induced famine and crossed a national border. As laid down in the *United Nations High Commissioner for Refugees* (UNHCR) charter of 1951, member countries were obliged to protect international refugees. National identity also became a key political tool in creating legal divisions between insiders and outsiders.

To be sure, the shift from absorption to expulsion was not absolute, and cannot be demarcated in time and space with precision, nor tied consistently to a singular explanatory framework. The systematic extermination of the Herero and Nama in German South West Africa (Namibia) by German invaders took place during the first decade of the 20th century, and was primarily rooted in colonial ideologies rather than competition over land and resources (Gewald 2003). British policies toward the Boers (Fourie, Chapter 7) are another early example of expulsion. In the post-colonial era, (non-state) militias have continued to pursue a strategy of absorption in their recruitment of (child) soldiers on a large scale (Laband 2017). Yet, despite these counter-examples, the long-run shift from absorption to expulsion, underpinned by processes of state formation and demographic growth, is clearly visible as a fundamental and consequential transition in the nature and perception of mobility in Africa.

5 A new global diaspora

It is important to emphasize that intra-African migration remains of huge significance today. By 2019, the great majority of African international migrants born south of the Sahara resided in Africa rather than outside the continent: about 19.7 million vs 8.7 million (Manning, Chapter 16). Nevertheless, the steady increase of African migration out of the continent in past decades signifies the end to an era in which the share of cross-border migrants from sub-Saharan Africa finding destinations within the continent exceeded those moving out of the continent by several orders of magnitude. As Table 1.1 shows, in 1960 a mere 0.13% of individuals born in Africa south of the Sahara had migrated out of the continent, against 2.60% within the region. By 2019, these shares were 0.81% and 1.85%, respectively. This means that the ratio of people from sub-Saharan Africa residing in a foreign country *within* the continent to those residing *outside* the continent reduced from 20:1 in 1960 to only 2.3:1 in 2019, a momentous shift. If we include North Africa, where migration was large and overwhelmingly extra-continental, the trend is much less extreme, but still visible, with a ratio declining from 2.6:1 to 1.1:1 in the same period. The gradual shift of migratory movements out of the continent from the 1960s onward cannot be missed: migrants out of Africa increased not only as a share of all African migrants, but also in absolute numbers, and in proportion to the total African population. Moreover, Table 1.1 only documents those who succeeded in realizing their migration aspirations, while

TABLE 1.1 Intra- and extra-continental migration from sub-Saharan Africa and Africa, including North Africa, 1960–2019 (emigrant stocks, numbers per 10,000 residents in Africa)

| | From sub-Saharan Africa | | | | From Africa, including North Africa | | | |
| | Intra-continental | | Extra-continental | | Intra-continental | | Extra-continental | |
	WB	UN	WB	UN	WB	UN	WB	UN
1960	260		13		207		80	
1970	235		23		186		110	
1980	201		40		160		126	
1990	160	262	44	54	128	213	129	117
2000	153	187	53	57	125	157	118	115
2010		163		74		139		141
2019		185		81		162		145

Sources: Migration data from World Bank *Global Bilateral Migration Database,* indicated as WB (Özden et al. 2011) and United Nations, indicated as UN, based on data provided in Patrick Manning's chapter. Population data from United Nations (2019).

Note: The data presented here are migrant stocks, not annual flows, and exclude refugees.

research has shown that there are millions of people across Africa – in some countries, including the Democratic Republic of Congo, Ethiopia, Ghana, and Nigeria, over 30% of the population – whose aspirations to settle abroad have remained unfulfilled, as of yet (Carling and Schewel 2018).

In the concluding epilogue of this volume, we further reflect on the drivers of increasing extra-continental migration of Africans by placing them in a long-run perspective, pointing at the role of fading opportunity gaps in Africa, the heightened restrictions on cross-country migration, and the growing accessibility of extra-continental destinations despite the erection of new barriers, as migration capabilities expand and diaspora networks strengthen (De Haas and Frankema, Chapter 17). Here, it suffices to conclude that while the resurging global diaspora of Africans signifies an end to the age of intra-African migration, this shift is only one in a series of *overlapping* but *distinct* patterns which have characterized African mobility since the early 19th century. Jointly, the chapters in this volume identify these shifting patterns and place them firmly in the view of those with both a historical and a contemporary interest in African migration.

Acknowledgment

We thank all contributors to this volume for their individual chapters and for discussion during author workshops in Wageningen (December 2018) and Barcelona (October 2019), which have crucially contributed to the ideas generated in this introduction. We thank Patrick Manning for his extensive comments on an earlier draft. Ewout Frankema gratefully acknowledges financial support from the Netherlands Organisation for Scientific Research for the project "South-South Divergence: Comparative Histories of Regional Integration in Southeast Asia and Sub-Saharan Africa since 1850" (NWO VICI Grant no. VI.C.201.062).

Notes

1 All references to chapters refer to chapters in "this volume," so we drop this addition from here on.
2 The intercontinental slave trades themselves produced substantial intra-continental mobility, related to raiding, flight, trading, and the overland transportation of enslaved people.
3 Numerous Africans went on pilgrimage to Mecca (Al-Naqar 1972) or served on the frontlines in Europe and Asia during the world wars (Killingray, Chapter 14). Several thousand obtained an education in colonial metropoles, especially since the 1950s. For the case of Africans in Britain, see Killingray (1994).
4 Even today approximately half of all African international migrants remain within their region, in contrast with Latin American and Caribbean international migrants, among whom only 15% stay within their respective regions (Lucas 2015, 1448).
5 In comparison, the shifting population shares of migrant-sending China and India and migrant-receiving Southeast Asia (excluding Japanese colonies, Thailand, and French Indochina) between 1820 and 1940 correspond with a net shift of 75 million people, or 7.4% of the region's total population (our calculations, based on data in Maddison, 2010), which resulted from both differences in natural increase and population mobility. This estimate does not address substantial population shifts *within* Southeast Asia.
6 Our discussion is necessarily condensed. A more comprehensive literature review can be pieced together from historiographical essays, including Swindell (1979), Sunseri (1996), Bilger and Kraler (2005), Bakewell and De Haas (2007), Cordell (2013), Guthrie (2016), Rossi (2018), and Pérez Niño (2019).
7 For example, according to Marfleet (2007, 137–8, also see Elie 2014, 23; Gatrell 2017), the field of refugee studies has even been averse to history, while policy circles "rarely show an interest in migrations of the past."
8 But note that we treat migration to urban areas as *cross-community migration*, because cities were distinct from rural areas with respect to several relevant markers (culture, economy, environment) of what makes up a community.
9 Much less so than in the Americas and Australasia, where indigenous populations were to a much larger extent displaced or exterminated through disease and violence.
10 It should be kept in mind that aspects of a migratory decision can be voluntary (such as the decision to migrate), while others are forced (such as the way the journey is undertaken or the choice of destination).
11 Migration systems typically also involve other important counterflows of information and remittances.
12 The UN bilateral migration data provide a strikingly smaller number (68,329 Chinese residents in Africa in 2019), but these are likely substantially underestimated as they are extrapolated from outdated census data (from before the expansion of Chinese presence in Africa), and because Chinese workers living in compounds may not have been accurately counted in censuses. Such discrepancies warrant caution with the UN data and highlight the need for further refinement of African migration statistics (also see Manning, Chapter 16, this volume).
13 For instance, recruits from Angola and Mozambique were stationed in Portuguese Timor, Gao, and Macau and the Dutch-recruited soldiers from the Gold Coast and Asante to fight in Java (Coelho 2002; Yarak 1997).
14 Colonial soldiers were a distinct type of migrants, but as Killingray (Chapter 14) notes, their enlistment was often motivated by similar incentives that drove voluntary rural and urban migrants.

References

Abaka, Edmund. 2009. "Traders, Slaves and Soldiers. The Hausa Diaspora in Ghana (Gold Coast and Asante) in the Nineteenth and Early Twentieth Centuries." In *Movements, Borders, and Identities in Africa*, edited by Toyin Falola and Aribidesi Usman, 185–99. Rochester, NY: University of Rochester Press.

Adepoju, Aderanti. 2003. "Migration in West Africa." *Development* 46(3): 37–41.

Aina, Tade Akin, and Jonathan Baker. 1995. "Introduction." In *The Migration Experience in Africa*, edited by Jonathan Baker and Tade Akin Aina, 11–25. Uppsala: Nordiska Afrikainstitutet.

Akyeampong, Emmanuel. 2000. "Africans in the Diaspora: The Diaspora and Africa." *African Affairs* 99(395): 183–215.

Allen, Richard. 2015. *European Slave Trading in the Indian Ocean, 1500–1850.* Athens: Ohio University Press.

Allina, Eric. 2012. *Slavery by Any Other Name: African Life under Company Rule in Colonial Mozambique.* Charlottesville: University of Virginia Press.

Al-Naqar, Umar. 1972. *The Pilgrimage Tradition in West Africa: An Historical Study with Special Reference to the Nineteenth Century.* Khartoum: Khartoum University Press.

Amin, Samir. 1972. "Underdevelopment and Dependence in Black Africa—Origins and Contemporary Forms." *The Journal of Modern African Studies* 10(4): 503–24.

Amin, Samir. 1974. "Introduction." In *Modern Migrations in Western Africa*, edited by Samir Amin, 3–126. London: Oxford University Press.

Amin, Samir. 1995. "Migrations in Contemporary Africa: A Retrospective View." In *The Migration Experience in Africa*, edited by Jonathan Baker and Tade Akin Aina, 29–40. Uppsala: Nordiska Afrikainstitutet.

Amselle, Jean-Loup, ed. 1976. *Les Migrations Africaines: Réseaux et Processus Migratoires.* Paris: Maspero.

Arrighi, Giovanni. 1970. "Labour Supplies in Historical Perspective: A Study of the Proletarianization of the African Peasantry in Rhodesia." *The Journal of Development Studies* 6(3): 197–234.

Asserate, Asfa-Wossen. 2018. *African Exodus: Migration and the Future of Europe.* London: Haus Publishing.

Bakewell, Oliver. 2014. "Relaunching Migration Systems." *Migration Studies* 2(3): 300–18.

Bakewell, Oliver, and Hein de Haas. 2007. "African Migrations: Continuities, Discontinuities and Recent Transformations." In *African Alternatives*, edited by Patrick Chabal, Ulf Engel and Leo de Haan, 95–118. Leiden: Brill.

Bassett, Thomas, and Matthew Turner. 2007. "Sudden Shift or Migratory Drift? Fulbe Herd Movements to the Sudano-Guinean Region of West Africa." *Human Ecology* 35(1): 33–49.

Berg, Elliot. 1961. "Backward-Sloping Labor Supply Functions in Dual Economies—The Africa Case." *Quarterly Journal of Economics* 75(3): 468–92.

Berriane, Mohamed, and Hein de Haas. 2012. *African Migrations Research: Innovative Methods and Methodologies.* Trenton: Africa World Press.

Bilger, Veronika, and Albert Kraler. 2005. "African Migrations: Historical Perspectives and Contemporary Dynamics." *Stichproben-Vienna Journal of African Studies* 5(8): 5–21.

Boone, Catherine. 2017. "Sons of the Soil Conflict in Africa: Institutional Determinants of Ethnic Conflict Over Land." *World Development* 96: 276–93.

Bozzoli, Belinda, and Mmantho Nkotsoe. 1991. *Women of Phokeng: Consciousness Life Strategy and Migrancy in South Africa, 1900–1983.* Portsmouth, NH: Heinemann.

Brown, Carolyn, and Marcel Van Der Linden. 2010. "Shifting Boundaries between Free and Unfree Labor: Introduction." *International Labor and Working-Class History* 78: 4–11.

Buell, Raymond. 1928. *The Native Problem in Africa.* New York: The Macmillan Co.

Cadbury, William 1910. *Labour in Portuguese West Africa.* London: Routledge.

Campbell, Gwyn, ed. 2004. *The Structure of Slavery in Indian Ocean Africa and Asia.* London: Frank Cass.

Campbell, Gwyn, ed. 2005. *Abolition and its Aftermath in Indian Ocean Africa and Asia.* London; New York: Routledge.

Carling, Jørgen, and Kerilyn Schewel. 2018. "Revisiting Aspiration and Ability in International Migration." *Journal of Ethnic and Migration Studies* 44(6): 945–63.

Cernea, Michael 1997. *African Involuntary Population Resettlement in a Global Context.* World Bank Environment Department Papers, Social Assessment Series 045.

Challenor, Herschelle Sullivan. 1979. Strangers as Colonial Intermediaries: The Dahomeyans in Francophone Africa. In *Strangers in African Societies*, edited by William Shack and Elliott Skinner, 67–84. Berkeley: University of California Press.

Clemens, Michael. 2020. "The Emigration Life Cycle: How Development Shapes Emigration from Poor Countries." Center for Global Development Working Paper 540.

Coelho, João Paulo Borges. 2002. "African Troops in the Portuguese Colonial Army, 1961–1974: Angola, Guinea-Bissau and Mozambique." *Portuguese Studies Review* 10(1): 129–50.

Cohen, Robin. 1995. "Part Six: Migration in Africa." In *Cambridge Survey of World Migration*, edited by Robin Cohen, 159–61. Cambridge: Cambridge University Press.

Cohen, Robin. 2019. "Strangers and Migrants in the Making of African Societies: A Conceptual and Historical Review." *Fudan Journal of the Humanities and Social Sciences* 12(1): 45–59.

Cooper, Frederick. 1996. *Decolonization and African Society: The Labor Question in French and British Africa.* Cambridge: Cambridge University Press.

Coquery-Vidrovitch, Catherine. 2005. *The History of African Cities South of the Sahara: From the Origins to Colonization.* Princeton, NJ: Markus Wiener Publishers.

Coquery-Vidrovitch, Catherine. 2021. "African Slavery in the Nineteenth Century: Inseparable Partner of the Atlantic Slave Trade." In *The Atlantic and Africa: the Second Slavery and Beyond*, edited by Dale Tomich and Paul Lovejoy, 7–17. New York: SUNY Press.

Cordell, Dennis 2013. "Interdependence and Convergence: Migration, Men, Women, and Work in Sub-Saharan Africa, 1800–1975." In *Proletarian and Gendered Mass Migrations. A Global Perspective on Continuities and Discontinuities from the 19th to the 21st Centuries*, edited by Dirk Hoerder, and Amarjit Kaur, 175–215. Leiden: Brill.

Cordell, Dennis, Joel Gregory, and Victor Piché. 1996. *Hoe and Wage: A Social History of a Circular Migration System in West Africa.* Boulder, CO: Westview Press.

Curtin, Philip 1984. *Cross-Cultural Trade in World History.* Cambridge: Cambridge University Press.

Curtin, Philip 1997. "Africa and Global Patterns of Migration." In *Global History and Migrations*, edited by Gungwu Wang, 63–94. Boulder, CO: Westview Press.

Curtin, Philip, Steven Feierman, Leonard Thompson, and Jan Vansina. 1995. *African History: From Earliest Times to Independence.* London and New York: Longman.

De Bruijn, Mirjam, and Han van Dijk. 2003. "Changing Population Mobility in West Africa: Fulbe Pastoralists in Central and South Mali." *African Affairs* 102(407): 285–307.

De Bruijn, Mirjam, Rijk van Dijk, and Dick Foeken, eds. 2001. *Mobile Africa: Changing Patterns of Movement in Africa and Beyond.* Leiden: Brill.

De Haas, Hein. 2008. "The Myth of Invasion: The Inconvenient Realities of African Migration to Europe." *Third World Quarterly* 29(7): 1305–22.

De Haas, Hein. 2010. "The Internal Dynamics of Migration Processes: A Theoretical Inquiry." *Journal of Ethnic and Migration Studies* 36(10): 1587–617.

De Haas, Hein. 2019. "Paradoxes of Migration and Development." International Migration Institute Working Paper 1957 (MADE Project Paper 9).

De Haas, Hein, Stephen Castles, and Mark Miller. 2020. "Migrations Shaping African History." Companion Website to *The Age of Migration: International Population Movements in the Modern World*, edited by Hein De Haas, Stephen Castles, and Mark Miller. London: Red Globe Press. Accessed 23 June, 2021. http://www.age-of-migration.com/additional-case-studies.

De Haas, Michiel. 2019. "Moving Beyond Colonial Control? Economic Forces and Shifting Migration from Ruanda-Urundi to Buganda, 1920–60." *Journal of African History* 60(3): 379–406.

De Wet, Chris. 1994. "Resettlement and Land Reform in South Africa." *Review of African Political Economy* 21(61): 359–73.

Deutsch, Jan-Georg. 2006. *Emancipation without Abolition in German East Africa, c. 1884–1914.* Woodbridge: James Currey Publishers.

Dinkelman, Taryn, and Martine Mariotti. 2016. "The Long-Run Effects of Labor Migration on Human Capital Formation in Communities of Origin." *American Economic Journal: Applied Economics* 8(4): 1–35.

Dougnon, Isaïe. 2007. *Travail de Blanc, Travail de Noir: La Migration des Paysans Dogon vers l'Office du Niger et au Ghana, 1910–1980.* Paris: Karthala.

Eldridge, Claire. 2016. *From Empire to Exile: History and Memory Within the Pied-Noir and Harki Communities, 1962–2012.* Manchester: Manchester University Press.

Elie, Jerome. 2014. "Histories of Refugee and Forced Migration Studies." In *Oxford Handbook of Refugee & Forced Migration Studies*, edited by Elena Fiddian-Qasmiyeh, Gil Loescher, Katy Long, and Nando Sigona, 23–35. Oxford: Oxford University Press.

Elkan, Walter. 1959. "Migrant Labor in Africa: an Economist's Approach." *American Economic Review* 49(2): 188–97.

Eltis, David. 1983. "Free and Coerced Transatlantic Migrations: Some Comparisons." *American Historical Review* 88(2): 251–80.

Eltis, David. 2000. *The Rise of African Slavery in the Americas*. Cambridge: Cambridge University Press.

Eltis, David. 2002. *Coerced and Free Migration: Global Perspectives*. Stanford, CA: Stanford University Press.

Erdal, Marta Bivand, and Ceri Oeppen. 2018. "Forced to Leave? The Discursive and Analytical Significance of Describing Migration as Forced and Voluntary." *Journal of Ethnic and Migration Studies* 44(6): 981–98.

European Commission, Joint Research Centre. 2018. *Many More to Come? Migration from and within Africa*. Publications Office of the European Union, Luxembourg.

Fay, Marianne, and Charlotte Opal. 2000. "Urbanization without Growth: A Not-So-Uncommon Phenomenon." World Bank Policy Research Working Paper 2412.

Ferenczi, Imre, and Walter Willcox. 1929. *International Migrations, Volume 1: Statistics*. New York: National Bureau of Economic Research.

Fernandez, Bina. 2013. "Borders and Boundaries: Containing African International Migration." In *Handbook of Africa's International Relations*, edited by Timothy Murithi, 134–44. London and New York: Routledge.

Findley, Sally. 1994. "Does Drought Increase Migration? A Study of Migration from Rural Mali during the 1983–1985 Drought." *International Migration Review* 28(3): 539–53.

Flahaux, Marie-Laurence, and Hein de Haas. 2016. "African Migration: Trends, Patterns, Drivers." *Comparative Migration Studies* 4(1): 1–25.

Fox, Sean. 2012. "Urbanization as a Global Historical Process: Theory and Evidence from Sub-Saharan Africa." *Population and Development Review* 38(2): 285–310.

Frankema, Ewout and Morten Jerven. 2014. "Writing History Backwards or Sideways: Towards a Consensus on African population, 1850–2010." *Economic History Review* 67(4): 907–31.

Frankema, Ewout, Jeffrey Williamson, and Pieter Woltjer. 2018. "An Economic Rationale for the West African Scramble? The Commercial Transition and the Commodity Price Boom of 1835–1885." *The Journal of Economic History* 78(1): 231–67.

Frederick, Katharine. 2020. *Deindustrialization in East Africa: Textile Production in an Era of Globalization and Colonization, c. 1830–1940*. London: Palgrave McMillan.

French, Howard. 2015. *China's Second Continent: How a Million Migrants are Building a New Empire in Africa*. New York: Alfred A. Knopf.

Freund, Bill. 2007. *The African City: A History*. Cambridge: Cambridge University Press.

Gatrell, Peter. 2013. *The Making of the Modern Refugee*. Oxford: Oxford University Press.

Gerold-Scheepers, Thérèse, and Wim van Binsbergen. 1978. "Marxist and Non-Marxist Approaches to Migration in Tropical Africa." *African Perspectives* 1: 21–35.

Geschiere, Peter. 2009. *The Perils of Belonging: Autochthony, Citizenship, and Exclusion in Africa and Europe*. Chicago, IL: University of Chicago Press.

Gewald, Jan-Bart. 2003. "The Herero Genocide: German Unity, Settlers, Soldiers, and Ideas." In *Die (koloniale) Begegnung: AfrikanerInnen in Deutschland (1880–1945), Deutsche in Afrika (1880–1918)*, edited by Marianne Bechhaus-Gerst, and Reinhard Klein-Arendt, 109–27. Frankfurt am Main: Peter Lang.

Gewald, Jan-Bart, Sabine Luning, and Klaas van Walraven, eds. 2009. *The Speed of Change: Motor Vehicles and People in Africa, 1890–2000*. Leiden: Brill.

Gupta, Sanjeev, Catherine Pattillo, and Smita Wagh. 2009. "Effect of Remittances on Poverty and Financial Development in Sub-Saharan Africa." *World Development* 37(1): 104–15.

Guthrie, Zachary. 2016. "Introduction: Histories of Mobility, Histories of Labor, Histories of Africa." *African Economic History* 44(1): 1–17.

Hance, William. 1970. *Population, Migration, and Urbanization in Africa*. New York: Columbia University Press.

Hanson, John. 1996. *Migration, Jihad, and Muslim Authority in West Africa: The Futanke Colonies in Karta*. Bloomington: Indiana University Press.

Harries, Patrick. 1981. "Slavery, Social Incorporation and Surplus Extraction; the Nature of Free and Unfree Labour in South-East Africa." *Journal of African History* 22(3): 309–30.

Harries, Patrick. 1994. *Work, Culture, and Identity: Migrant Laborers in Mozambique and South Africa, c. 1860–1910*. Portsmouth, NH: Heinemann.

Harries, Patrick. 2014. "Slavery, Indenture and Migrant Labour: Maritime Immigration from Mozambique to the Cape, c. 1780–1880." *African Studies* 73(3): 323–40.

Harris, John, and Michael Todaro. 1970. "Migration, Unemployment and Development: A Two-Sector Analysis." *American Economic Review* 60(1): 126–42.

Harris, Joseph, ed. 1993. *Global Dimensions of the African Diaspora* [second revised edition]. Washington, DC: Howard University Press.

Hatton, Tim, and Jeffrey Williamson. 1998. *The Age of Mass Migration: Causes and Economic Impact*. Oxford: Oxford University Press.

Hatton, Tim, and Jeffrey Williamson. 2003. "Demographic and Economic Pressure on Emigration out of Africa." *Scandinavian Journal of Economics* 105(3): 465–86.

Hatton, Tim, and Jeffrey Williamson. 2005. *Global Migration and the World Economy: Two Centuries of Policy and Performance*. Cambridge, MA: MIT Press.

Herbst, Jeffrey. 1990. "Migration, the Politics of Protest, and State Consolidation in Africa." *African Affairs* 89(355): 183–203.

Herbst, Jeffrey. 2000. *States and Power in Africa: Comparative Lessons in Authority and Control*. Princeton, NJ: Princeton University Press.

Hill, Polly. 1963. *The Migrant Cocoa-Farmers of Southern Ghana: A Study in Rural Capitalism*. Cambridge: Cambridge University Press.

Hoppe, Kirk Arden. 2003. *Lords of the Fly: Sleeping Sickness Control in British East Africa, 1900–1960*. Westport, CT: Praeger.

Horn, James, and Philip Morgan. 2005. "Settlers and Slaves: European and African Migrations to Early Modern British America." In *The Creation of the British Atlantic World*, edited by Elizabeth Mancke and Carole Shammas, 19–44. Baltimore, MD: Johns Hopkins University Press.

Huff, Gregg, and Giovanni Caggiano. 2007. "Globalization, Immigration, and Lewisian Elastic Labor in Pre-World War II Southeast Asia." *Journal of Economic History* 67(1): 33–68.

IOM. 2019. *Glossary on Migration*. Geneva: International Organization for Migration.

Jedwab, Remi, and Alexander Moradi. 2016. "The Permanent Effects of Transportation Revolutions in Poor Countries: Evidence from Africa." *Review of Economics and Statistics* 98(2): 268–84.

Kane, Abdoulaye, and Todd Leedy. 2013. *African Migrations: Patterns and Perspectives*. Bloomington: Indiana University Press.

Killingray, David, ed. 1994. *Africans in Britain*. London and New York: Routledge.

Klein, Herbert. 2010. *The Atlantic Slave Trade*. Cambridge and New York: Cambridge University Press.

Klein, Martin. 1998. *Slavery and Colonial Rule in French West Africa*. Cambridge: Cambridge University Press.

Kopytoff, Igor. 1987. "The Internal African Frontier: The Making of African Political Culture." In *The African Frontier: The Reproduction of Traditional African Societies*, edited by Igor Kopytoff, 3–84. Bloomington: Indiana University Press.

Kuper, Hilda, ed. 1965. *Urbanization and Migration in West Africa*. Oakland: University of California Press.

Laband, John. 2017. "The Slave Soldiers of Africa." *Journal of Military History* 81(1): 9–38.

Law, Robin, ed. 1995. *From Slave Trade to 'Legitimate' Commerce: the Commercial Transition in Nineteenth-Century West Africa*. Cambridge: Cambridge University Press.

Lee, Everett. 1966. "A Theory of Migration." *Demography* 3(1): 47–57.

Lewis, Arthur. 1954. "Economic Development with Unlimited Supplies of Labour." *Manchester School* 22(2): 139–91.

Lovejoy, Paul. 2005. *Slavery, Commerce and Production in the Sokoto Caliphate of West Africa*. Trenton, NJ: Africa World Press.

Lovejoy, Paul. 2012. *Transformations in Slavery: A History of Slavery in Africa*. Cambridge: Cambridge University Press.

Lovejoy, Paul, and Jan Hogendorn. 1993. *Slow Death for Slavery: The Course of Abolition in Northern Nigeria, 1897–1936*. Cambridge: Cambridge University Press.

Lubkemann, Stephen. 2008. "Involuntary Immobility: On a Theoretical Invisibility in Forced Migration studies." *Journal of Refugee Studies* 21(4): 454–75.

Lucas, Robert. 2015. "African Migration." In *Handbook of the Economics of International Migration, Volume 1B*, edited by Barry Chiswick, and Paul Miller, 1445–1596. Amsterdam: Elsevier.

Lucassen, Jan, and Leo Lucassen. 2009. "The Mobility Transition Revisited, 1500–1900: What the Case of Europe Can Offer to Global History." *Journal of Global History* 4(3): 347–77.

Lucassen, Jan, and Leo Lucassen, eds. 2014. *Globalising Migration History: the Eurasian Experience (16th–21st Centuries)*. Leiden: Brill.

Lucassen, Jan, and Leo Lucassen. 2017. "Migration over Cultural Boundaries: A Rejoinder." *International Review of Social History* 62: 521–35.

Lydon, Ghislaine. 2009. *On Trans-Saharan Trails: Islamic Law, Trade Networks, and Cross-Cultural Exchange in Nineteenth-Century Western Africa*. Cambridge: Cambridge University Press.

Mabogunje, Akin. 1968. *Urbanization in Nigeria*. London: University of London Press.

Mabogunje, Akin. 1970. "Systems Approach to a Theory of Rural-Urban Migration." *Geographical Analysis* 2(1): 1–18.

Machava, Benedito. 2019. "Reeducation Camps, Austerity, and the Carceral Regime in Socialist Mozambique (1974–79)." *Journal of African History* 60(3): 429–55.

Maddison, Angus. 2010. "Historical Statistics of the World Economy: 1–2008 AD." http://www.ggdc.net/maddison/oriindex.htm

Manchuelle, François. 1997. *Willing Migrants: Soninke Labor Diasporas, 1848–1960*. Athens: Ohio University Press.

Manning, Patrick. 1990. *Slavery and African Life: Occidental, Oriental, and African Slave Trades*. Cambridge: Cambridge University Press.

Manning, Patrick. 2006. Cross-Community Migration: A Distinctive Human Pattern. *Social Evolution & History* 5(2): 24–54.

Manning, Patrick. 2010. "African Population: Projections, 1851–1961." In *The Demographics of Empire. The Colonial Order and the Creation of Knowledge*, edited by Karl Ittmann, Dennis Cordell, and Gregory Maddox, 245–75. Athens: Ohio University Press.

Manning, Patrick. 2021. "The 'Second Slavery' in Africa: Migration and Political Economy in the Nineteenth Century." In *The Atlantic and Africa: The Second Slavery and Beyond*, edited by Dale Tomich and Paul Lovejoy, 203–15. New York: SUNY Press.

Manning, Patrick, with Tiffany Trimmer. 2020. *Migration in World History* (3rd edn). New York: Routledge.

Marfleet, Philip. 2007. Refugees and History: Why We Must Address the Past. *Refugee Survey Quarterly* 26(3): 136–48.

Mathys, Gillian. 2021. "Questioning Territories and Identities in the Precolonial (Nineteenth-Century) Lake Kivu Region." *Africa* 91(3): 493–515.

Matory, J. Lorand. 1999. "The English Professors of Brazil: On the Diasporic Roots of the Yorùbá Nation." *Comparative Studies in Society and History* 41(1): 72–103.

Mbembe, Achille. 2000. "At the Edge of the World: Boundaries, Territoriality, and Sovereignty in Africa," trans. By Steven Rendall. *Public Culture* 12(1): 259–84.

McKeown, Adam. 2004. "Global Migration, 1846–1940." *Journal of World History* 15(2): 155–89.

McKeown, Adam. 2010. "Chinese Emigration in Global Context, 1850–1940." *Journal of Global History* 5(1): 95–124.

Migrant Observatory. 2019. "Who Counts as a Migrant? Definitions and Their Consequences." *The Migration Observatory at the University of Oxford*. 10 July 2019. https://migrationobservatory.ox.ac.uk/resources/briefings/who-counts-as-a-migrant-definitions-and-their-consequences/.

Mitchell, Clyde. 1959. "Migrant Labour in Africa South of the Sahara: The Causes of Labour Migration." *Bulletin of the Inter-African Labour Institute* 6(1): 12–46.

Moch, Leslie Page. 1992. *Moving Europeans. Migration in Western Europe since 1650*. Bloomington: Indiana University Press.

Moyo, Innocent, Jussi Laine, and Christopher Changwe Nshimbi. 2021. *Intra-Africa Migrations: Reimaging Borders and Migration Management*. Abingdon: Routledge.

Mueller, Valerie, Clark Gray, and Douglas Hopping. 2020. "Climate-Induced Migration and Unemployment in Middle-Income Africa." *Global Environmental Change* 65: 102183.

Myint, Hla. 1958. "The 'Classical Theory' of International Trade and the Underdeveloped Countries." *The Economic Journal*, 68(270): 317–37.

Nicholson, Sharon, Amin Dezfuli, and Douglas Klotter. 2012. "A Two-Century Precipitation Dataset for the Continent of Africa." *Bulletin of the American Meteorological Society* 93(8): 1219–31.

Northrup, David. 1995. *Indentured Labour in the Age of Imperialism*. Cambridge: Cambridge University Press.

Nugent, Paul, and Anthony Asiwaju, eds. 1996. *African Boundaries: Barriers, Conduits, and Opportunities*. London: Pinter.

Ogura, Mitsuo. 1996. "Urbanization and Apartheid in South Africa: Influx Controls and Their Abolition. *Developing Economies* 34(4): 402–23.

Okia, Opolot. 2012. *Communal Labor in Colonial Kenya: The Legitimization of Coercion, 1912–1930*. New York: Palgrave Macmillan.

Orde-Browne, Granville St. John. 1933. *The African Labourer*. Oxford: Oxford University Press.

Oucho, John, and William Gould. 1993. "Internal Migration, Urbanization, and Population Distribution." In *Demographic Change in Sub-Saharan Africa*, edited by Karen Foote, Kenneth Hill, and Linda Martin, 256–96. Washington, DC: National Research Council, Committee on Population.

Özden, Çağlar, Christopher Parsons, Maurice Schiff, and Terrie Walmsley. 2011. "Where on Earth Is Everybody? The Evolution of Global Bilateral Migration 1960–2000." *World Bank Economic Review* 25(1): 12–56.

Penvenne, Jeanne Marie. 2015. *Women, Migration and the Cashew Economy in Southern Mozambique, 1945–1975*. Woodbridge: James Currey.

Pérez Niño, Helena. 2019. "Labour Migration." *General Labour History of Africa: Workers, Employers and Governments, 20th–21st Centuries*, edited by Stefano Bellucci and Andreas Eckert, 265–300. Woodbridge: James Currey.

Piché, Victor, and Dennis Cordell. 2015. *Entre le Mil et le Franc. Un Siècle de Migrations Circulaires en Afrique de l'Ouest: le Cas du Burkina Faso*. Québec: Presses de l'Université du Québec.

Potts, Deborah. 2012. "What Do We Know About Urbanisation in Sub-Saharan Africa and Does It Matter?" *International Development Planning Review* 34(1): v–xxii.

Prothero, Mansell. 1965. *Migrants and Malaria*. London: Longmans, Green & Co.

Razy, Élodie, and Marie Rodet, eds. 2016. *Children on the Move in Africa: Past and Present Experiences of Migration*. Woodbridge: James Currey.

Read, Margaret. 1942. "Migrant Labour in Africa and Its Effects on Tribal Life." *International Labour Review* 45(6): 605–31.

Reid, Richard. 2012. *Warfare in African History*. Cambridge: Cambridge University Press.

Richards, Audrey. 1954. *Economic Development and Tribal Change: A Study of Immigrant Labour in Buganda*. Cambridge: W. Heffer & Sons ltd.

Rigaud, Kanta Kumari, Alex de Sherbinin, Alex, Bryan Jones, Jonas Bergmann, Viviane Clement, Kayly Ober, Jacob Schewe, Susana Adama, Brent McCusker, Silke Heuser, and Amelia Midgley. 2018. *Groundswell: Preparing for Internal Climate Migration*. Washington, DC: World Bank.

Roberts, Andrew. 1962. "The Sub-Imperialism of the Baganda." *The Journal of African History* 3(3): 435–50.

Rockel, Stephen. 2006. *Carriers of Culture: Labor on the Road in Nineteenth-Century East Africa*. Portsmouth, NH: Heinemann.

Rodet, Marie. 2009. *Les Migrantes Ignorées du Haut-Sénégal (1900–1946)*. Paris: Karthala.

Ross, Edward Alsworth. 1925. *Report on Employment of Native Labor in Portuguese Africa*. New York: Abbott Press.

Rossi, Benedetta. 2014. "Migration and Emancipation in West Africa's Labour History: The Missing Links." *Slavery & Abolition* 35(1): 23–46.

Rossi, Benedetta. 2018. "Migration History and Historiography." In *Oxford Research Encyclopedia of African History*, edited by Thomas Spear. Oxford: Oxford University Press. https://oxfordre.com/africanhistory

Schapera, Isaac. 1947. *Migrant Labour and Tribal Life. A Study of Conditions in the Bechuanaland Protectorate*. Oxford: Oxford University Press.

Scheele, Judith. 2012. *Smugglers and Saints of the Sahara: Regional Connectivity in the Twentieth Century*. Cambridge: Cambridge University Press.

Schewel, Kerilyn. 2020. "Understanding Immobility: Moving Beyond the Mobility Bias in Migration Studies." *International Migration Review* 54(2): 328–55.

Schmidt-Soltau, Kai. 2003. "Conservation–Related Resettlement in Central Africa: Environmental and Social Risks." *Development and Change* 34(3): 525–51.

Siegelbaum, Lewis, and Leslie Page Moch. 2015. *Broad Is My Native Land: Repertoires and Regimes of Migration in Russia's Twentieth Century*. Ithaca, NY: Cornell University Press.

Smith, Stephen. 2019. *The Scramble for Europe: Young Africa on Its Way to the Old Continent*. Hoboken, NJ: John Wiley & Sons.

Stichter, Sharon. 1985. *Migrant Laborers*. Cambridge: Cambridge University Press.

Sunseri, Thaddeus. 1996. "Labour Migration in Colonial Tanzania and the Hegemony of South African Historiography." *African Affairs* 95(381): 581–98.

Sunseri, Thaddeus. 2018. "The African Rinderpest Panzootic, 1888–1897. In *Oxford Research Encyclopedia of African History*, edited by Thomas Spear. Oxford: Oxford University Press.

Swindell, Kenneth. 1979. "Labour Migration in Underdeveloped Countries: The Case of Subsaharan Africa." *Progress in Geography* 3(2): 239–59.

Tomich, Dale. 2004. "The Second Slavery: Bonded Labor and the Transformation of the Nineteenth-Century World Economy." In *Through the Prism of Slavery: Labor, Capital, and World Economy*, edited by Dale Tomich, 56–74. Lanham, MD: Rowmand & Littlefield.

UNHCR. 2016. "UNHCR Viewpoint: 'Refugee' or 'Migrant' – Which Is Right?" *United Nations High Commissioner for Refugees*, 11 July 2016. https://www.unhcr.org/news/latest/2016/7/55df0e556/unhcr-viewpoint-refugee-migrant-right.html.

UNDP. 2019. *Scaling Fences: Voices of Irregular African Migrants to Europe*. https://www.africa.undp.org/content/rba/en/home/library/reports/ScalingFences.html

United Nations. 2019. "World Population Prospects 2019: Highlights." United Nations: Department of Economic and Social Affairs, Population Division.

Usman, Aribidesi, and Toyin Falola. 2009. "Migrations in African History: An Introduction." In *Movements, Borders, and Identities in Africa*, edited by Toyin Falola and Aribidesi Usman, 1–34. Rochester, NY: University of Rochester Press.

Van Beusekom, Monica. 2002. *Negotiating Development: African Farmers and Colonial Experts at the Office du Niger, 1920–1960*. London: Heinemann.

Van Hear, Nicholas, Oliver Bakewell, and Katy Long. 2018. "Push-Pull Plus: Reconsidering the Drivers of Migration." *Journal of Ethnic and Migration Studies* 44(6): 927–44.

Van Leeuwen, Mathijs. 2001. "Rwanda's Imidugudu Programme and Earlier Experiences with Villagisation and Resettlement in East Africa." *Journal of Modern African Studies* 39(4): 623–44.

Van Onselen, Charles. 1976. *Chibaro: African Mine Labour in Southern Rhodesia, 1900–1933*. London: Pluto Press.

Van Waijenburg, Marlous. 2018. "Financing the African Colonial State: The Revenue Imperative and Forced Labor." *Journal of Economic History* 78(1): 40–80.

Vigneswaran, Darshan, and Joel Quirk, eds. 2015. *Mobility Makes States: Migration and Power in Africa*. Philadelphia: University of Pennsylvania Press.

Walker, Cherryl. 1990. "Gender and the Development of the Migrant System, c. 1850–1930: An Overview." In *Women and gender in Southern Africa to 1945*, edited by Cherryl Walker, 168–96. London: James Currey.

Walther, Olivier. 2015. "Business, Brokers and Borders: The Structure of West African Trade Networks." *Journal of Development Studies* 51(5): 603–20.

Williams, Christian A. 2020. "Editor's Introduction: African Refugee History." *African Studies Review* 63(3): 560–67.

Wolpe, Harold. 1972. "Capitalism and Cheap Labour-Power in South Africa: from Segregation to Apartheid." *Economy and Society* 1(4): 425–56.

Yarak, Larry. 1997. "New Sources for the Study of Akan Slavery and Slave Trade: Dutch Military Recruitment in Asante and the Gold Coast, 1831–72." *Source Material for Studying the Slave Trade and the African Diaspora*, edited by Robin Law, 35–60. Stirling: University of Stirling.

PART ONE

Slavery and Migration in the 19th Century

2

MIGRATION IN THE CONTEXTS OF SLAVING AND STATES IN 19TH-CENTURY WEST AFRICA

Gareth Austin

1 Introduction

In the scholarly literature, pre-colonial West Africa is noted for high spatial mobility, both in the positive sense proclaimed in Igor Kopytoff's celebrated essay of 1987, "The internal African frontier: the making of African political culture," and in the negative one encapsulated in depictions of lines of chained people being marched to market, for sale as slaves, whether their final destinations were within or without the region. Some wars produced a different kind of forced migration, where populations were uncaptured but displaced. There was also low-volume but commercially significant migration in the context of the religious and ethnic trading diasporas through which the long-distance trades of most of the region were conducted. The colonial occupation disrupted intra-regional trade, but the early years of the 20th century saw thousands of the displaced, and tens of thousands of former slaves, return home. This chapter examines the two major theories of migration, free and forced, that have been applied to pre-colonial West Africa. It does so in the context of the major drivers of change in the 19th century: the commercial transition in the Atlantic trade, from the export of captives to "legitimate commerce"; the Sufi jihads that swept over most of the savannas, establishing new states and, in the case of the Sokoto Caliphate, the largest market in West Africa; and, especially in the last decade of the century, the European colonization of the region (Liberia apart).

The substantive discussion is organized in five sections. The first enlarges the above introduction to the region and period. The second sets out four propositions, which I argue are broadly justified generalizations about the region in this period, as a framework for what follows. Two of these propositions are direct premises of the theories of free and forced migration: Kopytoff's model and the Nieboer-Domar hypothesis. These theories are presented and considered against the evidence in the third and fourth sections, respectively. The fifth section reviews further forms of migration and considers how the emergence of export agriculture began to change the hitherto prevailing "Nieboer-Domar conditions." It thereby points to a fundamental change in the nature of the predominant form of the labor market, and thereby of migration, that was to proceed further during the early decades of the 20th century.

DOI: 10.4324/9781003225027-4

2 The 19th century in West Africa: notes on times and spaces[1]

The 1807 British abolition act was the effective beginning of the end of the Atlantic slave trade from West Africa (as distinct from West-Central Africa) (Lovejoy 2012). That left the trans-Saharan slave trade, which is thought to have been at its most intense during the 19th century, declining only near the end of the century (and not yet stopping completely), after the French conquest of the Sahara.[2] Over the century as a whole (1801–1900), the best estimate is that nearly 2 million enslaved people were sold into either the Atlantic or Saharan trades from West Africa, the latter constituting 31.6% of the total (Austen 1979; Eltis et al. 2019). Just under a million of the 1,356,872 estimated to have been shipped from West Africa during the century departed after 1807. The last embarkations from the Windward Coast and Gold Coast were in 1840; the last of all from West Africa were from the Bight of Benin in 1863 (Eltis et al. 2019). Thus, the commercial transition from the export of human captives to that of agricultural commodities such as palm oil and groundnuts was protracted and locally varied (Hopkins 1973/2019, ch. 4; Law 1995; Lynn 1997; Swindell and Jeng 2006; Inikori 2009). The other great change of the early and middle 19th century came not from the coast but from the interior: a wave of Sufi jihads across the savanna and Sahel, which reached its greatest territorial and demographic extent in that period (Lovejoy 2016).

It is important to emphasize that, in West Africa, not only the period of the commercial transition, but the 19th century as a whole, was mainly pre-colonial. For nearly three-quarters of the century European territorial control in West Africa was confined to a few towns or small territories, on islands or on the coast. Even in Sierra Leone, which became a British colony in 1808, colonial authority was not extended to the hinterland until 1896. The first extension of British control beyond pinpricks on the coast had come in 1874, with the declaration of a protectorate over approximately the southern quarter of what is now Ghana. France had consolidated its control in the Lower Senegal Valley during 1854–65, by a mixture of trade, diplomacy, and force. But it was not until 1879 that the mechanism of interactive imperial aggression accurately described as the "Scramble" began, with the French setting out from their existing possessions in Senegal on a march of invasion eastward which eventually challenged their rivals to either join the land grab or see their trading interests fall under French sovereignty. Even so, the great majority of the people of West Africa, including "Nigeria" (Lagos excepted) and the other three-quarters of "Ghana," were free of colonial invasion until the 1890s. Indeed, John Hargreaves noted that "only in the 1890s did the gravity of the threat to African independence become generally apparent" (Hargreaves 1987, 405). The Borno kingdom and the Sokoto Caliphate, comprising what became Northern Nigeria, were conquered only in 1902 and 1903, respectively. At the conquest Northern Nigeria had probably at least a quarter of the whole population of West Africa, as it did when censuses became relatively reliable. When colonial occupation began, for most of the territories and even populations concerned, it was thin. Until well into the 20th century, for instance, the part of Gambia north of the river was administered by a "travelling commissioner," who, with no permanent base within the district, would simply tour it during the dry season.

Not surprisingly, the early colonial governments did not leave historians detailed numerical data on many things; still less did the independent indigenous polities that preceded them. We have some sources, but where information on migration *within* pre-colonial West Africa is precise, it is usually qualitative.

3 Land and population: a framework for analyzing pre-colonial migration in West Africa

An intriguing feature of pre-colonial migration as a subject of study is that the theories applied to it, Kopytoff's "internal African frontier" and the Nieboer-Domar hypothesis about the economics of slavery, start from similar premises yet seek to account for contrasting outcomes. This section sets out a framework for thinking about pre-colonial migration, in the form of four propositions. Proposition I is that average population density was low in West Africa until well into the 20th century. Proposition II, related but different, is that labor was scarce in relation to land (as well as to capital, as is true almost by definition in all but the most prosperous of pre-industrial societies). Thus, at least within a given year, the expansion of output in the major economic activity, agriculture, was constrained by the availability and cost of labor rather than of cultivable land. Proposition III is that the natural environment, while offering many possibilities for land-extensive methods in both arable and pastoral farming, offered major obstacles to land-intensive agriculture. To define the distinction, intensive agriculture involves high ratios of capital and/or labor per unit of cultivable land; extensive agriculture is the opposite. Proposition IV is that the first three conditions combined to make political centralization hard – though not impossible – to achieve. The first two of these propositions are explicitly given as premises of one or the other theory. The other two propositions reinforce the logic of the first pair.

All these propositions are broadly justified, I would argue. On the first, Patrick Manning has recently revised his estimates of population in African history, arguing that numbers were higher before 1900 than previously recognized (Manning 2014). This view has been challenged by the alternative estimates of Ewout Frankema and Morten Jerven (2014). But even Manning's figures imply a population density low enough to be consistent with Kopytoff's claim, to be discussed below, that open frontiers existed within West Africa.

The second proposition, about the land/labor ratio in pre-colonial West Africa, was presented and detailed in A. G. Hopkins' classic analysis of 1973 (Hopkins 1973/2019, ch. 2). In 2008 I reviewed it for sub-Saharan Africa as a whole, concluding that it continues to fit the evidence for the agricultural year as a whole, though I reinforced such qualifications as the availability of a labor surplus in the middle of the agricultural off-season, when labor was cheaply accessible for long-distance trading, mining, and handicraft production (Austin 2008). Again, in my view, even Manning's revised population estimates do not alter the conclusion that the labor/land ratio was low, though they amend its scale (see further, Frankema 2019). The northern belt of West Africa is desert. But even in relation to cultivable land, the supply-side constraint on the expansion of output in the region was labor. For instance, I have argued elsewhere that the "vent for surplus" models, which posit that the labor inputs that made possible the rapid growth of export agriculture during the early colonial period came out of a reserve of leisure, emphatically do not work for most of tropical Africa: with one notable exception, the labor inputs were re-allocated from existing activities (Austin 2014a, 2014b). The exception was the oil palm belt of southeast Nigeria, where, judging from Susan Martin's study of Ngwa district, the labor requirements of export agriculture were modest enough to be met from underemployed labor (Martin 1988). But one assumption of the "vent for surplus" models that does apply in most of early 20th-century West Africa, including the oil palm belt of southeast Nigeria, is that there was some sort of land surplus (Austin 2014a, 2014b).

40 Gareth Austin

The third proposition refers to a range of constraints that the physical environment imposed on economic activity in West Africa in this period. These included animal diseases, especially trypanosomiasis (the animal form of sleeping sickness), transmitted by the tsetse fly, which was present throughout the forests of West Africa, while fly belts occupied shifting portions of the savannas. Where the fly was present, large animals would die: hence cattle keeping tended to be limited to small, resistant breeds, and over much of the region animals were not available to pull plows, or as a means of transport. That increased the pain of the shortage of navigable rivers, at least until mechanized transport began to be introduced early in the colonial period. Finally, soil fertility was largely concentrated in a very thin layer of topsoil, most of the fertility actually being embodied in the vegetation. Soils were therefore very vulnerable to erosion, which ruled out the heavy plow, even had there been animals to pull it. Most West African farmers of this period had to be content with hoe agriculture, which they adapted effectively to their ecological and economic conditions, for example, by multi-cropping and avoiding clear felling. The limited opportunities for intensive agriculture limited the scope for food surpluses, but the abundance of cultivable land offered potential for land-extensive agricultural innovation.[3]

The fourth proposition, that centralizing political power – forming states, still more so forming large states – was difficult, is long established in the literature. The comparative historical anthropologist Jack Goody, the then-Marxist historian Catherine Coquery-Vidrovitch, and more recently the rational-choice political scientist Jeffrey Herbst have all argued that state construction was impeded by the difficulty in extracting agricultural surpluses sufficient to sustain a non-farming elite (Coquery-Vidrovitch 1969; Goody 1971; Herbst 2000). Unusually favorable locations, perhaps including the opportunity to draw revenue from taxing or participating in long-distance trade, permitted exceptions, from the long-lasting kingdom of Benin to the successive empires based on the Niger Bend cities until 1591 (Gomez 2018), and the smaller states that succeeded them in the same area, including in the 19th century the short-lived jihadist state of Masina (Johnson 1976). Indeed, the proportion of territory and population under the control of states appears to have increased gradually during and after the Atlantic slave trade.[4] Even on the eve of the Scramble, however, large proportions of the population of West Africa continued to live in stateless societies or mini-states.

The discussion was taken further in a 1985 essay by the geographers A. L. Mabogunje and Paul Richards, who implied that states in pre-colonial West Africa might be at least as well understood as networks rather than territories (Mabogunje and Richards 1985). The kingdom of Asante (Ashanti), centered in the northern part of the forest zone of what is now Ghana, was renowned in the 19th century for the coercive strength and administrative effectiveness of its government, both exerted partly through an impressive set of what Ivor Wilks called "great roads," radiating from the capital (Wilks 1989). Here, if anywhere, one would expect to meet discernible frontiers, and that was, in part, the case. Indeed, in 1881 a British official entered Asante, which was still recovering only seven years after a major military defeat, and reported that

> No sooner has one entered Ashanti and passed through one or two of the numerous small villages which dot the road than one is aware of having reached a new country. A system of some kind impresses itself upon the senses.[5]

Yet, when Wilks examined the Asante ruling elite's conception of the extent of space they controlled, his tentative conclusion was that it was strikingly stylized: the state was conceived as extending 20 days' standard walk in each direction. While roughly correct, in literal terms, as far as the northern limits of Asante control were concerned, to the south the sea was only ten days away, while, again, the state's military reach into the interior could exceed the 20 days (Wilks 1992).

Let us now turn to the theories themselves. The idea of abundant land, and by extension of an open land frontier, or rather – in this case – many local open frontiers (Kopytoff 1987), excites thoughts of both liberty and oppression. It might mean the existence of an exit option. Young adults might have the chance to escape patriarchy, in the sense of being able to relocate in order to bypass the normal wait for parental permission and material support to get married and found their own farming households.[6] For the general populace, as already noted, it offered some chance of escaping state-builders' demands for taxes or conscripts. Abundant land and open frontiers can be understood in forward-moving, entrepreneurial terms, as evoked in John Iliffe's memorable characterization of Africans as "the frontiersmen of mankind" (Iliffe 2007, 1). Against these egalitarian and pioneering visions, there is also the observation, encapsulated in the Nieboer-Domar hypothesis, that in the absence of technologies that create significant economies of scale, a relative abundance of land and scarcity of capital is precisely what makes it profitable for would-be employers to coerce labor.[7] That would provide a motive for the powerful either to immobilize labor, in the form of serfdom, thereby preventing migration, or to mobilize it, but in the form of slavery. The next two sections will enlarge on the contrasting approaches of Kopytoff and Nieboer-Domar, and consider them in the context of 19th-century West Africa.

4 Migration across Kopytoff's "internal African frontier": consensual repetition or conflictual dynamism?

The optimistic interpretation of pre-colonial migration – optimism, in his case, particularly as regards the implicit limiting of oppression and conflict – is most fully developed by Kopytoff, in perhaps the one model specifically formulated for that extremely long era of the continent's history. Citing "the last half century of Africanist scholarship" (before 1987), Kopytoff rejected the – already long discredited – notion of sub-Saharan Africa as "mired in timeless immobility" (Kopytoff 1987, 7). He went on to note that the peopling of Africa

> left the continent very sparsely populated – as much of it continued to be in historic times and even now. After the first thin spread of immigrants, large expanses remained available to settlement. Established societies were surrounded by large tracts of land that were open politically or physically, or both. Together, these tracts made up a continent-wide interstitial network of thousands of potential local frontiers.
>
> *(Kopytoff 1987, 10)*

Kopytoff proceeded to assert

> Settlers wishing to leave the established societies could move into this internal African frontier and set up their own social order in the midst of what was effectively an

42 Gareth Austin

> institutional frontier. It was under such frontier conditions that the dynamic of African social and political formation was played out over the past centuries.
>
> *(Kopytoff 1987, 10)*

Kopytoff's model incorporates important subsidiary propositions which largely apply in West Africa, even in the 19th century, such as that "(a) the frontier areas were unpoliced by the small metropoles from which the frontiersmen came, and (b) in most instances, the frontiersmen were not the advance agents of metropolitan expansion" (Kopytoff 1987, 11). Thus, in addition to starting from the proposition of low population density, Kopytoff assumes the truth of the fourth proposition discussed in the preceding section, about the difficulty of state construction.

Accepting Kopytoff's points in the last paragraph, there remains a basic problem with his analysis, namely, that his overall picture is not a story but a static, or rather endlessly reproduced, pattern: the frontier as "a force for culture-historical continuity and conservatism," the "reproduction" of "tradition" (Kopytoff 1987, 11 and sub-title). In his account, people leave existing polities, for a range of reasons and set up their own households or communities; some return to or are absorbed within the polity they left; others form new states, which, however, are culturally more or less reproductions of the one they left. Ironically, what Kopytoff's model suggests is not actually a story, but rather the "timeless immobility" he disavowed. Albeit, he rejected the idea of spatial immobility over time, whereas my objection is to his endorsement of the idea of institutional stasis. My view arises from viewing the matter from an economic and political economy perspective but it is also true of the history of political culture:[8] West Africa, at least, certainly since c. 1500, has been characterized by continual change, punctuated with watersheds (Austin, forthcoming).

The specifics of Kopytoff's model feature the proposition that "African societies were formed around an initial core-group developed under the relatively undramatic conditions of local frontiers," propelled by a variety of grievances or conflicts (Kopytoff 1987, quotation p. 7). The result was the systematic, "continuous reproduction of new frontier polities at the peripheries of mature African societies" (Kopytoff 1987, 7). Thus, "incipient smaller polities are produced by other similar and usually more complex societies" (Kopytoff 1987, 3).

Kopytoff's model is consistent with the account by Claude Hélène Perrot and her contributors, of settlement of land by lineage groups, often led (according to oral tradition) by a hunter who discovered the land in the first place (Perrot 2000, 9).[9] The first settlers then institutionalized their priority, on a principle often referred to today as the "sons of the soil": later migrants were welcome, as long as they accepted that the first-comers were the ultimate owners. Perrot was referring, within West Africa, to examples from stateless societies or mini-states in Côte d'Ivoire (Perrot 2000; further, Béké 2000). This process of "continuous reproduction" was surely part of the story. But, if it was as straightforward as the oral traditions suggest, I suspect it happened during "la période des premières migrations" (Gonnin 2000, 53), whenever that was, rather than more recently.

In the later centuries before colonial rule, at least, there was usually much more to the story, where it transpired at all. The most obviously different phenomenon in the 19th century was the Sufi jihads. These were the work of highly mobile clerics who participated in a network of Islamic scholarship and activism that stretched across the West African Sudan (Lovejoy 2016). Their armies were manned to a great extent by recruits from the mainly pastoral Fulani/Fulbe/Peul societies. They established large polities of rather different kinds. The most extended and most populous was the Sokoto Caliphate (1804–1903), which was created following Usman dan Fodio's call to jihad in 1804. The Caliphate eventually encompassed the whole of what is now northwestern and north-central Nigeria, and extending beyond to the north, west, and south. These jihads involved large-scale movement of armies, accompanied by enslavement and flight, and smaller-scale settlement of the conquerors and their families in the new states. The change sprang from originally small numbers of people who, contrary to Kopytoff's model, ended up living in states much larger than those in which they had been born. And certainly, they transformed the political culture of most of the savanna societies of West Africa, while, as we will now suggest for the Akan of the forest zone of southern Ghana (extending across what is now the international border into Côte d'Ivoire), the dynamics of political centralization also changed the local political cultures in a different direction in forest zone states.

On the face of it, the Akan case is much closer to Kopytoff's hypothesis. One of the strengths of his analysis is his astute observation of the combination of, and the need to reconcile, two contrasting motifs in African oral traditions: "we are from" somewhere else and "we were here first" (Kopytoff 1987, 25). This was (and is) indeed a widespread pattern in West African societies, including within the same society, politically centralized or otherwise, and indeed within the same village.

Let us consider the origins of the Akan states, focusing on what became the kingdom of Asante (c. 1701–1896), one of the largest forest-based states of West Africa. As in Kopytoff's model, most chiefs in Asante, from the Asantehene (the monarch) down to local level, presided over several lineage-based groups of people who had arrived in the area concerned at different periods. Upon arrival as newcomers, they were given use rights over defined portions of land, on condition that they accepted the control of the chieftaincy, and therefore ultimately of the lands, by the descendants of the very first inhabitants. This acceptance was to be reaffirmed annually by the presentation of token gifts in kind, and the pouring of libation (Austin 2005, ch. 5).

The Asante state emerged around the turn of the 18th century as or from an alliance of adjacent smaller states, which were themselves among a larger set of small polities which had emerged in the 16th and 17th centuries. Each was founded by an *obirempon* ("big man"), and all spoke some form of the Akan language and practiced other aspects of Akan culture, such as matrilineal inheritance (Wilks 1993). This sounds like the voluntary reproduction of an essentially uniform culture, exactly as Kopytoff had in mind. So it was: except for at least three things.

First, the settlers or colonists were not merely leaving home because of grievances or conflicts, though that may have been part of it. Rather, the figure of the *obirempon* in oral tradition was really a kind of far-seeing, armed, entrepreneur, who gathered followers around him for protection and collective ambition (Wilks 1993). The idea was to do more than create a home from home.

Second, the establishment of the Akan states required, or at least involved, the purchase of slaves. Some of them were originally captured in the savanna region to the north, and sold to the Akans by Juula traders (Kea 1982, 198, 200, 399; Wilks 1993). Many thousands of others – Raymond Kea suggests 40,000–80,000 – were imported by the sea route, between 1475 and the 1730s (Kea 1982, 200). The best-known episode in this story was the Portuguese buying slaves initially from the kingdom of Benin, shipping them along the coast and disembarking them at Elmina to sell to Akan buyers (Rodney 1969, 13; Kea 1982, 197–8, 399). This coast-wise trade in slaves to the gold-producing, Akan-speaking states of the forest zone was continued by the Dutch and Danish companies into the 18th century, as well as by African seaborne traders using the long canoes characteristic of the region (Kea 1982, 198–201, 399–401).[10] The Kopytoff of "the internal African frontier" is the Kopytoff of Kopytoff and Miers, who saw "slavery" (they preferred to put it in inverted commas) as a means of incorporating outsiders into a society, albeit in a low status (Kopytoff and Miers 1977; Kopytoff 1987, 46–8). The exploitation of slave labor to clear forest and establish the agricultural foundations of a new economy, and to mine for gold, is a much harsher story. Wilks suggested that the institution of the matriclans had served as a means of incorporating large numbers of enslaved foreigners; whereas when their descendants were partly assimilated into the society, the matriclans became vestigial, leaving the individual matrilineages as the basic units of Akan society (Wilks 1978). Given the much greater role of coercion in Wilks' than in Perrot's accounts, it is interesting that Perrot, too, has a hypothesis linking matriliny and slavery. She puts this forward as a generalization, citing Ivoirien examples such as the Anyi, that matrilineal societies suffer from a lack of heirs, and that this created an incentive for the acquisition of slaves, who could be assimilated over generations (Perrot 2000, 13–4).

Third, in contrast to Kopytoff's vision of movement and replication, Wilks' story is of movement, formation, and then largely *endogenous* expansion and complication: as several of the relatively new Akan states combined in opposition to an external foe to form a single confederation, which evolved into a rather centralized kingdom, Asante, which was qualitatively (politically, culturally, and indeed economically) different from its settler precedents (Wilks 1989). As with some other large states across Africa (the kingdom of Buganda, for example), the 18th and 19th centuries saw the monarchs working to enhance their authority and control over what became the provincial chiefs.[11] In the process, new centralized institutions were created, such as – in the Asante case – patrilineal chieftaincies, as instruments of the consolidation of the kingdom under the patronage of the ruler.[12] The Asante story illustrates that Kopytoff overlooked the potential dynamism of state formation, such that – rather than reproducing the same political culture – they could evolve into polities quantitatively and qualitatively different from their origin. The abundance of land, let alone the existence of open frontiers, hindered the formation and elaboration of states. But they did not preclude it. Where states were created, they could and did change the distribution of power and economic opportunities, including the attractiveness of migration.

5 Forced migration: the commercial transition and the Sokoto Caliphate in Nieboer-Domar conditions

What was introduced above as Proposition II, relative abundance of land, relative scarcity of labor as well as capital, defines Nieboer-Domar conditions: those in which systematic coercion of labor was likely to be profitable for prospective users of labor (Austin 2009b). I argue elsewhere that 19th-century West Africa fits the Nieboer-Domar hypothesis well.[13] In many cases, including Asante, the evidence suggests that regular wage labor was not an economic option: there was no price for labor which was in the mutual interest of both prospective employer and prospective employee to agree (the Domar version of the hypothesis) (Austin 2005, ch. 8). In less extreme cases, wage labor could be profitable but less so than slavery (the Hopkins version [Hopkins 1973/2019, ch. 2]).

The Nieboer-Domar hypothesis, however, is underdetermined in two senses. The first is that it says nothing about whether the political and cultural conditions for such coercion existed. Here, for reasons of space it will be simply noted that, while it was not unknown in West Africa to have a society without slaves (Searing 2002), it was highly exceptional, and, the difficulties facing would-be state-builders did not prevent the existence of widespread inequality in the distribution of coercive power, with hierarchies of power existing even in stateless and mini-state societies. The second sense in which the hypothesis is underdetermined is that it does not tell us which system of labor coercion (slavery, serfdom, *corvée*) would be likely to be the more profitable or feasible in particular circumstances. In West Africa, slavery was a more realistic ambition than serfdom or *corvée* for a would-be exploiter of labor (whether an individual master or a community). Propositions III and IV apply: as Goody observed, "unfree tenancies mean little unless land is highly valued and your peasantry has nowhere else to go" (Goody 1971, 31). Most land was not highly valued in economic terms, and the limited administrative capacities of many states meant that farming households might be able to move, at least locally. Given the relative weakness of most states, it was politically easier for masters to ally with their own commoners to exploit enslaved outsiders than to dispossess the majority of their own population and turn them into servile tenants or to demand from them large-scale labor services (Austin 2005, 158–60, 496–7). In world history, enslavement has usually been inflicted upon people considered outsiders. Thus, slavery as a system usually required forced immigration at the start and, almost always, for its continuation.[14]

Indeed, first-generation slaves in West African societies overwhelmingly tended to be foreigners, rather than being born within the society in which they were held. Some West African systems of slavery had a strong tendency toward the – at least partial – assimilation of descendants of slaves as junior members of the society. In Asante the children of slaves – who were almost invariably the offspring of a slave mother and free Asante father – had a higher status than their slave parent. Not all West African slave systems were assimilative. For the biggest slave-holding state, the Sokoto Caliphate, Mohammed Salau's recent book concludes that most slaves were not assimilated (Salau 2018, 158). In those slavery systems that were more assimilative, however, the result was that the demand for imported captives was reproduced in each generation (Austin 2005, ch. 8; Austin, forthcoming, ch. 6). Thus, the dependence of slave holding on forced immigration was especially high where there was an element of assimilation in the local system of slavery.

The majority of historians of West Africa follow Walter Rodney and Paul Lovejoy in accepting the "transformation thesis," that slave holding within the region was relatively low until stimulated by expanding demand for slaves from beyond the desert and (on a larger scale) the ocean (Rodney 1966; Lovejoy 2012).[15] Slave importation into societies within West Africa expanded as a joint product of the external trades: the same mechanisms of supply provided captives for purchase by owners within the region as by European or North African merchants. Ironically, the incidence of slave holding seems to have risen across most of West Africa, in both savanna and forest zones, during most of the rest of the century following 1807 (Lovejoy 2012).[16]

By the time of colonization at least 30% of the population of French West Africa appear to have been slaves (Klein 1998, esp. 252–6).[17] As a sample, French West Africa has the advantage of including large areas of all the major soil, vegetation, and climatic types of West Africa. If there is a sample bias, it is that – notoriously, as Lord Salisbury, the British prime minister, indicated at the time – the French territories were, on average, less commercially active at the time of colonization than the areas the British occupied. But, if anything, one would expect the richer areas to be importing more slaves, because they were mostly purchased on the market. Asante was a case in point, using its purchasing power from controlling gold mines and kola trees to buy slaves from traders bringing them from the north (Austin 2005). To generate a 30% incidence of slaves among the population, especially with this being the highest proportion ever, implying that a relatively high proportion of them were first-generation, indicates that the forced migration was both widespread and, over the century as a whole, large scale.

As before, the victims tended originally to be captured in wars or in raids directed at stateless societies or small states (raids from the Sokoto Caliphate targeted "pagans," who themselves took refuge where they could in hills or other relatively inaccessible areas).[18] States themselves, and their ruling elites, moved foreign captives in large numbers either to settle tracts of underpopulated land or to provide more labor for existing agricultural estates. The Asante kingdom and the Sokoto Caliphate are examples of this (Wilks 1989; Austin 2005; Lovejoy 2006). The British diplomat Thomas Bowdich, who visited Asante in 1817, reported that the Asantes sent newly imported slaves "to create plantations in the more remote and stubborn tracts" (Bowdich 1821: 18). Though Bowdich stated that this was "to prevent famine and insurrection" in the context of over-supply of new captives in the aftermath of the abolition of the Atlantic slave trade, the policy of out-settling slaves for agricultural purposes remained a feature of the kingdom afterward (Bowdich 1821, 18; Austin 2005, 120). In the Sokoto Caliphate, there was also a political dimension: slave plantations were established near fortifications which were themselves placed in the borderlands, in a sense to establish a frontier (Salau 2018).

What accounts for the 19th-century upsurge in slave holding, and therefore in forced migration? West African masters continued to have various reasons for acquiring slaves. But what was different in this century, to account for the rising incidence of slavery at a time when joint "production" of slaves for the Atlantic and intra-regional trades was declining or over? Albeit, joint supply continued at the desert edge, and perhaps on an enlarged scale, if we accept the generally held view that slave exports across the Sahara were larger than ever in the 19th century.[19] In societies deeply affected by the Atlantic trade, sex ratios presumably tended to equalize after 1807, given that the ratio of males to females among those embarked as captives into the Atlantic trade had been approximately two to one (Eltis et al. 2019). Patrick Manning has observed that this implies increased competition for women between men, increasing the demand for female slaves (Manning 1990, 142). This is probably part of the explanation. The growth of slavery seems to have been so general a phenomenon, however, across societies more and less and not at all involved in the Atlantic slave trade, that a general explanation is required.

The most plausible, I suggest, is that the demand for additional slaves in the 19th century was primarily a demand for their labor: specifically, their services in extra-subsistence production. This brings us back to the combination of the growth of "legitimate commerce" in the Atlantic market, and the impact of the jihads. The growth of exports of palm oil, and later palm kernels, especially from the Niger Delta but in this period also westward along the Guinea coast, was joined by groundnut exports from Guinea Bissau and Senegambia. To give a sense of scale, during 1880–84 annual groundnut exports from Senegal and the Gambia combined averaged 75,000 metric tons, while annual palm imports to Britain from

West Africa averaged 42,000 metric tons.[20] The 1880s brought the rubber boom, briefly stimulating the tapping (and felling) of wild rubber trees in forests from Nigeria to Guinea. In the 1880s and 1890s the first exports of cocoa beans took place from Lagos and Accra, though the scale was still small by 1900. All these export crops required labor in production and marketing, and there were multiplier effects, as rising incomes in the export-producing areas created markets for hinterland districts. The result was to give producers purchasing power to buy slaves, with the variation that in southeast Nigeria the main role of slave labor in the export economy was indirect. There, districts with relatively low population densities and high proportions of slaves in their populations produced foodstuffs and luxury cotton textiles for sale into the palm oil growing districts, which were more densely populated and (as the Nieboer-Domar hypothesis would predict) had lower proportions of slaves (Northrup 1979; Kriger 2006). The growth of effective demand for slaves is the most convincing explanation for the large, though partial, recovery of slave prices in West Africa from the initial fall caused by British abolition in 1807 (Lovejoy and Richardson 1995).

The commercial transition in the Atlantic trade was by no means the only driver of increased demand for labor to produce for the market. As Lovejoy and others have shown, the Sokoto Caliphate built on the market activity that had happened under the Hausa states defeated by the jihad, to become – by contemporary standards in the region – a huge producer of goods for the market based on slave labor, especially on plantations.[21] The latter supplied the raw cotton and vegetable dyes for the cotton textile industry of Kano and other towns, which not only clothed the inhabitants of the Caliphate, but were exported across a swathe of Western Africa, from Chad to an island off Mauretania. In turn, Kano and the Caliphate economy provided a market for salt producers in the Sahara and kola nut growers in animist Asante. These, too, were activities that drew heavily upon slaves, and thus on the slave trade within the region.

In this section I have argued that the Nieboer-Domar hypothesis is indeed valuable in elucidating the economics and political economy of the expansion of slavery in 19th-century West Africa. This was fed by an intra-regional slave trade, which was partly supported by the very fact that some societies in the region tended to assimilate the descendants of first-generation captives, thereby creating renewed demand for forced immigrants. The discussion points to the conclusion that forced migration was the dominant form of one-way mobility during the century. This was both because of its scale and because its very existence would have deterred people from leaving home voluntarily, except in defensible groups.

6 Legitimate commerce and other varieties of migration in 19th-century West Africa

This final substantive section is devoted to forms of migration other than the types we have discussed so far. Three kinds of migration will be discussed: voluntary migration to take opportunities created by "legitimate commerce," specifically the expansion of export agriculture; long-distance trading; and, briefly, displacement by war.

The 19th century was notable not only for the proliferation of intra-regional slave trading and slavery to an unprecedented level, but also for the first appearance of the form of mobility that would replace the slave trade: migration to access opportunities in the agricultural export economy. Though they were exceptional within the region as a whole, there were such movements. One was seasonal migration from Mali and the interior of Senegal to work in groundnut cultivation by the Senegal or Gambia rivers. Known as *navétanes*, from the Wolof word for rainy season, they could have grown the crop at home, but with no access to the seaborne market. To their employers or – more commonly – landlords they had the advantage over slaves of lower fixed costs: they could be set to work without prior payment (Manchuelle 1997, 53–9). Conversely, unlike the seasonal migrants, the slaves were available in the agricultural off-seasons, during which, on the north bank of the Gambia River, they were used as weavers, producing a particular kind of cloth used as local currency (Brooks 1975). So the migrants provided a no-fixed-cost supplement to the labor of slaves.

The *navétanes* were not the only free people moving in search of a share in the new agricultural export economy. In southern Ghana, Krobo farmers, who had taken refuge on a defensible "mountain" while their neighbors were prone to launch slave raids, took advantage of the diminution of danger after the end of the Atlantic slave trade in what is now the Eastern Region of Ghana, to come down the mountain and buy land cheaply from the much larger, and formerly slave-raiding, neighboring state of Akim Abuakwa (Johnson 1964; Austin 2007).

Both the *navétanes* and the Krobos took advantage of the growth of the overseas demand for crops that could be produced using appropriate land-extensive methods on West African soils (Austin 2008, 2014a, 2017]). In this they foreshadowed much larger movements in the early colonial period: the role of migrant cocoa farmers, including Krobos, in the cocoa take-off in southern Ghana (Hill 1997) and the growth of free migrant labor as a crucial part of, especially, the cocoa and groundnut sectors of West African economies (e.g., Austin 2005; Swindell and Jeng 2006).[22]

How was this possible, given the widespread risk of travelers being seized and sold into slavery? In much of West Africa, such as northern Ghana, the closure of the Atlantic slave market was accompanied or at least followed by an expansion of the local one, thereby giving specialists in violence the incentive to continue raiding. But in the case of Senegambia, the decline of what was anyway one of the smaller routes into the Atlantic slave trade was only partly offset by the growth of intra-regional slave trading, leaving the opportunity for migrants, traveling in bands for their own security, to make their way to and from the coast. With the Krobos, the situation was simpler: the Atlantic slave trade had stopped in their area, and their neighbors stood to gain more from selling surplus land to them than from kidnapping and selling them.

Various groups or communities of traders specialized in relay and long-distance commerce. In this period, on account of the insecurity, traders generally moved together, in caravan. Many of them included women. But the caravans of the Yoruba area of southwest Nigeria were notable for the traders being mostly women, accompanied by men who were most often in the roles of porters or guards. These caravans would often spend many days away from home, though not months – unlike the very long-distance traders, organized in trading diasporas (Falola 1991).

Most trade across linguistic and other cultural borders within West Africa was conducted by trading diasporas: defined as ethnic and/or religious groups in dispersal, for commercial ends. Two major "families" of diasporas, Juulas (Dioula) and Hausa, both Muslim, monopolized much of the long-distance trades (defined by commodity and/or route) of the Western Sudan (and western Guinea forest) and the Central Sudan, respectively. Both relied on members of the diaspora who settled "abroad" and provided accommodation, local information, and mediation to the itinerant merchants with whom they had shared affiliations, religious and ethnic, often reinforced by intermarriage (Curtin 1984). Their operations could lead to permanent migration and re-settlement along long-distance trade routes. This was likely to be so where the diaspora worked by having "landlords" dotted along the long-distance, cross-boundary, trans-cultural trade routes. Trading diasporas constituted moral communities whose existence can be seen as a response to the problems of information asymmetry and trust over distances that spanned cultural and political frontiers (Cohen 1971), and in the absence of modern communication technologies. In that sense, although ethnic trading diasporas can of course be found within modern states, their particular importance in pre-colonial West Africa can be seen as a response to the political disunity of much of the region: Proposition IV, on the difficulties of achieving political centralization. A large state, such as Asante, which had secured political control over the locally important trade routes, had the option – which Asante exercised – of excluding foreign traders, notably the members of the Muslim diasporas, in the interests of securing a domestic monopoly. As Emmanuel Terray noted, that option was costly for small states, because the traders might retaliate by bypassing them: so Asante's much smaller neighbor (and tributary), Gyaman, welcomed Dyula traders (Terray 1974).

The trading diasporas clearly participated in and benefited from upswings in trade, but especially from upswings in intra-regional trade, because that was where they primarily operated. Hausa traders, for example, were the intermediaries in the above-mentioned export of kola nuts from Asante to Kano; human captives were moved in the opposite direction (Lovejoy 1980).

Finally, the wars of the century produced a different kind of forced migration: the displacement of peoples, to escape capture or death. Asante civil wars in the late 19th century produced contrasting examples, which illustrate the possibilities. In 1875, after a failed attempt at seceding from Asante, a portion of the Juaben leadership and subjects crossed into British Protected Territory. Again, during the major Asante civil war of 1885–88 the south Asante state of Adanse was occupied by their northern neighbor, Bekwai, who was fighting on what became the winning side in the war as a whole. The Adanses, virtually as a whole, crossed into British territory (Wilks 1989, 91). Following the colonial occupation of Asante, the Adanses returned and reoccupied their territory, whereas the "New Juabens" generally stayed in the Gold Coast, having founded what became a new chieftaincy there. It may be too simple to say that the difference was purely a function of the length of exile, but that probably is part of the explanation.

7 Conclusion

This chapter has focused on the two main models of pre-colonial migration: Kopytoff's idea of internal African frontiers, across which small groups of settlers moved, and the Nieboer-Domar hypothesis about the conditions under which labor coercion would be profitable to masters. We also considered trading diasporas and war displacement. The main arguments can be summarized as follows.

Kopytoff's emphasis on incessant spatial mobility in pre-colonial Africa is thoroughly justified. However, if his model of local settlement reproducing existing cultural and political organization applied at any time, surely it was in a relatively peaceful era, certainly before the Atlantic slave trade intensified in the late 17th century.[23] Even in the 16th and 17th centuries, the use of slave labor was important in the establishment of the Akan states.

Kopytoff's model also overlooks the dynamics of state consolidation: once a would-be ruler did succeed in overcoming the fairly formidable obstacles to state formation, there was a logic favoring the expansion and centralization of the state, contrary to Kopytoff's schema. Crucially, the general problem with his approach is the institutional stasis it envisages, which is not supported by historical evidence. The 19th century should be seen as a very particular episode in the dynamic history of West Africa, rather than as the last chance to see "the reproduction of traditional African societies."[24] As against Kopytoff's classic model, this story of change arises from taking into account the endogenous dynamics of state building, the variety of state ideologies and ruling elite objectives, and the economic value of slaves to both their owners and the states.[25]

Nieboer-Domar's identification of the combination of land abundance with labor and capital scarcity as the conditions under which labor coercion would pay is well supported by the evidence from this century. The hypothesis needs further specification, however, to explain why the systematic coercion of labor took the form it did, directed not by a ruling elite against its own population, but by the elite and "free" subjects against outsiders: slavery. The 19th century saw striking growth in the incidence of slavery, and therefore of the slave trade, in West Africa as a whole. Forced migration was the dominant form of permanent personal mobility, not least because the risk of enslavement would have deterred voluntary migration in much of the region. However, there were exceptions, where people did move voluntarily in order to participate in the expanding economy of legitimate commerce.

Arguably, the most significant change of the 19th century, as far as migration and much else is concerned, was economic and ecological. With industrialization in Europe, markets were created for various crops that either were already grown in West Africa or could be adopted there. Crucially, they could be grown profitably with land-extensive techniques: the approach best suited to West Africa's resource environment, physical and demographic. It was a step on what I have suggested should be called the "land-extensive path of development." The choice of land-extensive techniques was not only rational under the prevailing circumstances of, say, 1800; it could also be a way forward (Austin 2008, 2013, 2017). While the immediate consequence of the emergence of overseas markets for West African farm produce was to stimulate growth in the demand for slaves, as the Nieboer-Domar hypothesis would predict, there were signs of change, starting with groundnuts in Senegambia and followed, at the end of the century, by the adoption – by African initiative – of cocoa cultivation. These crops could be and at first were grown profitably with slave labor, in Senegambia and Nigeria, respectively (Oroge 1985; Searing 1993, 187–8, 198, 244; Swindell and Jeng 2006, xxiii, 5–11, 243). But their advent weakened the hold of Nieboer-Domar conditions on West African agriculture, because they were sufficiently lucrative that free contracts could be made in the labor market: it was possible for a slave master to make the transition to being an employer of freed labor. This trend, a minority one in the 19th century, was to go much further in the first few decades of the 20th (Austin 2009a).[26]

Acknowledgment

This chapter is dedicated to Paul Lovejoy, great scholar of forced migration and long-distance trade in pre-colonial West Africa.

Notes

1 The best detailed overview of West Africa in the 19th century remains Ajayi and Crowder (1987, 1–484).
2 See Saleh and Wahby (Chapter 3, this volume).
3 Fora fuller discussion of environmental challenges see Austin (2017).
4 For an impression of this, see the successive maps of West Africa in Ajayi and Crowder (1985).
5 British Parliamentary Papers, C.3386, *Further Correspondence Regarding Affairs of the Gold Coast* (London 1882), "Report by Captain Rupert La Trobe Lonsdale, of his Mission to Coomassie, Salagha, Yendi, &c. October 1881 to February 1882", 59.
6 For a model of such a patriarchy, see Meillassoux (1972).
7 The hypothesis was introduced to West African history by Hopkins (1973/2019, ch. 2). It and its main variations are examined in Austin (2005, ch. 8).
8 For a study which pays attention to historical evidence and the sensitivity to context and change that is absent from Kopytoff's highly generalized and perhaps therefore schematic approach see McCaskie (1995).
9 On the role of hunters, see Gonnin (2000, 45–6).
10 On the indigenous maritime trade, see Smith (1970).
11 The process actually went back earlier, in some cases. Richard Reid commented that the "single most important theme of Ganda political history," 1500–1800, was "the gradual shift of political and territorial power from the ... clan heads to the *kabaka*" (king) (Reid 2002, 3). As in Asante, in Buganda political centralization was generally maintained or deepened long into the 19th century, with some qualifications. See Wilks (1989); Reid (2002); Médard (2007, 221–312). On East Africa, see, further, Pallaver (Chapter 4, this volume).
12 In first identifying this process of political centralization, Wilks argued that it was bureaucratic in a strict Weberian sense (impersonal, etc.). I am persuaded, rather, by the revisionist arguments of Arhin and Yarak that the new positions, and the system of authority as a whole, should rather be seen as patrimonial (Wilks 1966; Arhin, 1986; Yarak 1990).
13 Austin (2009b); and much more fully, Austin (forthcoming, ch. 6).
14 The US after the abolition of slave imports from 1 January 1808 was exceptional in world history, in that the slave population continued to grow without new imports.
15 For a different view, see Thornton (1998).
16 Lovejoy synthesized the literature in his *Transformations in Slavery*, first published in 1983. His view is supported by most of the specialist studies since, including Austin (2006, ch. 6).
17 Klein's estimate was for 1904, several years into colonial rule in much of French West Africa, so may understate the proportion of slaves at the time of colonization.
18 For a similar if late example, the Emir of Madagali kept raiding the nearby highland villages of northern Cameroon, and recorded his captures in his diary (Vaughan and Kirk-Greene 1995).
19 See Saleh and Wahby (Chapter 3, this volume).
20 Calculated from Swindell and Jeng (2006, 23–4); Searing (2002, 58, 187); Lynn (1997, 113).
21 This paragraph is based on the series of papers that began with Lovejoy (1978). They are collected in Lovejoy (2006); see, further, Lovejoy (2016). There have also been valuable contributions by other scholars, most recently Salau (2018).
22 Cash crop migration is discussed in this volume by De Haas and Travieso (Chapter 11).
23 There is an interesting comparison here with Schirmer and Keeton's argument in this volume (Chapter 6).
24 Referring again to the sub-title of Kopytoff, *African Frontier*.
25 Kopytoff's model remains heuristic, including apparently for the post-colonial era. See Korf, Hagmann, and Doevenspeck (2013).
26 See further De Haas and Travieso (Chapter 11, this volume).

References

Ajayi, J. F. A., and Michael Crowder, eds., with Paul Richards. 1985. *Longman Historical Atlas of Africa*. Harlow: Longman.

Ajayi, J. F. A., and Michael Crowder, eds. 1987. *History of West Africa* (vol. II, 2nd edition). Harlow: Longman.

52 Gareth Austin

Arhin, Kwame. 1986. "The Asante Praise Poems: The Ideology of Patrimonialism." *Paideuma* 32: 163–97.

Austen, Ralph 1979. "The Trans-Saharan Slave Trade: A Tentative Census." In *The Uncommon Market: Essays in the Economic History of the Atlantic Slave Trade*, edited by Henry A. Gemery and Jan S. Hogendorn, 23–76. New York: Academic Press.

Austin, Gareth. 2005. *Labour, Land and Capital in Ghana: From Slavery to Free Labour in Asante, 1807-1956*. Rochester, NY: University of Rochester Press.

Austin, Gareth. 2006. "The Political Economy of the Natural Environment in West African History: Asante and its Savanna Neighbors in the Nineteenth and Twentieth Centuries." In *Land and the Politics of Belonging in West Africa*, edited by Richard Kuba and Carola Lentz, 187–212. Leiden: Brill Academic Publishers.

Austin, Gareth. 2007. "Labour and Land in Ghana, 1879–1939: A Shifting Ratio and an Institutional Revolution." *Australian Economic History Review* 47(1): 95–120.

Austin, Gareth. 2008. "Resources, Techniques, and Strategies South of the Sahara: Revising the Factor Endowments Perspective on African Economic Development, 1500–2000." *Economic History Review* 61(3): 587–624.

Austin, Gareth. 2009a. "Cash Crops and Freedom: Export Agriculture and the Decline of Slavery in Colonial West Africa." *International Review of Social History* 54(1): 1–37.

Austin, Gareth. 2009b. "Factor Markets in Nieboer Conditions: Pre-Colonial West Africa, c.1500–c.1900." *Continuity and Change* 24(1): 23–53.

Austin, Gareth. 2013. "Labour-Intensity and Manufacturing in West Africa, c.1450–c.2000." In *Labour-Intensive Industrialization in Global History*, edited by Gareth Austin and Kaoru Sugihara, 201–30. London: Routledge.

Austin, Gareth. 2014a. "Explaining and Evaluating the Cash-Crop Revolution in the 'Peasant' Colonies of Tropical Africa: Beyond 'Vent-for-Surplus.'" In *Africa's Economic Development in Historical Perspective*, edited by Emmanuel Akyeampong, Robert H. Bates, Nathan Nunn and James Robinson, 295–320. New York: Cambridge University Press.

Austin, Gareth. 2014b. "Vent for Surplus or Productivity Breakthrough? The Ghanaian Cocoa Take-off, c.1890–1936." *Economic History Review*, 67(4): 1035–64.

Austin, Gareth. 2017. "Africa and the Anthropocene." In *Economic Development and Environmental History in the Anthropocene: Perspectives on Asia and Africa*, edited by Gareth Austin, 95–118. London: Bloomsbury Academic.

Austin, Gareth. Forthcoming. *Markets, Slavery and the State in West Africa Since 1500*. Cambridge: Cambridge University Press.

Béké, P. Zézé. 2000. "Les Nyabwa et les paradoxes de l'intégration (Côte d'Ivoire)." In *Lignages et territoire en Afrique aux xviii et xixe siècles: stratégies, compétition, intégration*, edited by Claude-Hélène Perrot, 23–37. Paris: Karthala.

Bowdich, Thomas. 1821. "Remarks on Civilisation in Africa." In his *The British and French Expeditions to Teembo with Remarks on Civilisation in Africa*, 3–26. Paris: J. Smith.

Brooks, George. 1975. "Peanuts and Colonialism: Consequences of the Commercialization of Peanuts in West Africa, 1830–70." *Journal of African History*, 16(1): 29–54.

Cohen, Abner. 1971. "Cultural Strategies in the Organization of Trading Diasporas." In *The Development of Indigenous Trade and Markets in West Africa*, edited by Claude Meillassoux, 266–81. London: Oxford University Press for the International African Institute.

Coquery-Vidrovitch, Catherine. 1969. "Recherches sur un mode de production africain." *Pensée*, 144: 3–20 (for an English translation see Martin A. Klein and G. Wesley Johnson, eds. *Perspectives on the African Past* [Boston: Little Brown, 1972]).

Curtin, Philip. 1984. *Cross-Cultural Trade in World History*. New York: Cambridge University Press.

Eltis, David, et al. 2019. *Voyages: The Transatlantic Slave Trade Database* www.slavevoyages.org (2019 edition accessed 11 August 2019).

Falola, Toyin. 1991. "The Yoruba Caravan System of the Nineteenth Century." *International Journal of African Historical Studies* 24(1): 111–32.

Frankema, Ewout. 2019. "Africa and the Demographic Consequences of the Columbian Exchange." *Asian Review of World Histories* 7: 66–79.

Frankema, Ewout, and Morten Jerven. 2014. "Writing History Backwards or Sideways: Towards a Consensus on African Population, 1850–2010." *Economic History Review* 67(4): 907–31.

Gomez, Michael. 2018. *African Dominion: A New History of Empire in Early and Medieval West Africa.* Princeton, NJ: Princeton University Press.

Gonnin, Gilbert. 2000. "Propriété foncière et parenté sociale en pays toura (ouest de la Côte d'Ivoire)." In *Lignages et territoire en Afrique aux xviii et xixe siècles: stratégies, compétition, intégration*, edited by Claude-Hélène Perrot, 39–54. Paris: Karthala.

Goody, Jack. 1971. *Tradition, Technology and the State in Africa.* London: Oxford University Press for the International African Institute.

Hargreaves, John. 1987. "The European Partition of West Africa." In *History of West Africa*, edited by J. F. A. Ajayi and Michael Crowder, (vol. II, 2nd edition.), 403–28. Harlow: Longman.

Herbst, Jeffrey. 2000. *States and Power in Africa: Comparative Lessons in Authority and Control.* Princeton, NJ: Princeton University Press.

Hill, Polly. 1997 (1963). *Migrant Cocoa-Farmers of Southern Ghana.* International African Institute and James Currey: Oxford; first published by Cambridge University Press.

Hopkins, A. G. 1973/2019. *An Economic History of West Africa.* London (2nd edition): Routledge (1st edition, Longman).

Iliffe, John. 2007. *Africans: The History of a Continent* (2nd edition). Cambridge: Cambridge University Press.

Inikori, Joseph. 2009. "The Economic Impact of the 1807 British Abolition of the Transatlantic Slave Trade." In *The Changing Worlds of Atlantic Africa: Essay in Honor of Robin Law*, edited by Toyin Falola and Matt Childs, 163–82. Durham, NC: Carolina Academic Press.

Johnson, Marion. 1964. "Migrant's Progress," Part I. *Bulletin of the Ghana Geographical Association*, 9: 4–27.

Johnson, Marion. 1976. "The Economic Foundations of an Islamic Theocracy – The Case of Masina." *Journal of African History* 17(4): 481–95.

Kea, Ray 1982. *Settlements, Trade, and Polities in the Seventeenth-Century Gold Coast.* Baltimore, MD: Johns Hopkins University Press.

Klein, Martin 1998. *Slavery and Colonial Rule in French West Africa.* Cambridge: Cambridge University Press.

Kopytoff, Igor. 1987. "The Internal African Frontier: The Making of African Political Culture." In *The African Frontier: the Reproduction of Traditional African Societies*, edited by Igor Kopytoff, 3–84. Bloomington: Indiana University Press.

Kopytoff, Igor, and Suzanne Miers. 1977. "Slavery as an Institution of Marginality." In *Slavery in Africa: Historical and Anthropological Perspectives*, edited by Suzanne Miers and Igor Kopytoff, 3–81. Madison: Wisconsin University Press.

Korf, Benedikt, Tobias Hagmann and Martin Doevenspeck. 2013. "Geographies of Violence and Sovereignty: The African Frontier Revisited." In *Violence on the Margins: States, Conflicts and Borderlands*, edited by Benedikt Korf and Timothy Raeymaekers, 29–54. New York: Palgrave Macmillan.

Kriger, Colleen. 2006. *Cloth in West African History.* Lanham, MD: AltaMira Press.

Law, Robin, ed. 1995. *From Slave Trade to 'Legitimate' Commerce: The Commercial Transition in Nineteenth-Century West Africa.* Cambridge: Cambridge University Press.

Lovejoy, Paul. 1978. "Plantations in the Economy of the Sokoto Caliphate." *Journal of African History* 19(3): 341–68.

Lovejoy, Paul. 1980. *Caravans of Kola: the Hausa Kola Trade, 1700–1900.* Zaria: Ahmadu Bello University Press.

Lovejoy, Paul. 2006. *Slavery, Commerce and Production in the Sokoto Caliphate of West Africa.* Trenton, NJ: Africa World Press.

Lovejoy, Paul. 2012. *Transformations in Slavery: A History of Slavery in Africa* (3rd edition). New York: Cambridge University Press.

54 Gareth Austin

Lovejoy, Paul. 2016. *Jihād in West Africa during the Age of Revolutions*. Athens: Ohio University Press.

Lovejoy, Paul, and David Richardson. 1995. "British Abolition and its Impact on Slave Prices along the Atlantic Coast of Africa, 1783–1850." *Journal of Economic History* 55(1): 98–119.

Lynn, Martin. 1997. *Commerce and Economic Change in West Africa: The Palm Oil Trade in the Nineteenth Century*. Cambridge: Cambridge University Press.

Mabogunje, A. L., and Paul Richards. 1985. "Land and People - Models of Spatial and Ecological Processes in West African History". In *History of West Africa* (vol. I, 3rd edition), edited by J. F. A. Ajayi and Michel Crowder, 5–47. Harlow: Longman.

Manchuelle, François. 1997. *Willing Migrants: Soninke Labor Diasporas, 1848–1960*. Athens: Ohio University Press.

Manning, Patrick. 1990. *Slavery and African Life: Occidental, Oriental, and African Trades*. Cambridge: Cambridge University Press.

Manning, Patrick. 2014. "African Population, 1650–2000: Comparisons and Implications of New Estimates." In *Africa's Development in Historical Perspective*, edited by Emmanuel Akyeampong, Robert H. Bates, Nathan Nunn and James A. Robinson, 131–50. New York: Cambridge University Press.

Martin, Susan. 1988. *Palm Oil and Protest: An Economic History of the Ngwa Region, South-Eastern Nigeria, 1800–1980*. Cambridge: Cambridge University Press.

McCaskie, T. C. 1995. *State and Society in Pre-Colonial Asante*. Cambridge: Cambridge University Press.

Médard, Henri. 2007. *Le royaume du Buganda au XIXe siècle*. Paris: Karthala.

Meillassoux, Claude. 1972. "From Reproduction to Production: A Marxist Approach to Economic Anthropology." *Economy and Society* 1: 93–105.

Northrup, David. 1979. "Nineteenth-Century Patterns of Slavery and Economic Growth in Southeastern Nigeria." *International Journal of African Historical Studies* 12(1): 1–16.

Oroge, E. Adeniyi. 1985. "*Iwofa*: An Historical Survey of the Yoruba Institution of Indenture." *African Economic History*, 14: 75–106.

Perrot, Claude-Hélène. 2000. "Introduction." In *Lignages et territoire en Afrique aux xviii et xixe siècles: stratégies, compétition, intégration*, edited by Claude-Hélène Perrot, 5–17. Paris: Karthala.

Reid, Richard. 2002. *Political Power in Pre-Colonial Buganda*. Oxford: James Currey.

Rodney, Walter. 1966. "Slavery and Other Forms of Social Oppression on the Upper Guinea Coast in the Context of the Atlantic Slave Trade." *Journal of African History* 7(4): 431–43.

Rodney, Walter. 1969. "Gold and Slaves on the Gold Coast." *Transactions of the Historical Society of Ghana* 10: 13–28.

Salau, Mohammed Bashir. 2018. *Plantation Slavery in the Sokoto Caliphate*. Rochester, NY: University of Rochester Press.

Searing, James. 1993. *West African Slavery and Atlantic Commerce: The Senegal River Valley, 1700–1860*. Cambridge: Cambridge University Press.

Searing, James. 2002. "'No Kings, No Lords, No Slaves': Ethnicity and Religion among the Sereer-Safèn of Western Bawol, 1700–1914." *Journal of African History* 43(3): 407–30.

Smith, Robert. 1970. "The Canoe in West African History." *Journal of African History* 11(4): 515–33.

Swindell, Kenneth, and Alieu Jeng. 2006. *Migrants, Credit and Climate: The Gambian Groundnut Trade, 1834–1934*. Leiden: Brill.

Terray, Emmanuel. 1974. "Long-Distance Trade and the Formation of the State: The Case of the Abron Kingdom of Gyaman." *Economy and Society* 3: 315–45.

Thornton, John. 1998. *Africa and Africans in the Making of the Atlantic World, 1400–1800* (2nd edition). Cambridge: Cambridge University Press.

Vaughan, James, and Anthony Kirk-Greene, eds. 1995. *The Diary of Hamman Yaji: Chronicle of a West African Muslim Ruler*. Bloomington: Indiana University Press.

Wilks, Ivor. 1966. "Aspects of Bureaucratization in Ashanti in the Nineteenth Century." *Journal of African History* 7: 215–32.

Wilks, Ivor. 1978. "Land, Labour, Capital and the Forest Kingdom of Asante: A Model of Early Change." In *The Evolution of Social Systems*, edited by J. Friedman and M. J. Rowlands, 487–534. London: Gerald Duckworth.

Wilks, Ivor. 1989 (1975). *Asante in the Nineteenth Century: The Structure and Evolution of a Political Order*. Cambridge (1st edition London): Cambridge University Press.

Wilks, Ivor. 1992. "On Mentally Mapping Greater Asante: A Study in Time and Motion." *Journal of African History* 33(2): 175–90.

Wilks, Ivor. 1993. *Forests of Gold: Essays on the Akan and the Kingdom of Asante*. Athens: Ohio University Press.

Yarak, Larry. 1990. *Asante and the Dutch, 1744–1873*. Oxford: Oxford University Press.

3

BOOM AND BUST

The Trans-Saharan Slave Trade in the 19th Century

Mohamed Saleh and Sarah Wahby

1 Introduction

While a voluminous literature exists on the trans-Atlantic slave trade, the trans-Saharan slave trade between sub-Saharan Africa and North Africa received much less attention. This is not a minor topic that only deserves the interest of the most curious historian, though. For one, trans-Saharan slave trade was a long-standing institution: it existed long before the trans-Atlantic slave trade, and it persisted long after the abolition of the latter (in 1807) until the beginning of the 20th century (Wright 2007, xiii). Over the centuries, the longer duration of the trans-Saharan slave trade created an intra-African forced migration system that altered the ethnic composition of local populations both south and north of the Sahara. For another, trans-Saharan slave trade was sizable in absolute numbers as well as a proportion of the total slave exports from sub-Saharan Africa, as can be seen in Table 3.1 drawing on the estimates of Lovejoy (2011).

The objective of this chapter is two-fold. The first objective is to document the main empirical facts about the trans-Saharan forced slave migration in terms of the trade volume, trade routes, and origins and destinations of the trade. We emphasize that slave trade was in essence a forced migration system that moved populations across the Sahara. The supply of slaves came from the enslaved population in the south of the Sahara that was destined to be either employed locally or exported across the Sahara to North Africa. Our focus in this

TABLE 3.1 Lovejoy's estimates of the percentage of slave exports by sector

Sector	1500–99	1600–99	1700–99	1800–99
Red Sea	9.2	3.6	2.6	8.0
Sahara	50.6	25.2	9.0	19.5
East Africa	9.2	3.6	5.1	7.2
Atlantic	31.1	67.6	83.3	65.4
Total	1,088,000	2,776,000	7,795,000	6,161,000

Source: Lovejoy (2011, 46 and 138).

DOI: 10.4324/9781003225027-5

chapter is on those who were forcibly migrated across the Sahara. The demand for slaves came from North Africa: current-day Egypt, Libya, Tunisia, Algeria, and Morocco. The key insight is that Egypt was the largest importer of slaves in North Africa during the 19th century. Furthermore, the trans-Saharan slave trade increased, albeit slightly, in Egypt, Morocco, and Libya, during the first half of the 19th century, before it declined in the middle of the century. It then surged again in Egypt during the 1860s, but this time at a much larger and somewhat unprecedented scale, at least judging by the region's history of slavery. It also surged in Morocco toward the end of the century.

The second objective of the chapter is to trace the drivers of these shifting patterns of intra-African forced slave migration. We attribute the shifting patterns of the trans-Saharan slave migration system to both supply and demand factors. The supply and demand effects were far from uniform, though, due to both the heterogeneity of the trans-Saharan trade routes and the segregation of the slave markets in the destination countries that were highly localized. Specifically, the slave trade between Egypt and the Nilotic Sudan and Ethiopia in the east was largely segregated from the trade between North Africa to the west of Egypt and sub-Saharan Africa west of present-day Sudan.

We discuss four potential drivers. First, the British abolition of the trans-Atlantic slave trade in 1807, and its subsequent relocation to the southwestern and southeastern regions of sub-Saharan Africa (Eltis 2021), arguably increased the supply of slaves in West Africa south of the Sahara during the first half of the 19th century. While this excess supply was primarily absorbed by the rising demand for slaves in sub-Saharan Africa (Lovejoy 2011, 161–2), a small share of the increased supply was probably absorbed via the increased demand for slaves in the Saharan oases and among the wealthier classes in North Africa that was going through a period of prosperity (Lydon 2009, 124–5; Austen 1979). The effect of the abolition of the trans-Atlantic slave trade varied by destination country, though. It was more pronounced in the trans-Saharan slave trade from sub-Saharan Africa to North African markets west of Egypt, in particular, Morocco and Libya, but (perhaps unsurprisingly) had less of an impact on the slave trade from the Nilotic Sudan and Ethiopia to Egypt.

Second, slave supply surged because of warfare in sub-Saharan Africa. For one, the *jihad* wars in the newly founded Muslim autocracies in sub-Saharan Africa may have contributed to the rising slave imports of Morocco and Libya, although most of the enslaved population was employed south of the Sahara. For another, Egypt's rising slave imports in 1820–45 can be attributed to Egypt's invasion of Sudan in 1820, which increased its supply of slaves.

Third, the surge in Egypt's slave imports in the 1860s can be traced to the rising demand for slaves that was driven by an exogenous export boom: the Lancashire cotton famine during the American Civil War in 1861–65 that increased the world demand for Egyptian cotton. The Egyptian cotton boom increased the demand for slaves in cotton-suitable villages in rural Egypt. This effect echoes contemporary export booms in other commodities in West Africa south of the Sahara that triggered an increase in the enslavement of the local population. The surge in Egyptian slave demand was met by increasing the supply of slaves via intensified slave raids in the Nilotic Sudan, causing a slight rise in (male) slave prices (Fredriksen 1977, 70–1). The effect of export price booms naturally varied by location owing to the initial suitability of a location to the production of the export commodity whose price surged. Hence, among North African countries, this effect was quite unique to Egypt.

Finally, the diplomatic pressure of European forces on North African countries to abolish slavery and their subsequent colonization led to the gradual decline of the trans-Saharan slave trade during the second half of the 19th century. The main exception was Morocco, which seemed to be more adept at resisting European forces and managed to circumvent both colonization and abolition for much longer than its neighbors (Wright 2007, 66). The rising slave trade in Morocco toward the end of the century can thus be attributed to the redirection of slave supply to its markets after the abolition of slavery in neighboring North African countries.

The chapter draws on two sources. First, it draws on secondary historical literature. Whenever possible, we will bring in quantitative evidence from the literature. Second, and perhaps more importantly, we draw on evidence from a primary archival source: Egypt's individual-level population census samples of 1848 and 1868, which were digitized by Saleh (2013) from the original Arabic hand-written manuscripts at the National Archives of Egypt. The Egyptian censuses are the most comprehensive, and the only known microdata source on the slave population not only in Egypt, but possibly in the entire Middle East and North African region, before the abolition of slavery and the emancipation of the slave population. In this regard, the chapter draws on Saleh (2021)'s findings on the impact of the Lancashire cotton famine in 1861–65 on the emergence of agricultural slavery in rural Egypt, and on the subsequent abolition of slavery in 1877.

The chapter is organized as follows. Section 2 first describes the key empirical facts about the trans-Saharan slave trade, drawing on secondary historical literature. We discuss the long-term trends of the trans-Saharan slave trade since 1800 by destination country, the sources of slave supply, the slave trade routes that crossed the Sahara, and the demand for slaves in North Africa. Section 3 discusses the potential drivers of the major shifts in the trans-Saharan slave trade that have been identified in Section 2. Specifically, it examines the effects of the abolition of the trans-Atlantic slave trade, warfare, the Egyptian cotton boom, and the abolition of the trans-Saharan slave trade. Section 4 concludes, where we highlight the long-term legacy of the trans-Saharan slave trade on today's world, in terms of its impact on the routes of current-day (illegal) immigration flows from sub-Saharan Africa to North Africa and Europe.

2 Trans-Saharan slave migration: the key empirical facts

2.1 Total volume and slave imports by country up to 1900

The trans-Saharan slave trade is a long-standing institution that existed long before the trans-Atlantic slave trade. Although it did not acquire its regularity until the Arab Conquests of North Africa in the 7th century, both the enslavement of people in the Sahara and the trans-Saharan slave trade had long existed before then. It can first be traced to Libyan Berbers, nomadic tribes who lived in the Sahara c. 2000 BCE, and who turned to raiding and enslaving other desert tribes or settled communities to adapt to their arid environment. The nomads' seasonal migration facilitated the development of a trade network across the desert that transported slaves among other commodities. The Arab Conquests furthered an already existing system of trade by creating a constant demand for larger numbers of slaves and more commercial incentives through intercontinental trade connections (Wright 2007, 3–18).

Estimating the volume of trans-Saharan trade is a particularly challenging task given the lack of documentation on the size and frequency of caravans crossing the Sahara. Perhaps

Austen (1979, 1992)'s attempt to estimate the volume of this trade is the most systematic and most exhaustive to date. He relies primarily on literary accounts and consular reports of Europeans who lived or traveled through the region at the time. Such accounts, while not always entirely reliable, are the most abundant sources of data that historians can rely on. Austen bolsters those literary accounts with more systematic customs records from slave markets in Cairo and Tripoli. He also evaluates the plausibility of these accounts in light of the source's experience with the region and the slave trade and filters out those inconsistent with systematic data or with more experienced sources. In addition, Austen uses available evidence on the slave population from census data as well as the historical evidence on spurts of demand for slaves for military or productive purposes to estimate the magnitude of trade comparatively throughout the centuries. Based on this careful analysis of available evidence he suggests that the 19th century, at least until 1880, witnessed an exceptional boom in the slave trade that is twice as large as the highest estimate in prior centuries (Figure 3.1).

Nevertheless, the estimates of the total volume of trade over a century mask the differences in slave imports across destination countries in North Africa. Figure 3.2 depicts Austen's estimates of annual slave imports by country in North Africa from 1700 to 1895. Two findings emerge. First, across North African countries, Egypt stands out as the largest importer of slaves, followed by Libya and Morocco. Slave imports were relatively low in Tunisia and Algeria. Second, across periods, there was a slight increase in slave imports in Egypt, Morocco, and Libya, during the first half of the 19th century. Egypt's annual slave imports rose from 2,600 slaves in 1800–10 to 10,400 slaves in 1811–40. Morocco's annual slave imports increased from 2,000 in 1700–1810 to 3,000 in 1811–40, whereas Libya's annual slave imports increased from 2,700 slaves in 1700–99 to 3,100 slaves in 1800–56. This

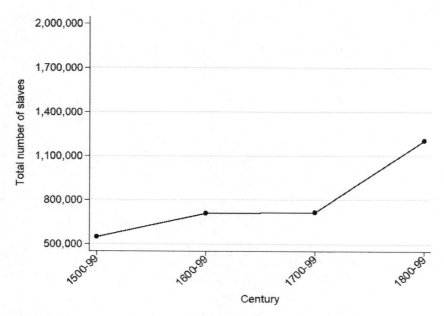

FIGURE 3.1 Estimate of the total number of slaves crossing the Sahara per century.
Source: Austen (1979, 66).

rise was followed by a subsequent decline, and then a final surge in slave imports both in Egypt in the 1860s and in Morocco toward the end of the century.

Austen did not have access to the Egyptian population censuses of 1848 and 1868, though. To complement Austen's estimates, Saleh (2021)'s census-based estimates of Egypt's slave population in 1848 and 1868 reveal that it tripled between these two years from around 55,000 to 173,000, which is consistent with Austen's estimates in Figures 3.1 and 3.2. Figure 3.3 shows estimates of the slave population (i.e., the stock) in Algeria, Egypt, and Libya during the 19th century, which are consistent with the flow estimates in Figure 3.2.

Overall, Figures 3.1–3.3 indicate that the trans-Saharan forced migration of slaves increased modestly during the first decades of the 19th century. It then witnessed an unprecedented surge during the middle decades of the 19th century, because of the Egyptian cotton boom in 1861–65. Finally, the rising European pressure to abolish slavery in North Africa led to its decline during the late decades of the 19th century, except for Morocco where slavery remained resilient for a longer period.

2.2 Supply of slaves in sub-Saharan Africa

Black slaves who were exported to Egypt came primarily from Eastern Africa: the Nilotic Sudan and Ethiopia, whereas those who were exported to North Africa west of Egypt originated from the northern savanna regions, extending from the African Atlantic Coast in the west to present-day Chad in the east, known as the "Sudan" or "Bilad es Sudan," which translates to the "land of the Blacks" (Map 3.1). Within this region, slaves primarily originated from the central Sudan, particularly from the Sokoto Caliphate (in Hausaland, in present-day Chad and Nigeria) and Bornu (in Kanem-Bornu that extends

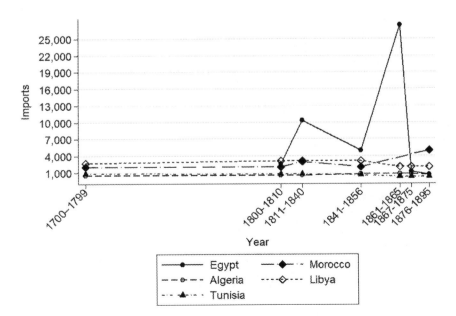

FIGURE 3.2 Slave imports (period annual averages) by country in North Africa (1700–1895). *Source*: Austen (1992, 227).

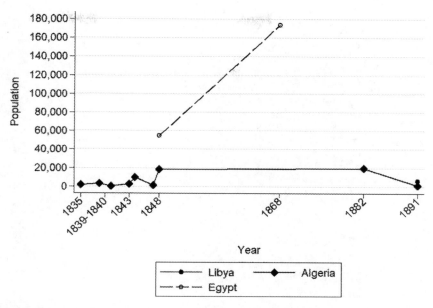

FIGURE 3.3 Slave population by country in North Africa (1835–91).
Sources: Austen (1992, 233–34) and Egypt's population census samples in 1848 and 1868.

in present-day Chad, Nigeria, and Libya) (Mahadi 1992, 111). Western Sudan also supplied the trans-Saharan trade, along with its larger trans-Atlantic trade outlet. Statistics on slaves who returned home after manumission in the beginning of the 20th century reveal that the largest proportion of slaves came from towns raided by two states in western Sudan: Samori (in present-day Guinea) and Sikasso (in present-day Mali) (Klein 1992, 46).

Warfare was the primary enslavement mechanism. Slaves were mostly war prisoners, enslaved either during large-scale slave raiding by centralized states of their vulnerable neighboring communities or during a war between neighboring states of relatively equal power. Other non-systematic enslavement mechanisms included kidnapping and small-scale raiding in lawless areas and the enslavement of convicted criminals as a method of punishment (Lovejoy 2011, 83–4).

2.3 Shifts in the trans-Saharan trade routes

Several routes spread across the Sahara creating a network linking the Sahara and North Africa with sub-Saharan Africa and enabling the trans-Saharan caravan trade. Trade routes were not fixed, though, and they often shifted depending on political conditions south of the Sahara, security conditions in the Sahara, climatic changes, and investment in the infrastructure by rulers in the region (Wright 2007, 14–5).

Caravans traveling from North Africa to the south of the Sahara carried European luxury commodities in addition to guns and ammunition, North African commodities, such as clothes, carpets, coarse silk, spices, perfumes, cowries, and beads, and Saharan exports such as tobacco, dates, and salt. Caravans going from sub-Saharan Africa to the Sahara and

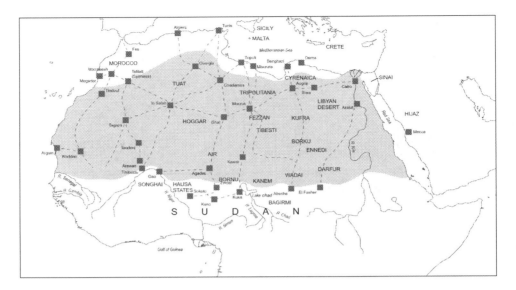

MAP 3.1 Trans-Saharan trade routes.
Source: Digitized by Stefan de Jong, based on Wright (2007, x).

North Africa carried mainly clothes, kola nuts, and most importantly (at least in the 19th century) slaves (Boahen 1962).[1]

In addition to the northern and southern termini, each route had a rendezvous where merchants could obtain camels and hire camel drivers and guides, and where financiers or their representatives resided. Moreover, fertile oases on the route acted as refreshment centers, where food and fresh water could be obtained, and an interchange of camels and guides could be made.

Five main routes crossed the Sahara to North Africa during the 19th century (see Map 3.1). (1) Perhaps the oldest was the **Tripoli-Fezzan-Bornu** route, starting south from Lake Chad, in Kukawa, capital of Bornu, and ending in the Regency of Tripoli. Murzuk in Fezzan (in present-day Libya) was the refreshment center on this route. While this route had historically carried most of the slave traffic coming from central Sudan to the north, it was losing its importance during the 19th century due to political tensions in the region and lack of security.

(2) The **Ghadames-Air-Kano** route, the central route, was situated to the west of the Tripoli-Fezzan-Bornu route. It started from Kano in the Hausa states, and went through Zinder and Agades in Air, arriving in Ghat, its main refreshment center. In Ghat, caravans would go either eastward to Murzuk or further to the north in Ghadames. This was the most important commercial route in the 19th century due to the shift of the political center of gravity from Bornu to the Sokoto Caliphate in the Hausaland. In addition, during the 19th century, this route was under the control of two of the most powerful branches of the Saharan tribe, the Tuareg. As their livelihood depended on caravan trade, they invested in route security (Boahen 1962).

Until the mid-19th century, Ghadames was the most important rendezvous point on this route (Wright 2007, 89). The Ghadamsi merchants played the role of middlemen between the northern trading centers and the entrepôts of western Sudan, and they were the main financiers of the trans-Saharan trade. They succeeded in establishing extensive business networks throughout central Sudan, and they invested a substantial part of the capital they advanced in slave trade (Mahadi 1992, 118). However, the abolition of the slave trade in Tunisia and the occupation of Algeria by France both led to the decline of Ghadames as a trading center. This worked in favor of Ghat, which, by the mid-19th century, became one of the busiest market centers in the Sahara and acted as a terminus for small caravans coming from the north or the south (Wright 2007, 97).

(3) The eastern route **Cyrenaica-Kufra-Wadai** was developed under the Senussi regime in Cyrenaica during the last quarter of the 19th century, as a substitute for the older eastern route. It went from the Sultanate of Wadai in the south to Benghazi in Cyrenaica in the north. Besides being a more direct route than its historical predecessor, the rulers of the Senussi regime gave it special attention by ensuring its safety, and by digging wells, and establishing *zawiyas* (lodges or hotels) along the route. This was the last operating trans-Saharan route by the beginning of the 20th century, before it came to a standstill following the French and Italian occupation of North Africa (Boahen 1962; Wright 2007, 70–2).

(4) The western route **Taghaza-Timbuctu** started south in Timbuctu and Gao and reached its main northern terminus in Mogador (in Morocco). Alternatively, caravans could diverge to its branch route through Tuat to reach Algiers, Constantine, and Tunis. Merchants were increasingly avoiding this route by the mid-19th century due to its deterioration in safety. This was largely due to tensions in western Sudan between the military states, and in the Sahara itself between different tribes fighting to gain control over the route. Morocco's demand for black slaves was catered instead by In Salah entrepôt in Tuat. Tuat owed its centrality in the slave trade to the emergence of Ghat as an alternative intermediate mid-Saharan source of supply, largely replacing Ghadames and Murzuk (Boahen 1962; Wright 2007, 142–3).

(5) Besides the aforementioned routes in western and central Sudan, slaves from the Nilotic Sudan and Ethiopia were transported to Egypt via several routes that crossed the Egyptian desert. The main route in this trade was **Darb al-Arba`in** (translates as the 40-days route), which started south in Kobbei in northern Darfur and reached its most northern destination in Asyut in the Nile Valley (Fredriksen 1977, 29–38). Slaves were then transported north along the Nile to Cairo and the Nile Delta. An alternative route started from Sinnar and crossed the Nubian desert to reach Aswan or Asyut in the Nile Valley. A third route started from Kordofan to Dongola, and from there either joined the Darb al-Arab`in or continued north along the Nile. The Nubians in southern Egypt controlled the slave trade within Egypt.

The trans-Saharan journey from the south to the north was a difficult one where death was inevitable for some of the slaves. The journey, whether in the west to Maghreb or in the east to Egypt, was approximately 1,000 km equivalent to a roughly 40-day march through an arid desert with few watering places or food sources (Alexander 2001). In the beginning of the journey, slaves were tied together and heavily guarded with armed men. However, once they reached the Sahara, slaves were usually not tied because the chance of them escaping was minimal and, in fact, their only chance to survive was to keep up with the caravan (Wright 2007, 51–2). Treatment of slaves differed greatly between different tribes. While the Tebu who traded in slaves from Bornu left their slaves hungry and naked, walked them by force, and whipped them, the Tuareg who traded in slaves from the Hausaland clothed and fed them and traveled by short journeys. This resulted in a significantly different death rate in the caravan between the Tuareg, 5%–10%, and the Tebu, 20%–50% (Wright 2007, 83). Once in the mid-Saharan entrepôts, slaves were usually prepared for northern markets by being cleaned, dressed, and encouraged to rest and gain weight. They were also taught a few words of Arabic and the basic tenets of Islam to increase their value in the market (Wright 2007, 120).

2.4 Demand for slaves in North Africa

Slavery was a long-standing institution in North Africa. Enslavement of foreign non-Muslims via raids (*ghazwas*) was permitted by Islamic law. Slavery was self-perpetuating in law; a slave's conversion to Islam did not result in emancipation, and the offspring of a male slave were automatically slaves. Concubinage was thus a means of integration in the society: a concubine who had borne her master's child could not be sold or given away, her children were free, and she was set free at her master's death (Hunwick 1992, 16).

Slaves in North Africa were mostly, but not entirely, from sub-Saharan Africa. Around 96% of slaves in Egypt in 1848 were blacks from the Nilotic Sudan (94%) and browns from Ethiopia (2%). The remaining 4% were whites from Circassia and Georgia.

Unlike slavery in the Americas, where many slaves reproduced and formed families in their own independent households, the slave population of North Africa was not sustainable by natural growth, and annual slave imports were necessary to meet the demand for slaves. This is due to the fact that most households owned either all-male or all-female slaves, as indicated by the Egyptian population census of 1848. As slaves mostly lived in their masters' households, and male slaves were permitted to marry only female slaves, there was a small probability for them to form families by marrying a female slave from another household. Also, many male slaves were castrated to be given access to their masters' households. In addition, slaves in North Africa had a short service life either because of early deaths due to diseases or because of manumission (Wright 2007, 2).

The distribution of slave ownership among the local population in North Africa was highly skewed, and more concentrated in urban areas. Prior to the cotton boom of 1861–65, the 1848 population census in Egypt reveals that only 3% of households in cities and less than 1% in rural provinces owned slaves. Slaves in rural areas in 1848 were relatively more concentrated in the non-cotton-growing provinces of Upper Egypt (Nile Valley). Importantly, most of Egypt's slave population resided in households headed by free individuals. Households headed by slaves (i.e., slaves forming their own families and living independently from their masters), which were widespread in the Americas, were quite rare in Egypt.

The distribution of slave ownership in Morocco was largely similar to Egypt prior to the Lancashire cotton famine, in the sense that it was more concentrated in cities, where the demand for slaves primarily came from relatively wealthy merchants and officials. The majority of slave owners had only one slave, while only the rich could afford to purchase more than one slave. Marriage was often an occasion to purchase a slave for newly married couples. Specifically, households preferred purchasing a slave to recruiting a free servant, because slave ownership signaled a household's higher social status and prestige (Ennaji 1999, 4).

Owning slaves in Morocco was not confined to urban households, though. Evidence suggests that households outside the urban centers purchased slaves too. According to Wright (2007), many slaves in caravans crossing the Sahara from western Sudan to the main Moroccan markets of Marrakesh and Fez never reached their final destinations and were instead purchased by local communities in the desert and oases, be it nomadic or settled in current-day Mauritania, Western Sahara, as well as in southern and rural Morocco. Perhaps unsurprisingly, the demand for slaves among these local communities depended both on slave prices and on the favorability of their local environmental conditions to herding and agriculture, which varied across years and locations.

2.5 Occupational and gender composition of slaves in North Africa

Slaves were employed in three main sectors: domestic service, military service, and agriculture and pasture. We do not have statistics on the occupational distribution of slaves across these three domains, as the Egyptian 1848 and 1868 population censuses do not record the occupation of slaves. It is likely, though, that Egypt's urban slaves in 1848 were employed as domestic servants, as they mostly resided in their masters' households. These urban slaves were 75% females. Similarly, the majority of slaves in Moroccan cities (around two-thirds) were females (Wright 2007), who were domestic servants. Local communities in rural Morocco, and nomadic tribes, also purchased female slaves for work in domestic service.

Domestic servants were employed in housework. Females also worked as nursemaids or wet nurses, and as concubines if they were owned by a male household head. Male slaves were employed to assist their masters in their commercial activities. They also played the role of messenger, and they would go to the market to fetch goods needed for their master's business and household. Domestic slaves had to take care of public and private rooms in the house (given the rigid segregation between female and male areas). Male slaves were also charged with the task of transporting animal husbandry, and they would accompany their male masters when they rode out to clear the way and protect them from aggressors (Hunwick 1992, 14–5).

The second sector that employed slaves was agriculture, pasture, and mining. However, the employment share of this sector was relatively limited in comparison to domestic service, prior to the cotton boom in Egypt in 1861–65. An early attempt at introducing agricultural slavery in southern Iraq under the Abbasids in the 9th century ended with a slave rebellion and hampered further introduction of agricultural slavery by the Abbasids and by subsequent Caliphates in the Middle East and North Africa. Perhaps more importantly, agriculture in North Africa (and in Egypt in particular) traditionally relied on the local population that was subject to a different form of labor coercion: restrictions on mobility. Coercing local labor in agriculture, whether directly by the state or by local tax farmers, persisted through the 19th century, and arguably mitigated the demand for slaves, because it was both cheaper and more productive to coerce locals. This does not mean though that agricultural slavery did not exist at all prior to the cotton boom. Black slaves in 1848 rural Egypt, where the sex ratio of slaves was balanced, were employed in the (non-cotton-growing) Nile Valley to work in state plantations and public works. Rural communities and nomadic tribes in Morocco also purchased male slaves who worked in agriculture and pasture.

Slave labor was also employed in pasture and mining. Saharan nomads such as the Moors in Western Sahara and the Tuareg in central Sahara employed black slaves for herding flocks, hewing wood, drawing water, and as a general workforce in their camps. In Western Sahara, slaves were used to work in the salt pans and to extract and smelt the copper. In Egyptian Nubia they were employed in gold mining (Hunwick 1992, 21).

The third sector that employed slaves was the army. While employing slaves in the military service was a long-standing tradition in the Middle East and North Africa, its importance declined during the 19th century. White slave soldiers (Mamluks) of mostly Turkic origin were first employed by the Abbasid Caliphate during the 9th century. Ahmed ibn Tulun, the Turkish autonomous viceroy of Egypt under the Abbasid Caliphate in 868–84, then introduced black slave troops into Egypt. They were also employed by the Ikhshidid dynasty in Egypt in 935–69. Turkic-origin Mamluks ruled Egypt and the Levant from 1250 until 1517 (Al-Sayyid Marsot 1984). Following the Ottoman conquest of Egypt in 1517, Mamluks continued as a military elite class. Muhammad Ali Pasha, the autonomous Ottoman viceroy of Egypt in 1805–48, massacred all Mamluk leaders in 1811, in order to consolidate his power, thus largely putting an end to their privileged status. Although he then attempted to recruit black slaves in the Egyptian army after his invasion of Sudan in 1820, his attempt was not successful, and so he turned instead to conscripting local Egyptians starting from 1822 (Helal 1999). In 1848 (resp. 1868), retired Mamluks constituted only 4% (resp. 6%) of the urban slave population in Egypt.

West of Egypt, black troops were first introduced to Tunisia in the 9th century under the rule of the Aghlabids. In Morocco, black troops were first introduced under the reign of Yusuf ibn Tashfin (1061–106), ruler of Almoravids, and were also used by Almoravids' successors, the Almohads (Hunwick 1992, 18–9). However, the most prominent incident of the use of black troops was under the reign of the second Alawid sultan, Mulay Ismail (1672–1727), who created an exclusively black slave army which was maintained via both the trans-Saharan slave trade and a reproductive program. In its heyday, this army reached 150,000 men. They were later dispersed in 1737 by Mulay Ismail's successor (Hunwick 1992).

3 Drivers of the major shifts in trans-Saharan slave migration

The key shifts in the 19th-century trans-Saharan slave trade can be summarized as follows. First, the slight rise in slave imports of Egypt, and to a lesser extent Morocco and Libya, during the first half of the century. Second, the unprecedented surge in Egypt's slave imports in the 1860s. Third, the abolition of the trans-Saharan trade and the rise in Morocco's slave imports toward the end of the century. In this section, we analyze a number of potential drivers of these shifting patterns of trans-Saharan slave migration.

3.1 Impact of the abolition of the trans-Atlantic slave trade

The abolitionist movement had made concrete victories by the beginning of the 19th century, and instituted abolition, first in Denmark in 1802, then in Great Britain and the US in 1807 and 1808, respectively. There are two possible impacts of the abolition of the trans-Atlantic slave trade, in the absence of any confounding shift in the demand for or the supply of slaves. First, slave supply may persist at the pre-abolition (high) level during the short to medium run. In the absence of an immediate supply response, the consequent excess supply of slaves will be redirected to both employment in sub-Saharan Africa and exportation to alternative destinations, including North Africa. Second, slave supply will likely respond in the longer run, by reducing enslavement of the local population. According to this analysis, we would expect the trans-Saharan slave trade to increase in the short to medium run in the aftermath of the abolition, before it declines to its pre-abolition levels.

Unfortunately, we are not able to disentangle these effects in detail due to the lack of yearly data on slave imports in North Africa. More importantly, a number of confounding shocks took place that make it difficult to isolate the impact of the abolition. As Figure 3.2 indicates, the trend of slave imports varied by destination country. Specifically, slave imports of Egypt, and to a lesser extent Morocco and Libya, appear to have increased during the first half of the 19th century.

The causes behind this increase in slave imports vary between Libya and Morocco on the one hand and Egypt on the other hand (see the discussion of the rise in Egypt's slave imports in 1820–45 in the next sub-section). The reason is that Libya and Morocco indeed imported slaves from western and central Sudan and were thus more exposed to the impact of the abolition of the trans-Atlantic slave trade that drew its slave supply from the same locations. Egypt, however, relied on slave imports from the Nilotic Sudan and Ethiopia, and only secondarily on slave imports from central Sudan (passing through Libya). The Nilotic Sudan and Ethiopia were too far to be important suppliers of slaves for the trans-Atlantic route.

There is some reason to believe that the observed (slight) rise in slave imports in Morocco and Libya, but not Egypt, is driven by the abolition of the trans-Atlantic slave trade. While the scarcity of data does not allow us to provide conclusive evidence on this point, the scant data on prices in West Africa provides suggestive evidence. Figure 3.4 depicts the evolution of slave prices in the Atlantic coast and West Africa. We plot data on slave prices in Morocco from the later period for comparison. We see that the prices had reached a peak in 1807, right before they declined sharply after the abolition (British laws instituted in 1807 became effective in 1808). While we do not have comparable records for prices in Morocco and Libya, it is likely that a decrease in the slave prices in the south of the Sahara was echoed in the north. Indeed, the later time-series data on slave prices from Morocco is

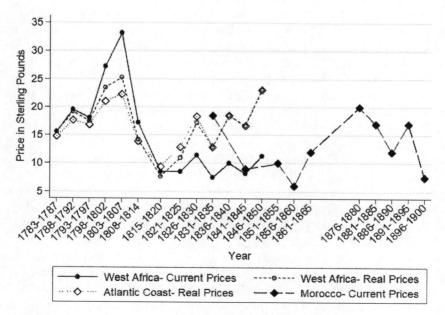

FIGURE 3.4 Prices of slaves in different markets of West Africa (1783–1900).
Sources: Lovejoy (2011, 139); Shroeter (1992, 194–6).

highly correlated with the series on slave prices in West Africa during the period in which we observe both series. The decrease in slave prices due to the abolition of the trans-Atlantic slave trade may thus explain why we observe a slight rise in slave imports in Libya and Morocco during this period.

The positive impact of the abolition of the trans-Atlantic slave trade on Libya's and Morocco's slave imports does not imply though that the trans-Saharan slave trade substituted for the forgone slave demand of the Americas. In reality, the fact that the observed increase in slave imports in Morocco and Libya is modest suggests that the post-abolition slave supply surplus was primarily absorbed by local demand in sub-Saharan Africa, and that it had less of an effect on the flow of slaves crossing the Sahara (Klein 1992, 41–3). We do not have data on the relative share of the slave export demand in the north, compared to the local demand for slaves in the south, during the first half of the 19th century. Travelers' observations during the second half of the 19th century suggest, however, that slave raiding was primarily motivated by the local demand in the south. Fisher (2001, 106) estimates the proportion of exported slaves to be at most 5% of slaves sold locally, based on both travelers' observations on the infrequency of northbound slave caravans and the size of the local slave market.

3.2 Impact of wars

The impact of the abolition of the trans-Atlantic slave trade on the trans-Saharan slave trade was confounded by another factor that had a large impact on the slave supply during the 19th century: warfare. Two important inter-state conflicts stand out: Egypt's invasion of Sudan in 1820 and the holy "jihad" wars in the south of the Sahara. Both conflicts resulted in an increase in slave supply, and to some extent, a rise in the trans-Saharan slave trade.

For one, the observed rise in Egypt's slave imports in 1820–45 was likely driven by Egypt's invasion of the Nilotic Sudan in 1820, which was motivated not only by territorial expansion but also by controlling and increasing the slave supply. Slave raiding even became a method of paying salaries to the officers of the Egyptian army, who captured slaves and sold them on the market. The process continued through the 1840s and was only hampered due to European pressure on the Egyptian state (Fredriksen 1977).

The warfare in central and western Sudan increased the slave supply west of Egypt. The Sokoto Caliphate, formed in 1804, was the largest theocratic state in central and western Sudan. It became a primary player in the jihad wars and a major slave supplier. Also, the transformation of the neighboring empire of Bornu (in present-day Chad and Nigeria) into an Islamic state and the consolidation of power in the hands of its ruler resulted in an increase in slave-raiding activities (Mahadi 1992, 115–6). In western Sudan, the symbiotic relationship between state leaders and trans-Saharan merchants in the burgeoning theocratic states following the example of the Sokoto Caliphate facilitated slave raiding and boosted the supply of slaves (Klein 1998, 2–3, Lydon 2009, 112–3).

While the consequent rise in slave supply was mostly absorbed locally (see Section 3.1), it probably contributed to the rise in the slave imports of Morocco and Libya during the first half of the 19th century. Again, we lack the detailed quantitative data that would allow us to test this hypothesis, but we have qualitative evidence for Libya. First, Tripoli (in present-day Libya) repeatedly invaded Baghirmi (in present-day Chad) to capture slaves. Baghirmi, a Sudanic state to the east of Bornu, had been an important supplier of slaves captured from southern non-Muslim states before 1800. It later fell victim to its neighbors' avidity for slaves. Starting

1806 it was repeatedly invaded by Bornu, Wadai (in present-day Chad), and Tripoli, hence turning into a source of captives itself (La Rue 2003, 38). Second, the Bornu empire consolidated its relationship with North African rulers and merchants and gave them a free hand to raid for slaves in the region, to resist the threat of the jihadist conquests from the expanding Sokoto Caliphate. The close relationship between Muhammad al-Kanemi, the ruler of the Bornu empire, and Yusuf Pasha Karamanli, the ruler of Tripoli (1795–1832), thus boosted the volume of trade (including slaves) between Bornu and Tripoli (Mahadi 1992, 115–7).

3.3 Impact of commodity export booms

Egypt witnessed an unprecedented surge in its slave imports in the 1860s due to the Lancashire cotton famine that was caused by the American Civil War in 1861–65, and the consequent increase in demand for slaves among Egyptian cotton farmers. Yearly slave imports increased to around 27,500 over this period. This is supported by the slave population that we observe in the Egyptian 1848 and 1868 population censuses, which suggest that the slave population tripled between 1848 and 1868 from 55,00 to 174,000 (Figure 3.3).

The boom in cotton prices caused Egypt, the largest cotton producer after the US and India in the 19th century, to quadruple its output and exports. Egypt's cotton production and exports remained at a high level, even after prices subsided. As a result, cotton's share in Egypt's exports jumped from 25% on the eve of the cotton famine to 80%, a level that was maintained until the oil boom in the 1970s. The increased cotton production led to the emergence of agricultural slavery in Egypt's cotton-suitable villages, where slavery was relatively rare prior to the famine. Specifically, the 1848 and 1868 population censuses reveal that there was a rise in household slaveholdings among landholding farmers and village headmen in cotton-suitable villages, in comparison to non-cotton-suitable villages (Saleh, 2021).[2] The increased demand for slaves was met via intensified slave raids in the Nilotic Sudan. Consistent with this interpretation, Figure 3.5 shows that prices of male black slaves in Egypt increased after the cotton boom. The gender composition of the slave population also changed with the cotton boom from traditionally female-majority slavery (in cities) prior to the cotton boom to male-majority slavery during the cotton boom. The impact on slaveholdings among farmers in the cotton-suitable villages is attributable to the surge of imports of male slaves in working age.

While the impact of the Lancashire cotton famine, or more broadly export price booms, on agricultural slavery is quite unique to Egypt among North African countries in the 19th century, it echoes similar effects on employment of slaves in sub-Saharan Africa. This was partially due to the efforts of the abolitionist movement itself (see the next section): while the movement sought to promote "legitimate trade" in commodities other than slaves to divert the focus of merchants from the, now considered illegal, slave trade, they did not expect that the expansion of the production of other commodities in itself will intensify the use of slaves. Accordingly, the increased demand on agricultural commodities produced by slaves led to an increased demand for slave labor (Lovejoy 2011, 136).

3.4 Impact of the abolition of the trans-Saharan slave trade

The increased effort to abolish the slave trade throughout the 19th century, first in the Atlantic basin and later across the Sahara, increased the local employment of slaves south of the Sahara, but had its effects on the trans-Saharan slave trade.

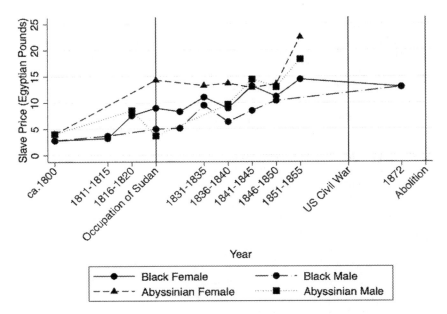

FIGURE 3.5 Slave prices in Cairo slave markets (1800–77).
Source: Saleh (2021).

First, Figure 3.2 shows that the slave imports of Egypt, Morocco, and Libya declined in the middle decades of the 19th century. This decline was probably due to the increased European pressure to abolish slave trade. This took the form of British diplomatic pressure on Egypt because of the British abolitionist movement (Fredriksen 1977, 157–80). As a result, Egypt stopped its state-sponsored slave raids around 1845, and slave imports to Morocco and Libya slowed down as well.

During the second half of the 19th century, the abolitionist movement achieved some success, although both slave supply and demand increased; the supply was boosted by the access of warlords and slave raiders in sub-Saharan Africa to more advanced weaponry that facilitated slaving and raiding, and the demand was boosted because of the Egyptian cotton boom. The abolitionist movement was actively seeking to abolish the slave trade either through gaining the buy-in of the rulers in the region or through imposed colonial rule. Official abolition was thus achieved in Tunisia (1841), Egypt (1877), and Ottoman Tripoli (1857) through diplomatic pressure on their independent rulers and the Ottoman Sultan-Caliph, respectively, and in Algeria (1848) and Morocco (1922) through direct French rule (Wright 2007, 64, 156, 163–4).

Slavery abolition led to the gradual decline of Egypt's slave imports in the 1870s as well, and its virtual disappearance in the 1890s. The Egyptian post-1877 population census data allow us to trace the emancipated slave population by examining the population share of Sudanese-origin individuals.[3] The data suggest that emancipated slaves moved out of the cotton-suitable districts to the less cotton-suitable districts. The emancipated slave population was (self-)identified as Egyptian in the censuses by 1927.

The official abolition of slavery in these countries was by no means rigorously enforced across their territories, and trafficking was widely exercised.[4] Nonetheless, these measures took a toll on the size of trade. For example, European travelers passing through Murzuk have estimated that the slave trade was one-third of its previous size in 1869 and that it had ended by 1877 (Wright 2007, 159).

However, the (legal) trans-Saharan slave trade persisted up to the beginning of the 20th century in Morocco, which managed to resist both colonization and the European pressure for abolition for much longer than its neighbors (Wright 2007, 66). This may explain why it witnessed a surge in its slave imports in 1876–95, probably as it remained the last legal destination of slave exports in North Africa.

4 Conclusion

This chapter documented the key empirical facts about the trans-Saharan slave trade and its long-term trend since 1800. It then analyzed four potential drivers of the shifting patterns of the trade since 1800: (1) abolition of the trans-Atlantic slave trade, (2) warfare, (3) export booms in other commodities, and (4) European pressure on North African countries to abolish the trans-Saharan slave trade. Each of these drivers has arguably impacted the slave trade crossing the Sahara, although this impact was far from uniform. It varied by destination country in North Africa, and across time periods.

The chapter opens two areas of research. First, while we identified potential drivers of the shifts of the trans-Saharan slave trade, detailed studies of the impact of each of these factors are essential. The feasibility of these studies is crucially dependent on the availability of data sources. Thus far, the literature on this trade has largely relied on European travelers' estimates and colonial censuses. While these are important sources of information, they are not sufficient for two reasons. For one, they do not provide information on the pre-colonial or pre-European-contact period. For another, they represent the viewpoint of one actor: the colonial administration or the European travelers. The literature arguably needs to include other viewpoints, even in the data construction process. This is not an easy task, however, because histories of the local populations in sub-Saharan Africa, and to a lesser extent, North Africa, are largely undocumented. There are ways around this, though. Examples of potential data sources include local archival pre-colonial sources, such as the Ottoman and Egyptian (state) population censuses and land tax records, as well as novel methods of quantifying local ethnographic and oral histories and surveys of descendants of agents of the slave trade (traders, raiders, slaves).

The second area of research is understanding the long-term legacy of the trans-Saharan slave trade. Following the colonization of the region which drew borders cutting across existing ethnic, cultural, commercial, and geographical networks, the trade routes lost their significance. However, in the late 20th century, successive droughts and conflicts in sub-Saharan Africa left behind migrants and refugees aspiring to make North Africa either their home or their transit to Europe. Old trade routes thus re-emerged as illegal migration routes, and historical trade centers regained their significance as migration hubs (Map 3.2). In migration hubs, migrants stop to finance and organize the next step of their journey, and businesses of migration-related services (accommodation, communications, money transfer, etc.) flourish. These hubs, therefore, play a similar role to what a refreshment center once played. Abéché (Chad), Kano (Nigeria), and Gao (Mali), once the southern termini of the eastern, central, and western routes, respectively, are now important migration hubs. This is also the case for historical refreshment centers such as Kufra (Libya) and Agadez (Niger) (De Haas 2006; Schapendonk 2010, 129–30). In fact, Agadez is one of the most prominent migration hubs

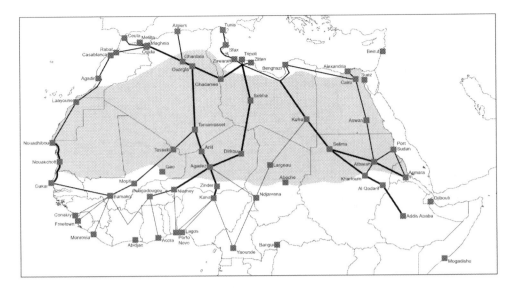

MAP 3.2 Present Trans-Saharan migration routes.
Source: Chart created by Stefan de Jong, based on De Haas (2006).

in Western Sahara since most of the overland migrants to the Maghreb traverse it in their journey (Bensaâd 2003). From Agadez, migrants can take the route to Sebha in southern Libya from where they go to Tripoli or other coastal cities or to Tunisia. Otherwise, migrants can take the route to Tamanrasset in southern Algeria and move northward to enter Morocco via Oujda (De Haas 2008). In the east of the Sahara, migrant workers and refugees from Sudan, Somalia, Eritrea, and Ethiopia either settle in Egypt or migrate to Libya, via Sudan, Chad, or Egypt. Similar to the central role that was once played by Saharan nomads in caravan trade in the past securing routes and providing guides, current-day smugglers, who are often former nomads themselves, facilitate the journey for refugees and migrants through their connections with local police and intermediaries to employers in Europe (De Haas 2006).

Notes

1 In 1858, the British Consul-General in Tripoli estimated that slave trade constituted more than two-thirds of the trans-Saharan caravan trade.
2 Saleh (2021) employs two measures of cotton suitability: (1) the Food and Agriculture Organization – Global Agro-Ecological Zones (FAO-GAEZ) cotton suitability index in irrigation-fed agriculture and the distance to the Damietta branch which determines access to summer irrigation canals.
3 While there was a sizable free Sudanese population in urban Egypt in 1848 and 1868, the vast majority of the rural Sudanese population was brought into Egypt as slaves.
4 Consular reports and explorers' accounts c. 1850s suggest that the annual number of slaves exported to North Africa west of Egypt was 9,500 during this period. It is believed that of these, 5,000 went to the Regency of Tripoli, 2,500 to Morocco, and the rest were smuggled into Algeria and Tunisia. Around 2,000 of the 5,000 sent into Tripoli were re-exported to other destinations (Boahen 1962).

References

Alexander, J. 2001. "Islam, Archaeology and Slavery in Africa." *World Archeology* 33(1): 44–60.

Al-Sayyid Marsot, Afaf. 1984. *A History of Egypt: From the Arab Conquest to the Present.* Cambridge: Cambridge University Press.

Austen, Ralph. 1979. "The Trans-Saharan Slave Trade: A Tentative Census." In *The Uncommon Market: Essays in the Economic History of the Atlantic Slave Trade*, edited by Henry Gemery and Jan Hogendorn, 23–76. New York: Academic Press.

Austen, Ralph. 1992. "The Mediterranean Islamic Slave Trade Out of Africa: A Tentative Census." In *The Human Commodity: Perspectives on the Trans-Saharan Slave Trade*, edited by Elizabeth Savage, 214–48. London: Frank Cass & Co. Ltd.

Bensaâd, Ali. 2003. "Agadez, carrefour migratoire sahélo-maghrébin." *Revue Européenne des Migrations Internationales* 19(1): 7–28.

Boahen, Adu. 1962. "The Caravan Trade in the Nineteenth Century." *Journal of African History* 3(2): 349–59.

De Haas, Hein. 2006. *Trans-Saharan Migration to North Africa and the EU: Historical Roots and Current Trends.* https://www.migrationpolicy.org/article/trans-saharan-migration-north-africa-and-eu-historical-roots-and-current-trends (accessed: 09-08-2020).

De Haas, Hein. 2008. *Irregular Migration from West Africa to the Maghreb and the European Union: An Overview of Recent Trends.* Geneva: International Organization for Migration.

Eltis, David. 2021. "A Brief Overview of the Trans-Atlantic Slave Trade." In *Slave Voyages: The Trans-Atlantic Slave Trade Database*, https://www.slavevoyages.org/voyage/about (accessed: 03-08-2021).

Ennaji, Mohammed. 1999. *Serving the Master: Slavery and Society in Nineteenth Century Morocco.* New York: St. Martin's Press.

Fisher, Humphrey. 2001. *Slavery in the History of Muslim Black Africa.* London: Hurst and Company.

Fredriksen, Borge. 1977. *Slavery and Its Abolition in Nineteenth-Century Egypt.* Bergen: Historisk Institutt Universitetet I Bergen.

Helal, E. A. 1999. *Al-raqiq fi misr fil qarn al-tasi' ashar* (Slavery in Egypt in the Nineteenth Century). Cairo: Dar-Al-Arabi Publishing House.

Hunwick, John. 1992. "Black Slaves in the Mediterranean World: Introduction to a Neglected Aspect of the African Diaspora." In *The Human Commodity: Perspectives on the Trans-Saharan Slave Trade*, edited by Elizabeth Savage, 5–38. London: Frank Cass & Co. Ltd.

Klein, Martin. 1992. "The Slave Trade in the Western Sudan during the Nineteenth Century." In *The Human Commodity: Perspectives on the Trans-Saharan Slave Trade*, edited by Elizabeth Savage, 39–60. London: Frank Cass & Co. Ltd.

Klein, Martin. 1998. *Slavery and Colonial Rule in French West Africa.* Cambridge: Cambridge University Press.

La Rue, Michael. 2003. The Frontiers of Enslavement: Baghirmi and the Trans-Saharan Slave Routes. In *Slavery on the frontiers of Islam*, edited by Paul Lovejoy, 31–54. Princeton, NJ: Markus Wiener Publishers.

Lovejoy, Paul. 2011. *Transformations in Slavery: A History of Slavery in Africa* (3rd edn). New York: Cambridge University Press.

Lydon, Ghislaine. 2009. *On Trans-Saharan Trails Islamic Law, Trade Networks, and Cross-Cultural Exchange in Nineteenth-Century Western Africa.* New York: Cambridge University Press.

Mahadi, Abdullahi. 1992. "The Aftermath of *Jihad* in the Central Sudan as a Major Factor in the Volume of the Trans-Saharan Slave Trade in the Nineteenth Century." In *The Human Commodity: Perspectives on the Trans-Saharan Slave Trade*, edited by Elizabeth Savage, 111–28. London: Frank Cass & Co. Ltd.

Saleh, Mohamed. 2013. "A Pre-Colonial Population Brought to Light: Digitization of the Nineteenth-Century Egyptian Censuses." *Historical Methods* 46(1): 5–18.

Saleh, Mohamed. 2021. *Globalization and Labor Coercion: Evidence from Egypt during the First Globalization Era*. CEPR Discussion Paper 14542.

Schapendonk, Joris. 2010. "Staying Put in Moving Sands: The Stepwise Migration Process of Sub-Saharan African Migrants Heading North." In *Respacing Africa*, edited by Ulf Engel and Paul Nugent, 113–38. Leiden: Koninklijke Brill NV.

Shroeter, Daniel. 1992. "Slave Markets and Slavery in Moroccan Urban Society." In *The Human Commodity: Perspectives on the Trans-Saharan Slave Trade*, edited by Elizabeth Savage, 185–213. London: Frank Cass & Co. Ltd.

Wright, John. 2007. *The Trans-Saharan Slave Trade*. London: Routledge.

4

SLAVES, PORTERS, AND PLANTATION WORKERS

Shifting Patterns of Migration in 19th- and Early 20th-Century East Africa

Karin Pallaver

1 Introduction

This chapter analyses the major shifting patterns of migration in East Africa over the 19th century and in the early 20th century. The analysis is structured around four historical processes that produced major shifts in migration patterns in East Africa. The development of the plantations on the coast and in Zanzibar led to the major quantitative and qualitative shift in the history of migration in 19th-century East Africa, which was the migration of enslaved people from the interior regions to the coast and Zanzibar. This gave rise to a migration system that supplied enslaved laborers to coastal and Zanzibar plantations, largely from the Congo area and from Southeast Africa. Another important historical process that involved East Africa in the 19th century was the expansion of ivory exports to global markets. As no other means of transport were available, waged porters were employed to carry ivory from the interior regions to the coast. Even if not quantitatively as relevant as the migration of enslaved people, the circular migration of porters gave rise to a migration system that survived well into the colonial period. The development of the long-distance trade in ivory and slaves stimulated the expansion of urban centers on the coast and in the interior to which people either moved voluntarily as free laborers or settlers or were forcibly moved after being enslaved. Finally, the establishment of European colonial rule in East Africa represented a major shifting pattern of migration, also in relation to the enforcement of the abolition of slavery. The chapter will discuss how European colonialism impacted and transformed the migration systems that had developed in connection to the ivory and slave trades.

The chapter combines qualitative sources and the limited available quantitative evidence in order to investigate the major drivers in shifting patterns of migration and provide a degree of magnitude of the main migration flows in East Africa in the 19th century and early 20th century. In order to unravel directions of change, the chapter adopts a geographical perspective that goes beyond present-day nation-state borders and look at East Africa as a region formed by present-day Kenya, Tanzania, southern Somalia, northern Mozambique, as well as parts of the Great Lakes region (Uganda, Eastern Democratic Republic of Congo

DOI: 10.4324/9781003225027-6

(DRC), Rwanda, Burundi). This broad geographical approach will allow us to show major trends and patterns in the ways in which people migrated or were forcibly moved across the region.

The first section of the chapter discusses how slavery changed in 19th-century East Africa and how these changes impacted migration within the region. Slavery was already a well-established institution and East Africa was a region of significant forced migrations from the 16th century onward. Even if people could be enslaved within their own societies as a result of indebtedness or in neighboring communities with the same language and cultural traits, almost all enslaved individuals were "outsiders," being obtained outside the receiving society (Campbell 2004, XV). This meant that these people were almost all cross-community migrants. With the establishment of a flourishing plantation economy along the Swahili coast and in Zanzibar in the 1810s, slave trading developed on an unparalleled scale in East Africa and gave rise to migration systems that supplied enslaved laborers to coastal and Zanzibar plantations from the Congo area and from Southeast Africa. Over the 19th century more than 750,000 people were forcibly moved to the coast. At the same time, the employment of enslaved workers also expanded in the interior regions, especially in the region of Unyamwezi in Western Tanzania (Deutsch 2006).

The second section of the chapter discusses the expansion of the ivory trade as a major driver of circular migration in 19th-century East Africa. With the expansion of the global demand for East African ivory at the beginning of the 19th century, new long-distance trade routes that connected the interior regions with the ports on the coast were established and pioneered by African traders who took their ivory to the coast with caravans formed by hundreds or even thousands of porters. Coastal traders followed, and settled in the main interior markets. The vast majority of porters were free waged workers, who voluntarily enlisted in commercial caravans. The majority of them were sojourners, as they returned home after spending months or even years away from home, whereas some of them settled permanently on the coast (Rockel 2006, 19–23). The expansion of long-distance trade created a migration system in which porters, especially from Unyamwezi, migrated to the coast. This system, as this chapter will discuss, persisted after the establishment of European rule and the construction of colonial railways, as workers from Unyamwezi continued to migrate to the coast, this time to be employed in European settlers' plantations. Connected to this migration system was the migration of people to the quickly expanding urban settlements that developed in connection to the ivory and slave trades.

The third section of the chapter will then analyze how new urban settlements emerged and expanded, both along the coast and in the interior, as a response to the demands of the ivory and slave trades. These towns became important drivers of migration in the second half of the 19th century as they became instrumental to the working of long-distance trade. Traders could use them to buy and store their goods, obtain fresh water, and attend rich markets offering a wide variety of food products needed to supply their caravans. These towns – such as Bagamoyo and Mombasa on the coast or Ujiji, Tabora, and the capital of Buganda Kingdom in the interior regions – had thousands of inhabitants and became attractive to people who migrated in search of new opportunities, and worked amongst others as small traders, smiths, tailors, or prostitutes (see Map 4.1).

The fourth section of the chapter analyses the early colonial period and the impact that the establishment of colonial rule had on pre-existing migration patterns. Toward the end of the 19th century, the abolition of slavery in Zanzibar and along the coast and

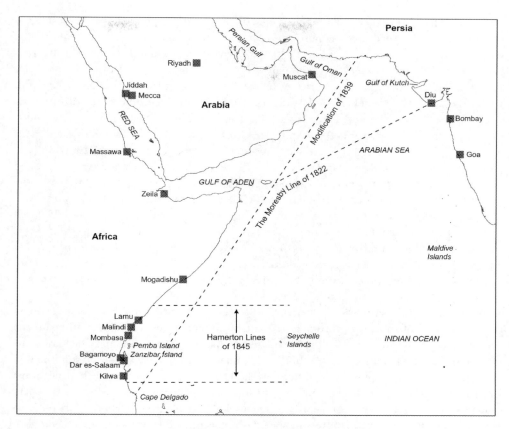

MAP 4.1 Legal slave trading zones in East Africa in the 19th century.
Source: Adapted from Harms, Freamon and Blight (2013), digitized by Stefan de Jong.

the establishment of European colonial rule created a new demand for migrant agricultural laborers. The wage labor colonial economy was built on established patterns of work that included porterage. Groups that had been involved in long-distance trade as porters, such as the Nyamwezi, appeared more willing to migrate to colonial plantations. The migration of laborers in the colonial period thus presented significant continuities from the point of view of motivations and origin of the migrants, with pre-colonial migration patterns, at least in the early colonial period.

2 Shifts in the migration of enslaved people in 19th-century East Africa

What Edward Alpers calls the "tyranny of the Atlantic" in slave studies has for a long time obscured how the structure of slavery and practices of enslavement in East Africa and the Indian Ocean World contrasted with that of the trans-Atlantic slave trade and plantation slavery in the Americas (Alpers 1997). These differences, as this section will discuss, had important consequences for the ways in which enslaved people were forcibly moved and/or freely migrated in 19th-century East Africa.

In East Africa and other Indian Ocean societies enslaved people could be – and actually often were – assimilated into the hosting society and their children could often obtain the status of non-slaves (i.e., were born free). As Gwyn Campbell points out, the distinction between freedom and slavery, even if analytically helpful in the Americas, does not fully apply to East Africa, where categories of hierarchy and dependency are more effective in analyzing slavery (Campbell 2004, VII–XXI). Another important difference with Atlantic slavery is that the majority of people enslaved in East Africa were women, who were valued for their reproductive power and attractiveness. Both within East Africa and in the regions where they were exported – the Arabic peninsula, the Persian Gulf, and Western India – enslaved people were largely employed as domestic servants, family helpers, concubines, and soldiers, whereas a limited number were employed as agricultural laborers. Owing to the variability that characterized their activities, their living and working conditions varied significantly from society to society. They were socially mobile, in that those enslaved by rich and wealthy people could acquire important positions as traders, guards, or overseers. This gave them freedom to move and even to migrate voluntarily. Before the establishment of plantations on the coast, East Africa had thus been a region of significant forced migrations, whose characteristics and conditions were highly diverse across the region and for which it is hard to isolate a common pattern (Médard 2007; Vernet 2009).

A first important shift in the structure of slavery and slave migration was caused in the second half of the 18th century by the establishment of sugarcane plantations in the French-occupied Mascarene Islands (Isle de France and Isle de Bourbon, present-day Mauritius and Réunion). This was a shift both in the quantity of slaves exported and in the way in which they were employed. The methods used to produce sugarcane in the Mascarene Islands were in fact very similar to those of Caribbean plantations, and it was here where enslaved East Africans were for the first time employed as plantation laborers. In 1787–88 there were 71,000 enslaved laborers in the Mascarene Islands, a number that increased to 133,000 in 1807–08 and 136,000 in 1815. The majority of these workers originated from East Africa and Madagascar, and small numbers from the Horn of Africa, West Africa, and India (Deutsch 2006, 34; Allen 2010; Lovejoy 2011, 151).

The Mascarene slave trade began to decline after the establishment of British colonial rule in Mauritius in 1810 and especially after 1822, when the Moresby Treaty was concluded between the Sultan of Muscat and Oman and the British. This treaty banned the export of slaves to the east and south of an imaginary line drawn from Cape Delgado in Mozambique to Diu in India, in this way prohibiting the purchase of captives by British and French citizens and subjects (see Map 4.2). As Abdul Sheriff points out, after the Moresby Treaty was signed, members of the Omani merchant class "realised that if slaves could not be exported, the product of their labor could" (Sheriff 1987, 48). The treaty produced a major shift in slave migrations in East Africa that has to be considered in relation to a changing regional economic system based on the production and export of cloves, coconut, sugar, and grains in Zanzibar, Pemba, and along the East African coast (Sheriff 1987, 60).

From the 1810s onward, following the introduction of the lucrative cultivation of cloves, large areas of Zanzibar previously devoted to the cultivation of food crops were converted into commercial clove plantations. The production of cloves was extended to Pemba in the 1840s. The production of this spice increased ten-fold between 1839/40 and 1846/47 when it amounted to about 1,500 tons. Production fluctuated, but reached 2,200 tons by 1850s and 3,900 tons by the 1870s. As the cultivation of cloves expanded, so did the demand for

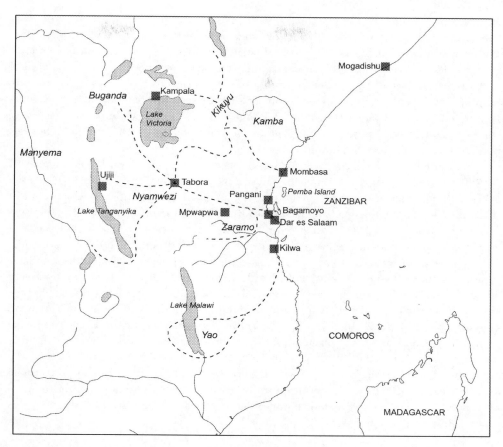

MAP 4.2 Main caravan roads and urban centers in 19th-century East Africa.
Source: Author's own, digitized by Stefan de Jong.

slave labor.[1] Various estimates exist on the number of enslaved laborers that were annually imported to Zanzibar and Pemba. By the 1810s, Zanzibar imported about 8,000 slaves per year. This number increased to 13,000 in the 1830s and 1840s, and peaked in the 1860s and 1870s with 15,000–20,000 imported per year (Sheriff 1987, 226). According to Paul Lovejoy (2011), out of a total of 1,650,000 slaves traded in East Africa during the 19th century, almost 50% were retained in the area for plantation work (see Figure 4.2). People imported to Zanzibar as agricultural laborers were largely men, who originated from the hinterland of Kilwa and the Lake Malawi region. This was a significant shifting pattern of migration, as men rather than women became the main migrants. At the peak of the slave trade, 95% of imported laborers came from this area, whereas only a small part originated from the northern interior, in present-day Kenya.[2] Slaves were also obtained in the regions around Lake Tanganyika and Lake Victoria, especially from the Manyema region in present-day Eastern DRC.

Given that more and more land in Zanzibar and Pemba was devoted to the cultivation of cloves, a new demand developed for imported grains and foodstuffs needed to feed the laborers of the plantations. Coastal planters employed slave labor to produce northern interior fruit, maize, sesame, millet, rice, and coconut that they then exported to Zanzibar and

Pemba. The so-called *shamba* (field) slaves worked for four or five days for their owners and then cultivated their own piece of land for subsistence for the rest of the week. The crops that they cultivated independently were divided between the enslaved and the enslaver (Clayton and Savage 1974, 2). There was an important difference between *waja* (newcomers) and *wazalia*, the latter being people born in captivity on the coast and who were generally employed as domestic servants in the house of their enslavers. Male *wazalia* often had a great deal of independence and could work outside the house as carpenters, builders, sailors, and dhow captains. They had to give one-half or one-third of their earnings to their enslavers and could retain the rest (Sunseri 2002, 30–1).

The peak of production on the coast was reached between 1875 and 1884, when about 45,000 enslaved laborers were reported to live in the coastal areas (see Figure 4.1) (Deutsch 2006, 39). The increase in the production and consequent slave imports was the result of two main factors. On the one hand, Zanzibari merchants and financiers invested their capital in the plantations on the coast after the decline of the clove price on the international markets and the economic stagnation in Zanzibar in the 1870s. On the other hand, the import of slave labor was favored by the decline in the price of slaves following the anti-slave treaties that the Sultan of Zanzibar signed with the British. After the 1822 Moresby Treaty mentioned above, in 1845 the area in which the slave trade was tolerated was further reduced by the Hamerton Treaty, which allowed trading within only the Sultan of Zanzibar's possessions (see Map 4.2). In 1873 slave markets in Zanzibar were closed. Even if an illegal trade continued to supply the plantations, the import of enslaved workers was significantly reduced and ended in the 1890s when the Germans obtained control of the ports on the coast. In 1897 slavery in Zanzibar – which since 1890 had become a British protectorate – was delegalized.[3] The abolition of slavery in Zanzibar, as will be discussed in the final section of this chapter, represented an important driver of shifting patterns of migration, as laborers migrated to Zanzibar to replace those freed from slavery.

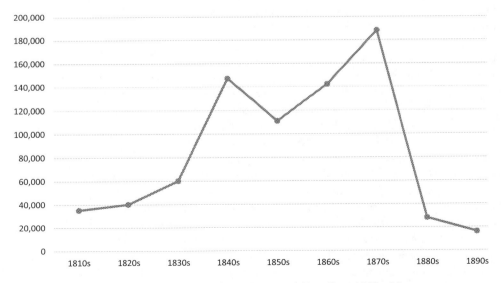

FIGURE 4.1 Slaves retained on the East African coast and Zanzibar, 1810s–90s.
Source: Lovejoy (2011, 151).

Slaves, Porters, and Plantation Workers 81

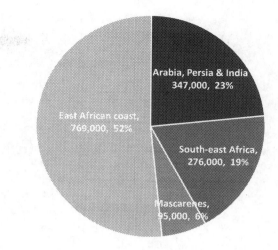

FIGURE 4.2 Destinations of the East African slave trade in the 19th century.
Source: Lovejoy (2011, 151).

The first census that reported the ethnic origin ("tribal designation") of the Zanzibar population was carried out by the British in 1924. Many identified themselves as Nyasa (10,570), Yao (6,623), Manyema (5,013), and Zaramo (6,170), which were the main ethnic groups from which the enslaved people exported to the coast during the 19th century originated (Zanzibar Protectorate 1924). For people freed from slavery the question of social identity was clearly a crucial aspect in the post-abolition era. They commonly asserted a "Swahili" identity, as a way to associate themselves with Islam and the coastal culture. However, many of them also decided to reject Islam and identify with their homeland ethnic group. The significant number of people who identified as "Manyema" confirms this aspect, as the region of Manyema was not involved in colonial migration processes and Manyema people had migrated to Zanzibar during the 19th century as enslaved laborers (Cooper 1980, 166; Zöller 2019) (Figure 4.2).

The East African slave trade boomed in the 19th century. While exports to Arabia, Persia, and India increased, the main driver of expanding slave migrations was the development of plantations within East Africa, in Zanzibar, and along the coast. At the same time, slave trading and slavery were also significant drivers of forced migration in the interior regions of East Africa. At the time of the establishment of German colonial rule in Tanzania, it was estimated that about 10% of the total population of the colony consisted of enslaved people, who were largely concentrated on the coast (Sunseri 2002, 27). The first German explorer who reached the region of Unyamwezi in the 1880s estimated that between 70% and 75% of the population of the region was enslaved (Reichard 1889, 277). These numbers are very likely exaggerated and motivated by the abolitionist spirit of the time, but nevertheless testify to the great presence of enslaved people in the region. Thomas Vernet guesstimates that in the 19th century about 10% to 15% of the people living in the interior – meaning the commercial hinterland of Zanzibar – were enslaved (Vernet 2013, 5). Among the most important areas were the Kingdom of Buganda and the urban centers that developed along the main caravan roads, such as Tabora, Ujiji, and Mwanza in present-day Tanzania.

In Buganda the institution of slavery was critical to social and economic life. Captives were obtained by the Baganda mainly from Bunyoro and Busoga (see Map 4.1). Women and girls became wives or concubines, performed agricultural tasks and domestic work, and also tended the grounds of the shrines providing food for the spirit mediums and priests. Men and boys were employed in the Buganda army, as well as in agricultural work and domestic service. The position of enslaved people in Ganda society depended on hierarchies determined both by the task performed and by the length of their stay in Ganda society. Compared to newcomers, long-term residents were more likely to be integrated into the household and less likely to be sold (Reid 2002, 116–24). Children of enslaved mothers were regarded as free as long as their fathers were not enslaved (Twaddle 1988, 126). Enslaved persons were also incorporated into state or private armies. Women were married into local families, and even in the royal family, testifying to the social mobility of enslaved people in many interior societies, as has been previously described for the coast. Mobility was also favored by the fact that clans were very large and it was easy for an enslaved person to move from one place to another without being detected, as the Ganda state put little energy in searching for fugitive slaves (Unomah 1972, 110–3; Médard 2007, 29).

The Baganda were also exporters of slaves, who rarely reached the coast and were mainly bought by Nyamwezi and coastal traders and farmers in the area of Tabora (see below). The export of slaves in Buganda increased in the 1860s and 1870s and reached its peak in the 1880s, when the Kingdom of Buganda exported about 1,000 slaves per year. This peak occurred at the same time when the export from the interior regions to the coast was declining, as a consequence of the prohibition of slave markets in Zanzibar in 1873. The restrictions posed on slavery had "the effect of internalizing that sector," in the sense that the slave trade shifted from export to the coast to intensified use of slave labor in the interior regions (Sheriff 1987, 35). As a consequence, the slave trade increased from the 1880s and peaked in the 1890s, especially in the Great Lakes region. With the expansion of the slave trade, Buganda leaders sold their own people. Between 1889 and 1892, 20,000 Ganda captives were sold to Bunyoro in exchange for food, guns, and cloth (Hanson 2003, 97–8; Médard 2007, 18–9). Even if the destinations of these people are not all known, many of them were sent to the chiefdom of Unyanyembe and its capital, Tabora, in present-day west-central Tanzania (Reid 2002, 161). Here, coastal settlers as well as local residents employed enslaved agricultural laborers, as we will see in Section 3. The migration of enslaved people within the interior regions was partly connected to processes of urbanization in the interior of 19th-century East Africa which, in turn, were the result of the development of ivory exports to global markets.

3 The expansion of the ivory trade and the circular migration of porters

Along forced slave migrations, the 19th century witnessed the migration of free laborers in connection to the development of the ivory trade. In the 19th century, East African ivory began to be widely requested in Europe and America by a growing middle class, for which ivory-made luxury products, such as carved figures, parts of instruments, combs, billiard balls, and so on, became one of the symbols of high living standards (Beachey 1967, 274). The global demand for East African ivory had the effect of pushing up its price in Zanzibar by about 6% per year between 1823 and 1873 (Sheriff 1987, 102–3). The trade in ivory being very lucrative, new commercial caravan roads were established that connected the interior regions with the coast. Among them, the most important in terms of the volumes traded was the so-called central caravan road that connected Lake Tanganyika to the town of Tabora, in Western Tanzania and then to the port of Bagamoyo on the Swahili coast.

In many parts of East Africa, the use of draft and pack animals was severely hindered by the presence of the tsetse fly, whose bite causes sleeping sickness, a disease fatal to many animals. Therefore, the only way to transport ivory and other goods was by human carriers. African porters successfully transported goods across deep-rooted trade networks and played a critical role in creating the conditions for the participation of East Africa in the global economy. Porters originated from different areas of the interior as well as from the coast, but the biggest part of them were Kamba from present-day Kenya; Nyamwezi from present-day Western Tanzania; and Yao, from present-day Southern Tanzania/northern Mozambique. All the groups that enrolled as porters came from regions that were crossed by the main caravan roads and were therefore strategically located for long-distance trade (Rockel 2000, 177). Reasons for working as porters varied per group, and were largely connected to social and economic conditions in the sending regions from which porters were recruited. For the Kamba, for example, enrolment as porters at the end of the 18th century was a response to recurrent famines that led them to engage in hunting and trade and put them in contact with the coast (Cummings 1973, 11, 1975, 277; Håkansson, Chapter 5, this volume). Porters generally enrolled freely for wages and for the prestige that derived from the experience of travel, as was the case for the Nyamwezi. Employment in the caravans was a way for personal socio-economic improvement. Wages obtained during commercial expeditions created the conditions for the accumulation of wealth in the form of imported commodities, especially cloth, that were then employed in the payment of bridewealth and the purchase of cattle. Wages could thus be transformed into social prestige, and well-experienced porters could exploit their knowledge of the caravan routes, their personal relationships, and their skills to finance their own caravans (Cummings 1973, 12; Rockel 2006, 77). As a class of wage laborers, porters acted individually and collectively to defend their common interests. When the wages were not considered appropriate they refused to continue their march until conditions of employment were renegotiated.

Travel and porterage had great social prestige among many East African societies, and this provided an important motivation for joining the caravans. For the Nyamwezi, for example, it was a long-term tradition and involved pride and skills. The region of Unyamwezi had already been central to a network of interregional trade in iron and salt before the development of long-distance trade with the coast (Roberts 1970). Thanks to this experience and the central position of Unyamwezi in the trading system of the interior regions, Nyamwezi porters profited from the new opportunities that emerged from the expansion of the ivory trade. It has been estimated that in the 1890s one-third of the total male population of Unyamwezi was engaged in the caravans (van der Burgt 1913, 309). Women also traveled with the caravans as porters, traders, and partners of men. They enrolled voluntarily as a way to get individual access to paid labor or to accompany their husbands. They provided domestic and sexual services, and also carried small loads, such as kitchen utensils (Rockel 2006, 118–27).

In the first part of the 19th century, porterage was a seasonal occupation and porters remained circular migrants. They traveled with the caravans only in the dry season from May to November, when agricultural labor was less demanding and could be carried out by women, and then went back to their fields at the beginning of the rainy season. When the ivory trade reached its peak in the 1870s, however, porterage became a more permanent occupation. The need for laborers increased owing to the growing demand for ivory, and porters could negotiate higher wages and spent longer periods away from home. They could spend years in the caravans before returning home. For some of them it became a lifetime occupation and they became permanent migrants (Deutsch 2006, 24). Nyamwezi men could move over great distances and be away for long periods for a variety of reasons. On the one hand, Nyamwezi people did not own large herds of cattle. Cattle was herded by Tutsi immigrants, who sold milk and butter to the main markets of Unyamwezi (Rockel 2019). On the other hand, women took care of the fields while men were away with the caravans. Women were helped in their agricultural tasks by enslaved laborers, the number of which increased significantly over the 19th century (Rockel 2000, 177). Money earned with caravan work or trade was in fact used to buy slaves needed to help women in the fields. This long-term development of labor specialization is confirmed for many interior societies, including not only the Nyamwezi, but also the Kamba (Cummings 1973, 116).

About half the able-bodied Nyamwezi men participated in porterage during the second half of the 19th century. Estimates for the second half of the 19th century range from 15,000 to 30,000 porters reaching the coast each year (Rockel 2006, 33). According to German colonial statistics, the number of porters traveling in German East Africa (GEA) in 1892 was 100,000, and these data only considered those porters who reached and departed from the coast (Sunseri 2002, 56–7). In Bagamoyo, the main coastal terminus of the caravan road that connected Lake Tanganyika with the coast, Nyamwezi porters established semi-permanent settlements and while waiting to be enrolled by the caravans found work in the plantations or tended small gardens on their own (Deutsch 2006, 23). The development of urban centers such as Bagamoyo was a response to the demands of trade, and these towns became in turn drivers of shifting patterns of migration, as discussed in the next section.

4 New urban centers as drivers of migration in 19th-century East Africa

The establishment and growth of urban settlements represented an important driver of shifting patterns of migration in 19th-century East Africa. As is well known, the Swahili coast had a long tradition of urbanism since its origins in the latter part of the first millennium AD. In the 19th century, with the expansion of the ivory and slave trade, settlements on the coast, such as Bagamoyo, Pangani, and Kilwa Kivinje, expanded as terminus of the caravan roads coming from the interior (see Map 4.1) (Burton 2002, 8). During the trading season their population swelled and these settlements became in themselves drivers of migration as they attracted people for economic reasons, including porters, traders, prostitutes, and slaves.

The development of urban settlements in the interior regions was also related to issues of security. The intensification of slave raiding, the insecurity caused by the arrival of the Ngoni from Southern Africa in the 1840s (Keeton and Schirmer, Chapter 6, this volume), and the emergence of expansionist political leaders such as Mirambo or Nyungu ya Mawe in what today is Tanzania led to the proliferation of fortified and more concentrated settlements, especially starting from the mid-19th century (Burton 2002, 14).

The main driver of urbanization in the interior regions continued to be long-distance trade. Commercial towns developed along the main caravan roads and were inhabited by thousands of people who moved to these towns mainly for economic reasons. Along the main caravan road through which ivory was exported to the coast, three main settlements developed: Bagamoyo on the coast, Ujiji on Lake Tanganyika, and Tabora in the region of Unyamwezi. In the second half of the 19th century, Bagamoyo became the most important port on the coast. Its population was around 4,000–6,000 people in the 1880s, a number that swelled when caravans arrived from the interior regions. Porters remained in town for up to three or four months waiting for a caravan for the interior to be reorganized. Besides porters, Bagamoyo attracted merchants, financiers, farmers, and craftsmen, who moved to the town thanks to the commercial opportunities it offered. Enslaved people were also present in large numbers and were employed as domestic servants and family helpers. They accounted for 15% of the population in the 1890s (Fabian 2013).

Tabora was the most important town in the interior of East Africa. Established in the 1840s following the collaboration between local political authorities and coastal merchants, in the 1870s it had a population of about 5,000 inhabitants, increasing to 20,000 in the 1890s (Pallaver 2020). Tabora was populated by a large number of enslaved people, for the biggest part coming from the Lake Victoria region and Eastern Congo, who were employed by coastal merchants and by local families to produce food. Traders from the coast, of both Swahili and Omani origin, had migrated to Tabora to deal in ivory, but later also engaged in food production for caravans and landless people in town, such as merchants and artisans. They imported slaves, the majority being women, whom they employed in the production of rice and cassava amongst others. Between 100 and 300 enslaved people lived on the estates of important merchants, where they were employed as domestic servants, concubines, and/or agricultural laborers. Local families also bought slaves to improve their productive capabilities and for domestic service. The number of enslaved people that entered Unyamwezi from Buganda, Bunyoro, and Karagwe was "substantial" and led to a "remarkable increase in population and economic prosperity" (Unomah 1972, 113–4). The attractiveness of these towns was related to the resulting opportunities to trade, for example, of foodstuff for passing caravans. In Unyamwezi, for example, grain, rice, sweet potatoes, and cassava were produced by immigrants from Buha and Burundi, by Nyamwezi women, and by agricultural enslaved laborers, and then carried to the market of Tabora (Deutsch 2006, 25).

The capital of the Kingdom of Buganda was unique in the East African interior for its size, population, and political and religious significance. It had a population of about 10,000 in the early 1850s, half of which were soldiers and members of the royal entourage (Reid and Médard 2000, 100). The transformation of its urban environment was related to the development of long-distance trade, and the expansion of foreign religions in the second half of the 1880s. With the development of long-distance trade in the 1850s, the capital of the kingdom that had been itinerant until that moment became more permanently anchored to the area around modern-day Kampala, a convenient location for the control of trade (Reid and Médard 2000, 99–103). Foreign traders from the coast as well as from neighboring regions visited the capital and this enhanced its commercial centrality. People moved to the quickly expanding settlement attracted by trade opportunities, and the capital extended into suburban areas. The first Christian missionaries – first French Catholics and then British Protestants – reached Buganda in the 1870s. Both the Roman Catholics and the British Protestants built big cathedrals in the capital, and in the 1890s – after the religious wars – the town became the most important Christian center in the interlacustrine region. At the time of the 1911 British census, the population of the town had increased to 32,000 (Burton 2002, 15).

Enslaved people formed a significant part of the population of these urban settlements. They were imported by traders and farmers from neighboring regions or from the coast. But they also migrated freely from the coast. Enslaved people from the coast were often slave artisans (*fundi*) and worked as blacksmiths, tinkers, masons, carpenters, tailors, potters, rope makers, and guards (Unomah 1972, 113). They paid their enslavers a percentage of their earnings that was set at between one-third and two-thirds (Clayton and Savage 1974, 2). Finally, concubines (*suria*) also traveled and moved with their enslavers from the coast to all parts of Eastern Africa, as far as the Eastern Congo (Wright 1993).

The presence of markets and the opportunities offered by long-distance trade also attracted free migrants to these towns. As already mentioned, coastal traders migrated to interior towns and created trading diasporas in Ujiji, Tabora, Mwanza, and in the region of Manyema. At the same time, free people moved to these towns in search for opportunities and advantages, including small traders, caravan staff, and artisans who came from both the coast and neighboring regions, such as modern-day DRC, Uganda, and Zambia. They brought with them their material culture, their language, their way of dressing, and their religion (Pallaver 2020). As a consequence, these urban settlements shared important similarities. They had similar immigrant groups; they shared similar commercial practices, including the use of glass beads and cloth as currency; and, finally, they acquired a common cultural life expressed linguistically with the use of Kiswahili as *lingua franca*, and religiously with the introduction of Islam. Together, these towns formed a network of "places where people met, mixed and traded goods and ideas" and became nodal points within a wider social and economic system (Coquery-Vidrovitch 1993, 213).

5 The impact of the establishment of colonial rule on migration patterns

The establishment of European colonial rule in East Africa was another important driver of shifting mobility patterns. The creation of plantations together with the building of colonial railways produced a new demand for migrant laborers all over East Africa. Laborers recruited locally were not sufficient to satisfy the needs of colonial enterprises and they were often not available to work for Europeans. For this reason, the colonial states had to turn to migrant laborers. This was particularly true for Kenya and GEA, where the demand for labor from settler-led plantations created the conditions for the development of new migration flows, but also for Zanzibar and its clove plantations. In Uganda, on the contrary, the production of the most important export crop, cotton, was left to chiefs and local peasants and remained largely a household production rather than a plantation crop (Hanson 2003, 169–70).[4] It was only after 1910, when cotton became the most important export product of Uganda, that Buganda attracted migrant laborers from Ruanda-Urundi, Eastern Congo, and other parts of Uganda, thanks to its better wages and labor conditions (Reid 2017, 269–70; De Haas 2019). It was, however, only after the First World War and the abolition of forced labor in the early 1920s that migration took off (Powesland 1957).

The demand for free migrant laborers on the coast was also the result of the abolition of slavery, which in the pre-colonial period had been the main way of mobilizing labor, as already discussed. The British abolished slavery in Zanzibar in 1897 and in Kenya in 1907. After abolition, it became difficult to make freed people work in the settlers' plantations, as they preferred to cultivate their own land. This created a new demand for wage laborers that was satisfied by the promotion of labor migration from the interior regions.

Contrary to the British, the Germans in GEA did not delegalize slavery. As a way to deal with labor shortages, the Germans used enslaved people as a ready source of labor for the plantations. German planters made contracts with both the enslaved laborers and their enslavers, according to which the plantation owner paid the redemption of the worker, who in turn had to work to pay for his/her ransom for about two/three years. As a matter of fact, in GEA, enslaved laborers in the plantations outnumbered wage laborers. In 1914, there were 180,000 enslaved laborers in the colony and 172,000 wage laborers. Besides slave ransoming, the Germans used penal labor and indentured labor to increase the number of available workers (Sunseri 2002, 27). In Tanzania, slavery was only abolished in 1922, by the British administration following Germany's loss of its colonies after the First World War.

In order to manage recurrent labor shortages, at the beginning of the colonial period both the British and the Germans hired indentured laborers to build colonial infrastructures, especially railways. In 1896 the British began the construction works for the Uganda railway that connected Mombasa on the coast to Kisumu on Lake Victoria. They hired 3,948 laborers from India. At the time of the completion of the railway in 1902, their number had reached 31,983 (Clayton and Savage 1974, 11). Indian laborers received higher wages compared to African laborers. Wages for Africans were in the range of 4–5 rupees per month, whereas Indian laborers received 12 rupees per month, and skilled craftsmen could even obtain 45 rupees per month. Hiring Indian laborers had the advantage that they would stay for longer periods compared to African workers, who were both unfamiliar with waged labor and did not have enough incentives to move for long periods. They worked for short periods and their presence was temporary as it was connected to the seasonality of agricultural labor. But indentured labor was expensive and difficult to obtain, and could not be a viable solution for the demand for laborers in the plantations.

For this reason, both the Germans and the British turned to long-distance migrants. The entire colonial period was characterized by incessant labor shortages, as the colonial state failed to mobilize the required number of workers. This forced the colonial state into a perpetual search for labor that in GEA became to be known as the *Arbeiterfrage*, the "labor question." In order to control the sources of uncertainty and instability in the labor supply, the colonial state used coercion and expanded the scope and intensity of its intervention (Berman 1990, 68). However, this could not suffice, as the availability of laborers was connected to the level of taxation, the rhythms of the subsistence agricultural production, and the attractiveness of wages. As discussed above, in the pre-colonial period waged labor, such as porterage, could be combined with agricultural labor and followed the seasonality of agricultural production. Contracts in the plantations or for railway construction implied a form of more permanent labor, longer periods away from home, and, ultimately, less negotiating power for African laborers.

The establishment of African reserves in Kenya was an important factor pushing up the migration of laborers, especially after the beginning of the expansion of European settler production from 1908. Unskilled migrant laborers were recruited in the reserves by labor recruiters, local chiefs, and the settlers themselves. African laborers left the reserves out of land shortages, cash need, and the pressures of chiefs who recruited laborers for the colonial state or the settlers. As many settler areas were located near to the most populous reserves, laborers moved back and forth between the reserves and the plantation areas, giving birth to "a relative brief cycle of labor migration to the estates with regular return to the reserves" (Berman 1990, 223).

The Kikuyu, the group that was more dramatically affected by the presence of British settlers in Kenya, moved more permanently out of the reserves and became squatters on European plantations. Kikuyu laborers were allowed to settle on the farmer's land with their families, to cultivate a small plot of land, and to herd their cattle. In exchange, they had to provide a certain amount of labor for the settler, or services or rent in kind. It was calculated that in the early 1930s one-fifth (110,000) of the total Kikuyu population were living outside the reserves, the biggest number of them as squatter laborers on settlers' plantations (Berman 1990, 229). Thus, squatting became a new pattern of migration in colonial Kenya – a pattern characterized by short-distance and permanent migrations within the colony that also characterized other regions of the continent in which there was a strong presence of European settlers, such as South Africa.[5]

In Zanzibar, the establishment of colonial rule and the abolition of slavery became important drivers of long-distance labor migration. There, the British government recruited clove pickers from Kenya and GEA on three-month contracts. They were 819 in 1905 and 1,600 in 1907. The migration of these laborers was, however, temporary. Many migrants stayed for two or three picking seasons and many for less than six months. According to Frederick Cooper, in the period 1924–26, 13,546 arrived in Zanzibar and 9,233 left (Cooper 1980, 106–7). The 1924 census in Zanzibar – the first census that listed occupations and the ethnic origin of laborers – showed that the Nyamwezi were the largest group of "weeders" (2,075) in the clove plantations. Many Nyamwezi women (1,406) also migrated to Zanzibar with their husbands (Zanzibar Protectorate 1924).[6] They worked in the plantations picking cloves from the lower branches and separating the cloves from the stems (Sheriff et al. 2016, 40). The Nyamwezi started to migrate to Zanzibar in 1905 and their number increased significantly after the First World War (Cooper 1980, 106). They migrated voluntarily, through a communication network that was not controlled by the colonial state.

Compared to Kenya, the German colonial state was less coercive in terms of labor recruitment. The Germans established plantations on the coast and in the northeast of the colony, especially in the region of Usambara. The main products were cotton, coffee, sisal, copra, and coconut. The aim of the German colonial state was to base the development of the colonial economy on large-scale plantations, what Thaddeus Sunseri calls the "plantation imperative" (Sunseri 2002, 55). The employment of workers in the vicinity of plantations was complicated by the fact that it was more profitable to produce grain and vegetables to feed the laborers of the plantations, rather than being employed by German planters over long-term contracts. To satisfy the "plantation imperative," the colonial state initially employed enslaved people and later convict laborers. However, toward the end of the 1910s, the colonial state ceased to be the main mobilizer of labor in the colony and migrant laborer moved more freely to the plantations (Sunseri 2002, XXV–XXVII). In 1902, European farms in GEA employed between 4,000 and 5,000 workers; in 1905–06, 36,000 workers; and in 1912–13, 90,000 workers (Koponen 1988, 367). Contracts were signed for 180 days and they could be renewed. Upon termination of the contract, about half of the workers went home, 25% remained on the plantations, and the remaining 25% moved to other plantations (Calvert 1916, 88). In 1913, the new labor statuses introduced the 240 days-per-year contract, or a minimum of 20 days of work per month, and this produced more stabilized communities of migrants in the coastal areas and in Usambara, where German-owned plantations were concentrated (Koponen 1988, 394).

Slaves, Porters, and Plantation Workers **89**

In terms of numbers, the most significant group of migrant workers in the colony in the early colonial period were, again, the Nyamwezi. They represented the majority of migrant workers in Usambara, as well as on the coast. They were also employed as dock-workers in Dar es Salaam, Mombasa, and Kisumu, and they even migrated to the mines in South Africa (Koponen 1988, 168). According to one missionary, in 1913 the male population of Unyamwezi was reduced by one-third compared to 1892, owing to perma-nent migrations to the plantations (van der Burgt 1913, 706). As Deutsch points out, this was in part due to the restructuring process that took place in the caravan trade after the establishment of colonial rule and the building of colonial railways (Deutsch 2006, 225). In 1912, the Central Railway from Dar es Salaam to Tabora was completed. This reduced the number of porters traveling along the central caravan route as the new railway basically followed their route. In 1900, 35,000 porters reached Bagamoyo on the coast and 43,880 left for the interior. After the opening of the railway, the number of porters drastically declined: in 1912, 851 porters arrived at the coast and only 193 left for the interior (Iliffe 1980, 280). The pre-colonial tradition of traveling contributed to the willingness of the Nyamwezi to migrate to colonial plantations and shows an important continuity between the pre-colonial and early colonial periods from the point of view of the origin and mo-tivation of migrants.

6 Conclusion

This chapter has discussed the four main drivers of shifting patterns of migration in East Africa during the 19th century and the early 20th century: (1) slavery and its abolition; (2) porterage; (3) urbanization; and (4) European colonialism. Among them, the most import-ant, both quantitatively and in terms of the legacy for the societies involved, was slavery. The establishment of plantations in Zanzibar and along the Swahili coast gave rise to a new migration system that developed "out of a more diffuse form of slavery" that had character-ized the region (Cooper 1979, 112). The variability of the status of slavery that characterized coastal societies complicated the trajectories of enslaved migrants. As this chapter has dis-cussed, enslaved people were not only forced to migrate, but they could move voluntarily, with their enslaver's permission, from the coast to the urban centers that developed along the main caravan roads. When looking at slavery in 19th-century East Africa, it is possible to identify different migration flows that overlapped and did not just follow the direction interior regions-coastal plantations.

British attempts to limit slavery and the slave trade in the Indian Ocean contributed to an important shift within the slave migration system, as the slave trade shifted from export to the coast to a major use of enslaved workers in the interior regions. Following this relocation, more enslaved people migrated within the interior regions and to the urban centers that had developed along the main caravan roads in connection with the ivory trade. These settlements had thousands of inhabitants and were characterized by the presence of immigrant groups both from the coast and from the interior region. The expansion in the ivory trade gave rise to another migration system, formed by free laborers who traveled the caravan roads. As the journey from the coast to Lake Tanganyika and back generally took from four to six months, they spent long periods away from home and became circular migrants.[7]

Changes brought about by the establishment of colonial rule were important drivers of shifting patterns of migration. The restructuring of the caravan trade in GEA after the building of the Central Railway, the pressure of white settlers and the coercive nature of the colonial state in Kenya, and the abolition of slavery created the conditions for the emergence of a new migration system that supplied waged laborers to European plantations. External factors cannot be held solely responsible for migrations. Even if forced recruitment was not absent, these migrations were the result of choices of groups and individuals who responded to changing socio-economic conditions.

Notes

1 On the history of the introduction of cloves to Zanzibar, see Sheriff (1987, 49–51), and for exports and prices (62–3).
2 Lovejoy (2011, 151–2) estimates it at 47.5%.
3 Slavery continued, however, to be tolerated in the coastal areas by colonial authorities, who needed slaves as manpower for the plantations; see below.
4 This was due to the 1900 land agreement between the Baganda and the British that limited the land available for settlers in Buganda. Cotton seed were distributed by the government to local chiefs, who in turn distributed them to peasants. See De Haas (2017) and Wrigley (1959). On migration flows connected to cash-crop production in Uganda see De Haas and Travieso (Chapter 11, this volume).
5 On South Africa see Keeton and Schirmer (Chapter 6, this volume) and Fourie (Chapter 7, this volume).
6 The total population of Zanzibar at the time was 115,016 (Zanzibar Protectorate 1924).
7 The average was 60–5 days from the coast to Ujiji on Lake Tanganyika and 45 from Tabora to the coast (Cummings 1973, 114).

References

Allen, Richard. 2010. "Satisfying the "Want for Laboring People": European Slave Trading in the Indian Ocean 1500–1850." *Journal of World History* 21(1): 45–73.

Alpers, Edward. 1997. "The African Diaspora in the Northwestern Indian Ocean: Reconsideration of an Old Problem, New Directions for Research." *Comparative Studies of South Asia, Africa and the Middle East* 17(2): 62–81.

Beachey, Raymond. 1967 "The East African Ivory Trade in the 19th century." *Journal of African History* 8(2): 269–90.

Berman, Bruce. 1990. *Control & Crisis in Colonial Kenya: The Dialectic of Domination*. London: James Currey.

Burton, Andrew, ed. 2002. *The Urban Experience in Eastern Africa c. 1750–2000*. Nairobi: British Institute in Eastern Africa.

Calvert, Albert F. 1916. *The German African Empire*. London: T.W. Laurie.

Campbell, Gwyn, ed. 2004. *The Structure of Slavery in Indian Ocean Africa and Asia*. London: Frank Cass.

Clayton, Anthony and Donald Savage. 1974. *Government and Labour in Kenya, 1895–1963*. London: Frank Cass.

Cooper, Frederick. 1979. "The Problem of Slavery in African Studies." *Journal of African History* 20(1): 103–25.

Cooper, Frederick. 1980. *From Slaves to Squatters: Plantation Labor and Agriculture in Zanzibar and Coastal Kenya, 1890–1925*. New Haven, CT: Yale University Press.

Coquery-Vidrovitch, Catherine. 1993. *The History of African Cities South of the Sahara. From the Origins to Colonization*. Translated by Mary Baker. Princeton, NJ: Markus Wiener.

Cummings, Robert. 1973. "A Note on the History of Caravan Porters in East Africa." *Kenya Historical Review* 1(2): 109–38.

Cummings, Robert. 1975. *Aspects of Human Porterage with Special Reference to the Akamba of Kenya: Towards an Economic History, 1820–1920*. PhD Thesis, University of California.

De Haas, Michiel. 2017. "Measuring Rural Welfare in Colonial Africa: Did Uganda's Smallholders Thrive?" *Economic History Review* 70(2): 605–31.

De Haas, Michiel. 2019. "Moving beyond Colonial Control? Economic Forces and Shifting Migration from Ruanda-Urundi to Buganda, 1920–1960." *Journal of African History* 60(3): 379–406.

Deutsch, Jan Georg. 2006. *Emancipation without Abolition in German East Africa, c. 1884–1914.* Oxford: James Currey.

Fabian, Steven. 2013. "East Africa's Gorée: Slave Trade and Slave Tourism in Bagamoyo, Tanzania." *Canadian Journal of African Studies* 47(1): 95–114.

Hanson, Holly. 2003. *Landed Obligation. The Practice of Power in Buganda.* Portsmouth: Heinemann.

Harms, Robert, Bernard Freamon, and David Blight, eds. 2013. *Indian Ocean Slavery in the Age of Abolition.* London: Yale University Press.

Iliffe, John. 1980. "Wage Labour and Urbanisation." In *Tanzania under Colonial Rule*, edited by Martin Kaniki, 276–306. London: Longman.

Koponen, Juhani. 1988. *People and Production in Late Pre-colonial Tanzania. History and Structures.* Helsinki: Finnish Society for Development Studies.

Lovejoy, Paul. 2011. *Transformations in Slavery. A History of Slavery in Africa.* Cambridge: Cambridge University Press.

Médard, Henri. 2007. "Introduction." In *Slavery in the Great Lakes Region of East Africa*, edited by Shane Doyle and Henri Médard, 1–37. Oxford: James Currey.

Pallaver, Karin. 2020. "A Triangle. Spatial Processes of Urbanization and Political Power in 19th-century Tabora, Tanzania." *Afriques. Debàts, methods et terrains d'histoire* 11, http://journals.openedition.org/afriques/2871.

Powesland, Philip. 1957. *Economic Policy and Labour. A Study in Uganda's Economic History.* Kampala: East African Institute of Social Research.

Reichard, Paul. 1889. "Die Wanjamuesi." *Zeitschrift der Gesellschaft für Erdkunde zu Berlin* 24: 246–60; 304–31.

Reid, Richard. 2002. *Political Power in Precolonial Buganda: Economy, Society and Warfare in the Nineteenth Century.* Oxford: James Currey.

Reid, Richard. 2017. *A History of Modern Uganda.* Cambridge: Cambridge University Press.

Reid, Richard and Henri Médard. 2000. "Merchants, Missions and the Urban Environment in Buganda." In *Africa's Urban Past*, edited by David Anderson and Richard Rathbone, 98–108. Oxford: James Currey.

Roberts, Andrew. 1970. "Nyamwezi Trade." In *Pre-colonial African Trade in Central and Eastern Africa before 1900*, edited by Richard Gray and David Birmingham, 39–74. London: Oxford University Press.

Rockel, Stephen. 2000. "'A Nation of Porters': The Nyamwezi and the Labour Market in nineteenth-century Tanzania." *Journal of African History* 41(2): 173–95.

Rockel, Stephen. 2006. *Carriers of Culture. Labor on the Road in Nineteenth-century East Africa.* Portsmouth: Heinemann.

Rockel, Stephen. 2019. "The Tutsi and the Nyamwezi: Cattle, Mobility, and the Transformation of Agro-Pastoralism in Nineteenth-Century Western Tanzania." *History in Africa* 46: 231–61.

Sheriff, Abdul. 1987. *Slaves, Spices and Ivory in Zanzibar. Integration of an East African Commercial Empire into the World Economy 1700–1873.* Oxford: James Currey.

Sheriff, Abdul, Vijayalakshmi Teelock, Saada Omar Wahab, and Satyendra Peerthum. 2016. *Transition from Slavery in Zanzibar and Mauritius. A Comparative History.* Dakar: CODESRIA.

Sunseri, Thaddeus. 2002. *Vilimani. Labour Migration and Rural Change in Early Colonial Tanzania.* Portsmouth: Heinemann.

Twaddle, Michael. 1988. "The Ending of Slavery in Buganda." In *The End of Slavery in Africa*, edited by Suzanne Miers and Richard Roberts, 119–49. Madison: University of Wisconsin Press.

Unomah, Alfred Chukwudi. 1972. *Economic Expansion and Political Change in Unyanyembe, c. 1840–1900.* PhD Thesis, University of Ibadan.

Van der Burgt, Joannes. 1913. "Zur Entvölkerungsfrage Unjamwesis und Usumbwas." *Koloniale Rundschau* 12: 705–28.

Vernet, Thomas. 2009. "Slave Trade and Slavery on the Swahili Coast (1500–1750)." In *Slavery, Islam and Diaspora*, edited by Behnaz Asl Mirzai, Ismael Musah Montana and Paul Lovejoy, 37–76. Trenton: Africa World Press.

Vernet, Thomas. 2013. "East Africa: Slave Migrations." In *The Encyclopedia of Global Human Migration*, edited by Immanuel Ness, 1–8. Oxford: Wiley Blackwell.

Wright, Marcia. 1993. *Strategies of Slaves and Women: Life Histories from East/Central Africa*. London: James Currey.

Wrigley, Christopher. 1959. *Crops and Wealth in Uganda: A Short Agrarian History*. Kampala: East African Institute of Social Research.

Zanzibar Protectorate. 1924. *Report on the Native Census, 1924*. Zanzibar: Government Printer.

Zöller, Katharina. 2019. "Crossing Multiple Borders: 'The Manyema' in Colonial East Central Africa." *History in Africa* 46: 299–326.

PART TWO

Frontiers, Connections, and Confrontations in the 19th Century

5

CATTLE, CLIMATE, AND CARAVANS

The Dynamics of Pastoralism, Trade, and Migration in 19th-Century East Africa

N. Thomas Håkansson

1 Introduction

This chapter explores the expansion of pastoralism in East Africa from the 18th to the early 20th centuries in relation to the ivory trade, climate, and migrations. The main thesis is that the ivory trade amplified an economic field of exchange that funneled cattle from the north to central East Africa. The increasing number of cattle, in turn, accelerated migrations from agricultural areas into pastoralist societies and spaces, increasing the size and scope of the latter mode of production. All of these movements were influenced by a major and a minor drought that took place during this period.

Migrations were enmeshed in, and responsive to, ecological factors such as climate and disease, the dynamics of regional and global trade arrangements, and wealth accumulation. The historical and anthropological study of East African pastoralists has largely focused on local or regional adaptations to the natural environment only rather than on their dependence on trade and world-system relationships (e.g., Dyson-Hudson and Dyson-Hudson, 1980; Marshall, 1990; Spencer, 1998). For example, in an article addressing the long-term dynamics of pastoralism in prehistoric East Africa, Marshall (1990) claims that, unlike in the Near East where pastoralism was strongly dependent on trade and irrigated agriculture, pastoralists in East Africa were oriented toward subsistence production. However, recent historical and ethnographic studies of East Africa stress that, for as far back in time as we have evidence, pastoralist societies were part of changing and fluid regional economies, productive specializations, and long-distance trade (Håkansson 2008a; Waller 1985a). Furthermore, the reasons for migrations during the colonial period continued to be conditioned by the same goals of social reproduction through cattle accumulation, social networks, and family expansion.

Ivory was paid for in beads, metals, and cloth, all of which became currencies that were used to buy cattle from the Great Lakes region, and from what is today northern Kenya, southern Ethiopia, and Somalia. The increasing infusion of cattle through trade from these areas to central Kenya and northern Tanzania resulted in a long period of population transfer from cultivation and foraging into pastoralism. The demographic and spatial expansion

DOI: 10.4324/9781003225027-8

of pastoralism was based on two main forms of cattle accumulation: trade and raiding. Cultivators and foragers that were successful in obtaining large herds through trade merged with pastoralists, increasing both human and cattle populations. Established pastoralists used three strategies to increase their herds: they exchanged ivory either directly for cattle or for coastal goods that could be used to buy cattle and they raided cultivators or other pastoralists. Raiding thus contributed to the spread of cattle outside the trade routes.

An influential structural approach argues that migrations in Africa transitioned from traditional to modern migrations, from one of migrations of peoples in the pre-colonial period to a shift to migrations of labor (Amin 1995). This theory focuses on how the process of economic and political peripheralization of Africa in the global capitalist system induced modern migrations. I argue, in contrast, that far from being part of what is often dismissed as a single, uniform traditional, pre-colonial migration pattern, pastoral mobility in the 19th century was flexible and adapted to complex configurations of ecology and political economy (see also De Haas and Frankema, Chapter 1; Austin Chapter 2, this volume).

While colonialism and increasing incorporation into the capitalist world system significantly influenced the movement patterns and adaptations of pastoralists, I also argue that there was no clear break between pre-colonial and colonial patterns of migration (cf. Manchuelle 1998). Indeed, the effects of world-system changes on migrations were not uniform, but were conditioned by specific regional economic, ecological, and social contexts through which modes of exploitation and region-specific factors combined.

Environmental factors such as climate change and weather also played an important role in affecting migrations, shaping the trajectories of social institutions, exchange, and trade through time (Håkansson 2019). Because of the recent developments in paleo-ecological research on prior climate in East Africa it is possible to construct a tentative timeline for decades of long fluctuations in rainfall from the late 18th to the 20th centuries. Following Anderson (2016), I relate the catastrophic droughts during the early 19th century to a virtual cessation of viable pastoralism in central and northern Kenya and central Uganda. The new era of pastoralism, which started around 1830, was book-ended by the Rinderpest cattle epidemic at the beginning of the 1890s, which together with drought and smallpox in the human population led to a collapse of the pastoral economy again. The subsequent restoration of pastoralism took place in the context of a new colonial political economy.

The chapter begins with an overview of the interrelationships between productive specializations, ethnicities, and migrations. I then describe the principles of the expansive pastoralist political economy. After a brief outline of the history of pastoralism in the second millennium AD, I devote the next section to the effects of the long dry period in the 18th and early 19th centuries on pastoralists. I then outline my central argument about the influence of trade on the accumulation of cattle and migrations in East Africa followed by an analysis of the connection between the recursively related intensification of cultivation, pastoralism, and migration between communities engaged in different productive specializations.

2 Shifting livelihoods and ethnic identities

Pastoralism is not a fixed ethno-economic identity but rather a specialized livelihood strategy linked to social status, ethnic identification, and ecology, and one into which and out of which people can move. The way that long-term climate change as well as shorter drought events affected the spatial movement of pastoralist people in East Africa was shaped by a triangular pattern of exchange and movement between three basic modes of production: agriculture, pastoralism, and gathering/hunting. These three productive specializations were not exclusive but represented the ends of a continuum along which members of different communities moved. Ethnicities were situational and based on productive specializations, and the shifting of ethnic identities was common (Galaty 1982). Finally, the wider networks of regional and long-distance trade facilitated local cattle accumulations and structured shifting ethnic relationships between foragers, cultivators, and pastoralists.

Specialized pastoralism is by necessity a regionally dependent mode of production. Because a purely pastoral economy cannot produce enough food to feed the population, specialized pastoralists had to exchange livestock for crops from cultivating neighbors (Berntsen 1976; Schneider 1979; Galvin, Coppock, and Leslie 1994). Thus, pastoral societies and economies were part of regional systems of interaction and their productive specialization depended on access to agricultural products and/or wild resources. Indeed, the expansion of pastoralism was recursively linked to the spread of "islands of intensive agriculture" in East Africa (Map 5.1).

Pastoralists in East Africa moved in seasonal patterns to pastures and water, resources that varied temporally and spatially. Often the settlements were divided into clusters of households where the married women and men and young children lived, and cattle camps where the young unmarried men followed the cattle to pastures and water sources. The movements of pastoralists over large distances included the seasonal encampments between dry and rainy seasons within territories that were divided between sections of the society. Pastoralists also expanded geographically and demographically, especially in the case of the Maasai and their related groups of Maa-speakers. Historical linguistics offer reconstructions of what seem like large-scale migrations of Maa-speakers from the area of Lake Turkana south through the Rift Valley to Kilimanjaro in Tanzania already in the 1600s and possibly earlier.

However, a closer examination of such movements reveals a more complex picture than simple movements of people outward from an original point. Among the reasons that pastoralist societies were inherently expansive was that cattle is a form of wealth that grows under suitable environmental conditions and husbandry. Thus, migrations tended to take place as a result of searches for more pasture. But the success of herd expansion was mutually related to, and dependent on, the expansion of labor to tend the herds. What on the surface looks like a steady migration was actually a continuous absorption of people from local agricultural and foraging groups in different geographical areas into the pastoral sphere. In addition, such expansion continued into new areas already occupied by pastoralists that were either pushed away or absorbed into a new ethnic umbrella of more powerful groups such as the Maasai.

3 Growth and expansion in pastoral economies

The expansionist tendencies were built into the social structures of these societies. Through natural reproduction and the application of labor, cattle are a form of capital, the expansion of which depends on an ever-increasing access to good grazing pastures during the dry season (Waller 1985b). There was an institutionalized tension between older men who controlled cattle necessary for bridewealth payments and their sons and wives who desired

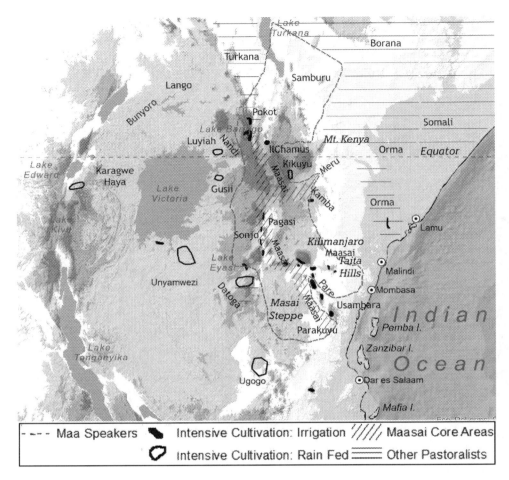

MAP 5.1 Pastoralism and intensive cultivation in East Africa.

Notes: Areas with intensive cultivation are shown for central Kenya to central Tanzania. The map is a work in progress.
Sources: Map drawn by Ryan Kelly, based on Börjeson (2004); Håkansson (1994, 2008a, 2008b); Höhnel (1894, 302); Kjekshus (1977, 36, 42–3); Petek and Lane (2017); Thomson (1885, 177, 284); Waller (1985a); Widgren and Sutton (2004). The pastoralists in northern Kenya were integrated into regional trade networks that encompassed southern Ethiopia and Somalia from where they obtained agricultural products and other goods (Robinson 1985, 342–4; Sobania 1991).

to accumulate their own cattle in order to establish households independent of their fathers and husbands. Thus, the mother-centered households had strong incentives to amplify cattle accumulation through raiding and trade, in order to provide livestock for the sons' early marriages independently of the husbands' cattle.

Social reproduction depended on the role of cattle as a key symbol and was central as a metaphor and a value that related numerous aspects of social structure and culture among East African societies (cf. Ortner 1973). Cattle are economic assets that symbolize and create social relationships and elaborate cosmological links between human and plant fertility. All economic activities were ultimately connected through cattle as the primary prestige good and investment. Agricultural production, land use, and gathering-hunting can therefore be traced to political and economic strategies directed toward access to and control of cattle.

Pastoralist societies exhibit cyclical demographic characteristics of human and livestock populations that move up and down in a saw-tooth profile of steady growth offset at irregular intervals by a sharp and devastating loss (Spencer 1998, 41; Waller 1999). Repetitive pre-colonial disasters are documented in oral traditions (Spencer 1998, 208). For example, an earlier, historically known, widespread destruction of Maasai herds took place in the 1830s (Waller 1999). Droughts and stock disease periodically decimated cattle herds (Taylor, Robertshaw and Marchant 2000). Human epidemics also reduced labor availability, which in turn affected herd managements. Those who suffered large losses either migrated to agricultural areas where they took up cultivation or joined foraging bands, in order to survive and to build up new cattle herds through the exchange of foodstuffs or ivory for livestock with the remaining stock owners (Spear 1997; Waller 1985a). Once they had enough cattle for a pastoral existence, they would again move onto the plains and a new cycle of herd growth would ensue until environmental and social factors precipitated new declines in their herds. Such periodic and frequent herd reductions have also been documented in contemporary northern, semi-arid Kenya, where droughts are frequent (Fratkin 1997).

4 The historical dynamics of pastoralism

The available evidence from historical linguistics suggests that very few communities in East Africa practiced specialized pastoralism at the end of the first millennium AD. The historical linguistic work of Ehret shows a prevalence of mixed economies where cattle-keeping groups practiced cultivation and foraging as well (Ehret 1971, 1984, 2002). The emergence of specialized pastoralism seems to be associated with Southern Nilotic speakers who, during the 12th and 13th centuries, spread south from northern Kenya and adjacent areas to northern Tanzania along the Rift Valley (Ehret 1971, 60–2; Sutton 1990, 41). This was a slow process that lasted c. 300 years and by 1500 AD they were settled as far south as the modern city of Dodoma in Tanzania. The western Rift Valley escarpment remained a barrier for the South Kalenjin and the Datoga-dominated crater highlands (Ehret 1984).

After the spread of the Southern Nilotes, the next phase of pastoral expansion derives from the Maa cluster northwest of Mount Kenya. The proto-Maasai began to make inroads into the lands of the South Nilotic Kalenjin along the Rift Valley in central Kenya as early as the early 16th century. In Kenya, Maa-speaking pastoralists dominated from north of Lake Baringo southward to the Rift Valley and surrounding plateaus (Galaty 1993). By the mid-1600s they had expanded as far as the northern edges of Tanzania and Kilimanjaro (Ehret 1984; Galaty 1993).

In Uganda specialized pastoralism may have emerged in the beginning of the second millennium (Schoenbrun 1998, 76). Until the mid-18th century pastoralism and agro-pastoralism dominated the plateaus of central Uganda from Lake Albert south to the Kagera River. This dry savanna region was utilized for cattle, millet, and sorghum cultivation, as well as iron and salt industries (Chretien 2003, 142).

Sometime during the second half of the 18th century, precipitation declined and much of modern Kenya, Uganda, and northern Tanzania became much dryer than it is today. Evidence from paleo-ecological data, oral traditions, and historical linguistics point to a period of increasingly dry climate, which culminated in a severe drought during the first decades of the 19th century (Bessems et al. 2008). Several lakes in Kenya and Uganda completely dried out, indicating that the climatic anomaly of severe drought was widespread over equatorial East Africa (Bessems et al. 2008; De Cort et al., 2013). Authors such as Chretien have used oral traditions alone to date droughts and climate events in the Great Lakes region (Chretien 2003, 142). According to this view the regular droughts began at the beginning of the 18th century.

Much of the data that is used for such reconstructions derive from sediments that reflect water levels in lakes over time. However, problems with the dating of lake sediments still make detailed chronologies impossible (Bessems et al. 2008). In their sediment study of four lakes in Kenya and Uganda, Bessems et al. (2008) find that dried-out lakes began being filled with water again around 1830, signaling the beginning of a wetter climate. According to Verschuren, Laird, and Cumming, the second half of the 19th century was a period of increasing precipitation and presumably more favorable conditions for cultivation (Verschuren, Laird, and Cumming 2000; see also Petek and Lane 2017). This trend was interrupted by a regionally significant drought during the 1870s (Anderson 2016). These dates and qualitative assessments must be understood with the caveat that the spatial distribution of the severity and durations of dry conditions varied within East Africa during the time period under consideration.

Indeed, oral traditions from many different societies confirm that a long catastrophic drought occurred at the time the paleo-ecological data indicate. We do not know exactly how this dry period affected the pastoralists, only what happened after it ended. According to Anderson (2016), prior communities and social formations broke down, instigating a wholesale remaking of identities and cultures, and probably caused starvation and migrations to places where food could be obtained by foraging and cultivation.

The dry period ended quite abruptly around 1830 followed by a wetter climate after which many communities reconstituted and either built new social institutions or reinvigorated old forms. The return to pastoralism by the Maa-speakers seems to have been rapid because soon they were involved in internecine wars between different sections called the "Iliokop Wars." The speed with which this reconstitution took place indicates that there must have been refugia where sizable numbers of former pastoralists survived. The conflict can be divided into three phases that lasted between the 1830s and 1870s (Anderson 2016). The first phase of conflict between Maa-speaking pastoralists began at the end of the 1830s and probably ended by 1850 and coincided with a speedy environmental recovery after the great catastrophe. A second phase began at the end of 1840s and was partly caused by pressures from Turkana and Pokot who expanded into Maasai areas from the south and the east. The final phase, in the 1860s and 1870s, saw the decline in the dominance and final dissolution of Laikipiak Maasai by attacks from the southern Maasai sections. Anderson (2016) attributes the cause of this long-lasting conflict to competition between sections for new pastures during the improved environmental conditions.

5 Trade and expansion of pastoralism

The reconstruction of the history of pastoralism during the second millennium is mainly based on historical linguistics and to some extent oral traditions and chronologies provided by their age-set systems. The archaeology of the Pastoral Iron Age is still spotty and has yet to provide a more complete understanding. Hence, it is not until the 19th century that a more detailed picture emerges that delineates expansion of pastoralism set within a context of regional and extra-regional economic and political processes. Between the 1830s and 1850s economic interactions with the coast experienced fundamental and unprecedented transformations. Beginning at the end of the 18th century markets for ivory expanded in Western Europe and the US where it was used for a variety of consumer goods such as combs, piano keys, and billiard balls. From having been largely an enterprise controlled by interior communities, in the mid-19th century there was a shift to coastal control that led to the expansion of markets and trading settlements in the interior of East Africa. During the second half of that century slave trade became an important component of trade, adding additional social upheaval and suffering (Pallaver, Chapter 4, this volume). The pastoralists in East Africa were directly involved in the ivory trade (see below), which affected their economic strategies and relationships with other populations that practiced agriculture or foraging, and such specialized production as iron or salt (Håkansson 2004).

The vast and steady accumulation of cattle in the region between northwestern Kenya east to southern Somalia and then south and west to northern Tanzania and the Rift Valley was based on exchange advantages that emerged from the networks of trade. In addition to trade, local accumulation of cattle by cultivators also stimulated cattle raiding by pastoralists, thus further distributing cattle into areas outside the main trade circuits. Fischer and Baumann reported that the Maasai regularly raided cattle near Mombasa on the Kenyan coast, south of Lake Victoria, and what is now Western Kenya (Fischer 1882–83, 57, 70, 89; Baumann 1891, 148–9).

With a few exceptions, our knowledge of the complex trade and exchange networks crisscrossing East Africa is fragmentary but obviously more detailed toward the end of the 19th century (cf. Pallaver, Chapter 4, this volume). Nevertheless, I believe it is possible to formulate a basic model for the value chains in the indirect regional trade that interfaced with the coastal trade (cf. Schneider 1979, 98). Communities in the interior were strongly engaged in trade and profited by exploiting price differences of cattle and other goods in different localities. Traders based on the coast paid for the ivory, brought to them by caravans originating in the hinterland, in imported goods such as cloth, beads, and metals. Later on, by the mid-19th century, the coastal emporia themselves sent large caravans into the interior. They comprised several thousand members who carried imported goods and provisions. The regional traders who exchanged directly with these caravans in turn exchanged such goods for cattle even further inland. Parallel to engaging in the ivory trade, many communities conducted a thriving business in selling food to caravans in exchange for coastal goods, which were also bartered for livestock in other areas outside the caravan routes (Farler 1882; Fischer 1882–83, 68, 75; Reichard 1892, 259; Volkens 1897, 240). Finally, those members of inland communities who had access to beads and cloth used these to exchange for food during shortages caused by drought instead of using livestock in such transactions, thereby avoiding dispensing of livestock and preserving their herds.

However, close to the main caravan routes there were signs in the 1840s of a growing disinterest in trading for coastal goods, which continued until the end of the century. More and more Kamba traders refused to sell ivory for cloth and beads and demanded cattle instead (Krapf, Journal, 11–28–1849; Ambler, 1988, 103). Similar trends of devaluation of cloth and beads are reported in other parts of East Africa. According to Moore, Chagga chiefs had to pay elephant hunters in cattle. Likewise, in Karagwe, ivory could only be bought with cattle (Beachey, 1967; Moore, 1986, 28).

102 N. Thomas Håkansson

I have identified three tributaries along which cattle moved through complex networks of transactions to this region: (1) from cattle-rich areas in Uganda/Rwanda (Wissman 1889, 235–40), (2) from northern Kenya/southern Ethiopia (Robinson 1985, 307–9), and (3) from southern Somalia (Fischer 1878–79). The increasing infusion of cattle through trade from these areas to central Kenya and northern Tanzania resulted in a long period of population transfer from cultivation and foraging into pastoralism.

5.1 Uganda/Rwanda

Explorers in the mid-19th century reported that the kingdoms of Nyoro and Karagwe possessed large herds of cattle, which they obtained through trade with northern neighbors such as Lango and Teso (Uzoigwe 1970). In the mid-1800s, King Kamrasi of Nyoro was frequently visited by traders who bought ivory, cattle, and slaves (Grant 1864, 289). According to Burton, cattle were sold for 500 to 1,000 cowries that were brought from the coast by Nyamwezi caravans (Burton 1860, 185 and 198). South of Nyoro, the kingdom of Karagwe had emerged as a center of trade during the 19th century and was reported to have more cattle than other kingdoms (Stanley 1878, 459). Grant reported that the king, Rumanika, was part of an established trade network and acted as a supplier of coastal goods to the societies further north from which he received cattle, ivory, or slaves in exchange for, e.g., ornaments in brass or copper or porcelain cups (Grant 1864, 144).

Through trade, large numbers of cattle ended up in Unyamwezi, the chiefdoms of which had been involved in the ivory trade since the end of the 18th century. During the 19th century they invested their gains from the ivory trade in cattle obtained from Karagwe but also the BuHa chiefdoms to the south of Karagwe (Rockel 2019). Passing through Unyamwezi, Speke (1864, 286) commented on the enormous herds of cattle that he observed and the large numbers of them that were sold at cattle markets in Unyamyembe near Lake Eyasi (Speke 1864, 268), close to Maasai territory (see Map 5.2). From these markets cattle were further traded northward along the eastern coast and hinterland of Lake Victoria (Hartwig 1976, 110). While the main route of the cattle trade was directed to the south, another path toward Western Kenya seems to have existed during the 19th century (Hobley 1898; Cohen 1988; Cohen and Atieno Odhiambo 1989, 69).

5.2 Northern Kenya/southern Ethiopia

Several pastoralist groups, such as Turkana, Samburu, and Borana, that were integrated into coastal trade networks prior to the 19th century, including southern Ethiopia, the Benadir coast, and central Kenya, inhabited this region (Robinson 1985, 300). The dry savannas, rivers, and highlands formed ecological zones that offered varying resources supporting both pastoralism and cultivation. Communities were connected through a regional network of exchange, which in turn interfaced with the coastal trade. From this area a trade route connected pastoralists with the Mount Kenya communities of Kikuyu, Embu, and Meru. The details of this trade are sketchy and do not provide a complete picture of what was exchanged and with whom. Samburu traded hides and skins, and brought cattle for sale at Meru on Mount Kenya (Kerven 1992, 19). The Boran traveled to a marketplace east of Naivasha where they exchanged cattle for other goods and valuables (Robinson 1985, 308). This is probably the same market mentioned by Joseph Thomson as a place where Dorobo

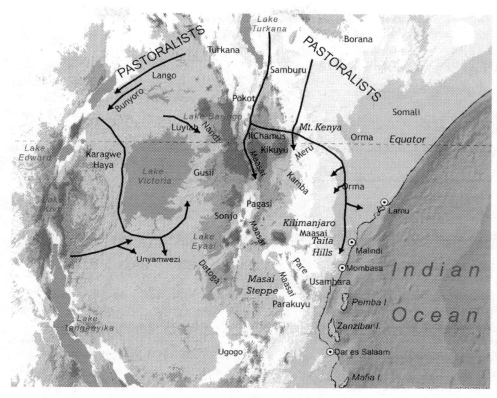

MAP 5.2 Trade routes for the dispersal of cattle from northern East Africa to central Kenya and northern Tanzania in the 19th century.
Source: Author's own, drawn by Ryan Kelly.

villagers "subsist entirely by buying vegetable food from the Wa-kikuyu and sell it again to the Masai" (Thomson 1885, 262).

5.3 Northeastern Kenya/southern Somalia

During the 19th century Somali traders were conspicuously active in the region, connecting and cooperating with communities in Somalia and northern Kenya such as the Borana, Samburu, Gabbra, and Rendille. Somali caravans traded for many goods but especially cattle and ivory for which the Somali exchanged such items as clothing, tobacco, coffee, and metal implements (Robinson 1985, 308).

Traders capitalized on differences in exchange rates between different locations in the interior and the coast. The Somali traders were the first stage in a chain of exchanges that moved cattle to the Kenyan coast. In northeastern Kenya, the Orma, culturally and linguistically related to the Borana, were the dominant pastoralists. They used cloth and money obtained from their sale of ivory and cattle on the coast to buy both cattle and ivory further inland at favorable exchange rates. First, the Somali obtained cattle from the Borana, and sold these to Orma for Maria Theresa dollars, which Orma had obtained from the sale of cattle on the coast where prices were the highest (Fischer 1878–79). Near the Sabaki River, in the hinterland of Malindi, the pastoralist Orma traded cattle to the Swahili and Mijikenda on the southern coast of Kenya for cloth (Krapf, June 24, 1845), which was probably among the goods they used in their trade with Samburu pastoralists undertaken at the upper reaches of the Tana River (Fischer 1878–79).

In the Kenyan coastal hinterland, many agricultural communities converted their gains from the coastal trade into cattle. During the first half of the 19th century, the Giriama north of Mombasa and the Digo to the south were expanding their cattle herds and moved further inland in search of grazing (Baumann 1891, 148–9). The Giriama were practically an agro-pastoral group by the middle of the 19th century (Parkin 1991, 22). South of the Digo, on the Tanzanian coast, the Zigua communities also accumulated cattle through ivory trade and the sale of grain to the coast and expanded their villages westward toward the Pangani (Giblin 1992, 26 and 33).

6 Pastoralism, intensive cultivation, and population movements

The Rift Valley and the surrounding highlands were lined with agricultural communities practicing intensive cultivation, which served as sources of agricultural products and as refuges for pastoralists during severe stock losses (see Map 5.1). Eastern Africa's Rift Valley stretches from Kenya's Lake Turkana area, running southward through the Kenya Highlands into Tanzania. Near Lake Turkana, the valley floor tapers down to less than 500 meters above sea level, but southward it rises steadily to nearly 2,000 meters near Lake Naivasha from which it drops to approximately 660 meters in Tanzania (Morgan 1973). Escarpments and highlands that provide variations in rainfall, temperature, surface water, and vegetation surround the valley. The valley floor and the foothills are interspersed with grass savanna and excellent pastures, while at the higher elevations, with higher levels of precipitation, and streams, irrigated agriculture was practiced. The Rift Valley and surrounding highlands were the incubators of specialized pastoralism in East Africa during the last millennium.

These agricultural systems were capable of producing sizable surpluses that were used for the exchange of crops for livestock, which, in turn enabled cultivators to build cattle herds that allowed them to move into pastoralism (Berntsen 1976; Håkansson 2008a; Petek and Lane 2017). Some authors have incorrectly suggested that I view the provisioning of caravans as a major cause of agricultural intensification in East Africa (Biginagwa 2012, 70; Petek and Lane 2017). I do not. As I have explained in several publications, I view the emergence and maintenance of intensive cultivation as based on regional exchange of surplus crops before the expansion of the caravan trade (e.g., Håkansson 2004, 2008a, 2009; see also Waller 1985b).

The 19th-century AD saw the peak of a Maa-language expansion, at which point it was spoken widely between southern Ethiopia and central Tanzania, a territory of some 60,000 square miles (Galaty 1991), encompassing an array of geographical, ecological, and economic zones, as well as self-identified non-Maasai populations (Sommer and Vossen 1993). On the periphery of Maasailand were several groups of agro-pastoralists, including the Pokot, Nandi, Arusha, and Il Chamus, in various stages of advance toward, or retreat from, pastoralism.

One example of how such smaller agro-pastoral groups developed into specialized sections of cultivators and pastoralists is the Pokot in the Kerio Valley who pursued a generalized agro-pastoral livelihood in the 18th century. Possibly as a response to the drying conditions the population moved up into the Cherangani and Seker Hills on the west side of the valley. There, at the turn of the 19th century, they developed large-scale irrigated cultivation, which was followed by the emergence of a section of Pokot practicing specialized pastoralism. Thus, agricultural intensification and pastoral specialization developed through mutually reinforcing exchange of crops and livestock. The pastoralist wing expanded throughout the century absorbing immigrants from neighboring groups (Davies 2012; Bollig 2016).

On the surface, this expansion of specialized pastoralism and its concomitant socio-cultural attributes could be interpreted as the result of a large-scale population movement of bounded ethnic groups. However, this was not the case. Rather, the spread of the Maasai and allied groups was the result of the assimilation of successful cattle accumulators from neighboring cultivators and foragers into a cultural package of language, social organization, and ritual (Sutton 1990, 54; see also Ehret 2002, 394; Homewood 2008, 38). Manning (2013) classifies this form of population movement over relatively short distances *cross-community migration*, which refers to the selective movement of individuals or sub-groups between communities. As pastoral and cattle populations increased, they moved into previously uninhabited areas or absorbed extant inhabitants into their communities. This type of migration corresponds to Manning's notion of a movement that involves the replication of a community into new areas. The combined forms of migrations were made possible by the existence of agricultural communities all along the Maasai core territory (see Map 5.1) where the pastoralists and cultivators constituted mutually dependent parts of a spatially wider socio-ecological system. For example, around Mount Kenya along the Maasai borderland, semi-pastoral Kikuyu and Meru populations developed through the movement of successful cattle accumulators into the areas where cultivation and forest merged into pastures (Lawren 1968; Waller 1985; Fadiman 1993, 91).

The process of removing people from the agricultural to the pastoral sector may seem to contradict the expansion of labor-intensive cultivation. The demographic and economic effects of the two opposite migration patterns must be further investigated. However, there are several possible solutions to this apparent contradiction. First, the territorial expansion of successful pastoralists led to warfare against other pastoralists whose cattle were appropriated, forcing destitute former pastoralists to join agricultural communities (cf. Waller 1985; Spear 1997). Second, the spatial spread of population movement into pastoralism is much greater than the reverse change of land use to cultivation. That is, the labor requirements for herd growth are much less than for intensive cultivation. Hence, a relatively small number of people moving into pastoralism with thousands of cattle would produce a significant territorial bumper car effect. Third, there was a regional slave trade to the interior, mainly in women from the coast and the Maasai whose offspring were assimilated into the agricultural communities (Ambler 1988, 70–2).

The process of assimilation was different for women and men. Women from cultivating societies such as the Kikuyu often married Maasai men, thereby also creating networks of kinship relationships between the two groups. Frequent intermarriage between pastoralist and cultivating communities created enduring kinship networks that enabled flexibility in group membership and economic activities. For men, assimilation into the pastoral community depended on the ability to accumulate enough cattle to transfer into a fully pastoral existence. Young men from the Kikuyu and Meru in Kenya and from the Pare Mountains in Tanzania dressed like Maasai warriors and could join

Maasai initiation rituals and age sets (Kenyatta 1938, 209–10; Lawren 1968; Berntsen 1976; Håkansson 2008b).

Further south in the Rift Valley, in southern Kenya and northern Tanzania, the Pagasi and Sonjo irrigation communities were, as the inhabitants expressed it, "a school for Maasai" where cultivators became Maasai through the accumulation of herds. During periods of significant cattle losses, Maasai pastoralists also utilized the system. Large numbers of them lived in Pagasi between 1850 and 1870, and again in the 1890s after the Rinderpest epidemic. The farming population contracted as climate conditions improved and allowed people to return to pastoralism (Berntsen 1976).

The extensive networks of friendship, marriage, and kinship between cultivators and pastoralists that was conducive for recruiting new members into the herding economy also enabled pastoralists to seek refuge during times of loss of cattle. The relationship between Maa-speaking pastoralists and cultivators was complex and entailed both peaceful exchange and raiding. The warrior age sets subsisted mainly on livestock products – milk, blood, and meat. These young men frequently conducted raids on the cultivators' cattle in order to build up their own herds and ability to marry. The older married generations of men and women maintained peaceful relationships and were dependent on the cultivators for plant food. The trade between the Maasai and cultivators was completely in the hands of women who were allowed safe passage even if the men were fighting (Thomson 1885, 178; Lawren 1968).

The Arusha on Mount Meru in the Pangani Valley provide an example of how such population interchange could function. In the early 19th century the slopes of Mount Meru were settled by Maa-speakers who practiced irrigated agriculture, intermarried with the Maasai, and maintained a flourishing exchange of pastoral and agricultural products.

A common form of migration was a result of droughts and other events that reduced the herds, making a pastoral life style untenable. The destitute pastoralists could move either to friends and relatives in neighboring agricultural areas or to local Dorobo foragers, where they could accumulate cattle through trade. These were usually short-distance movements rather than long treks. Dorobo was a collective term used by pastoralists and cultivators for gatherer-hunter groups that inhabited forested and wooded areas of East Africa (Van Zwanenberg 1976). They were central actors in the regional and extra-regional trade systems exchanging natural products, including ivory, for livestock, beads, iron implements, and cultivated plant food. For example, Dorobo hunters sold ivory to their Maasai patrons who in turn traded with coastal caravans.

Spear (1997, 52) describes the processes of changing from a pastoral existence to cultivation in a host community, cattle accumulation, and return to the livestock economy among the agricultural Arusha and pastoral Maasai in northern Tanzania. The agricultural Arusha were (and are) linguistically and culturally closely related to the Maasai and occupied the highlands of Mt. Meru where rainfall was ample and streams provided water for irrigation. Hence, the Arusha almost never experienced the effects of droughts, or the spread of cattle disease, because their cattle were kept on isolated highland pastures. When the Maasai experienced a period of relative prosperity they often had a surplus of cattle relative to available labor. During periods of prosperity among the Maasai, Arusha women married Maasai men in exchange for cattle as bridewealth. Such transactions were mutually beneficial to both groups in that the Maasai gained women and children while ridding themselves of surplus cattle to the gain of the Arusha who were almost always in need of cattle for marriages. Through marriage the Maasai also gained Arusha affines who could provide herdboys, access to agricultural products, and potential refuge in times of need. The Arusha, who had a shortage of pasture land on the mountain, could gain access to pasture on the plain through affinal connections with the ultimate goal of establishing themselves as pastoralists on the plains when they wished to do so.

Conversely, during periods of drought or cattle diseases, cattle herds were reduced, making it impossible for the Maasai on the plains to maintain their diet based on livestock as the major food source. Women and children sought refuge among Arusha affines and age mates during famines while the men remained on the plains to care for the remaining cattle and to rebuild herds with stock from Arusha and elsewhere.

7 Uganda

The development of pastoralism in the Great Lakes area differed radically from the rest of East Africa. Instead of a geographical division of labor into different socio-ecological niches, pastoralists, cultivators, and foragers became parts of stratified social formations. Access to and control over cattle were in the hands of pastoral elites who dominated the farmers and foragers in various kingdoms. In Rwanda, the pastoral Tutsi constituted the ruling group and in other kingdoms the pastoral Hima formed the ruling groups. Thus, while wealth and prestige was distributed horizontally in Kenya and Tanzania between politically independent groups, in Uganda foragers, cultivators, and pastoralists were arranged in political hierarchies within societies.

Several authors ascribe the growth of hierarchy based on control over cattle to climate change and migrations during the 18th and 19th centuries (Steinhart 1981; Chretien 2003, 145). As the climate became drier and droughts became more common in southeastern Uganda, cultivators moved westward to higher rainfall areas. By the mid-19th century all the cultivating communities had moved to the west of the 1200 mm isohyet, abandoning the drier eastern side to the pastoralists (Spinage 2012, 135). These authors argue that more than half a century of declining precipitation had differential effects on cultivators and pastoralists. While the latter preserved their herds by moving cattle to wetter areas, the decline in agricultural production forced the cultivators to obtain food and protection from pastoralists. The new social relationship favored the pastoralists who established political domination over the farmers. The periodic drought cycles that occurred throughout the western lacustrine zone may also have led to direct competition with pastoralists for water and land (Steinhart 1981). However, this explanation is not tenable because it ignores the fact that pastoralists cannot survive without access to plant food. Hence, giving cattle to starving farmers would not help them very much and food shortage among the cultivators meant that the pastoralists would also experience famine. We are therefore still at a loss to explain the difference in the political economy of pastoralism in the Great Lakes region and the rest of East Africa.

8 Conclusions

Compared to earlier centuries (as far as we know), there was a formidable expansion of pastoralism in terms of people and livestock during the 19th century, which was driven by the growth of the international ivory trade. This growth may have reached a plateau around the 1880s, only to collapse during the catastrophes of massive cattle disease, human disease, and droughts during the end of the 1880s and the beginning of the 1890s.

The overall effect of the Maasai expansion both into and within present-day Tanzania seems to have included a transfer of people from the northern part of Maasailand and the absorption of successful cattle accumulators from other agro-pastoral and agricultural populations from northern Kenya to the Pangani Valley in Tanzania. As the pastoralist population expanded, so did the concomitant cultivation and the building of landesque capital in the form of irrigation systems and semi-permanent fields in the highlands, as well as in enclaves on the plains (Waller 1985; Widgren and Sutton 2004; Håkansson 2008a).

At the end of the 19th century, the wider economic and political contexts for pastoralism changed. The immediate effect of colonialism on pastoralism was the establishment of tribal reserves and the suppression of armed conflict and raiding. Pastoralist movements were curtailed but smaller groups experienced relief from the depredation by larger neighbors.

The colonial states of Kenya and German East Africa were established after the severe epidemics that reduced both human and cattle populations across East Africa. Colonial administrators failed to see that this decline was temporary and that the pastoralists were still on the move. Administrative boundaries froze the pastoralist populations within tribal ethnic boundaries. Boundaries and territories cut across the ecological resources necessary for successful pastoralism, denying them access to dry and wet season pastures and watering holes. In addition, the Maasai saw themselves cut into two halves by the international border between Kenya and German East Africa (Homewood 1996). A part of the latter became the British protectorate of Tanganyika after 1918. Despite being governed by the same colonial power, the two colonies pursued different policies that affected pastoralists. This was especially problematic in Kenya where large swaths of prime grazing land were alienated to European ranches (Waller 2012, 55).

The creation of administrative boundaries and ethnic categories by the colonial authorities contributed to a decline in the old system of relief for impoverished pastoralists through migration to agricultural enclaves. By 1940, the pre-colonial flexible social networks between communities that had enabled pastoralists to move between cultivation and cattle keeping had declined. Notwithstanding these colonial changes, the cross-community migrations of successful cattle accumulators to pastoralist groups from cultivators and foragers continued (Cronk 2002; Håkansson 2008b). However, in Kenya the establishment of large European ranches and farms provided the colonial equivalent for such refuge settlements. Squatting in the White Highlands made it possible for households with livestock to accumulate cattle in more favorable environments than existed in the reserves. In addition, pastoralist men were sought after as herders and paid twice as much than other farm laborers, usually in stock, which allowed them to rebuild their herds (Waller 1999). Thus, pastoralists have exhibited a remarkable resilience in trying to maintain their way of life despite the restrictive policies enacted by colonial and post-colonial governments alike.

Acknowledgments

Several people have read and re-read various versions of this manuscript on its journey to the final version. The editors Ewout Frankema and Michiel de Haas have skillfully steered this project to its end. Their constructive comments and suggestions significantly improved the chapter. Likewise, Monica Udvardy tirelessly read and expertly caught my sometimes dense prose, and her comments on several versions significantly improved the final product. I would also like to thank my friend, geographer Ryan Kelly, who worked hard to draw the maps based on my primitive sketches.

References

Ambler, Charles H. 1988. *Kenyan Communities in the Age of Imperialism*. New Haven, CT: Yale University Press.

Amin, Samir. 1995. "Migrations in Contemporary Africa: A Retrospective View." In *The Migration Experience in Africa*, edited by J. Baker and T. Akin Aina, 29–40. Uppsala: Nordiska Afrikainstitutet.

Anderson, David. 2016. "The Beginning of Time? Evidence for Catastrophic Drought in Baringo in the Early Nineteenth Century." *Journal of Eastern African Studies* 10(1): 45–66.

Baumann, Oscar. 1891. *Usambara und seine Nachbargebiete*. Berlin: D. Reimer,

Beachey, R. W. 1967. "The East African Ivory Trade in the 19th Century." *Journal of African History* 8(2): 269–90.

Berntsen, John. 1976. "The Maasai and their Neighbors: Variables of Interaction." *African Economic History* 2: 1–11.

Bessems, Ilse, Dirk Verschuren, James M. Russell, Jozef Hus, Florias Mees, and Brian F. Cumming. 2008. "Palaeolimnological Evidence for Widespread Late 18th Century Drought across Equatorial East Africa." *Palaeogeography, Palaeoclimatology, Palaeoecology* 259: 107–20.

Biginagwa, Thomas John. 2012. *Historical Archaeology of the 19th Century Caravan Trade in North-Eastern Tanzania: A Zooarchaeological Perspective*. PhD Dissertation, University of York.

Bollig, Michael. 2016. "Adaptive Cycles in the Savannah: Pastoral Specialization and Diversification in Northern Kenya." *Journal of Eastern African Studies* 10: 21–44.

Börjeson, Lowe L. 2004. *A History under Siege. Intensive Agriculture in the Mbulu Highlands, Tanzania, 19th Century to the Present*. Stockholm: Almqvist & Wiksell International.

Burton, Richard. 1860. *The Lake Regions of Central Africa*, Vols. I and II, London: Longman.

Chretien, Jean-Pierre. 2003. *The Great Lakes of Africa*. New York: Zone Books.

Cohen, David W. 1988. "The Cultural Topography of a 'Bantu Borderland': Busoga, 1500–1850." *Journal of African History* 29(1): 57–79.

Cohen, David, and Atieno Odhiambo. 1989. *Siaya*. London: James Currey.

Cronk, Lee. 2002. "From True Dorobo to Mukogodo Maasai: Contested Ethnicity in Kenya." *Ethnology* 41(1): 27–49.

Davies, Matthew. 2012. "Some Thoughts on a 'Useable' African Archaeology: Settlement, Population and Intensive Farming among the Pokot of Northwest Kenya." *African Archaeological Review* 29(4): 319–53.

De Cort, Gijs, Ilse Bessems, Edward Keppens, Florias Mees, Brian Cumming, and Dirk Verschuren. 2013. "Late-Holocene and Recent Hydroclimatic Variability in the Central Kenya Rift Valley: The Sediment Record of Hypersaline Lakes Bogoria, Nakuru and Elementeita." *Palaeogeography, Palaeoclimatology, Palaeoecology* 388: 69–80.

Dyson-Hudson, Rada, and Neville Dyson-Hudson. 1980. "Nomadic Pastoralism." *Annual Review of Anthropology* 9: 15–61.

Ehret, Christopher. 1971. *Southern Nilotic History*. Evanston, IL: Northwestern University Press.

Ehret, Christopher. 1984. "Between the Coast and the Great Lakes." In *The UNESCO General History of Africa 12th -16th Centuries*, edited by D. J. Niane, 481–97. Berkeley: The University of California Press.

Ehret, Christopher. 2002. *The Civilizations of Africa*. Charlottesville: University of Virginia Press.

Fadiman, Jeffrey. 1993. *When We Began There Were Witchmen: An Oral History from Mount Kenya*. Berkeley: University of California Press.

Farler, J. P. 1882. "Native Routes in East Africa from Pangani to the Masai Country and the Victoria Nyanza." *Proceedings of the Royal Geographical Society* 4: 730–53.

Fischer, Gustav. 1878–79. "Das Wapokomo-Land und seine Bewohner." *Mittheilungen der Geographischen Gesellschaft in Hamburg* 3: 1–57.

Fisher, Gustav. 1882–83. "Bericht uber die im Auftrage der Geographischen Gesellschaft in Hamburg unternommene Reise in das Massai-Land." *Mittheilungen der Geographischen Gesellschaft in Hamburg*, 36–99; 189–279.

Fratkin, Elliot. 1997. *Ariaal Pastoralists of Kenya: Studying Pastoralism, Drought, and Development in Africa's Arid Lands*. Needham Heights, MA: Allyn and Bacon Publishers.

Galaty, John. 1982. "Being "Maasai"; Being "People of Cattle": Ethnic Shifters in East Africa." *American Ethnologist* 9(1): 1–20.

Galaty, John. 1991. "Pastoral Orbits and Deadly Jousts: Factors in the Maasai Expansion." In *Herders, Warriors, and Traders: Pastoralism in Africa*, edited by John Galaty and Pierre Bonte, 171–98. Boulder, CO: Westview Press.

Galaty, John. 1993. "Maasai Expansion and the New East African Pastoralism." In *Being Maasai*, edited by Thomas Spear and Richard Waller, 61–86. London: James Currey.

Galvin, Kathleen, Layne Coppock, and Paul Leslie. 1994. "Diet, Nutrition, and the Pastoral Strategy." In *African Pastoralist Systems*, edited by Elliot Fratkin, Kathleen Galvin, and Eric Abella Roth, 113–32. Boulder, CO: Lynne Rienner.

Giblin, James. 1992. *The Politics of Environmental Control in Northeastern Tanzania, 1840–1940*. Philadelphia: University of Pennsylvania Press.

Grant, James. 1864. *A Walk across Africa*. London: William Blackwood.

Håkansson, Thomas. 1994. "Grain, Cattle, and Power: The Social Process of Intensive Cultivation and Exchange in Precolonial Western Kenya." *Journal of Anthropological Research* 50: 249–76.

Håkansson, Thomas. 2004. "The Human Ecology of World Systems in East Africa: The Impact of the Ivory Trade." *Human Ecology* 32(5): 561–91.

Håkansson, Thomas. 2008a. "The Decentralized Landscape: Regional Wealth and the Expansion of Production in Northern Tanzania before the Eve of Colonialism." In *Economies and the Transformation of Landscape*, edited by Lisa Cligget and Christopher Pool, 239–65. Walnut Creek, CA: Altamira Press.

Håkansson, Thomas. 2008b. "Regional Political Ecology and Intensive Cultivation in Colonial South Pare, Tanzania." *International Journal of African Historical Studies* 41: 433–59.

Håkansson, Thomas. 2009. "Politics, Cattle And Ivory: Regional Interaction and Changing Land-Use Prior To Colonialism." In *Culture, History and Identity: Landscapes of Inhabitation in the Mount Kilimanjaro Area, Tanzania*, edited by Timothy Clack, 141–54. BAR International Series 1966.

Håkansson, Thomas. 2019. "Criticizing Resilience Thinking: A Political Ecology Analysis of Droughts in Nineteenth-Century East Africa." *Economic Anthropology* 6(1): 7–20.

Hartwig, Gerald. 1976. *The Art of Survival in East Africa: The Kerebe and Long-Distance Trade, 1800–1895*. New York: Africana Publishing Company.

Hobley, C. W. 1898. "Kavirondo." *The Geographical Journal* 12(4): 361–72.

Höhnel, Ludwig von. 1894. *Discovery of Lakes Rudolph and Stefanie*, vol. I. London: Longmans, Green.

Homewood, Katherine. 1996. "Ecological Outcomes of Boundary Formation in Maasailand." In *African Boundaries*, edited by Paul Nugent and A. I. Asiwaju, 87–110. London: Pinter.

Homewood, Katherine. 2008. *Ecology of African Pastoralist Societies*. Oxford: James Currey.

Kenyatta, Jomo. 1938. *Facing Mount Kenya*. London: Harwill Secker.

Kerven, Carol. 1992. "Customary Commerce: A Historical Reassessment of Pastoral Livestock Marketing in Africa." *ODI Occasional Agriculture Paper* 15. London: Overseas Development Institute, 19.

Kjekshus, Helge. 1977. *Ecology Control and Economic Development in East African History*. Berkeley: University of California Press.

Krapf, J. Ludwig, Journals (1845–49). CMS (The Church Missionary Society Archives).

Lawren, William. 1968. "Masai and Kikuyu: An Historical Analysis of Culture Transmission." *Journal of African History* 9(4): 571–83.

Manchuelle, Francois. 1998. *Willing Migrants: Soninke Labor Diasporas, 1848–1960*. London: James Currey.

Manning, Patrick. 2013. *Migration in World History*. New York: Routledge.

Marshall, Fiona. 1990. Origins of Specialized Pastoral Production in East Africa. *American Anthropologist* 92: 873–94.

Moore, Sally. 1986. *Social Facts and Fabrications*. Cambridge: Cambridge University Press.

Morgan, William. 1973. *East Africa*. London: Longman.

Ortner, Sherry. 1973. "On Key Symbols." *American Anthropologist* 75(5): 1338–46.

Parkin, David. 1991. The *Sacred Void*. Cambridge: Cambridge University Press.

Petek, Nik, and Paul Lane. 2017. "Ethnogenesis and Surplus Food Production: Communitas and Identity Building among Nineteenth- and Early Twentieth-Century Ilchamus, Lake Baringo, Kenya." *World Archaeology* 49(1): 40–60.

Reichard, Paul. 1892. *Deutsch-Ostafrika. Das Land, und seine Bewohner, seine Politische und Wirtschafliche Entwicklung*. Leipzig: Otto Spamer.

Robinson, Paul. 1985. *Gabbra Nomadic Pastoralism in Nineteenth and Twentieth Century Northern Kenya: Strategies for survival in a Marginal Environment*, vol. 1. PhD Dissertation, Northwestern University.

Rockel, Stephen. 2019. "The Tutsi and the Nyamwezi: Cattle, Mobility, and the Transformation of Agro-Pastoralism in Nineteenth-Century Western Tanzania." *History in Africa* 46: 231–61.

Schneider, Harold. 1979. *Livestock and Equality in East Africa*. Bloomington: Indiana University Press.

Schoenbrun, David. 1998. *A Green Place, A Good Place: Agrarian Change and Social Identity in the Great Lakes Region to the 15th Century*. Portsmouth, NH: Heinemann.

Sobania, Neil. 1991. "Feasts, Famines and Friends: Nineteenth Century Exchange and Ethnicity in the Eastern Lake Turkana Region." In *Herders, Warriors, and Traders. Pastoralism in Africa*, edited by John G. Galaty and Pierre Bonte, 118–42. Boulder, CO: Westview.

Sommer, Gabriele, and Rainer Vossen. 1993. "Dialects, Sectiolects, or Simply Lects? The Maa Language in Time Perspective." In *Being Maasai*, edited by Thomas Spear and Richard Waller, 25–37. London: James Currey.

Spear, Thomas. 1997. *Mountain Farmers*. London: James Currey.

Speke, John. 1864. *What Led to the Discovery of the Source of the Nile?* Edinburg: William Blackwood and Sons.

Spencer, Paul. 1998. *The Pastoral Continuum*. London: Oxford University Press.

Spinage, Clive. 2012. *African Ecology: Benchmarks and Historical Perspectives*. New York: Springer.

Stanley, Henry. 1878. *Through the Dark Continent*, vol. I. New York: Harper and Brothers.

Steinhart, Edward I. 1981. "From 'Empire' to State: The Emergence of the Kingdom of Bunyoro-Kitara: c. 1350–1890." In *The Study of the State*, edited by Henri Claessen and Peter Skalnik, 363–70. Berlin: De Gruyter, Inc.

Sutton, John. 1990. *A Thousand Years of East Africa*. Nairobi: British Institute in Eastern Africa.

Taylor, D., Robertshaw, P., and Marchant, R.A. (2000). Environmental Change and Political-Economic Upheaval in Precolonial Western Uganda. *The Holocene* 10(4): 527–36.

Thomson, Joseph. 1885. *Through Masai Land*. London: Sampson Low, Marston, Searle & Rivington.

Uzoigwe, G. N. 1970. "Inter-Ethnic Co-Operation in Northern Uganda in the 19th Century." *Tarikh* 3(2): 69–77.

Van Zwanenberg, Roger. 1976. "Dorobo Hunting and Gathering: A Way of Life or a Mode of Production?" *African Economic History* 2: 12–24.

Verschuren, Dirk, Kathleen R. Laird, and Brian F. Cumming. 2000. "Rainfall and Drought in Equatorial East Africa during the Past 1,100 years." *Nature* 403: 410–13.

Volkens, Georg. 1897. *Der Kilimandscharo*. Berlin: Dietrich Reimer.

Waller, Richard. 1985a. "Economic Relations in the Central Rift Valley: The Maa-speakers and Their Neighbors in the Nineteenth Century." In *Kenya in the Nineteenth Century*, edited by Bethwell Ogot, 83–151. Nairobi: Bookwise.

Waller, Richard. 1985b. "Ecology, Migration, and Expansion in East Africa." *African Affairs* 84(336): 347–70.

Waller, Richard. 1999. "Pastoral Poverty in Historical Perspective." In *The Poor Are Not Us*, edited by David Anderson and Vigdi Broch-Due, 20–49. Oxford: James Curry.

Waller, Richard. 2012. "Pastoral Production in Colonial Kenya: Lessons from the Past." *African Studies Review* 55(2): 1–27.

Widgren, Mats, and John Sutton, eds. 2004. *Islands of Intensive Agriculture: In Eastern Africa*. London: James Currey.

Wissman, H. von. 1891. *My Second Journey through Equatorial Africa*. London: Chatto & Windus.

6

MIGRATION AND STATE FORMATION IN PRE-COLONIAL SOUTH AFRICA

Why the 19th Century Was Different

Lyndal Keeton and Stefan Schirmer

> To move was a socially constructed reflex; a natural, accepted way of seeking to exploit the environment. A tradition of migration was ingrained in everyday patterns of life ...
>
> Patrick Harries, 1994, 17

1 Introduction

Drawing inspiration from the seminal work of Patrick Harries,[1] this chapter seeks to make sense of migration patterns in pre-colonial South Africa. It focuses primarily on the northeastern parts of the country where migration, shifting links with global markets, and processes of state formation were deeply rooted. The question we want to shed light on is, why did processes of migration and state formation change so drastically in the 1750s?[2] Migration and state formation were interrelated: migration influenced socio-political interactions and patterns of state formation, and as processes of state formation changed, so too did the nature of migration. Our focus is on shifting patterns of migration, but we also unpack and analyze interrelated changes in state formation, social norms, and economic interactions.

Prior to 1750, migration can mostly be characterized as voluntary, economic migration, which was a primary strategy to deal with the general precariousness and unpredictability of farming communities' lives. In Manning's (2020) terms, *cross-community migrants*, both sojourners and settlers, as individuals and in groups, were pervasive throughout the pre-1750 period. Migration influenced the emergence of a powerful cultural emphasis on cooperation and mutual support, weak and unstable political systems, and a tendency toward peaceful interactions between regions and communities rather than violent conflict and coercion. However, around 1750 (and until approximately 1830 when colonial interference intensified), the nature of migration changed. Invaders in the form of groups of people who could both seize and dominate a local population became very prominent. Hence, migration after 1750 can be characterized as forced displacement, both of individuals and of whole communities, by violent, centralizing polities.[3]

DOI: 10.4324/9781003225027-9

Migration and State Formation **113**

This chapter begins by outlining the evidence for widespread migration, the existence of cooperative cultures, and relatively peaceful polities, like the Mapungubwe and the Pedi, in the period before 1750. We call this the era of the "Mapungubwe Equilibrium," with reference to the relatively peaceful emergence, flourishing, and then dissipation of the Mapungubwe state (Chirikure, Ntsoane, and Esterhuysen 2016). We point to other state systems or polities that emerged before 1750 that can be characterized in the same way.

We then outline major forces of change, such as changing values of arable land, trade routes, slaves, and improved military technology, which disrupted this equilibrium from around 1750 onward. As migration and state formation were transformed fundamentally, we label this the "Mfecane Equilibrium." Mfecane means "crushing" in Zulu and is the term that historians have used to describe the violence, forced migrations, and recurrent political centralization associated with the rise of Mthetwa, Ndwandwe, Swati, Ndebele, and, especially, Zulu polities. During the Mfecane, the extent and intensity of invasion and forced migrations escalated in an unprecedented way (e.g., Makhura, 2006; Wright 2009). Never before had migrations been forced to this extent by either belligerent bands representing centralized polities or entire militant migrating polities like the Ndebele, subjugating people into involuntary subservience (Lye 1969). Women, children, and even adult men were uprooted from their homes and forcibly taken elsewhere. Others fled and became refugees, desperately seeking safe havens elsewhere. Evidence of this period is documented from the experience of the Pedi (Delius 2010). Consequently, during the Mfecane Equilibrium, migration evolved into strategic migration of newly centralized, militarized polities and forced migration of refugees fleeing these polities.

To model the earlier Mapangupwe Equilibrium and the later Mfecane Equilibrium, we employ one of the earliest evolutionary game theory models, the Hawk-Dove model (Maynard Smith and Price 1973; Maynard Smith 1982). This model allows us to consider how interactions between different types of polities and the net payoffs from those interactions can influence the types of polities that emerge or persist over time. Setting these choices out in this way does not imply that every person made these individualistic choices in every instance. Instead, what we are pointing to are broad tendencies, which we believe helped to cement in place certain norms and a cultural order that constrained the everyday choices people made.

In the Hawk-Dove model (detailed in the Appendix), polities can be characterized as either violent and aggressive hawks or peaceful and cooperative doves. Interaction of two dove polities results in cooperative sharing of resources. In contrast, when two hawks interact, violence ensues, and the winning hawk expropriates resources. Violent interactions are costly, however, and reduce the net payoff. When a dove and a hawk interact (or vice versa), the hawk wins and subjugates the dove taking all the resources. Whether a polity chooses to be a hawk or a dove depends on the value of available resources (e.g., land, trade routes, slaves) relative to the cost of a violent interaction.

There is little evidence of violent interactions prior to 1750 (Wilson, 1969b). We can think of Mapungubwe and the Pedi during this time as characteristic doves. Other communities did not necessarily form polities but still are generally considered cooperative. Communities built cooperation through repeated interactions. This outcome is consistent with a context of abundant land with a few areas of relatively good quality soil and sufficient rainfall, such as the area around Mapungubwe from the 11th to the 13th century (Dubois and Giraldeau 2003; Hauert et al. 2006). Resources held value but violence could only be a short-term strategy. Over the long term, violence would likely prove too costly in the face of the pervasiveness of migration and cooperation institutionalized through repeated inter-actions. The main form of migration, by individuals, small groups, and even whole communities, was both voluntary and of an economic nature, primarily in pursuit of resources.

From 1750, the relative value of resources and the returns from violence changed. Largely due to greater competition, land and trade routes became more valuable. Simultaneously, violence became less costly due to conscription and improved military technology. Hence, aggressive, violent hawk states began to emerge, along with two new forms of migration: entire hawk states started migrating while migration of individuals and smaller groups of people shifted from voluntary to forced.[4]

2 Migration in South Africa: the long view

Migration has always been a pervasive feature of South Africa. The first people were hunter-gatherers who pursued resources and game by moving around. They avoided over-using natural resources by decamping when shortages loomed, and they would sometimes pursue large animals for days before delivering the killer blow. Later, when some acquired cattle, they continued to move around in pursuit of the best pastures (e.g., Parkington 1972; Parkington and Hall 2009).

In the early years of the first millennium, people possessing iron tools and knowledge about how to grow crops like millet and sorghum migrated to South Africa from the north. They gradually moved along the coast and settled in parts of what is today KwaZulu-Natal (Evers 1975; Hall 1987, 30–8; Hall 2009). Once settled in permanent villages, they cultivated fields. While they migrated less than the hunter-gatherers who preceded them, migration was still required as the crops they grew could not provide all the nutrients needed, and the environment they inhabited did not permit dense settlement. The environment was relatively precarious, with regular droughts and diseases like malaria and African trypanosomiasis (sleeping sickness) preventing anyone from becoming too complacent about the security of sedentary life. Those who lived in villages had to supplement their diets by hunting and, where possible, fishing. They also traded whenever possible with those who could provide resources that were not available inside the village (Beinart 2000, 269–302).[5] At the same time, people moved between different forms of production depending on circumstance, including abandoning agriculture when that was the only viable option (Hall 2009, 122).[6]

During the 5th century, sedentary farming practices began to spread into low-lying inland valleys where soil was fertile, rainfall regular, and rivers plentiful. These agricultural communities kept some stock, mostly sheep and goats, but gradually acquired cattle. Hunting and gathering remained crucial, as did regular interactions with more mobile pastoralists and hunter-gatherer communities (Evers 1975; Hall 1987, 39–42; Huffman 1990).

During this era when farmers had few cattle and depended heavily on hunting and gathering for additional sources of nutrition, people remained generally stateless and culturally homogeneous over a large area or frontier (Hall 2009, 121–2). To ensure survival, this frontier produced cultural norms about reciprocal obligation. When drought or disease struck in one area, to survive, affected communities depended on the assistance and hospitality of others from unaffected areas. Rather than depend on arbitrary goodwill, farmers developed a culture of mutual aid that incorporated all the communities living along the east coast and throughout the escarpment during the first millennium. Those against whom nature had turned could count on the help of others.[7]

Through trade with pastoralists and stock accumulation, early farming communities were gradually able to acquire large cattle herds, which enabled them to break away from the coastal areas and fertile valleys. Cattle, therefore, made migration into the interior possible, resulting in settlement across the large inland plateau that is known as the "highveld" (see Map 6.1) in the second millennium. Its largely treeless environment, coupled with unpredictable weather, was unsuitable for people who depended primarily on sorghum and millet crops. But, as these eastern communities adopted mixed farming, they could exploit the valuable grazing land of the highveld.[8] Settlements took the form of villages comprising a few hundred families. Those villages built largely from stone became larger and more densely settled (Hall 1987, 46–55). Cattle production lowered the need for widespread cooperation across ecologically diverse regions, simultaneously enabling people to spread more widely and to populate the eastern half of South Africa more intensively. Consequently, social systems emerged in which reciprocal interactions *within* geographically defined communities became more evident than the interactions *between* communities. This is reflected in the divergence of pottery styles, which previously had been homogenous across vast distances (Hall 1987, 72).

However, despite the changes reflected in archaeological evidence, the local culture of cooperation and mutual aid across large regions continued to form an important foundation of Southern African societies' survival strategies (Hall 2009, 142). Anthropologists have long pointed to powerful cooperative norms within the cultural traditions of these pre-colonial societies, and there is now widespread acceptance that such societies were not stable entities organized around hereditary leaders and ancient lineages. Instead, as we will see, identities, leadership, and the size and makeup of various kinds of communities were all extremely fluid.[9]

Ongoing migrations, especially of groups of people from East Africa moving south, can be detected in the archaeological records from the 13th century to the 16th century.[10] Practices of recurrent cross-community migration were incorporated into cultural norms (e.g., Harries 1994, 5–7; Hall 2009, 131–2). According to John Wright (2009, 219), "[i]dentities in all these societies were not fixed features with a timeless history; they cohered under particular circumstances and they might be remade under different circumstances." People identified according to the community they were attached to or to the chief they paid tribute to, both of which could change from time to time as environmental or economic circumstances changed. As Harries (1994, 6) has put it:

> The continual movement of people and ideas caused the material culture of the chiefdom to change continually through adaptation, borrowing, and innovation. Political identity was rooted in the chiefdom, but it needs to be stressed that this identity was not based on a shared kinship or membership of a lineage or clan. The chiefdom was an open institution attracting and incorporating outsiders prepared to kondza [pay tribute] to the chief.

Social and economic interactions between groups of people with different economic specializations were also ancient and extensive. Crops were traded for cattle, and cattle and the products of the hunt were traded for iron, salt, and other technological goods (Parkington and Hall 2009, 89). Trade routes crisscrossed the Southern African interior, from very early in its history (see Map 6.1). Goods were transported from Indian Ocean ports such as Chibuene and Delagoa Bay, along trade routes that followed the rivers inland. Areas of South Africa rich in salt, such as Eiland on a tributary of the Letaba River, specialized in

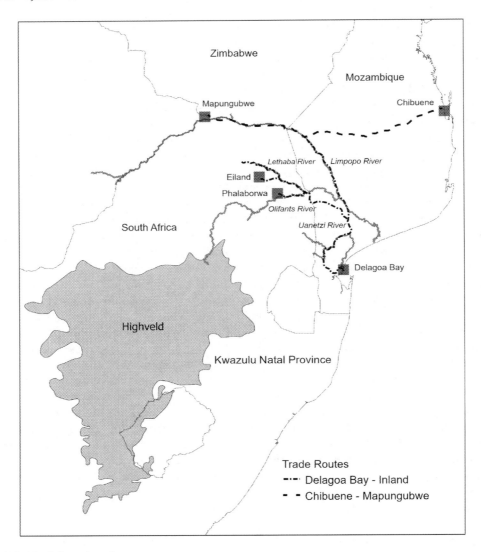

MAP 6.1 Selected trade routes.
Source: Authors' own, digitized by Stefan de Jong.

trading this essential good across a wide radius. In Phalaborwa, copper and iron were mined and then forged into wire, beads, bracelets, arrows, spears, woodworking tools, and agricultural hoes (Harries 1994, 15).

On the east coast of Africa, communities acted as middlemen between, on the one hand, hunters, farmers, and manufacturers in the interior, and, on the other, Arabs who plied their wares in settlements like Chibuene, as shown in Map 6.1. Visits from Arab traders to this region were not regular, but they were frequent enough to boost the prosperity of local communities well placed to take advantage of trading opportunities. These communities were, in turn, an important source of demand for the agricultural producers and manufacturers of the interior. Arab traders brought in glass beads, exotic cotton cloth, and golden artifacts, thereby channeling rare and valuable goods into South Africa, initially mainly to regions bordering the Limpopo River (Hall 1987, 78).

A well-established commercial network (see Map 6.1) linked the coastal plain with the South African interior. Long caravans of hunter-traders and porters made their way along the rivers linking the escarpment to the coast. The mineral springs on the Nkomatie River bend served as a meeting ground for traders making their way from the east coast to the Uanetzi and Olifants rivers. From the Olifants, three routes led into the northern interior through the rich copper- and iron-producing Phalaborwa area as well as across the Letaba River to the salt mines at Eiland and to various hunting grounds (Harries, 1994, 15).

Trading activities and trade routes shifted over time, waxing and waning in intensity. At no time were the routes controlled by a state system that could have provided the order and protection that traders typically require before they invest in the risky and costly exercise of transporting and trading goods over vast distances.[11] This suggests the pre-existence of a relatively peaceful environment, in which communities tended to cooperate rather than succumb to the temptation of appropriating the goods being transported by force. When trading activities intensified, channeling valuable goods, they permitted some urbanization and intensification of centralized structures of power and control, like Mapungubwe.

3 Migration and socio-political systems prior to 1750

Prior to 1750, cross-community migration was a continuous phenomenon in which the structures and identities associated with these migrations came and went in response both to changing circumstances and to complex interactions between incoming groups and more settled populations. Throughout this time, it must also be remembered, the majority of South Africans lived in what can broadly be described as stateless communities.

Patrick Harries was responsible for developing a highly persuasive picture of pre-colonial African cultures and societies in which cooperative interactions were encouraged across geographical regions. One of the sources on which he drew to make this case was a collection of traditional African folk tales, collected in the 19th century in the area around Delagoa Bay. As Harries shows, for the people in the folk tales,

> famine remains an ever-present menace to which people respond by moving – to a nearby hillside or to the commonage, where they pick wild fruit and vegetables. Others move much further and kondza [pay tribute] to a distant chief whose patronage allows them to grow wealthy and famous; having succeeded in life they sometimes return to their village of origin.
>
> *(Harries 1994, 16–7)*

The tales depict traveling as dangerous, eventful, and character-building, but they usually end up in a better life and self-fulfillment. There are also frequent admonishments against staying put, close to one's family and village of origin. Harries concludes:

> the picture created by folk tales reinforces the vision produced by everyday behavior. To move was a socially constructed reflex; a natural, accepted way of seeking to exploit the environment. A tradition of migration was ingrained in everyday patterns of life.
>
> *(Harries 1994, 15)*

The idea that African systems were open to incoming migrants, who could take up a variety of fluid positions in relation to existing leaders, but could also, over time, secure control over land and other resources, can be found in a large number of ethnographies on groups such as the Tswana, the Lobedu, the Pedi, and the Nguni in the eastern parts of South Africa.[12]

Within these systems economic accumulation, migration, and political power were intimately intertwined. Outstanding economic skills or access to trade goods or the best grazing land allowed people to become powerful by attracting dependents who could be from the immediate vicinity, but given the prevalence of mobility, also from distant regions. In this way, more centralized political structures could be established, which allowed the powerful to maintain their economic superiority by demanding tribute from the people they controlled. However, the ability of people outside the formal positions of power to accumulate cattle,[13] or to migrate to alternative centers of prosperity and power, and the natural ecological fluctuations between regions, all ensured that there were frequent changes in who controlled large numbers of followers, and where they were located. Migration continued to be extensive and vital for survival. The socio-political systems built up in this context were highly unstable. As Hall (1987, 63–4) puts it:

> One of the characteristics of the chiefdom is a tension between the forces of centralization, which allow individuals to build up political and economic power, and competition for authority by rivals. Thus through time, chiefdoms are constantly fragmenting and reforming as factions gain power, build up strength and subsequently lose control to other groups.[14]

Anthropological research has emphasized the importance of reciprocity and redistribution in the pre-colonial societies of South Africa. The wealthy were expected to make their resources available to the less fortunate. Emphasis was on security rather than on advancement at the expense of others. Individual families pursued wealth and power, but they were expected to ensure that their own success benefited everyone in the society. Cattle loans and other forms of support were not just a way to build up political influence; they were a moral duty. There were strong mechanisms, such as witchcraft accusations, that could be used to punish those who did not fulfill their duty. These kinds of cultural obligations were usually not proscribed in terms of a narrowly defined ethnic identity; they applied equally to strangers and familiars (Wilson 1969a, 114).

4 The Mapungubwe Equilibrium

At the beginning of the second millennium some areas linked to global trade routes saw the emergence of urban centers of which the town of Mapungubwe (Map 6.1) was the most important. This town was a center of trade and of manufacturing and became the residence of powerful regional rulers. The commodities manufactured at Mapungubwe included ivory armbands, finely crafted bone tools, and cotton textiles, which were produced by groups of specialist craftsmen. Sufficient quantities of the commodities were produced to achieve surpluses that could be traded. The most important form of trade was between the Limpopo region and the coastal region to the east (Hall 1987, 80).

The state system whose center of power was located in the town of Mapungubwe was able to exert significant extent of control over the beads, cloths, and artifacts brought into the region by trade. These commodities became symbols of status. As wealth increased, the rulers developed a system in which they lived in symbolically constructed stone enclosures on top of Mapungubwe Hill, made accessible only by an elaborate staircase and divided up to represent the different levels of status within the royal family and its entourage. The town formed the hub of a system of centralized control, with other groups and polities in the surrounding regions pledging allegiance to the center (Hall 2009, 120).

Lesser chiefs saw this central form of power based on the control of rare commodities as a way to stabilize their power. They paid tribute to the new rulers at Mapungubwe. In return "their high status would be signified by ownership and display of the rare and valuable trade goods from the Indian Ocean" (Hall 2009, 118). However, research confirms that the influence of the center was, in fact, extremely weak, and that groups within the Mapungubwe system retained control over their daily lives (Antonites 2012). There is also evidence that conflicts emerged over the control of trading goods between the Mapungubwe center and alternative centers of power as they emerged (Huffman 2015, 15–27).

Overall, though, evidence points to the relative absence of conflict and coercion. Archaeological digs have uncovered a general absence of arms and armed retinues that could have been employed to create more coercive forms of centralized power (Hall 1987, 89). The power of the Mapungubwe state was almost certainly based to a large extent on spiritual and ritual forms of power. The Mapungubwe king and parts of his retinue were regarded as having highly regarded rain-making powers, with the prosperity of the region depending heavily on paying tribute to these leaders to ensure adequate rainfall (Hall 2009, 80).

From the beginning of the 10th century until the end of the 13th century, both temperatures and rainfall rose in the region. Annual rainfall in this period is estimated to have been approximately 500 mm, which is sufficient to grow crops like sorghum (Huffman 1996, 57). It is likely, therefore, that this period of higher and more reliable than usual rainfall coincided with the intensification of trade in these parts of South Africa. Trade then permitted greater centralization and political stability, which, in turn, stimulated economic improvements and enabled greater population densities. In a context where migration toward centers of prosperity was encouraged and there were cultural imperatives to be welcoming toward migrants, the population numbers in and around Mapungubwe increased at an accelerated pace for a relatively long period (Chirikure, Ntsoane, and Esterhuysen 2016). A virtuous cycle ensued. Population increase in what had been an under populated area then drove prosperity forward and enhanced opportunities for further centralization. This, in turn, encouraged further migrations to the area, more economic activity, and greater volumes of tribute, allowing even more centralization and power.

In the early 13th century, the focus of trade moved further north, toward a new center of power in present-day Zimbabwe. This likely coincided with economic difficulties resulting from failing rains and lower temperatures (although the evidence for this is not clear), as well as increased population pressure in Mapungubwe. It is easy to see what the consequences could have been. Prosperity decreased, people left, and the rain-making powers of the king and his retinue were questioned. It became difficult for people to appreciate the virtues of centralization compared to looser political arrangements. The virtuous economic and political cycles in this region came to an end. At some point in the 13th century, the Mapungubwe system collapsed (Hall 2009, 84). Overall, and in contrast to many other examples of state formation, both elsewhere in the world and later in South Africa, the rise and fall of Mapungubwe appears to have been remarkably peaceful (Chirikure, Ntsoane, and Esterhuysen 2016). As much as resources had initially attracted voluntary migrants to Mapangubwe, the ability to freely migrate also contributed to its collapse.

During the 17th century, similarly peaceful processes of centralization and prosperity emerged in more easterly regions as they integrated into trade networks. According to oral traditions, processes of centralization that were initiated by a number of migrations were marked by peaceful cooperation, in marked contrast to the rising levels of violence that began to emerge 100 years later (Delius 1983).

In his seminal study of the Pedi, Delius (1983) stresses the importance of migration, cooperation, and shifting economic advantages in making sense of patterns of state formation. The Pedi (or Maroteng) were originally a sub-group of Kgatla people, who moved north from an area around present-day Tshwane to an area just south of the Olifants River (see Map 6.1). As the Pedi were adept at iron smelting and manufacturing, they had an economic advantage which allowed them to exercise political influence soon after their arrival. By the mid-17th century, the Pedi started establishing themselves as a kind of state.[15] Trade that connected to coastal ports brought in Indian, Chinese, and Arabian goods that fed into these processes, raising the stakes and enabling more centralization than would otherwise have been possible.

Local traditions describe the period before the late 18th century as an era of tranquility, "a time when the chiefdom grew rich in cattle, not taken from other tribes but peacefully bred in the splendid grazing of the Steelpoort Valley" (Delius 1983, 15). Delius estimates that it took at least four generations before the Pedi established a dominant position in the area, arguing that the cultural homogeneity of the 19th century, i.e., the people identifying as Pedi and speaking a similar language later classified as Northern Sotho, was due to a long history of local interactions rather than a defined period of dominance. Thus, rather than the Pedi being a product of a powerful group forcefully establishing a chieftainship or state, the evolution of regional identities and loyalties took place in an organic, decentralized fashion as groups of people moved into the area, cooperated, and pledged allegiance to those who had both political and economic power.[16]

From the evidence of Mapungubwe and the Pedi, among others, in the long era before the 1750s there was a broad tendency of the people of pre-colonial South Africa to employ a peaceful strategy, influenced by both conscious and unconscious calculations about the personal payoffs that these strategies generated in their specific context. This influences our interpretation of the evidence throughout the descriptions above, and we now set out more explicitly how the choices we have described above could be modeled.

In the Hawk-Dove model (see Appendix), in which people choose between violent, aggressive hawk strategies and peaceful, cooperative dove strategies, we can see that in contexts such as those that were prevalent around the formation of Mapungubwe (when resources such as land which were freely available and therefore not considered particularly valuable and the costs of violence were particularly high) there was a prevalence of cooperative dove-type polities over violent hawk-type polities. While practices of raiding and enslaving neighboring people occurred, the extent to which this took place was muted by imperatives for cooperation and peaceful interactions, as well as difficulties associated with controlling people in a context of weak, dove-type states and abundant land. The prevailing strategy before the 19th century, therefore, was one of cooperation as the payoff of violence was relatively low and only undertaken in exceptional circumstances. Moreover, as the land values were generally low, repeated peaceful interactions were the norm, and, crucially, people would remember previous interactions through oral tradition. These repeated interactions would reinforce a cooperative dove strategy.[17]

This kind of context where cooperation is the norm rather than the exception, furthermore, creates a low incentive to form polities, helping to explain why unique forms of centralization like the Mapungubwe system formed as peacefully as it did, and why, apart from some internal tensions, other competing polities did not emerge and seek to prey on the resources being generated within the Mapungubwe system. Stable dove strategies are more likely in contexts where one state system faces very limited competition from other systems, low rewards for violence, and repeated interactions.

5 Violence, state formation, and migration in the northeast from 1750 to 1830

In 2010, Delius published a paper in which he set out details of interviews that German missionaries conducted in the 1870s with ordinary Pedis. These relate horrific levels of violence, chaos, and forced movements, which, even if they contain exaggerations and biases inserted by the Europeans who transcribed them, depict patterns that contrast sharply with the cooperative norms and patterns of interaction detailed above. Take, for example, an informant named Mochayane, who explained that when he was 12 years old, around 1820, the "Zulah swamped the land," his father was killed, and he was forced to flee with his mother, brother, and sister to the north. On the way he was separated from his mother and sister and never saw them again. Later he returned home with his brother, but they lived in constant fear of "enemies in the area." As a result, they had to live in small groups scattered across the hills surrounding their original homeland. One day, living in these circumstances, the group he was with suddenly found themselves surrounded by a gang of armed men, who rushed upon them with terrible screams. He was caught along with his brother and another male. After killing his brother and, he claimed, eating him, this gang led him away with several other captives to "the land of the Makhema." He was then forced into servitude by one of the leaders of the gang. His narrative goes on to describe the great cruelty with which other captives were treated; many were brutally murdered for the smallest mistakes. He also claimed that cannibalism was common within this group, and that he was frequently forced to eat human flesh (Delius 2010, 10).

After describing similar stories, Delius (2010, 11) concludes,

> [t]he world that these narratives describe is one terrifyingly turned on its head. In a context of famine and anarchy, cultivation becomes impossible, people are treated like cattle, marriage takes place without bridewealth or wider family bonds, cruel punishments are inflicted without due process, people eat people, and children literally feast on adults.

The breakdown of order in the first two decades of the 19th century was extreme, but violence had been rising for a while and the nature of order had been shifting since, approximately, the mid-18th century.

The shifts in the character of the social and political order are also evident in the lands of the Tswana, broadly to the west of the Pedi area of influence. Parsons (1995) and Morton (2012) have identified the emergence of new Tswana military institutions and the rise of the raiding state occurring during the period from the 1780s to the 1820s. Wright (2009, 213) echoes their arguments, explaining that the consensus amongst historians is that, while conflicts between chiefdoms were probably present in the region during earlier periods, "in the later eighteenth century they seem to have acquired a new dynamic." State formation and rising conflict emerged, corresponding to rising trade with global trading centers like Delagoa Bay to the east, along with demands and disruptions emanating from the impact of European colonialism to the south, in the Cape Colony. An additional source of violence in the region came from raiding groups of San, Khoekhoen, Griquas, runaway slaves, bandits, and migrants with various origins from the Cape and Orange Free State regions. By the 1780s, Wright claims, these groups were "making depredations on Tswana communities to the north" (see Map 6.2) (Wilson 1969b, 165; Wright 2009, 215).

Consequently, as trade intensified, "goods passed back and forth between numerous trading networks dominated by political leaders who sought to use new forms of wealth brought by trade with the outside world to increase their status and power" (Wright 2009, 216). This led to frequent conflicts between Tswana chiefs, as well as the emergence of large, urban-like settlements, reflecting both the growth of centralized forms of political control and the need to cluster together to protect against escalating raids (e.g., Delius 1983; Mason 1995; Hall 2009). Parsons (1995, 52) has observed that by 1820 "warfare was so widespread amongst the western Tswana that hardly a chiefdom had not seen its chief killed in battle."

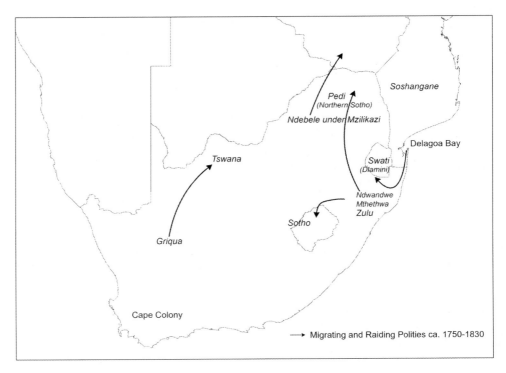

MAP 6.2 Mfecane Equilibrium polities and migration.
Source: Authors' own, digitized by Stefan de Jong.

In the east, from the 1760s, especially in the areas close to Delagoa Bay, similar patterns emerged. Escalating levels of trade seem to have played a role in encouraging competing forms of state formation and rising levels of violence.[18] Consequently, the Tembe and Mabhudu chiefdoms were drawn into increasing competition with each other as they sought to control the routes to ivory- and cattle-producing regions to the south and the west. Similarly, in the regions that are now part of northern KwaZulu-Natal, two competing centers of power emerged: the Ndwandwe and Mthethwa kingdoms (see Map 6.2). As was the case amongst the new Tswana polities, these new formations used the institution of "age sets of young men" in a newly militarized context.[19] Increasingly, age sets were employed as fighting, raiding, and policing units under the centralized control of a chief. Consequently, as Wright puts it, "generally speaking, in the business of raiding and fighting, those chiefs who had *amabutho* age regiments at their disposal had a major advantage over those who did not" (Wright 2009, 223).

There is an unresolved debate that stretches back to the early 1980s about whether these processes of state formation and escalating violence in KwaZulu-Natal were a product of defensive reactions to change and violence emanating from elsewhere or part of an aggressive process of state building emanating from within the polities themselves. Surely, the answer is that both happened simultaneously: as competition for resources rose, so power became more concentrated and some leaders sought to take advantage of these opportunities. Some were better placed and more able to do so than others. These leaders were able to use their advantages in raiding to capture people and forcibly turn them into subservient followers. At the same time, in this context of rising violence and competition for power, individuals could no longer rely on cooperative norms to secure order and their safety. They were increasingly compelled to turn to powerful leaders with military capacity to defend against the rising violence. Dove-type polities and decentralized areas without much military capacity disappeared as they had no defense against constant raiding. This process, for example, led to the disappearance of the loosely organized Bokoni, who before the 1820s had cultivated terraced fields for centuries along the escarpment stretching from present-day Nelspruit to Carolina.

6 Violence, state formation, and new patterns of migration

As we saw in the Pedi stories collected in the 1870s, this was a period of dramatic and almost constant movement. Migration was no longer voluntary. People were now forced to move away from areas of instability, either temporarily or permanently, but the latter case often required settlement in different parts of their original homelands, especially areas that were more rugged and easier to defend. The main purpose of forced migration was to avoid capture and subjugation by raiding bands from violent hawk polities. What was new in the period around the turn of the 19th century was the extent to which migration was accompanied or caused by coercion, and the extent to which communities became more centralized, stratified, and internally coercive. Map 6.2 shows the approximate locations and migrations of these polities during this period.

An important part of this story is the extent to which enslavement became a much larger feature of the landscape than it had been in previous periods. Only when hawk states started to emerge could slavery intensify, as stronger states had the capability to subjugate people.[20] In addition, as happened intensively and for long periods of time especially in West and

Central Africa, slaves were traded through east African ports from early times. It is likely that the southeastern parts of Africa were minimally impacted by the global slave trade prior to the 18th century (Thompson 1995). However, during the 18th and early 19th centuries, the Indian Ocean slave trade, specifically from Mozambique, intensified (Hooper and Eltis 2013). A major source of demand for the slaves exported from Delagoa Bay were the sugar plantations on the French-controlled island of Mauritius. There is evidence of slaves being sold in the pre-1820s period, but the numbers have not yet been quantified (Chewins and Delius 2020, 19–20). It appears that a significant escalation of slaving occurred through Delagoa Bay precisely during the time that rising violence and newfound raiding capabilities were emerging in what are today parts of KwaZulu-Natal, Mpumalanga, Limpopo, and North West Provinces (Chewins and Delius 2020).[21]

The evidence for the 1820s is clearer, and it reveals that groups from northern KwaZulu-Natal were migrating to the bay and selling a variety of trade goods, including slaves. Raiding armies under the control of hawk states like the Soshangane, Zwadeng-aba, and Shaka moved north toward the bay, creating destruction and destitution in their wake, in the early 1820s and possibly earlier. Once they got there, they continued their raiding activities, "spreading terror and panic in the hinterland," forcing people to flee or be captured.[22] The Portuguese authorities were "on good terms with the raiders" and did nothing to stop their destructive activities in these parts of Mozambique. They clearly had a strong interest in encouraging the Zulu army's scorched earth policy as the subsequent famine produced forced migration of "large numbers of destitute people who could be enslaved relatively easily and cheaply." In the decade from 1825 to 1835, Delius and Chewens conservatively estimate that around 50,000 slaves were exported from Delagoa Bay (Chewins and Delius 2020, 21).

Slavery, it would appear, was both a cause and a consequence of the rising violence and the emergence of militaristic, raiding states in the KwaZulu-Natal region. What also emerges from this evidence is that other states emerging, migrating out of KwaZulu-Natal, and beating a destructive path north – into Mozambique, in the case of Soshangane, and into Zimbabwe, in the case of Mzilikazi's Ndebele – need to be understood as more than just reacting to competition from an all-powerful Zulu state. Instead, they were part of a broader process of migration in which tightly organized raiding states rampaged widely in pursuit of bounty, followers, and slaves. Major forced migrations of individuals and dove-type polities were sparked in response to the movements of these states in various directions. Soshangane's hawk-like migration north, and eventual settlement in southern Mozambique, for example, engendered a significant migration of more peaceful dove-like Shangaan communities into what is now Mpumalanga, where they "tended to attach themselves to Pulana, Pai, Kutswe, Ngomane and Mahlalela groupings" (Makhura 2006, 119). Later, tensions arose between these incoming migrants fleeing from Mozambique and the earlier inhabitants of the Mpumalanga region.[23]

The Dlamini formed another migrating hawk polity, under the leadership of Sobhuza. They had originally moved south from the broad vicinity of Delagoa Bay, but were then forced northward again under pressure from Ndwandwe competition and eventually established the Swati/Swazi polity between what is now northern KwaZulu-Natal and southern Mpumalanga (see Map 6.2). The group originally moved into fortified caves in the area around present-day Mbabane, and then gradually expanded their influence over smaller chiefdoms in the area that is now southern Eswatini. In doing so, they also forced many Sotho living in the area to migrate northward (Wilson 1969b, 164). By the 1830s, Sobhuza had extended his influence as far north as the Sabi River. This emerging Swati polity was organized along similar lines as neighboring states, with militarized age sets at its core, and, despite their origins in southern Mozambique, a distinction between the original Dlamini aristocracy, who were called the "first people," and other subjugated or incorporated groups – who had often been in the area longer than the Dlamini. These followers were called "those who go ahead" (Bonner 1978; Delius and Cope 2006). From these foundations, the Swati evolved into a classic 19th-century polity. While still undertaking extensive raids across the Mpumalanga and Limpopo regions, the Swati continued to provide refuge for those displaced by the rising violence as the earlier cultural norms regarding the acceptance of migrants persisted.[24]

Perhaps the most dramatic example of the new migrating hawk states' propensity to rampage and cause further forced migration amongst the people they came into contact with is Mzilikazi's Ndebele. In about 1820, in the wake of the breakup of the Ndwandwe kingdom, a group originating from several distinct Khumalo chiefdoms in the area around the Mfolozi River decided to migrate in a northwesterly direction. They settled for a time along the northern banks of the Vaal River, and built up their power and resources by seizing grain and cattle from the surrounding regions and by absorbing Sotho, Tswana, and Ndwandwe seeking refuge from the escalating violence in their vicinities. This group, labeled Ndebele or Marauders by local Sotho speakers, started moving in a northwesterly direction near the end of the 1820s in pursuit of greater safety from other hawk-type competitor states as well as fresh cattle and people to raid and absorb into their growing entity (see Map 6.2).

During this time, they may have come into contact with the Pedi in Limpopo province. They then moved to the Marico area in the North West Province and eventually settled in southern Zimbabwe. Everywhere they went, chaos, destruction, and forced migration resulted. Labeled the "migrant kingdom" by Rasmussen (1978), the Ndebele rampaged through significant sections of the territories west of the Drakensberg mountains and south of the Limpopo. The following description by Lye (1969, 89–90) provides a sense of the violence and chaos these raiding migrations engendered,

> "Mzilikazi destroyed his village [on the Vaal] and moved to the lands of the Kwena, where he established his people. Here Mzilikazi built two military kraals … at the confluence with the Crocodile. Once established, the Ndebele raided in every direction. Five regiments crossed the Limpopo after cattle of the Shona people. In 1827 the Ndebele returned [sic] to the Steelpoort, where they avenged themselves against the Pedi. These Pedi were sent to construct a palisade around Mzilikazi's royal residence. No tools were provided and no food was given them. As one group dropped from exhaustion, more Pedi were impressed. They were called Hole by the Ndebele, which became the Ndebele equivalent for slave. Other Ndebele armies subjugated the Phuthing living north of the Vaal and other Sotho communities to the south, east and west. They drove Moletsane's Taung south of the Vaal."

7 The Mfecane Equilibrium

The choice to voluntarily migrate in a context of land abundance across many parts of Africa and for long periods of its history largely explains the relative absence of centralization and well-developed, stable states, especially prior to 1750 (Herbst 2000, 26). The fundamental

126 Lyndal Keeton and Stefan Schirmer

change that emerged in this late pre-colonial period just before significant contact with colonial settlers was the emergence of numerous competing and aggressive raiding polities. The reasons why this happened are complex but can largely be ascribed to three interacting factors. The first was the emergence of, at least the beginnings of, circumscription. Circumscription limited people's choice to migrate from the regions in which they were living, which was crucial for the emergence of centralization and processes of state formation (Carneiro 2012).

The second factor was rising economic prosperity and accompanying population increases which shifted relative costs in favor of land. These trends were underpinned by increases in agricultural output during the 18th century, which were probably the result of a combination of better weather, more intensive farming practices, and perhaps the introduction of maize (Gump 1989; Smale and Jayne 2003).

The most dramatic and third factor came out of Delagoa Bay in the form of rising demand for slaves for export (Delius 2010). The impact of this may not have been as dramatic as in other parts of Africa. But it likely played a role in creating new incentives for leaders and some of their followers to transform themselves into more mobile, tightly organized, militarized entities ready to engage in raiding at a new level of intensity. In this context, the norms of cooperation, despite their widespread application and their long-term persistence, could not stand up to the countervailing imperatives to raid.

The period from the 1750s until the 1830s witnessed the emergence of significant changes to the payoffs associated with interactions between different groups, as well as interactions between individuals and groups. These changes, although not incredibly sudden or very dramatic in themselves, fundamentally changed the character of migration and state formation processes. The underlying cause of the changes was the gradual rise of the value of resources caused by greater competition over resources, combined with reduced shareability of previously relatively abundant land due to rising populations, and the benefits to be gained from control of trade routes. This increased the payoffs from violent interactions and encouraged the emergence of new institutions suited to both increased raiding and defense against rising violence. These institutions, especially the formation of age regiments, then reduced the cost of violence as polities started to specialize in tactical warfare. The insertion of a growing demand for slaves into this context then ensured the rise of a number of raiding states in the vicinity of this demand. Another change occurred when the African societies started to interact with white migrants (often called *Voortrekkers*) from the Cape Colony from the late 1830s onward.[25]

As we can see in Figure 6.1, prior to 1750, the cost of conflict exceeded the value of the resource (arable land, a trade route, a slave) that could be gained during the conflict ($V(t) < C(t)$). Hence, interactions between different polities tended to be peaceful and cooperative. Tied to these interactions was migration which tended to be voluntary. However, after 1750 the relative values of resources and conflict reversed. The cost of conflict fell, most likely due to conscription and improved military technology, and the value of resources rose so that the value of the resources exceeded the cost of the conflict ($V(t) > C(t)$). It then became worthwhile to engage in the lower-cost conflict in order to capture the greater-valued resources. The strategic choice for any polity encountering another polity was to play a hawk strategy. Hawk polities became more prevalent, conquering dove polities and fighting other hawk polities. The evolutionary stable strategy[26] from 1750 until the 1830s was one of violence due to the high net payoff, leading either to the formation

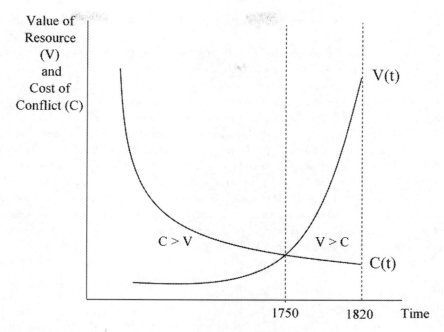

FIGURE 6.1 Changes in resource value and the cost of conflict.

of more hawk polities or to forced migration to avoid them. Hence, there were two shifts: an increase in the number of hawk polities (in response to the changing environmental and political incentives) and a change from voluntary to forced migration (people not attached or subjugated to these hawk polities started to flee from them and their ensuing conflicts).

We can see that numerous factors (both costs and benefits) combined to change the context from one in which peaceful migrations and interactions were possible to one in which these were unlikely. Then, in a self-reinforcing fashion, the subsequent emergence of violence-orientated polities acted as a cause of their persistence and intensification. When, as was the case during the Mapungubwe Equilibrium, there was one center of power during a time of rising prosperity, the benefits of absorbing more people and refraining from attacking and stealing from others were relatively easily to calculate. The nature of these calculations was completely transformed when many competing units emerged with the capacity to overpower others. Such circumstances created a strong incentive to be the first to attack. Violence reinforced even more violence, which then overwhelmed the influence of established norms of cooperation. Conflict between hawk-type polities (some of them highly mobile) became the new normal, as did forced migration of individuals and dove-type polities.

8 Conclusion

A fundamental transformation in the nature of migration occurred in the northeastern regions of South Africa during a period that broadly began in the 1750s and, to an extent, concluded in the 1830s, when African societies in the northern interior had to confront incoming white settlers for the first time. We used the logic of evolutionary game theory, both to lend credence to our explanation for why this change happened and to structure our narrative.

Migration is critical for understanding pre-colonial South Africa. It was fundamental in allowing individuals and communities to cope with their environment, and it played a huge role in determining the nature of African culture, chiefdoms, states, and ethnic identities. The nature of migration was transformed in the early 19th century. That was a time when people moved because they wanted to raid other communities, because they were looking for refuge and safety in a context of rising violence, or because they were forced to move as captives or slaves. That, as Delius has put it, was a world turned on its head. Prior patterns of migration had been mostly voluntary, driven much more by economic needs, and they took place in a relatively cooperative and peaceful environment. The mid-18th and early 19th century fundamentally changed that situation. Whole aggressive polities started migrations in search of resources, while individuals and groups were forced to flee these aggressive migrating polities as well as other stationary aggressive polities who were sending groups of raiders to defeat rivals and collect people for various purposes.

Notes

1 Patrick Harries (1950–2016) was one of the foremost historians in South Africa. His monograph, *Work, Culture and Identity: Migrant Labor in Mozambique and South Africa, c. 1860–1910* (1994), stands out for its close consideration of transnational migration between South Africa and Mozambique.
2 This turning point, marking the start of changes in state formation, trade, and migration in South African history, has been narrated in oral records (e.g., Hall 2009; Wright 2009).
3 These changes were taking place coetaneously to those in the Cape Colony as detailed by Fourie (Chapter 6, this volume).
4 Gareth Austin (Chapter 2, this volume) finds a similar shift in the nature of migration in the context of 19th-century West Africa.
5 Note that this does not ignore the realities that disease vectors shifted regularly, nor that African communities and cattle probably developed some resistance to these diseases. See also Prins (1994) and Hall (1987, 33–4).
6 For similar strategies in East Africa, see Håkansson (Chapter 3, this volume).
7 Archaeological evidence shows similar pottery styles adopted by far-flung communities. "The span of similarly decorated ceramics is quite incompatible with any ethnic or tribal model of shared social system but it is consistent with a wide-ranging network of shared obligations" (Hall 1987, 71). See also Hall (1984), Maggs (1994), and Whitelaw (1994).
8 This is a generalized picture. Some parts of the highveld that were more hospitable than others (e.g., Etherington, 2001).
9 For anthropological studies that emphasize the importance of internal cooperation and a readiness to absorb clients, see Sansom (1974), Wilson (1982a), Wilson (1982b), and Silberbauer and Kuper (1966).
10 For evidence of cultural patterns that link pottery with settlements associated with Sotho-Tswana and Nguni groups, see Hall (2009, 136–42).
11 This may, in part, have been due to the trade routes being within areas of similar ecology (Fenske 2014).
12 For anthropological evidence, see Morelli (2019, 47) and Beinart, Delius, and Hay (2017, 16).
13 For details of the importance of cattle accumulation, see Guy (1987).
14 For a more detailed argument employing the logic of expected utility theory see Keeton (2016).
15 Another group, the Tau, who migrated to the area at a similar time as the Pedi, were able to establish themselves as a regional power for a while. Oral tradition describes the process: "[w]hen we first arrived some local groups bartered skin carosses for cattle. We [the Tau] lived in peace with them, and then just swallowed them up without any fighting" (Delius 1983, 15). Note that skin carosses are joined animal skins used as clothing and/or blankets.

16 Delius and Schirmer (2014) also explore the archeological evidence of extensively terraced, partially irrigated, field systems at Bokoni that existed from about 1500 until the early 19th century on the escarpment on the eastern boundary of the Pedi heartland. The large-scale investments, in the form of many kilometers of stone terraces, could not have taken place without some form of socio-political order. However, the underlying political economy of these terraces suggests that the Koni were able to specialize in the production of field crops without devoting extensive resources to centralized political systems or organized military defenses. Hence, the Koni likely formed another example of a loosely organized dove-type polity.

17 As predicted with an iterated Hawk-Dove model (Dubois and Giraldeau 2003).

18 For how the introduction of maize crops and the expansion of cattle grazing land contributed to these changes, see Gump (1989).

19 These groups were originally brought together temporarily for rites of circumcision and some form of collective service, such as hunting. Delius and Schirmer (2014, 124) speculate that the Koni used similar institutional forms to mobilize the collective labor required to construct the stone terraces.

20 While land abundance and a labor shortage meet two of the Nieboer-Domar conditions for slavery, what is missing in this context is the presence of extensive agriculture. For example, cocoa in Austin's West African context (Chapter 2, this volume).

21 For a broader and earlier exploration of colonial interactions with surrounding African communities around Delagoa Bay see Chewins (2015).

22 Similarly, Austin shows that slavery was the main driver of the change from voluntary to forced migration in West Africa (Chapter 2, this volume).

23 Rather than being the single catalyst for these complex processes, the Zulu state under the leadership of Shaka was a similar kind of hawk entity. He and his followers were able to expand their power in the wake of succession disputes and other sources of weakness within the pioneer Mthethwa and Ndwandwe states, and were then able to exert control over the KwaZulu-Natal region during the 1820s. It is important not to exaggerate the extent of Shaka's control and centralization. While he introduced new institutions that promoted centralization, like age regiments for women, he remained dependent on the goodwill of chiefs in charge of local groups who were incorporated into the Zulu polity during this time of instability (e.g., Wright 2009, 250).

24 For details on these raids and the dislocations they produced, see Makhura (2006, 111–9).

25 The reasons for the migration of the Europeans are explored by Fourie (Chapter 7, this volume).

26 An evolutionary stable strategy is one that is followed by almost all members of the population. Any person or polity trying to employ a strategy that is different to the evolutionary stable strategy will find the payoff to be too low to make it worthwhile. For example, when a hawk strategy is evolutionarily stable, anyone employing a dove strategy will find the net return from a peaceful interaction too low to make it worthwhile to employ again. Once a hawk strategy is evolutionarily stable, a significant shift in resources and/or environment is needed to revert back to the equilibrium of the period prior to 1750 (e.g., Maynard Smith 1982).

27 Dubois and Giraldeau (2003).

28 The dynamic replicator equation has been applied in different contexts, such as learning by doing and population genetics. For an application to policy experimentation, see Garzarelli and Keeton (2018, 949–74).

References

Antonites, Alexander. 2012. *Political and Economic Interactions in the Hinterland of the Mapungubwe Polity, c. AD 1200–1300, South Africa.* PhD diss., Yale University.

Beinart, William. 2000. "African History and Environmental History." *African Affairs* 99(395): 269–302.

Beinart, William, Peter Delius, and Michelle Hay. 2017. *Rights to Land: A Guide to Tenure Upgrading and Restitution in South Africa.* Johannesburg: Jakana.

Bonner, Philip 1978. "Factions and Fissions: Transvaal/Swazi Politics in the Mid-Nineteenth Century." *Journal of African History* 19(2): 219–38.

Carneiro, Robert. 2012. "The Circumscription Theory: A Clarification, Amplification, and Reformulation." *Social Evolution & History* 11(2): 5–30.

Chirikure, Shadreck, Otsile Ntsoane, and Amanda Esterhuysen. 2016. *Mapungubwe Reconsidered: A Living Legacy: Exploring Beyond the Rise and Decline of the Mapungubwe State*. Johannesburg: Real Africa Publishers.

Chewins, Linell. 2015. *Trade at Delagoa Bay: The Influence on Political Structures, 1721–179*. Master's thesis, University of the Witwatersrand.

Chewins, Linell, and Peter Delius. 2020. "The Northeastern Factor in South African History: Re-evaluating the Volume of the Slave Trade Out of Delagoa Bay and Its Impact on Its Hinterland in the Early Nineteenth Century," *Journal Of African History* 6(1): 89–110.

Delius, Peter. 1983. *The Land Belongs to Us: The Pedi Polity, The Boers and the British in the Nineteenth Century Transvaal*. Johannesburg: Ravan Press.

Delius, Peter. 2010. "Recapturing Captives and Conversations with 'Cannibals': In Pursuit of a Neglected Stratum in South African History." *Journal of Southern African Studies* 36(1): 7–23.

Delius, Peter, and Richard Cope. 2006. "Hard Fought Frontiers: Mpumalanga 1845–1883." In *Mpumalanga: Reclaiming the Past, Defining the Future*, edited by Peter Delius, 137–200. Durban: University of KwaZulu-Natal Press.

Delius, Peter, and Stefan Schirmer. 2014. "Order, Openness and Economic Change, In Precolonial Southern Africa: A Perspective from the Bokoni Terraces." *Journal of African History* 55(1): 37–54.

Dubois, Frédérique, and Luc-Alain Giraldeau. 2003. "The Forager's Dilemma: Food Sharing and Food Defense as Risk-Sensitive Foraging Options." *American Naturalist* 162(6): 768–79.

Etherington, Norman. 2001. *The Great Treks: The Transformation of Southern Africa, 1815–1854*. Harlow: Longman.

Evers, T. M. 1975. "Recent Iron Age research in the Eastern Transvaal, South Africa." *South African Archaeological Bulletin* 30(119/120): 71–83.

Fenske, James. 2014. "Ecology, Trade, and States in Pre-Colonial Africa." *Journal of the European Economic Association* 12(3): 612–40.

Garzarelli, Giampaolo and Lyndal Keeton. 2018. "Laboratory Federalism and Intergovernmental Grants." *Journal of Institutional Economics* 14(5): 949–74.

Gump, James. 1989. "Ecological Change and Pre-Shakan State Formation." *African Economic History* 18: 57–71.

Guy, Jeff. 1987. "Analysing Pre-Capitalist Societies in Southern Africa." *Journal of Southern African Studies* 14(1): 18–37.

Hall, Martin. 1984. "Pots and Politics: Ceramic Interpretations in Southern Africa." *World Archaeology* 15(3): 262–73.

Hall, Martin. 1987. *The Changing Past: Farmers, Kings and Traders in Southern Africa, 200–1860*. London: James Currey.

Hall, Simon 2009. "Farming Communities of the Second Millennium: Internal Frontiers, Identity, Continuity and Change." In *The Cambridge History of South Africa Volume 1: From Early Times to 1885*, edited by Carolyn Hamilton, Bernard Mbenga, and Robert Ross, 112–67, Cambridge: Cambridge University Press.

Harries, Patrick. 1994. *Work, Culture, and Identity: Migrant Laborers in Mozambique and South Africa, C. 1860–1910*. London: Pearson Education.

Hauert, Christoph, Franziska Michor, Martin A. Nowak, and Michael Doebeli 2006. "Synergy and Discounting of Cooperation in Social Dilemmas." *Journal of Theoretical Biology* 239(2): 195–202.

Herbst, Jeffrey. 2000. *States and Power in Africa: Comparative Lessons in Authority and Control*. Princeton, NJ: Princeton University Press.

Hooper, Jane and David Eltis. 2013. "The Indian Ocean in Transatlantic Slavery." *Slavery & Abolition* 34(3): 353–75.

Huffman, Thomas N. 1990. "Broederstroom and the Origins of Cattle Keeping in Southern Africa." *African Studies* 49(2): 1–12.

Huffman, Thomas N. 2015. "Mapela, Mapungubwe and the Origins of States in Southern Africa." *South African Archaeological Bulletin* 70(201): 15–27.

Keeton, Lyndal. 2016. *Essays on the Political Economy of State Formation and of Laboratory Federalism*. PhD diss., University of the Witwatersrand.

Lye, William F. 1969. "The Ndebele Kingdom South of the Limpopo River." *Journal of African History* 10(1): 87–104.

Maggs, Tim. 1994. "The Early Iron Age in the Extreme South: Some Patterns and Problems." *Azania: Archaeological Research in Africa* 29(1): 168–78.

Makhura, Tlou. 2006. "Early Inhabitants." In *Mpumalanga: Reclaiming the Past, Defining the Future*, edited by Peter Delius, 91–136. Durban: University of KwaZulu-Natal Press.

Manning, Patrick, with Tiffany Trimmer. 2020. *Migration in World History* (3rd edn). New York: Routledge.

Mason, Andrew. 1995. "Conflict in the Western Highveld/Southern Kalahari, c.1750–1820." In *The Mfecane Aftermath: Reconstructive Debates in Southern African History*, edited by Carolyn Hamilton, 357–8. Johannesburg: Wits University Press.

Maynard Smith, John. 1982. *Evolution and the Theory of Games*. Cambridge: Cambridge University Press.

Maynard Smith, John, and George Price. 1973. "The Logic of Animal Conflict." *Nature* 246(5427): 15–8.

Morelli, Ettore. 2019. "Have You Ever Captured Anything for Your Parents? War Captivity and Slavery on the Pre-Colonial Southern African Highveld, c. 1800–71." *Journal of African History* 60(1): 45–65.

Morton, Fred. 2012. "Mephat: The Rise of the Tswana Militia in the Pre-Colonial Period." *Journal of Southern African Studies* 38(2): 301–18.

Parkington, John. 1972. "Seasonal Mobility in the Late Stone Age." *African Studies* 31(4): 223–44.

Parkington, John, and Simon Hall. 2009. "The Appearance of Food Production in Southern Africa 1,000 to 2,000 Years Ago." In *The Cambridge History of South Africa Volume 1: From Early Times to 1885*, edited by Carolyn Hamilton, Bernard Mbenga, and Robert Ross, 63–111. Cambridge: Cambridge University Press.

Parsons, Neil. 1995. "Prelude to *Difaqane* in the Interior of Southern Africa, c.1600–c.1822." In *The Mfecane Aftermath: Reconstructive Debates in Southern African History*, edited by Carolyn Hamilton, 329–35. Johannesburg: Wits University Press.

Prins, Frans 1994. "Climate, Vegetation and Early Agriculturist Communities in Transkei and Kwazulu-Natal." *Azania: Archaeological Research in Africa* 29(1): 179–86.

Rasmussen, R. Kent. 1978. *Migrant Kingdom: Mzilikazi's Ndebele in South Africa*. London: Rex Collings.

Sansom, Basil. 1974. "Traditional Economic Systems." In *The Bantu Speaking Peoples of Southern Africa*, 2nd edn, edited by W.D. Hammond Tooke, 135–76. London: Routledge.

Silberbauer, George and Adam Kuper. 1966 "Kgalagari Masters and Bushman Serfs: Some Observations." *African Studies* 25(4): 171–80.

Smale, Melinda and Thom Jayne. 2003. "Maize in Eastern and Southern Africa, Seeds of Success in Retrospect." Environment and Production Technology Division International Food Policy Research Institute Discussion Paper No. 9, Washington D.C.

Thompson, Leonard. 1995. "Southern Africa to 1795." In *African History: From Earliest Times to Independence*, edited by Phillip Curtin, Steven Feierman, Leonard Thompson, and Jan Vansina, 277–303. New York and London: Longman.

Whitelaw, Gavin. 1994. "Towards an Early Iron Age Worldview: Some Ideas from KwaZulu-Natal." *Azania: Archaeological Research in Africa* 29(1): 37–50.

Wilson, Monica. 1969a. "The Nguni People." In *The Oxford History of South Africa, Volume 1*, edited by Monica Wilson and Leonard Thompson, 75–130. Oxford: Oxford University Press.

Wilson, Monica. 1969b. "The Sotho, Venda, and Tsonga." In *The Oxford History of South Africa, Volume 1*, edited by Monica Wilson and Leonard. Thompson, 131–82. Oxford: Oxford University Press.

Wilson, Monica. 1982a. "The Nguni People," In *A History of South Africa to 1870*, edited by Monica Wilson and Leonard Thompson, 75–130. London: Routledge.

Wilson, Monica. 1982b. "The Sotho, Venda and Tsonga." In *A History of South Africa to 1870*, edited by Monica Wilson and Leonard Thompson, 131–82. London: Routledge.

Wright, John. 2009. "Turbulent Times: Political Transformations in the North and East, 1760s-1830s." In *The Cambridge History of South Africa Volume 1: From Early Times to 1885*, edited by Carolyn Hamilton, Bernard Mbenga, and Robert Ross, 211–52, Cambridge: Cambridge University Press.

APPENDIX

HAWK-DOVE MODEL

Consider that there are two types of polity strategies in a context abstracted from the complex historical realities we outlined above, namely, hawk strategies (H) and dove strategies (D). Hawk strategies are violent and aggressive, attempting to dominate control over the resource, while dove strategies are peaceful and cooperative, preferring sharing of the resource. Polities are competing over natural resources, such as fertile land, game, cattle, and people. Each interaction for a particular resource is between two polities. The winner receives the value of the resource ($V = V(R)$) while any violent interaction incurs a future cost of limiting the possibility for peaceful interactions (C). This provides us with three possible outcomes from an interaction (shown in Figure 6.A1):

1. A hawk polity migrates and meets a dove polity (or vice versa). The hawk polity takes the resource at full value (V) without any cost, while the dove polity gets nothing and has to flee.

2. Two dove polities meet. They choose to cooperate and to share the resource equally, each receiving half the value $\left(\dfrac{V}{2}\right)$.

3. Two hawk polities meet. Violence ensues. Each can expect, with a probability of 50%, a gain of the shared value of the resource $\left(\dfrac{V}{2}\right)$ less the cost of the violence $\left(\dfrac{C}{2}\right)$, i.e., a net gain or loss $\left(\dfrac{V-C}{2}\right)$.

	hawk	dove
hawk	$\frac{V-C}{2}; \frac{V-C}{2}$	$V;0$
dove	$0;V$	$\frac{V}{2}; \frac{V}{2}$

FIGURE 6.A1 Payoffs for hawk and dove strategies.

134 Lyndal Keeton and Stefan Schirmer

The returns to each strategy depend on the relative value of the resource compared to the cost of a violent interaction. If $V < C$, then neither strategy dominates and the evolutionary stable strategy is a mixed strategy: a hawk strategy with probability ρ or the dove strategy with probability $1-\rho$, where $0<\rho<1$. This mixed strategy yields the result $\rho = \dfrac{V}{C}$, i.e.,

the proportion of hawk polities (or the probability of a polity playing a violent hawk strategy) is equal to the value of the resource divided by the cost of a violent interaction. Thus, the lower the V or the higher the C, the fewer hawk-type polities emerge. Hence, the prevalence of cooperative dove-type polities over violent hawk-type polities and the prevailing strategy before the 19th century being one of cooperation as the payoff of violence is relatively low and, hence, only undertaken in exceptional circumstances.

However, the Hawk-Dove interaction is generally a single interaction game. This cooperative outcome is reinforced by the repeated interactions of small numbers of people who would meet at the rare parts of Southern Africa where land was both arable and rainfall sufficient for survival. An iterated Hawk-Dove game becomes very similar to an iterated Prisoners' Dilemma. Hence, over time and multiple interactions the dove strategy is reinforced.[27]

Taking the Hawk-Dove model further, as $V > C$, a dove strategy is now strictly dominated and the evolutionary stable strategy is to play hawk only. Moreover, if $V = C$, then a dove strategy is weakly dominated and the evolutionary stable strategy is hawk. In this period, while $V \geq C$, the strategic choice for any polity encountering another polity during a migration is to play a hawk strategy. Thus, the evolutionary stable strategy of cooperation falls away, leading a dominant strategy of violence and aggression.

In the long run we can examine the dynamics of the polities of Southern Africa in terms of a simple dynamic replicator equation[28]:

$$\dot{\rho} = \frac{1}{2}\rho(1-\rho)[V-C\rho]$$

(6.A1)

The dynamic replicator (6.A1) shows that the change in the population of hawks over time $(\dot{\rho})$ depends on the number of hawks in a particular time period $\left(\rho = \rho(t) = \dfrac{V}{C}\right)$, the number of doves in a time period $(1-\rho)$, and the difference between the value of the contested resource (V) and the cost of fighting for that resource multiplied by the number of potential hawks to fight $(C\rho)$. Underlying this equation is that as the net payoff for hawkish behavior increases, so too do the number of hawk polities. Essentially, if $V = C\rho$ then the number of hawks will be stable over time. If $V < C\rho$ the number of hawks will decrease over time. And, if $V > C\rho$, then the number of hawk-type polities will grow over time.

We can thus see a greater number of smaller, passive dove-type polities during the Mapungubwe Equilibrium, while $V < C\rho$. However, once $V > C\rho$ (c. 1750) then the number of hawk-type polities start to increase over time, which can explain the growth in the number of violent states we see during the Mfecane Equilibrium.

7

THE SETTLERS OF SOUTH AFRICA

Economic Forces of the Expanding Frontier

Johan Fourie

"Trek verder!" So klink dit
die môre heel vroeg;
en laat in die aand:
"Nog nie ver genoeg!"
  - Totius, *Trekkerslied*, 1913

"Trek on!" it rings out
at the crack of dawn;
and at sundown:
"Yet further still!"
  - Totius, *Trekkerslied*, 1913

1 Introduction

The first "Fourie" to settle at the southern tip of Africa was a man by the name of Louis Fourie. Born in the Dauphiné, a former province of southeastern France, Fourie fled his country after the revocation of the Edict of Nantes in 1685. Like many Huguenots of his time, he found his way to Amsterdam. Then, perhaps more adventurous than the thousands of his compatriots who headed for England or North America, Fourie chose to head south. On 27 July 1688 he allegedly boarded the *Wapen of Alkmaar*. Six months later, on 27 January 1688, at the age of 20, he set foot on African soil for the first time.

We know little about his first few years in the Cape Colony. He reported three heads of cattle in the 1692 tax census. In 1695 he married Suzanne Cortier. But a decade after his arrival, when he was given a farm by the governor, Willem Adriaan van der Stel, the story begins to gather detail. On this farm, *De Slangerivier* ("Snake River") in the *Wagenmakersvallei*, which is today the town of Wellington, he remained for the next five decades, until his death in 1750.

Fourie was not a very prosperous farmer by Cape standards. The tax censuses report that he owned 37 head of cattle in 1700 and by 1702 he had planted 4,000 vines, though he was predominantly a wheat farmer, sowing around six *mudden* in each of the tax censuses and reaping between 25 and 70 *mudden*.[1] His productivity seems to have increased over the course of his life. But he is perhaps better known for productivity of another kind: he had 21 children, more than any other Cape Huguenot, and 99 grandchildren. After his first wife died in 1714, leaving him with five young children (five more died in infancy), he married 18-year-old Anne Jourdan, with whom he had another 11 children.[2]

DOI: 10.4324/9781003225027-10

136 Johan Fourie

Like so many other Cape settlers of European origin, almost all of Fourie's sons would move across the Cape mountains that separated the fertile Cape peninsula from the drier interior in search of better opportunities. His eldest, Louis Jnr, settled in Swellendam, a district east of Cape Town, and became a wealthy farmer and local *Heemraad*.[3] His wife, Susanna, owned a stock farm in Outeniqualand, even further east. They and their siblings all followed the incessant push toward the east. In fact, when the elder Louis died in 1750, not one of his sons wanted to return to *De Slangerivier* and the farm was sold.

Louis Fourie's story exemplifies that of many Dutch and French settlers who arrived at the Cape during the second half of the 17th century and dispersed into the interior during the eighteenth. By 1806, when the Cape became a British colony, they inhabited a vast area of mostly sparsely populated pastoral farms. Three decades later, those on the frontier migrated deeper into the interior, starting a wave of colonization that would ripple through southern Africa for much of the 19th and 20th centuries.

The European settlers' internal migration affected African demography and biogeography not only locally but far beyond the borders of the colony. They brought with them a commercial, market-oriented society that made many of them remarkably wealthy. To make this wealth possible, they imported slaves. They brought wheat and vines and other winter-rainfall crops, new livestock species, and more productive farming methods, boosting agricultural productivity and population growth. They brought Christianity and literacy, and new kinds of property rights, the Roman-Dutch law, and a new form of government. And, of course, they brought "guns, germs and steel"; it would be guns and germs that would, within the first few decades of settlement, decimate the Khoesan (Diamond 1998).

The patterns of 18th-, 19th-, and early 20th-century settler migrations can shed light on later African migrations. The descendants of the first Dutch and French farmers, later known as Afrikaners, were following *a strategy of resistance against and flight from colonial policies* when they trekked into the South African interior. As the introductory chapter notes, this was the strategy of many internal migrations elsewhere on the continent, although the reasons underpinning these treks were often different: the frontier settlers feared expropriation (of their slaves) and limitations on freedom, while African migrants often escaped (land) dispossession and (labor) exploitation. The "Great Trek," as this settler migration into the interior became known, was not a single event but a series of haphazard migrations that ultimately resulted in two independent republics where *the definition of citizenship and control over state bureaucracy* was of vital import. Others would later migrate beyond the Limpopo for reasons similar to those of the Voortrekkers. But not all migration was rural to rural; in the 1960s, black Africans would move to the cities for the same reasons that white Africans were *urbanizing* half a century earlier.

None of these migrations can be easily categorized as a specific migration type. The European settlers were *invaders, settlers,* and, to some extent, *sojourners* as *cross-community migrants,* but at various stages could also be considered part of Manning's *colonization* or even *home-community* migration types. The experiences of the Cape settlers demonstrate the complexity and diversity of migration systems. One consistent thread throughout the chapter, though, is the *economic motive* for migrating. Despite the political, cultural, or religious rhetoric, in essence the settlers migrated, as many South Africans do today, in pursuit of a better life.

In this chapter I discuss four stages of European settler migration in southern Africa: the 18th-century migration of Dutch and French settler farmers beyond the first mountain ranges of the Cape peninsula; the early 19th-century migration of their descendants into the South African interior; the further expansion of these descendants into southern Africa in the later 19th century; and finally the 20th-century migration of whites to the cities. The much larger migration of black Africans to the cities that followed later is beyond the scope of this chapter.

2 European settlers in Africa and the early frontiers

When the first crew of Dutch officials and workmen stepped ashore at the Cape in April 1652, the plan was not to colonize the African interior. They were there to establish a re-freshment station. The *Dutch East India Company* (VOC) aimed to reduce the shipping costs between Amsterdam and the spice islands in the East Indies. The Cape would supply passing ships with fresh fruit, vegetables, water, meat, and fuel.

The Cape made sense for a number of reasons. It was about halfway between Europe and the East Indies. It had fresh water and was sparsely inhabited. Settling here was easy compared with subduing the more densely settled indigenous populations further along the east coast. And it was also free from the deadly diseases that characterized much of Africa, such as malaria, trypanosomiasis, or sleeping sickness, for example (Alsan 2015). Had settler mortality been high at the Cape, European settlement might have taken a very different form (Acemoglu, Johnson and Robinson 2001).

But the future growth of what would become the Cape Colony was not immediately obvious. Soon after settlement, Jan van Riebeeck, the first commander, ran into trouble. Almost 6,000 soldiers and sailors arrived in Table Bay every year and the small refreshment station could not produce even enough to satisfy its own needs (Boshoff and Fourie 2008). A new plan was needed, and so, in 1657, nine Company servants were released to become free settlers. In Manning's taxonomy, *sojourners* became *settlers*. Van Riebeeck had envisaged a small, densely settled farming community, much in the style of the Netherlands, with farmers producing wheat and vegetables and selling these at fixed prices to the fort in Cape Town, which would then resell, at inflated prices, to the passing ships. The small community never materialized. Farm sizes soon increased on the windswept Cape peninsula, meat instead of wheat was the preferred produce, and a region that Van Riebeeck had thought would accommodate thousands of small farmers was soon taken over by a few dozen.

These early settler farmers had many problems to deal with: not just the southeasterly winds and the tough Cape vegetation, but also retribution from the indigenous Khoesan, dispossessed of their grazing and hunting lands.[4] After several decisive victories against Gonnema's Cochoqua, a Khoesan clan, in the 1670s, the fertile land below the encircling mountain ranges was opened for VOC settlement. It was the promise of this fertile land that attracted about 180 French Huguenots to the Cape. Fleeing persecution, they were given farms between those of the Dutch settlers so that they would assimilate as quickly as possible. This they did, although they seem to have maintained their advantage in making wine, a staple of the sailor's diet at the Cape (Fourie and Von Fintel 2014).

By 1700, then, the Cape had a population of about 3,000 people, 40% of whom were settlers, and half of these were children. Another 20% were Company servants and *knechten*.[5] The final 40% were slaves, imported from the Indian Ocean regions of modern-day Malaysia, Indonesia, India, Madagascar, Mauritius, and Mozambique, of whom 30% belonged to the VOC and 70% to the settlers (Baten and Fourie 2015).

By this time, too, most of the available land west of the first mountain ranges was occupied and so farmers began to move beyond the mountains to the north and northeast, into the dry interior, or along the coast below the southern mountain ranges. At first, this was only seasonal migration to find grazing for their livestock – *sojourners*. But the pasture seeking soon became a permanent migration eastward, taking with it the sons of Louis Fourie. Again, *sojourners* became *settlers*.

At the end of the 17th century the border of the colony was about 80 km east of Cape Town; by the end of the 18th century it had moved more than 800 km further east (Giliomee 1990). The eastward migration finally came to a halt when the settlers met groups of amaXhosa pastoralists, who were slowly migrating westward, in an area between the Sunday's River and the Kei River, later known as the Cape's eastern frontier.

The repeated eastward migration of the Cape frontier farmer, the *trekboer*, is well documented in South Africa historiography. In his extensive study,[6] P. J. van der Merwe noted that a "combination of game hunting and the requirements of extensive stock farming kept the pioneers in a state of great mobility" (Van der Merwe 1995, 43). Their lifestyle, he suggested, was very similar to that of the Khoesan: "half-nomadic, carnivorous hunter-stock farmers – the migrant farmer," in a world of solitude and simplicity (Van der Merwe 1995, 43).

The history of the frontier farmers has informed an ongoing debate about whether the migrating settlers were pushed or pulled eastward – whether they moved from necessity or to take advantage of opportunity (Newton-King 1999). The standard view is that they were pushed. Agricultural land close to Cape Town began to be in short supply. High fertility rates meant that the settlers' many sons had little chance of inheriting enough land to secure their survival, let alone their upward mobility. Instead, they chose to marry and then migrate eastward in search of a means of survival. The subsistence lifestyles of those on the frontier, reported by European travelers and documented by scholars like Van der Merwe, support the "push" view (Harris and Guelke 1977).

An alternative view, first proposed by Neumark, suggests that the high returns these young farmers could obtain on the frontier pulled them eastward (Neumark 1957). Meat was a sought-after commodity at the Cape, supplying both a growing local market and the passing ships. Their rudimentary pastoral lifestyle may mask a flourishing and lucrative commercial trade in livestock, a very different picture from that of the isolated frontier subsistence farmer.

A new historiography, based on micro-level evidence, provides support for this "pull" view. Using probate inventories, I have shown that the average farmer in the Cape Colony attained levels of wealth comparable to those of Europe or the US (Fourie 2013). Recent work using newly transcribed tax censuses confirms the surprisingly high levels of output

TABLE 7.1 Average ownership and production by district, 1790

District	Number of farms	Household members	Slaves	Wheat	Wine	Horses	Cattle	Sheep
Drakenstein	1011	3.13	4.02	4.32	3.27	4.48	16.43	99.74
Stellenbosch	360	3.20	5.92	2.53	5.05	5.92	13.33	43.79
Graaff-Reinet	747	3.73	0.86	*NA*	*NA*	1.88	41.53	318.84

Source: J109 (Graaff-Reinet) and J218 (Stellenbosch and Drakenstein), Cape Town Archives.

(Fourie and Green 2015; Fourie and Garmen 2020). Table 7.1 shows the average levels of ownership and production for three districts in 1790 – Stellenbosch and Drakenstein, both close to Cape Town, and Graaff-Reinet, on the frontier.

Two differences are immediately apparent. The Stellenbosch and Drakenstein settlers owned far more slaves than the settlers on the frontier (Worden 1985). The frontier farmers, on the other hand, owned far more cattle and sheep. The averages of 42 and 319 are not just due to outliers: the medians are 32 and 200.

But there were nevertheless considerable disparities in wealth on the frontier, even among the landholders, as Giliomee (1990, 455) noted more than three decades ago. Newton-King (1999, 158), using a small sample of probate inventories, confirmed that some frontier households were extremely poor and others extremely wealthy (by the standards of the day). Using new data sources and more sophisticated methods, others have found similarly large wealth differentials (Fourie and Von Fintel 2010). The point here is that although *some* settler farmers were poor, the frontier was not characterized by widespread poverty; a large subsistence class would be unlikely to reflect such extreme differences. Despite the distance from Cape Town, the settlers not only were part of the commercial economy but responded to market conditions (Ross 1990, 253).

In the expanding agricultural economy of the 18th and 19th centuries, the frontier farmers' migrations were driven by the availability of cheap land, cheap labor, and a reliable market for their produce. The Khoesan's weakened resistance to settler intrusion, from conflict and disease, made private enforcement of settlers' territorial claims cheaper. This relaxation of the rules for property rights was an important reason why, according to Dye and La Croix (2018), the colony could expand so rapidly.[7] The new system of property rights, developed within a very specific early 18th-century setting, would travel more than a century later with the frontier farmers on their exit from the colony.

The migrating settlers were not only interested in land – they also needed labor. The Company had banned the enslavement of the Khoesan, to prevent settlers from raiding a potential trading partner.[8] Absent a large pool of European labor, and given the complementary skills the Khoesan brought with them, notably herding and handling of draft animals, the subjugation of the Khoesan not only opened vast lands for settlement but also provided a ready supply of labor, especially in the frontier districts (Links, Fourie and Green 2019).

Khoesan labor was not the main source of labor, of course. The Cape was a slave economy. Between 1652 and 1808 the Cape imported an estimated 63,000 slaves (Shell 1994). Although a large number were housed in the Slave Lodge in Cape Town and worked on Company projects, most were purchased by settlers and used in agriculture. Slave ownership at the Cape was widespread. Eighteenth-century settler households owned, on average, five slaves (Fourie 2013). The numbers reported in Table 7.1 suggest higher averages for wheat and wine farmers.

Yet slaves were not only used as laborers. In the absence of a formal credit market, settlers had developed an intricate informal financial network with slaves as capital. The weak property rights of the loan farms and the liquidity of slaves as assets meant that slaves were the most convenient collateral in loan agreements. Using the credit and debit entries in probate inventories, Fourie and Swanepoel show that loans were not only mortgaged against slaves, but slave purchases were the most likely reason for entering a loan agreement (Swanepoel and Fourie 2018). At the time of emancipation in 1834, the numerous volumes of slave mortgage rolls attest to the widespread practice of using slave men and women as collateral

(Ekama 2020). Only after the payment of partial compensation and the establishment of a formal banking sector would this practice end.

The emancipation of almost 38,000 slaves – and the partial compensation for what was then considered to be the settlers' most important asset class at the Cape – brought substantial changes in the distribution of wealth in colony. Many slave owners received only a fraction of the true value, resulting in widespread bankruptcy and poverty (Ekama et al. 2021).

This was also true for the Fourie family. Louis Fourie owned slaves and so did his children and grandchildren. In 1776, the year that Adam Smith published *The Wealth of Nations*, another grandchild, David Hermanus Fourie, was born to the now long-dead patriarch. In 1797, two years after the first British takeover, David Hermanus married the 20-year-old Jacoba Hendrina Heyns and settled in the Langkloof, in the district of George. When the commissioners who were appointed to appraise the value of the slaves moved through the colony in 1834, this is where they recorded David Hermanus' seven slaves: six men, Mey, aged 44, Albertus, aged 42, Mawira, aged 42, Adam aged 26, Damon, aged 19, and Frans, aged 13, and one woman, Regina, aged 44.[9] Their total value was £907.10. When compensation was calculated, David Hermanus was offered only £260.11.05, or 29% of the total value. Given his father's large losses when compensation was paid, it is no surprise that Stephanus Johannes Fourie, the eldest son of David Hermanus, moved to the district of George close to the present-day town of Oudtshoorn, naming his new farm *Armoed* – "Poverty." Map 7.1 plots the 5,503 farms in the Cape Colony in 1850. Polygons in black show the 37 farms owned by farmers with the Fourie surname.

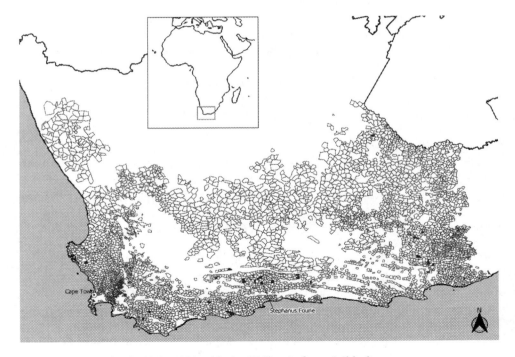

MAP 7.1 Cape settler farms in 1850 with the 37 Fourie farms in black.
Source: Le Roux, Niemandt and Olivier (2012).

3 The Great Trek

The loss of labor and the loss of capital when the slaves were emancipated in 1834 may have been two pressing reasons why bands of frontier farmers, by the mid-1830s, were organizing to trek beyond the borders of the colony. Piet Retief, a well-known leader of the Voortrekkers, wrote in his Manifesto that the trek was necessary "to preserve the proper relations between master and servant."[10] *Ordinance 50* of 1828, which protected the Khoesan from the coercive labor practices that had become common by the early 19th century, combined with the emancipation of the slaves, resulted in severe labor shortages on the frontier and complaints from farmers (Peires 1990). The Voortrekkers also complained that they had lost "up to four-fifths of the market value of their slaves" because the British government paid out the compensation money in Britain rather than in South Africa (Peires 1990, 505). While the difference between the market value and the cash compensation was largely due to the way Britain appraised the slaves and not the location of pay-outs, there is little doubt that some slave owners, heavily in debt and with their slaves as their only collateral, were financially ruined.

Yet if emancipation did play such a critical role in the settlers' decision to migrate deeper into the interior, then one would expect that either those who were the largest slave owners or those with the largest losses would be the most likely to do so. The slave emancipation rolls and the list of Voortrekkers migrants have not yet been matched, but the geographic origin of the migrants – from the frontier regions of Somerset and Graaff-Reinet – suggest that they owned few slaves and were unlikely to be those most affected by the inadequate compensation. The Voortrekkers themselves acknowledged this. In her diary, Anna Steenkamp, the niece of Piet Retief, stressed social and, as can be expected of a God-fearing people, religious reasons for trekking:

> The disgraceful and unrighteous freedom given to the slaves did not drive us away as much as the equality with us as Christians, which is contrary to God's laws and to nature. It was simply too intolerable for any decent Christian to carry such a load, which is why we would rather leave [the Colony] so as to preserve our faith in its pure form.
>
> *(Steenkamp 1939, 10; own translation)*

Given South Africa's later history, such political and racial segregationist rhetoric is often foregrounded when discussing the reasons for the interior migrations. But segregation was only part of the story. After the Cape came under British rule in 1795 and again in 1806 (after three years of rule by the Batavian Republic), the institutions set up by the VOC a century earlier had served their purpose. In 1813, a quitrent land system was introduced with the purpose of increasing the colonial revenue through taxation. Many settlers complained about the new system and were, to some extent, protected by the inability of the new British government to enforce the new laws (Peires 1990). A provisional system of "request-places" soon became a popular form of land tenure but caused some insecurity, especially when the new governor, Lord Bathurst, withdrew the property rights of 120 farmers (Peires 1990, 503). Almost all of these 120 would eventually join the Great Trek.

Not only were the rights to land increasingly contentious, but so was access to land. The open frontier of the 18th century had closed by the second decade of the 19th century.

During the 1770s colonists with little or no capital could still acquire land and start raising cattle, but by 1798 only 26% of the colonists owned farms, and by 1812 only 18% (Giliomee 1990, 450). This situation was further exacerbated by the arrival, in 1820, of around 4,000 settlers from Britain. Colonial officials hoped that these British settlers would help not only to anglicize the eastern frontier, but also to placate the Dutch-speaking settlers who were in constant conflict with groups of Khoesan and Xhosa. But the effect was exactly the opposite.

Not only were new groups of settlers arriving but, around 1823, waves of black migrants were arriving on the frontier too (Muller 1974). Where the Fingo – or Mfengu – came from is still debated, although there is little doubt that the cause of their arrival was the Mfecane, a period of warfare that ravaged much of the interior of South Africa from 1815 to 1840. As Keeton and Schirmer (Chapter 6) argue in this book, the reasons for the Mfecane are interrelated: the emergence of circumscription that limited movement, the introduction of maize that gave rise to larger populations, and an increase in the intensity of slave trade in Delagoa Bay. Another strand of recent scholarship suggests that the cause of the Mfecane was resource shortages due to a serious drought caused by the eruption, in 1815, of Tambora, an Indonesian volcano (Garstang, Coleman and Therrell 2014). Whatever the reasons for it, the incoming Mfengu further complicated an already volatile situation on the Cape Colony's eastern frontier. Muller emphasizes their continued mobility: "These immigrants remained mobile on the Cape frontier. It is exactly this special mobility that contributed to increased frontier conflict and caused the Great Trek" (Muller 1974, 134; own translation). Black mobility helps to explain white mobility.

This may be true for an altogether different reason too. South African historians have focused almost exclusively on push factors to explain the Great Trek. Yet it is perhaps useful, as Neumark did for the 18th-century frontier farmers, to also consider pull factors (Neumark 1957). Apart from the political and religious sentiment that permeates Voortrekker rhetoric, there is no doubt that the prospect of sparsely populated land beyond the Orange River, with abundant resources, would have contributed to their decision. It is not as if the region beyond the colony's borders was completely unknown to the frontier farmers. One consequence of the depopulation of the interior was the return of large herds of game. Muller notes that, from 1819, large hunting expeditions, led by men like G. P. N. Coetzee, O. J. van Schalkwyk, J. H. Snyman, and L. J. Fourie, visited the region almost annually. He says that by 1830 several routes to the north were already known and this "attractive, easily accessible region" was considered "mostly depopulated," a region where, apart from some Khoesan, only "some roaming blacks" could be found (Muller 1974, 229).[11] News about the relatively open interior and its abundant resources would have reached frontier farmers, and hunters, by the 1830s.

The Mfecane pushed war refugees and other migrants into the already densely populated eastern frontier, where the rugged terrain offered security (as did the Drakensberg mountains where Moshoeshoe gathered war refugees into the Basuto Kingdom). The Mfecane may explain why, by the 1830s, blacks in South Africa were mostly concentrated in the rugged regions of what would later become the Transkei, Zululand, Lesotho, and Swaziland (now Eswatini) (Von Fintel and Fourie 2019). It has been argued that African settlement patterns were a consequence of the slave trade; in Southern Africa, the violence of the Mfecane may instead explain why Africans opted for rugged terrain (Nunn and Puga 2012).

The migration of several thousand settlers to the interior was thus driven by a combination of push factors – such as a general dissatisfaction with the British authority at the Cape and its new labor, regulatory, and fiscal institutions that undermined the autonomy of the

The Settlers of South Africa **143**

frontier farmer – and pull factors – particularly the opportunity to acquire fertile land relatively cheaply in the interior. The exact number of these settlers depends on the definition of the period and who would be included in the count: Peires suggests that up to 15,000 "Afrikaners" left, about a fifth of the total settler population (Peires 1990).

What is clear is that the first half of the 19th century was a period of flux. The Great Trek has perhaps been overemphasized – it was just one of many migrations in search of a better life. The Mfecane and its (forced) migrations displaced millions of people across Southern Africa, outnumbering the Great Trekkers by at least a factor of 100. Etherington (2014, 344) agrees, noting that the Great Trek was "only one of many treks undertaken by people of differing leaders... seeking different homelands." It has no special claim to be called "Great."

History may have cast the Voortrekkers as instigators, lead actors that shaped the course of South African history. But that is an oversimplification. Just like the Ndebele under Mzilikazi had trekked north or the Mfengu that fled west in response to Zulu aggression, so too did the Voortrekkers migrate in response to events in both Cape Town and the interior. And where they arrived, just like the Ndebele and Mfengu and the many other groups that were on the move, they caused enmity and exodus amongst the local inhabitants, sparking another cycle of migrations that would repeat again and again, echoing throughout Southern Africa. The Great Trek, from this perspective, was just another wave in an endless sea of migrations.

For the settlers, though, the Great Trek was special. Yes, on the one hand, the trek was just the continuation of a migratory existence in search of better economic opportunities that characterized frontier life. But, on the other hand, this trek was different – for the Voortrekkers, there was no going back. The frontier farmers of the Cape Colony remained dependent on the commercial capital, Cape Town, and later, Port Elizabeth, and could return closer to these centers if their existence was threatened on the frontier, and many did so. But very few Voortrekkers who left for the Southern African interior ever returned to the Cape.

Arguments about the differing significance of the South African migrations can perhaps be clarified by defining their types. In Manning's taxonomy, the Voortrekkers could be classified as a special case of itinerants, moving from place to place before ultimately settling down. Because many of them settled in sparsely settled areas, avoiding the more densely settled, rugged areas, their migration could also be classified as *colonization* as Manning defined it.[12] One might even make a case for them to be classified as *invaders*, who seize and dominate the local population, although this is probably more reflective of their actions in the second half of the 19th century and into the 20th century.

Ultimately, though, the Voortrekkers are best described as *settlers* in the category *cross-community migration* – moving but remaining segregated from the groups they would meet. A grandchild of Louis Fourie, David Stephanus Fourie, provides a good example of this type.[13] Leading a large party who left the colony in 1838, Fourie purchased land between the Modder and Vaal rivers from the mixed-race Korana leader David Danster on 15 May 1839. He called his farm Van Wyksvlei, after a Griqua who used to farm there. The farm later became the town of Boshof, named after the second president of the Orange Free State. It became a municipality in 1872.

4 Waves of expansion

As David Stephanus Fourie's story demonstrates, the migration of settler farmers into the interior in the 1830s and 1840s resulted in a political transformation of the interior. The trek followed a haphazard process, with each band of Voortrekkers following its own route and with its own leader, sometimes combining and at other times separating, and sporadically clashing with Bantu-speaking groups, notably the Zulu at the Battle of Blood River on 16 December 1838. The most prominent leaders were Hendrik Potgieter (1835), Gerrit Maritz (1836), Hans van Rensburg (1835), Louis Tregardt (1835), and Piet Retief (1837). The routes they are thought to have taken are shown in Map 7.2.

One immediate consequence was that the Boers – as they would become known – established the Republic of Natalia in 1839, although this proved to be short-lived as Britain annexed it in 1843 as the Colony of Natal. Many Boers, frustrated with the continual political intervention by Britain, moved north, into the highveld, and founded several independent Boer republics, with the two most prominent being the South African Republic (the ZAR, *Zuid-Afrikaansche Republiek*, later the Transvaal) in 1852 and the Orange Free State in 1854. Smaller republics, like the Republic of Utrecht and the Republic of Lydenburg, joined the ZAR in 1860.

The establishment of independent Boer republics did not mean an abrupt end to trekking within and beyond the borders of the new territories. From at least the early 18th century, the search for minerals and better living conditions drew migrants toward the deserts and semi-deserts of South West Africa, today's Namaqualand, and into the former German South West Africa, now Namibia. Gustav Preller describes, for example, the trek of Hendrik Smith of Piquetberg who in 1890 began to trek northward, a trek that would last four years and end in German South West Africa's Swakopmund (Preller 1941).

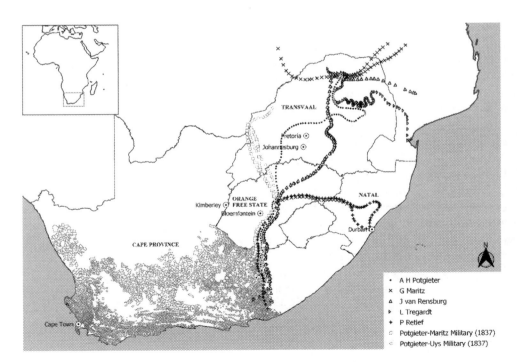

MAP 7.2 Cape settler farms in 1850 with Voortrekker routes and 1910 South African provinces.
Source: Von Fintel and Fourie (2019).

The Settlers of South Africa **145**

One of the most notorious, and arguably the best-known, treks beyond South Africa's borders, was the Thirstland Trek of 1874. Several scholars have studied this ill-fated trek, but it is Nicol Stassen's monumental study, *The Thirstland Trek*, that gives us a full picture of the miseries these migrants endured (Stassen 2016). The immediate reason for trekking seems to have been a religious dispute. The ZAR president, Thomas François Burgers, was perceived by many Boers belonging to the Dopper or Reformed Church, a more conservative faction of Afrikaner Calvinism, as "too liberal." But although these Boers may have left to escape the "false religious perceptions" of the president and in quest of "an earthly paradise or New Jerusalem," there were probably others reasons too: the lack of freely available land, fear of equalization with black Africans, and fear of new forms of taxation (Stassen 2016). These echo the economic motivations of earlier trekkers.

Terrible tragedy befell the Thirstland trekkers. Leaving Pretoria in May 1874, the migrants slowly moved in the direction of the Kalahari Desert, collecting more families along the way. The trek, eventually consisting of 480 trekkers in 128 wagons, halted at Rietfontein, bordering the Kalahari. A tale of misery and near catastrophe then befell them, as drinkable water here was so scarce that it "had to be given by the spoonful." Fever and the consumption of poisonous fruit killed nearly half their cattle. Thirty-seven trekkers succumbed to the harsh conditions.

While some decided to return to the Transvaal, others diverted to Damaraland and the Okavango River, where at Rustplaas in the Etosha Pan they found abundantly flowing springs. Here the trek halted temporarily, providing relief for the tired trekkers. Some built houses and cultivated gardens. Those who returned to the Transvaal pleaded for funds to be raised to aid the trekkers. Nonetheless, because of their desire to be self-reliant, some continued to trek further north, into Angola, establishing a new settlement at Humpata. Although their relationship with the local Portuguese settlers was amicable, the Portuguese authorities never recognized their citizenship and in 1928 many were repatriated to South West Africa. According to Stassen, on repatriation, the descendants of the trekkers were praised for "almost a century-long stay in Angola" that "played a decisive role in the road network development in southern Angola" (Stassen 2016, 460).

As the encounter with the Portuguese settlers in Angola makes obvious, the Boer settlers were not the only settlers of European descent in Southern Africa. As the zeitgeist of imperialism swept through Africa, the British embarked on a more organized and coordinated series of annexations in an attempt to build an empire from the Cape to Cairo. Much of this interest in the Southern African interior was kindled by the discovery of minerals – first diamonds, in 1867, and then the discovery of the much more lucrative gold, in 1886, on the Witwatersrand. These discoveries transformed the interior, bringing in thousands of prospectors in a diamond and gold rush. The growth of these mining towns was spectacular; by 1891, for example, Kimberley was the second-largest city in the Cape Colony, with 40,231 inhabitants; 17.8% of its population was foreign-born compared to 3.4% for the entire colony.

British migrants came not only to make money but also to convert souls. Hunting and trading expeditions paved the way toward the Zambezi and missionaries followed. Following in the footsteps of men like David Livingstone, Reverent François Coillard set out on a missionary expedition in 1877 beyond the Limpopo River, settling eventually on the banks of the Zambezi (Mackintosh 1950). Others followed. The Hully-Cawood Trek of 1896 was the largest missionary trek into Rhodesia, and one that experienced, much like the

Thirstland trekkers, intense suffering (Boggie 1962). Missionary activities like these actively contributed to bringing Southern African territories under Britain's sphere of influence, becoming protectorates like Nyasaland (present-day Malawi) in 1907.

It was Rhodesia, in particular, that would become a popular destination for settlers moving beyond South Africa's borders. In 1890, after protracted negotiations with Chief Lobengula, Cecil John Rhodes, diamond magnate and Prime Minister of the Cape Colony, and his *British South Africa Company* (BSAC), prepared the Pioneer Column for settlement in the lands beyond the Limpopo. The Pioneer Column was to be "a selection of one in ten from the 2000 applicants who were deliberately designated to constitute a cross-section of Cape Colonial society, with a strong emphasis on the English side" (Blake 1973, 4). As Rhodes envisaged a long-term occupation of the northern territories, his Pioneer Column was to "attract plenty of men from good families with a love of adventure" (Blake 1973, 4). On 12 September 1890, in 65 heavily laden wagons, the Column embarked on their journey of 400 miles toward Mashonaland. After two and a half months of trekking, they arrived at their destination, Fort Hampton (which became the capital, Salisbury, renamed Harare in 1982). There they raised the Union Jack flag in Cecil Square – marking the formal annexation of Rhodesia.

The imperial ambition that drove the annexation of Rhodesia was, of course, closely tied to the prospect of profits from extracting mineral resources. Rumors soon spread of the discovery of a rich copper reef across the Zambezi, which attracted the interests of BSAC. According to Brelsford, it was Rhodes' conviction that the Royal Charter extended to Northern Rhodesia and so he instructed the pioneers to "just go in and take the place" (Brelsford 1965, 43). To that end, the BSAC police extended their influence to northeastern Rhodesia, and some of them were enlisted in the North-Eastern Rhodesia Police. In 1901, the last formal trekking movement, the Northern Rhodesia Expedition under the leadership of George Grey, set off. Grey planned not only to prospect for copper but also to develop the area of Kansanshi. The expedition comprised 15 European settlers chosen from more than 400 applicants (Brelsford 1965).

The opening up of the territories north of the Limpopo for settlers spurred on what has been described as a "Second Great Trek." Boer commissions preceded the treks to evaluate the feasibility of agricultural production. The *Paarl Mashonaland Commission* negotiated with Rhodes for a possible permanent settlement within the newly colonized territories. Rhodes, regarding the Afrikaners as pioneers in agricultural development, longed for their presence in Rhodesia, though not merely for economic reasons but also to strengthen the number of Europeans under British rule in the Manica and Gazaland areas in Southern Rhodesia as a buffer against possible Portuguese infiltration from Mozambique.

As an economic incentive, Rhodes initiated the Land Settlement Scheme in Gazaland. Although the scheme stipulated an advance payment, none of the farms were larger than 3,000 morgen, and all mining and mineral rights belonged to the BSAC; this was an attractive proposition for many Boers (Olivier 1943). Despite the obvious economic motives, the rhetoric of the time was of a revived *trekgees* ("trek spirit"). Some of the leaders spoke of the "drywende gees van trek in ons harte" ("incessant desire to trek in our hearts") (Preller 1941). Newspapers echoed this sentiment. *Die Afrikaanse Patriot* of 3 May 1894 said: "Trekken moet en trekken zal men dus weder. Er is een trekgeest ontwaakt" ("One must and shall trek again. A trek spirit has awoken").[14]

But this spirit may have been partly a front for the economic motive. The Boers considered poverty a great embarrassment. Trekking was considered an "escape mechanism," a way to relieve the pressures felt by inhabitants of the Cape Colony and the Boer republics (Hendrich 2010). Just as the vision of empty land beyond the Orange attracted frontier farmers in the 1830s, and just as the vision of prosperity attracted thousands to the diamond mines of Kimberley in the 1860s, so the vision of open land beyond the Limpopo in the 1890s sparked the interest of people who could scarcely eke out a living. Uneven spatial opportunities, then, partly explain the waves of migration that simultaneously pulled and pushed settlers deeper into the African interior.

Again, the migrants traveled in groups. The first Boer trek, the Adendorff Trek to establish a Republic of Banjaland in Matabeleland, was short-lived. On 24 June 1891 this trek, with some 2,000 to 3,000 trekkers, departed toward Florisdrift on the Limpopo River. Again, the "trek spirit" was given as the reason: it appeared to be a repeat of the Great Trek – the circumstances were different, but the call to trek was apparent everywhere (Blok 1928, 42). Despite the optimism, the Adendorff Trek ended prematurely when President Kruger and his Volksraad, or People's Council, decided at the last minute to urge the trekkers to return in order to avoid any direct confrontation with Rhodes.

Others soon followed. The size of these treks varied between 10 and a 100 families. When Marthinus Jacobus Martin, a Member of Parliament of the Orange Free State, heard that he would receive eight farms as a prize for bringing settlers to Rhodesia, he hastily organized a trek that would become the largest of all the Boer treks into Rhodesia (Groenewald 1978). On 19 April 1894 the Martin Trek, consisting of 104 men with fully laden oxwagons, departed from Fouriesburg, a town in the eastern Free State named after Christoffel Fourie, a sixth-generation Fourie and nephew of Louis Johannes Fourie.

5 Migration to the cities

Fouriesburg served as a temporary capital for the Orange Free State during the Second Boer War (1899–1902) and, given its strategic importance, was almost completely destroyed. So, too, were many of the farms in the former Boer republics, with many families forced to move to the temporary internment camps set up by the British. The numbers of people interned were not inconsequential. Well over 100,000 Afrikaner men, women, and children were moved to the camps (Du Plessis and Fourie 2016). An estimated 26,000 of them died. Of the 114,315 individuals in a dataset that Elizabeth van Heyningen has meticulously reconstructed from camp records, 1,453 (1.3%) had a Fourie surname; 295 of them died in the camps (Van Heyningen 2009).

One consequence of the devastation caused by the war was increasing white urbanization. The goldmines of the Witwatersrand and the industries that developed around them required labor, both white and black. Many white *bywoners*, landless farm workers, were displaced by the war and had little alternative but to move to these industrial centers. As Map 7.3 shows, it was especially the eastern districts of the Cape Province and the western districts of the Orange Free State that depopulated between 1911, the year of the Union of South Africa's first population census, and 1936. Almost all of South Africa's major cities, bar Kimberley, were destination regions for these rural migrants, with the Witwatersrand region, with Johannesburg at its center, the most popular.

Although it was mostly men who moved first, women soon followed. From the beginning of the 20th century, white English female immigration and settlement in Cape Town was encouraged and the *British Women's Emigration Association* was established with the specific aim to increase this demographic (Bickford-Smith, Van Heyningen, and Worden 1999). In the 1920s, white Afrikaner women from agricultural areas moved into jobs in the emerging textile, clothing, and food industries in Johannesburg and Cape Town, bolstering the suffragette movement as they did so (Walker 1990). In the wake of the Great Depression, young women arriving in the cities were happy to take any employment opportunity (Brink 1990). Women had generally been outnumbered by men but this began to change around the middle of the century. In Cape Town, colored and white women outnumbered men by the time of the 1946 census (Bickford-Smith, Van Heyningen, and Worden 1999). Women's migration to the cities is an example of what Manning would classify as *home-community migration*.

Not all migration was to the cities, though. As is clear from Map 7.3, many rural areas of the Transvaal attracted white settlement too. One reason for this was the 1913 *Land Act* that dispossessed black farmers and sharecroppers of their land and tenure. This was not a new phenomenon: 18th- and 19th-century settler expansion in the Cape Colony and

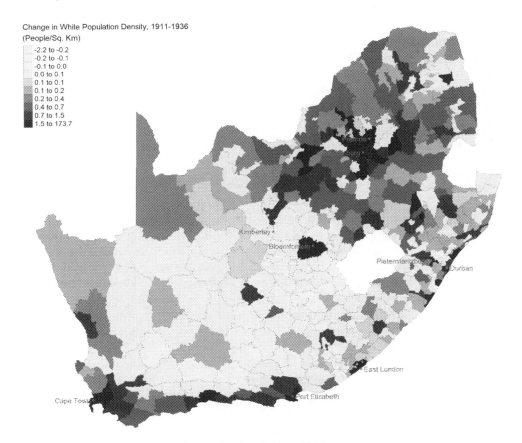

MAP 7.3 Change in white population density, 1911 to 1936.
Source: South African censuses, 1911 and 1936.

beyond had inevitably involved land dispossession and exclusion. The *Land Act* of 1913 (and its later amendments) was different in being the first to designate regions where only white residents could own land. In fact, the *Land Act* allocated less than 7% of the country for black ownership.

In 20th-century South Africa, legislative segregation shaped the migration of the whites, and later the blacks, who sought to take advantage of the increasing prosperity of South Africa's rapidly industrializing cities. The laws introduced by the National Party, after its narrow victory in the 1948 all-white elections, further segregated all aspects of South African public life on the basis of race. But it was the *Groups Areas Act* of 1950 that most effectively enforced spatial segregation. The Act split towns and cities into areas for whites, coloreds, Indians, and blacks. One implication of these laws was that black ownership was circumscribed, a decision that affected migration and settlement. The repercussions are evident in South Africa today: leafy, suburban, formerly white neighborhoods stand in sharp contrast to the miserable living conditions in black "townships" on the periphery of cities.

Segregation turned into "self-development." The *Promotion of the Black Self-Government Act* of 1959 was intended to turn the traditional areas allocated to black farmers by the various Land Acts into independent countries, a scheme that became known as "grand apartheid." More than 3 million black residents of what became known as "white South Africa" were forcibly resettled in the under-resourced "homelands." Pass laws were introduced to regulate the system of temporary labor migration into white South Africa, a policy known as "influx control." Although costly to the economy, the system persisted until 1986 for reasons of political economy: it protected unskilled and semi-skilled white workers (voters) against competition from black workers (who were not allowed to vote). Of those white voters who were registered on the voters' roll in 1984, 0.7% had the surname Fourie.[15]

The abolition of influx control opened up opportunities for black South Africans to settle permanently in former white areas. Their rights to free movement and residence were enshrined in the country's new constitution after its first democratic elections in 1994. The expectation was that the temporary labor migration would be replaced by permanent settlement. Yet the evidence suggests that temporary internal labor migration did not decline and may have actually increased (Posel 2004). The reason for this is the rapid rise in female labor migration. In contrast to white migrants moving during the early 20th century, black migrants to the cities retain ties with their original households and continue to return to their original homes. In Manning's taxonomy, they could be classified as a mix between *sojourners* and *itinerants* within *cross-community migration*. Whether these cultural norms are a consequence of land dispossession, economic insecurity, and exclusion under apartheid or a phenomenon deeply embedded in histories of pastoral life and seasonal migration is an intriguing question that should invite future research.

6 Trekking on

Despite rapid white urbanization during the 20th century, the trekking spirit has never entirely disappeared. Whereas Southern Africa was a destination for white immigration until the mid-20th century, the situation has now been reversed. Deteriorating economic and physical security have been important push factors. The disruptions and conflict of the independence movements across Southern Africa caused many settler descendants to emigrate to Europe or to offshoots of the former British Empire. After Zimbabwe's *Land Reform*

Programme of 2000, large numbers of white farmers left that country for South Africa, England, or Australia. Although there is some evidence to suggest that white South Africans have emigrated in large numbers, it is difficult to verify any estimates because Statistics South Africa does not record emigration statistics. One estimate is that between 2001 and 2015 almost 400,000 South Africans emigrated, most of them white (Kaplan and Höppli 2017). What we do know is that in 2011, the most recent census year, the census found that South Africa was home to 4.5 million white residents, 8.9% of the total population. That figure is larger than the 1996 census figure of 4.4 million and the 2001 census figure of 4.3 million, although both those figures are disputed. With the numbers in doubt, it is even more difficult to discern the motivations for leaving.

Of relevance to the early migrant story this chapter has related is the fact that, of the 4.5 million whites in 2011, 2.7 million, or 61%, recorded Afrikaans as their first language, a rough proxy for the ancestors of the 17th- and 18th-century settlers. For most, the trekker spirit lives on only in popular culture. One of the most popular lifestyle magazines in Afrikaans is *Weg!* (also published as *Go!*), focusing on the outdoors. In his 2009 album *Afrikanerhart* ("Heart of an Afrikaner"), Afrikaans artist Bok van Blerk recalls the Afrikaner's trekker spirit in his love song: *Tyd om te Trek?* – "Time to Trek?" Totius, one of the first Afrikaner poets, who often used the trek as a metaphor for life, would have been proud.

Some, though, have rekindled the trekking spirit of their ancestors more literally. In August 1997, *The Economist* reported on a "second Great Trek":

> Some 150 years after Afrikaners left the Cape to set off on their Great Trek north, their descendants are embarking on another odyssey. This time they are not travelling in canvas-covered ox-wagons. They go by scheduled flight from Johannesburg, their pick-up trucks and motorbikes following by container ship. Over the past two years, several dozen Afrikaner farming families have set off from South Africa for Congo-Brazzaville and Mozambique. Battered by years of drought, they pack up their belongings and leave for the promise of more fertile lands north of the Limpopo. "It was amazing," recalls Jan Tromp of his first impressions of Congo-Brazzaville. "The country had a beautiful climate, yet this kind of land was still lying in Africa without anybody using it."[16]

What is most striking about *The Economist* news report is the shift in motivation: the religious rhetoric of yesteryear and the nationalistic fervor of historians past have been replaced with an overt economic motive. The 2019 Afrobarometer, a pan-African survey, confirms these economic motives for all South Africans. Of those interviewed in South Africa who said they had considered emigrating (31% of the sample), 40% said their main motivation was to find work. Only 8% cited concerns with peace and security as their main motivation. When Wynand Fourie moved to Amsterdam in 2018, it was to take up a lucrative new job and career prospects, much like his ancestor Louis Fourie did ten generations ago when he moved in the opposite direction.[17]

South Africa is a country of immigrants. As this chapter has shown, the European settlers who arrived during the 17th, 18th, and 19th centuries joined a society in flux, one where migration was a way of life rather than an aberration. These settlers sometimes followed but most often caused the migrations of the people they encountered. Rather than pursuing a deliberate goal to subjugate and conquer (even though that was often the outcome), settler migration was, more often than not, a way to survive the harsh conditions of the South African landscape, a way, real or perceived, to improve their standards of living.

This quest reverberates across Africa today. Millions of immigrants from other African countries have arrived in South Africa during the past three decades, repelled by the harsh economic realities of their countries of origin and drawn by the bright lights of Jozi and dreams of a better life.[18] Just as past expanding frontiers caused disruption and dislocation, so, too, will these African settlers steer their destination country in a new direction.

Notes

1 A *mud* is approximately 100 liters.
2 I am a descendant of Fourie's 20th child, Stephanus, born in 1734.
3 "Home-advisor," similar to an alderman.
4 "Khoesan" is a composite term for the Khoe pastoral farmers and the San hunter-gatherers.
5 European wage laborers.
6 Van der Merwe's formidable corpus of work was, sadly, never published. Today, his unprocessed research material is preserved at the Western Cape Archives in Cape Town as the PJ van der Merwe Collection, occupying almost 22 meters of shelving.
7 Although the de jure property rights of loan farms were indeed weaker than those of the free tenure farms close to Cape Town, Swanepoel and Fourie show, using an innovative identification strategy, that there was little difference between tenure and loan farms in their de facto property rights. See Swanepoel and Fourie (2018).
8 Settler-Khoesan relations varied across time and space. Elphick and Malherbe note that travelers had seen settlers who "were brutal and serenely indifferent to suffering and death among their Khoesan employees" but also "happy farms where Khoesan received considerate treatment and looked to their employers with evident affection" (Elphick and Malherbe 1990, 29).
9 The spelling of these names is subject to uncertainty owing to the poor handwriting in the original source.
10 *The Graham's Town Journal*, 2 February 1837.
11 Louis Johannes Fourie, born in 1797 in the Swellendam district, was the first born of the fifth generation of Fouries. Author's translation.
12 In line with Manning and Trimmer (2020) we define *colonization* as the replication of a community in space (De Haas and Frankema, Chapter 1, this volume).
13 David Stephanus Fourie was not the only Fourie who joined the Great Trek. In the most authoritative study of Voortrekker families to date, Visagie records the names of 2,313 male and 2,183 female migrants who left the Cape Colony between 1834 and 1845. Thirty of these men (or 1.3%) and 26 of the women (or 1.2%) have the surname Fourie (Visagie 2000).
14 *Die Afrikaanse Patriot*, 3 May 1894.
15 21,682 of the 2,944,105 white voters.
16 *The Economist*. 28 August 1997. https://www.economist.com/international/1997/08/28/afrikaners-on-a-second-great-trek
17 Wynand Fourie is the brother of the author.
18 Jozi is a colloquial term for Johannesburg.

References

Acemoglu, Daron, Simon Johnson, and James Robinson. 2001. "The Colonial Origins of Comparative Development: An Empirical Investigation." *American Economic Review* 91(5): 1369–401.

Alsan, Marcella. 2015. "The Effect of the Tsetse Fly on African Development." *American Economic Review* 105(1): 382–410.

Baten, Joerg, and Johan Fourie. 2015. "Numeracy of Africans, Asians, and Europeans during the Early Modern Period: New Evidence from Cape Colony Court Registers." *Economic History Review*, 68(2): 632–56.

Bickford-Smith, Vivian, Elizabeth Van Heyningen, and Nigel Worden. 1999. *Cape Town in the Twentieth Century: An Illustrated Social History*. Cape Town: David Philip Publishers.

Blake, L. R. N. W. 1973. *The Pioneer Column: Its Origins and Implications*. Grahamstown: 1820 Settlers National Monument Foundation.

Blok, Thomas. 1928. *Die Adendorff-trek*. Nasionale Pers, Beperk.

Boggie, Jeannie. 1962. *First Steps in Civilizing Rhodesia*. Bulawayo: Kingstons.

Boshoff, Willem, and Johan Fourie. 2008. "Explaining Ship Traffic Fluctuations at the Early Cape Settlement 1652–1793." *South African Journal of Economic History* 23(1–2): 1–27.

Brelsford, William. 1965. *Generation of Men: The European Pioneers of Northern Rhodesia*. Salisbury; Rhodesia: Stuart Manning for the Northern Rhodesia Society.

Brink, Elsabe. 1990. "Man-made Women: Gender, Class and the Ideology of the Volksmoeder." In *Women and Gender in Southern Africa to 1945*, edited by Cherryl Walker, 273–92. Cape Town: David Philip.

Diamond, Jared. 1998. *Guns, Germs and Steel: A Short History of Everybody for the Last 13,000 Years*. London: Random House.

Dye, Alan, and Sumner La Croix. 2018. "Institutions for the Taking: Property Rights and the Settlement of the Cape Colony, 1652–1750." *Economic History Review* 73(1): 33–58.

Ekama, Kate. 2020. "Bondsmen: Slave Collateral in the Cape Colony". Mimeo: Stellenbosch University.

Ekama, Kate, Johan Fourie, Hans Heese, and Lisa-Cheree Martin. 2021. "When Cape Slavery Ended: Introducing a New Slave Emancipation Dataset." *Explorations in Economic History* Volume 81, July, 101390.

Elphick, Richard and V. Malherbe. 1990. "The Khoisan to 1828." In *The shaping of South African society*, edited by Richard Elphick and Herman Giliomee, 3–65. Maskew Miller Longman.

Etherington, Norman. 2014. *The Great Treks: The Transformation of Southern Africa 1815–1854*. Oxford: Routledge.

Fourie, Johan. 2013. "The Remarkable Wealth of the Dutch Cape Colony: Measurements from Eighteenth-Century Probate Inventories." *Economic History Review* 66(2): 419–48.

Fourie, Johan, and F. Garman. 2020. "The Settlers' Fortunes: Comparing Tax Censuses in the Cape Colony and Early American Republic." *Mimeo*.

———. 2018. "Building the Cape of Good Hope Panel." *History of the Family* 23(3): 493–502.

Fourie, Johan, and Dieter von Fintel. 2010. "The Dynamics of Inequality in a Newly Settled, Pre-Industrial Society: The Case of the Cape Colony." *Cliometrica* 4(3): 229–67.

———. 2014. "Settler Skills and Colonial Development: The Huguenot Wine-Makers in Eighteenth-Century Dutch South Africa." *Economic History Review* 67(4): 932–63.

Garstang, Michael, Anthony Coleman, and Matthew Therrell. 2014. "Climate and the Mfecane". *South African Journal of Science* 110(5–6): 01–06.

Giliomee, Herman. 1990. "The Eastern Frontier, 1770–1812." In *The Shaping of South African Society*, edited by Richard Elphick and Herman Giliomee, 421–71. Maskew Miller Longman.

Groenewald, Christo. 1978. *Ons Afrikaners in Rhodesia*. Bloemfontein: C.J.O. Groenewald.

Harris, R. C., and L. Guelke. 1977. "Land and Society in Early Canada and South Africa." *Journal of Historical Geography* 3(2): 135–53.

Hendrich, Gustav. 2010. *Die Geskiedenis van die Afrikaner in Rhodesie (1890–1980)*. PhD thesis. Stellenbosch: University of Stellenbosch.

Kaplan, David, and Thomas Höppli. 2017. "The South African Brain Drain: An Empirical Assessment." *Development Southern Africa* 34(5): 497–514.

Le Roux, J.G., Niemandt, J.J. and Olivier, M. 2012. *Bewaarders van ons erfenis: Indeks van plase en plaaseienaars in die Kaap Kolonie 1850*. Drakenstein Heemkring. Available online: https://www.drakensteinheemkring.co.za/_Bewaarders.html.

Links, Calumet, Johan Fourie, and Erik Green. 2019. "The substitutability of slaves: Evidence from the eastern frontier of the Cape Colony." *Economic History of Developing Regions* 35(2): 98–122.

The Settlers of South Africa **153**

Mackintosh, Catharine. 1950. *Some Pioneer Missions of Northern Rhodesia and Nyasaland*. Livingstone: Rhodes-Livingstone Museum.

Manning, Patrick, with Tiffany Trimmer. 2020. *Migration in World History* (3rd edn). New York: Routledge.

Muller, C. F. J. 1974. *Die oorsprong van die Groot Trek*. Cape Town: Tafelberg.

Neumark, Daniel. 1957. *Economic influences on the South African frontier, 1652–1836*. PhD thesis. Stanford University Press.

Newton-King, Susan. 1999. *Masters and Servants on the Cape Eastern Frontier*. Cambridge University Press.

Nunn, Nathan, and Diego Puga. 2012. "Ruggedness: The Blessing of Bad Geography in Africa." *Review of Economics and Statistics* 94(1): 20–36.

Olivier, S. P. 1943. *Die pionierstrekke na Gazaland*. Pretoria: Unie-Volkspers.

Peires, J. 1990. "The British and the Cape, 1814–1834." In *The shaping of South African Society*, edited by Richard Elphick and Herman Giliomee, 472–518. Maskew Miller Longman.

Du Plessis, Sophia du and Johan Fourie. 2016. ""'n Droewige laslap op die voos kombers van onreg": 'n Statistiese analise van konsentrasiekampbewoners." *Tydskrif vir Geesteswetenskappe* 56(4–2): 1178–99.

Posel, Dorrit. 2004. "Have Migration Patterns in Post-Apartheid South Africa Changed?" *Journal of Interdisciplinary Economics* 15(3–4): 277–92.

Preller, Gustav. 1941. *Voortrekkers van Suidwes; geskiedenis van die land en sy volke met hul oorloe; van die Dorslandtrek; die Smit-trek uit Piketberg en die Duitse en Britse veroweringe met 'n oorsigsketskaart*. Cape Town: Nasionale Pers.

Ross, Robert. 1990. "The Cape of Good Hope and the World Economy, 1652–1845." In *The Shaping of South African Society*, edited by R. Elphick and H. Giliomee, 243–80. Cape Town: Maskew Miller Longman.

Shell, Robert. 1994. *Children of Bondage: A Social History of the Slave Society at the Cape of Good Hope, 1652–1838*. Johannesburg: Witwatersrand University Press.

Stassen, Nicol. 2016. *The Thirstland Trek, 1874–1881*. Pretoria: Protea Book House.

Steenkamp, Anna. 1939. *Die Dagboek van Anna Steenkamp en fragmentjies oor die Groot Trek*. Pietermaritzburg: Natalse Pers.

Swanepoel, Christie, and Johan Fourie. 2018. "Why Local Context Matters: Property Rights and Debt Trading in Colonial South Africa." *Studies in Economics and Econometrics* 42(2): 35–60.

The Economist. 28 August 1997. https://www.economist.com/international/1997/08/28/afrikaners-on-a-second-great-trek.

Van der Merwe, Petrus. 1995. *The Migrant Farmer in the History of the Cape Colony, 1657–1842*. Athens: Ohio University Press

Van Heyningen, Elizabeth. 2009. "The Concentration Camps of the South African (Anglo-Boer) War, 1900–1902." *History Compass* 7(1): 22–43.

Visagie, J. C. 2000. *Voortrekkerstamouers, 1835–1845*. Universiteit von Suid-Africa.

Von Fintel, Dieter, and Johan Fourie. 2019. "The Great Divergence in South Africa: Population and Wealth Dynamics over Two Centuries." *Journal of Comparative Economics* 47(4): 759–73.

Walker, Cherryl. 1990. "The Women's Suffrage Movement: The Politics of Gender, Race and Class." In *Women and Gender in Southern Africa to 1945*, edited by Cherryl Walker, 313–45. Cape Town: David Philip.

Worden, Nigel. 1985. *Slavery in Dutch South Africa*. Vol. 44. Cambridge: Cambridge University Press.

PART THREE

Colonial Policies and Labor Mobility

8

FORCED LABOR AND MIGRATION IN BRITISH EAST AND WEST AFRICA

Shifting Discourses and Practices during the Colonial Era

Opolot Okia

1 Introduction: forced labor and migration in colonial Africa

A long-standing literature has come to view forced labor and migration in colonial Africa, and especially Southern and Portuguese Africa, as joint outcomes of coercive labor practices that pushed Africans into the wage labor market to serve the extraction of primary commodities (Duffy 1967; Wilson 1972; Van Onselen 1976; Nzula, Potekhin and Zusmanovich 1979; Zegeye and Ishemo 1989; Penvenne 1994; Isaacman 1996; Sundiata 1996, 2003; Rubert 1998; Hochschild 1999; Allina 2012; Higgs 2012; Ball 2015; Cleaveland 2015; Guthrie 2018). In particular, studies by Samir Amin (1972, 1973, 1974) and Giovanni Arrighi (1973), which were published almost 50 years ago, have imbued the literature with a critical perspective, typical of World Systems or Dependency Theory, on the pivotal role of labor coercion to facilitate capitalist development under colonial rule. Much remains to be learned, however, about the manifold interconnections between evolving patterns of coercive labor practices and shifting patterns of labor migration, and how these are situated in their local and regional contexts, particularly in British (and French) Africa. This chapter pursues this aim by historicizing the interplay between labor migration and coercive labor practices in British East and West Africa: Uganda, Kenya, and the Gold Coast (Ghana). Kenya and Uganda offer an interesting contrast of the migration and forced labor nexus in a colony dominated by European settlers versus a colony predicated upon the African peasant model of export production (Brett 1973; De Haas 2017). The case of the Gold Coast allows for a comparison of deeper ideological fissures regarding acceptable labor practices in colonial dependencies that were part of the same colonial framework. The comparison with the Gold Coast also helps to clarify the differences in forced labor and migration between East and West Africa.

Control of labor was of paramount importance in the development of economies of extraction across colonial Africa in the early 20th century. Cash-strapped colonial states sought supplies of cheap African labor for the development of a rudimentary infrastructure of roads, railways, ports, and centers of administration, as well as for the extraction and transportation of sub-soil, forest, and agricultural commodities, such as cotton, copper,

DOI: 10.4324/9781003225027-12

gold, and rubber (Van Onselen 1976; Isaacman 1996; Rubert 1998; Hochschild 1999; Juif, Chapter 10, this volume). In settler colonies, like Kenya and Southern Rhodesia, European farmers became dependent on considerable amounts of inexpensive labor to squeeze out profit margins (Mungeam 1966; Arrighi 1973; Mosley 1983).

Labor scarcity was a predominant feature of nearly all of the European colonies south of the Sahara, especially during the early period of colonial rule from the 1880s up to the 1930s. Colonial labor demands were partially satisfied by an expanding a web of voluntary African labor migration flows, but such supplies were often insufficient. Initial extra-market drivers of labor migration such as direct taxes, in the form of hut and poll levies, proved inadequate to fulfill the demand for cheap, commodified labor (Arrighi 1973, 194). In a land-abundant context, African peasants could often expand production of livestock or crops to meet the tax requirements (Kitching 1980; Mosley 1983; Rubert 1998; Fibaek and Green 2019). Those who did migrate to offer their labor avoided (long-term engagement with) expatriate employers, and instead favored circular migration and sharecropping or wage labor for African employers as a means to obtain cash (Miracle and Fetter 1970; Fall and Roberts 2019; De Haas and Travieso, Chapter 11, this volume). Although colonial employers were thus saved from the costs of complete proletarianization, since they only paid a so-called "bachelor wage" which sustained the worker but the family remaining in the rural areas (Freund 1988), labor market involvement remained transient and the aggregate labor supply precarious.

Across colonial Africa, the answer to insufficient labor supply was typically coercion, which took the form of various types of direct forced labor recruitment (Fall and Roberts 2019), as well as more indirect forms of coercion, involving the engineering of extra-market forces to push people into the (migratory) labor market, such as unequal agricultural, marketing, and railway policies – and, in settler colonies, land alienation. Workers were employed on government projects as well as by private expatriate employers. In some cases they were paid a wage; in other cases forced labor was treated as a form of in-kind taxation. Even when they received wages, coerced workers were paid below the market rate for voluntary labor (see, for example, Van Onselen 1976). If not employing forced labor themselves, colonial administrations were typically indirectly involved in recruitment, through coopted traditional chiefs, which further reduced labor costs for business owners (Meillassoux 1981, 92).

In the early period of colonial rule until the 1930s, forced labor and coercive pressures had a major impact on the formation of wage labor markets and migration. Across French, Portuguese, and Belgian Africa, expatriate-run plantations and mines relied to a very large extent on the inflow of forcibly recruited labor (Higgs 2012; Ball 2015; Guthrie 2018; also see Ribeiro da Silva and Alexopoulou; Juif, Chapters 9 and 10, this volume). Infrastructural development was even more heavily dependent on labor coercion. In French Africa, for example, major public works, such as the construction of the Congo-Océan Railway, the Thiès-Kayes Railway, and the *Office du Niger* irrigation scheme, each involved the forced migration of tens of thousands or even over a 100,000 workers, under the guise of military service and with massive toll in human lives and welfare (Fall and Roberts 2019:89–90). Labor coercion also had a major *indirect* effect on labor market formation and migration. Government-forced labor created an economic advantage for private employers. Men already in wage labor could obtain exemptions from corvée or forced employment below the market wage rate. As a result, the supply of (migrant) labor increased, and the cost of wages declined (Powesland 1957, 18–34; Brass 1997, 61). Flight from zones of coerced recruitment, often to areas where better working conditions and wages prevailed, was a common African response to coerced recruitment (Asiwaju 1976; Hanson 2003, 176–7; De Haas 2019, 398; De Haas and Travieso, Chapter 11, this volume).

By the late 1940s, the dynamics had shifted. With the exception of the Portuguese territories (Ribeiro da Silva and Alexopoulou, Chapter 9, this volume), forced labor for private purposes was curtailed. At the same time extra-market forces increasingly meshed with economic factors, driven by Africans themselves, like the desire for cash, bridewealth, clothes, and bicycles (Stichter 1982, 80–9; Mitchell 1989, 37–43; De Haas and Travieso, Chapter 11, this volume). Additionally, the increased exploitation of female domestic, agricultural and communal labor freed up men to engage in voluntary labor migration, which reduced the private sector's reliance on direct, paid forced labor by males (Akurang-Parry 2010, 33–5). In settler colonies, the effort-cost involved in participation in peasant agricultural production increased in comparison to working for wages in the European sector of the economy (Arrighi 1973, 206–7; Mosley 1983, 118–225). For the colonies discussed in this chapter, the gradual rise in wages made wage employment more attractive, particularly when incorporated into the seasonal agricultural cycle in the rural areas through migrant or casual labor (Stichter 1982, 84; Mosley 1983, 118; Frankema and van Waijenburg 2012, 901–4; De Haas 2017, 621–7). At the same time, despite the decline in direct, private sector coercive labor practices, various forms of paid government-forced labor continued.

By the 1950s, in both the British and French dependencies, colonial administrations suppressed the use of paid government-forced labor for large infrastructure projects. Still, colonial administrations continued to exploit unpaid so-called "traditional" labor for village infrastructure and roadwork in the rural areas. This coercive labor practice did not involve a lot of geographic mobility since the workers usually toiled on projects within the vicinity of their villages. However, in some cases, the habitual labor requirement led to flight as village residents moved to escape the work requirement. At its core, "traditional" labor involved female labor in the rural areas, which further reinforced migrant labor by lessening the impact of the loss of male workers.

2 Shifting global discourses on colonial forced labor

Changes in forced labor and labor migration patterns in colonial Africa occurred against a backdrop of changing international discourses concerning acceptable labor practices in dependent territories. Although European nations, like Britain, France, and Portugal, had profited tremendously from the trans-Atlantic slave trade, by the late 19th century, slavery was viewed as an archaic form of labor organization that was morally objectionable and less efficient than voluntary wage labor (Davis 1984, 61; Cooper 2000, 113–5). It is important to note, however, that European colonial powers often discarded this professed antipathy toward slavery when practical abolition potentially represented a threat to political or economic interests (Miers and Roberts 1988). The impact of several forced labor scandals, like the period of "Red Rubber" in the Belgian Congo (1885–1908), "Chinese Slavery" in South Africa (1902–10), and the "Chocolate Island Slavery" in Portuguese-held São Tomé and Principe (1901–13), solidified the moral opposition of humanitarian organizations, like the *Congo Reform Association* and the *Anti-Slavery and Aborigines Protection Society*, to slavery and conditions of work analogous to slavery (Miers 1998; Grant 2005; Higgs 2012).

160 Opolot Okia

By the 1920s, the international discourse concerning human rights had evolved to the point where slavery and forced labor for private business interests (but not government-forced labor) were viewed as morally objectionable (Newbury and Newbury 1976; Miers 1998; Grant 2005). This ideological shift was part of what Frederick Cooper called a "reformist critique of imperialism" (Cooper 2000). The *League of Nations Slavery Convention* of 1926 called for the end of all forced labor, with the exception of government-forced labor, but provided no legal framework for its suppression. It also established international norms regarding forced labor, one of which was that there existed a moral gulf between forced labor for private purposes, which was categorically sanctioned, and forced labor for public projects (ILO 1929, 19–20).

After the *Slavery Convention*, the passage of the *Forced Labour Convention* in 1930 occasioned a re-evaluation of the use of forced labor since it, specifically, banned signatory nations from using forced labor for private purposes. However, it only called for signatory nations to progressively end government-forced labor, without any specific time frame. In addition, there were various exemptions to the definition of forced labor in the Convention. Minor communal services ("traditional" labor), military labor, civil obligations of citizens of self-governing countries, prison labor, and work performed in the context of an emergency (war, famine, fire, flood, earthquake, disease, pests) were all defined as exemptions to the definition of forced labor. The *Forced Labour Convention* was an example of one of the earliest in a series of attempts to establish global human rights law in the West (Viljoen 2009, 9). It was also part of the International Labour Organization's (ILO's) *Native Labour Code* that targeted the social impacts of labor migration of workers in colonial territories. The ILO's *Native Labour Code*, specifically, sought to protect workers in colonial territories from the potential consequences of participation in private and public labor markets. At th same time, it intentionally excluded workers in colonial territories from protections included in conventions that applied to workers in Western countries (Maul 2007, 481–3). Under the umbrella of the *Native Labour Code*, the ILO passed the *Recruiting of Indigenous Workers Convention*, followed by the *Contracts of Employment (Indigenous Workers) Convention* (1936) and the *Penal Sanctions (Indigenous Workers) Convention* (1939). The *Recruiting of Indigenous Workers Convention* was intended to prevent colonial administrations from recruiting workers for private companies (Maul 2012, 26). Under the *Contracts of Employment (Indigenous Workers) Convention*, long-term labor contracts were required to be written and fall under the supervision of administrative authorities. The *Penal Sanctions (Indigenous Workers) Convention* called for the abolition of legal penalties for breaching a labor contract, like fines and imprisonment.

3 British African case studies

Unlike in South Africa, Southern Rhodesia, and parts of the Congo, agricultural production predominated over mining in British East Africa. At the labor destination zones, Africans were organized through wage labor or tenancy. Migrant labor systems became firmly established during the first quarter of the 20th century. The southern central region of Uganda where African smallholding predominated, and the White Highlands in Kenya's Rift Valley, where the agricultural sector was dominated by white settlers, were major labor-importing regions. Less developed areas within, and adjacent to, these respective colonies exported labor. In contrast to French West Africa and Portuguese Africa, during the early 1920s, most of the British colonies in Africa effectively abolished forced labor for private purposes. In 1921, the Colonial Office specifically forbade the use of forced labor for private purposes. Afterward, in the commodity production zones there would be an increasing reliance upon women and child workers, in addition to migrant laborers from neighboring colonies. By the late 1920s, though, with the exception of wartime, emergency, and the practice of human porterage, the prevalence of certain forms of paid government-forced labor had also begun to decline across British Africa (Stichter 1982, 40; Mosley 1983, 142).

3.1 Uganda

The British formed the Uganda Protectorate in 1894. With the exception of ivory, the region that encompassed Uganda was not immersed in the production of "legitimate" cash crops, like palm oil, prior to colonial rule (also see Pallaver; De Haas and Travieso, Chapters 4 and 11, this volume). This meant that the British administration needed to sink more resources into the creation of the export sector and the concomitant labor market to support it. As the Protectorate expanded to its ultimate geographic boundaries, the colonial administration faced chronic labor scarcity for the construction of roads, bridges, and other types of infrastructure. European planters competed with for workers the administration as well as with missionary bodies and African proprietors, which drove up the cost of labor in Uganda (Kaberuka 1990, 109). As a result, until 1922, the administration occasionally forcibly recruited African laborers for European planters (Hansen 1993, 189). The growth of the colonial economy, particularly in more developed areas like Buganda Province in the south-central portion of the Protectorate and to a lesser extent, Eastern Province, drew more African workers into the wage labor market for the production of cash crops like cotton, coffee, tobacco, and sim sim (sesame). Labor-sending areas included the Mount Elgon region, Western Province, and the West Nile and Bunyoro areas further north. African farmers began to produce cotton for export 1903, and expanded the cultivation of Robusta coffee on a large scale in the 1920s (Hanson 2003; De Haas 2017). Although there was also a small outcropping of European settlers in the Uganda Protectorate, who demanded cheap laborers, the colonial administration favored peasant agriculture but without the significant technological innovation and institutional support that was granted to European planters in neighboring Kenya (Brett 1973; Van Zwanenberg and King 1975, 64).

Taxation was one of the earliest extra-market stimulants used to raise the supply of wage labor for private interests and government projects. In 1900, the administration introduced a hut tax of three rupees per year, followed by a poll tax of two rupees in 1905 that was levied on African males who did not pay the hut tax (Hansen 1984, 177; Maxon 1992, 63–75; Mwangi 2001). In 1909 the administration abolished the hut tax but retained the poll tax. Since the tax required payment in cash, African males needed to enter the wage labor market or produce agricultural or animal surplus. The tax regime was also linked to cotton production, the leading early export. In 1906, 1910, and 1920 peasant cotton production expanded following increases in taxation (Kaberuka 1990, 56). In their function as administrative officials, chiefs also required peasants to plant a certain amount of the cash crop (Kaberuka 1990, 79).

Defaulting on poll tax payments was not uncommon. Deliberate nonpayment of taxes during this early phase of colonial rule represented the limits of taxation as an effective means of drawing men into the wage labor market and was a form of resistance. The colonial state responded with the introduction of tax labor in 1905. By 1909, African males 18 years and older who failed to pay their poll tax of five rupees were required to extinguish the monetary balance of their tax through work on various government infrastructure projects for two months (Hanson 2003, 177). This tax labor was Uganda's earliest systematic form of government-forced labor. The administration, mainly the Public Works Department, which was the largest government employer, usually paid below market rates for unskilled African labor but included rations with the pay (Powesland 1957, 35). Unlike the paid government-forced labor, *kasanvu*, that we will discuss shortly, the tax laborers usually worked within the vicinity of their homes. The provincial administrations in the Uganda Protectorate gradually stopped using poll tax labor after 1924, with the 1930 *Forced Labour Convention* providing an official seal to this process (Okia 2017, 64).

The colonial administration also occasionally redirected government-forced labor to fulfill the labor needs of European planters, African chiefs, and even missionaries (Hansen 1993, 189). However, similar to the Gold Coast, the administration never displayed the same energy for coercing Africans to work for Africans as it did in forcing them to work for Europeans in Kenya. The main thrust of coercive labor practices was directed toward the administration's own needs. Starting in 1909, the colonial administration also used a variant of government-forced labor, known as *kasanvu,* for infrastructure development projects (Vincent 1982, 215). *Kasanvu* literally means "seven thousand," after the number of men requisitioned for an early project (Hanson 2003, 170). Exempting workers who were engaged in wage employment, the law governing *kasanvu* required African males to perform one month, later extended to two months, of paid work per year on certain government projects (Hansen 1993, 189). Much of this work related to roadwork, bridgework, and porterage for administrators on tour (Hansen 1993, 178–9). The men were usually paid three rupees per month. This wage was below the market rate for unskilled labor, which, at the time, was approximately five rupees per month (Powesland 1957, 20). The exemptions and the lower wage scale paid to *kasanvu* workers were designed to push young men into the private wage labor market. *Kasanvu* involved extensive worker mobility. Peasants who were forced to perform *kasanvu* at times neglected the cultivation of their own food crops due to the work requirements which required them to travel long distances to work sites.[1] The labor requirement also caused some young men to flee Buganda Province in order to escape the labor requirement (Hanson 2003, 176–7).[2] African farmers were never able to benefit from *kasanvu* labor. Alongside exploiting family labor and enforcing customary duties, like *busulu* (rent) *and envujo* (tithe), their only means of attracting labor was to offer higher wages, better rations, and domiciles. According to Powesland, Baganda planters were noted for paying higher wages and giving larger food portions to their workers than expatriate employers (Powesland 1957, 38). Most migrant laborers from Ruanda worked as casual laborers without contracts (Powesland 1957, 71). This gave planters more financial flexibility. In exceptional cases, African farmers in Buganda Province employed as many as 100 workers, but most of the largest African planters retained about 12 to 20 workers. More commonly, commercially minded farmers employed one or two laborers, while the majority did not hire labor at all (Mamdani 1976, 155–6).

Reflecting the overall trend in Britain's colonies, the administration abrogated *kasanvu* in 1922, though it percolated sporadically into the late 1920s (Hansen 1993, 201). An important factor in the administrative impetus toward the abolition of *kasanvu* was its extreme unpopularity among the African populace. Another factor that influenced abolition was the ripple effect of a forced labor crisis in Kenya in 1920–21 that we will discuss in the next section. The abandonment of *kasanvu* impacted the labor market. Powesland asserts that it was not coincidental that the cessation of *kasanvu* by the administration also coincided with the eventual economic decline of the ephemeral European planter class in Uganda, which lost its ability to compete in the labor market without the collusion of the administration (Powesland 1957, 32). In addition, with the abolition of *kasanvu*, the local population intensified its cotton cultivation efforts. Wages increased, as did labor migration, especially from Ruanda-Urundi (De Haas 2019, 380; De Haas and Travieso, Chapter 11, this volume). In 1923 the colonial administration established a labor bureau to more effectively recruit labor into central Uganda from outlying areas in Western and Northern Uganda (Kaberuka 1990, 111). As was the case for West Africa, migrants from Ruanda-Urundi had to travel great distances of up to 300 miles to arrive at their destinations in Uganda (Rutabajuka 1996, 31).

Uganda's burgeoning cash-crop economy during the 1920s also played a role in the demise of *kasanvu* (De Haas 2019, 391–6). According to Powesland, the increased number of exemptions given to Africans who worked full-time for wages actually diminished the labor pool available for *kasanvu* work (Powesland 1957, 20). By the 1920s, the attraction of consumer goods also stimulated labor participation. Specifically, the growth of peasant cotton production led to an increased demand for various consumer goods, like bicycles. Most of the bicycle imports into East Africa were shipped via Mombasa on Kenya's coast to Uganda, where there was a larger market and demand. For example, in 1,927 out of 4,852 bicycles imported into Kenya Colony, 3,133 were shipped to the Uganda Protectorate (Kenya Colony 1929, 36). For comparison, in 1929 4,313 bicycles were imported into the Gold Coast, which had approximately the same population size as Uganda (Gold Coast Protectorate 1930, 17) (Table 8.1).

While the Uganda administration abolished *kasanvu*, it retained unpaid "traditional" labor (Okia 2017). *Luwalo* was customary unpaid forced labor required of African males, ages 15 to 45, for up to 30 days per year. Every African who resided in Uganda, including immigrants, was liable to be called up for work on roads, bridges, building chief's camps, and other assorted projects. Similar to communal labor employed in the neighboring Kenya and Tanganyika colonies, *luwalo* workers were not supposed to be employed more than 5 miles from their homes. *Luwalo* was subject to abuse of power by chiefs and the exploitation of female labor. For instance, chiefs would reroute *luwalo*

TABLE 8.1 Import of bicycles into Kenya Colony

Year	Number of bicycles
1923	2,761
1924	17,430
1925	23,928
1926	11,629
1927	4,852
1928	6,152
1929	10,976
1930	7,056

Source: Colony and Protectorate of Kenya, *Annual Reports for 1923 to 1930.* London: His Majesty's Stationary Office.

labor on to their personal estates. Elite men, who often commanded many dependents in their compounds, could simply pass their obligations on to peripheral female members of their household (Vincent 1982, 215). As a result, poor people, women, and children populated *luwalo* labor projects. The 5-mile radius restriction sometimes became a source of tension when women engaged in *luwalo* labor were required to stay overnight at worksites.

The 5-mile restriction on African mobility was in many cases illusory anyway. In the mid-1920s the administration's labor inspector discovered that some *luwalo* laborers were taken 20 to 40 miles from their homes for work and were not given adequate food during their employment (Okia 2017, 62). In addition, in 1929 a public scandal over the use of corporal punishment involving *luwalo* workers led to the discovery that the administration actually used the labor for railway construction, which transported the men beyond the 5-mile "traditional" perimeter. Africans who failed to turn out or absconded from *luwalo* work were subject to fines, imprisonment, and floggings (Okia 2017, 60).

As was the case with *kasanvu*, Africans typically resisted *luwalo* through absenteeism and exodus to outlying areas. Another means of evading the *luwalo* requirement in less developed parts of the Uganda Protectorate involved African males migrating into areas of southern Uganda, like Buganda Province, that allowed higher rates of *luwalo* cash commutation than their home provinces. Unlike in Kenya, in Uganda Africans could commute their *luwalo* responsibility through a fee of sh.10 (10 East African shillings) which was roughly equivalent to the yearly poll tax, or a month's wage in Kampala in the early 1920s and 1930s (De Haas 2019). Opportunities for commutation of the labor requirement in other areas of the Protectorate accelerated after the passage of the *Forced Labour Convention*.[3] By 1935, 75% of African male workers eligible for *luwalo* were commuting the labor obligation with a cash payment.[4] In essence, as was the case earlier with *kasanvu,* the rising level of commutations was an indicator of the ongoing growth in the wage labor market that would, in fact, make abolition possible.[5] The administration officially, though not completely, abolished *luwalo* in 1939 and completely stopped using it in 1943. Afterward, taxation increased. In 1939, the administration introduced a new *Native Administration Tax* that essentially replaced the value of *luwalo* commutation (Okia 2017, 66).

Reflecting Uganda's expanding voluntary but highly transient labor market, in 1938 the *Report of the Committee of Enquiry into the Labour Situation in the Uganda Protectorate* recommended the creation of a large class of permanent workers (Powesland 1957, 63). However, at this point, the administration was not prepared to support labor stabilization due to fears concerning rising wages.[6] The push for labor stabilization would pick up after the Second World War with the passage of the *Employment Ordinance* and *Employment Rules* of 1946, which established a baseline of minimum standards concerning worker treatment in regard to housing, medical treatment, rations, and welfare (Powesland 1957, 75). During the 1950s, as real wages rose substantially, laborers in urban areas became more settled and increasingly brought their families along (De Haas 2017, 621).

The rise of voluntary labor migration and decline of paid forced labor were mutually reinforcing processes. The gradual increase in labor migration into Uganda, especially from the Belgian colony of Ruanda-Urundi, helped facilitate the transition in the labor market away from outright coercion. As in French West Africa (Asiwaju 1976), the intensity of forced labor in Ruanda (Rwanda) was a push factor for migrants, in addition to the lure of comparatively better paid unskilled jobs in Buganda Province (De Haas 2019, 393–4).

3.2 Kenya

The British constituted the East Africa Protectorate, later called Kenya Colony and Protectorate, in 1895. In contrast to Uganda, Kenya's large class of European émigrés played a significant role in the development of the forced labor migration nexus. Kenya developed a notorious reputation for the abusive exploitation of African laborers due to the presence of European settlers (Berman 1990, 79). The dual economy, comprising both African peasant and European settler production, led to tensions between the two sectors and eventual struggles over the control of labor. Periodic labor shortages during the early period of colonial rule in Kenya precipitated calls for more labor coercion and other extra-market means to force Africans into the wage labor market. The perception of labor shortages between 1909 and 1939 precipitated subsequent calls from European settlers for more coercive labor measures to augment the labor supply (Kitching 1980, 247). In the early period, the administration instituted various labor migration drivers, including taxation and forced labor. By the late 1920s, the administration abolished private sector-forced labor and seriously curtailed government-forced labor.

Starting in 1903, the administration alienated land, known as the White Highlands, which constituted part of the Central Highland and Rift Valley regions of Kenya exclusively for European settlement, while placing Africans into reserve areas (Sorrensen 1968). The White Highlands and the coastal areas became core destinations for migrant labor from ethnic groups in the western portion of Kenya and the Central Highland area. To alleviate land hunger, Africans also engaged in squatting on the various European plantations in the Central Highland areas and the Rift Valley (Zeleza 1992, 177).

As in the Uganda Protectorate, the administration introduced taxation to force African men into wage employment. An early governor of Kenya, Sir Henry Belfield (1912–17), stated, "we consider that taxation is the only possible method of compelling the native to leave his reserve for the purpose of seeking work" (Taurus 2005, 123). The administration required married African men to pay a hut tax in 1902, followed by a poll tax in 1908 on young unmarried males above the age of 16. The initial monetary payment for both taxes was three rupees, and by 1921 it was eight rupees or 16 shillings (Stichter 1982, 35, 42). Indeed, in contrast to British West Africa, Africans in British East African colonies had to work much longer in order to pay the yearly direct taxes (Frankema and van Waijenburg 2012, 916–8). In contrast to Uganda, Kenyan workers had fewer options to earn their taxes through cash-crop cultivation in self-employment, and hence were more reliant on the migrant wage labor market.

From 1903 to 1923, the number of African migrant laborers gradually grew to around 120,000 men out of a total estimated workforce of 134,500, excluding women, children, and squatters or resident laborers (Stichter 1982, 30, 61), and a population of approximately 3.7 million people in 1920 (Frankema and Jerven 2014). Young African males were mostly engaged in long-distance migration, either to the coast or to the Central Highland area, typically involving journeys of 300 km and sometimes up to 800 km. However, if men lived within the plantation zones, or if the laborers were women or children, who also participated in wage labor, the sojourn to work was usually concluded within a day.

The Kenyan administration did impose in-labor taxation, similar to *luwalo*, which was justified as an indirect outgrowth of general cultural practices of most pre-colonial tribal units. This was known as communal labor. Communal labor in Kenya (see below) gave the administration greater flexibility in deploying forced labor without having to keep official records or inform the Colonial Office. Moreover, with the notable exception of Wanga Kingdom in Western Kenya, there were no centralized political kingdoms in pre-colonial Kenya that could have possibly provided the direct customary legal template for the administration to co-opt and manipulate forced labor during the colonial period. The more limited use of paid government-forced labor prevented the colonial administration from enervating the private sector labor market by siphoning off workers.

Wage statistics before the 1950s are not precise because it is difficult for scholars to calibrate colonial-era African wages since they varied according to the duties performed, the sex of the workers and their age, and the particular industry where they were employed. However, generally, wages for unskilled African farm labor were low up to the Second World War (Van Zwanenberg 1975, 36). In essence, the settlers had a state-supported monopsony and were able to depress wages despite rising productivity on the farms (Collier and Lal, 1986, 32). With the exception of the competition from some Indian settlers, the European settlers basically had a monopoly on buying labor in the market at low wages. The reality of persistently low wages is starkly reflected in the research by Ewout Frankema and Marlous van Waijenburg, who show that African wages in Kenya were at the subsistence level for much of the colonial period and were much lower in comparison to African wages in West Africa (Frankema and van Waijenburg 2012, 902, 910). In 1915, it took about 11 workdays to accrue enough wages to pay off the hut tax but by 1920 the duration of work required had increased to over a month (Fibaek and Green 2019, 83–4).

Due to the low wages and despite the institution of direct taxes, European settlers were not able to attract enough African workers without direct state intervention during this early period (Collier and Lal 1986, 34). Indeed, outright coercion was another factor in the transition toward a voluntary labor market. Although the Colonial Office officially disproved of the use of forced labor for private purposes in dispatches to the governor of Kenya in 1908 and 1912, in the early period administrative forced recruitment of African labor for Europeans was widespread. African traditional authorities, in their capacity as salaried administrators who could be removed from office by the district commissioners, were the officials who actually carried out the bulk of forced recruitment at the ground level. European administrative officers would also write circular letters to chiefs requesting that they "encourage," which was a euphemism for coercion, African males in their locals to go out and work.[7] In some cases, professional labor recruiters raided villages, with the connivance of chiefs, and held women hostage to get the men to agree to labor contracts (Zeleza 1992, 163).

In 1919, the governor of Kenya, Sir Edward Northey, publicly stated in an administrative circular that administration officers should "encourage" Africans to work in the private sector. This call elicited an outcry from various humanitarian organizations in England and various missionary bodies involved in Kenya and culminated in a debate in the House of Lords in 1920. Due to the reverberations of this "Northey Forced Labour Scandal," as it came to be known, in 1921 the Colonial Secretary, Winston Churchill, issued a dispatch that categorically prohibited forced labor for private purposes and seriously curtailed government-forced labor by requiring Colonial Office approval, which affected all of the colonies (Okia 2008). After Churchill's dispatch, outside of wartime, there would be no government recruitment of African labor for private business interests. In addition, in 1923 the administration also reduced the hut and poll tax rates from sh.16 back to sh.12 following intense African protests (Stichter 1982, 80).

From 1923 to 1938, there were habitual European demands for African labor. However, in most cases settler demands for more labor did not lead to coercion but instead were resolved in the market, resulting in an eventual rise in African wages (Mosley 1983, 128). As in Uganda, this reflected the impact of the market on wage labor engagement. Ultimately, coercive labor practices designed to augment the private labor market also incurred a cost due to the high rates of desertion and the resources used for surveillance (Freund 1988, 31).

Despite the official disavowal of coercion, the administration deployed a labor identification system in 1920 called the *kipande*, which was designed to control the mobility of wage laborers and suppress wages. The relegation of forced labor for private business interests also led to greater reliance upon women and children as casual laborers, mostly on the coffee estates, in the Central Highland region in the 1920s (Mosley 1983, 141). The women and child laborers engaged in seasonal work and normally lived close to the plantations (Presley 1986, 262). Due to the close proximity to their homesteads, the women were still engaged in subsistence production even though the peak demand for labor on the coffee plantations clashed with the agricultural cycle in the African reserve area (Presley 1986, 262). Moreover, women were the main laborers under communal forced labor in the rural areas. Unskilled coffee laborers were among the lowest paid workers in Kenya Colony, and, with the exception of child laborers, women were the lowest paid workers, compared to men (Collier and Lal 1986, 34). As evidence of the scale of female and child labor, in 1925 there were 5,477 women and 11,315 children engaged in officially recorded wage work, generally (Clayton and Savage 1974, 124).

The period from 1924 to 1930 was also a period of expansion of settler production and increased African employment (Collier and Lal 1986, 34). In the 1920s, more African men were drawn into the labor market seeking to fulfill various material needs, in addition to taxation. As mentioned earlier, it took approximately one month of work to pay the hut or poll tax, but men typically worked for six months (Pallaver 2018, 314). This indicates that they stayed in employment for longer periods to acquire more cash for material needs, like clothes, school fees, and bridewealth, and also to reinforce low household incomes in the rural areas. According to Claude Meillassoux, the bridewealth payment represented one of the ways that the capitalist sector, or wage economy, exploited the rural sector, since the value of the bridewealth payment was based upon ideological prestige (Meillassoux 1981, 114–5). In essence, migrant labor innervated but sustained the rural sector. During this time, periodic labor shortages persisted, but labor migration from Uganda and Tanganyika increased (Clayton and Savage 1974, 124). Africans from Uganda migrated to Kenya and worked primarily as cooks, domestic servants, and clerks, jobs that required more skills. Kenyans migrated to Uganda for work as well, often working in the transportation and urban construction sector (Elkan 1960, 86).

Although the administration conclusively abolished private sector-forced labor in 1921, it continued to use paid government-forced labor until 1925. African men aged 18 to 45 could be required to do paid work for up to 60 days per year on state infrastructure projects building heavy roads, dams, bridges, railways, as porters, or for emergencies. Due to the location of some work sites, workers were required to travel great distances from their home. For example, during the construction of the Uasin Gishu extension of the Uganda Railway, recruited laborers were required to travel approximately 40 miles from their home area to the worksite.[8] As in Uganda, compulsory government labor actually placed more pressure on African men to go into wage employment (Stichter 1982, 81). The wages were always

168 Opolot Okia

below the local market rate for unskilled labor. In addition, men who worked for Europeans for at least three months in the preceding year were exempt from coercion. Africans who failed to comply with coercion were subject to fines and imprisonment.

As mentioned earlier, Churchill's dispatch in 1921 only curtailed paid government-forced labor. In 1925 following another dispatch, the Colonial Office required the colonial administration to limit the number of men who could be forcibly requisitioned for paid labor to 4,000 men, per request.[9] Due to this stipulation, coupled with the requirement to seek formal approval, with a few exceptions, the administration stopped employing paid forced labor for infrastructure projects but continued to force African men to carry loads. Forced porterage did not require Colonial Office approval. As can be seen from Table 8.2, the administration coerced 14,901 men per year, primarily for porterage, during the eight years following the abolition of forced labor for private purposes. Forced porterage persisted due to the dearth of paved roads in the colony and the cheaper cost of using men to carry loads. In certain areas, district officers found it cheaper to use porterage, over a short distance, even if wheeled transport was available.[10]

Forced porterage was at the intersection of mobility and coercion. Men could be forced to carry up to 50-pound loads and walk up to 15 miles a day in support of administrative officers and chiefs on safari.[11] One hundred miles was the maximum distance men could be forced to carry loads away from their homes. The labor was exacting. Discussing forced porterage an administrative official admitted candidly that "by no stretch of the imagination can their engagement be regarded as voluntary, so unpopular and unremunerated is the work of porterage."[12] In Kenya, men resisted forced porterage through desertion.[13] From a high of 25,501 men, mainly forced to carry loads in 1923, the administration gradually weaned itself of forced porterage, as the numbers of men forced to carry loads gradually declined until abolition in 1951.

The termination of paid government-forced labor did not signal an end to coercive labor practices. The passage of the *Forced Labour Convention* in 1930, as mentioned earlier, permitted certain exemptions to the definition of forced labor, one of which was minor communal services or communal labor. After the passage of the Convention, Kenya relied more upon communal labor as the main form of coercion for general infrastructure development (Okia 2012; Okia 2019). Colonial chiefs and headmen had the power to coerce able-bodied men for so-called "communal" work for up to 24 days a year. Under communal labor, Africans in the village areas were required to work, without payment, on road maintenance and

TABLE 8.2 Paid forced labor in Kenya Colony

Year	Number of men
1922/23	10,547
1923/24	25,501
1924/25	19,323
1925/26	15,240
1926/27	13,228
1927/28	12,809
1928/29	12,897
1929/30	9,663

Source: Clayton and Savage (1974, 153, Appendix 1, Table 3).

construction, water courses, building minor irrigation schemes, light dams and bridges, and footpaths that were deemed to be part of the traditional obligations of an ethnic group and, hence, a communal responsibility. Although, legally, only males were required to perform communal labor, women and children often did the work as well. Communal labor reinforced the male wage labor market by sustaining a labor force of women and children in the rural sectors. Africans could gain exemptions through various means, including providing evidence of wage employment for Europeans. Moreover, the preservation of the rural sector buoyed the justification for low wages paid to migrant laborers. Unlike peasants in Uganda and French West Africa, Africans were not allowed to commute their communal labor requirement through a cash payment.

In contrast to the French territories, Africans did not engage in wholesale flight in order to avoid the work requirement. The most common form of resistance was desertion and, in some cases, work stoppage. Probably the most well-known account of African resistance to communal labor was the so-called "Revolt of the Women" in 1948 where approximately 2,500 women in Central Province refused to do communal labor and, instead, marched in protest to the district commissioner's headquarters (Mackenzie 1998, 164–5). The administration eventually broke up the demonstration and punished the women through fines. Communal labor persevered until independence in 1963, which reflects its fiscal importance in preserving rural areas.

3.3 The Gold Coast (Ghana)

The British established the Gold Coast Protectorate in 1874. After the defeat of the Asante Confederation in 1900–01, the administration expanded its political control and embarked on infrastructure development in the interior. The colonial administration of the Gold Coast promoted the growth of an export-oriented economy, which had its roots in the commercial transition of the 19th century (Austin; De Haas and Travieso, Chapters 2 and 11, this volume). The booming cocoa sector turned the Gold Coast into one of Britain's most lucrative African colonies (Amin 1973, 42; Hopkins 1973, 179). The colonial state also supported private European business interests, specifically in the gold mining sector, but, similar to the Uganda Protectorate, African commodity production buoyed the economy and was the engine that drove migrant labor (Grier 1992, 316). In comparison to East Africa, laborers often migrated over greater distances within West Africa. Regarding coercive labor practices, the administration did not need to forcibly recruit Africans to work on cocoa farms due to the lively African engagement in wage employment but also the pervasiveness of family and servile labor. However, the administration utilized paid and unpaid forced labor for public development projects that involved mobility and, indirectly, served as inducements into the wage labor market for men.

In contrast to Kenya and Uganda, the British administration initially (until 1937) did not develop a hut and poll tax system to push African men into wage labor (Buell 1928, 796). The implementation of poll taxes incurred higher administrative and social costs than taxing international trade, which precluded its earlier deployment (Frankema 2011, 141) Moreover, the Gold Coast accrued much of their revenue from customs duties, as was the case across British West Africa (Frankema and van Waijenburg 2012, 915). In addition, the administration implemented taxation through unpaid forced labor for infrastructure projects, mainly roads, under the aegis of Indirect Rule, or labor that was routed through the traditional political structures (Wiemers 2017a, 92; Kunkel 2018, 4–8).

Despite the absence of direct taxation, areas that produced commodities were also the areas that attracted migrant labor (Freund 1981, 75). Overall, the West African labor force developed a high degree of geographic mobility that was enhanced during the colonial era with the proliferation of transport networks and wage labor (Hopkins 1973, 224). Labor migrants traveled great distances to work in the cocoa fields in the Gold Coast from territories as far as Sierra Leone, Liberia, Nigeria, and French West Africa, specifically Upper Volta, which functioned as a labor reserve colony for all of French West Africa (De Haas and Travieso, Chapter 11, this volume). For instance, migrant laborers traveling from Nigeria to the Gold Coast would travel approximately 700 miles, which required a 35-day journey of 20 miles a day (Prothero 1957, 257).

French West Africans migrated to the Anglophone zones due to the attraction of higher wages and the desire to escape the harsh regime of forced labor in the French territories (Asiwaju 1976; Watson 2017, 158). The desire for consumer goods was a factor in the growth of wage labor. Under colonial rule, despite the abolition of slavery, the retention of various forms of servitude also helped to facilitate the transition to voluntary wage labor. Although the administration did not forcibly recruit workers for cocoa farms, chiefs, through their traditional powers, did use local forced labor from their own communities on cocoa farms in the early period of colonial rule (Austin 2005, 239–40). Moreover, the administration forcibly recruited laborers for railways and for private European gold mines (Akurang-Parry 2000, 3–4). In 1920, European gold mines received approximately one-third of the government-recruited labor force (Thomas 1973, 97). The administration also instituted anti-desertion laws to ensure that Africans remained in wage employment (Buell 1928, 827). Outside of the mining sector, European coastal exporting companies also used children and women, who held servile status, as porters for cocoa, palm oil, and palm kernels (Akurang-Parry 2001, 33–4).

Although the British officially abolished slavery in 1874, this proclamation only affected the legal status of slavery and did not apply to concubines (Dumett and Johnson 1988, 79–80). This legal casuistry meant that slave owners could not use the court system or legal machinery to retain people as slaves. However, if slaves were unaware of their new rights, or, for various practical and social reasons, chose to remain on, or near, the owner's homestead, then their practical condition of servitude did not really change. Though slavery was technically, in terms of the legal status, illegal after 1874 and the institutions of slavery and pawning were prohibited after 1908 in Asante, various forms of female and child servitude persisted in the Gold Coast until the 1930s (Austin 2005, 206–7; Akurang-Parry 2010, 33–5). The colonial administration was not keen to aggressively affect the wholesale release of slaves due to fears that abolition would undermine the economy.

Prior to the extension of paved roads and railways in the 1920s, most of the harvested cocoa beans were transported to the coast via human porters (Grier 1992, 320). African cocoa farmers used pawns and female child forced laborers as porters transporting goods from interior regions, like Akuapem close to the Togo border, to coastal cities, like Accra (Akurang-Parry 2001, 32–4). Females were the traditional source of labor in agriculture and were the majority of slaves. The use of female children as porters was consistent with the customary exploitation of labor. The child laborers ranged in age from 9 to 14 years old and would have been required to carry loads ranging from 10 to 40 pounds while walking up to 10 miles per day (Akurang-Parry 2001, 39). As with other coerced laborers, girls forced to carry loads also resisted through flight, or, in some cases, villages prevented recruitment of girls for porterage (Akurang-Parry 2001, 34). Similar to Kenya Colony, after 1921 the colonial administration began to eliminate some aspects of forced labor associated with children and forced labor for private purposes in general (Akurang-Parry 2001, 42). For example, employing children under the age of 14 was prohibited under the *Master and Servants Ordinance* (Gold Coast 1939, 59).

The Gold Coast experienced a cocoa boom after the First World War, supplying about half of the world's production in the 1920s (Gold Coast 1920, 35). Austin argues that the rise in cocoa farming from 1890 to the 1920s led to more wage labor for men and higher incomes as wealthy farmers were inclined to hire labor (Austin 2005, 243). The banning of slave trading drove up the cost of slaves since they were now harder to acquire. This caused a gradual decline of coercive labor practices like male slavery by the 1930s. The expansion of paved roads also contributed to a decline in the use of forced labor (Thomas 1973, 103). This gradual decline in the prevalence of servitude did not necessarily impact female slavery, which persisted into the 1940s (Austin 2005, 247; Austin 2007, 114–5). In fact, Akurang-Parry contends that during the 1930s in the Gold Coast female servitude became more institutionalized (Akurang-Parry 2010, 31). With rising class differentiation, the voluntary wage labor market expanded for men. However, these male wage earners increasingly employed domestic female workers as house servants whose status as free was often questionable, specifically in the case of pawns (McSheffrey 1983, 362). In addition, despite the expansion of wage labor, cocoa farming in the plantation zones often involved family, particularly up to 1916, servile, and forced labor (Austin 2005, 239–40; Austin 2009, 21).

The expansion of road, railway, and port construction in the southern portion of the Gold Coast in the early 20th century led to wide-scale use of government-forced labor (Wiemers 2017a, 89–90). With the expansion of cocoa production, the administration gradually built a network of roads that linked the cocoa-producing areas and the coast. From 1919 to 1924 under a ten-year development plan designed to raise investment in infrastructure, the administration made a concerted effort to recruit workers for railways and porterage (Thomas 1973, 90). However, reflecting the wider changes in colonial policy after 1921, the administration began to shift toward the use of more voluntary wage labor on public works projects.[14] After the passage of the *Forced Labour Convention*, the administration continued this process by increasing the use of paid wage labor for road maintenance, but only for main roads.[15]

Although the administration gradually shifted toward paid labor for main roads, the chiefs continued to use unpaid communal forced labor for the construction of "political" or, so-called, "native" roads, because these were justified as customary duties that fell under the purview of chiefs (Phillips 1989, 40). These were the smaller untarmacked roads, or even footpaths, that connected the villages to the wider infrastructural grid. Under the aforementioned ten-year development plan of Governor Frederick Guggisberg, the expansion of road networks also included the heavy use of unpaid communal labor for maintenance on untarmacked roads (Wiemers 2017a, 96).

African men were required to perform up to 24 days per year of unpaid road maintenance work or other types of public works (Wiemers 2017b, 244). Male workers were organized into groups or "companies" (non-kin associations) and performed the work on specific days during the course of the year. The justification was that this labor requirement was analogous to traditional Akan forms of collective labor. Chiefs also forced women to do communal labor. Certain tasks, like weeding or clearing and sweeping roads, were actually considered women's work (Ayesu, Gbormittah and Adum-Kyeremeh 2016, 8). According to Thomas, in 1919 Governor Guggisburg, through a conference held to organize labor recruitment for various public works and railways, called for the use of communal labor for railway construction (Thomas 1973, 94–5).

As with *prestations* in French West Africa, workers were only supposed to be deployed locally within the vicinity of their villages. However, in sparsely populated districts roadwork involved considerable travel to the work sites (Wiemers 2017a, 104). In addition, prior to the passage of the *Forced Labour Convention*, chiefs used communal labor for roadwork extending between villages, which lengthened the travel of laborers beyond the 5-mile "traditional" radius.

Africans who failed to perform communal labor when ordered were subject to fines and imprisonment. Africans resisted the forced recruitment through desertion or failure to show up for work (Akurang-Parry 2000, 9). Flight was a common method of resisting some of the excesses of communal labor. During the 1920s in certain areas in the Northern Territories the demands for communal labor became oppressive enough for people to flee in such large numbers as to cause food insecurity (Wiemers 2017a, 98). Flight, in some cases, became more permanent as Africans fled into neighboring districts that utilized communal labor with less frequency and attempted to establish farming rights in the new locale (Wiemers 2017a, 99). Although colonial officials tried to control this internal flight, they also confronted them with the limits of their power, particularly in areas that were more sparsely populated (Wiemers 2017a, 101).

Sarah Kunkel argues that the Gold Coast administration strategically shifted to using more communal labor for road maintenance after the passage of the Convention (Kunkel 2018, 462–5). In contrast to Uganda, where the administration eventually abolished *luwalo* "traditional" labor, the passage of the *Forced Labour Convention* did not lead to the abolition of political labor in the British territories, even though it was a coercive labor practice, since it was deemed an exemption to forced labor, as a minor communal service (Freund 1981, 137). As mentioned earlier, this was also the case in Kenya. The only significant change in the use of communal labor following the *Forced Labour Convention* related to the mobility of workers. After the Convention, communal labor was restricted to work on roads within a village area.

4 Conclusion

This chapter has sought to fill a gap in the historiography of African colonial labor migration studies through the prism of labor coercion. Forced labor was intertwined with the shifting patterns of labor migration within colonies and in the wider regional context between the different colonial zones. Coercive labor practices were drivers of migrant labor. Mobility defined the contours of both migrant labor and the different historical phases of labor coercion in colonial Africa. In response to the imposition of coercion, Africans responded through flight or migration.

During the colonial period in British West and East Africa, the labor markets were part of an interconnected system of forced labor and labor migration. Forced labor for private business interests was one of the early drivers of labor migration, but the precise interaction varied across region and time period. By the early 1920s, the British colonial administration stopped relying upon forced labor for private purposes. At this point, market

Forced Labor and Migration **173**

transformations encouraged the rise in voluntary wage labor migration, but there was also more reliance upon female and child labor, plus the input of migrant labor from neighboring colonies. Moreover, colonial administrations continued to use paid government-forced labor, which was also a driver of labor migration and involved extensive geographic mobility of workers.

By the 1930s, following the passage of the *Forced Labour Convention*, paid government-forced labor was seriously curtailed. However, colonial administrations rerouted coercive labor practices through "traditional" labor, which was one the exemptions to the definition of forced labor contained in the Convention. Communal labor flourished after the passage of the *Forced Labour Convention* and served as an indirect driver of migration through the preservation of the rural sector. Ultimately, changes in the international conception of acceptable labor practices bounded, ideologically, the colonial system of forced labor and migration in Africa.

Notes

1 Andrea L. Kimbugwe to Provincial Commissioner Cooper, 15 July 1918, Papers of Sir Robert Thorne Coryndon, Box 14, Rhodes House Library, Oxford.
2 Kabaka Daudi Chwa to Provincial Commissioner Cooper, 15 July 1918, Papers of Sir Robert Thorne Coryndon, Box 14, Bodleian Library, Oxford.
3 Uganda Protectorate: Report on the Convention Concerning Forced or Compulsory Labour for Period June 3rd to September 30th 1939, Eighth Annual Report, Forced Labour Convention 1930 (N. 29): Returns from British African Colonies, 1932–63, D 614/3002/25, ILO Archives, Geneva, Switzerland.
4 Provincial Commissioner, Buganda, B. Ashtain-Waverly to Chief Secretary, 16 June 1936, Box 20, Luwalo Abolition (30 May 1936–10 September 1937) C22861 (IV), Secretariat: C Series, UNA, Entebbe.
5 Conversely, in her research on *prestations*, a form of unpaid forced labor that was used in French West Africa, Marlous van Waijenburg found that, although commutation of *prestations* was expanded for Africans during the 1920s and 1930s, very few were able to take advantage of it (Van Waijenburg 2018, 51).
6 For transitions toward labor stabilization elsewhere in colonial Africa see Juif; Frederick and Van Nederveen Meerkerk (Chapters 10 and 12, this volume).
7 "Letter to the Editor by a White Highland Farmer," *East African Standard,* 27 November 1930, AG/25/6, KNA, Nairobi.
8 Minute by W. Bottomley, 17 March 1925, CO 533/330. This affected Luyia residing in Kerio Province.
9 This dispatch became Parliamentary Command Paper 2464 of July 1925.
10 District Commissioner, W. Marchant to Provincial Commissioner, Nyanza Province, 1 October 1933, District Commissioner [hereafter DC]/Kisumu [hereafter KSM]/1/17/20, KNA Nairobi.
11 V. Fisher, Principal Labour Inspector to All Senior Commissioners, 1 June 1928, AG/25/4, KNA, Nairobi.
12 R. Ryland, Acting Provincial Commissioner Rift Valley Province, 10 January 1949, PC/NKU/3/8/2, KNA, Nairobi.
13 C. Wood, Provincial Commissioner, Nyanza Province to P. Larkin, District Commissioner, 13 January 1928, PC/NZA/3/32/1, KNA, Nairobi.
14 Forced Labour Convention 1930 (N. 29): Returns from British Colonies, Reports on the Convention Concerning Forced or Compulsory Labour, Gold Coast and Gambia, 1936–37, D 614/3002/25, ILO, Geneva, Switzerland.
15 Forced Labour Convention 1930 (N. 29): Returns from British Colonies, Reports on the Convention Concerning Forced or Compulsory Labour, Gold Coast and Gambia, 1936–37, D 614/3002/25, ILO, Geneva, Switzerland. Overall, by the 1940s, the Gold Coast administration used primarily voluntary labor for public works projects.

References

Akurang-Parry, Kwabena. 2000. "Colonial Forced Labor Policies for Road-Building in Southern Ghana and International Anti-Forced Labor Pressures, 1900–1940." *African Economic History* 28: 1–25.

———. 2001. "'The Loads are Heavier than Usual': Forced Labor by Women and Children in the Central Province, Gold Coast (Colonial Ghana), CA. 1900–1940." *African Economic History* 30: 31–51.

———. 2010. "Transformations in the Feminization of Unfree Domestic Labor: A Study of Abaawa or Prepubescent Female Servitude in Modern Ghana." *International Labor and Working Class History* 79(1): 28–47.

Allina, Eric. 2012. *Slavery by Another Name: Life Under Company Rule in Colonial Mozambique.* Charlottesville: University of Virginia Press.

Amin, Samir. 1972. "Underdevelopment and Dependence in Black Africa: Origins and Contemporary Forms." *Journal of Modern African Studies* 10(40): 503–24.

———. 1973. *Neo-Colonialism in West Africa.* Harmondsworth, Middlesex: Penguin Books.

———. 1974. "Introduction." In *Modern Migrations in Western Africa*, edited by Samir Amin, 3–126. London: Oxford University Press.

Arrighi, Giovanni. 1973. "Labor Supplies in Historical Perspective: A Study of Proletarianization of the African Peasantry in Rhodesia." In *Essays on the Political Economy of Africa*, edited by Giovanni Arrighi and John Saul, 180–236. New York: Monthly Review Press.

Asiwaju, Anthony I. 1976. "Migrations as Revolt: The Example of the Ivory Coast and the Upper Volta before 1945." *Journal of African History* 17(4): 577–94.

Austin, Gareth. 2005. *Labour, Land and Capital in Ghana: From Slavery to Free Labour in Asante, 1807–1956.* Rochest, NY: University of Rochester Press.

———. 2007. "Labour and Land in Ghana, 1874–1939: A Shifting Ratio and An Institutional Revolution." *Australian Economic History* 47(1): 95–120.

———. 2009. "Cash Crops and Freedom: Export Agriculture and the Decline of Slavery in Colonial West Africa." *International Review of Social History* 54(1): 1–37.

Ayesu, Ebenezer, Francis Gbormittah, and Kwame Adum-Kyeremeh. 2016. "British Colonialism and Women's Welfare in the Gold Coast Colony." *Africa Today* 63(2): 3–30.

Ball, Jeremy. 2015. *Angola's Colossal Lie: Forced Labor on a Sugar Plantation, 1913–1977.* Leiden; Boston: Brill.

Brass, Tom. 1997. "Some Observations on Unfree Labour, Capitalist Restructuring and Deproletarianization." In *Free and Unfree Labour: The Debate Continues*, edited by Tom Brass and Marcel Van Der Linden, 37–76. New York: Peter Lang.

Brett, E.A. 1973. *Colonialism and Underdevelopment in East Africa: The Politics of Economic Change, 1919–1939.* London: Heinemann.

Buell, Raymond. 1928. *The Native Problem in Africa, V1.* New York: The Macmillan Company.

Clayton, Anthony, and Donald Savage. 1974. *Government and Labour in Kenya, 1895–1963.* London: Frank Cass.

Cleaveland, Todd. 2015. *Diamonds in the Rough: Corporate Paternalism and African Professionalism on the Mines of Colonial Angola, 1917–1975.* Athens: Ohio University Press.

Collier, Paul, and Deepak Lal. 1986. *Labour and Poverty in Kenya, 1900–1980.* Oxford: Clarendon Press.

Colony and Protectorate of Kenya. 1929. *Colonial Reports-Annual: Report for 1927.* London: His Majesty's Stationery Office.

Cooper, Frederick. 2000. "Conditions Analogous to Slavery: Imperialism and Free Labor Ideology in Africa." In *Beyond Slavery: Explorations of Race, Labor, and Citizenship in Postemancipation Societies*, edited by Frederick Cooper, Thomas Holt and Rebecca Scott, 107–49. Chapel Hill: University of North Carolina Press.

Davis, David. 1984. *Slavery and Human Progress.* Ithaca, NY: Cornell University Press.

De Haas, Michiel. 2017. "Measuring Welfare in Colonial Africa: Did Uganda's Smallholders Thrive?." *Economic History Review* 70(2): 379–406.

———. 2019. "Moving Beyond Colonial Control? Economic Forces and Shifting Migration from Ruanda-Urundi to Buganda, 1920–60." *Journal of African History* 60(3): 379–406.

Duffy, James. 1967. *A Question of Slavery: Labour Policies in Portuguese Africa and British and British Protest, 1850–1920*. Oxford: Oxford University Press.

Elkan, Walter. 1960. *Migrants and Proletarians: Urban Labour in the Economic Development of Uganda*. London: Oxford University Press.

Fall, Babacar and Richard Roberts. 2019. "Forced Labour." In *General Labour History of Africa*, edited by Stefano Bellucci and Andreas Eckert, 77–118. Woodbridge: James Currey.

Fibaek, Maria, and Erik Green. 2019. "Labour Control and the Establishment of Profitable Settler Agriculture in Colonial Kenya, c. 1920–45." *Economic History of Developing Regions* 34(1): 72–110.

Frankema, Ewout. 2011. "Colonial Taxation and Government Spending in British Africa, 1880–1940: Maximizing Revenue or Minimizing Effort?" *Explorations in Economic History* 48(1): 136–49.

Frankema, Ewout, and Marlous van Waijenburg, 2012. "Structural Impediments to African Growth? New Evidence from Real Wages in British Africa, 1880–1965." *Journal of Economic History* 72(4): 895–926.

Frankema, Ewout, and Morten Jerven. 2014. "Writing History Backwards or Sideways: Towards a Consensus on African Population, 1850–2010." *Economic History Review* 67(4): 907–31.

Gold Coast. 1920. *Colonial Reports-Annual: Report for 1919*. London: His Majesty's Stationary Office

———. 1930. *Colonial Reports-Annual: Report for 1929–30*. London: His Majesty's Stationary Office.

———. 1939. *Colonial Reports-Annual: Report for 1937–38*. London: His Majesty's Stationary Office, 1939.

Grant, Kevin. 2005. *A Civilised Savagery: Britain and the New Slaveries in Africa, 1884–1926*. New York: Routledge.

Grier, Beverly. 1992. "Pawns, Porters, and Petty Traders: Women in the Transition to Cash Crop Agriculture in Colonial Ghana." *Signs: Journal of Women in Culture and Society* 17(2): 304–28.

Guthrie, Zachary K. 2018. *Bound for Work: Labor, Mobility, and Colonial Rule in Central Mozambique, 1940–1965*. Charlottesville: University of Virginia Press.

Hansen, Holger. 1984. *Mission, Church and State in a Colonial Setting: Uganda, 1890–1925*. London: Heinemann.

———. 1993. "Forced Labour in a Missionary Context" A Study of *Kasanvu* in Early Twentieth-Century Uganda." In *Wages of Slavery: From Chattel Slavery to Wage Labour in Africa, The Caribbean and England*, edited by M. Twaddle. London and Portland: Frank Cass.

Hanson, Holly. 2003. *Landed Obligation: The Practice of Power in Buganda*. Portsmouth: Heinemann.

Higgs, Catherine. 2012. *Chocolate Islands: Cocoa, Slavery, and Colonial Africa*. Athens: Ohio University Press.

Hochschild, Adam. 1999. *King Leopold's Ghost: A Story of Greed, Terror, and Heroism in Colonial Africa*. New York: Mariner Books.

Hopkins, Antony. 1973. *An Economic History of West Africa*. New York: Columbia University Press.

Isaacman, Allen. 1996. *Cotton Is the Mother of Poverty. Peasants, Work, and Rural Struggle in Colonial Mozambique, 1938–1961*. Portsmouth: Heinemann.

Kaberuka, Will. 1990. *The Political Economy of Uganda, 1890–1979: A Case Study of Colonialism and Underdevelopment*. New York: Vantage Press.

Kenya, Colony and Protectorate of. 1929. Report for 1927. London: His Majesty's Stationary Office.

Kitching, Gavin. 1980. *Class and Economic Change in Kenya: The Making of an African Petite-Bourgeoisie*. New Haven, CT: Yale University Press.

Kunkel, Sarah. 2018. "Forced Labour, Roads, and Chiefs: The Implementation of the ILO Forced Labour Convention in the Gold Coast." *International Review of Social History* 63(3): 449–76.

Mackenzie, A. Fiona D. 1998. *Land, Ecology and Resistance in Kenya, 1880–1952*. Edinburgh: Edinburgh University Press for the International African Institute,

Mamdani, Mahmood. 1976. *Politics and Class Formation in Uganda*. New York: Monthly Review Press.

Manchuelle, François. 1997. *Willing Migrants: Soninke Labor Diasporas, 1848–1960*. Athens: Ohio University Press.

Maul, Daniel. 2007. "The International Labour Organization and the Struggle against Forced Labour from 1919 to the Present." *Labour History* 48(4): 477–500.

———. 2012. *Human Rights, Development and Decolonization: The International Labour Organization, 1940–1970*. New York: Palgrave Macmillan, 2012.

Maxon, Robert. 1992. "The Establishment of the Colonial Economy." In *An Economic History of Kenya*, edited by William Ochieng and Robert Maxon, 63–74. Nairobi: East African Educational Publishers.

McSheffrey, Gerald. 1983. "Slavery, Indentured Servitude, Legitimate Trade and the Impact of Abolition in the Gold Coast, 1874–1901: A Reappraisal." *Journal of African History* 24(3): 349–68.

Miers, Susan. 1998. "Slavery and The Slave Trade as International Issues, 1890–1939." In *Slavery and Colonial Rule in Africa*, edited by Susan Miers and Martin Klein, 16–37. London: Routledge.

——— and Richard Roberts, eds. 1988. *The End of Slavery in Africa*. Madison, WI: University of Wisconsin Press.

Miracle, Marvin P., and Bruce Fetter. 1970. "Backward-Sloping Labor-Supply Functions and African Economic Behavior." *Economic Development and Cultural Change* 18(2): 240–51.

Mitchell, J. Clyde. 1989. "Causes of Labor Migration." In *Forced Labour & Migration: Patterns of Movement within Africa*, edited by Adebe Zegeye and Shubi Ishemo, 28–56 London: Hans Zell.

Meillassoux, Claude. 1981. *Maidens, Meal and Money: Capitalism and the Domestic Community*. Cambridge: Cambridge University Press.

Mosley, Paul. 1983. *The Settler Economies: Studies in the Economic History of Kenya and Southern Rhodesia, 1900–1963*. Cambridge: Cambridge University Press.

Mungeam, G. 1966. *British Rule in Kenya, 1895–1912*. Oxford: Clarendon Press.

Mwangi, Wambui. 2001. "Of Coins and Conquest: The East African Currency Board, the Rupee Crisis, and the Problem of Colonialism in the East Africa Protectorate." *Comparative Studies in Society and History* 43(4): 763–87.

Newbury, Gertrude, and Colin Newbury. 1976. "Labor Charters and Labor Markets: The ILO and Africa in the Interwar Period." *Journal of African Studies* 3(3): 311–27.

Nzula, A.T., Potekhin, I. I., and A. Z. Zusmanovich. 1979. *Forced Labor in Colonial Africa*. London: Zed Press.

Penvenne, Jeanne. 1994. *African Workers and Colonial Racism: Mozambican Strategies and Struggles in Lourenco Marques, 1877–1962*. Portsmouth: Heinemann.

Presley, Cora Ann. 1986. "Labor, Unrest among Kikuyu Women in Colonial Kenya." In *Women and Class in Africa*, edited by Claire Robertson and Iris Berger, 255–73. New York: Africana Publishing Company.

Okia, Opolot. 2012. *Communal Labor in Colonial Kenya: The Legitimization of Coercion*. New York: Palgrave-Macmillan.

———. 2008. "The Northey Forced Labor Crisis, 1920-1921: A Symptomatic Reading." *The International Journal of African Historical Studies* 41(2): 263–293.

———. 2017. "Virtual Abolition: The Economic Lattice of *Luwalo* Forced Labor in the Uganda Protectorate." *African Economic History* 45(2): 54–84.

———. 2019. *Labor in Colonial Kenya after the Forced Labor Convention, 1030–1963*. New York: Palgrave-Macmillan.

Pallaver, Karin. 2018. "Paying Cents, Paying Rupees in Colonial Currencies, Labour Relations, and the Payment of Wages in Early Colonial Kenya." In *Institutional Change and Shifts in Global Labour Relations*, edited by Karin Hofmeester and Pim de Zwart, 295–326. Amsterdam: Amsterdam University Press.

Phillips, Anne 1989. *The Enigma of Colonialism: British Policy in West Africa*. London: James Curry.

Powesland, Philip. 1957. *Economic Policy and Labour*. Kampala: East African Institute of Social Research.

Prothero, R. Mansell. 1957. "Migratory Labour from North-Western Nigeria." *Africa* 27(3): 251–61.

Rubert, Steven. 1998. *A Most Promising Weed: A History of Tobacco Farming and Labor in Colonial Zimbabwe, 1890–1945*. Athens: Center for International Studies Ohio University.

Rutabajuka, Simon. 1996. "Migrant Labour in Masaka District, 1900–62: The Case of Coffee Shamba Labourers." In *Uganda Studies in Labour*, edited by Mahmood Mamdani, 11–52. Dakar: CODESRIA.

Sorrensen, Maurice. 1968. *Origins of European Settlement in Kenya*. Nairobi: Oxford University Press.

Stichter, Sharon. 1982. *Migrant Labour in Kenya: Capitalism and African Response, 1895–1975*. Essex: Longman, 1982.

Sundiata, Ibrahim. 1996. *From Slaving to Neoslavery: The Bight of Biafra and Fernando Po in The Era of Abolition, 1827–1930*. University of Wisconsin Press, 1996.

———. 2003. *Brothers and Strangers: Black Zion, Black Slavery, 1914–1940*. Durham, NC: Duke University Press.

Thomas, Roger. 1973. "Forced Labour in British West Africa: The Case of the Northern Territories of the Gold Coast 1906–1927." *Journal of African History* 14(1): 79–103.

Van Onselen, Charles. 1976. *Chibaro: African Mine Labour in Southern Rhodesia, 1900–1933*. London: Pluto Press.

Van Zwanenberg, R.M.A., with Anne King. 1975. *An Economic History of Kenya and Uganda, 1800–1970*. London: Macmillan Press.

Viljoen, Frans. 2009. "International Human Rights Law: A Short History." *UN Chronicle* 1(2): 8–13.

Vincent, Joan. 1982. *Teso in Transformation: The Political Economy of Peasant and Class in Eastern Africa*. Berkeley: University of California Press.

Watson, J. 2017, "Protecting Empire from Without: Francophone African Migrant Workers, British West Africa and French Efforts to Maintain Power in Africa." in *Britain, France and Decolonization of Africa: Future Imperfect*, edited by Chris Jeppesen and Andrew Smith, 156–71. London: UCL Press.

Wiemers, Alice. 2017a. "'It Is All He Can Do to Cope with the Roads in His Own District': Labor, Community and Development in Northern Ghana, 1919–1936." *International Labor and Working Class History* 92(Fall): 89–113.

———. 2017b. "'When the Chief Takes an Interest': Development and the Reinvention of 'Communal' Labor in Northern Ghana." *Journal of African History* 38(2): 239–7.

Wilson, Francis. 1972. *Labour in the South African Gold Mines, 1911–1969*. Cambridge: Cambridge University Press.

Zegeye, A., and S. Ishemo, eds. 1989. *Forced Labour and Migration: Patterns of Movement within Africa*. London; New York: Hans Zell Publishers.

Zeleza, Paul. 1992. "The Colonial Labour System." In *An Economic History of Kenya*, edited by William Ochieng and Robert Maxon, 347–70. Nairobi: East African Educational Publishing.

9

GOVERNING FREE AND UNFREE LABOR MIGRATION IN PORTUGUESE AFRICA, 19TH–20TH CENTURY

Filipa Ribeiro da Silva and Kleoniki Alexopoulou

1 Introduction

On 4 January 1953, Maria Joana Gomes, *serviçal* in São Tomé stated: "Look Brother we are not at all, as the paper said, and you and our brothers should never think of coming to this land, because you have no idea how much I have cried."[1] Maria's emotional words, addressed to her brother Marcelino, resident in the island of Santo Antão, Cabo Verde, are a clear testimony to the ordeals that African migrant workers went through in major parts of Portuguese Africa. However, most of the scholarship on migration within the Portuguese empire during the 19th and 20th centuries has focused on the movement of Europeans from the metropole to the colonies, the circulation of white workers serving the colonial administration in different parts of the empire, or of free skilled workers and students (Castelo 2007).

The migration history of Africans within the Portuguese empire, and in particular between different Portuguese African colonies (including Cabo Verde, Guinea-Bissau, São Tomé and Príncipe, Angola, and Mozambique), has not been widely researched, despite the fact that its long-term legacies have been noted in recent studies by sociologists, anthropologists, and ethnographers (Berthet 2011, 2016; Bussotti and Martins 2019). Most of the historical literature on migration of Africans has focused on movements out of the so-called "labor reservoirs" (Amin 1972) of Angola and Mozambique into the mining areas of Southern Africa, in the context of labor agreements signed with other European colonial powers and the semi-autonomous countries of South Africa and Southern Rhodesia (Harries 1981, 2014; First 1977). These outward migrations have been largely explained by harsher working conditions in Portuguese Africa, the extensive use of violence by employers and the state, and lower wages, among other factors. These partly involuntary migrations were promoted and controlled by the Portuguese colonial authorities.

How did the colonial state govern the allocation of African labor in the different colonies that made up the Portuguese empire as a whole? And why did the Portuguese colonial state promote the migration of workers out of its territories, while these states were confronted

DOI: 10.4324/9781003225027-13

with endemic local labor shortages (Penvenne 1984; Ishemo 1989, 1995; Allina 2012; Alexopoulou and Juif 2017)? So far, these questions have been only partially addressed by a handful of case studies of specific intra-African labor flows, such as the migration of coerced and skilled workers from various parts of the empire to the cacao- and coffee-producing centers in São Tomé and Príncipe. Indeed, these studies signal the existence of a complex system of labor recruitment and migration within Portuguese Africa, but with a focus on São Tomé and Southern Africa (Harries 1981, 2014; Nascimento 1998, 2001, 2002a, 2002b, 2004a, 2004b, 2012; Tornimbeni 2005; Kagan-Guthrie 2011; Cahen 2015; Bussotti and Martins 2019). Two complementary questions have also largely remained unaddressed: how was this system structured, organized, and governed and why did the Portuguese colonial state develop such complex recruitment and transportation systems? Finally, there is the observation that, compared to other African colonies, Portuguese Africa attracted very few workers from other parts of the continent, and the question why this was so awaits a more comprehensive answer as well.

This chapter aims to fill part of these gaps by offering an overview of free and coerced labor migration of Africans *within* Portuguese Africa as well as to neighboring colonies and countries from the late 19th till the late 20th century. We focus on four main aspects. First, we study the overall labor migration system in Portuguese Africa, its different flows and regional sub-systems, paying special attention to the following: (i) rural-rural and rural-urban migration within the colonies; (ii) migration between colonies within Portuguese Africa, especially to plantations and mines; and (iii) migration from Portuguese colonies to other parts of Central and Southern Africa. Second, we analyze the legal and administrative frameworks regulating these movements. Third, we look into the various forms of recruitment used by the colonial authorities, private concessionary companies,[2] and private recruitment agencies that were allowed to operate across Portuguese Africa, such as the *Witwatersrand Native Labour Association* (WNLA). Finally, we explore the main structural drivers (environment, economy, and violence) of the different migrant flows, and discuss how these drivers played out differently for free and unfree and for skilled and unskilled migrant workers.

By looking into the contractual arrangements underpinning transport, payment, and repatriation, we also seek to shed more light on the different degrees of agency and freedom enjoyed by various groups of migrant workers. This is of special importance as in many studies free, forced, and compelled labor migration often appear under the same, uniform banner of coerced migration. Forms of recruitment also tend to be labeled indiscriminately as "coercive," with little distinction being made between workers who have been recruited by an agency and have volunteered to work in a specific region and others who have been coerced to sell their labor, or simply been arrested by the colonial authorities for petty crimes and minor offenses and sentenced to exile and forced labor (punitive labor).

For this study we rely on historical sources on (i) Portuguese legislation on colonial labor and labor migration and (ii) correspondence between colonial authorities in the metropole and the colonies. These materials are complemented by information from (iii) official state bulletins, (iv) population censuses, and (v) statistical yearbooks. Most of these written sources are available in Portuguese and other European archives and libraries, but we have also used the collections of the National Historical Archives of former Portuguese-African countries, as well as archival collections deposited in Southern Africa.

2 Patterns of migration in Portuguese Africa

As Ishemo (1995, 162) states, "throughout the history of Portuguese colonialism, forced labor constituted a form of labor migration and, invariably, labor migration was in effect an attempt to escape from forced labor." Coerced migration within Portuguese Africa can be traced back to the late 15th century, when Portuguese ventures to the Senegambia and Guinea-Bissau started to capture, enslave, or purchase Africans for transportation to the Atlantic Islands of Madeira, the Azores, and Cabo Verde. In these islands enslaved Africans were used to clear the land and prepare the fields for sugarcane cultivation and various other profitable export crops (Carreira 1983; Vieira 1991; Green 2011; Machado 2014). Another flow connected the Slave Coast (also called Bight of Benin) and the West Central African coast (present-day Congo and Angola) to the islands of São Tomé and Príncipe. As in Madeira and Cabo Verde, African slaves were use in cane production and for the construction of basic infrastructures to facilitate sugar exports (Vogt 1973). With the development of higher-quality sugar factories in the Americas, the movement of enslaved Africans in Portuguese Africa declined in the early 17th century and shifted to increasing trans-Atlantic trades (Burnard 2012).

Migration of Africans within and between Portuguese colonies as well as to neighboring countries would start to grow again in the 19th century. This shift was directly related to the loss of Brazil (1821), and the turn in Portuguese economic interests toward Africa, through renewed promotion of commercial agriculture in Angola, Mozambique, Cabo Verde, and São Tomé. Another factor contributing to this shift was the ending of the slave trade in the Southern Atlantic in the 1850s and the subsequent phase-out of slavery in Portuguese Africa after official abolition in 1858 (Nascimento 2004; Allina 2012).[3] Forced recruitment and long-distance migration thus were long-lasting, common phenomena in Portuguese Africa. Workers recruited in the interior of Guinea-Bissau could be found working on commercial farms near the larger urban centers such as Farim or Bissau (INEP, Secretaria dos Negócios Indígenas, C1.6/01.010). Cabo Verdeans recruited in the poorest and least economically developed islands were found at the plantations of São Tomé and Príncipe. Angolans and Mozambicans migrated in large numbers to non-Portuguese colonies, and especially the mining areas of South Africa, Zimbabwe, and the Congo (see also Juif, Chapter 10, this volume).

Labor migration *within* the colonies assumed different forms. The first type of migration was from rural villages to new or expanding colonial cities (see Table 9.1). Most migrant workers, including both voluntary and coerced migrants, ended up in domestic services, in the construction of transport infrastructure or the logistics associated with colonial trades. The census of Lourenço Marques (present-day Maputo) in Mozambique, carried out in 1912, recorded 3,225 *serviçais* (i.e., servants, more often than not under forced labor contracts).[4] Migrants also moved from rural areas to the outskirts of colonial cities to work on farms and plantations oriented toward export markets (see Table 9.1). These migrations in most cases had a seasonal character dictated by agricultural seasons, with workers returning to their villages at the end of the harvest. The 1912 Census of the outskirts of Lourenço Marques counted 7,928 *serviçais* working and living in the outskirts of the city.[5] This type of migration was especially common in Mozambique, Angola, and Guinea-Bissau, but Table 9.2 (further below) shows that in all Portuguese colonies such forms of rural-urban migration occurred.

Governing Free and Unfree Labor Migration

TABLE 9.1 Migration within the colonies

Colony	Types of migration
Guinea-Bissau	• From rural areas to the cities • Areas of traditional agriculture to areas of commercial agriculture
Cabo Verde	• From most arid islands to those best agriculturally and economically developed, with the islands of Santiago and São Vicente being the main destinations • From rural areas to main cities • Migration to rural areas to promote internal colonization
Angola	• From rural areas to the cities • From areas of traditional agriculture to areas of commercial agriculture • From rural areas to the mines (in Angola) – diamonds
Mozambique	• From rural areas to the cities (mainly Beira and Lourenço Marques, present-day Maputo) • From areas of traditional agriculture to plantation areas

Source: Authors as based on sources and literature.

A second type of migration consisted of state-controlled rural–rural migration (see Table 9.1). In Cabo Verde and Guinea-Bissau labor migration between rural areas was organized to promote internal colonization through the development of agricultural production schemes.[6] In the 1850s and 1860s, the colonial state issued several bills regulating the concession of state lands to private entrepreneurs and companies to support export crop production. This practice continued in the following decades.[7]

In Angola, a third form of migration headed to the diamond mines explored by Diamang (*Companhia de Diamantes de Angola*) (see Table 9.1). Diamang was granted a concession for diamond mining in 1917, which it maintained until independence. It had exclusive mining and labor supply rights and became the colony's largest commercial operator as well as its leading revenue generator. Over the years, hundreds of thousands of African laborers were forcibly recruited to work in the mines (Cleveland 2015). The districts of Lunda Sul and Lunda Norte in northeastern Angola, where the diamonds were mined, were remote and sparsely populated inland areas far off the main overland transportation routes. The expansion of cities in Lunda was largely planned and administered by Diamang, in cooperation with colonial authorities (Udelsmann Rodrigues and Tavares 2012, 688). Diamang fostered urbanization through enclosed residential compounds for mineworkers, such as the town of Dundo (Cleveland 2008).

Estimating the volume of these internal migration flows is a challenging task, as many of the workers involved in these circular migration systems were seasonal and casual workers who left very little paper trail in the colonial archives. However, the analysis of the size of the recruited workforce in certain enterprises provides us with some indicative figures. The annual average workforce size of Diamang in late 1920s was 5,000 workers, a figure that had doubled ten years later, and further rose to about 27,000 on the eve of Angolan independence (Cleveland 2008, 83–4). According to Ball, between the late 1920s and early 1930s, the Cassequel sugar plantation located between Lobito, Benguela, and Catumbela employed between 3,000 and 6,000 workers, most of them recruited in the neighboring provinces of Benguela, Huambo, Bie, and Huíla (Ball 2015, 86). Thus, in the 1920s, these two firms alone employed at least 8,000 workers per year in Angola. Ten years later their numbers had increased to 16,000, and by the early 1970s it can be safely assumed that they employed at least 30,000 workers per year. Even if we assume that 50% of these workers were rehired every year and, therefore, did not have to relocate/migrate, we estimate that Diamang alone recruited about 250,000 new workers between the 1920s and 1970s.[8] If we take into account that agricultural firms, the railways, the army, and the public works also recruited at least 5,000 workers each, we may safely assume that at least 1 million workers migrated within the colony during the half century between the 1920s and 1970s. Information on Mozambique points to a comparable order of magnitude. Adding all up, migration of African workers within the colonies must have involved at least 1 million but perhaps up to 3 million people in Angola and Mozambique together, including the full spectrum of voluntary to forced migrants.

Regarding the movement of workers across the borders of Portuguese African colonies and beyond, we identify at least three major systems: (i) the São Tomé system; (ii) the Congo-Katanga system; and (iii) the Rand system. The São Tomé system consisted of sizable flows of workers from Angola, Mozambique, Cabo Verde, and Guinea-Bissau to São Tomé and Príncipe (see Table 9.2). As Figures 9.1 and 9.2 show, Angola and Mozambique were the main suppliers of unskilled labor to these islands during most of the 20th century (see also Appendix Tables 9.A1 and 9.A2). For the period 1870s–1960s, the total recorded number of workers that arrived in São Tomé is about 300,000, and we may safely assume that the actual number must have been closer to half a million.

The Congo-Katanga and Rand systems connected Angola and Mozambique to the copper mines in the southeastern parts of the (Belgian) Congo and the gold mines in the Rand (South Africa). These labor migrants were accompanied by workers from present-day Zimbabwe and Malawi. These large spatial systems of circular migration consisted mainly of

TABLE 9.2 Migration between Portuguese colonies and to neighboring countries

Colony of origin	Colony of destination	Type of labor	Colony function
Cabo Verde Angola Mozambique Guinea-Bissau	São Tomé and Príncipe	Unskilled	Labor reservoir of unskilled labor for São Tomé and Príncipe
Angola	Kongo-Katanga	Unskilled	Labor reservoir of unskilled labor for neighboring colonial territories
Mozambique	Rand region Zimbabwe Malawi	Unskilled	Labor reservoir of unskilled labor for neighboring colonial territories
Cabo Verde	Guinea-Bissau Angola Mozambique (less)	Skilled	Labor reservoir of skilled labor for several colonies of Portuguese Africa
Portuguese India	Mozambique (mainly)	Skilled	Labor reservoir of skilled labor mainly for Portuguese East Africa

Source: Authors as based on sources and literature.

unskilled workers (Juif, Chapter 10, this volume).[9] In the case of Mozambique, outmigration started in the late 19th century. Between 1913 and 1952, 2.2 million workers migrated to the Rand, and 2.1 million were repatriated. In view of this we estimate that this circular migration flow involved at least 2.5 million to 3.5 million workers prior to independence. Migration figures for Southern Rhodesia were more modest, but still significant. For the period 1930–52, more than 200,000 workers migrated from Mozambique to this region and about 95,000 returned home. Assuming that migration flows remained on par with the figures we have for the early 1950s (approximately 20,000 migrants per year), we estimate that some 700,000 to 1 million Africans migrated to Southern Rhodesia up to independence.[10] Hence, at least 3.5 million, but perhaps close to 5 million Africans, migrated from Mozambique to the Rand and Southern Rhodesia.[11] Information on outmigration from Angola to Congo-Katanga is scarcer but the numbers were probably smaller. Our best guess would put it at approximately 2.5 million. If this is not too far off, total outmigration from Portuguese colonies to neighboring regions must have involved the voluntary and forced movement of about 7.5 million Africans.

Workers contracted to work outside the colony of recruitment underwent a rather complicated bureaucratic and logistic procedure. First, they were relocated from the place of recruitment to the local dependency of the respective *curadoria*, and later to its headquarters, where they signed their labor contracts.[12] This often implied walking for several days in the absence of a nearby railway. Once workers arrived at the agency of the *curadoria* labor contracts would be formalized and transport to the colony of destination arranged. Then the recruited workers would be transported either over sea or over land by available railways or by foot. Both Portuguese Mozambique and Angola invested in transportation for various economic and political purposes, facilitating migration within and outside the imperial borders. In the case of Mozambique, which was culturally more diversified and less integrated in socio-economic terms, a complex railway network served mineral and agricultural clusters as well as native labor migration and colonial settlements. In addition, there were also significant flows of skilled migrant labor in Portuguese Africa, who were mainly employed in government administration or private enterprises. Skilled workers from Cabo Verde moved to Guinea-Bissau and to a lesser extent to Angola and Mozambique. Most of these migrants were free and moved for reasons of career advancement.

As Figure 9.3 shows, in 1950, many migrant workers residing in Angola were *mestiços*, meaning of mixed descent, coming mainly from other Portuguese African colonies, but also from Brazil and even from Greece. Most of these people were working in skilled occupations for the colonial administration, in public services or infrastructure projects. Another major group of migrants were white settlers who originated mainly from Portugal. They were often employed as clerks or were involved in commerce and farming. There was also some mobility of whites, *mestiços,* and black people within Angola, moving across districts or *conselhos* (municipalities) (see Figure 9.4). Mozambique received skilled migrant labor from Portuguese India, who found employment in the colonial administration and the commercial sector. According to the 1930 census of the indigenous population of Mozambique, only 1.7% of the population originated from other Portuguese colonies or foreign countries. In 1950 most migrants in Mozambique came from other Portuguese colonies or other foreign countries besides Portugal (see Figure 9.5). The numbers coming from the metropole were small.

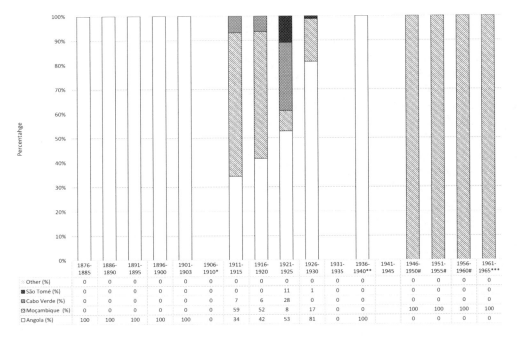

FIGURE 9.1 Arrivals of workers (*Serviçais*) in São Tomé and Príncipe according to their place of origin, 1876–1965 (percentage).

Source: See Table 9.A1 in appendix to the chapter.

Notes: ★ Data for only 1910; ★★ data for only 1937; ★★★ data for only Mozambican workers, 1961; # data for only Mozambican workers.

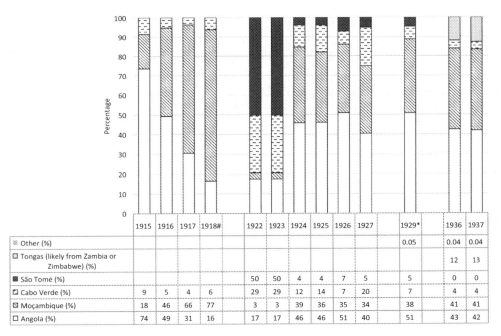

FIGURE 9.2 Contracted and re-contracted workers (*Serviçais*) in São Tomé and Príncipe according to their place of origin, 1915–37 (percentage).

Source: See Table 9.A2 in appendix to the chapter.

Notes: # Data for only the first semester of the year; ★ Youngsters under 14 years old accounted for 4,554 in São Tomé and for 837 in Príncipe; if we add them to the total number of workers above 14 years we get to a total of 46,657 individuals.

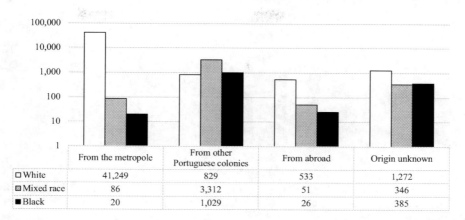

FIGURE 9.3 Skilled migrant workers in Angola according to their place of origin and "race," 1950.

Source: Província de Angola (1955), 84–109.

Note: The data refer to the so-called "civilized," non-indigenous population of the colony.

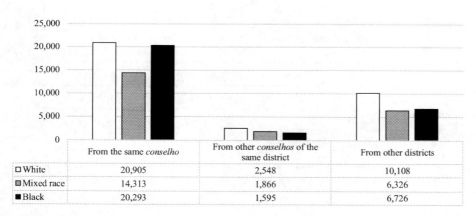

FIGURE 9.4 Skilled workers in Angola according to their place of origin and "race," 1950.

Source: Província de Angola (1955), 84–109.

Note: The data refer to the so-called "civilized," non-indigenous population of the colony.

Finally, Africans from various parts of the empire were recruited to serve in colonial police forces and the army. Policemen and soldiers were often assigned service in a colony other than their place of origin (see Table 9.3). This became standard practice after the outbreak of the Portuguese colonial war against the different Liberation Movements as a strategy to prevent desertion of African soldiers or their transfer to the Liberation forces.

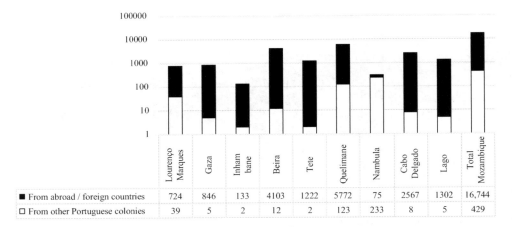

FIGURE 9.5 Migrant workers in Mozambique per district and according to their place of origin, 1950.

Source: Província de Moçambique (1955), 112–7.

Note: The data refer to the so-called "non-civilized," indigenous population of the colony.

TABLE 9.3 Armed forces in Portuguese Africa (1910–30): total size and share per 1,000 inhabitants

Portuguese colonies	Total size of armed forces		Soldiers per 1000 inhabitants	
	1910	1930	1910	1930
Angola	11,000	6,740	4.1	2.2
Mozambique	4,600	3,500	1.1	0.8
Guinea-Bissau	250	412	0.2	0.2

Source: Army size data from Killingray (1982), Appendix 1, pp. 424–5; population from Frankema and Jerven (2014).

3 Governing labor migration in Portuguese Africa: legislation and administrative structure

Following the abolition of the slave trade and slavery in Portuguese Africa in the 1850s, a Committee for the Protection of Slaves and Freed Peoples (*Junta Protectora dos Escravos e Libertos*) was established in 1856. The aim of the *Junta* was, at least in the spirit of the law, to protect former slaves from abuses from former masters and to oversee the transition from slavery to the infamous apprenticeship system, which tied former slaves to their workplace for a period of 20 years in return for housing and meals. In practice, the *Junta* did less to safeguard the interests of former slaves than it did to secure the labor needs of former masters.[13]

In 1863 the Portuguese Secretary of the Navy and Overseas territories (*Secretaria da Marinha e Ultramar*) began to authorize the migration of former slaves and freed workers from Cabo Verde to São Tomé. Many of these workers were offered free passage, their travel expenses being covered by the state. The *Junta* mediated this migration flow (Correia, 2001, 13). Demand for African migrant workers grew considerably in the following years due to the emergent cocoa boom in São Tomé. This motivated legislation in 1875 to transfer freed slaves from the jurisdiction of the *Junta* to the newly established General Committee for the Protection of the African servants and settlers (*Curadoria geral dos Serviçais e Colonos Indígenas*). In 1878 the government in Lisbon issued the first regulation of labor contracts for Africans stipulating conditions for employment and migration.[14]

Multiple terms were used to distinguish categories of recruited workers, including *serviçais, colonos, contratados, compelidos, evadidos,* and *voluntários*. *Serviçais* were African workers aged 14 and above who were declared fit to work. This term was often used interchangeably with *contratados*, who were contracted by the colonial state for public works or were allocated to private employers, concessionary companies, and foreign recruitment agencies. *Compelidos* were people of age 14+ without occupation, and who were compelled to work by the authorities. If *contratados* or *compelidos* left their jobs before the end of their contract, they were designated as *evadidos*. Those who engaged with the wage labor market on a voluntary basis were known as *voluntários*. This group of mostly skilled workers tended to be better paid and had better working conditions. The term *colono* referred to farmers who were assigned a plot of land.[15]

The *Curadoria* centralized the registration of African workers and kept records of migration to destinations outside the colony. This administrative body also supervised the compliance of laws regarding labor protection, payments, and aided poor African workers, including judicial support, in case of abuse. The *Curadoria* also surveilled the repatriation of workers at the end of their contract periods. Two main types of contracts were issued, the first was to provide labor services and the second gave land concessions to European and African workers for farming. Each colony had its own *Curadoria* with multiple agencies in its different administrative districts (see Figure 9.6).

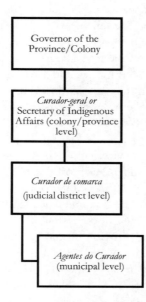

FIGURE 9.6 Structure of the *Curadorias* in Portuguese Africa and beyond (19th–20th century).

Source: Authors as based on legislation published in the Official Bulletins of Cabo Verde, São Tomé and Príncipe, Angola, and Mozambique, and sources from the Curadoria Geral of Cabo Verde and São Tomé deposited in the AHNCV and AHNSTP.

In the years following their establishment, the *Curadorias* appear to have done little to defend the interests of African migrant workers, and matters got worse after the issuing of the new *Indigenous Labor Code* (*Regulamento do Trabalho Indígena*) in 1899.[16] According to this new labor code Africans had "the legal and moral obligation to work." The *Curadorias* were given the jurisdiction to compel all people who were expected to work, including (i) those who owned no capital or property, or whose income could not guarantee their survival; (ii) those who were not merchants, industrialists, or did not have a liberal profession, or occupation; (iii) those who did not cultivate their own land; (iv) those who did not work as journeymen or for a wage for a certain number of months/days per year; and (v) those who had been sentenced to correctional labor for various crimes.[17] Hence, the *Curadorias* could issue labor contracts between vast numbers of impoverished, landless workers and private Portuguese or foreign-owned companies, as well as with owners or tenants of agricultural estates, industrialists, or merchants.

In most cases the recruitment of workers was done at the village level. Recruiters, known as *engajadores*, were in their vast majority Africans commissioned by the European recruiters in charge of the recruitment offices set up under the jurisdiction of the *curadorias* (see Figure 9.7). Village chiefs also acted as recruiters, as they had the authority to determine who was fit and expected to work, and who could be sentenced to work as punishment for criminal offenses and tax evasion (Keese 2013). Chiefs could also be involved in agreements with the recruiters in a system of "indirect" rule.[18] The geographic scope of these recruitment networks was vast, and often not limited to a single colony, nor even to Africa. In the case of labor recruitment for São Tomé and Príncipe, it encompassed several colonies located in different continents, with agencies established in Angola, Mozambique, Guinea-Bissau, Cabo Verde, Portuguese India, and Macau, including various delegations in each of these colonies (Nascimento 2004b) (Figure 9.8).

The *Curadorias* monitored compliance of the contract, and punished employers and employees who breached the clauses. The employers would be called upon in cases of failure in payment of wages; detention of the *serviçal* after the end of the contract; firing the *serviçal* without a fair cause; other abuses of the *serviçal*. The *serviçais*, on the other hand, would be called to come before the *Curadorias* if they would leave the workplace without reason; refused to do the work described in the contract; in cases of disobedience, insubordination, aggression, or damage caused to the property or assets of the employer; or if misbehavior disadvantaged third parties. Finally, the *Curadorias* were expected to mediate or solve labor conflicts between employers and *serviçais*.

Concerning labor contracts for service outside the colony or province, the *curadorias* registered all contracts pertaining to individual workers and families, including children. The *Curadorias* issued a duplicate of the contract to be handed over together with the *serviçal* to the *curadoria* of the migrant workers' destination. The identification card that the *serviçal* was supposed to carry at all times included a description of the contract.

Labor contracts could have the duration of one up to five years, contracts of two and three years being the most common. Wages were in general meager. According to the first diploma regulating contract labor in São Tomé and Príncipe dating from the 1878, a male *serviçal* was to be paid at least 2.5 *réis* and a female 1.8 *réis*. Employers were expected to pay half of the monthly salary to the employees, whereas the other half was to be deposited in the *cofre da repatriação* (Coffer of Repatriation). This amount could be used in two possible

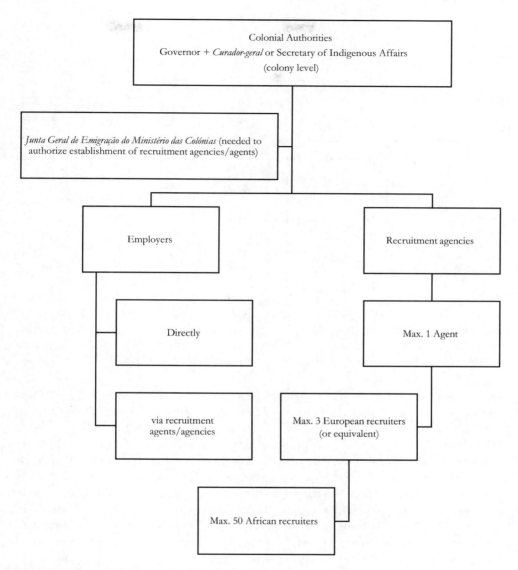

FIGURE 9.7 Recruitment process.

Sources: Authors as based on legislation published in the multiple Official Bulletins of Cabo Verde, São Tomé and Príncipe, Angola, and Mozambique and sources from the Curadoria Geral of Cabo Verde and São Tomé and Príncipe deposited in the AHNCV and AHNSTP. For details on the collections concerning Cabo Verde's Curadoria, see Correia 2001.

ways. It could be accumulated and given to the worker upon arrival at his/her home colony after repatriation – the so-called *bonus*; or it could be used to guarantee the livelihood of the worker's family back home through a system of deferred payment.[19] These amounts were kept by the Treasury/Coffer for Labor and Repatriation of each colony (*Cofre do Trabalho e da Repatriação*) and supervised by the colony's Exchequer. Remuneration was not limited to

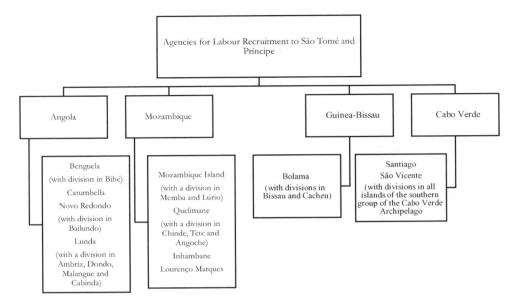

FIGURE 9.8 Agencies for labor recruitment to São Tomé and Príncipe.

Sources: Authors as based on legislation published in the multiple Official Bulletins of the colonies of Cabo Verde, São Tomé and Príncipe, Angola, and Mozambique and source materials related to the Curadoria Geral of Cabo Verde and São Tomé and Príncipe deposited in the AHNCV and AHNSTP.

wage as employers were expected to provide each worker with clean housing, food, clothing, adequate medical care free of charge, infant care for children of *serviçais* under seven years old.

Workers who had completed their contract term were officially entitled to a paid ticket to return to their home colony. Very often, however, *serviçais* ended up not receiving their wages and return tickets, due to lack of payment by employers and corruption on the part of the officials of the *curadorias* or equivalent entities. As a consequence, many workers were forced to accept a new or renewed contract. This situation is to a certain extent illustrated in the data gathered for São Tomé and Príncipe, as the number of workers under contract was always rather high compared to the number of newly arrived workers, and those repatriated back home (see Figures 9.1, 9.2, and 9.9 as well as Appendix Tables 9.A1, 9.A2, and 9.A3).

In the course of the 20th century, the laws and policies governing labor migration in Portuguese Africa underwent several reforms. The *Curadorias* continued to operate in each of the territories, as well as in South Africa, to control the flow of workers heading to the Rand region. However, from 1914, they came under the jurisdiction of the Secretary of the Indigenous Affairs (*Secretaria dos Negócios Indígenas*) of each province/colony, and in some colonies, including São Tomé, also of the Colonial Committee for Labor and Emigration (*Junta colonial do Trabalho e da Emigração*). The issuing of labor contracts to serve outside of the colony (either within or beyond the Portuguese empire) now had to be approved by a Central Committee for Labor and Emigration (*Junta Central do Trabalho e da Emigração*) under the auspices of the metropolitan government. After the issuing of the *New Indigenous Labor Code* in 1928, the full jurisdiction over labor contracts of "indigenous workers" who migrated outside their home colony (province) was transferred to the *Junta Central* in Lisbon.[20] Meanwhile, the labor recruitment system also experienced important changes. From

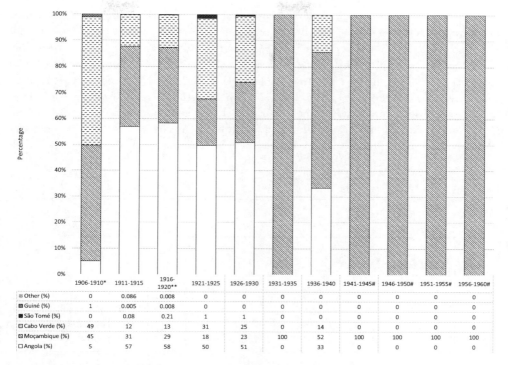

FIGURE 9.9 Workers (*Serviçais*) repatriated from São Tomé and Príncipe to their place of origin, 1906–60 (percentage)

Sources: See Table 9.A3 in appendix to the chapter.

Notes: * Data for only the years of 1908–10; ** data for only the years of 1916–18; # data for only Mozambican workers.

as early as the 1930s, forceful recruitment of African labor would take new forms with the introduction of the forced cultivation systems, in particular of rice and cotton, in various regions in Mozambique, Angola, and Guinea-Bissau (Pitcher 1991; Isaacman 1992).

These reforms by the central government in Lisbon served two main purposes. First, the government sought to reduce situations of abuse by local colonial governments, even though these remained commonplace up to the 1970s.[21] Second, the Portuguese colonial state aimed to have a tighter control over labor resources in the African colonies in order to pursue its broader economic development plans focusing on the construction of infrastructure, the implementation of forced cultivation schemes, and recruitment for the armed forces. Yet, forced recruitment was not the only mechanism to make African laborers meet their "legal and moral obligation to work." As early as the mid-19th century the hut tax (*imposto da palhota*) was introduced in Portuguese Africa to generate state revenue, to promote the monetization of the economy, and to push Africans onto the wage labor market to meet their tax obligations (Havik, Keese and Santos 2015; Alexopoulou and Juif 2017). Whenever Africans were unable to pay the hut tax, they were easy targets for recruiters, who could force them to "pay" their tax in labor.

These forms of state-directed compulsion were not always needed though. Many Cabo Verdean workers voluntarily moved to work in the plantations of São Tomé and Príncipe, in order to escape extreme poverty on islands that were frequently plagued by droughts and famine, and where local employment possibilities were virtually absent. The migration statistics of São Tomé clearly show that the number of *serviçais* arriving from Cabo Verde swelled in periods of drought and famine, such as 1920–22, when approximately 25,000 people in Cabo Verde died from famine (see Figure 9.2). Floods and famines also drove Mozambicans into voluntary labor migration to other parts of the Portuguese empire, including São Tomé and Príncipe, as well as neighboring colonies and countries. As we indicate in Table 9.4, labor recruitment was influenced not only by the coercive arm of the state, but also by environmental problems and related uneven economic opportunity structures that

TABLE 9.4 Drivers of migration within Portuguese Africa and to neighboring colonies

Main type of drivers	*Specific drivers*	*Migration flow*
Environmental drivers	Drought	Cabo Verde – São Tomé and Príncipe
	Famines	
	Disease	Cabo Verde – São Tomé and Príncipe
	Floods	Cabo Verde – São Tomé and Príncipe; Mozambique – neighboring colonies
		Mozambique – neighboring colonies
Economic drivers	Monetization and direct taxation	All colonies
	Higher wages	Mozambique – Rand; Mozambique – Congo-Katanga
	Better working conditions (or the hope for)	Cabo Verde – São Tome and Príncipe Mozambique – Rand; Mozambique – Congo-Katanga
	Improvement or progress in career	Applies only to skilled workers
	Labor demand (employer's side)	All colonies
	False/illusive offers of private recruitment agencies to work in commercial agriculture and mines in other Portuguese colonies and neighboring African colonial spaces	Cabo Verde – São Tomé and Príncipe Kongo-Katanga
Coercive drivers	Sentenced to labor by local African authorities due to customary laws	Guinea-Bissau; Angola; Mozambique
	Sentenced to exile and/or forced labor by administrative decision by the colonial authorities	Cabo Verde–São Tomé; Angola–São Tomé; Mozambique–São Tomé
	Compelled to work for colonial authorities by the African local authorities as means to pay taxes and other fiscal obligations	Guinea-Bissau (internal migration); Angola (internal migration); Mozambique (internal migration)
	Compelled to work for colonial authorities in the regimes of compulsive agricultural production to meet required quotas of production, e.g., cotton	Angola (internal migration); Mozambique (internal migration)

Sources: Authors own, based on a wide range of sources and literature.

were shaped in large part by the availability of jobs, the level of wages, tax regulations, and the seasonality of varying cultivation systems.

Finally, recruiters also lured workers into signing written contracts or consent to verbal agreements based on vague "success stories" or false promises of high wages and decent working conditions. In a letter dating from 22 December 1952, Mr. Pires, *serviçal* in São Tomé, wrote to his mother in Cabo Verde: "Life here is not how I imagined; here they fool us [...]. Tell Tomás [Thomas] not to think of [contacting] that agent or other individuals."[22]

4 Extracting labor from within and raising revenue from abroad

Compared to other European empires in Africa, the migration policies and practices pursued in Portuguese Africa were unique in several respects. First, the complexity and geographic scope of the recruitment system had no parallel with other colonies, with the possible exception of the Belgian Congo. Second, Portugal was unable to attract African migrant workers to its territories, unlike most other African colonies, including the Belgian Congo (Juif and Frankema 2018). Third, Portugal fostered the development of outward migration flows to neighboring territories in clear contrast with policies adopted by other colonies and countries in sub-Saharan Africa. These distinct features raise important questions regarding the rationale of large-scale, state-directed recruitment for external destinations in a context of internal labor scarcities.

To better understand the specific recruitment and migration policies of the Portuguese colonies in Africa we first need to recognize that control over labor and its mobility played a key role in the process of colonial state formation. Control over labor and mobility were fundamental to raise the revenues (through direct and indirect taxes) necessary to finance the colonial state, as well as to recruit able-bodied men for the armed forces, and for the development of state infrastructure and zones of export production.

A second key factor was the scarcity of local population in several parts of Portuguese Africa with economic potential. Local scarcity forced the state and private employers to look for laborers elsewhere. São Tomé and Príncipe was a prominent example, as the local population was too small to meet the labor demand of the islands' cocoa plantations in the 19th and 20th centuries. In Angola and Mozambique the size of the population was larger, but overall densities were low and unevenly distributed. In the primary mining region of Angola that was granted to Diamang for exploration, recruitment soon had to be extended to neighboring areas as well. Companies operating in certain areas of Mozambique faced similar challenges. In 1930, for example, the territories of Manica and Sofala alone recruited more than 1,000 labor migrants from other parts of the colony, while over 2,000 migrant workers were repatriated at the same time.[23] Yet, Portugal was never able to attract the level of investment to its territories that other European powers did, which limited economic development opportunities and growth. Portuguese investors who did invest in Portuguese Africa were, more often than not, accustomed to practices of labor coercion, including the use of violence and the payment of below-market wage rates in order to limit costs and create windows for profit.

This situation created a catch-22: widespread labor coercion reduced the willingness of local laborers to work for Portuguese employers or the state and it diminished the chances of recruiting voluntary foreign African migrant workers from neighboring colonies and independent countries. At the same time, it enhanced expectations of labor migration that external destinations would offer better prospects. According to J. Serrão de Azevedo, head of the *Curadoria* of Johannesburg in 1913, the average monthly wage of workers in several

South African mines was between 2 and 3 pounds, i.e., 9,000 and 13,500 *réis* (1 pound = 4,500 *réis*), and the highest wages paid varied between 5 and 7 pounds, i.e., 22,500 and 31,500 *réis*, respectively.[24] These average wages were four to six times larger than the minimum monthly wage paid to a male *serviçal* in São Tomé in 1909, who earned a meager 2,500 *réis*, equivalent to roughly half a pound.[25] Evidence from the 1930 to the 1950s also shows that wages in the Rand gold mines were much higher than those paid to unskilled wage workers employed by the state or private companies in Mozambique (Alexopoulou and Juif 2017: 233, 250).

As low levels of investment limited the capacity of the state to raise revenue, state-controlled recruitment for external migration was necessary to float the entire system of labor recruitment, which after all required substantial investments in coercive forces (e.g., army and police). Authorizing African laborers to work outside the Portuguese empire enabled the state to generate revenue indirectly, that is, through the management of workers' wages paid in deferral and the control over remittances sent by workers from abroad, increasing the monetization levels of the economy, the possibilities of workers' families to comply with the payment of the hut tax, and the financial reserves of the colonies. In other words, forced internal migration was difficult to organize without the revenues obtained through external migration.

As early as the 1890s, Portugal started to regulate migration of African workers from Mozambique to South Africa. This was followed by a series of agreements between Portugal and several colonial and independent neighboring states, such as, for example, the *Mozambique-Transvaal Convention* from 1901. According to the regulations for the recruitment of African workers from Mozambique to South Africa issued in 1897, the Portuguese colonial state should collect fees from recruiters, employers, or employees at different stages of the recruitment process. For every contract of a maximum of 100 workers the recruiters had to pay a fee of 4,500 *réis* in gold. To move to South Africa each worker needed a pass. Each pass issued by the Portuguese state cost 1,680. To work in South Africa, they also needed a working visa. These were issued by the Portuguese *curador* in Johannesburg. Each visa cost 2.6 shillings. This was to be paid either by recruiters or by workers. Mozambiquan workers in South Africa who wished to get a new contract needed to acquire a new pass costing 10 shillings. Migrant workers who sought to change employers also needed a new visa of 20 shillings.[26] In addition, all Portuguese African workers whose contracts ended and were repatriated to Mozambique had to pay a fee of 10 shillings to the state, the so-called *taxa de regresso*.

During the years 1910–12, the operations of the *Curadoria* in Johannesburg generated between 60,000 and 79,000 pounds per year and a total of 218,075 pounds for the three-year period.[27] The *Curador* J. Serrão de Azevedo stated in 1913: "the [financial] movement [of the *Curadoria*] was very important and [its] checking account [...] can be put on the same footing as of any of the big commercial houses of the Transvaal."[28] In the following decades revenue from migration to the Transvaal, including the profits not only from the *Curadoria* in Johannesburg but also from other dependencies continued to increase. By 1926, the annual revenue was more than 180,000 pounds, and by the late 1930s it had almost doubled to over 340,000 pounds per year. These figures were topped with fees from labor migration to Southern Rhodesia. During the 1930s alone, Portugal generated about 70,000 pounds from this migration flow. Hence, in the 1930s the fees from migration to the Transvaal and Southern Rhodesia together generated approximately 3 million pounds in revenue for the colonial treasury of Mozambique.[29] Revenue from external labor migration in the 1940s and 1950s represented around 20% of total direct tax revenue in Mozambique alone (Alexopoulou and Juif 2017, 232).[30] Without these financial sources it must have been very difficult to organize such an extensive bureaucratic system of labor recruitment in the first place.

5 Conclusion

The evidence presented and discussed in this chapter reveals how, and to some extent also clarifies why, the Portuguese set up such an intricate system of labor recruitment and migration since the closing decades of the 19th century, a system that regulated the supply of labor within each colony, between Portuguese African colonies, and catered to a series of political agreements with other European colonial powers regarding the supply of African labor. These three meta-patterns of migration are likely to have contributed to the free movement and coerced displacement of an estimated number of 9 to 14 million workers between 1900 and independence: half a million to São Tomé and Principe, 1–6 million within the colonies of Angola, Mozambique, and Guinea-Bissau, and 7.5 million to the neighboring colonies.

What seems to set labor migration patterns in Portuguese Africa apart from neighboring colonies is, first, the rather low number of workers of foreign origin (foreign is here used as meaning from outside of the Portuguese colonial spaces) found laboring and living in the colonies, as the figures from the 1950 censuses of Angola and Mozambique clearly show; and, second, the combined functioning of Angola and Mozambique as labor reservoirs for external labor markets as well as internal labor markets. This indicates how widespread the recruitment system has been, and how much stress this must have placed on workers, on their families, and on countless local communities.

In our view this particularly intensive and coercive system was rooted in a combination of three specific conditions: (a) the labor market conditions, partly shaped by limited investment opportunities, were not sufficiently attractive to workers outside the colony, who found better employment opportunities elsewhere; (b) the levels of labor coercion and the working conditions in Portuguese Africa did not only deter labor immigration, but they also enhanced labor emigration, which was partly forced, partly voluntary; and (c) the development of the Portuguese colonial state (and especially Mozambique) soon depended on the revenue it generated from the circulation of migrant workers within and beyond imperial borders.

Each of these three propositions deserves further consideration in future research on the topic of free and forced migration in Portuguese Africa in relation to the intensified use of coercive recruitment policies and labor exploitation. The legacies of these forms of short- and long-distance displacement are still very much present across Southern and Central Africa as many of the millions of migrant workers ended up somewhere else without being given a chance to return back home.

Notes

1 "Irmão, olha nós não estamos nada como o papel dizia, e tu e os irmãos, nunca vocês pensem em vir a esta terra porque vocês não calculam tanto que eu tenho chorado," Letter obtained from Arquivo Histórico Nacional de Cabo Verde (AHNCV), Repartição Provincial dos Serviços de Administração Civil (RPSAC) (A2), box 428, process 118: "Averiguação a que procedeu o Inspector Superior de Administração Ultramarina em São Tomé acerca das cartas que alguns trabalhadores Cabo Verdeanos aqui enviaram a seus parentes em Santo Antão." Translation by the authors.

2 Several private companies financed by both Portuguese and foreign investors were granted permission by the Portuguese state to carry out economic activities as well as govern sizable areas of colonial territories. The Mozambique (1891–1942) and Nyassa (1891–1929) companies operating in Portuguese East Africa were the two most prominent examples.

3 Slavery did continue to exist first in the form of a 20-year apprenticeship and later in modified and disguised forms up to the First World War, and some would argue up to the 1960s.

4 Census of Lourenço Marques, 1912, published in *Boletim Oficial de Moçambique (BOM)* 12, 1913.

5 Census of Lourenço Marques outskirts, 1912, published in *BOM* 12, 1913. For further details on the different terms and types of contracted and forced workers employed in Portuguese Africa see Section 3 of this chapter.

6 In the collection of the Secretary of Indigenous Affairs for Guinea-Bissau currently deposited in the archive of the *Instituto Nacional de Estudos e Pesquisa (INEP)* (Bissau), there is plenty of evidence of this practice. We refer to correspondence concerning the recruitment of workers for the farms near Farim between the secretary, the military command in the region of Papel, the secretary general for the Ministry of the Colonies, the administration of the civil division of Farim, and the military command in the region of the Balantas. INEP, *Secretaria dos Negócios Indígenas*, C 1.6/01.010.

7 *Boletim Oficial de Cabo Verde (BOCV)*, no. 9, 10, and 11 (1857); *BOCV*, no. 20 (1843); no. 47 (1865). An example of this type of land concessions can be found in the *BOCV* of 1863, no. 49. Examples of this type of land concessions can be found in the *BOCV* (1867), nos. 15, 20, 23, 25, 26, 27, 28, 32, 34, 41; *BOCV* (1868), nos. 4, 6, 7, 8, 9, 20, 24; and BOCV (1870), no. 10.

8 Estimates by the authors based on figures from Ball (2015) and Cleveland (2008).

9 Adepoju (in Kok et al. 2006, 32) states:

> The 1926 Angolan decree, taking its cue from a labour agreement signed between Portuguese administrators and South Africa in 1908, declared all unemployed adult males liable to contract labour for up to six months within Angola, or six to twelve months outside the country. Apart from the massive internal migration it induced, the law also provoked large-scale clandestine emigration to neighboring countries to escape forced-labour recruitment and the abuses associated with its implementation. By 1962, when the decree was reviewed and renewed, an estimated one million Angolans had already emigrated clandestinely to Botswana, Zambia, Zaire and South Africa (ECA 1981).

10 Colónia de Moçambique (1926–52).

11 Data underpinning this estimate are available upon request.

12 For further details on the *Curadorias*, see Section 3, this chapter.

13 There were many cases of abuse where enslaved Africans continued working for their former masters after their period of apprenticeship had ended, even though they were formally free to leave their master and their workplace (Nascimento 2002b, 2004a).

14 1878/12/2: Regulamento para os contratos de serviçais e colonos nas províncias da África Portuguesa, in *Boletim do Conselho Ultramarino, Legislação Novíssima*, Vol. IX, pp. 701–11.

15 In the collection of the Secretary of Indigenous Affairs at the INEP, multiple examples of this type of concessions can be found. Here we cite a set of documents concerning the land concessions to local people in Bissau free of charge. INEP, C1.6?01/1118.

16 1899/11/9: Regulamento do Trabalho Indígena, in *BOCV. Suplemento*, no. 30, 1900, pp. 3–8.

17 In the collection of the Secretary of Indigenous Affairs for Guinea-Bissau, currently deposited in the archive of the INEP, we retrieved two cases of individuals from Guinea-Bissau condemned to exile in São Tomé, and others from Angola sentenced to exile in Guinea-Bissau. INEP, Secretaria dos Negócios Indígenas, C1.6/01.013; C1.6/05.099.

18 Indirect rule was also used for tax collection purposes, population counts, and military recruitment.

19 Legislation published in the multiple Official Bulletins of the colonies of Cabo Verde, São Tomé and Príncipe, Angola, and Mozambique and source materials related to the *Curadoria Geral de Cabo Verde* and São Tomé and Príncipe deposited in the AHNCV and Arquivo Histórico Nacional de São Tomé and Príncipe (AHNSTP).

20 "Indigenous workers" were defined as "individuals of black race or of black descent, that in view of their education and costumes, do not differentiate themselves from the common individuals of that race." Código do Trabalho dos Indígenas nas Colónias Portuguesas na África, in *BOCV. Suplemento*, no. 5, 1932, pp. 1–39 (article 2)

Governing Free and Unfree Labor Migration **197**

21 Only after the 1960s did the International Labour Organisation (ILO) play a considerable role in reforming labor policies and practices in Portuguese Africa, as Monteiro shows (2018).
22 "A vida não era como eu formava, aqui eles entrujava-nos [...] Diga ao Tomás que não pense no tal [a]gente nem em outros indivíduos," AHNCV, RPSAC, (A2), box 428, proc. 118: "Averiguações [...]". Translation by the authors.
23 República Portuguesa (1926–52), (1930): 380.
24 República Portuguesa (1913): 55 and ss.
25 República Portuguesa (1913): 50; Ministério da Marinha e Ultramar (1909): 31–5.
26 Regulamento para engajamento dos indígenas da província de Moçambique para o trabalho na República Sul-Africana," 18/11/1897. According to J. Serrão de Azevedo, head of the *Curadoria* in Johannesburg, South Africa, in 1913: "the main sources of income [...] [were] generated from the fiscalization [of labor migration]: passes 20 shillings or 5 shillings (for duplicates), registration fees per worker 10 shillings and renewal or new contracts 1,6 shillings per every three months or fraction." Translation by the authors.
27 For the period 1910–12 see República Portuguesa (1913), for the period 1926–40 see Colónia de Moçambique (1926–52). For data after the 1940s see Alexopoulou and Juif (2017).
28 República Portuguesa (1913): 42. Translations by the authors.
29 Data underpinning this estimate are available upon request.
30 It must be noted here that migration within the Portuguese colonies was also a source of revenue for the state.

References

Adepoju, Aderanti. 2006. "Internal and International Migration within Africa". In *Migration in South and Southern Africa: Dynamics and Determinants*, edited by Pieter Kok, John Oucho, Derik Gelderblom and Johan Van Zyl, 26–46. HSRC Press.

Aguiar, A. Corrêa de. 1919. *O Trabalho Indígena nas ilhas de S. Tomé e Príncipe*, S. Tomé: Imprensa Nacional.

Alexopoulou, Kleoniki, and Dacil Juif. 2017. "Colonial State Formation without Integration: Tax Capacity and Labour Regimes in Portuguese Mozambique (1890s–1970s)." *International Review of Social History* 62 (02): 215–52.

Almeida, Pedro Ramos de. 1979. *História do Colonialismo Português em África. Cronologia Séc. XX.* Lisboa: Ed. Estampa.

Allina, Eric. 2012. *Slavery by Any Other Name. African Life under Company Rule in Colonial Mozambique.* Charlottesville and London: University of Virginia Press.

Amin, Samir. 1972. "Underdevelopment and Dependence in Black Africa. Origins and Contemporary Forms." *Journal of Modern African Studies* 10(4): 503–24.

Ball, Jeremy. 2015. *Angola's Colossal Lie: Forced Labor on a Sugar Plantation, 1913–1977.* Leiden, Boston: Brill.

Berthet, Marina. 2011. "Emigração Caboverdiana em São Tomé e Príncipe (1940–1970): Uma Apropriação do Tempo e dos Espaços." *Anais do XXVI Simpósio Nacional de História*, 1–13. São Paulo: ANPUH.

Berthet, Marina. 2016. "À Sombra do Cacau: Representações sobre Trabalho Forçado nas ilhas de São Tomé e Príncipe." *Revista do Arquivo Geral da Cidade do Rio de Janeiro* 11: 343–56.

Burnard, T. January 01, 2012. "Atlas of the Transatlantic Slave Trade - By David Eltis and David Richardson." *Economic History Review* 65(2): 822–3.

Bussotti, Luca, and Teodora Martins. 2019. "Marcas do Desterro. Moçambicanos deportados para São Tomé e Príncipe (1947–1961): história, estórias, atualidade." *Tempo e Argumento*, Florianópolis 11(27): 8–42.

Cahen, Michel. 2015. "Seis ^Teses sobre o Trabalho Forçado no Império Português Continental em África." *África* (35): 129–55.

Carreira, Antonio. 1983. *Cabo Verde: Formação e Extinção de uma Sociedade Escravocrata (1460–1878).* Lisbon: A. Carreira.

Castelo, Cláudia. 2007. *Passagens para África. O Povoamento de Angola e Moçambique com Naturais da Metrópole*. Porto: Edições Afrontamento.

Centro de Estudos Africanos da Universidade do Porto. 2006. *Trabalho Forçado Africano. Experiências Coloniais Comparadas*. Porto: Campo das letras.

Cleveland, Todd. 2008. *Rock Solid: African Laborers on the Diamond Mines of the Companhia de Diamantes de Angola (Diamang), 1917–1975*. Minneapolis, University of Minnesota, PhD Dissertation.

Cleveland, Todd. 2015. *Diamonds in the Rough: Corporate Paternalism and African Professionalism on the Mines of Colonial Angola, 1917–1975*. Athens: Ohio University Press.

Colónia de Moçambique, Repartição Técnica de Estatística. 1926–1952. *Anuário Estatístico*. Lourenço Marques: Imprensa Nacional de Moçambique.

Colónia de S. Tomé e Príncipe. Serviço de Estatística. 1938. *Elementos Estatísticos. Ano de 1937*. São Tomé: Imprensa Nacional.

Correia, Cláudia. 2001. *Para o Estudo da Curadoria dos Serviçais e Colonos em Cabo* Verde. MA dissertation. Porto: Centro de Estudos Africanos, Faculdade de Letras, Universidade do Porto.

Duffy, James. 1967. *A Question of Slavery (Labor politics in Portuguese Africa and the British Protest, 1850–1920)*. London: Clarendon Press/ Oxford University Press.

First, Ruth & Universidade Eduardo Mondlane. 1977. *The Mozambican miner: A Study in the Export of Labor*. Maputo, Mozambique: IICM.

Frankema, Ewout, and Morten Jerven. 2014. "Writing History Backwards or Sideways: Towards a Consensus on African Population, 1850–2010." *Economic History Review* 67(4): 907–31.

Green, Toby. 2011. *The Rise of the Trans-Atlantic Slave Trade in Western Africa, 1300–1589*. Cambridge: Cambridge University Press.

Harries, Patrick. 1981. "Slavery, Social Incorporation and Surplus Extraction; the Nature of Free and Unfree Labor in South-East Africa." *Journal of African History* 22(3): 309–30.

Harries, Patrick. 2014. "Slavery, Indenture and Migrant Labor: Maritime Immigration from Mozambique to the Cape, c.1780–1880." *African Studies* 73(3): 323–40.

Havik, Philip, Alexander Keese, and Maciel Santos. 2015. *Administration and Taxation in Former Portuguese Africa 1900–1945*. Newcastle upon Tyne: Cambridge Scholars Publishing.

Isaacman, Allen. 1992. "Coercion, Paternalism and the Labor Process: The Mozambican Cotton Regime 1938–1961." *Journal of Southern African Studies* 18(3): 487–526.

Ishemo, Shubi. 1995. "Forced Labor and Migration in Portugal's African colonies." In *The Cambridge Survey of World Migration*, edited by Robin Cohen, 162–65. Cambridge: Cambridge University Press.

Ishemo, Shubi. 1989. "Forced labour, mussoco (taxation), famine and migration in Lower Zambezia, Mozambique, 1870-1914". In *Forced Labour and Migration : Patterns of Movement Within Africa*, edited by Abebe Zegeye and Shubi Ishemo, 109–158. London: Hans Zell Publishers.

Juif, Dacil, and Ewout Frankema. 2018. "From Coercion to Compensation: Institutional Responses to Labour Scarcity in the Central African Copperbelt." *Journal of Institutional Economics* 14(SI 02): 313–343.

Kagan-Guthrie, Zachary. 2011. "Repression and Migration: Forced Labor Exile of Mozambicans to São Tomé, 1948–1955." *Journal of Southern African Studies* 37(3): 449–62.

Keese, Alexander. 2013. "Searching for the Reluctant Hands: Obsession, Ambivalence and the Practice of Organising Involuntary Labor in Colonial Cuanza-Sul and Malange Districts, Angola, 1926–1945." *Journal of Imperial and Commonwealth History* 41(2): 238–58.

Killingray, David. 1982. *The Colonial Army in the Gold Coast: Official Policy and Local Response, 1890–1947*. Doctoral dissertation. London: University of London.

Machado, Margarida Vaz do Rego. 2014. *El Papel de los Esclavos en la Sociedad del Antiguo Régimen en las Azores / The Role of Slaves in Azorean Society in the Old Regime - O Papel dos Escravos na Sociedade Açoriana no Antigo Regime*. Gran Canaria: Cabildo de Gran Canaria.

Ministério da Marinha e Ultramar, Direcção Geral do Ultramar. 1909. *Serviço de Emigração e recrutamento dos operários, serviçais e trabalhadores para a província de São Tomé e Príncipe*. Lisboa: Imprensa Nacional, pp. 31–5.

Monteiro, José Pedro. 2018. ""One of Those Too-Rare Examples": The International Labor Organization, the Colonial Question and Forced Labor (1961–1963)." In *Internationalism, Imperialism and the Formation of the Contemporary World*, edited by Miguel Jerónimo and José Pedro Monteiro, 221–49. New York: Palgrave Macmillan.

Nascimento, Augusto. 1998. "O Recrutamento de Serviçais Moçambicanos para as Roças de S. Tomé e Príncipe (1908–1921)." In *Seminário: Moçambique: Navegações, Comércio e Técnicas*, edited by Faculdade de Letras da Universidade Eduardo Mondlane de Maputo and Comissão Nacional para as Comemorações dos Descobrimentos Portugueses. Lisboa: CNCDP.

Nascimento, Augusto. 2001. "Representações Sociais e Arbítrio nas Roças: As Primeiras Levas de Caboverdianos em S. Tomé e Príncipe nos Primórdios de Novecentos." *ARQUIPÉLAGO HISTÓRIA*, 2a série (5): 325–70.

Nascimento, Augusto. 2002a. *Desterro e Contrato. Moçambicanos a Caminho de S. Tomé e Príncipe (anos 1940–1960)*. Maputo: Arquivo Histórico de Moçambique.

Nascimento, Augusto. 2002b. *Poderes e Quotidiano nas Roças de S. Tomé e Príncipe de Finais de Oitocentos a meados de Novecentos*. PhD Dissertation. Lisbon: Universidade Nova de Lisboa.

Nascimento, Augusto. 2004a. "Escravatura, Trabalho Forçado e Contrato em S. Tomé e Príncipe nos Séculos XIX-XX: Sujeição e Ética Laboral." *Africana Studia* 7: 183–217.

Nascimento, Augusto. 2004b. "A Passagem de *Coolies* por S. Tomé e Príncipe." *Arquipélago – História, 2ª serie* (8): 77–112.

Neves, Carlos Agostinho das. 1980. *S. Tomé e Príncipe: Antes e Depois do Estado Novo, 1910–1933/1933–1953*. MA dissertation. Lisbon: University of Lisbon.

Penvenne, J. 1984. "Labor Struggles at the Port of Lourenço Marques, 1900–1933." *Review (Fernand Braudel Center)* 8(2): 249–85.

Pitcher, Anne. 1991. "Sowing the Seeds of Failure: Early Portuguese Cotton Cultivation in Angola and Mozambique, 1820–1926." *Journal of Southern African Studies* 17(1): 43–70.

Província de Angola, Repartição de Estatística Geral. 1955. *Recenseamento Geral da População, 1950*. Luanda: Imprensa Nacional.

Província de Moçambique, Repartição Técnica de Estatística. 1955. *Recenseamento Geral da População em 1950*. Lourenço Marques: Imprensa Nacional de Moçambique.

República Portuguesa, Curadora dos Indígenas Portugueses no Transvaal 1913. *Relatório do Curador. J. Serrão de Azevedo. Ano Económico de 1912–1913*. Lourenço Marques: Imprensa Nacional.

República Portuguesa, Governo da Colónia de S. Tomé e Príncipe. 1929. *Curadoria Geral dos Serviçais e Colonos: Elementos Estatísticos de S. Tomé e Príncipe: 1922–1927*. São Tomé: Imprensa Nacional.

República Portuguesa, Governo da Colónia de S. Tomé e Príncipe. 1930. *Curadoria Geral dos Trabalhadores Indígenas: Elementos Estatísticos de S. Tomé e Príncipe: 1929*. São Tomé: Imprensa Nacional.

Tornimbeni, Corrado. 2005. "The State, Labor Migration and the Transnational Discourse – A Historical Perspective from Mozambique." *Stichproben. Wiener Zeitschrift für kritische Afrikastudien* 8: 307–28.

Udelsmann Rodrigues, Cristina, and Tavares, Ana Paula. 2012. "Angola's Planned and Unplanned Urban Growth: Diamond Mining Towns in the Lunda Provinces." *Journal of Contemporary African Studies* 30(4): 687–703.

Vieira, Alberto. 1991. *Os Escravos no Arquipélago da Madeira, Séculos XV a XVII*. Funchal: Secretaria Regional do Turismo, Cultura e Emigração: Centro de Estudos de História do Atlântico.

Vogt, John. 1973. "The Early São Tomé-Principe Slave Trade with Mina, 1500–1540." *International Journal of African Historical Studies* 6(3): 453–67.

APPENDIX

TABLE 9.A1 Arrivals of workers in São Tomé and Príncipe according to their place of origin, 1876–1965

Periods	Angola (no.)	Mozambique (no.)	Cabo Verde (no.)	São Tomé (no.)	Other (no.)	Total (no.)
1876–85	12,601					12,601
1886–90	14,304					14,304
1891–95	11,106					11,106
1896–1900	17,858					17,858
1901–03	11,135					11,135
1906–10★						413
1911–15	4,882	8,375	965	0	0	14,222
1916–20	7,785	9,725	1,180	0	0	18,690
1921–25	157	25	83	32	0	297
1926–30	9,602	2,056	34	111	0	11,803
1931–35	0	0	0	0	0	946
1936–40★★	11	0	0	0	0	11
1941–45						
1946–50#	0	6,669	0	0	0	6,669
1951–55#	0	8,852	0	0	0	8,852
1956–60#	0	8,187	0	0	0	8,187
1961–65★★★						775
Total	**89,441**	**43,889**	**2,262**	**143**	**0**	**137,869**

Sources:

- 1876–1903: Almeida (1979), 11 and 29.
- 1906–10: Neves (1980), 35.
- 1911–20: Aguiar (2019), 312–9.
- 1921–30: República Portuguesa (1929), 5 and 14; Neves (1980), 35; Nascimento (2002a), 16.
- 1931–45: Colónia de São Tomé e Príncipe (1938), 8.
- 1946–65: Nascimento (2002a), 55.

Notes: ★ Data for only 1910; ★★ data for only 1937; ★★★ data for only Mozambican workers, 1961; # data for only Mozambican workers.

TABLE 9.A2 Contracted and re-contracted workers in São Tomé and Príncipe according to their place of origin, 1915–61

Years	Angola (no.)	Mozambique (no.)	Cabo Verde (no.)	São Tomé (no.)	Tongas (likely from Zambia or Zimbabwe) (no.)	Other (no.)	Total (no.)
1915	1,533	371	179				2,083
1916	1,797	1,661	190				3,648
1917	2,818	6,065	340				9,223
1918#	645	3,043	242				3,930
1922	3,717	6,298	1,215	424			11,654
1923	2,301	409	3,864	6,628			13,202
1924	6,409	5,423	1,626	532			13,990
1925	5,206	4,064	1,590	443			11,303
1926	3,557	2,446	484	498			6,985
1927	1,865	1,592	923	237			4,617
1929★	20,930	15,666	2,741	1,909		20	41,266
1936	12,016	11,663	1,175	0	3,391	11	28,256
1937	11,477	11,333	1,049	0	3,509	11	27,379
1940							28,459
1941★★							6,679
1945		7,310					7,310
1946		5,640					5,640
1947		5,640					5,640
1948		7,541					7,541
1949		4,959					4,959
1950							24,060
1950		5,739					5,739
1951		9,200					9,200
1952		9,470					9,470
1953		7,792					7,792
1954		6,362					6,362
1955		7,502					7,502
1956		7,960					7,960
1957		7,957					7,957
1958		7,558					7,558
1959		7,824					7,824
1960		7,110					7,110
1961		5,545					5,545
Total	**74,271**	**191,143**	**15,618**	**10,671**	**6,900**	**42**	**298,645**

Sources:

- 1915–18: Aguiar (1919), 334–7.
- 1922–27: República Portuguesa (1929), 3 and 14.
- 1929: República Portuguesa (1930), 3 and 17.
- 1936–37: Colónia de S, Tomé e Príncipe (1938), 8.
- 1940 and 1950: Nascimento (2002b), 137.
- 1941–61: Nascimento (2002a), 56.

Notes: # Data for only the first semester of the year; ★ youngsters under 14 years old accounted for 4,554 in São Tomé, and for 837 in Príncipe; if we add them to the total number of workers above 14 years old we get a total of 46,657 individuals; ★★ Data for workers from only Mozambique.

202   Filipa Ribeiro da Silva and Kleoniki Alexopoulou

TABLE 9.A3 Workers repatriated from São Tomé and Príncipe to their place of origin, 1906–60

Periods	Angola (no.)	Mozambique (no.)	Cabo Verde (no.)	São Tomé (no.)	Guinea (no.)	Other (no.)	Total (no.,)
1906–10*	82	708	783	0	18	0	1,591
1911–15	11,938	6,460	2,553	17	1	18	20,987
1916–20★★	7,220	3,585	1,552	26	1	1	12,385
1921–25	710	258	440	21	0	0	1,429
1926–30	2,632	1,199	1,311	27	0	0	5,169
1931–35	0	546	0	0	0	0	546
1936–40	492	773	211	0	0	0	1,476
1941–45#	0	432	0	0	0	0	432
1946–50#	0	6,787	0	0	0	0	6,787
1951–55#	0	7,537	0	0	0	0	7,537
1956–60#	0	4,103	0	0	0	0	4,103
Total	**23,074**	**32,388**	**6,850**	**91**	**20**	**19**	**62,442**

Sources:

- 1906–20: Aguiar (1919), 407–8.
- 1921–30: República Portuguesa (1929), 5 and 14; República Portuguesa (1930), 3 and 17; Neves (1980), 35.
- 1931–60: Nascimento (2002), 57–8; Colónia de S, Tomé e Príncipe (1938), 8 and 11; Nascimento (2002a), 16.

Notes: ★ Data for only the years of 1908–10; ★★ data for only the years of 1916–18; # data for only Mozambican workers.

10

MIGRATION AND STABILIZATION

Mining Labor in the Belgian Congo, Northern Rhodesia, and South Africa

Dácil Juif

1 Introduction

The mining of metals and precious gems has been the most important industry for the Southern and Central African region since the late 19th century. Industrial mining in this area began with the discovery of large diamond deposits in Kimberley in 1867 and gold in the Witwatersrand in 1886, both in South Africa. These copious findings and the prospects of further mineral wealth were a primary impetus for the European scramble for Africa in the late 19th century (Cleveland 2014). A few decades later, when the value of copper and other non-precious metals in international markets rose, the Central African Copperbelt, located in the British protectorate of Northern Rhodesia and the Belgian Congo, emerged as a second major industrial mining region.

The discovery and extraction of minerals set in motion unprecedented magnitudes of population movement to supply the mines with labor. The migration systems that emerged after mineral discoveries partly reinforced existing migration ties – such as between Mozambique and South Africa – but also led to the creation of new migration routes. This chapter compares the shifting patterns in the migrant labor systems directed to Southern and Central African mines with a focus on four major migrant-receiving industrial mining areas in three different countries: the Kimberley diamond and Rand gold mines of South Africa and the copper mines in Northern Rhodesia (Copperbelt province) and the Congo (Katanga province). Certainly, other Southern and Central African regions developed mining industries that attracted African migrants from rural areas and from across territorial borders as well, but these fall outside the scope of this chapter. Even though the labor recruitment strategies of company and state constitute the main focus of this chapter, I also consider migrants' motivations and agency when exploring the causes and directions of large and continuous migrations flows.

One aim of this chapter is to explain the differences between mining areas in their reliance on stabilized versus circular migrant labor.[1] In all studied mining centers, African workers started out as temporary, circular migrant laborers, housed in single-men barracks, while their families continued farming in their rural homelands. But longer-term work relations with corresponding company investments in workers' training and welfare and

DOI: 10.4324/9781003225027-14

the settlement of black mineworkers with their families in mining towns were eventually favored by mining companies, and either tolerated or promoted by states. However, the timing of this "stabilization" varied, with Katanga taking the lead from the early 1920s, followed by the Northern Rhodesian Copperbelt from the late 1940s, and lastly South Africa in the 1970s. According to Brown (2019, 164), the decision of companies and the state to rely on either stabilized or circular migrant labor "was shaped by population densities, production technologies, the relative costs and ratio of skills and the geographical composition of the ore field." I argue that colonial governance ideology and geopolitical considerations played an important role as well.

A second, related, aim of this chapter is to explain the changes over time and differences in geographical scope of the recruitment catchment area, which was much wider in the case of the South African gold mines than for the diamond mines or the Central African copper mines. The gold mines relied on a sophisticated system of organized recruitment to continuously replenish its transient workforce, including agreements with foreign governments and recruitment stations throughout Southern Africa, as far as Nyasaland and Northern Rhodesia (Pérez Niño 2019). This system was developed and expanded throughout the 20th century. At the peak in the early 1970s, 70% of the workforce in the Rand gold mines was foreign, while the numbers of foreign workers had increased from 100,000 in the 1920s to 265,000 in 1970 (Pérez Niño 2019, 275). The Congolese mining company *Union Minière du Haut Katanga* started out with a much tighter catchment area which initially included neighboring countries but became completely internally oriented as its reliance on recruitment diminished in the 1920s. When industrial mining took off in Northern Rhodesia, the copper mining companies tapped into the domestic labor pool, which had supplied the mines of Katanga (as well as Southern Rhodesia) for over a decade, and complemented it with foreign migrant workers from neighboring colonies who reached the mines on their own account.

This chapter is structured as follows. Section 2 describes the period of discovery and consolidation of mines. Section 3 delves into the formation and evolution of labor systems specific to each mining area until the 1960s when most sub-Saharan African nations had attained independence. Section 4 examines comparatively the stabilization undertaken belatedly in the Rand after 1970, as well as the effect of the copper crisis on labor migration. Section 5 concludes with comparative remarks.

2 Discovery and consolidation of industrial mines

2.1 Gold and diamonds in South Africa: from individual prospecting to amalgamation

The history of large-scale mining in Southern Africa starts with the discovery of diamonds in 1867 near the confluence of the Vaal and the Orange River, in Griqualand West, a territory that lay north of the British Cape Colony and west of the "Boer" republics of Orange Free State and the South African Republic (Transvaal colony after 1902 and until 1910).[2] Griqualand had been granted protection and right of self-government by the British in 1834. The Griqua (descendants from Khoikhoi and European colonists of the Cape) were the main inhabitants of this area.

Diamond mining started on a relatively small scale: in 1870, some 5,000 people camped along the river diggings (Herbert 1972, 25). Digging and washing were carried out mostly by Boers from the Orange Free State and the South African Republic, sometimes with the help of a black employee, while women and children usually took care of the sorting (Hofmeester 2017). Claims were 20 square feet (approximately 37 m^2) large. Local rules limited the number of claims per digger to one and dictated the loss of the claim when the holder was absent for more than three workdays in a row.

The discovery of much vaster diamond deposits on two white farms (Dorstfontein and Bultfontein) about 100 miles (about 160 km) from the river diggings in 1870 led to a diamond rush. The next year, some 50,000 diggers were working on what were called dry diggings on those farms, around 20,000 of whom were of European descent, the rest black. In July 1871 the richest mine, Kimberley (which became famous as the "Big Hole"), was discovered. That same year, Britain annexed the diamond fields and much additional territory of Griqualand West, which had been claimed by the neighboring Boer nations. The area became a Crown Colony and the mining region became known as Kimberley. From the early 1870s, a group of London diamond merchants bought one farm after another from the Boers and became owners of the mines, which they let out to individual diggers (Worger 1987, 17).

However, in the mid-1870s, the diamond industry was already into depression, given the saturation of the diamonds market, the exhaustion of surface deposits, and the problem of constantly collapsing sides of the shafts due to the large quantity of small, deep claims (Worger 1987, 19).

The use of more sophisticated technology (like dynamite, water pumps, and steam engines to pull the diamantiferous soil out of the hole and wash it) could make mining profitable again but required the amalgamation of claims for scale economies. In 1877, the colonial governor of Griqualand West repealed the claim limitation and invited foreign investors to buy claims and land. This precipitated the end of individual prospecting and the rise of oligopolistic large-scale mining. From 1880 onward, the remaining claim holders transformed their firms into joint-stock companies, selling part of the shares to the public (Hofmeester 2017). In 1885 only three companies (*Kimberley Central*, the *Compagnie Française,* and Cecil Rhodes' *De Beers Mining Company*) controlled the diamond mines. By 1888, De Beers had a monopoly.

The discovery of South Africa's main gold reefs took place in 1886 in what was at the time the Boer Republic of Transvaal, in the Witwatersrand scrap. Initially, as with diamonds, the working of the gold outcrops was carried out by individual prospectors, many of whom had been bought out in the course of amalgamation of the diamond fields (Katzenellenbogen 1975, 363). In 1889 it was discovered that more gold lay deep underground but was embedded in a pyritic rock that required sophisticated and expensive technology to be extracted. The consequent shift to deep-shaft mining in the 1890s propelled the process of amalgamation in the gold fields. Small claimholders gradually gave way to conglomerates, especially the *Rand Mines Company,* formed in 1893, and the *Consolidated Gold Fields of South Africa,* formed in 1887. *Anglo American Corporation*, a South African conglomerate, was founded in 1917 by Ernest Oppenheimer with British and American capital, and became a dominant producer of gold, and – by taking over De Beers – diamond as well. After the Second World War, prospecting by this company yielded the discovery of further large gold deposits in the Orange Free State.

Soon the industry acquired the characteristics of a monopoly. There was little or nothing to be gained by competition among companies regarding wages or technology because the demand for gold was infinitely price elastic and because the selling price could not be changed by the companies (it was fixed internationally). Until the early 1960s, there was complete collusion among the companies to keep African wages low (Austen 1987, 163).

2.2 Central African copper: from European discovery to main colonial export

Large-scale copper extraction on the Copperbelt began on the Congolese side (Katanga province) in the first decade of the 20th century. The rich copper deposits that lay on the surface had been mined by locals for centuries, but from the late 19th century British prospectors showed increasing interest (Larmer 2017).

In the Leopoldian tradition of state-monopoly policy, the Congolese state granted the *Comité Spécial du Katanga* (CSK) the right to prospect copper (Peemans 1975, 178). The CSK had been entrusted with the administration of large land concessions in Katanga in 1900, and the state received two-thirds of the profits generated by the CSK, the other third going to a Belgian chartered company. As the CSK was unable to attract Belgian prospectors, Robert Williams, a Scottish engineer who had also obtained prospecting rights in Northern Rhodesia, acquired a 40% interest in Katanga's mineral wealth in 1900. In 1906, the *Union Minière du Haut Katanga* (UMHK) was formed by the CSK in cooperation with Williams' *Tanganyika Concessions Ltd.*

When the Belgian state took formal control over the Congo from King Leopold II in 1908, the UMHK retained its copper mining monopoly until copper was nationalized in 1967 by independent Congo's president Mobutu. Through its holdings in the CSK, the colonial government kept the right to approximately 60% of all profits generated by the mines. Production started in 1912, two years after the railway reached Elisabethville and connected the mines to the port of Beira in Mozambique, from where the product was exported. Smelting plants were set up near the mines to carry out at least the early stages of refinement, to save on transport costs. By the late 1920s Belgian Congo had become the world's third-largest copper exporter (Perrings 1979).

In the mid-1920s, systematic prospecting yielded extensive underground copper reserves on Northern Rhodesia's side of the Copperbelt. The average copper content of the ores in the British colony was much lower (3%–4%) than in Katanga (about 15%) – though higher than in the American ore. However, a new processing method, called flotation, made mining of these lower grade ores profitable. Two large investment groups were attracted by the *British South Africa Company* (BSAC), which administered the territory of Northern Rhodesia until 1924, to prospect and exploit the copper reserves: Chester Beatty's *Selection Trust Limited* (reorganized in 1926 as *Rhodesian Selection Trust*), a British concern with American financial and technical backing, and *Anglo American Corporation*, mainly South African. By 1930, several mines were under construction and commercial production started soon after. Those two parent companies (individual companies were floated for the different mines) retained a monopsony over copper mining until copper was nationalized in 1970 by President Kaunda.

3 The migrant mining labor system until the independence era

3.1 Making the mining labor force in 19th-century South Africa

Labor migration was crucial for the functioning of the mines. Most black laborers in Kimberley did not originate from the immediate surroundings but had traveled more than 150 miles. The largest group of workers belonged to the Pedi tribe from the South African Republic in the Northeast. Second in numbers were the Tsonga people who came from Southern Mozambique (Tsonga from Mozambique were also called Shangaans). For instance, in 1878, Shangaans from Gaza district in Mozambique made up about 30% of the workforce on the diamond diggings (Harries 1994). In 1885, over two-thirds of laborers were Pedi and Tsonga, who traveled 600 to 1,000 miles on foot to the mines (Worger 1987, 109). The Southern Sotho from Basutoland were the third-largest group in the early years, but they and the Tswana from Botswana overtook the former two in the 1890s when the Pedi and Tsonga turned to the gold mines of Transvaal (Turrell 1987, 169). Other ethnic groups (like Tlhaping, Kalanga, Natal Zulu) supplied lower numbers of workers (see Map 10.1).[3]

Africans from the mentioned areas had sought work on farms or public works in the British and Boer republics decades before the onset of mining. In the 1850s and 1860s, rising

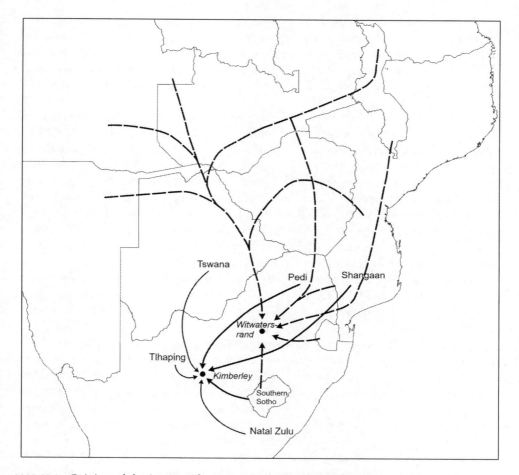

MAP 10.1 Origin and destination of migrants to the South African mines.

Sources: Author's own, based on Crush, Jeeves and Yudelman (1991, 35), Worger (1987, 65ff). Digitized by Stefan de Jong.

Notes: For the gold mines (Witwatersrand), the arrows denote actual major migration routes. For the diamond mines (Kimberley), the arrows merely connect the mines to their major sending regions.

ecological pressures in large parts of Southern Africa (due to the spread of livestock diseases and droughts), as well as the Boers' territorial expansion and wars against Pedi, Tlhaping, and Sotho, had impoverished some of these peoples and increased social stratification, which probably pushed people into labor migration (Worger 1987, 65). Young men belonging to the Sotho and Pedi sought temporary work for some months in the Cape Colony and obtained desired goods like cattle, guns, ammunition, or blankets, to improve their individual economic situation upon return, as well as that of their chiefs, since a proportion of those goods were used to pay taxes.[4] The Tsonga from Southern Mozambique had traveled to Natal (a British colony until 1910) to work on the sugar fields since the 1850s and 1860s, usually for about two years, and returned with sterling pounds. Cash was used to buy goods imported from Europe via Delagoa Bay (now Maputo Bay) and became the main medium of bridewealth from around 1870 (Van den Berg 1987). The diamond mines opened another opportunity to work that paid higher wages than other types of employment, and to acquire desired goods, pay for a bride, and reinvest in the rural economy (purchasing livestock, plows, or wagons).[5]

On the other hand, the diamond mines' high demand and prices of perishable food and firewood, which were too expensive or short-lived to transport over long distances at least until the railway from the Cape reached Kimberley in 1885, provided a market opportunity for Africans who occupied land in the immediate surroundings, like the Griquas, Korannna, and Tlhaping (Worger 1987, 82–3).

In the early stages of mining, a few black Africans were claim holders in the diamond diggings, or independent share-workers of the claims, though most were already wage laborers. The wage workers traveled on their own account for several hundred miles on foot to work with pick and shovel under the supervision of white diggers, usually for short periods of three to six months, upon which they returned to their rural homes. Given the high demand of wage workers during the rushes on the diamond mines, their wages were relatively high and rising in the early years. Between 1871 and 1875, weekly wages quintupled from 5 shillings per week to 25 shillings per week plus food (Worger 1987, 87). Clearly, workers' wages, when determined freely and competitively, had to compensate the long and dangerous journey on foot, as well as the high costs and daily insecurity of living around the mines (Harries 1994, 53). Reflecting miners' agency, when mining faced a deep crisis in 1876, black workers resisted the 50% wage cuts that white claim holders aimed to introduce, and instead left en masse to their rural areas or sought wage work in the Cape. Soon after, wages shot up again.

The situation of black mine labor took a turn for the worse after diamond mining changed hands from individual prospectors to large-scale oligopolistic firms. Less labor was required due to increasing mechanization (Table 10.1), and companies were able to exert pressure on the administration to help them increase the supply of wage workers from South Africa, by reducing their subsistence basis and opportunities to market their produce, and by imposing or increasing financial obligations in the form of taxes.[6] For instance, Britain's annexation of Griqualand West went hand in hand with dispossessions of the local population in favor of whites, confining Griquas to plots of land often too small to be self-sufficient. Additionally, in 1879 the administration raised a hut tax on the native population (Worger 1987, 94–6). Land annexations by British or Boers elsewhere, such as in Basutoland in 1882 and Bechuanaland (today's Botswana) in 1885, had the same effect of pushing black Africans to seek wage labor in the mines (and elsewhere). The companies also colluded over wages to limit the bargaining power of workers (Worger 1987, 107).

TABLE 10.1 Number of black mineworkers by mine in Kimberley in the 1880s

Mine	1881	1882	1883	1884	1885
Kimberley	3,000	4,000	2,000	1,500	1,500
De Beers	2,000	2,000	1,260	1,700	1,700
Dutoitspan	8,000	3,235	2,800	3,300	4,500
Bultfontain	4,000	2,685	2,300	2,500	3,600
Total	17,000	11,920	8,360	9,000	11,300

Source: Worger (1987, 103).

Large diamond mine owners managed to obtain significant political influence to impose laws that facilitated the exertion of control over their labor force. In 1880, the Cape Colony annexed the Crown Colony of Griqualand West and made the Cape Parliament directly responsible for enacting legislation in the territory. In 1881, J. B. Robinson, one of the major shareholders of the Kimberly mines, and Cecil Rhodes of the *De Beers Mining Company* were both elected for Kimberley in the Cape Parliament. At their suggestion, the Parliament enacted the *Diamond Trade Act* in 1882. Under this Act, people accused of illicit diamond trade were presumed guilty until they could prove their innocence and heavy punishments were imposed on diamond thieves. The Act also allowed the mining companies to perform intimate body searches on black workers when entering or leaving the diamond mines. Furthermore, extra police were appointed to enforce the pass laws, increasing the number of arrests and convicts.[7] In 1883, De Beers negotiated with the Cape government to establish a privately controlled convict labor station, whose inmates carried out compulsory work in the mines.

From 1885, all miners were housed in compounds, built by the three mining companies that effectively controlled the diamond production, following the example of the De Beers' convict labor station. The aim of compounds was to avoid illicit diamond trade and to eliminate drunkenness and absenteeism. Miners were not allowed to leave the compound except to work, and they did so through a tunnel connecting the compound with the mines. Food was sold in the company store and alcohol was prohibited in the early years. Diseases like pneumonia and dysentery prevailed under the unsanitary conditions and inadequate housing of the compounds. Hospital facilities for black workers were very deficient.[8] However, an uprising in 1890 in response to a reduction of wages led to some improvements in labor conditions, such as the implementation of eight-hour shifts and better medical and sanitary services in compounds (Hofmeester 2017, 100).

Still not content with the supply and price of labor, the mining companies sought to actively recruit labor in farther rural areas from 1885. Until then, black wage workers had arrived in Kimberley largely on their own account, in accord with demands of the agricultural cycle, and white diggers contracted them at the outskirts of the town. Following a depression of the industry in 1883, thousands of workers were dismissed. Afterward, the three companies started to hire men recruited through direct negotiations with chiefs in rural areas or through established labor agents, who generally had unsavory reputations. They also colluded to pay only half the pre-crisis wage and offer only longer (six months to one year) contracts (Worger 1987, 107). In contrast to the gold mines, since the early 20th-century diamond mines used independent recruiters (as opposed to a monopolistic recruitment organization) and could rely to a larger extent on workers who presented themselves on their own accord (Katzenellenbogen 1975, 412). It is unclear to what extent miners at the turn of the 20th century were still combining mine work with farming. According to Turrell, the large number of women and children who resided around the diamond compounds and were dependent on miners in 1903 suggests that an increasing number were landless and did not return to their rural homesteads between contracts (Turrell 1987, 169).

3.2 Twentieth-century expansion of South Africa's labor catchment area

Initially, the demand for unskilled black labor in the gold mines was met by the men who had supplied the diamond mines: the Pedi from Transvaal and the Shangaans (Tsonga) from Mozambique. However, the gold rush of the 1890s accelerated labor demand so that at the turn of the century, 100,000 black Africans worked in the Rand mines, up from 14,000 in 1890, a number that increased further in the following decades (Wilson 1972, 4).

The mobilization of large numbers of unskilled and low-paid laborers from poorer distant areas throughout Southern Africa (and even for a short time between 1904 and 1907 from China) probably became crucial for the survival of the South African gold mining industry (Crush, Jeeves, and Yudelman, 1991, 1). Ore deposits, though large, turned out to be of lower quality than expected and lay deep underground. The geological characteristics demanded expensive equipment for deep-shaft mining and also favored the use of a large number of unskilled labor.[9] Since the price of gold was fixed internationally, production costs could not be passed on to consumers (Figure 10.1). Saving on labor costs was the only strategy left to increase the profit margins. Thus, while the white workers' positions and wages were protected by racial policies and trade unions, the real value of black mineworkers' cash earnings probably fell over the period from 1911 to 1969. Black miners' wages also lost value against black wages in the South African manufacturing sector, which did not tap into foreign countries' labor pools (Feinstein 2005, 67).

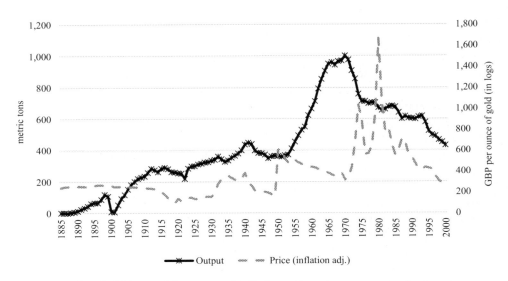

FIGURE 10.1 South African gold output and inflation-adjusted average annual price.
Sources: South African gold output in metric tons and UK inflation (for CPI): https://clio-infra.eu/Indicators/Inflation.html; price of gold (London Market Price): Officer and Williamson (2021).

The *Chamber of Mines*, formed in 1889, coordinated the Randlords' initiatives to secure sufficient labor at a low cost (Wilson 1972, 2–3). In 1896, it created the *Rand Native Labor Association* to curtail the competition in labor recruitment by the different mines and keep wages low. Its successor since 1900, the *Witwatersrand Native Labor Association* (WNLA), retained a monopsony over African labor recruitment outside South Africa and the protectorates. Initially WNLA recruited only in Mozambique, which supplied most foreign workers throughout the history of Rand gold mining, but it expanded its catchment area in the following decades.

WNLA recruitment outside South Africa was regulated by inter-state agreements that secured at least some profit for the labor-exporting countries. The first official Labor Agreement between the Portuguese colonial government and the *Chamber of Mines*, the Modus Vivendi, was signed in 1901. This agreement and its later amendments granted WNLA monopolistic permission to recruit labor in Mozambique. For its part, the Lusitanian colonial government charged recruitment licenses as well as administrative fees for each Mozambican employee to the recruiting organization. Workers were to travel by train to Johannesburg and be repatriated after completion of their fixed-term contracts, to ensure Mozambique was not permanently deprived of its working population. This way, miners contributed to the monetization of the home economy and paid hut taxes levied by the Portuguese administration (Alexopoulou and Juif 2017).

The length of stay of foreign circular migrant workers in the mines – also stipulated in the inter-state agreements – varied by origin and in time but was never more than two years in a row. For Mozambicans, contracts were of 12 months, extendable by a further 6 months. Black South African workers were mostly engaged for fixed contracts of 270 shifts (around ten and a half months) by the *Native Recruiting Corporation* (NRC). Following the example of Kimberley's diamond mines, black workers in the Witwatersrand were housed as single men in barracks for the duration of their contracts. Until the 1970s, a mere 3% of black workers were placed in family housing (Crush, Jeeves, and Yudelman 1991, 13).[10]

Table 10.2 shows the origin of black gold mineworkers from the 1890s to the 2000s. Before the *Native Recruiting Corporation* (NRC) was set up in 1912, to recruit in South Africa, Lesotho, Swaziland, and the southern parts of Botswana, almost 70% of black mineworkers were recruited in Mozambique by WNLA. About another 8% originated from "tropical Africa," including Angola, Northern Rhodesia, and Nyasaland. However, due to the appalling pneumonia death rates among the latter groups of workers, in 1913 (and until 1933) the British and South African governments banned recruitment in any area above 22 degrees south latitude.

Labor shortage was relieved in the 1920s and 1930s and the mines temporarily cut down on recruitment in foreign countries. A sharp decline in real gold prices after the First World War threatened to render several mines unprofitable, and many workers were laid off. The Great Depression, which freed workers from other sectors, made labor even more abundant. By 1932, the share of – recruited – foreign black workers had come down to less than 40% (Crush, Jeeves, and Yudelman 1991, 232).

From 1940 to 1970, the increasing wages and proletarianization outside mining raised pressure on African miners' wages, which was met by a renewed push of recruitment northward. In fact, the African miners reacted to the refusal of the Chamber to increase wages by illegally forming the *African Mine Workers' Union* in 1941 and inciting a strike in 1946, which the state and Chamber ruthlessly suppressed (Crush, Jeeves, and Yudelman 1991, 12). The mining industry even tried in the post-Second World War period to cut its total wage bill by partly stabilizing its South African black labor force and weakening the "color bar,"

TABLE 10.2 Black workers in the South African mines, totals and percentages

Panel A: Total numbers (yearly average)

Year	South Africa	Mozambique	Nyasaland	Southern Rhodesia	Northern Rhodesia	German East A.	Angola	Botswana	Lesotho	Swaziland	Other	Tropical	Total
1896–98[a]	19,170[b]	32,508	270					2106					54,000
1906[c]	18,000	53,000						300	2,000	600		6,000[d]	79,900
1920	74,452	77,921	354	12				2,112	10,439	3,449	5,484		174,402
1930	92,772	77,828		44		183		3,151	22,306	4,345	5		200,634
1940	179,708	74,693	8,037	8,112	2,725		698	14,427	52,044	7,152	70		347,766
1950	121,609	86,246	7,831	2,073	3,102	5,495	9,767	12,390	34,467	6,619	4,826		294,425
1960	141,806	101,733	21,934	747	5,292	14,025	12,364	21,404	48,842	6,623	844		375,614
1970	105,169	93,203	78,492	3			4,125	20,461	63,988	6,269	972		370,312
1980	233,088	39,539	13,569	5,770			5	17,763	96,309	8,090	1,404		415,537
1989	243,556	42,807	2,212					16,051	100,529	16,730			421,885
2000	99,575	57,034						6,494	58,224	9,360			230,687

TABLE 10.2 *(continued)*

Panel B: Percentages

Year	South Africa	Mozambique	Nyasaland	Southern Rhodesia	Northern Rhodesia	German East A.	Angola	Botswana	Lesotho	Swaziland	Other	Tropical[b]	Total
1896–98[a]	35.5	60.2	0.5					3.9					100
1906[c]	22.5	66.3						0.4	2.5	0.8		7.5[d]	100
1920	42.7	44.7	0.2	0.0				1.2	6.0	2.0	3.1		100
1930	46.2	38.8		0.0		0.1		1.6	11.1	2.2	0.0		100
1940	51.7	21.5	2.3	2.3	0.8		0.2	4.1	15.0	2.1	0.0		100
1950	41.3	29.3	2.7	0.7	1.1	1.9	3.3	4.2	11.7	2.2	1.6		100
1960	37.8	27.1	5.8	0.2	1.4	3.7	3.3	5.7	13.0	1.8	0.2		100
1970	28.4	25.2	21.2	0.0			1.1	5.5	17.3	1.7	0.3		100
1980	56.1	9.5	3.3	1.4			0.0	4.3	23.2	1.9	0.3		100
1989	57.7	10.1	0.5					3.8	23.8	4.0			100
2000	43.2	24.7						2.8	25.2	4.1			100

Sources: Crush, Jeeves, and Yudelman (1991, 234–5); Feinstein (2005, 65); Wilson (1976, 456); Crush, Peberdy, and Williams (2006, 10).

[a] Includes labor in gold and coal mines in Transvaal.

[b] Includes Lesotho and Swaziland.

[c] Data from Witwatersrand Native Labour Association (WENELA) Annual Reports (rounded numbers), cited in Wilson (1976, 456).

[d] Includes Malawi, Angola, Zambia.

so as to replace some of the increasingly expensive white miners by cheaper black ones, but these attempts failed due to government opposition (Crush, Jeeves, and Yudelman 1991, 83). Similar agreements as the one with Mozambique had been reached with Northern and Southern Rhodesia and Nyasaland in 1938, and several new WNLA recruitment stations refurbished the mines in the following decades. Map 10.1 shows the main migration streams in 1940 to 1970. From about 1970, labor migrancy to South Africa's mines entered a new phase (see Section 4).

To sum up, the gold mines in South Africa relied for a long time, until the 1970s, on a system of circular migration from distant rural places and foreign countries. Labor-supplying governments, rural chiefs, and white workers (voters) preferred this system, which was, most times, also not at odds with the mining industry's interests, over the stabilization of workers and their families around mines.

Recruiting in distant poor areas allowed mining companies to hire men with a low reservation wage. A workforce whose members oscillate between rural and urban areas could "justifiably" be paid below the urban subsistence level as it was assumed that the worker got additional support from his native village (Wilson 1972, 121). A migrant workforce was also easier to control, as insurgent workers could be removed by returning them to their home areas, and could be fragmented politically.[11]

The high turnover of black mineworkers helped ensure that they did not compete with white miners in terms of training and skills, providing justification for the color bar, which became entrenched in South Africa's racial state ideology both before and during the apartheid regime (after 1948). Under the later pass laws including the 1923 *Natives (Urban Areas) Act* and its subsequent amendments, urban areas were deemed as "white," and black South Africans were granted only temporary permission of residence for the duration of their contracts. The circular labor migration system made sure that black people did not reside and work long enough without interruption in the city to qualify for permanent residency in the metropolitan area (Ogura 1996).

For their part, labor-sending colonial governments did not wish to be deprived permanently of their working and tax-paying population and received their share from "lending" their workforce. Rural chiefs and village elders generally insisted on their followers' allegiance to traditional leadership structures and gained, for instance, from taxing returning mineworkers and cashing in on bridewealth. As to migrants themselves, the circulation between mines and rural areas may have been their preferred arrangement in the beginning, particularly when there was no minimum contract length, which allowed men to work long enough to meet a set target while their help was not needed at home for farming. But after years of movement and increasing landlessness or deterioration of traditional livelihoods, they might have preferred to settle permanently with their families near their workplace. However, in the Rand mines this option was cut off by the law (Wilson 1972, 5).

The sending rural areas were certainly affected as a consequence of the periodical deprivation of a significant share of their young adult male population, but the effects may have varied from place to place. In the view of many scholars writing in the 1960s and 1970s, South African mine labor migrancy in the 20th century undermined the peasantry and intensified poverty in the African reserves (e.g., Moyana 1976; Bundy 1979). The absence of able-bodied men may have resulted in lower yields in some instances, but logically the total income in the communities, including cash wages, must have increased in the short run, as men would probably have decided to stay put otherwise (Wilson 1972, 131). Still, income distribution, agricultural practice, culture, or institutions may have suffered disruptions induced by labor migration (Sanderson 1961; Van den Berg 1987).

On the other hand, some studies emphasize African agency, and hold that, although some migrants used their earnings to gain independence from parental or chief control or to satisfy newly acquired tastes of consumption goods, many have also used such earnings to support their rural homesteads. For instance, Beinart (2014) argues that most migrant miners returning to Mpondoland – where in 1936 over 40% of all 15–40-year-old males were absent at any time of the year – reinvested their wages (which until 1910 were sometimes even paid in cattle) into the rural economy, thereby raising agricultural productivity. He provides evidence based on agricultural censuses and surveys of a positive rather than an inverse relationship between mine wage income, livestock holdings, and smallholder output – at least until the 1960s. In the latter part of the 20th century, when the share of households deriving their incomes from farming declined and unemployment rose, transfers of income from mineworkers were probably vital for some rural households in sending areas.

3.3 From international recruitment to stabilization in Katanga until the Great Depression

Securing sufficient labor for the construction and operation of the mines in Katanga was the largest challenge faced by the UMHK in the first decades of its existence. The mining area was sparsely populated given its unfavorable geographic and climatic characteristics. Moreover, the Congolese population probably had little incentive to work for Europeans, due to the bad reputation it earned during the rubber exploitation under King Leopold's rule, the high morbidity and mortality of miners, and the possibilities to sell food produce to the mines.[12]

In the early years, the mines, in cooperation with the Belgian colonial state, resorted to organized and often forceful recruitment in relatively distant areas of the Congo as well as in surrounding colonies. From 1910, a government-assisted recruiting agency, the *Bourse du Travail du Katanga* (BTK), controlled by UMHK, Katanga Railways, and other enterprises, recruited labor in Belgian colonial territory, particularly in the province of Kasai in the center of the Congo and in the Lomami district of Katanga. After neighboring Ruanda-Urundi became a League of Nations-*mandated territory* under Belgian administration, the BTK recruited there as well.

The colonial state legitimized moral and fiscal pressure to work exerted on natives by a need to defeat presumed "African laziness" (Juif and Frankema 2018). It set quotas of able-bodied men who could be recruited in each village, to be selected by local chiefs and handed over to recruiters. Although the Belgian foreign office voiced some concerns about violent and fraudulent practices by the semi-private recruitment agencies in the late 1910s, and legislation attempted to safeguard recruits from those abuses, little was done to enforce it (Buell 1928, 538). Around 10% of recruits, many of whom had been compelled to sign work contracts, deserted on their way to the mines or shortly after arrival in the early 1920s (in South Africa the desertion rate was around 2%) (Buell 1928, 554). Government assisted employers in retrieving deserted workers by introducing a dactyloscopic (fingerprint-based) identification system in 1919, and in 1922 decreed the termination of employment before contract expiration as illegal, punishable with prison and fines (Buell 1928, 553). Until the Great Depression, an important but decreasing share of African mineworkers was recruited outside the Belgian territories, in neighboring British Northern Rhodesia (also Nyasas were recruited there), and Portuguese Angola (see Table 10.3). The "foreign" share was almost 50% until the mid-1920s, and most of them were contracted through private recruiting companies like *Robert Williams and Company* or *Correa Freires*. Other than the vast catchment area of South Africa's recruiters, the majority came from neighboring countries (see Map 10.2), and organized recruitment ceased to be the main instrument to secure labor after 1930.

Like between South Africa and other sending countries, labor migration to Katanga was regulated by inter-state contracts. The agreement with Northern Rhodesia included the posting of a permanent Inspector of Rhodesian Labor at the largest mine, the "Star of the Congo" at Lumumbashi, and granting *Robert Williams and Company* the exclusive right of labor recruitment in the northeast of Northern Rhodesia. These contracts also stipulated that workers had to be repatriated to their home village at the end of their terms, where they would receive the last part – about two-thirds – of their wage according to what was known as the "deferred pay system." This clause ensured that "exported" laborers fulfilled their domestic tax obligations. The wages of mine labor migrants were the main source of tax revenue raised by the BSAC. The BSAC also permitted labor recruitment for Katanga because the mines provided traffic for the Rhodesian railway which it had built. The duration of contracts was usually 180 working days (ca. 7 months) or, after 1922, 240 days.[13]

TABLE 10.3 Origin of laborers at the UMHK in total numbers and percentages

Panel A: Total numbers (period averages)

Years	Northern Rhodesia	Barotse[a]	Angola	Congo	Nyasaland and others	Ruanda-Urundi	Total of foreigners	Sum total
1920–22	6,182	241	355	5,472	431		7,195	12,680
1923–25	6,380	77	401	8,167	385		7,243	15,410
1926–27	4,834	920	577	13,303	535	1,241	6,844	21,409
1928–30				11,672		2,860	4,922	19,454
1931–40				10,214		707	1,502	12,423
1941–50				17,709		239	1,952	19,900
1951–60				19,954		3,481	1,816	25,252

Panel B: Percentages

Years	Northern Rhodesia	Barotse[a]	Angola	Congo	Nyasaland and others	Ruanda-Urundi	Total of foreigners	Sum total
1920–22	48.8	1.9	2.8	43.2	3.4		56.8	100
1923–25	41.4	0.5	2.6	53.0	2.5		47.0	100
1926–27	22.6	4.3	2.7	62.2	2.5	5.8	32.0	100
1928–30				60.0		14.7	25.3	100
1931–40				82.3		5.7	12.1	100
1941–50				88.9		1.2	9.8	100
1951–60				79.1		13.8	7.2	100

Source: Rapports Annuels UMHK-MOI, various years.
[a] Barotseland was a part of Western Northern Rhodesia which enjoyed special autonomy.

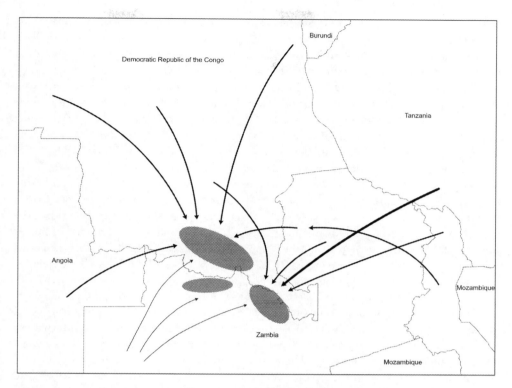

MAP 10.2 Origin of migrants to the Congolese and Northern Rhodesian Copperbelt mines.
Sources: Author's own, based on Rapports Annuels UMHK-MOI, various years; Northern Rhodesia Chamber of Mines Annual Reports, 1950s and 1960s. Digitized by Stefan de Jong.

Note: The destinations are approximate; the arrows do not signify the specific destination of migrants within the Copperbelt.

Arguably, thanks to some of the conditions stipulated in these agreements, the morbidity and mortality of Rhodesian workers in Katanga was lower than among the Congolese recruits.

Recruitment for the UMHK had important consequences for the sending regions in and outside the Congo. Perrings (1977) documents a short period of organized recruitment by *Robert Williams and Company* in the Angolan province of Moxico (about 300 to 500 miles from the mines) between 1917 and 1921. Even though stipulated differently in an inter-state agreement with the Portuguese, outright coercion was employed in the recruitment and deserters were brutally punished. As a consequence of the deplorable recruitment practices and the high morbidity in the mine camps, out of the 3,479 Angolans recruited in this period, 536 men died on company premises, and a further 778 deserted. One year after the recruitment operation started, the territory was recorded to have been left abandoned by Africans following the disruptions of these activities. Williams' concession was not renewed the following year, but some Angolans continued to be recruited until 1921; afterward, they came on a voluntary basis.

Beginning in 1918 and until 1930, the UMHK withdrew from the Southern African migrant labor system, which continued to furnish African recruits for other industries and farms of the region (Higginson 1989). As Table 10.3 shows, the share of "foreign" workers in the Katanga mines decreased from about 60% in the early 1920s to about 10% in the

218 Dácil Juif

1940s. As it turned its back on foreign labor, mine management freed itself from the considerable costs of organized recruitment in foreign territory. In 1931, as the Great Depression had diminished the demand for labor, the UMHK decided to stop actively recruiting outside Belgian territory altogether. At the same time, the company resolved to cut down on recruitment within the Congo, also due to pressure from missionaries and some civil servants who denounced the social disruption caused by the departure of young men to the emerging urban centers (Peemans 1975, 190). While in 1922 76% of all UMHK black workers had been actively recruited, in 1935 the share was only 15% – all recruited in Katanga's Lomami district – and by the mid-1940s it had declined to around 5%.[14]

One reason for giving up on foreign African labor recruitment was its costs relative to Congolese labor. After the First World War, the value of the Belgian franc against the British pound dropped abruptly, raising the wage bill for black African workers from British colonies – as well as for white workers – who had to be paid in sterling. On top of that, the incipient mining industry and consequent rise in labor demand on the Rhodesian side of the Copperbelt border disrupted the labor supply for Katanga. In 1929, the British colonial government prohibited recruitment by the UMHK in Northern Rhodesia upon request of the new domestic mining companies.

The UMHK management's decision to dissolve its dependence on large-scale labor recruitment in and outside Belgian territory went hand in hand with the implementation of a policy of stabilization, which involved a search for improved productivity and paternalistic and authoritarian welfare policy. The UMHK sought to reengage Congolese workers immediately after their contracts expired and offered longer contracts. After 1927, the company hired workers only for three-year contracts. While in 1928 45% of the workforce had a contract for a duration of three years, 98% had one in 1931 (Mottoulle 1946, 53). In the vein of paternalism, a very large share of labor costs was not spent on cash wages but on food for workers and their families, hospital and children's welfare, amortization of housing construction, clothes, and firewood, in total about 50% to 70% until the 1950s (Juif and Frankema 2018). The company had realized that married workers were healthier, more productive, and more likely to stay for the three years or longer. Thus, the UMHK strongly encouraged the presence of wives in camps, even advancing wage payments for bridewealth to unmarried workers when signing their work contract (Mottoule 1946, 19). Infrastructure in mining compounds was improved dramatically during the 1920s and Catholic missionaries were put in charge of the provision of wide-ranging welfare services. Workers' death rates declined from 35 per 1,000 in 1920 to less than 2 per 1,000 in 1930 and thereafter, remaining higher for underground workers than for surface miners (see Table 10.4).

TABLE 10.4 Stabilization in Katanga

Years	mortality per thousand workers	% workers married	% non-recruited workers	Desertion % (contract breach)
1920–24	32.5	14.8[a]	25.6	9.5
1925–29	1.6	25.8	45.1	5.5
1930–34	1.2	52.0	72.0	n.d.

Sources: Rapports Annuels UMHK-MOI, various years; 1930 Report of the Health Inspector of Northern Rhodesia on Native Labor in Katanga. National Archives of Zambia, Lusaka. SEC 2/165.
[a] In 1924.

A motivation for the UMHK's investment in longer-term work relations was its decision that it was economical to invest in African workers' training. Trained black workers were to complement increasingly used machinery and to replace more expensive (semi-)skilled white mineworkers. Increased labor productivity and mechanization resulted in an increase of UMHK's finished copper production from about 19,000 tons in 1920 to 147,500 in 1930, while the African workforce was merely doubled (see Figures 10.2 and 10.3). Soon, the children of the stabilized workers were also educated and trained to make up the future labor force, whereby Benedictine missionaries with the help of African *moniteurs* inculcated in them the traits of obedience and work ethic (Juif 2019). In the Congo, other than in the British territories of Southern and Central Africa, given the absence of European trade unions which demanded equal pay for equal work, technically qualified Africans could be promoted to skilled jobs and could replace Europeans (for a much lower pay). Already in 1919, after a failed strike by – mainly South African – white miners, many of the white workers had been dismissed and were replaced by black Africans (Higginson 1989, 42). The range of wage scales for African workers was thus higher in the Congolese than in the Rhodesian mines, because it included, for instance, overseers (Juif and Frankema 2018, 24).

Worker insurgencies among UMHK-stabilized workers were probably kept at bay by a tight net of control, including camp police and church-sponsored associations, and in general an appeasing paternalistic labor system. Following black workers' strikes in 1941, during the Second World War, motivated by a rise in food prices, the Belgian government introduced a further series of improvements in working conditions, like minimum wages and legalization of trade unions in 1946; compensation for accidents at the workplace in 1949; family allowances in 1951; paid vacations in 1954; as well as an eight-hour day in 1958 (Larmer 2017). The Katangese indigenous miners' trade union turned out to be disinclined to strike – also compared to its Rhodesian counterpart – and only a small share of workers affiliated. In the words of Ralph Austen: "miners in Katanga became a black labor aristocracy but one very much under the control of *Union Minière* and lacking political, social or [...] economic influence comparable to the position of white south African workers" (Austen 1987, 167).

Stabilization was well established in the 1950s and 1960s, and the UMHK had a large pool of experienced and trained workers, even if it continued its recruitment missions within the Congo (in Kasai and Lomami) and Ruanda-Urundi (Rwanda and Burundi) to supply a small part of the "fresh" labor (except in the 1930s, when the Great Depression did away with labor shortage). By 1951, the average term of employment in Katanga mines was 11 years.[15] Out of the workers who were newly engaged (i.e., in their first three-year contract) the share that had been actively recruited by the UMHK recruitment missions ranged between 13% in 1956 and 35% in 1961. The rest were engaged onsite.[16]

3.4 Hesitant urbanization in Northern Rhodesia's Copperbelt

When mining operations started out in Northern Rhodesia, labor scarcity was a challenge, given that the population was used to seeking work abroad. On the other hand, the mining companies had the advantage that they were able to tap into a domestic pool of labor that was experienced with copperminework in Katanga. The costs that could be saved on organized recruitment were invested in workers' wages to compete with the UMHK. In 1928, for instance, all workers had come to the mines on their own account in Bwana Mkubwa

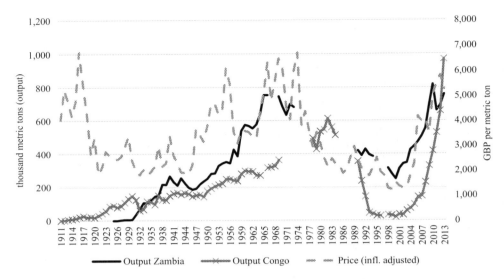

FIGURE 10.2 Congolese and Zambian copper output and inflation-adjusted average annual price.
Sources: Congo output up to 1990: Statistical Year Books of Belgium and the Belgian Congo, various years, Perrings (1979, 248–9), Rapport Annuel Banque National du Congo 1970, République du Zaïre: conjoncture économique, années 1985–86; Zambia output up to 1990: Blue Books of Northern Rhodesia, Northern Rhodesian Chamber of Mines Year Books, Annual Report of the Mine Department 1973 (for 1969–73); Congo and Zambia output after 1990: https://www.usgs.gov/; copper price (at London Metal Exchange or COMEX): Berger (1974, 238) before 1942, Northern Rhodesia Chamber of Mines Year Books from 1942 until 1959; after 1960, https://www.macrotrends.net/1476/copper-prices-historical-chart-data; CPI for United Kingdom (GBP) from https://clio-infra.eu/Indicators/Inflation.html.

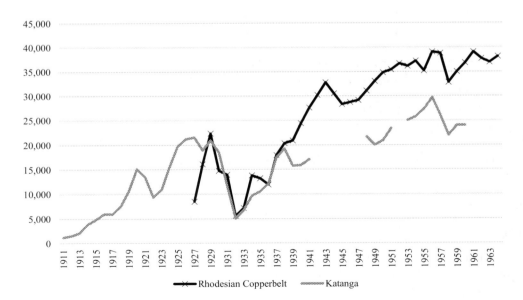

FIGURE 10.3 Number of workers, Katanga and Copperbelt, 1911–64.
Source: Juif and Frankema (2018, 319).

(a lead and zinc mine in Central province) and 88% at the Roan Antelope copper mine (Ferguson 1999, 49). Only during the mine construction boom, which required the mobilization of huge numbers of workers in a short period (31,941 in the peak in September 1930), was part of the labor obtained by recruitment agencies, sometimes through coercion (some 30% to 40%) (Ferguson 1999, 49).

The height of the Northern Rhodesian mine construction boom coincided with the onset of the Great Depression, which hit the copper industry hard. The price of copper declined by half in the years after 1929 (see Figure 10.2), resulting in the temporary closure of mines and a hold on mine construction work. With the crisis, the problem of labor scarcity had been solved and organized recruitment was done away with altogether, in favor of an all-voluntary labor force (Parpart 1986, 47). Even though mining companies did not have to resort to proactive recruitment, they did complain at times about the government failing to raise higher barriers on outmigration to Southern Rhodesia and South Africa.[17]

Like in the other cases studied here, most of the African workers did not originate from the areas immediately surrounding the mines, but, in the case of Northern Rhodesia, from the agriculturally poorer areas in the Northeast about 300 to 500 miles away, where the Bemba-speaking people lived. A 1945 memorandum on native labor of the most important mining companies reads that 50% came from Northern province (Bemba territory); Southern and Western provinces supplied 2–3% of miners each; Barotse province in the west supplied 3% of labor; and the remaining provinces contributed about 8% in total. The rest, around 30% to 40%, came from outside Northern Rhodesia. The 1960 *Chamber of Mines Year Book* records that 25% of all workers came from outside Northern Rhodesia, 30% from Northern province (main Bemba territory), 16% from Luapula province, 10% from Eastern province, 8% from Central province, and the rest from Northwestern, Barotse, Western, and Southern province.[18]

The Northern Rhodesian mining companies looked at both South Africa and Katanga for models of labor systems. Mine management may at first have favored a men-only, circular migrant labor force, following the example of South Africa, as it allowed the companies to save on the cost of housing and on feeding workers' families (Parpart 1986). On the other hand, Chauncey (1981) has argued that the policy of the mine managers almost from the start was to gain a competitive advantage over labor markets in South Africa and Southern Rhodesia by allowing the presence of wives and children. Even though companies did not build enough suitable houses or provide sufficient food rations for families until after the Second World War, often resulting in crowded living conditions, the possibility to bring their wives was attractive for many workers, and compound managers soon also recognized the advantages of the presence of women. The share of married workers in the camps of Katanga and the Rhodesian Copperbelt was not dissimilar in the late 1920s (about 30%), though afterward Katanga was always ahead of Northern Rhodesian by around 10% to 20% (see Table 10.5).

Still, compared to Katanga, mining companies probably had lower incentives to invest in longer-term relations with their African workers. A *legal* color bar was never introduced in Northern Rhodesia, as the Colonial Office opposed it, and European settlers as well as white South African workers lacked the political power or incentives to impose it, also because they were small in numbers and their turnover was high (Money 2016). Still, a de facto color bar was embedded in company policy. This meant that all skilled and semi-skilled positions were reserved for the white workforce, deterring companies from training Africans. As Table 10.6 shows, whereas Katanga gradually replaced white workers by Africans, the black to

TABLE 10.5 Percentage of workers married

	Rhodesian Copperbelt	Katanga
1929	28.4	33.7
1935	41.0	50.4
1940	52.1	57.7
1945	48.3	69.7
1950	53.3	78.2
1955	68.8	82.2
1960	75.0	84.9

Source: Ferguson (1999, 59), Rapports Annuels UMHK-MOI, various years.

TABLE 10.6 Black–white mineworker ratio (black miners per white miner)

	Rhodesian Copperbelt	Katanga
1930	8.75	9.49
1932	5.81	7.63
1934	7.62	17.58
1936	7.52	15.23
1938	8.09	22.11
1940	8.31	16.16

Source: Perrings (1979), Rapports Annuels UMHK-MOI, various years.

white miners' ratio remained constant in the Northern Rhodesian mines. At the same time, there was less scope for mechanization in the mostly underground mines of Northern Rhodesia, comparably favoring the use of more untrained workers. Thus, while in 1938 almost all African workers in Katanga had three-year contracts and the majority reengaged after contracts expired, a ticket system whereby miners were paid after 30 completed shifts (one ticket) was still in place in the Northern Rhodesian mines (and over 90% of the workforce had been in service for less than three years).

Different from the Belgian Congo government, Northern Rhodesia's colonial rulers shunned what they called detribalization, or the complete severance of indigenous peoples from their tribal roots (Ferguson 1999, 50 ff). They continued for years to fear a depression similar to the one of 1931, which left thousands of urban unemployed who had to be taken care of. The provision that the mining industry would die out someday discouraged the presence of children in compounds who would know of no employment other than mining. Further, permanent urbanization and the loss of support from rural kin would require the provision of costly retirement pensions and adequate urban welfare facilities. Therefore, in the 1940s the Rhodesian government demanded that Copperbelt mining companies retain a part of miners' salary and remit it to their tribal villages at the end of their contracts, to ensure that workers returned and spent their cash there.[19] Legal restrictions to African settlement in urban areas were set in place as well and not lifted completely until independence in 1964, although they were certainly not enforced as effectively as in South Africa.

Despite the often-conflicting interests between the colonial administration on the one hand and company managers (and Africans) on the other, in 1945 and 1946 the decision was taken by ruling elites to invest in a stabilized workforce. The government's goal to invest in urban development was recorded in the *Ten-Year Development Plan for Northern Rhodesia* approved in 1947 (Heisler 1971).[20] African mining townships in the Copperbelt were supplied with water-borne sanitation, paved roads, street lighting, proper houses for nuclear families, and some schools. Until 1950, all African workers were housed and fed at the expense of the mining companies, while afterward they were gradually brought into an "inclusive wage scheme," which consisted of wages being paid exclusively in cash, and in which they paid rents themselves. As part of the stabilization program, the Northern Rhodesian *Chamber of Mines* decreed that Africans in their industrial capacity could be represented by trade unionists and most improvements in mine labor conditions were introduced after strike actions, particularly after the creation of the indigenous trade union in 1949, and the state remained at the fringes of it. As mining companies made high profits in the post-war reconstruction period, wages were raised, turning Copperbelt miners into some of the best-paid manual workers in sub-Saharan Africa (Juif and Frankema 2018).

4 Post-independence and the oil crises

When across sub-Saharan Africa, including the areas of recruitment of the South African mines, colonies started gaining independence one after another, some governments of newly independent nations prohibited the recruitment of workers in their territories. WNLA recruiters had always been banned from Angola (Angolans were recruited in Northern Rhodesia, see Map 10.1), and inter-state agreements with the Portuguese colonial administration included the prohibition to recruit above 22° latitude in Mozambique, except for a short time between 1908 and 1913 (Alexopoulou and Juif 2017). After independence in the 1960s, Zambia and Tanzania withdrew their workers from the mines (Wilson 1976). Migration from Mozambique was curtailed in the 1970s when the Frelimo independence movement closed several recruitment centers operated by the WNLA. Most "tropical" recruits came from Malawi before the Malawian president withdrew workers consequent to the crash of a WNLA plane that was carrying migrants to the Rand mines in 1972 (Wilson 1976).

As the events of the 1960s and 1970s revealed the vulnerability derived from depending almost entirely on foreign workers, South African mining companies decided to change their labor and production policy. This shift involved attracting black South African labor by raising wages to make them competitive with other South African industries and at the same time introducing more mechanized production techniques on deeper-level mines to reduce the labor needs (Moodie and Ndatsche 1994). The steep rise in gold prices in 1973–74 (see Figure 10.1) made this wage increase and investments in technology easily bearable (James 1992, 20). In the 1970s companies experimented with stabilization, incentivizing workers to reengage immediately after terminating their contracts, under threat of being replaced (this was a moment of general economic crisis and unemployment outside the gold mining sector). In 1986, almost two-thirds of all miners had been working in the mines for five to ten consecutive years, which contrasted sharply with the high labor turnover before the 1970s (De Vletter 1987).

Stabilization in South Africa was driven partly by the same motives as in Katanga in the 1920s, in particular the increasing insecurity of foreign labor supplies. It also went hand in hand with large investments in technology to reduce the demand for labor. However, neither companies nor the state wholeheartedly invested in family housing and welfare services in workers' camps, in that sense bearing more resemblance with Northern Rhodesia before the late 1940s (De Vletter 1987). Other than in the Belgian Congo, stabilization was certainly not fully backed by the state. Instead, the apartheid regime maintained – at least partly for racial-ideological reasons – high barriers to the permanent settlement of black people in urban centers in the form of pass laws, which were lifted only after 1986 (Ogura 1996, 415).

Different from South Africa's gold mines, the copper mining industry experienced a calamitous bust in the decade after Zambia's and the Democratic Republic of Congo's independence. Copper price crashed after 1974 and did not recover for almost three decades. In the years following the oil shock of the mid-1970s, the terms of trade for copper exporters declined sharply, pushing both countries, which had become heavily dependent on copper, into prolonged economic crises. Throughout the 1980s and 1990s, mining regions were in sustained decline, leading to counter-urbanization, that is, urban to rural migration, and the adoption of rural-based economic activities like charcoal production or agriculture (Potts 2005, 604). In Katanga, some retrenched mineworkers turned to artisanal mining as a survival mechanism (Larmer 2017). Zambia had reached an unusually high level of urbanization for sub-Saharan Africa, with 40% of the population classified as urban in 1980, about half of which was in the Copperbelt (Potts 2005). Fraser and Larmer (2010, 50) explain the return to rural areas this way:

> While developing distinct urban cultures and outlooks, Copperbelt Zambians were never separated in any meaningful sense from their rural kin and areas of origin: indeed, what really defined Zambia was not urbanization per se but the dynamic exchanges between town and village that it enabled.

As a result of structural adjustment programs, the state-owned mining companies *Gécamines* (Congo) and the *Zambia Consolidated Copper Mines Limited* (ZCCM, Zambia) sold their assets to private bidders from the 1990s onward. The growing Chinese demand for copper raised prices from the early 2000s and led to a renewed rise in production. This relatively recent re-emergence of copper mining activities has brought about new types of immigration including Chinese mineworkers, formally contracted by Chinese-owned mining companies; as well as the irregular immigration from neighboring countries of sex workers and workers engaged in the informal sector surrounding mines (Coderre-Proulx, Campbell, and Mandé 2016).

5 Conclusion

This chapter highlighted and compared the strategies used by the major mining companies of Southern and Central Africa to meet their demand for black labor over the 20th century.

At the beginning of mining activities, all mining companies relied on a circular migrant labor force. Where the recruitment of the temporary mineworkers took place depended on the relative costs of labor (including recruitment costs) and the willingness of "labor reserve" governments to allow recruitment in their territory. Eventually, employers throughout Southern and Central Africa deemed it economically sensible to stabilize the labor force, despite the costs – at least partly borne by companies – of retirement pensions, unemployment benefits, urban housing for families, and modern health and education services. These costs probably balanced out the returns on investments in job training, made worthwhile for employees with long-term contracts, and the waning recruitment costs (Austen 1987, 165). The timing of the transition from a continuous migration-based labor system to a stabilized workforce varied from one place to another, which has been explained with reference to different geological conditions of the mines which determined their suitability for a more mechanized production, as well as the relative costs of national to foreign labor, the latter of which could generally not be stabilized.

However, the states' stances toward stabilization, which were informed by both economic and political considerations (including voters' power and preferences), played a major role as well, and were relatively path dependent. Governments' influence on urban workers' stabilization extended to other urban employers than the mines as well (Frederick and Van Nederveen Meerkerk, Chapter 12, this volume). There were clearly different ideological conceptions of the advantages and disadvantages of stabilization not only regarding the net returns to investing in urban development but also regarding the socio-economic consequences for the rural sending areas and the migrants themselves. Northern Rhodesia's government clung to considering "detribalization" as a problem for all parties involved until the late 1940s, when mining companies pressured for stabilization and the state realized urbanization was already under way and irreversible. The Congolese government, in cooperation with employers, experimented early on with stabilization, and positive results strengthened their confidence in the system. South Africa's policy of racial segregation culminating in its apartheid system prevented the promotion of Africans into (semi-)skilled jobs and disincentivized training investments by mining companies. Moreover, the state aimed to reserve central urban areas for white South African residents. Under the circular migrant labor system granting permanent residency permit to black workers and their families could be avoided.

Notes

1 Frederick and Van Nederveen Meerkerk (Chapter 12, this volume) address the early shift to permanent settlement of migrants in Belgian Congolese towns compared to the much more persistent transient character of rural-urban migration in Southern Rhodesia.
2 See Fourie, Chapter 7, this volume) on the Boer expansion in South Africa.
3 The black societies that did not or hardly participated in wage work on the diamond mines, like the Zulu, Mfengu, or Pondo, had relatively prosperous farming conditions and local markets (Turrell, 1987, 19).
4 For many years, diamond miners' wages were also payable directly in guns or ammunition (Katzenellenbogen 1975, 412).
5 As for Mozambicans, escaping worse paid forced work at home, consolidated by the Portuguese forced labor provisions of 1899, probably contributed to push men to enroll for minework in Kimberley and Rand mines (Wilson 1972, 128–9). On labor and migration in Mozambique, also see Ribeiro da Silva and Alexopoulou (Chapter 9, this volume).
6 For similar dynamics in British colonial Africa, see Okia (Chapter 8, this volume).
7 Under the pass laws (which had been introduced in 1872 in Kimberley) the black "servant" received a pass with his name, wage, and the duration of his contract. When he wished to leave the diamond fields, the worker had to present a discharge certificate or a pass attesting to his conduct to be able to leave (Hofmeester 2017, 96).
8 The high morbidity together with the frequency of deadly accidents at work produced a death rate among black people in Kimberly of 80 per 1,000 around 1880 (Worger, 1987, 100).
9 The use of many unskilled workers was more economic for a longer time in the underground Rand gold mines than in the open pit mines of Katanga, where the extraction process soon became more mechanized (Austen 1987).

10 The Rand compounds were not completely closed as theft was not as problematic as in the diamond mines, but closely surveyed.

11 Interestingly, however, Wilson (1972, 125) suggests that a stable workforce should be less prone to industrial unrest, and Northern Rhodesian and Congolese mine companies may have thought so as well.

12 In 1913–17 annual mortality rates of mining workers ranged from 70 to 140 per 1,000 (Roberts 1976, 178).

13 Rapport Annuel du Department de la Main d'Oeuvre Indigène (UMHK-MOI), 1922, 17. Archives générales du Royaume 2 – dépôt Joseph Cuvelier, Brussels.

14 Rapports Annuels UMHK-MOI, several years.

15 Rapport Annuel UMHK-MOI, 1951.

16 Rapports Annuels UMHK-MOI, 1950s and 1960s.

17 "1945 Memorandum on native labor of the most important mines (Mufulira Copper mines Ltd, Nchanga Consolidated Copper Mines, Ltd., Rhokana Corporation Ltd., Roan Antelope Copper Mines Ltd.)". ZCCM (Zambia Consolidated Copper Mines Limited) Archives, Ndola, 10.7.10B.

18 Northern Rhodesian Chamber of Mines Year Book of 1960, ZCCM Archives.

19 Note that this provision was similar to those made with foreign employers receiving Northern Rhodesian laborers.

20 *Ten-Year Development Plan for Northern Rhodesia,* section XVII: African Urban Housing.

References

Alexopoulou, Kleoniki, and Dácil Juif. 2017. "Colonial State Formation without Integration: Tax Capacity and Labour Regimes in Portuguese Mozambique (1890s–1970s)." *International Review of Social History* 62(2): 215–52.

Austen, Ralph. 1987. *African Economic History: Internal Development and External Dependency.* London: James Currey.

Beinart, William. 2014. "A Century of Migrancy from Mpondoland." *African Studies* 73(3): 387–409.

Berger, Elena. 1974. *Labour, Race, and Colonial Rule: the Copperbelt from 1924 to Independence.* Oxford: Clarendon Press.

Brown, Carolyn. 2019. "Mining." In *General Labour History of Africa: Workers, Employers and Governments, 20th–21st Centuries,* edited by Stefano Bellucci and Andreas Eckert, 151–76. Woodbridge: James Currey.

Buell, Raymond. 1928. *The Native Problem in Africa, Vol. II.* New York: Macmillan and Company Limited.

Bundy, Colin. 1979. *The Rise and Fall of the South African Peasantry.* London: James Currey.

Chauncey Jr, George. 1981. "The Locus of Reproduction: Women's Labour in the Zambian Copperbelt, 1927–1953." *Journal of Southern African Studies* 7(2): 135–64.

Cleveland, Todd. 2014. *Stones of Contention: A History of Africa's Diamonds.* Ohio: Ohio University Press.

Coderre-Proulx, Mylène, Bonnie Campbell, and Issiaka Mandé. 2016. *International Migrant Workers in the Mining Sector.* Geneva: International Labour Office.

Crush, Jonathan, Alan Jeeves and David Yudelman. 1991. *South Africa's Labor Empire: A History of Black Migrancy to the Gold Mines.* Cape Town: David Philip Publishers.

Crush, Jonathan, Sally Peberdy, and Vincent Williams. 2006. *International Migration and Good Governance in the Southern African Region.* Southern African Migration Project, Migration Policy Brief No. 17.

De Vletter, Fion. 1987. "Foreign Labour on the South African Gold Mines: New Insights on an Old Problem." *International Labour Review* 126(2): 199–218.

Feinstein, Charles. 2005. *An Economic History of South Africa: Conquest, Discrimination and Development.* Cambridge: Cambridge University Press.

Ferguson, James. 1999. *Expectations of Modernity: Myths and Meanings of Urban Life on the Zambian Copperbelt* [first edition in 1959]. Berkeley: University of California Press.

Fraser, Alastair, and Miles Larmer. 2010. *Zambia, Mining, and Neoliberalism: Boom and Bust on the Globalized Copperbelt*. Cham: Springer.

Harries, Patrick. 1994. *Work, Culture, and Identity: Migrant Laborers in Mozambique and South Africa, c. 1860–1910*. London: James Currey, Johannesburg: Witwatersrand University Press, Portsmouth: Heinemann.

Heisler, Helmuth. 1971. "The Creation of a Stabilized Urban Society: A Turning Point in the Development of Northern Rhodesia/Zambia." *African Affairs* 70(279): 125–45.

Herbert, Ivor. 1972. *The Diamond Diggers: South Africa 1866 to the 1970's*. Tom Stacey Limited.

Higginson, John. 1989. *A Working Class in The Making: Belgian Colonial Labor Policy, Private Enterprise, and the African Mineworker, 1907–1951*. Madison: University of Wisconsin Press.

Hofmeester, Karin. 2017. "Economic Institutions and Shifting Labour Relations in the Indian, Brazilian, and South African Diamond Mines." In *Colonialism, Institutional Change, and Shifts in Global Labour Relations*, edited by Karin Hofmeester and Pim de Zwart, 67–108. Amsterdam: Amsterdam University Press.

James, Wilmot Godfrey. 1992. *Our Precious Metal: African Labour in South Africa's Gold Industry, 1970–1990*. Bloomington: Indiana University Press, Cape Town: David Philip, and London: James Currey.

Juif, Dácil. 2019. "Mining, Paternalism and the Spread of Education in the Congo since 1920." In *Cliometrics of the Family*, edited by Claude Diebolt, Auke Rijpma, Sarah Carmichael, and Charlotte Störmer, 305–32. Cham: Springer.

Juif, Dácil and Ewout Frankema. 2018. "From Coercion to Compensation: Institutional Responses to Labour Scarcity in the Central African Copperbelt." *Journal of Institutional Economics* 14(2): 313–43.

Katzenellenbogen, Simon. 1975. "The Miners' Frontier, Transport and General Economic Development." In *Colonialism in Africa, 1879–1960, Volume 4: The Economics of Colonialism*, edited by Peter Duignan and L.H. Gann, 360–426. Cambridge: Cambridge University Press.

Larmer, Miles. 2017. "Permanent Precarity: Capital and Labour in the Central African Copperbelt." *Labor History* 58(2): 170–84.

Money, Duncan. 2016. *'No Matter How Much or How Little They've Got, They Can't Settle Down': A Social History of Europeans on the Zambian Copperbelt, 1926–1974*. Doctoral dissertation, University of Oxford.

Moodie, T. Dunbar, and Vivienne Ndatsche. 1994. *Men, Mines, and Migration: Going for Gold*. Berkeley and Los Angeles: University of California Press.

Mottoulle, Léopold. 1946. *Politique Sociale de l' Union Minière Du Haut-Katanga pour sa Main D'oeuvre Indigène et ses Résultats au Cours De 20 Années D'application*. Brussels: G. Van Campenhout.

Moyana, J. Kombo. 1976. "The Political Economy of the Migrant Labour System: Implications for Agricultural Growth and Rural Development in Southern Africa." *Africa Development/Afrique et Développement* 1(1): 34–41.

Officer, Lawrence, and Samuel Williamson. 2021. "The Price of Gold, 1257–2014," *MeasuringWorth* [URL: http://www.measuringworth.com/gold/]

Ogura, Mitsuo. 1996. "Urbanization and Apartheid in South Africa: Influx Controls and their Abolition." *Developing Economies* 34(4): 402–23.

Parpart, Jane. 1986. "The Household and The Mine Shaft: Gender and Class Struggles on the Zambian Copperbelt, 1926–64." *Journal of Southern African Studies* 13(1): 36–56.

Peemans, Jean-Philippe. 1975. "Capital Accumulation in the Congo under Colonialism: The Role of the State." In *Colonialism in Africa, 1879–1960, Volume 4: The Economics of Colonialism*, edited by Peter Duignan and L.H. Gann, 165–212. Cambridge: Cambridge University Press.

Pérez Niño, Helena. 2019. "Labour Migration." In *General Labour History of Africa: Workers, Employers and Governments, 20th–21st Centuries*, edited by Stefano Bellucci and Andreas Eckert, 265–98. Woodbridge: James Currey.

Perrings, Charles. 1977. "'Good Lawyers but Poor Workers': Recruited Angolan Labour in the Copper Mines of Katanga, 1917–1921." *Journal of African History* 18(2): 237–59.

Perrings, Charles. 1979. *Black Mineworkers in Central Africa. Industrial Strategies and the Evolution of an African Proletariat in the Copperbelt 1911–1941*. London: Heinemann.

Potts, Deborah. 2005. "Counter-Urbanisation on the Zambian Copperbelt? Interpretations and Implications." *Urban Studies* 42(4): 583–609.

Roberts, Andrew. 1976. *A History of Zambia*. New York: Africana Publishing and Co.

Sanderson, F. E. 1961. "The Development of Labour Migration from Nyasaland, 1891–1914." *Journal of African History* 2(2): 259–71.

Turrell, Rob. 1987. *Capital and Labour on the Kimberley Diamond Fields, 1871–1890*. Cambridge: Cambridge University Press.

Van den Berg, Jelle. 1987. "A Peasant Form of Production: Wage-Dependent Agriculture in Southern Mozambique." *Canadian Journal of African Studies/La Revue canadienne des études africaines* 21(3): 375–89.

Wilson, Francis. 1972. *Labour in the South African Gold Mines 1911–1969*. Cambridge: Cambridge University Press.

Wilson, Francis. 1976. "International Migration in Southern Africa." *International Migration Review* 10(4): 451–88.

Worger, William. 1987. *South Africa's City of Diamonds: Mine Workers and Monopoly Capitalism in Kimberley, 1867–1895*. New Haven, CT and London: Yale University Press.

PART FOUR

Shifting Patterns of Circulation and Settlement in the 20th Century

11

CASH-CROP MIGRATION SYSTEMS IN EAST AND WEST AFRICA

Rise, Endurance, Decline

Michiel de Haas and Emiliano Travieso

1 Introduction

For much of the 20th century, African economies relied heavily on the export of cash crops that were grown, harvested, and sometimes processed by self-employed and often small-scale African producers. Exports of groundnuts in the Senegambia and palm oil along the West African coast took off in the first half of the 19th century. Cocoa rapidly diffused in the West African forest from the 1890s onward. Cotton and coffee expanded across East Africa in the early 20th century. In most cases agricultural exports peaked in the mid-20th century, after which volumes per capita declined sharply. The cash-crop economy crucially sustained the budgets of colonial states, stimulated African demand for European manufactures, and supplied strategic raw materials for European colonizers. Still, the most successful cases of commercial agriculture did not result from colonial planning and policy, but hinged on African initiative, as indigenous farmers chose to adopt new crops and outcompeted the European settlers who tried. Yet members of households and communities in well-endowed and accessible farming regions were not the only Africans who sought new economic opportunities. Annually, hundreds of thousands of rural migrants cultivated and harvested cash crops as seasonal laborers, sharecroppers, or aspiring settlers. They are the protagonists of this chapter, which seeks to explain not only how these cash-crop migrations emerged, but also why they endured over decades, and what finally caused their undoing.

At the apex of the "cash-crop revolution" during the first half of the 20th century, tropical Africa's areas of export agriculture attracted more immigrants than urban centers and mining areas together, and the vast majority of these rural migrants were absorbed by the indigenous economy rather than the "formal," European-controlled wage economy. Migrants made long and perilous journeys, often covering hundreds of kilometers by foot over weeks or even months. In the 1970s, "underdevelopment" theorists argued that migrant-sending areas were deliberately and successfully reduced to impoverished "reserve regions" to serve "capitalist development" in the cash-crop zones (Amin 1974). More recent work, however, has emphasized how this perspective places undue strategic insight and administrative control in the hands of European colonizers, and underplays the choices of

DOI: 10.4324/9781003225027-16

migrants themselves. African migrants proved highly receptive to rapidly emerging spatial disparities of opportunity, often defying their designated roles in colonial economic blueprints, or moving beyond colonial control altogether by crossing borders (Asiwaju 1976; Manchuelle 1997; De Haas 2019). On the receiving end, as long as labor demand outweighed supply, rural communities exhibited a remarkable ability and willingness to attract and absorb newcomers, especially in temporary and subordinated roles.

Despite the scale and importance of "uncontrolled" or "nondirected" migration toward cash-crop regions in colonial and post-colonial Africa, research on this topic is notably fragmented, and our understanding remains limited as a consequence. In the pages that follow, we attempt to overcome that fragmentation by bringing together the four largest cash-crop migration systems in the continent. Section 2 describes their contours, while Section 3 explains their shared origins in the emergence of a migratory labor market brought about by emancipation from slavery. Section 4 presents quantitative estimates of evolving wage gaps between sending and receiving regions that motivated rural-rural migration flows. Sections 5 and 6 examine competing explanations for the endurance of these flows, respectively considering pressures in sending regions and opportunities in receiving areas. Before the conclusion, Section 7 identifies the causes behind the transformation of cash-crop migrations, as (semi-)settled immigrant populations grew and flows abated, and their ultimate decline.

2 The contours of cash-crop migration systems

Our four migration systems encompass the most important zones of export agriculture in 20th-century Africa in terms of total output, all of which experienced substantial and sustained immigration, with flows peaking near or well above 100,000 people per year. Map 11.1 provides the locations of sending and receiving regions; Figure 11.1 shows the population-adjusted volumes of the most important crops exported from the latter relative to their peak year.

First, from west to east, the **Senegambia estuary**, which encompassed British colonial Gambia and coastal French colonial Senegal, had long attracted migrants from a wide hinterland, harboring a major Atlantic port. During the 19th century, the region emerged as Africa's leading exporter of groundnuts (peanuts), the demand for which had risen substantially due to the oil's use in industrial processes. Commercial groundnut farming was inextricably linked to migration from its very onset. From the 1840s onward, migrants converged upon the riverine systems of the groundnut-producing zones, where they were known as "strange farmers" or "navétanes" (Jarrett 1949; David 1980). In the first half of the 20th century, Gambian officials repeatedly estimated that migrants produced about half of the colony's groundnut output (Jarrett 1949, 650; Sallah 2019, 127). Over a period spanning from the mid-19th into the late 20th century, the groundnut sector attracted tens of thousands of seasonal migrants annually from vast swathes of the western Sahel. Recorded migration peaked in the interwar era, with up to some 90,000 recorded immigrants arriving annually (David 1980, 470).

The **Ghanaian forest zone** had also long been a center for regional mobility, notably through the forced migration of enslaved people from the northern savanna over the 19th century. Following the adoption of cocoa in the 1890s, it attracted voluntary seasonal migrants as well as settlers from northern Ghana (the British Gold Coast's Northern Territories), but also from neighboring French colonial territories, notably Burkina Faso (Haute Volta) (Austin 2005, 412–24).[1] From the 1920s onward, these flows widened to include migrants

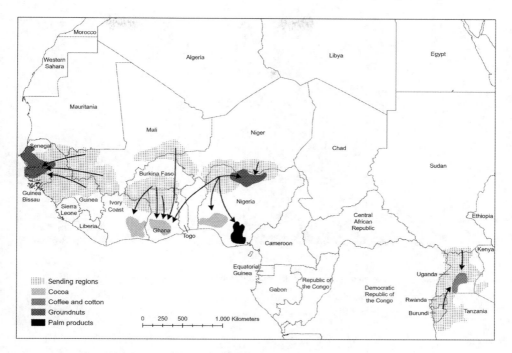

MAP 11.1 Location of four cash-crop migration systems.

Sources: Drawn by the authors on the basis of Gold Coast Government (1955) and previous maps in Hance, Kotschar, and Peterec (1961), Hopkins (2020[1973]), Richards (1973[1954]), Swindell (1982), and Austin (2009a).

Notes: Approximate locations only. Present-day borders shown for orientation purposes.

from northern Côte d'Ivoire to northwestern Nigeria. Annual flows reached 100,000 migrants in the 1930s (Dickinson 1938). By the early 1950s, flows had again increased, to well over 200,000 (Gold Coast Government, 1955, 14; Hopkins, 2020[1973], 275). During the 1960s, the center of cocoa production and labor migration shifted from Ghana to southern Côte d'Ivoire, where it was sustained into the late 20th century, by when the other major cash-crop migration systems had long collapsed (Cordell, Gregory and Piché 1996). This longevity explains why Côte d'Ivoire had the highest intra-African immigration intensity of all large African countries between 1960 and 2000, and the largest immigrant population after South Africa (Flahaux and De Haas 2016, 11).

Third, **colonial Nigeria** saw the development of various cash-cropping systems during the late 19th and early 20th century, which were associated with large labor mobility within and out of the interior savanna (Swindell 1984; Lovejoy and Hogendorn 1993, 200–22). Here, population movements had a long pre-colonial history associated with slave raids as well as free circular migration, but the "cash-crop revolution" brought about new spatial inequalities and expanded old ones, resulting in greater migration flows than ever before. While many migrants traveled to Ghana, most of them worked as rural laborers within colonial Nigeria, which saw rising exports of cocoa beans form the southwest, palm oil from the southeast, and groundnuts in parts of the center-north. About 190,000 migrants were counted traveling southward from northwestern Nigeria in the dry season of 1952–53 (Prothero 1959).

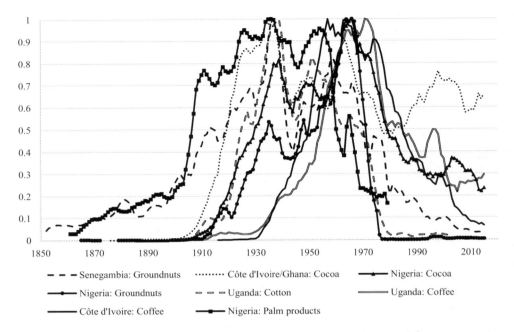

FIGURE 11.1 Per capita volumes of cash-crop exports, 1850–2017 (centered five-year moving averages, peak year=1).
Sources: 1850 to 1940/45: Frankema, Williamson, and Woltjer (2018). 1941/48–1960: De Haas (2017a) for Uganda; David (1980, 460–1) for Senegal; Mitchell (1995) for Côte d'Ivoire; unpublished extensions of the African Commodity Trade Database (ACTD), for the remaining missing points, Mitchell (1995) for other countries. From 1961 onward: ACTD extensions for Nigeria; FAOSTAT for other countries.

Lastly, the British-controlled areas of bimodal rainfall around Lake Victoria, and **Buganda** in particular, became a center of cotton and coffee export under colonial rule. Buganda was the economic and administrative center of the Uganda Protectorate, and was situated in a wider region with a longstanding history of population mobility (Reid 2017). Export-oriented agriculture only became feasible when the Uganda railway reached Lake Victoria in the early 1900s. Within 20 years, cotton had spread throughout the Protectorate, encompassing an area with a wide variety of agro-ecological characteristics and socio-political structures (De Haas 2017a, 2017b, 132–3). It took until the early 1920s for labor migration to take off on a substantial scale, considerably later than in the other cases discussed here. Migrants arrived in Buganda from all directions, but especially from Belgian-controlled Ruanda-Urundi. By the late 1930s, when migrant flows peaked, annual arrivals from Belgian territory had likely swelled to over 100,000 (De Haas 2019).

Alongside these four major cases, there were numerous other cash-crop zones across tropical Africa that did not attract large-scale migrant labor. In some cases, the reasons were obvious. For example, African cotton production in French Equatorial Africa, the Belgian Congo, and Portuguese Mozambique was directed by state-sanctioned concessionary companies, took place under harsh conditions, and was poorly remunerated. In such contexts, cash cropping triggered flight rather than immigration (Isaacman 1996, 209–12; Stürzinger, 1983, 225; Likaka 1997, 110–5). There were also cases of cash-crop cultivation that relied on African initiative, but did not attract sustained flows of voluntary migrants, such as cocoa production in southwestern Cameroon (Eckert 1996) and in the island of Bioko off Equatorial Guinea (Sundiata 1996), or cotton cultivation in the Shire Valley in Malawi (Frederick 2020). That these cash-crop economies remained small is explained by their particular island or riverine ecologies, but is also a consequence of not attracting migrants. Finally, in some places, such as Kenya and Southern Rhodesia, cash crops were grown on European settler farms, which relied on African migrant labor, but did not attract voluntary migrants on the same scale as the migration systems we discuss here (Mosley 1980; Frederick and Van Nederveen Meerkerk, Chapter 12, this volume).

In the major zones of export agriculture, migration and cash-crop production came to reinforce and ultimately depend upon each other. Migrants would not have left their homes for extended periods and in large numbers had cash-crop economies not provided them with distinctly better economic prospects. At the same time, continued expansion of cash-crop output in land-abundant and labor-scarce contexts such as the West African forest belt or Buganda relied crucially on the mass attraction of strangers to contribute to cultivation, harvesting, and processing. Yet, the emergence of cash-crop production cannot sufficiently explain the rise of rural migration, or vice versa. Suitable environmental endowments and access to export markets allowed some regions to take up the production of cash crops, often experiencing a take-off well before large-scale immigration began. Protracted emigration, all the while, was at least partly sustained by dynamics in sending regions that had no direct link to the cash-crop economy, as Section 4 will show. As for the initial rise of cash-crop migrations, its explanations are found in longer trajectories of socio-economic change that preceded the colonial period, and to which we now turn.

3 Emergence of cash-crop migration

Each of the four major cash-crop migration systems emerged in a context of agricultural commercialization, the protracted abolition of slavery, and the formation of free labor markets. Into the 19th century, human captives had been the main export product from mainland tropical Africa. Most African slaves were transported across the Atlantic to produce cash crops on New World plantations, most infamously sugar and cotton (Curtin 1990). Africa's own export agriculture, in the meanwhile, was mostly limited to provisioning of slave caravans and ships (Dalrymple-Smith and Frankema 2017).

Between the British abolition of the slave trade in 1807 and the colonial "scramble" in the 1880s, the barter terms of trade of tropical commodities underwent a sustained rise, incentivizing production on the continent (Frankema, Williamson, and Woltjer 2018). Already by the 1830s, the value of agricultural commodities exported from West Africa exceeded the value of slaves, and continued to grow rapidly afterward. Europeans experimented with export-oriented plantation agriculture along the West African coast using free African labor, but without much success (Law, Schwartz, and Stickrodt 2013). Most successful moves toward what was at the time known as "legitimate commerce" in contrast with "illegitimate" slave trades shared at least one of the following two characteristics: they were initiated by Africans and they (ironically) relied on slavery (Law 1995; Pallaver, Chapter 4, this volume). To understand the emergence of cash-crop migration systems, we must look closely at the connections between indigenous agricultural commercialization, slave emancipation, and labor mobility.

Agricultural commercialization in 19th-century Africa was a response to the decline of the oceanic *slave trades*, not the institution of *slavery* as such. Indeed, the transition to "legitimate commerce" did not immediately produce freedom but provided new ways for African slave traders and owners to profit from their captives, who were redirected from the Atlantic export market toward commodity production. Slaves played an important role in the emergence of export-oriented groundnut cultivation in the Senegambia and palm oil production across West Africa in the first half of the 19th century (Swindell 1980; Miott 1989; Lynn 1997). Slavery (and human pawning) also provided crucial sources of labor for the production of gold, rubber, and kola, and subsequently cocoa among the Asante in the Ghanaian forest zone, and groundnuts around early-colonial Kano in Northern Nigeria (Austin 2009a; Salau 2010). In fact, cash-crop systems came to rely to such an extent on slave labor that colonial states were hesitant to enforce their abolitionist policies in the early 20th century, worried about undermining agricultural export economies (Austin 2009a). Even in Buganda, where cotton was introduced after formal slavery had been suppressed, the initial uptake by chiefs relied on reconfigured forms of labor coercion, enabled by the colonial government (De Haas 2017b: 133–6).

The widespread use of slave labor in pre-colonial West Africa was predicated on a strong economic logic. In a context of land abundance, free workers commanded high wages as the returns to dependent employment had to outweigh those of independent family cultivation (self-employment) (Hopkins 2020[1973], 68–71). Thus, before the "cash-crop revolution," for most of the year and in most places "there was no wage rate which would have been mutually profitable for an employer to offer and for a worker to accept" (Austin 2009b, 42). Despite their initial reliance on slave labor, cash crops came to play an essential role in the development of free labor markets in tropical Africa. The surplus generated by increasingly lucrative commercial crops gave employers and employees more room to negotiate. Free labor markets emerged in places where independent cash-crop farming was not equally accessible to everyone (Austin 2009a). In some host communities, property or use rights to land suitable for export-oriented agriculture were strongly differentiated by geographical and ethnic origin, effectively excluding foreigners. Local authorities in the Asante and Yorubaland forest zones, for example, prevented strangers from clearing land to grow their own cocoa trees, so they could only participate in the agricultural export economy as laborers or sharecroppers (Agiri 1984, 102; Austin 2006). Access to capital (bearing trees in these cases) or credit was also difficult for "strangers" who could not rely on local networks, or borrow against the next cash-crop harvest.

The abolition of slavery and subsequent emancipation of slaves was a prolonged process, which took hold in the 1880s and in many places lasted into the 1930s. Ex-slaves were certainly not the only, nor the first, to engage in free cash-crop migration. In the Senegambia, from the 1840s onward, enslaved people cultivated groundnuts alongside free migrants who themselves built on their commercial experience in the slave trade, for example, as provisioners of grain to slave caravans (Manchuelle 1997, 53–9; Swindell and Jeng 2006). Emancipation, however, generated large new labor supplies within cash-crop migration systems, which was crucial for a major expansion of output (Figure 11.2), which occurred despite the fact that terms of trade for tropical commodities had turned for the worse after c. 1890 (Frankema, Williamson, and Woltjer 2018). Emancipated slaves were highly motivated to migrate, not only because participation in the cash-crop economy provided new avenues to greater economic freedom, but also because mobility allowed them to shed the social stigma of slavery and start anew elsewhere (Rossi 2014). Even when they moved within their broad region of origin, emancipated people played crucial roles in cash-crop production. In Northern Nigeria, for example, they often entered tenancy agreements with former masters that allowed them to grow groundnuts, especially in the populous Kano emirate, where most of the region's export agriculture was based (Lovejoy and Hogendorn 1993, 211–3).

On the migrant-receiving end, abolition cut off the supply of outside labor to African producers and compounded labor scarcity, exactly at a time when infrastructural development increased the potential to put such labor to profitable use. Moreover, and perhaps counter-intuitively, the legacy of slavery generated favorable conditions for free immigration in host communities. One striking similarity of our cash-crop migration systems is that the receiving societies had a history of incorporating foreign slaves into their rural economy. Post-abolition, this legacy contributed to their ability to absorb large numbers of strangers, even if these were now free migrants rather than slaves. In the Gambia, arrangements between local hosts and migrant farmers indeed drew from earlier slave work regimes (Swindell and Jeng 2006, 125). Buganda also showed a remarkable ability to absorb strangers, relative to neighboring polities which had not previously relied on slaves to a similar extent.[2] Even though Buhaya (coffee) and Busoga (cotton) were equally involved in cash-crop cultivation, they were mostly bypassed by migrants who instead walked an extra 100 miles to seek employment in Buganda (Richards 1973[1954], 218). In the Ghanaian forest zone, most free migrant laborers arrived from savanna regions where slaves had been captured before, but their bargaining power was substantially larger and they used it to change labor arrangements with the introduction of sharecropping (Austin 2005, 424–7, 545).

To understand why the formation of free labor markets in post-abolition tropical Africa came to involve such a large degree of mobility, we must also consider the fact that the potential for export agriculture was immensely varied, and that cash-crop production was largely confined to small spatial "enclaves" (Map 11.1; also see Roessler et al. 2020). Access to external markets was vital for profitable export agriculture, but transportation infrastructure was extremely limited in much of Africa's vast interior. Tellingly, groundnut production in Northern Nigeria and cotton production in Buganda, both over 800 kilometers removed from a coast, took off only (and very soon) after a railroad arrived. Uneven agro-ecological conditions also mattered greatly. Soils and rainfall patterns in Africa's savannas did not allow for the cultivation of cocoa, coffee, or oil palm, and their short unimodal rainfall regimes created seasonal bottlenecks that limited farmers' ability to combine food crop cultivation and labor-intensive cash crops suitable for the savanna, such as cotton and groundnuts (Tosh 1980; Austin 2014; De Haas 2021). Most cash crops took off in regions with abundant fertile land. Thus, the "cash-crop revolution" generated growing spatial disequilibria in labor demand and supply, increasing the scope for large-scale mobility.

4 Measuring opportunity gaps

Why was voluntary long-distance migration toward cash-crop zones sustained on such a large scale, and over a period of many decades? A first step toward answering this question is to evaluate the magnitude and evolution of opportunity gaps. Figure 11.2 shows the ratio of unskilled wages between sending and receiving regions, which is the closest we can get to systematically quantifying and comparing such gaps. Since urban and rural employers competed for the same pool of unskilled migrant labor, these ratios are roughly indicative of returns to agricultural wage labor (or sharecropping) in the indigenous cash-crop sector. The comparison becomes more problematic in the 1950s, when public sector minimum wage policies began to distort this market mechanism (De Haas 2017a), although the rising cost of urban housing may at least have partially attenuated a growing rural-urban gap (Westland 2021). For this analysis, we assume that potential wage distortions were of the same magnitude in sending and receiving regions and thus had limited impact on the ratios presented here. Because we compare nominal wages, these ratios directly translate into differences in purchasing power of imported goods (after taking into account the cost of migration itself, and assuming that trade costs and import duties were similar in sending and receiving regions).[3]

Figure 11.2 shows that wage ratios between receiving and sending regions were sizable but varied. In southern Ghana nominal wages were, on average, over twice as high as in Burkina Faso in the period from 1920 to 1970 (a ratio of 2.3). In neighboring Côte d'Ivoire, the ratio was much smaller, but increased and overtook Ghana's in the 1950s. The ratio between coastal Senegal and the Gambia, both migrant-receiving, and migrant-sending Mali averaged out at 2. The wage differential between the Nigerian cash-crop regions and their major sending areas (northwestern Nigeria and Niger) was even larger. Buganda offered a much less impressive wage ratio of 1.5 overall, which nevertheless still corresponded with a wage premium of 50%.[4]

Overall, these figures suggest that cash-crop migration was profitable for a sustained period, but they in turn must be explained. Were these gaps driven by low wages in the sending regions, or by high ones in host communities? The next two sections systematically evaluate both possibilities and their possible causes. Moreover, how and why did opportunity gaps close over time? Section 6 will pick up this question.

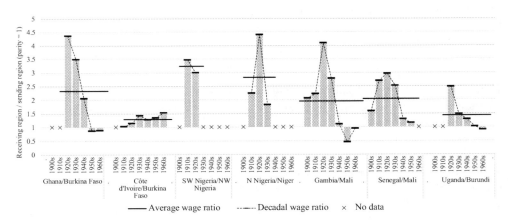

FIGURE 11.2 Unskilled nominal wage ratio between sending and receiving regions, 1900–69.

Sources: Unskilled nominal wages (averages of rural and urban wages if observed separately) for Burkina Faso, Côte d'Ivoire, Gambia, Ghana, Mali, Niger, Senegal, and Southwestern Nigeria from Frankema and Van Waijenburg (2019), for Uganda and Burundi from De Haas (2019), and for central Northern Nigeria from Travieso and Westland (2021). The franc-sterling exchange rate used to convert wages into pound sterling from MeasuringWorth.org and unpublished extensions of the ACTD (Frankema, Williamson, and Woltjer 2018). From 1945 onward, wages are converted from CFA to franc (1 CFA = 1.7 franc in 1946–48; 2 francs in 1949–60).

5 Pressures in the sending regions

The endurance of labor migration systems in the process of capitalist development is often associated with declining access to land and livelihoods in sending regions. In Arthur Lewis' (1954) foundational "dual-sector model," cheap labor for developing capitalist sectors comes forth when the marginal productivity in an economy's subsistence sector approaches zero. This happens in situations where land is so densely and intensively used that it cannot accommodate any more productive labor, resulting in incomes close to survival level, widespread underemployment, and landlessness. However, these conditions were not in place in most of tropical Africa during the era of cash-crop migration. As was first systematically pointed out by Hla Myint (1958), African rural economies were generally not land-constrained, and did not operate at their productive limits. Widespread access to land meant that rural self-employment should have been sufficiently remunerating and livelihoods secure enough to prevent a rural exodus of low-wage workers.

However, the generalized premise of "Myintian" land abundance in African agriculture needs qualification. This premise certainly does not apply to Ruanda-Urundi, the major sending region for Buganda's cash-crop migration system, which was by far the most densely settled territorial unit in colonial Africa, and experienced rural poverty and recurrent subsistence crises before Europeans arrived (De Haas 2019, 388–90). Consistent with the high incidence of rural poverty, up until the 1940s wages in Ruanda-Urundi rank at the very bottom of all sending and receiving areas. That Ruanda-Urundi migrants offered their labor in Buganda despite comparatively modest wage gaps (Figure 11.2) is a testament to rural poverty in the sending area.

Nigeria's migration system was also influenced by land scarcity. The northwestern Sokoto Province, which supplied most of Nigeria's labor migrants, was densely populated despite the low carrying capacity of its savanna soils. In such conditions, high densities could only be sustained through short fallow periods, heavy manuring, and the intensive farming of riverine floodplains (Swindell 1986). As population grew in the early 20th century, increasingly marginal soils were brought under cultivation. When traditional methods of rising yields or expanding acreage were exhausted, the scarcity of floodable land put livelihoods at risk and motivated large-scale outmigration (Goddard 1974; Watts 1983). The wage observations we have for northwestern Nigeria and Niger rank at the low end of the wage distribution, confirming that rural livelihoods were close to survival level.

In the other major sending regions of the four cash-crop migration systems, the presumption largely holds that land was sufficiently abundant to sustain growing rural populations. Facing limited voluntary labor supplies, colonial states could draw from a register of strategies to push down reservation wages and force people to offer themselves for employment, either by exerting direct force or by deliberately disrupting rural livelihoods (Okia; Ribeiro da Silva and Alexopoulou, Frederick and Van Nederveen Meerkerk, Chapters 8, 9, and 12, this volume). Indeed, both Lewis (1954, 149–50) and Myint (1958, 326–7) suggest that such strategies were widely adopted by colonial governments in Africa to generate a cheap labor supply for capitalist development, for example, through large-scale land alienation in Kenya, Rhodesia, and South Africa. But can colonial interventions to overcome labor scarcity in a context of land abundance explain cash-crop migration?

There can be little doubt that colonial governments envisioned controlling a pool of cheap labor, and committed scant investment into infrastructure, education, or livelihood diversification in what would become the primary sending regions of cash-crop migrants.[5] Moreover, colonial administrations could use the introduction of monetary and labor taxes as a powerful instrument to push people onto the labor market (Okia, Chapter 8, this volume). A monetary tax generates a migratory labor supply when the required cash can only be obtained through wages, as was often the case in non-cash-crop regions. Additionally, a tax pushes up local labor supply, suppressing wages and thus incentivizing people to look for income elsewhere. Colonial labor and monetary taxes were introduced in most of the sending regions. In Ruanda-Urundi, the onset of large-scale migration coincided with the institution of a colonial poll tax (De Haas 2019, 392). In Northern Nigeria direct colonial taxation preceded cash-crop migration, but during times of hardship in the 1930s tax pressure was more harshly felt and may have encouraged mobility (Ochonu 2009, 90–3). In other sending regions, like the Senegalese interior, Mali, and northern Ghana, migration preceded the legal imposition of monetary and labor taxes, but expanded as the tax burden increased and enforcement was strengthened (Asiwaju 1976; Manchuelle 1997; Van Waijenburg, 2018).

Nevertheless, viewing taxation as the prime trigger of migration is problematic in several ways. First, the personal taxes that were instituted in sending regions were often not high enough to fuel mass migration. For example, at prevailing unskilled wage rates, a laborer in northern Côte d'Ivoire in 1925 could fulfill his yearly tax obligation in less than five days, while his counterpart in Ruanda-Urundi required less than four days in 1929.[6] Second, while the unevenness of taxation across space certainly played a part in some of our cases, it was far from a necessary condition for migration, as a comparison between two sending regions in the Ghanaian migration system shows. The increasing head taxes imposed by the French colonial administration in Burkina since 1906 contributed, as did the threat of forced labor and military conscription, to Burkinabè migration to the Ghanaian forest zone, where direct taxation was introduced much later (Coulibaly 1986). But a substantial share of migrant laborers in the cocoa farms came from northern Ghana even before direct taxation was imposed in 1936 (Thomas 1973).

Third, even if generating a labor supply was part of the reason why taxes were instituted, the direction of migration as it subsequently emerged largely defeated such purpose, even resulting in a loss of labor to colony and empire. Migrants from Burkina Faso, which the French designated as their prime "labor reservoir," did not offer their labor cheaply to the European plantations in Côte d'Ivoire but preferred to work on the native cocoa farms in neighboring Ghana, a British colony. The key migration destination began to gravitate toward Côte d'Ivoire only when forced labor was abolished in French West Africa in the late 1940s. Still, French colonial subjects continued to account for over 40% of people crossing the river Volta into Ghana up to the 1950s, as well as of immigrants present in Ghanaian cocoa-producing regions in the 1960 census (Gold Coast Government 1955, 14; Ghana 1962).

Moreover, forced labor policies and the imposition of cash crops in the sending regions, such as cotton in Mali, northern Côte d'Ivoire, and Burkina Faso, or coffee in Ruanda-Urundi, tended only to contribute to people's decisions to work or even live elsewhere (Asiwaju 1976, 590; De Haas 2019, 398–400). While many migrants from the French-controlled Upper Senegal Valley went to coastal Senegal, others chose to go to the Gambia, again a British colony. Most migrants from Ruanda-Urundi did not move to the European plantations and mines in the Congo, but to native cotton and coffee farms in Uganda, yet again under British control. Part of the cash that migrants earned was used to pay taxes on return, and colonial authorities ratcheted up tax rates in response to migration. As such, colonial states certainly reaped some benefits from cash-crop migration. Yet, rural-rural mobility hardly took on the shape that colonial governments had envisioned and hoped for, and French authorities in West Africa and Belgian authorities in Ruanda-Urundi only reluctantly accepted a massive labor flow toward British territories outside their control (Roberts 1996, 173; De Haas 2019, 397).

In conclusion, pressures in the sending regions partially explain the supply of cash-crop migrants, serving as a contextual driver of migration in densely populated rural areas in Ruanda-Urundi and northwestern Nigeria. Still, the logic of colonial taxation as a prime driver of migration holds up at most only partially when confronted with the historical evidence, and gives at least some credence to Manchuelle's (1997, 90) stark claim, formulated in the context of the Senegambian migration system, that

> Taxation did not create labor migration in the Soninke homeland nor was it intended for that purpose by the French administration. Far more significant in this period than the taxation or other nonexistent coercion and economic disruption was the attraction of high wages and incomes in an expanding coastal Senegambian economy.

In the next section, we will scrutinize the latter component of this claim, by evaluating the role of opportunities in the four cash-crop migration systems.

6 Opportunities in receiving regions

Seasonality was at the core of rain-fed agriculture across tropical Africa, and thus became an important ingredient in migratory decisions. Even where land was abundantly available, it could not be profitably cultivated during the dry season, resulting in agricultural un(der) employment during that part of the year (Tosh 1980; Austin 2008). Food availability was also seasonal, with surpluses after the harvest but shortages toward the end of the dry season. In such conditions, sending off household members to work elsewhere during the agricultural off-season was a rational strategy, as long as "elsewhere" offered better opportunities to use labor productively during this time of the year. To evaluate the extent of potential complementarities, Figure 11.3 shows the intra-annual distribution of rainfall for the sending and receiving regions of the four migration systems.

Seasonal complementarities were most pronounced in the Ghanaian and Nigerian migration systems, where migrants moved latitudinally, cutting through ecological zones. By outmigrating during the long dry season, also known as the "hungry season," and returning to sow crops before the first rains, villagers from the Sahel fringes in the Sokoto Province in Nigeria temporarily relieved their families of seasonal nutritional stress (Swindell 1984; Lovejoy and Hogendorn 1993, 199–200). A similar complementarity was found in Ghana, where migrants entered seasonal contracts and received their wages once the cocoa harvest was sold, approximately six months after they had started work (Cordell, Gregory and Piché 1996, 109; Austin 2005, 360).

In the Senegambia, on the other hand, migrants moved longitudinally between savanna systems with synchronized rainfall distributions. Even though absent migrant farmers could not contribute to cultivation in the sending region, their mobility could still benefit households' subsistence position. Food tended to be most scarce at the start of the wet season, before the first food crops were harvested. This meant that migrant-sending families had fewer mouths to feed at this critical time, while migrants were able to consume imported rice in the receiving regions (Van Beusekom 2002, 21–5; Swindell and Jeng 2006).

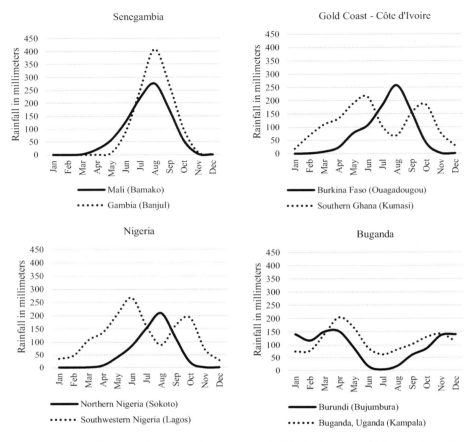

FIGURE 11.3 Rainfall seasonality in sending regions (solid lines) and receiving regions (dotted lines).
Sources: Average monthly rainfall estimates for the period 1931–60 from the World Bank Climate Knowledge Portal (https://climateknowledgeportal.worldbank.org).

Seasonal cash-crop migration arose as a new and effective strategy of savanna households to mitigate recurrent episodes of dry-season hunger. It is telling that between the two world wars, male heights increased even more in Ghana's northern savanna than in the forest zone, indicating an improvement in the biological standard of living in the migrant-sending regions (Moradi 2008, 1115–6). In Northern Nigeria, growing population densities and reduced fallow periods in migrant-sending savanna areas also testify to the benefits of circular migration (Goddard, Mortimore and Norman 1975). That migrants exploited agricultural seasonality to their benefit, a strategy that moreover predated the onset of colonial rule, also undermines the idea that pressures in the sending regions due to colonial policies were the prime, let alone single, driver of cash-crop migration.

But was there perhaps a marked decline in income-earning opportunities during the dry season in the colonial era that triggered people to opt for circular mobility in such large numbers? Across the West African savanna, encompassing the sending regions of three of the migration systems discussed here, pre-colonial dry-season labor was employed in a range of non-agricultural economic activities, notably producing cotton fabrics which were traded in extensive regional markets. The traditional argument that cheap imported European manufactures successfully destroyed local circuits of production and exchange has been widely contested, and most scholars now stress the remarkable resilience of local handicraft industries (Frederick 2020). Soninke migrants even took local cloth with them to the coast to arbitrage price differences (Manchuelle 1997, 101, 188).

If the wage disparities observed in Figure 11.2 were not driven primarily by declining (seasonal) incomes in the sending regions, we should turn to the opportunities that attracted migrants to cash-crop zones beyond seasonal complementarity. Key was the accumulation of textile fabrics and other imported consumer goods, which returning migrants used to improve their social status, marry, or set up a home (Swindell 1984; Manchuelle 1997, 172; Austin 2005, 51–2; De Haas 2019, 394–5). In the receiving areas, imported products were easier to obtain, and especially could be earned faster, because nominal wages were so much higher – and in most cases substantially above barebones subsistence level (Frankema and Van Waijenburg 2012). Migrants engaged in price arbitrage, exploiting price and wage gaps between the sending and receiving regions, which opened up as a result of currency fluctuations and regional price imbalances, especially of locally produced goods with low tradability, such as liquors, handicrafts, livestock, and local building materials.

To exploit such opportunities, migrants often lived frugal lives in the receiving areas to maximize their savings, and brought back consumer goods for resale in their home communities (Manchuelle 1997, 120; Swindell and Jeng 2006, 60–1; De Haas 2019). As Swindell points out for the case of migrants from Sokoto Province, toward the end of the dry season people went from being migrant laborers elsewhere to traders in their own communities, selling the consumer goods they had brought with them in the return journey, and finally went back to being farmers (Swindell 1984). Colonial officials in Ruanda-Urundi saw migrants returning home loaded with textiles, which were used for bride price and to accumulate livestock. Migrants here also engaged in a lively currency trade (De Haas, 2019, 394).

At the same time, it is important to not overstate the opportunities available to cash-crop migrants. The returns to migrant labor gradually deteriorated between the late 19th and mid-20th century, as the price of agricultural commodities (and African real wages) declined precipitously relative to imported manufactured goods (Martin 1989). During the 1920s and 1930s, producers in East and West Africa had to work about twice as long to obtain the same amount of imported textiles as during the first two decades of the 20th century.[7] In French and Belgian territories, the loss of purchasing power was further compounded by substantial depreciation of their respective currencies to the pound sterling in the 1920s. In most cases, the Belgian and French francs made up lost ground during the 1930s, which reduced (but not erased) wage gaps with receiving regions in British territories (Figure 11.2).

That cash-crop migration systems, nevertheless, continued to be shaped by migrants' own aspirations is illustrated by savanna migrants changing their destination from southern Ghana to Côte d'Ivoire from the 1950s onward in response to changing wage premiums (Figure 11.4). This spatial shift was linked to currency alignments as well as the fortunes of the two countries' cocoa sectors. Ghana's cocoa farming began a decisive decline from the mid-1960s onward, as reserves of fertile land depleted and the Nkrumah government used the cocoa sector as a cash cow for the state coffers. In Côte d'Ivoire, virgin forest was still available and the opportunities for indigenous entrepreneurship expanded with the Houphouet-Boigny Law of 1946, which abolished forced labor. To boost the country's

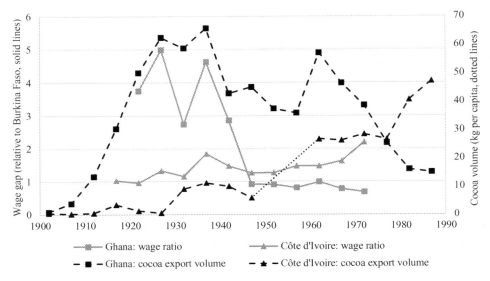

FIGURE 11.4 Wage ratios and cocoa exports in Ghana and Côte d'Ivoire (five-year-centered averages).
Sources: see Figure 11.1 and 11.2.

emerging cocoa sector, Côte d'Ivoire's post-colonial Houphouet-Boigny government welcomed rural migrants and facilitated their access to resources. The response of migrants, the majority of whom came from the country's northern regions, Mali, and Burkina Faso, was impressive. Between 1950 and 1965 the number of African international immigrants working in Côte d'Ivoire rose from 100,000 to 950,000, two-thirds of whom settled in the forest region (Bassett, 2001, 95). As one migrant from northern Côte d'Ivoire recalled in 1992: "we would be gone for 6 months, sometimes a year, and come back with a bicycle. Everyone saw that you could earn some money if you left the village, so people left to work for a bike." He also noted that "it wasn't like that during [the preceding regime of] forced labor; if the workers returned, they were in poor health" (quoted in Bassett 2001, 98).

Finally, cash-crop migrants also exerted their agency when choosing, if such options were available, whether to work for African smallholders, large African farmers, or expatriate employers in the same regions. While independent, small-scale family farmers widely took up cash crops, the development of export agriculture in receiving regions also underpinned economic differentiation among rural producers, allowing some to achieve substantial scale (Austin 2009, 34; Hopkins 2020[1973], 292). As Austin has observed for the case of Ghana, migrant workers could play different roles in small and large farms. Cocoa smallholders did not see migrant workers as an alternative to family labor, but as a way to supplement it in times of peak demand; very large cocoa farmers, on the other hand, required so much labor to look after many thousands of trees that they had to rely on migrants to a much larger extent (Austin 2005, 406–8). In some districts of southern Yorubaland, in southwestern Nigeria, inflows of migrant laborers concentrated on larger cocoa-bearing farms and made their expansion possible (Agiri 1984, 99–100). In Buganda, native farmers, operating at various sizes, proved more attractive employers than expatriate (Asian and European) planters, as the former offered, according to one colonial official, "conditions and inducements with which the private [sic] employers cannot compete" (Richards 1973[1954], 29).

In conclusion, opportunities in receiving regions were a key driver of voluntary cash-crop migration. Such opportunities arose from seasonal complementarities, which predated colonial rule but were compounded by the colonial-era "cash-crop revolution" in the receiving regions, while sending regions lacked similar dynamism. Migrants proved highly responsive to opportunities in receiving regions. They lived frugal lives in order to accumulate savings and consumer goods and engaged in price arbitrage, even though the returns to their efforts deteriorated over time. When opportunities in receiving regions changed, for example, as the center of gravity of cocoa production shifted from Ghana to Côte d'Ivoire, migrants responded with alacrity and en masse. In the final substantive section of the chapter, we will evaluate how cash-crop migration systems became less circular and eventually declined, while nevertheless leaving profound legacies.

7 Transformation and decline of cash-crop migration

Initially, cash-crop migration was characterized by the temporary and often circular mobility of adult men. Migrants typically moved for a few months and sometimes up to a few years, before going home to establish or return to a family holding. Over time, many extended their trips, and expanded their involvement in a wider range of economic activities in receiving regions. In the early 1970s, close to half of the migrants who were surveyed in the Gambia had already been present during the previous agricultural season, spending the dry season working in the docks, groundnut processing facilities, or setting up small businesses. For many, groundnut cultivation had become a means to accumulate capital, with the ultimate aim of setting up an urban business (Swindell 1977). In Buganda, the average length of migrant trips increased substantially in the 1940s, and women and children began to migrate alongside (and sometimes without) spouses, typically with the aim to move permanently. As migrants stayed longer, they also adopted new ethnic identities and married into receiving societies. The proportion of migrants who settled at their destination increased (De Haas 2019, 401–5).

Migrant settlement had profound demographic consequences, contributing to a major population shift even before migrants increasingly sought out booming cities after 1950 (Meier zu Selhausen, Chapter 13, this volume). As shown in Table 11.1, Buganda's population share with migrant origins rose spectacularly, from 12.8% in 1931 to 42.2% in 1959, about half of which was of non-Ugandan origin (predominantly Ruanda-Urundi). That the majority of migrants ended up in the countryside, and that this is not (yet) a story of urbanization, is illustrated by the fact that in the latter year only 6.8% of Buganda's African population lived in an urban or peri-urban context (Uganda Protectorate 1960). In rural Ghana, communities of settled immigrants also grew, as they successfully negotiated for longer-term arrangements as permanent laborers or, increasingly, as sharecroppers (Hill 1997[1963]; Robertson 1982). Most of these migrants were directly involved in cash-crop cultivation: foreign migrants came to represent 47% of permanent workers in cocoa farms in the 1960s (Addo 1974, 73). However, as Table 11.2 shows, the recorded growth of immigrant communities in southern Ghana was not as spectacular as in Buganda. This contrasts to a massive inflow of migrants in neighboring Côte d'Ivoire, where foreigners comprised 22% of the forest regions' rural population (and 35% of the male rural population) by 1965,

246 Michiel de Haas and Emiliano Travieso

TABLE 11.1 Enumerated migrant population of Uganda's cash-crop zone

		Total African population	Total African migrants	African migrants, by origin		
				Internal, other regions	International, within Empire	International, outside Empire
1931	Total counted	682,893	87,611	56,522	13,039	18,050
(May)	% of population		12.8%	8.3%	1.9%	2.6%
1948	Total counted	1,302,162	455,009	162,024[a]	40,506[a]	252,479[a]
(August)	% of population		34.9%	12.4%	3.1%	19.4%
1959	Total counted	1,834,128	773,645	355,570	51,044	367,031
(August)	% of population		42.2%	19.4%	2.8%	20.0%
1969	Total counted	2,617,609	723,508	319,308	108,444	295,756
(August)	% of population		27.6%	12.2%	4.1%	11.3%

Sources: Uganda Protectorate (1933); East African Statistical Department (1950); Uganda (1960); Uganda (1974).

Notes: The cash-crop zone comprises Buganda Province's constituent districts. Data for 1931, 1948, and 1959 pertain to individuals' ethnicity. Non-Ganda have been labeled as migrants, except for Banyoro in Mubende district. Data for 1969 pertain to individuals' birthplace and are therefore not strictly comparable to the other years (De Haas 2019, corrigendum 2021, 179–80).
a   The sub-division by origin in 1948 is the authors' approximation.

TABLE 11.2 Enumerated migrant population of Ghana's cash-crop zone

		Total African population	Total African migrants	African migrants, by origin[a]		
				Internal, other regions	International, within Empire	International, outside Empire
1931	Total counted	2,152,472	248,650	54,806	60,190	133,654
(April)	% of population		11.6%	2.5%	2.8%	6.2%
1948	Total counted	2,862,668	297,429	196,890	45,600	54,939
(Jan/Feb)	% of population		10.4%	6.9%	1.6%	1.9%
1960	Total counted	4,369,904	689,803	301,283	94,380	289,640
(March)	% of population		15.8%	6.9%	2.2%	6.6%
1970	Total counted	6,021,704	596,783	462,691	26,971	104,358
(March)	% of population		9.9%	7.7%	0.4%	1.7%

Sources: Gold Coast (1932); Gold Coast (1950); Ghana (1962); Ghana (1975).

Notes: The cash-crop zone includes all administrative areas except for Volta, Togo mandated territory, Northern and Upper. Data pertain to individuals' birthplace. Data for 1960 suggests that the number of individuals with non-Ghanaian "origins" is about 50% higher than individuals with non-Ghanaian "birthplace," so these figures give a conservative estimate of the "migrant" population.
a   Since the origin of a small portion of migrants is unknown, the sub-division by origin may not add up to the total migrants.

compared to only 2.5% in 1950 (Bassett 2001, 95). In the Gambia, settlement also increased, and some villages were even made up entirely of immigrants. However, over three in four immigrants enumerated in the Gambia in the early 1970s indicated they wished to return to their sending regions, which suggests that the Senegambian migration system remained comparatively circular (Swindell 1982).

It should not come as a surprise that an increasing share of migrants aspired to settle as they gradually adapted to the culture and institutions of receiving societies and expanded their networks. One major benefit of settlement is its compatibility with a stable family life, but the economic pay-offs to rural settlement could also be substantial. As migrants were increasingly able to obtain (often informal) land rights, they were able to secure their own food supply, and no longer had to share their agricultural output with hosts or employers. In the Yorubaland forest belt, in southwestern Nigeria, migrants' decision to settle permanently depended crucially on whether they could obtain land rights as tenants or freeholders. Where they could, migrants readily settled as independent cultivators, as in the case of farmers from communities in the Nigerian Middle Belt who moved to the eastern districts of the Yorubaland forest belt to plant cocoa in the 1940s and 1950s (Berry 1985, 56). Where they could not, circular migration remained dominant (Agiri 1983, 102). Pay-offs to settlement also varied substantially from case to case. In Asante, southwestern Nigeria, and Buganda, settlement enabled migrants to invest in their own tree crops (cocoa or coffee). In the Senegambia and in north-central Nigeria, peanut cultivation did not benefit to a similar extent from a multi-annual investment, which may be one factor contributing to limited settlement.

While (semi-)settled migrant populations increased, flows eventually began to dry up. As shown in Figure 11.5, the flows of migrants to Buganda and the Senegambia (expressed as a share of the host population) gradually abated. In the Buganda-centered migration system, male circularity became less attractive as opportunities for price arbitrage declined with the equalization of wages and prices in sending and receiving areas. In response, migrants

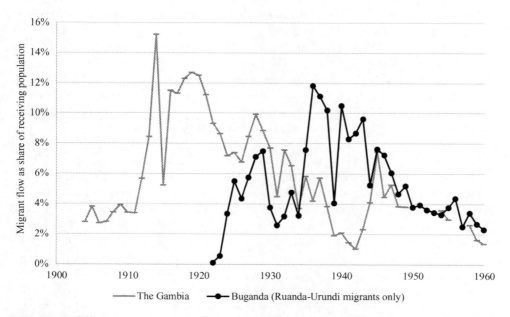

FIGURE 11.5 Migrants coming annually to the Gambia and Buganda relative to total receiving population, 1904–60.

Sources: Migration into the Gambia from David (1980, 467–8), Ruanda-Urundi migration into Buganda from De Haas (2019). Population estimate from the Gambia from Frankema and Jerven (2014) and Buganda interpolated from census data (see Table 11.2), assuming constant annual growth rates between census years.

either stopped making trips to Buganda or moved there once (more) to resettle on a more permanent basis (De Haas 2019, 401–5). In the early 1950s, a survey in three Buganda villages found that only one in seven migrants had plans to return to the sending region, and these were usually migrants from poorer sending regions, such as eastern Rwanda (Richards 1973[1954], 274; De Haas 2019, 404). In the Senegambia, the arrival of circular migrants also diminished, except from independent Guinea, which suffered badly from French economic retaliation, despite attempts by the Sékou Touré government to stave off an exodus (Swindell 1977). In the forest zones of Côte d'Ivoire, Ghana, and Nigeria, large opportunity gaps between sending and receiving regions, partly driven by nominal wage gaps and partly by the seasonal dynamics of these migration systems, continued to attract temporary migrants, as long as their cocoa economies thrived (Walker 2000).

To understand why the circulation that characterized cash-crop migration systems ultimately came to a halt we should evaluate the role of both increasing opportunities in sending regions and declining opportunities in the receiving areas. Many of the migrant-sending regions were gradually incorporated into the orbit of cash-crop cultivation themselves, as transportation and marketing infrastructure improved, and new agricultural technologies helped break labor bottlenecks in the savanna areas. In Ruanda-Urundi, the Belgian forced coffee campaign of the 1930s began to yield returns after the Second World War, and especially during the early 1950s, when commodity prices boomed. Cash crops not only brought in money to cultivators, but the increased export earnings also generated government revenues and enabled wages to rise and converge toward Ugandan levels (De Haas 2019, 401–2). As a result of coordinated efforts to provide inputs, including new seed varieties and improved marketing infrastructure, from the 1950s onward, cotton production expanded markedly in the sending regions of both the Senegambian and the Ghanaian/Ivoirian migration systems (Bassett 2001; De Haas 2021) The ability to grow and market cash crops locally raised the bar for people to choose migration over local employment, but since Côte d'Ivoire came to offer increasingly attractive conditions for migrants, the trip continued to be worthwhile for many.

During the second half of the 1940s, various coercive colonial institutions were dismantled in French and Belgian Africa, which also changed the dynamics of migration. In Ruanda-Urundi, corvée labor and chiefs' extractive powers were significantly scaled back in 1949, which reduced people's incentives to engage in labor migration. This effect was counteracted, to some extent, by the introduction of affordable buses and recruiters' lorries, which migrants could use to travel to Buganda (Richards 1973[1954], 56–63; De Haas 2019, 404). In the French West African colonies, the abolition of forced labor in 1946 had a rather different effect. Despite formal abolition of slavery half a century earlier, many captives' descendants had been retained in subordinate positions as domestic servants. This lack of emancipation was condoned by the colonial state, as "house captives" provided much of the forced labor requisitioned by the authorities for local public works and the settler plantations in southern Côte d'Ivoire. With the threat of forced labor gone, this system broke down, and former slaves in the sending regions began to engage in profitable migrant labor, alongside other young men, echoing similar developments just half a century earlier (Bassett, 2001, 96). The initial effect of the abolition of forced labor, therefore, was to extend people's capabilities to migrate, resulting in an uptick of the flow, which perhaps also contributed to the post-war increase of the migration flow into the Senegambia (Figure 11.5).

While opportunity structures in migrant-sending regions improved, they tended to worsen in the receiving regions. This was partly a cumulative feedback effect of migrant

Cash-Crop Migration Systems   **249**

settlement. Settlers took up land, which had long been amply available in the Senegambia, Buganda, and the Ghanaian and Nigerian forest zones but became increasingly scarce, especially in the most commercially attractive parts of each of these regions. Moreover, as migrants began to settle in larger numbers while circular migration abated, local farmers lost their access to a cheap migrant labor force. These developments contributed to growing hostility toward migrants, whose rights to be present and access land had been poorly codified by colonial governments and were contingent on the support of local hosts. In the early 1950s, smallholders in Buganda began to express their grievances about the fact that migrants were increasingly taking up tenancies and were no longer willing to work for them, a trend that was enabled by large landowners who encouraged migrants to settle and open up their uncultivated land (Richards 1973[1954], 194–200).

As Ghana's agricultural export economy declined in the mid-1960s, the economic position of undocumented foreign migrants was increasingly compromised: years of voluntary immigration ended, for many, with the shock of forced displacement under the Aliens Compliance Order of 1969 (Addo 1974; Frankema, Chapter 15, this volume). In neighboring Côte d'Ivoire, instead, immigrants were drawn to the cocoa and coffee economy by the independent government's promise that "land belongs to those who make it bear" (Chauveau and Léonard 1996). However, in the 1980s, as the Ivoirian cash-crop frontier closed, strangers' land rights also became increasingly questioned by locals, leading to intense conflict (Chauveau 2006; Lentz 2006). The increasing pace of population growth in the second half of the 20th century intensified these struggles over resources, even if such competition preceded the height of the demographic transition in most cash-crop areas. Meanwhile, the expanding scale of African cities encouraged rural migrants to choose urban destinations (Meier zu Selhausen, Chapter 13, this volume).

Some of the cash-crop migration systems began to decline while the cash-crop economies themselves were still flourishing. In all cases, however, the sharp reduction of agricultural exports from the receiving regions from the 1960s onward marked their definitive undoing. The colonial-era "cash-crop revolution" had been predicated on extensive growth, converting increasing amounts of land and labor inputs into exports, with very limited technological change beyond the adoption of new cultigens and varieties. As land frontiers were closing, this type of growth was increasingly untenable. The cocoa take-off in southern Ghana and southwestern Nigeria was particularly dependent on fresh supplies of virgin land which sustained a "forest rent": the surplus derived from cultivating cocoa in cleared primary forest in comparison with planting it in land previously used for other crops (Ruf 1995).

Agricultural exports also became the cash cow of colonial states, and increasingly elaborate systems were put in place to tax rural production and export. From the 1930s onward, colonial states devised marketing boards which had the mandate to stabilize prices. However, marketing boards often accumulated large reserves, especially during the price boom of the early 1950s, which were used for development projects outside the agricultural sector. In Uganda, cotton and coffee prices were kept at an artificially low level during the late 1940s, which suppressed rural incomes. As world market prices worsened during the 1960s, Ugandan cash-crop farmers increasingly began to fall behind their wage-earning counterparts (De Haas 2017a). In the Senegambia, marketing boards had a similar effect on farmers' earnings (Swindell 1977). In Ghana, the marketing board monopoly of cocoa exports since 1939 imposed low real producer prices for cash-crop farmers during the late colonial period, and would do so again after independence in the 1970s and early 1980s (Alence 2001). In

Nigeria, the overvaluation of the naira following the oil boom since 1973 further penalized agricultural exports, reducing the exchange value of cocoa, groundnuts, and palm products, and thereby the profit margins of cash-crop farmers (Collier 1988, 761). Deteriorating economic conditions in the countryside created a fertile ground for resentment toward strangers who were increasingly perceived as taking up scarce land and jobs. It is no coincidence that mass expulsions such as those from Ghana (1969), Uganda (1969, 1972, 1982), and Nigeria (1983, 1985) often took place in the wake of economic decline (Frankema, Chapter 15, this volume).

8 Conclusion

This chapter brought together experiences of rural labor migration that shaped the development of export agriculture in East and West Africa. Between the late 19th and the mid-20th centuries, the "cash-crop revolution" presented rural communities across these regions with massive economic disparities. As this chapter strove to show, individuals and households in ecologically frailer or geographically isolated environments did not merely watch from afar as the new export economy brought prosperity to other places. In a colonial policy environment that was sometimes reluctant and often indifferent to their efforts, hundreds of thousands of Africans chose to embark on long, uncertain journeys to secure a material share of international agricultural trade. They did so balancing significant costs and benefits to familiar and communal livelihoods, and often at great personal risk. The result were cash-crop migrations signaled by dramatic inequalities and struggles for livelihoods, but also extremely rich in displays of creativity and economic initiative.

By looking at the interactions between sending and receiving regions in a comparative framework, we aimed to identify the defining features of this era of intense and widespread rural migration and understand the forces that brought it into existence, the factors which made it endure, and the causes behind its final decline. Like many other experiences of labor mobility in global history, cash-crop migrations were effective responses to large and protracted economic opportunity gaps, and were sometimes also a way out of rural poverty and seasonal hunger. But, unlike most examples of large-scale labor migration elsewhere, cash-crop migrations emerged in connection with, and decisively contributed to, a fundamental change in the nature of labor itself: the momentous transition from slavery to free labor. Their routes were also particularly fine-tuned to environmental opportunities and bottlenecks: African export-oriented agriculture was, in the 19th and for most of the 20th century, narrowly confined by nature, physical infrastructure, and farming technologies to specific places and seasons, and so only a handful of receiving regions accounted for extremely large and varied catchment areas. Finally, cash-crop migration systems declined as incomes between sending and receiving regions converged, partly as a result of the quickness with which previous generations of migrants had responded and partly because of the limits of the cash-crop economies themselves, faced with the closing of the agricultural frontier and decreasing producer prices for tropical agriculture.

The "do-it-yourself" nature of the cash-crop revolution, which economic historians of Africa attribute chiefly to the market responsiveness of indigenous farmers in export zones, was also defined by these entrepreneurial migrants through their bottom-up decision-making, at the individual, household, and village level. Their strategies went beyond choosing to offer their agricultural labor elsewhere, and encompassed small-scale trading and price arbitrage, wage contract and sharecropping negotiations, as well as deciding between alternative forms of mobility, from circular migration to permanent resettlement. In so doing, they ushered in a new kind of large-scale, long-distance, voluntary economic migration: a powerful response to yawning inequalities in material living standards across rural spaces. When seen in the long history of African mobility, their quest for economic opportunity foreshadowed future journeys that would lead many away from the rural world and into big cities in Africa and far beyond.

Acknowledgment

We thank Ewout Frankema for his comments and suggestions.

Notes

1 Henceforth, we use the names of independent African countries also when discussing the colonial period, provided their boundaries broadly coincide.
2 On slavery in Buganda, see Richards (1954); Twaddle (1988); De Haas (2019).
3 A wage ratio of 2 means that wage labor in the receiving region provided double the purchasing power in imported goods compared to the sending region.
4 For comparison, wage ratios between the migrant-receiving New World and migrant-sending Europe during the 1850s (the onset of the "Age of Mass Migration," see De Haas and Frankema, Chapter 1, this volume) were between 1.7 (Britain) and 3.7 (Norway). In the 1870s, indentured Indian workers in British Guiana, the West Indies, or Hawaii earned over five times as much as they would at home, while Chinese moving to Siam navigated a wage ratio of 3 (Hatton and Williamson 2005, 136–7).
5 For northern Ghana and Burkina Faso, the extent to which such "underdevelopment" was actively used to generate labor supplies has been extensively debated; see, for example, Destombes (2006) and Cordell and Gregory (1982).
6 For Côte d'Ivoire, see tax rate in Bassett (2001, 66) and wage rate in Van Waijenburg (2018); for Ruanda-Urundi, see De Haas (2019, 398).
7 This estimate is based on the wage rates in Figure 11.2 and textile prices in eight British African markets from Frankema and Van Waijenburg (2012).

References

Addo, N. O. 1974. "Foreign African Workers in Ghana." *International Labour Review* 109(1): 47–68.
Agiri, B. A. 1984. "The Development of Wage Labour in Agriculture in Southern Yorubaland 1900–1940." *Journal of the Historical Society of Nigeria* 12(1/2): 95–107.
Alence, Rod. 2001. "Colonial Government, Social Conflict and State Involvement in Africa's Open Economies: The Origins of the Ghana Cocoa Marketing Board, 1939–46." *Journal of African History* 42(3): 397–416.
Amin, Samir. 1974. "Introduction." In *Modern Migrations in Western Africa*, edited by Samir Amin, 3–126. London: Oxford University Press.
Asiwaju, Anthony. 1976. "Migrations as Revolt: the Example of the Ivory Coast and the Upper Volta before 1945." *Journal of African History* 17(4): 577–94.
Austin, Gareth. 2005. *Labour, Land, and Capital in Ghana: From Slavery to Free Labour in Asante, 1807–1956*. Rochester: University of Rochester Press.
Austin, Gareth. 2006. "The Political Economy of the Natural Environment in West African History: Asante and Its Savanna Neighbours in the Nineteenth and Twentieth Centuries." In *Land and the Politics of Belonging in West Africa*, edited by Richard Kuba and Carola Lentz, 187–212. Leiden: Brill.

Austin, Gareth. 2008. "Resources, Techniques, and Strategies South of the Sahara: Revising the Factor Endowments Perspective on African Economic Development, 1500–2000." *Economic History Review* 61(3): 587–624.

Austin, Gareth. 2009a. "Cash Crops and Freedom: Export Agriculture and the Decline of Slavery in Colonial West Africa." *International Review of Social History* 54(1): 1–37.

Austin, Gareth. 2009b. "Factor Markets in Nieboer Conditions: Pre-Colonial West Africa, c. 1500–c. 1900." *Continuity and Change* 24(1): 23–53.

Austin, Gareth. 2014. 'Explaining and Evaluating the Cash Crop Revolution in the 'Peasant' Colonies of Tropical Africa, ca. 1890–ca.1930: Beyond 'Vent for Surplus.'" In *Africa's Development in Historical Perspective*, edited by Emmanuel K. Akyeampong, Robert H. Bates, Nathan Nunn and James A. Robinson, 295–320. New York: Cambridge University Press.

Bassett, Thomas. 2001. *The Peasant Cotton Revolution in West Africa: Côte d'Ivoire, 1880–1995.* Cambridge: Cambridge University Press.

Berry, Sara. 1985. *Fathers Work for Their Sons. Accumulation, Mobility, and Class Formation in an Extended Yorùbá Community.* Berkeley: University of California Press.

Chauveau, Jean-Pierre, and Eric Léonard. 1996. "Côte d'Ivoire's Pioneer Fronts: Historical and Political Determinants of the Spread of Cocoa Cultivation." In *Cocoa Pioneer Fronts since 1800. The Role of Smallholders, Planters and Merchants*, edited by William G. Clarence-Smith, 176–94. London: Macmillan.

Chauveau, Jean-Pierre. 2006. "How Does an Institution Evolve? Land, Politics, Intergenerational Relations and the Institution of the Tutorat Amongst Autochthones and Immigrants (Gban region, Cote d'Ivoire)." In *Land and the Politics of Belonging in West Africa*, edited by Richard Kuba and Carola Lentz, 213–40. Leiden: Brill.

Collier, Paul. 1988. "Oil Shocks and Food Security in Nigeria." *International Labour Review* 127(6): 761–82.

Cordell, Dennis, and Joel Gregory. 1982. "Labour Reservoirs and Population: French Colonial Strategies in Koudougou, Upper Volta, 1914 to 1939." *Journal of African History* 23(2): 205–24.

Cordell, Dennis, Joel Gregory, and Victor Piché. 1996. *Hoe and Wage: A Social History of a Circular Migration System in West Africa.* Boulder, CO: Westview Press.

Coulibaly, Sidiki. 1986. "Colonialisme et Migration en Haute Volta (1896–1946)." In *Démographie et Sous-Développement dans le Tiers-Monde*, edited by Danielle Gauvreau, Joel Gregory, Marianne Kempeneers, and Victor Piché, 73–110. Montreal: McGill University Press.

Curtin, Philip. 1990. *The Rise and Fall of the Plantation Complex: Essays in Atlantic History.* Cambridge: Cambridge University Press.

Dalrymple-Smith, Angus, and Ewout Frankema. 2017. "Slave Ship Provisioning in the Long 18th Century. A Boost to West African Commercial Agriculture?" *European Review of Economic History* 21(2): 185–235.

David, Philippe. 1980. *Les Navétanes: Histoire des Migrants Saisonniers de L'arachide en Sénégambie des Origines à Nos Jours.* Dakar: Nouvelles Éditions Africaines.

De Haas, Michiel. 2017a. "Measuring Rural Welfare in Colonial Africa: Did Uganda's Smallholders Thrive?" *Economic History Review* 70(2): 605–31.

De Haas, Michiel. 2017b. *Rural Livelihoods and Agricultural Commercialization in Colonial Uganda: Conjunctures of External Influences and Local Realities.* PhD dissertation. Wageningen University.

De Haas, Michiel. 2019. "Moving Beyond Colonial Control? Economic Forces and Shifting Migration from Ruanda-Urundi to Buganda, 1920–60." *Journal of African History* 60(3): 379–406; corrigendum in 62(1) (2021): 179–80.

De Haas, Michiel. 2021. "The Failure of Cotton Imperialism in Africa: Seasonal Constraints and Contrasting Outcomes in French West Africa and British Uganda." *Journal of Economic History* 81(4): 1098–136.

Destombes, Jérôme. 2006. "From Long-Term Patterns of Seasonal Hunger to Changing Experiences of Everyday Poverty: Northeastern Ghana c. 1930–2000." *Journal of African History* 47(2): 181–205.

East African Statistical Department. 1950. *African Population of Uganda Protectorate [1948].* Nairobi: East African High Commission – Statistical Department.

Eckert, Andreas. 1996. "Cocoa Farming in Cameroon, c.1914–c.1960: Land and Labour." In *Cocoa Pioneer Fronts since 1800. The Role of Smallholders, Planters and Merchants*, edited by William Clarence-Smith, 137–53. London: Macmillan.

Flahaux, Marie-Laurence, and Hein de Haas. 2016. "African Migration: Trends, Patterns, Drivers." *Comparative Migration Studies* 4(1): 1–25.

Frankema, Ewout, and Marlous van Waijenburg. 2012. "Structural Impediments to African Growth? New Evidence from Real Wages in British Africa, 1880–1965." *Journal of Economic History* 72(4): 895–926.

Frankema, Ewout, and Marlous van Waijenburg. 2019. *The Great Convergence. Skill Accumulation and Mass Education in Africa and Asia, 1870–2010*. CEPR Discussion Paper No. 14150.

Frankema, Ewout, Jeffrey Williamson, and Pieter Woltjer. 2018. "An Economic Rationale for the West African Scramble? The Commercial Transition and the Commodity Price Boom of 1835–1885." *Journal of Economic History* 78(1): 231–67.

Frederick, Katherine. 2020. *Deindustrialization in East Africa: Textile Production in an Era of Globalization and Colonization, c. 1830–1940*. London: Palgrave McMillan.

Ghana, Republic of. 1962. *1960 Population Census of Ghana: Advance Report of Volumes III and IV*. Accra: Census Office.

Ghana, Republic of. 1975. *1970 Population Census of Ghana: Volume III - Demographic Characteristics of Local Authorities Regions and Total Country*. Accra: Census Office.

Goddard, A.D. (1974) "Population movements and land shortages in the Sokoto close-settled zone, Nigeria", In *Modern Migrations in Western Africa*, edited by Amin, Samir, 258–280. Oxford: Oxford University Press.

Goddard, A.D. Mortimore, M.J., and Norman, D.W. 1975. "Some Social and Economic Implications of Population Growth in Rural Hausaland." In *Population Growth and Socioeconomic Change in West Africa*, edited by John Caldwell, 321–36. New York: Columbia University Press.

Gold Coast Government. 1955. *Report on the Ministry of Labour for the Year 1953–54*. Accra: Government Printer.

Gold Coast, the. 1932. *Appendices: Containing Comparative Returns and General Statistics of the 1931 Census*. Accra: Government Printer.

Gold Coast, the. 1950. *Census of Population 1948: Report and Tables*. Accra: Government Printing Department.

Hance, William, Vincent Kotschar, and Richard Peterec. 1961. "Source Areas of Export Production in Tropical Africa." *Geographical Review* 51(4): 487–99.

Hatton, Tim, and Jeffrey Williamson. 2005. *Global Migration and the World Economy: Two Centuries of Policy and Performance*. Cambridge, MA: MIT Press.

Hill, Polly. 1997[1963]. *The Migrant Cocoa-Farmers of Southern Ghana: a Study in Rural Capitalism*. Oxford: LIT Verlag, James Currey.

Hopkins, Anthony G. 2020[1973]. *An Economic History of West Africa* (2nd edn). London: Routledge.

Isaacman, Allen. 1996. *Cotton is the Mother of Poverty: Peasants. Work and Rural Struggle in Colonial Mozambique 1938–1961*. Portsmouth, NH: Heinemann.

Jarrett, H. Reginald. 1949. "The Strange Farmers of the Gambia". *Geographical Review* 39(4): 649–57.

Law, Robin, ed. 1995. *From Slave Trade to 'Legitimate' Commerce: The Commercial Transition in Nineteenth-Century West Africa*. Cambridge: Cambridge University Press.

Law, Robin, Suzanne Schwarz, and Silke Strickrodt, eds. 2013. *Commercial Agriculture, the Slave Trade and Slavery in Atlantic Africa*. Woodbridge: Boydell & Brewer.

Lentz, Carola. 2006. "Land Rights and the Politics of Belonging in Africa: An Introduction." In *Land and the Politics of Belonging in West Africa*, edited by Richard Kuba and Carola Lentz, 1–34. Leiden: Brill.

Lewis, W. Arthur. 1954. "Economic Development with Unlimited Supplies of Labour." *Manchester School* 22(2): 139–91.

Likaka, Osumaka. 1997. *Rural Society and Cotton in Colonial Zaire*. Madison: University of Wisconsin Press.

Lovejoy, Paul, and Jan Hogendorn. 1993. *Slow Death for Slavery: The Course of Abolition in Northern Nigeria, 1897–1936*. Cambridge: Cambridge University Press.

Lynn, Martin. 1997. *Commerce and Economic Change in West Africa: The Palm Oil Trade in the Nineteenth Century.* Cambridge: Cambridge University Press.

Manchuelle, François. 1997. *Willing Migrants: Soninke Labor Diasporas, 1848–1960.* Athens: Ohio University Press.

Martin, Susan. 1989. "The Long Depression: West African Export Producers and the World Economy, 1914–45." In *The Economies of Africa and Asia in the Inter-War Depression*, edited by Ian Brown, 74–94. London: Routledge.

Mitchell, B. R. 1995. *International Historical Statistics: Africa, Asia & Oceania 1750–1988, Second Revised Edition.* New York: Stockton.

Moradi, Alexander. 2008. "Confronting Colonial Legacies—Lessons from Human Development in Ghana and Kenya, 1880–2000." *Journal of International Development* 20(8): 1107–21.

Mosley, Paul. 1980. *The Settler Economies: Studies in the Economic History of Kenya and Southern Rhodesia 1900–1963.* Cambridge: Cambridge University Press.

Myint, Hla. 1958. "The 'Classical Theory' of International Trade and the Underdeveloped Countries." *The Economic Journal* 68(270): 317–37.

Ochonu, Moses. 2009. *Colonial Meltdown: Northern Nigeria in the Great Depression.* Athens: Ohio University Press.

Prothero, R. Mansell. 1959. *Migration Labour from Sokoto Province, Northern Nigeria,* Kaduna: Government Printer.

Reid, Richard. 2017. *A History of Modern Uganda.* Cambridge: Cambridge University Press.

Richards, Audrey, ed. 1973[1954]. *Economic Development and Tribal Change: A Study of Immigrant Labour in Buganda* (Revised Edition). Oxford: Oxford University Press.

Roberts, Richard. 1996. *Two Worlds of Cotton: Colonialism and the Regional Economy in the French Soudan, 1800–1946.* Redwood City, CA: Stanford University Press.

Robertson, Alexander. 1982. "Abusa: The Structural History of an Economic Contract." *Journal of Development Studies* 18(4): 447–78.

Roessler, Philip, Yannick Pengl, Robert Marty, Kyle Sorlie Titlow, and Nicolas van de Walle. 2020. *The Cash Crop Revolution, Colonialism and Legacies of Spatial Inequality: Evidence from Africa.* Working Paper WPS/2020-12, Centre for the Study of African Economies, University of Oxford.

Rossi, Benedetta. 2014. "Migration and Emancipation in West Africa's Labour History: The Missing Links." *Slavery & Abolition* 35(1): 23–46.

Ruf, François. 1995. "From Forest Rent to Tree Capital: Basic 'Laws' of Cocoa Supply." In *Cocoa Cycles: The Economics of Cocoa Supply*, edited by François Ruf and P.S. Siswoputranto, 1–53. Cambridge: Woodhead Publishing.

Salau, Mohammed Bashir. 2010. "The Role of Slave Labor in Groundnut Production in Early Colonial Kano." *Journal of African History* 51(2): 147–65.

Sallah, Tijan. 2019. "'Strange Farmers' and the Development of The Gambia's Peanut Trade." *African Economic History* 47(2): 117–38.

Stürzinger, Ulrich. 1983. "The Introduction of Cotton Cultivation in Chad: The Role of the Administration, 1920–1936." *African Economic History* 12: 213–25.

Sundiata, Ibrahim. 1996. *From Slaving to Neoslavery: The Bight of Biafra and Fernando Po in the Era of Abolition, 1827–1930.* Madison: University of Wisconsin Press.

Swindell, Kenneth. 1977. "Migrant Groundnut Farmers in the Gambia: The Persistence of a Nineteenth Century Labor System." *International Migration Review* 11(4): 452–72.

Swindell, Kenneth. 1980. "Serawoollies, Tillibunkas and Strange Farmers: The Development of Migrant Groundnut Farming Along the Gambia River, 1848–95." *Journal of African History* 21(1): 93–104.

Swindell, Kenneth. 1982. "From Migrant Farmers to Permanent Settler: The Strange Farmers of the Gambia." In *Redistribution of population in Africa*, edited by John Clarke and Leszek Kosinski, 96–101. Portsmouth, NH: Heinemann.

Swindell, Kenneth. 1984. "Farmers, Traders, and Labourers: Dry Season Migration from North-West Nigeria, 1900–1933." *Africa*, 54(1): 3–19.

Swindell, Kenneth. 1986. "Population and Agriculture in the Sokoto-Rima Basin of North-West Nigeria: A Study of Political Intervention, Adaptation and Change, 1800–1980." *Cahiers d'Etudes Africaines* 26(101/102): 75–111.

Swindell, Kenneth, and Alieu Jeng. 2006. *Migrants, Credit and Climate: The Gambian Groundnut Trade, 1834–1934.* Leiden: Brill.

Thomas, Roger G. 1973. "Forced Labour in British West Africa: The Case of the Northern Territories of the Gold Coast 1906–1927." *Journal of African History* 14(1): 79–103.

Tosh, John. 1980. "The Cash-Crop Revolution in Tropical Africa: An Agricultural Reappraisal." *African Affairs* 79(314): 79–94.

Travieso, Emiliano, and Tom Westland. 2021. *Deindustrialization in the Savanna? Northern Nigerian Textiles from Caliphate to Colonial Rule.* Unpublished manuscript. Typescript.

Twaddle, Michael. 1988. "The Ending of Slavery in Buganda." In *The End of Slavery in Africa*, edited by Susan Miers and Richard L. Roberts, 119–49. Madison: University of Wisconsin Press.

Uganda Protectorate. 1933. *Census Returns 1931.* Entebbe: Government Printer.

Uganda Protectorate. 1960. *Uganda Census 1959: Non-African Population.* Nairobi: East African High Commission – Statistical Department.

Uganda, Republic of. 1974. *Report on the 1969 Population Census: Volume III – Additional Tables.* Entebbe: Statistics Division – Ministry of Finance, Planning and Economic Development.

Van Beusekom, Monica. 2002. *Negotiating Development: African Farmers and Colonial Experts at the Office du Niger, 1920–1960.* Portsmouth, NH: Heinemann.

Van Waijenburg, Marlous. 2018. "Financing the African Colonial State: The Revenue Imperative and Forced Labor." *Journal of Economic History* 78(1): 40–80.

Walker, Ezekiel. 2000. "Structural Change, the Oil Boom and the Cocoa Economy of Southwestern Nigeria, 1973–1980s." *Journal of Modern African Studies* 38(1): 71–87.

Watts, Michael. 1983. *Silent Violence: Food, Famine and Peasantry in Northern Nigeria.* Berkeley: University of California Press.

Westland, Tom. 2021. "The Fruits of the Boom: Real Wages and Housing Costs in Dakar, Senegal (1914–1960)." AEHN Working Paper No. 60, African Economic History Network.

12

FROM TEMPORARY URBANITES TO PERMANENT CITY DWELLERS?

Rural-Urban Labor Migration in Colonial Southern Rhodesia and the Belgian Congo

Katharine Frederick and Elise van Nederveen Meerkerk

1 Introduction

In many parts of sub-Saharan Africa, the foundations of early urban development were laid prior to colonial rule and the introduction of industrial capitalism (Freund 2007). However, colonialism would constitute a "virtually continent-wide rupture" that altered the course of African urbanization. Whether European colonists established new cities or expanded existing urban areas, African cities served as business hubs for European economic and political interests and attracted large numbers of African workers from rural areas (Coquery-Vidrovitch 2005, 4, 27–8). Varying by colonial context, the experiences of African migrants traveling to burgeoning cities differed considerably. Some settled permanently in town, while others labored temporarily in cities before returning home. This chapter evaluates the intriguing differences between the relatively early shift from temporary to more permanent settlement of African migrants in Belgian Congolese towns as opposed to the more persistently transient character of rural-urban migration in Southern Rhodesia.

These two colonies offer excellent cases for comparison, sharing some distinct similarities, along with significant differences that together affected the nature of their respective migration systems during the early 20th century. In terms of similarities, first, both colonies had relatively sparse urban settlements during the 19th century. In what would eventually become colonial Southern Rhodesia, the Kingdom of Great Zimbabwe had displayed impressive urbanization from the 11th to 15th century; however, by the late pre-colonial period, the only major extant indigenous city was Bulawayo. In the Congo, nearly all substantial cities were founded by the Belgian colonizers, except for the pre-colonial town of Boma (Heymans 1952, 9–10). Second, migrants began flowing to urban centers in both colonies relatively early and quickly, exceeding average sub-Saharan African urbanization rates (14.7%), reaching 23% (Belgian Congo) and 17% (Southern Rhodesia) in 1961 (see Table 12.1) (Kamer der Volksvertegenwoordigers 1958, 69; Gargett 1977, 38, Table 12.2).[1]

Third, both colonies developed relatively diversified economies, with significant mining, commercial farming, and manufacturing sectors. They would ultimately rank among the most industrialized colonies in sub-Saharan Africa. By the 1960s, manufacturing comprised

DOI: 10.4324/9781003225027-17

TABLE 12.1 Urbanization rates in Southern Rhodesia
and Congo, 1936–61

Year	Southern Rhodesia (%)	Belgian Congo (%)
1936	3.6	8.9
1946	5.9	14.7
1949	10.0	18.3
1951	12.7	20.2
1956	14.3	22.9
1961	17.0	23.0

Sources: Southern Rhodesia: *Report* 1958, 162; Gargett 1977, 38;
Zinyama and Whitlow 1986, 378; Congo: *Annual Reports
Congo*, 1938–58.

Notes: Urbanization rates for Southern Rhodesia imputed from
the available indexes. Congo: 1936 = 1938.

16% of GDP in Southern Rhodesia and 14% in the Belgian Congo, trailing only behind
South Africa's 20% (Austin, Frankema and Jerven 2017, 346, 353, Table 14.1). In both colonies, urban growth and industrialization progressed in tandem, as African laborers poured
into emerging cities to work in the growing industrial sector, while others found urban
employment in services. In East and West African cities, in contrast, opportunities in manufacturing were less decisive in stimulating rural-urban migration, with trade and (informal)
services playing a more pronounced role.[2]

Amid rapid industrial and urban growth, colonial officials in both Southern Rhodesia
and the Congo expressed concern over mounting urban pressures. Consequently, attempts
were (eventually) made to stabilize the urban labor force by encouraging African male laborers to permanently settle in town with their families. Here, however, outcomes differed
markedly. In the Belgian Congo, the percentage of working-age men in the total urban
population declined substantially from the 1940s onward, from 46.8 in 1938 to 31.1 in
1958, suggesting a steady increase in the settlement of families in urban zones (Kamer der
Volksvertegenwoordigers 1939–58). In the mining region of Katanga (e.g., contemporary
Lubumbashi, then Elizabethville), "labor stabilization" dates back further to the 1920s.[3] By
contrast, in the two main cities of Southern Rhodesia, working-age men comprised 48%
(Salisbury) and 46% (Bulawayo) of the population by 1962, reflecting a still predominately
migratory labor force of mostly single men with tenuous urban ties (Central Statistical Office 1964).

This chapter aims to uncover *how and why rural-urban migration patterns shifted* more rapidly toward permanent urban settlement in the Belgian Congo compared with Southern
Rhodesia. We argue that the specific geopolitical circumstances of the two colonies affected the timing and character of their industrial take-offs and the degree of integration
of each colony with surrounding territories, both of which influenced the nature of their
urban labor markets and migratory flows. Meanwhile, the different colonial contexts of the
semi-autonomous settler colony of Southern Rhodesia relative to the more metropolitan-
controlled Belgian Congo influenced colonial institutions and social policies. This affected
rural and urban opportunity structures, thus impacting the decision-making of potential
African migrants in profoundly different ways.

Thematically, we predominantly study *rural-urban migration to manufacturing centers*, although rural-rural migration and migration to mining areas feature as part of the broader colonial migration systems in our case studies (Section 2). Geographically, we focus on the main industrial urban centers in each colony: Salisbury[4] and Bulawayo in Southern Rhodesia and Leopoldville,[5] Elizabethville,[6] and Stanleyville[7] in the Belgian Congo. Our analysis begins in the 1920s, when the Congo received its initial industrial impulse, and continues to mid-century, when both colonies were undergoing substantial industrial and urban growth. While analysis of the Belgian Congo concludes with its independence in 1960, our discussion of Southern Rhodesia, which declared independence in 1965, moves beyond that point to analyze the persistence of temporary urban migration well past the early industrial boom years.

The next section provides an overview of the most important migration systems in Congo and Southern Rhodesia. Section 3 then sketches differing opportunity structures in rural and urban labor markets in the two colonies, which would result in divergent labor stabilization patterns. The remaining sections unpack the underlying drivers of those differing opportunity structures.

2 Migration systems in colonial Southern Rhodesia and the Belgian Congo

Rural-urban migration can best be understood as a dynamic "system" consisting of sending and receiving zones – rural and urban "sub-systems," respectively – that exist within a broader "environmental" context, encompassing institutions, policy, market conditions, and technological characteristics, which affect the migratory system (Mabogunje 1970, 4). African migration in colonial Southern Rhodesia and the Belgian Congo was broadly typified by three often overlapping systems that provided alternative opportunities to would-be migrants: rural-rural migration, rural-mining area migration,[8] and rural-urban migration. To understand the development of the rural-urban migration systems in our two cases, we must also consider competition and interactions *between* systems in each colonial context.

The rural-rural migration system in colonial Southern Rhodesia predated significant rural-urban migration flows in the colony. After the foundation of Southern Rhodesia in 1889, African migration remained predominantly rural-rural in nature, involving movements either to European settler farms or to the Native Reserves established in 1903 (Section 5). As labor shortages began to emerge, indigenous peasants whose land had been heavily alienated by the colonial government regularly labored on commercial farms. The majority of black Southern Rhodesians remained active in subsistence agriculture, but many necessarily supplemented household incomes with rural wage labor or – increasingly after the Second World War – employment in urban settings (Pilossof 2014, 252–3). Meanwhile, labor for all sectors was increasingly drawn from other nearby British territories, particularly Northern Rhodesia and Nyasaland. Between 1904 and 1922, the proportion of "foreigners" in the colony's total black wage labor force rose to 68% (Arrighi 1970, 208–10). From the 1930s, the Southern Rhodesian government even operated a *Free Migrant Labor Transport Service*, which included rest stops and food depots, to efficiently funnel labor into the colony (Scott 1954, 36; Clarke 1974, 25). The share of extra-territorial workers in agriculture would remain high until the late 1950s. Likewise, the Wankie coal mines and gold fields attracted migrants from beyond Southern Rhodesia, especially Northern Rhodesia and, secondarily, Nyasaland and Mozambique (Scott 1954, 42–5).

Rural-urban migration forms the main focus of this chapter. Most Southern Rhodesian cities were established as forts or early mining towns soon after the *British South Africa Company* (BSAC) obtained mineral rights in the area from the British government in 1889. Salisbury, in the northeast, was founded by settlers in 1890 and would become the eventual seat of government and a major industrial center. Bulawayo, which would become the colony's second largest city and manufacturing center, forms an exception. It was established in the 1840s in Matabeleland as the seat of the Ndebele king and came under settler control only after it was captured in 1893. From around 1900, settlers increasingly clustered in these growing towns, where 58% of the colony's non-African population (mostly of European origin) lived (Smout 1975 80, 82). Almost immediately, relatively small numbers of Africans took up urban employment – primarily in workshops and services. Most early urban laborers were male migrants, working for roughly two-month stints before returning home (Urban African Affairs Commission 1958, 6). Consequently, most African urban inhabitants were men, comprising 94–95% of the African population of Salisbury in the early 1900s. Like much of the colony's agricultural and mining labor force, many urban labor migrants came from abroad, with more than half of Salisbury's African inhabitants hailing from neighboring colonies until the 1950s (see Table 12.2) (Yoshikuni 1991, 134–6).

We now turn to the migration systems in the Belgian Congo. Here, rural-rural mobility traditionally involved movement into "internal frontiers," stimulated by shifting agriculture.[9] Following the establishment of the Congo Free State by Belgian King Leopold in 1885, colonial land occupation for cash-crop production and the imposition of forced cultivation disturbed existing shifting cultivation practices, which Europeans deemed backward (Jewsiewicki 1983, 112–3). Consequently, the colonial government introduced policies to prevent shifting agriculture. A distinctive colonial-era rural-rural migration system emerged with the introduction of European plantations, often run by concession companies. The *Huileries du Congo Belge*, for instance, employed thousands of people in the Eastern Province. Many were migrant workers recruited by force, as low wages and poor working conditions formed a disincentive to move to European plantations voluntarily (Northrup 1988 132, 148, 164–6). Due to similar abysmal working conditions in the mines,

TABLE 12.2 Africans in employment in Southern Rhodesian towns, 1956

Town	Country of birth					Total	% Foreign migrants
	Southern Rhodesia	Northern Rhodesia	Nyasaland	Portuguese territories	Other		
Salisbury	41,203	2,181	28,987	28,972	701	**102,044**	**59.6%**
Bulawayo	42,841	7,928	10,262	5,224	1,150	**67,407**	**36.4%**
Umtali	7,496	93	618	5,568	77	**13,852**	**45.9%**
Gwelo	8,737	425	1,030	517	77	**10,768**	**19.0%**
Que Que	2,890	474	960	457	15	**4,796**	**39.7%**
Gatooma	2,049	460	1,137	584	35	**4,265**	**52.0%**
Fort Victoria	3,031	41	116	167	17	**3,372**	**10.1%**
Total	*108,247*	*11,602*	*43,110*	*41,489*	*2,072*	***206,520***	***47.6%***

Source: Report 1958, 16, Table VII.

recruitment problems also arose in the sparsely populated copper fields of Katanga. Until 1925, the mining areas relied on laborers from surrounding British and Portuguese African territories, predominantly Northern Rhodesia. Most were circular contract migrants, who returned to their colony of origin after a specified number of shifts. However, after the discovery of new copper and sulfide deposits in Northern Rhodesia, the flows of "foreign" migrant workers to Katanga dried up. In 1929, the monopolist concession company *Union Minière du Haut Katanga* decided to exclusively recruit workers from the Congo and Belgian-mandated Ruanda and Urundi. In the same period, mining real wages started to rise, and there were serious attempts to stabilize the workforce in Katanga from the mid-1920s (Juif and Frankema 2018, 321–2, 327).[10] Measures were taken to secure a steadier, healthier workforce maintained in newly built houses with running water, sewerage, and cooking facilities (Elkan and van Zwanenberg 1975, 657).

Finally, rural-urban migration formed an integral part of the Congo's broader migration system. In 1881, commissioned explorer Henry Morton Stanley established Leopoldville, the eventual colonial capital of the Congo, on the west coast (Taylor 1959, 352). Several other towns were soon established, including Elisabethville (1910) and Jadotville[11] (1917) in the mining region of Katanga in the south and the smaller towns of Stanleyville (1883) and Albertville (1892) in the east. Around 1920, about 5% of the Congolese population lived in an urban environment (Marzorati 1954, 106), and the migration of black Congolese to urban areas steadily increased over the next decades (see Table 12.1).

Rural-urban migration in the Belgian Congo included comparatively few "foreigners." Around 1950, the majority of urban dwellers in the Congo's three largest cities came from rural areas within the colony (Figure 12.1). In geographically isolated Stanleyville, a notable percentage was born in town and a large share arrived from nearby areas, suggesting short-distance migrations. In contrast, the larger cities of Leopoldville and Elisabethville attracted migrants from across the Congo, but also from other colonies, probably partly due to their relative proximity to the colonial border, which offered economic opportunities

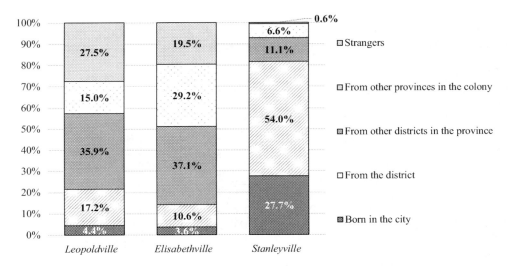

FIGURE 12.1 Background of laborers in Leopoldville, Elisabethville, and Stanleyville, 1951.
Source: AA, 3ème DG, dossier 379, Rapport de la sous-commission des problèmes sociaux, 1952.

to cross-border migrants (Jewsiewicki 1983, 109). In Leopoldville, most of these *étrangers* ("strangers") originated from nearby Portuguese Angola (about 23%) (Capelle 1947, 29–30). Compared with Southern Rhodesian cities, however, both Leopoldville and Elisabethville attracted relatively *few* foreign migrant workers.

The character of rural-urban migration in the Belgian colony differed markedly from Southern Rhodesia in one other crucial respect: in the Congo, a shift toward permanent urban settlement of laborers emerged considerably earlier. Just as in Southern Rhodesia, early rural-urban migration in the Congo consisted primarily of circular migration of rural men, who returned to their home villages after laboring in town for a few months or years. In the early 20th century, colonial authorities and private European enterprises in the Congo favored this temporary character of migration and discouraged the permanent settlement of Africans in "European towns" (Northrup 1988, 210). However, because of the vast distances between their rural homelands and places of urban employment, some migrants began settling in cities in the 1920s (Pons 1969, 35). By the 1940s, colonial policy shifted decisively in favor of boosting urban labor stabilization, which would proceed more rapidly than in Southern Rhodesia, where stabilization of the urban African population began only after 1960.

The differing pace of stabilization in the two colonies is reflected in their urban sex ratios (see Table 12.3). Congolese cities experienced a decline in sex ratios during the 1940s, suggesting a reduction in the circular nature of the colony's rural-urban migration system and an increase in urban settlement. Whereas the share of adult men in all "extra-customary centers" (which included urban zones) had been almost 47% in 1938, this had declined to just over 30% by 1958. The proportion of adult women declined slightly, from 28% to 24%, whereas the share of children rose from 25% to 45%. Thus, urban areas increasingly consisted of settled families (Kamer der Volksvertegenwoordigers 1939–58). There was, however, some variation between Congo's cities. Leopoldville and Elisabethville, which attracted more cross-border migrants, exhibited more skewed sex ratios than Stanleyville as migrants from abroad were less likely to settle permanently in Congolese towns. In both of Southern Rhodesia's main cities, sex ratios in the early 1960s were considerably more skewed than

TABLE 12.3 Sex ratios in a number of cities, Congo, 1952, and Southern Rhodesia, 1962

Year	Locality	Number of men per 100 women (total population)	Number of men per 100 women (age >16)
1952	Leopoldville	150	184
1952	Elisabethville	127	140
1952	Stanleyville	116	119
1952	*All Congo*	*99*	*93*
1962	Salisbury	186	276
1962	Bulawayo	163	211
1962	*All Southern Rhodesia*	*108*	*111*

Sources: Southern Rhodesia: *Final report* 1964, 45; Congo: AA, 3ème DG, dossier 701, Fonds; dossier 800, Documentation; *Annual report Congo* 1952, 69; Pons 1969, 43–6, 60 (note 15).

Notes: Figure for Leopoldville age >16: 1950. Figure for Elisabethville age >16: 1948.

even the most gender-imbalanced Congolese towns. Here, urban living remained a temporary stage in the life cycle for most rural–urban labor migrants, with persistently low levels of urban family settlement decades after urban populations began to swell.

3 Uneven rural and urban opportunity structures

The proximate cause of different labor stabilization developments in the Belgian Congo relative to Southern Rhodesia lies in the different opportunity structures for both rural and urban laborers that arose in the two colonies despite some similarities in urban wage developments. In both cases, urban wages rose beyond agricultural wages, drawing men to urban employment. In the Belgian Congo, empirical wage data are scattered, and some studies provide only rough indications of wage indexes over time and between regions (Dupriez et al. 1970, 270–3),[12] but we can reconstruct relative rural and urban wages for Leopoldville and Elisabethville between the 1920s and late 1950s (Figure 12.2).

During the 1920s, which saw an initial industrial impetus in the colony, urban nominal monthly wages rose dramatically – far above those offered by (usually European-owned) agricultural firms – inducing the first wave of (still mostly temporary) rural-urban migrants. Soon, however, the Great Depression caused urban unemployment and prompted the return of laborers to their home villages, indicating strong remaining rural-urban ties (Dupriez et al. 1970, 369). But thereafter, the economic boom of the 1940s led to higher nominal wages in *all* regions, and even faster wage growth on plantations and European farms than in cities. Based on supply-and-demand principles, the substantial flow of migrants from rural to urban areas in this period likely led to a relatively strong demand for remaining labor in

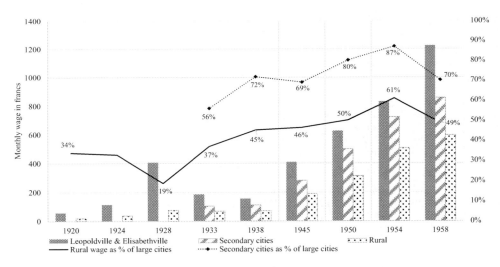

FIGURE 12.2 Nominal monthly wage of unskilled male day labor in the Belgian Congo, 1920–58. *Sources*: Kamer der Volksvertegenwoordigers (1933, 155–6); AA, 3ème DG, dossier 379, Commission; Dupriez et al. (1970, 271, 273).

rural areas, which may partly explain why agricultural wages rose so quickly and even surpassed the rate of growth for urban nominal wages, which also continued to rise.

Importantly, the purchasing power of wages in both Congolese cities *and* the countryside had risen considerably by the late 1950s. The improvement in urban purchasing power, particularly in the 1930s and early 1940s, played a crucial role in the decline of circular migration and increase in permanent settlement in cities. Prior to this period, an unskilled wage worker could barely support a wife and children without any additional income, creating a barrier for urban family settlement. Instead, men migrated alone, leaving family members in rural areas to tend their land, which generated much-needed additional household income. Women remaining in rural areas were under increased pressure to provide subsistence food for the family (as they had traditionally done) and produce for local markets to supplement household incomes (Dupriez et al. 1970, 308–9).[13] Indeed, home farms formed an important safety valve for urban migrant workers during economic slumps and unemployment, such as the Great Depression (Kamer der Volksvertegenwoordigers 1931, 7; 1933, 131; 1934, 10). However, by the late 1930s urban nominal wages in Congolese cities had risen much faster than prices, providing both the means and the incentive for rural migrants to permanently settle in town with their wives and children (Figure 12.3). This process began earliest in Elisabethville in the Katanga mining region, where real wages grew with impressive momentum, allowing families to settle in cities in the 1920s (Elkan and van Zwanenberg

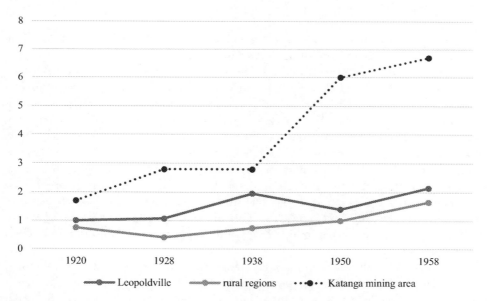

FIGURE 12.3 Welfare ratios of unskilled wages (Leopoldville & rural regions) and mining wages (Katanga) in the Belgian Congo, 1920–58 (1 = subsistence level for a family of 4).
Sources: Leopoldville and rural regions: Dupriez et al. (1970, 370); AA, 3ème DG, dossier 379, Rapport de la sous-commission des problèmes sociaux, 1952; Kamer der Volksvertegenwoordigers (1951). Katanga: Juif and Frankema (2018, 325).

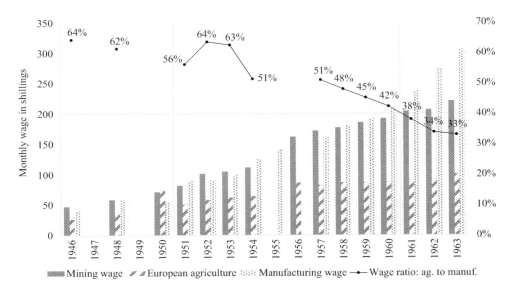

FIGURE 12.4 Average nominal wages for African labor, Southern Rhodesia, 1946–63.
Source: Mosley (1983, 160, Table 4.9b). Note: the agriculture-manufacturing wage ratio for the outlier year 1950 has been excluded to more clearly illustrate the broader trend.

1975, 657). Similarly, living standards in the industrial city of Leopoldville would double between 1928 and 1938, underpinning urban family settlement.

In Southern Rhodesia, urban and rural wage developments followed a different pattern (see Figure 12.4). As in the Belgian Congo, urban wages showed upward momentum from the early years of industrialization in the 1940s, exceeding rural agricultural wages and eventually even outstripping mining wages by the 1960s. Rising wages consequently drew many male migrant laborers from the countryside to cities from the 1940s onward. Unlike the Belgian Congo, however, rural wage rates would *not* show a marked improvement in the ensuing decades and thus fell increasingly behind urban manufacturing wages. Consequently, rural men were drawn in ever-larger numbers to wage work in urban areas where they competed fiercely for employment. The strong, increasing differential between rural and urban wages intensified the instability of urban tenure for migrants by keeping the urban labor supply high, resulting in high levels of unemployment and uncertainty in cities, even as wages rose.[14]

Meanwhile, although wages for black urban laborers rose, they remained far too low to support a family in town, perpetuating the much higher share of single male laborers in urban Southern Rhodesia relative to the Belgian Congo. Similarly, as Meier zu Selhausen highlights in his comparison of rural-urban migration in East and West Africa (Chapter 13, this volume), low wages in East African cities – generally set at rates to sustain a single male worker – deterred urban family settlement for much of the colonial period, resulting in distorted urban sex ratios; West African urban wages, in contrast, were nearly double, enabling families to settle in towns, thus engendering more balanced urban sex ratios.

For Southern Rhodesia, a 1958 commissioned study on the poverty datum line in Salisbury found that most African laborers could not maintain a family in urban environs, and those who did typically struggled immensely. Wages for married men were often higher

Rural-Urban Labor Migration 265

TABLE 12.4 Percentage of households in income brackets relative to the Poverty Datum Line (PDL), Salisbury, 1957

	Extremely impoverished (%)	Below PDL (%)	Within PDL (%)	Above PDL (%)	Extremely affluent (%)
Single men	5	22	37	17	13
Families in New Highfield	47	18	20	2	13
Families in "other areas"	57	19	17	3	3

Source: Bettison (1958, Tables 1, 6, and 7).

than for single men, but these earnings could not offset the increased expense of urban family living, relegating a large share of black urban families to poverty (Table 12.4). While only 27% of single African laborers in the Salisbury sample fell below the poverty datum line, this number increased to 65% for families residing in the township of New Highfield – which housed "in general a wealthier class of African" – and reached 76% among families located in "other areas" of Salisbury. Moreover, 47% of the families in New Highfield fell under the category "extremely impoverished," reaching 57% in "other areas." Even in comparatively affluent New Highfield, the incidence of "extreme impoverishment" increased substantially with each additional child (Bettison 1958, 188, 193). Consequently, the vast majority of urban laborers continued to venture to the city alone as temporary migrants, maintaining a "dual existence," noted already by officials in the late 1940s, characterized by "part-time employment in the European [urban] areas and part-time farming in the Native Reserves" (cited in Phimister 1993, 231).

The position of married laborers residing in town with their families remained precarious for decades, even as nominal wages increased through the 1950s and 1960s. A 1974 poverty datum line study found that 89% of black industrial laborers in Southern Rhodesia still fell below the monthly wage required to support a family of six (Harris 1975, 149). The capacity to comfortably establish a family in urban areas thus remained out of reach for most Africans in Southern Rhodesia decades after the initial industrial boom had stimulated urban migration. In the remainder of this chapter, we explore the underlying causes of the divergent opportunity structures that perpetuated the transient character of rural–urban migration in Southern Rhodesia, while labor stabilization proceeded much earlier in the Belgian Congo.

4 Two colonial economies: Southern Rhodesia and the Congo in wider geopolitical context

Key differences between Southern Rhodesia and the Belgian Congo derived from their colonial origins and geopolitical circumstances, which influenced European settler behavior and differing degrees of economic integration with surrounding colonies. This, in turn, affected the relative pace and nature of industrial development, along with the rural and urban opportunity structures that subsequently developed in each colony.

Following a series of unsuccessful revolts by the Ndebele against encroaching white settlers, Southern Rhodesia was largely brought under British control by 1900, and settlers began establishing both mines and farms. Over the succeeding decades, what had initially been founded as a mining colony, largely controlled by the BSAC, increasingly transformed into a settler farming colony, steadily attracting European immigrant farmers and their families (Phimister 1988, 4–20, 100–1). The political voice and legislative capacity of these settlers was bolstered by the British government's acquiescence to allow semi-autonomous "Responsible Government" in the colony from 1923. The resulting political control of the relatively large settler community in Southern Rhodesia contrasted sharply with metropolitan-controlled Belgian Congo, which drew comparatively smaller numbers of European settlers, who typically remained for relatively short stints.

Since the founding of Southern Rhodesia, white settler politics had been largely framed in opposition to the economic agency of black Africans in the colony. The establishment of mining ventures and embryonic cities by the turn of the 20th century had initially brought new agricultural trading opportunities for the indigenous Shona and Ndebele, who began producing foodstuffs for the market (Phimister 1988, 25). White settlers were consequently confronted not only with competition for settler-grown produce but also labor shortages since Africans who could generate incomes from peasant production were unwilling to work for wages in mines or on European farms. A number of measures were consequently taken to minimize African agricultural marketing opportunities and funnel African labor toward European enterprises (see next section) (Arrighi 1970, 209–10). Once settler political control was strengthened in 1923, these processes intensified. A policy of segregation and land alienation was institutionally solidified with the *Land Apportionment Act* of 1930, which allotted less than 29.8% of the colony's land to Africans, who comprised 95% of the population (Table 12.5) (Zinyama and Whitlow 1986, 368–9). Rural Africans were thus under immense economic pressure by the 1940s, when the colony rapidly began to industrialize, prompting rural–urban migration.

In the early 20th century, the colonial government championed the mining industry and commercial settler agriculture but showed comparatively limited interest in manufacturing

TABLE 12.5 Population development, Southern Rhodesia and the Belgian Congo, 1901–60

	Southern Rhodesia					*Belgian Congo*				
	Black African population		*Population of European descent*		*Total population*	*Black African population*		*Population of European descent*		*Total population*
1901	1,107,415	99.0%	11,032	1.0%	1,118,447			n.d.		9,355,140
1911	1,291,789	98.2%	23,606	1.8%	1,315,395			n.d.		8,495,725
1921	1,508,870	97.8%	33,620	2.2%	1,542,490	8,152,779	99.9%	9,361	0.1%	8,162,140
1931	1,847,656	97.4%	49,910	2.6%	1,897,566	9,275,871	99.8%	22,482	0.2%	9,298,353
1941	2,315,053		n.d.		2,315,053	10,511,169	99.7%	29,735	0.3%	10,540,904
1951	2,697,902	95.2%	136,017	4.8%	2,833,919	12,407,692	99.4%	69,204	0.6%	12,476,896
1960	3,526,000	94.0%	225,000	6.0%	3,751,000	15,332,997	99.2%	118,003	0.8%	15,451,000

Sources: Black African population: AEHN, Frankema-Jerven African Population Database, v. 1.0, pertaining to Frankema and Jerven 2014; European population Southern Rhodesia: McEwan 1963, 429 (Table 12.1); European population Belgian Congo: *Congo Annual Reports* 1921; 1931; 1939–44; 1951; 1958.

Note: While early colonial census data for African populations represent guesstimates, they provide a rough picture of early population shares and developments.

(Clarence-Smith 1989, 173–5). Urban industries did grow gradually, particularly in the years after the Great Depression when enhanced mining profits encouraged domestic demand for manufactured goods. However, much of this demand was met with imports from Britain or early-industrializing South Africa, with whom Southern Rhodesia traded extensively, limiting incentives to expand Rhodesian manufacturing (Phimister 1988, 240). The Southern Rhodesian government's lukewarm attitude toward broader industrial development shifted during the Second World War when the need for domestic industry to fill supply bottlenecks became painfully apparent. The government threw its support behind industrial development and by 1940 provided funds for essential industrial projects, including a state-sponsored ordnance factory, spinning mill, and nationalized iron and steel works. The number of factories increased from 294 to 473 within a decade, with average annual output growth reaching 24.4% between 1944 and 1948. Thereafter, the governments of South Africa and Southern Rhodesia negotiated a Customs Union agreement that offered Southern Rhodesian consumer goods free access to the large South African market, while providing Southern Rhodesia access to South African capital goods. Investors, particularly from Britain and South Africa, flocked to develop Southern Rhodesia's consumer goods sector, situated primarily in Salisbury and Bulawayo (Phimister 1988, 239–57).

Regional exporting spurred the expansion of Southern Rhodesia's manufacturing sector, facilitated by the colony's economic ties with neighboring British colonies. Textile and clothing exports alone, sent primarily to South Africa and secondarily to Northern Rhodesia and Nyasaland, grew swiftly – from £65,000 in 1948 to £988,000 in 1949, reaching over £4 million in 1953 (Phimister 2007, 437). By the early 1950s, the Southern Rhodesian manufacturing sector matched and even surpassed net earnings in both mining and settler agriculture (Urban African Affairs Commission 1958, 9). Demand for industrial labor consequently boomed, stimulating rural-urban migration, with urbanization rates more than tripling between 1936 and 1951 (see Table 12.1). Many cross-border "voluntary" labor migrants (as opposed to contracted migrants, who were typically directed toward farms and mines) were attracted to the comparatively high wages and better conditions of Southern Rhodesia's urban centers, especially Salisbury. In the mid-1950s, 53% of black African laborers employed in secondary industries came from beyond Southern Rhodesia, particularly from the British colony of Nyasaland. While voluntary labor migrants were not under contractual obligation to return to their colony of origin, migrants from Nyasaland typically ceased working in the colony within five years (Scott 1954, 45–6). Consequently, the presence of foreign manufacturing employees undoubtedly influenced the far more temporary character of urban tenure in Southern Rhodesia compared to the Belgian Congo, at least during the 1940s and 1950s, when the number of foreign migrants in Southern Rhodesian cities reached its peak.

As in Southern Rhodesia, early colonial rule and economic development in the Belgian Congo was characterized by exploitation of African colonial subjects. To maximize resource extraction, King Leopold installed a violent regime in which concession companies displaced entire villages and created harsh work regimes, most notably for harvesting wild rubber. A brutal system of taxation and force was imposed to extract labor (Harms 1974, 11–4; Hochschild 1998). However, ensuing financial troubles, along with international indignation over these atrocities, led the Belgian state to become increasingly involved in the Congo and finally annex it – against Leopold's will – in 1908 (Vanthemsche 2012, 21–6). Under international scrutiny, the Belgian state developed a less violent and comparatively more humane approach to colonial rule. This is not to suggest in any way that Belgian colonialism became benevolent: resource extraction still remained the colonial state's primary objective. There were few freedoms or benefits for the majority of the black population, particularly before the 1940s, and although forced labor declined, it continued to exist throughout the colonial period, especially for public works (Exenberger and Hartmann 2013, 27–8). However, as noted, the white settler population of the Belgian Congo remained comparably small and unattached to the colony. Thus, unlike in Southern Rhodesia, the colonial government was not beholden to the vested interests of a large settler community competing for (and with) African labor.

Moreover, in contrast with Southern Rhodesia, the Belgian Congo was relatively isolated, situated between the African empires of Britain, France, and Portugal, and had been mandated a free trade and navigation area at the Berlin Conference. This prevented Belgium from favoring industrial imports from the metropole via preferential tariffs and ultimately incentivized domestic manufacturing within the colony (Clarence-Smith 1989, 193). Consequently, the Congo began to industrialize in the mid-1920s, relatively early for the African colonial context, bolstered by Belgian investments in export processing industries, food processing, and textile manufacturing (Brixhe 1953, 110–2). Emerging employment opportunities drew rural Africans to manufacturing towns, initially mostly as temporary or circular migrants, although increasing numbers began settling around the "European" city centers.

Rural-urban migration gained further steam following a brief downturn during the Great Depression (Vandewalle 1966, 31). The Second World War boosted industrial development in the Congo when isolation from the German-occupied metropole caused shortages of consumer product imports during the war (Taylor 1959, 353). The post-war economic boom led to a rise in indigenous living standards, further inducing internal consumer demand for Congo-made products (Dienst voor de Voorlichting 1960, 38). By 1946, industrial textile production – which began in Leopoldville in 1925 – supplied a quarter of the domestic market, a uniquely high share in colonial Africa (Clarence-Smith 1989, 194). Manufacturing soon received further stimulus as European capitalists, fearing a Third World War, funneled their money toward Congolese industries. The Congo became one of the most developed industrial regions in sub-Saharan Africa and began catching up with earlier-industrializing South Africa due to exceptional growth in Congolese industrial output.[15] This fed back into increasing demand for urban industrial labor, resulting in an uptick in post-war rural-urban migration and rising urbanization (see Table 12.1).

5 Colonial policies and the development of uneven opportunity structures

Alongside (and related to) geopolitical and colonial characteristics, an array of specific institutions and policies would have profound implications for the development of migration systems in our two case studies. From the early stages of colonization, both the British in Southern Rhodesia and the Belgians in the Congo restricted the economic agency of rural Africans. This interference served at least three purposes: first, the exploitation of African land to extract natural resources, including cash crops and minerals; second, the creation of a wage labor force by narrowing alternative economic opportunities; and, third, the reduction of competition for European agricultural enterprises from African farmers seizing new commercial opportunities arising from settler consumer demand. Typically, colonial authorities employed three main methods to create a cheap and transient African labor force directed either to European farms and mines or to cities: restricting African access to land, imposing rural and urban segregation policies, and levying taxes in money or labor services. Alternatively, authorities could seek to *stabilize* the wage labor force by improving living conditions, thus diminishing incentives to migrate. We argue that the choice of policies, and their relative "success," played a decisive role in creating distinctive rural and urban opportunity structures in Southern Rhodesia and the Belgian Congo, which led to fundamentally different labor stabilization outcomes in both rural and urban zones.

At the turn of the 20th century, Southern Rhodesia created the first Native Reserves for African settlement. This land alienation strategy started a process of African-European segregation that progressively eroded the economic position of most black Southern Rhodesians. Reserve lands often had poor soil quality and inadequate water supplies and were typically located far from emerging urban centers and railways, leaving peasant producers disconnected from growing markets.[16] By 1909 Africans still living outside the reserves were obligated to pay land rents – to which grazing fees were added in 1912 – to the BSAC, pushing many toward the reserves. Others were evicted from their land to supply farms to white settler immigrants. In 1922, 63.5% of Southern Rhodesia's black inhabitants already resided in the reserves (Phimister 1988, 65–7, 83). The 1930 *Land Appropriation Act* further segregated the colony into the existing *Native Reserves*, a *Native Purchase Area* (available only to wealthier Africans), various unassigned zones, and a *European Area*. While white European settlers made up no more than 5% of the colony's population, the *European Area* ranged over 51% of the colony (Floyd 1962, 577). Africans were forbidden to reside in *European Areas*, including all urban centers, unless employed by a white employer. The geographic mobility of black Southern Rhodesians was consequently sharply curtailed. Meanwhile, space on the reserves steadily dwindled, from 19 hectares per person in 1931 to only 9 by the early 1950s, as populations increased (Phimister and Pilossof 2017, 217).

Alongside land alienation, taxation further diminished peasant incomes. Hut tax, levied on Africans from 1893, was doubled by 1904, and additional taxes were introduced (Phimister 1988, 83). While the fiscal burden was placed on black peasants, investments in white settler agriculture "became one of the major items on the Government budget" (Arrighi 1970, 210). Moreover, in the 1930s, the *Maize Control Acts* sharply depressed grain prices paid to most African cultivators, which diminished their capacity to pay rents and taxes and pushed poorer peasants onto the wage labor market.[17] The proportion of black male inhabitants of Southern Rhodesia engaged in wage labor grew from around 20% in 1920 to about 60% in 1951 (Arrighi 1970, 204, 221–2). From the 1940s, many were heading to urban centers, as industrial employment opportunities expanded, rather than to European farms, where wages were considerably lower.

A systematic depression of agricultural wages in Southern Rhodesia – which accentuated the rural-urban wage gap and perpetuated competition for better-paying urban jobs – was linked to a steady inflow of cheap contract labor from neighboring colonies. From the early 20th century, contracted migrant laborers flowed into Southern Rhodesia and were channeled toward commercial farms and mines by the Rhodesia Native Labour Bureau (RNLB), which was established in 1903 to redirect labor away from the Transvaal and toward Southern Rhodesian enterprises (Phimister 1988, 50, 85). Labor recruitment agreements between Southern Rhodesia, Northern Rhodesia, and Nyasaland lubricated the inflow of migrant workers (Secretary for Labour, Social Welfare and Housing 1961, 11–2).[18] By the 1950s, numerous recruits hailed from Nyasaland, stimulated by local job scarcity, population pressures, and taxation, while others came from Portuguese Mozambique (Scott 1954; Clark 1974, 39). Most contracted laborers were destined for rural employment, and their influx helped keep rural wages stagnant, even as urban wages continued to rise. This rural-urban wage differential was exacerbated by the restrictive *Masters and Servants Act*, which diminished agricultural worker rights, and the powerful Rhodesia National Farmers Union, which lobbied against wage regulations (Clarke 1974, 43–4). In contrast, strike action by black industrial laborers during the 1940s had resulted in the *Native Labour Boards Act* (1947), which instituted labor dispute machinery. This led to upward momentum of manufacturing wages, although wages paid to black workers still remained far below those earned by white workers (see discussion below).

Relative to Southern Rhodesia, colonial-era land alienation policies were milder in the Belgian Congo. Still, colonial interventions resulted in an urban push effect for many rural dwellers. Before the colonial period, land tenure systems were based on shifting cultivation within corporate groups (e.g., chiefdoms, villages, and lineages) and consisted of temporary individual rights on cultivated land and communal hunting and gathering rights on uncultivated land (Harms 1974, 1–2). When Leopold's Congo Free State was founded, it generally recognized rights over cultivated land but ignored communal rights on uncultivated land, which it claimed for settlement, cultivation, and natural resource extraction (Harms 1974, 11–4). Land alienation for plantations was relatively limited, but when it did occur, the most fertile arable lands were targeted (Jewsiewicki 1983, 111).

As in Southern Rhodesia, extractive colonial policies stimulated the development of a rural-urban migration system. Contemporary anthropologists noted that compulsory cultivation, combined with harsh *corvée* labor in some rural areas, incentivized rural-urban migration (Pons 1969, 48–9). Initially, the Belgian colonial authorities tightly controlled the Congolese wage labor market. Recruitment for public and private works – largely rural in nature – was primarily handled by the government as of the 1920s, while forced labor kept a check on wage levels. Although measures were introduced to break this stringent regime – for instance, by limiting forced labor in certain sectors, such as railroad construction, and for private enterprises – officials often bent the rules to aid European entrepreneurs. At the same time, low wages and poor working conditions in European mines and plantations did little to stimulate voluntary wage labor in these sectors (Northrup 1988, 158–60). In contrast, more remunerative wage-earning opportunities in growing urban centers had become increasingly attractive to many (young) men from the 1920s onward.

By the 1940s and 1950s, living standards were gradually improving in rural areas (Figures 12.2 and 12.3). Wage workers were still better off in cities than in rural zones, but this difference declined from the late 1940s. Part of this shift in rural fortunes was related to a reorientation of rural policies. Before the Great Depression, colonial agricultural policies had generally favored large concession companies, like the *Congo Cotton Company* (*Cotonco*), that produced export crops, while African farmers were pushed onto marginal lands and often forced to produce food crops for the non-agricultural labor force. During the economic crisis of the 1930s, the colonial state expanded its forced peasant cultivation strategy to include cash crops, such as cotton, coffee, and palm oil (Jewsiewicki 1983, 100–1). By the 1940s, it had become clear that forced cultivation led to soil exhaustion and an exodus to the cities. Consequently, the colonial government abandoned forced cultivation and introduced the *paysannat* scheme, allotting individual rectangular plots to be cultivated in fixed rotations (cash crops, food crops, and fallowing), thereby binding Congolese peasants to their farms (Brixhe 1953, 64–7). However, the plan did not account for substantial local differences in soil quality. In poorly endowed regions, many farmers soon left, fearing that soil depletion would lead to starvation. Instead of providing greater security through fixed land tenure, the introduction of the *paysannat* led to increasing rural insecurity and migration to cities (Harms 1974, 18). Government policies in the early 1950s therefore shifted (with greater success) to improving living conditions in rural areas to prevent excessive urban migration and promote greater stability throughout the colony. For example, efforts were made to decrease the cultivation of soil-depleting export crops and introduce less land-exhaustive agricultural techniques.[19]

Despite often ineffective and disruptive colonial interventions and the dismissal of communal land rights, cultivatable land was generally more accessible for peasants in the Congo than in Southern Rhodesia. Moreover, Belgian colonial authorities had recognized relatively early on that balanced urban *and* rural development was vital to the broader development of the colony. This helped prevent land alienation policies similar to those faced by Southern Rhodesian peasants. This was a crucial condition for the eventual convergence of living standards in rural and urban areas in the Congo, which in turn promoted labor stabilization in *both* rural and urban zones. Improvements in rural living conditions diminished earlier incentives for peasants to flee to urban areas in search of better economic opportunities; meanwhile, improvements in urban wages not only enabled family settlement, but likely also reduced the necessity of maintaining close rural-urban kinship ties for support in times of economic distress. The greater reluctance of the Belgian colonial state to divest rural Africans of access to land, compared with Southern Rhodesia, was undoubtedly tied to the fact that there were far fewer European settlers in the Congo. As the next section illustrates, the government of Southern Rhodesia had to reckon with the interests of a vocal white settler community in the cities. This undermined policies directed toward stabilizing the African wage labor force in the settler colony, whereas in the Congo, this process proceeded more smoothly.

6 Labor stabilization policies in urban context

In the early 20th century, colonial officials – particularly in British settler colonies – were preoccupied with concerns that industrial development would lead to "detribalization" if African laborers began settling permanently in urban areas, which were generally reserved for Europeans. In their view, this would undermine colonial efforts to establish "institutional segregation," along with "territorial segregation," which was widely demanded by white settlers. Consequently, temporary urban migration of African male laborers was generally favored over family migration and permanent urban settlement (Mamdani 1996, 6–7). However, colonial attitudes and official policy regarding urban labor stabilization shifted markedly after the Second World War. Imperial powers had become increasingly concerned with the consequences of what they deemed the "abnormal" (i.e., largely transient) movement of black laborers into urban areas. In the post-war years, stabilization was widely promoted to instill so-called "modern" behavior among Africans, who, according to paternalistic colonial rhetoric, were too attached to "tribal" values and culture that perpetuated backwardness and unproductivity. Fear of a potential rise in social unrest and political instability among the African population further fueled stabilization efforts. Colonial administrations broadly agreed that providing urban wages sufficient to support a family, along with adequate housing and social services, was key to stabilizing the urban workforce (Cooper 1996, 365–7).

Of course, colonial officials' juxtaposition of African workers as being either "tribal" or "urbanites" was far too simplistic and disregarded the capacity of migrants to flexibly adjust to multiple social realities and contexts, as late-colonial anthropologist J. Clyde Mitchell observed in his work on Tanganyika and the Rhodesias (Mitchell 1951, 1958). Moreover, while, in theory, colonial policies pursued stabilization of the urban African workforce, in practice, these aims were complicated "by diverse social linkages and conflicting interests; they remained contradictory and unrealizable projects" (Cooper 1996, 381). With respect to our two cases, the contradictory nature of colonial stabilization projects was most prominent in Southern Rhodesia, where white settler interests were often at odds with the material interests of both rural and urban black Africans. However, in both colonial contexts, segregationist ideologies defined urban space and restricted African movement.

In the Congo, increasing rural-urban migration prompted state-led designation of particular African quarters. These *Centres Extra-Coutumiers* (CECs – extra-customary centers), established in 1931, were located mainly around white urban centers and were distinguished from the customary centers – those areas where Africans lived as peasants.[20] The CECs were carefully separated from European city centers by a *cordon sanitaire* of airports, military bases, and other non-residential areas for purported "hygienic and safety reasons" that were grounded in racist ideology. Africans were forbidden to live in the centers but permitted to work there, with a day pass, until dusk (Van Bilzen 1993, 25–6). With the influx of migrants into towns after the Great Depression, concerns grew about the social and moral pitfalls associated with predominately male urban populations, including prostitution in the CECs.[21] The colonial government consequently disseminated policy suggestions to urban employers to address emerging socio-economic problems in Congolese cities. First, the government appealed to urban employers to provide affordable housing for their workers, suitable for accommodating wives and children. Although compliance remained mixed, housing improved in the 1940s, sometimes subsidized by employers, particularly in Elisabethville and Stanleyville. Colonial authorities remained preoccupied with providing adequate housing and social provisions, even developing an early pension system.[22] By the early 1950s, a special committee recommended that urban employers be obliged to maintain a share of 60% married employees among their total staff. In Elisabethville and Stanleyville, this prescribed ideal was (approximately) achieved by 1951, with percentages of married male workers reaching 63% and 55%, respectively.[23]

Ultimately, the government intervened more directly. The development of public provisions constituted part of the ambitious Ten Year's Plan designed after the Second World War to facilitate Congolese economic development and reduce the colony's dependence on exports and vulnerability to world market fluctuations (Dienst voor de Voorlichting 1960, 69). Considerable funds were allotted to economic development from 1950 to 1959, initially budgeted at $500 million but ultimately doubling to nearly $1 billion over the decade. Although the majority of this budget was spent on improving infrastructure, including roads and electricity, more than 25% was intended for social provisions (Huge 1955, 66). Along with investments in agricultural innovations to aid rural peasants, funds were also earmarked for improvements in public healthcare, education, and housing for urban African laborers and their families. To this end, *Offices des Cités Africaines* (offices for African quarters) were established in the colony's major cities. The plan was to construct 40,000 houses by 1959. Although by the mid-1950s a considerable shortage of adequate housing reportedly remained,[24] over 8,000 new urban houses had been built using government funds (Huge 1955, 69).

As in the Belgian Congo, Rhodesian cities were highly segregated. The *Land Apportionment Act* of 1930 had designated cities as "European areas," and later acts would stipulate "where Africans shall live in urban areas and how control shall be exercised over them there" (Mitchell 1954, 5). Among white settlers, segregationist ideology and anxiety about blacks and whites living closely together fostered a preference for temporary African urban tenure, with wives and children left on the reserves or in their colony of origin (Gray 1960, 256). However, as the urban African labor force continued to grow, Southern Rhodesian officials became concerned, like their Belgian counterparts, about the "overwhelming preponderance of men [dominated by] the fluid mass of the irresponsible 18–35 age group," supposedly undermining industrial productivity and leading to widespread prostitution (Howman Committee 1945, 11–3). By the early 1950s, the government began a series of interventions intended to increase urban labor stabilization and simultaneously cope with ever-worsening overcrowding on rural reserves.[25]

Whereas the Belgians sought to reduce transitory rural-urban flows by simultaneously improving rural living conditions and providing the means for urban workers to settle their families in town, Southern Rhodesia pursued a radical – and far less effective – solution under the *Native Land Husbandry Act* of 1951, which ultimately produced greater insecurity in both rural and urban areas. The colony's black African subjects were to be divided into either rural peasants, situated on tenured land, or industrial laborers, settled with their families in urban zones.[26] The urban African industrial worker, it was envisioned, would have "his tentacles pulled out of the soil" and lose access to reserve lands (quote from Phimister 1993, 231). Meanwhile, married women were prohibited from owning land in rural areas, even if their husbands had migrated for a shorter or longer period to work, thus increasing their economic precarity (Boserup 1970, 60). By the end of the 1950s, the *Land Husbandry Act* had reportedly been applied to roughly 42% of the African reserves, creating an estimated 102,000 landless families (Phimister 1993, 236). This did little to correct rural or urban gender imbalances, with on average only 28 men per 100 women in the age category 20–35 reported in Southern Rhodesian villages in 1956 (Mitchell 1961, 80). Meanwhile, a recession in the late 1950s reduced urban employment opportunities, generating crises for urban labor migrants.[27] The Act, a disruptive failure, was abandoned by the early 1960s.

The Southern Rhodesian government implemented additional interventions to achieve urban labor stabilization. The *Foreign Migratory Labour Act* of 1958 sought to reorient the colony's cross-border migration system by banning the employment of "foreign Africans" in urban zones, with the exception of mining areas. This legislation was, first, intended to minimize competition between foreign-born and indigenous African workers in Southern Rhodesian cities; second, it sought to redirect cheap foreign labor from Nyasaland and, increasingly, Mozambique to European plantations and mines (Clarke 1978, 51). Within a decade, the share of black urban laborers of Southern Rhodesian origin increased rapidly: from 52% in 1958 to 67% in 1963, reaching 82% by 1969 (Urban African Affairs Commission 1958, Table VII, 16; Central Statistical Office 1964, 27; Harris 1974, 13).

However, even as native-born Southern Rhodesians formed an increasing share of the black urban labor force, white settler interests continued to hinder the permanent settlement of black families in cities for decades. Well into the 1970s, insufficient wages would remain the single greatest barrier to the development of a substantial permanent urban African labor force in Southern Rhodesia (Harris 1974; Gargett 1977). Low wages, according to Bettison, were in line with a Southern Rhodesian "subsistence wage" tradition for black labor – that is, wages primarily determined not by market mechanisms but essentially fixed at a level sufficient to provide subsistence for a *single worker*.[28] White workers, in contrast, earned considerably higher wages. The racial wage gap grew from the 1940s onward and persisted, with white workers of European origin earning nearly 11 times more than black workers in 1972, even *after* the relative gap had showed modest improvement from 5% in 1938 to 14% in 1966 (see Figure 12.5) (Harris 1974, 11). While white laborers comprised no more than 20% of the manufacturing labor force between 1938 and 1966, they claimed on average nearly 70% of the sectoral wage bill.

Colonial officials claimed that lower wages for black African laborers were a consequence of their lower productivity (e.g., Urban African Affairs Commission 1958, 73). In reality, the racial wage gap was effected and perpetuated by institutional factors, particularly strong bargaining power among white Southern Rhodesian workers and legislation that diminished African access to skilled and semi-skilled occupations, creating pronounced occupational segregation (Arrighi 1967, 49–50). Tellingly, a number of jobs were reportedly "reserved" at "European" wage rates – principally in state-run organizations – to "provide

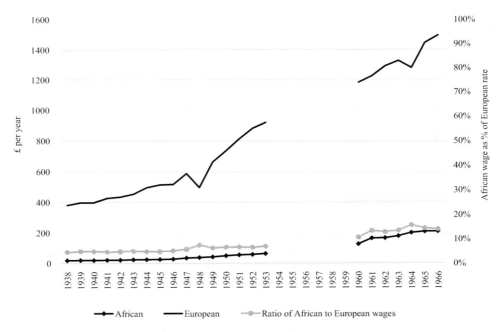

FIGURE 12.5 Average annual white European and black African nominal wages per worker, Southern Rhodesian manufacturing sector, 1938–66.
Sources: Central African Statistical Office (1955, 26, 34, Tables II and III); Central Statistical Office (n.d., 53, Table 6). Note: "European" category includes a small number of "Asian" and "Colored" laborers for the years 1960–66.

assurance that any unskilled members of [white] families will not have to compete directly with similarly unskilled blacks for employment" (Harris 1974, 15–6). Thus, the presence of a well-organized community of blue-collar settler workers in urban areas accounted for both occupational segregation and racial wage discrimination, which depressed black urban wages well into the 1970s.

Alongside inadequate wages, black laborers faced perpetual housing shortages and poor living conditions in Southern Rhodesia's manufacturing centers, with many forced to "live in hovels and places not fit for human habitation" (Ibottson 1946, 79). The *Natives (Urban Areas) Accommodation and Registration Act* (1946, 1951) sought to tackle the housing crisis by requiring employers to provide housing for laborers in approved accommodations. However, in practice, this legislation further restricted African urban tenure by linking accommodation with official employment, thus diminishing African workers' ability to remain in town in the event of temporary unemployment. Meanwhile, the broad powers afforded by the Act enabled city officials to identify women co-habiting with men without official marriage certificates, who were "deemed to be living 'illegally' in the city" and became "the main target of increasingly frequent police raids" in the 1950s (Phimister and Raftopoulos 2000, 311–2).

Moreover, new housing projects concentrated primarily on providing hostel accommodations for *single men*, particularly in Salisbury, which did little to improve the lot of urban African families (Urban African Affairs Commission 1958, 50). While the Belgian Congo had succeeded in improving living conditions for urban African households by the 1940s (and earlier in mining areas), black Southern Rhodesians faced urban housing shortages and inadequate wages into the 1970s. Economic precarity perpetuated the persistence of a circular rural-urban labor migration system and slowed the evolution toward more permanent rural-urban movements that had developed decades earlier in the Belgian Congo. Family settlement in towns would increase by the 1970s, concurrent with rising wages, but the majority of black laborers earned wages below the minimum required to support an average-sized family. Among those urban families that managed to settle in town, most consequently remained heavily dependent upon connections with rural areas for economic assistance, maintaining the rural-urban ties that had loosened decades earlier in the Belgian Congo (Gargett 1977, 20, 25, 29).

7 Conclusion

In both Southern Rhodesia and the Belgian Congo, uneven opportunity structures stimulated the development of rural-urban migrations during the first half of the colonial 20th century. However, the migration systems that arose would evolve very differently. Circular migration remained dominant in Southern Rhodesia deep into the early post-colonial era. In the Belgian Congo, rural-urban ties had instead been gradually disengaged and urban tenure increasingly secured from the 1940s onward. Our comparative analysis shows that a combination of geopolitical and institutional factors was decisive in explaining the differentiated evolution of rural-urban migration and labor stabilization patterns that developed amid early industrialization in the two colonies.

First, the relative geopolitical isolation of the Belgian Congo stands out in contrast to the much firmer integration of Southern Rhodesia in the British Southern African imperial context. The position of the Belgian Congo as a mandated free trade zone helped incentivize Belgian investment in local industries, as did a large internal market for manufactured goods, stimulating early industrialization and rural-urban migration flows in the region. Moreover, the colony had less tangible links with broader migration systems beyond its colonial borders compared with Southern Rhodesia, which had long bound its own migration system with a broader institutionalized labor migration system encompassing nearby British colonies. This initially underpinned a greater degree of transience in Southern Rhodesian urban centers – since many laborers were temporary migrants from abroad. This intertangling of cross-border migration systems would also help perpetually depress rural wages in commercial agriculture, motivating many rural young men to migrate to cities, despite high urban unemployment.

Second, there were noticeable dissimilarities in colonial policies in both regions. In Southern Rhodesia, policies were overwhelmingly influenced by the vested interests of white settlers, including farmers, miners, industrialists, and white urban laborers. These interests, which at times were contradictory, strongly influenced institutional developments. The establishment of Responsible Government in 1923 effectively allowed the semi-autonomous government to craft policies that catered to the demands of the white settler community, often to the detriment of the colony's African inhabitants. A combination of increasing urban industrial wages and perpetually depressed rural wages drew Southern Rhodesian men to cities. However, direct interventions into land and labor markets shaped economic possibilities within rural and urban zones, keeping *both* rural and urban wages low – particularly relative to high settler wages – making it difficult for urban African laborers to sustain a family in the city. This would perpetuate the circular nature of the colony's rural-urban migration system.

Initially, European interests in plantations and mines were likewise safeguarded in the Belgian Congo via forced labor and the alienation of common land in the early colonial period. However, the relatively small number of European settlers (and often temporary nature of their settlement), combined with a largely metropolitan-controlled colonial government, eventually led to the development of colonial wage labor markets that were more sensitive to supply-and-demand changes compared with Southern Rhodesia. Wage rates in industrializing urban areas were higher than in rural areas, but this differential declined as rural wages rose, in line with a broader colonial policy that favored improvement in urban *as well as* rural living conditions. Where the Belgian Congo could respond with relative dexterity to urban African development issues, the Southern Rhodesian government was beholden first and foremost to settler interests, which were often at odds with those of African laborers.

These differing contexts affected the consumption capabilities of Congolese and Rhodesian laborers, which, in turn, influenced migration choices. In the Congo, substantial upticks in nominal *and* real wages allowed for more family migration to urban areas from the 1940s onward as men were increasingly able to provide for their wives and children. This fundamentally changed the existing rural-urban migration system into a system increasingly characterized by one-way migrations. Conversely, in Southern Rhodesia, the "subsistence wage" tradition for African labor, which helped subsidize high white settler wages, forced black urban migrants to retain close ties to the poor but vital reserves, where their families often remained. Moreover, in the Congo, urban settlement was further stimulated by efforts to improve housing facilities and social provisions for urban families. Meanwhile, in Southern Rhodesia, urban accommodations remained woefully insufficient, particularly for families. Taken together, these factors informed and (re)directed migrant flows, producing a marked divergence in the character of rural–urban migration and urbanization in the Belgian Congo and Southern Rhodesia by the close of the colonial period.

Acknowledgment

The authors would like to thank Ewout Frankema, Michiel de Haas, and the participants of the African Economic History Network conference in Barcelona (2019) for their useful comments on earlier drafts of this chapter. This research was carried out as part of the ERC-funded project *Race to the Bottom?* (acronym TextileLab, ERC-CoG grant number 771288).

Notes

1 For average sub-Saharan Africa rates in 1960, see the World Bank website: https://data.world-bank.org/indicator/SP.URB.TOTL.IN.ZS.
2 For rural–urban migration in East and West Africa, see Meier zu Selhausen, Chapter 13, this volume.
3 In this chapter, we use "labor stabilization" to denote the process of increasing permanence of the labor force in urban settlements. We are aware that this term was used by colonial authorities in connection with urbanization ambitions and concerns about male predominance in colonial cities. We employ the term as a synonym for permanent urban settlement but do not intend to reproduce the moral or socioeconomic anxieties of colonial authorities.
4 Current-day Harare. Given the periodization of our analysis, colonial city names are used here.
5 Current-day Kinshasa.
6 Current-day Lubumbashi.
7 Current-day Kisangani.
8 Rural-mining area migration often overlapped with rural-urban migration as mining towns developed into major urban centers, as in the Belgian Congo.
9 On "frontier" land in sub-Saharan Africa, see Kopytoff (1987), and for a critique Austin, Chapter 2, this volume.
10 For a comparison of labor recruitment, migration, and stabilization in Katanga relative to the mining areas of Northern Rhodesia and South Africa, see Juif, Chapter 10 in this volume.
11 Current-day Likasi.
12 The authors do not provide the nominal data on which they base their indexes. However, their growth rates correspond with archival data and colonial reports for several points in time (1933, 1938, and 1950), so we have applied these growth rates to the actual average urban and rural wages we found and extrapolated them to years for which we lack information.
13 On traditional subsistence production by women, see Boserup (1970, 16–22).
14 In the early 1960s, "general unemployment on a large scale" was reported in urban areas, while demand for labor exceeded supply in rural areas (Secretary for Internal Affairs and Chief Native Commissioner 1963, 32).
15 Congolese industrial production multiplied over 12.5 times between 1938 and 1957, whereas South African and Southern Rhodesian output expanded 3.8 times and 7.5 times, respectively. A growth index (1949=100) reveals that Congo's industrial expansion exceeded all other African colonies (Lacroix 1967, 22–3).
16 Initially, Africans could theoretically purchase land beyond the reserves, but few had the means to do so. The segregation-oriented *Land Apportionment Act* of 1930 would later specify particular areas where black Africans were allowed to purchase land, separate from European zones (Zinyama and Whitlow 1986, 368–9).
17 While white farmers received on average 8 shillings per bag of maize between 1934 and 1939, African farmers received between 2 shillings and 6 pence and 6 shillings and 6 pence (Phimister 1988, 185–9).
18 Contracted migrant laborers typically remained in Southern Rhodesia for the duration of their contract (between 12 and 18 months) before returning to their home colony, where they received final settlement of their wages under a deferred payment system (Clarke 1974, 39–40).

19 Brussels, *Archives Africaines* (AA), 3ème Directorat Général (3ème DG), dossier 379, Note de M. le Gouverneur Général sur le problème de la M.O.I. au Congo Belge, 1952.
20 The CECs obtained a limited degree of administrative autonomy, which according to Northrup (1988, 210), points to the acceptance of permanent urban migration by the colonial authorities early on.
21 AA, Affaires Indigènes (AI), dossier 1994, Protection de la femme noire.
22 For housing, see AA, 3ème DG, dossier 379, Rapport de la sous-commission des problèmes sociaux, 1952. Pensions were associated with labor cards introduced in the 1940s (Capelle 1947, 14).
23 AA, 3ème DG, dossier 1123, Commission de la main-d'oeuvre et du travail indigènes.
24 AA, AI, dossier 1396, Amélioration des conditions de vie matérielle des indigènes.
25 Already by 1943, it was reported that 62 of the 98 reserves were overpopulated, with 19 of those overpopulated by at least 100% (Phimister 1988, 237–8).
26 For the official philosophy underlying this plan, see Urban African Affairs Commission (1958, 21).
27 Some historians suggest that the recession of 1957/58 was a key determinant in the demise of the *Land Husbandry Act* as demand for labor dropped among urban employers, reducing interest in stabilizing the industrial labor force (Palmer 1977, 243–4).
28 The concept of the "subsistence wage" was initially identified by Bettison (1960) and subsequently expanded upon by Arrighi (1970).

References

Arrighi, Giovanni. 1967. *The Political Economy of Rhodesia*. The Hague: Mouton.
Arrighi, Giovanni. 1970. "Labour Supplies in Historical Perspective: A Study of the Proletarianization of the African Peasantry in Rhodesia." *Journal of Development Studies* 6(3): 197–234.
Austin, Gareth, Ewout Frankema, and Morten Jerven. 2017. "Patterns of Manufacturing Growth in Sub-Saharan Africa. From Colonization to the Present." In *The Spread of Modern Industry to the Periphery since 1871*, edited by Kevin O'Rourke and Jeffrey Williamson, 345–73. Oxford: Oxford University Press.
Bettison, David 1958. "The Socio-economic Circumstances of a Sample of Africans in Salisbury, July, 1957." In *Report of the Urban African Affairs Commission, 1958*, edited by Robert Percival Plewman, William Margolis, Leslie Benjamin Fereday, James Scott Brown, and Herbert Wiltshire Chitepo, 180–94. Salisbury: Government Printer.
Bettison, David. 1960. "Factors in the Determination of Wage Rates in Central Africa." *The Rhodes-Livingstone Journal* 28: 22-46.
Boserup, Ester. 1970. *Women's Role in Economic Development*. London: Allen & Unwin.
Brixhe, A. 1953. *De Katoen in Belgisch-Congo*. Brussels: Directie van Landbouw.
Capelle, Emmanuel. 1947. *La Cité Indigène de Léopoldville*. Elisabethville: C.E.P.S.I.
Central African Statistical Office. 1955. *Thirteenth Report on the Census of Industrial Production, 1938–1953*. Salisbury: Central African Statistical Office.
Central Statistical Office. 1964. *Final Report of the April/May 1962 Census of Africans in Southern Rhodesia*. Salisbury: Central Statistical Office.
Central Statistical Office. n.d. *The Census of Production in 1966. Mining, Manufacturing, Construction, Electricity and Water Supply*. Salisbury: Central Statistical Office.
Cooper, Frederick. 1996. *Decolonization and African Society: The Labor Question in French and British Africa*. Cambridge: Cambridge University Press.
Coquery-Vidrovitch, Catherine. 2005. *The History of African Cities South of the Sahara. From the Origins to Colonization*. Princeton, NJ: Markus Wiener Publishers.
Clarence-Smith, William-Gervase. 1989. "The Effects of the Depression on Industrialization in Equatorial and Central Africa." In *The Economies of Africa and Asia in the Interwar Depression*, edited by Ian Brown, 170–202. London/New York: Routledge.
Clarke, Duncan. 1974. *Contract Workers and Underdevelopment in Rhodesia*. Gwelo: Mambo Press.
Clarke, Duncan. 1978. "International Labour Supply Trends and Economic Structure in Southern Rhodesia/Zimbabwe in the 1970s." Working Paper World Employment Programme WEP2–26/WP20.

Dienst voor de Voorlichting. 1960. *Kent u Belgisch-Congo?* Brussels: Dienst voor de Voorlichting en de Publieke Relaties van Belgisch-Congo en Ruanda-Urundi.

Dupriez, Leon, Nicolas Bardós Feltoronyi, Georges Szapary, and Jean-Philippe Peemans. 1970. *Diffusion du Progrès et Convergence des Prix. Volume II. Congo-Belgique 1900–1960.* Louvain/Brussels: Editions Nauwelaers.

Elkan, Walter, and Roger Van Zwanenberg. 1975. "How People Came to Live in Towns." In *Colonialism in Africa 1870–1960. Volume 4. The Economics of Colonialism*, edited by Peter Duignan and L.H. Gann, 655–72. London/Cambridge: Cambridge University Press.

Exenberger, Andreas, and Simon Hartmann. 2013. "Extractive Institutions in the Congo: Checks and Balances in the Longue Durée." In *Colonial Exploitation and Economic Development: The Belgian Congo and the Netherlands Indies Compared*, edited by Ewout Frankema and Frans Buelens, 19–40. London/New York: Routledge.

Floyd, Barry. 1962. "Land Apportionment in Southern Rhodesia." *Geographical Review* 52(4): 566–82.

Frankema, Ewout, and Morten Jerven. 2014. "Writing History Backwards and Sideways: Towards a Consensus on African Population, 1850-Present." *Economic History Review* 67(S1): 907–31.

Freund, Bill. 2007. *The African City. A History.* Cambridge: Cambridge University Press.

Gargett, Eric. 1977. *The Administration of Transition. African Urban Settlement in Rhodesia.* Gwelo: Mambo Press.

Gray, Richard. 1960. *The Two Nations. Aspects of the Development of Race Relations in the Rhodesias and Nyasaland.* London: Oxford University Press.

Harms, Robert. 1974. *Land Tenure and Agricultural Development in Zaire, 1895–1961.* Unpublished Thesis, University of Wisconsin.

Harris, Peter. 1974. *Black Industrial Workers in Rhodesia. The General Problems of Low Pay.* Gwelo: Mambo Press.

Harris, Peter. 1975. "Industrial Workers in Rhodesia, 1946–1972: Working-class Élites or Lumpenproletariat?" *Journal of Southern African Studies* 1(2): 139–61.

Juif, Dácil, and Ewout Frankema. 2018. "From Coercion to Compensation: Institutional Responses to Labour Scarcity in the Central African Copperbelt." *Journal of Institutional Economics* 14(2): 313–43.

Heymans, G.R. 1952. *Urbanisme in Belgisch Kongo.* Brussels: De Visscher.

Hochschild, Adam. 1998. *King Leopold's Ghost: A Story of Greed, Terror and Heroism in Colonial Africa.* London: Macmillan.

Howman Committee. 1945. "Report on Urban Conditions in Southern Rhodesia." *African Studies* 4(1): 9–22.

Huge, J. 1955. "Economic Planning and Development in the Belgian Congo." *The Annals of the American Academy of Political and Social Science* 298: 62–70.

Ibottson, Percy. 1946. "Urbanization in Southern Rhodesia." *Africa* 16(1): 73–82.

Jewsiewicki, Bogumil. 1983. "Rural Society and the Belgian Colonial Economy." In *History of Central Africa*, edited by David Birminghan and Phyllis M. Martin, 95–125. London/New York: Longman.

Kamer der Volksvertegenwoordigers. 1923–1959. *Verslag over het Beheer van Belgisch-Congo gedurende het Dienstjaar 1921* (various issues, 1921–1958). Brussels: Kamer der Volksvertegenwoordigers.

Kopytoff, Igor (ed.). 1987. *The African Frontier: The Reproduction of Traditional African Societies.* Bloomington: Indiana University Press.

Lacroix, Jean Louis. 1967. *Industrialisation au Congo. La Transformation des Structures Économiques.* Paris/The Hague: Mouton.

Mabogunje, Akin. 1970. "Systems Approach to a Theory of Rural-Urban Migration." *Geographical Analysis* 2(1): 1–18.

Mamdani, Mahmood. 1996. *Citizen and Subject. Contemporary Africa and the Legacy of Late Colonialism.* Princeton, NJ: Princeton University Press.

Marzorati, A.F.G. 1954. "The Political Organisation and the Evolution of African Society in the Belgian Congo." *African Affairs* 53(211): 104–12.

McEwan, Peter. 1963. "The European Population of Southern Rhodesia." *Civilisations* 13(4): 429–44.

Mitchell, Clyde. 1951. "A Note on the Urbanization of Africans on the Copper Belt." *Rhodes-Livingstone Institute Journal* 12: 20–27.

Mitchell, Clyde. 1954. "Urbanization, Detribalization and Stabilization in Southern Africa: A Problem of Definition and Measurement". Working Paper Conference on the Social Impact of Industrialization and Urban Conditions in Africa, Abidjan, 1954. https://unesdoc.unesco.org/ark:/48223/pf0000156173.

Mitchell, Clyde. 1958. *Gazetteer of Tribes in the Federation of Rhodesia and Nyasaland.* Salisbury: University College of Rhodesia and Nyasaland, Department of African Studies.

Mitchell, Clyde. 1961. *An Outline of the Sociological Background to African Labour.* Salisbury: Ensign Publishers.

Mosley, Paul. 1983. *The Settler Economies.* Cambridge: Cambridge University Press.

Northrup, David. 1988. *Beyond the Bend in the River. African Labor in Eastern Zaire, 1865–1940.* Athens: Ohio University.

Palmer, Robin. 1977. *Land and Racial Domination in Rhodesia.* Berkeley/Los Angeles: University of California Press.

Phimister, Ian. 1988. *An Economic and Social History of Zimbabwe, 1890–1948: Capital Accumulation and Class Struggle.* New York: Longman.

Phimister, Ian. 1993. "Rethinking the Reserves: Southern Rhodesia's Land Husbandry Act Reviewed." *Journal of Southern African Studies* 19(2): 225–39.

Phimister, Ian. 2007. "Secondary Industrialisation in Southern Africa: The 1948 Customs Agreement between Southern Rhodesia and South Africa." *Journal of Southern African Studies* 17(3): 430–42.

Phimister, Ian, and Rory Pilossof. 2017. "Wage Labor in Historical Perspective: A Study of the De-Proletarianization of the African Working Class in Zimbabwe, 1960–2010." *Labor History* 58(2): 215–27.

Phimister, Ian, and Brian Raftopoulos. 2000. "'*Kana Sora Ratswa Ngaritswe*': African Nationalists and Black Workers – The 1948 General Strike in colonial Zimbabwe." *Journal of Historical Sociology* 13(3): 289–324.

Pilossof, Rory. 2014. "Labor Relations in Zimbabwe from 1900 to 2000: Sources, Interpretations, and Understandings." *History in Africa* 41: 337–62.

Pons, Valdo. 1969. *Stanleyville: An African Urban Community under Belgian Administration.* London: International African Institute.

Scott, Peter. 1954. "Migrant Labour in Southern Rhodesia." *Geographical Review* 44(1): 29–48.

Secretary for Internal Affairs and Chief Native Commissioner. 1963. *Report of the Secretary for Internal Affairs and Chief Native Commissioner for the year 1962.* Salisbury: Government Printer.

Secretary for Labour, Social Welfare and Housing. 1961. *Report of the Secretary for Labour, Social Welfare and Housing for the year ended 31st December, 1960.* Salisbury: Government Printer.

Smout, M.A.H. 1975. "Urbanisation of the Rhodesian Population." *Zambezia* 4(2): 79–91.

Taylor, Marjory. 1959. "The Belgian Congo Today: Background to the Leopoldville Riots." *World Today* 15(9): 351–64.

Urban African Affairs Commission. 1958. *Report of the Urban African Affairs Commission, 1958.* Salisbury: Government Printer.

Van Bilzen, Jef. 1993. *Kongo 1945–1965. Het Einde van een Kolonie.* Leuven: Davidsfonds.

Vandewalle, Gaston. 1966. *De Conjuncturele Evolutie in Kongo en Ruanda-Urundi van 1920 tot 1939 en van 1949 tot 1958.* Gent: Hogere School voor Handels- en Economische Wetenschappen.

Vanthemsche, Guy. 2012. *Belgium and the Congo, 1885–1980.* Cambridge: Cambridge University Press.

Yoshikuni, Tsuneo. 1991. "African Harare, 1890–1925: Labor Migrancy and an Emerging Urban Community." *African Study Monographs* 12(3): 133–48.

World Bank, World Development Indicators. https://data.worldbank.org/indicator/SP.URB.TOTL.IN.ZS.

Zinyama, Lovemore, and Richard Whitlow. 1986. "Changing Patterns of Population Distribution in Zimbabwe." *GeoJournal* 13(4): 365–84.

13

URBAN MIGRATION IN EAST AND WEST AFRICA SINCE 1950

Contrasts and Transformations

Felix Meier zu Selhausen

1 Urban growth in sub-Saharan Africa

Sub-Saharan Africa[1] is the least urbanized region in the world. Yet, home to the world's youngest and fastest-growing population, Africa has recorded faster urban growth than any other world region since 1960. Its urban population has been growing at an average annual rate of 4%–5% since 1960, at much lower income levels than Asia or Latin America. The United Nations forecasted that Africa's urban population is likely to nearly triple between 2018 and 2050. Cities are viewed as important engines of African economic growth, generating a much larger share of countries' GDP than their share of the population (McKinsey 2011; UN-Habitat 2016a). Cities are thus attractive to those in search for economic opportunity. Cities not only offer higher wages than rural areas, but urban housing, schools, and health facilities also tend to be superior. Such perspectives of urban privilege, upward social mobility, and opportunity remain dominant motivations for rural–urban migration in Africa.

Such enthusiasm should not mask the fact that, whereas in other parts of the world urban agglomeration generally has been associated with structural economic change and a move into more productive (formal) jobs, in Africa urban centers are often built around consuming the rents extracted from natural resources. Cities, therefore, have become dominated by locally consumed low-value (informal) services and goods, rather than tradable goods or services (Gollin, Jedwab, and Vollrath 2016). Over the second half of the 20th century Africa's rapid urbanization process (see Maps 13.1 and 13.2), amidst a comparatively poor economic performance, has therefore resulted in rising urban poverty with the majority of urban residents living in slums (Marx, Stoker, and Suri 2013).

However, for most of African history, until the mid-20th century, rural-to-rural migration has been of greater prevalence than rural-to-urban flows.[2] Yet, throughout Africa, the onset of colonial rule accelerated urban growth and structural change, fueled by rural migrant flows (Coquery-Vidrovitch 2005, 4).[3] Maps 13.1 and 13.2 as well as Figure 13.1 illustrate those dynamics over the second half of the 20th century. Maps 13.1 and 13.2 show each African city with a population exceeding 10,000 in 1950 and 2015, respectively.

DOI: 10.4324/9781003225027-18

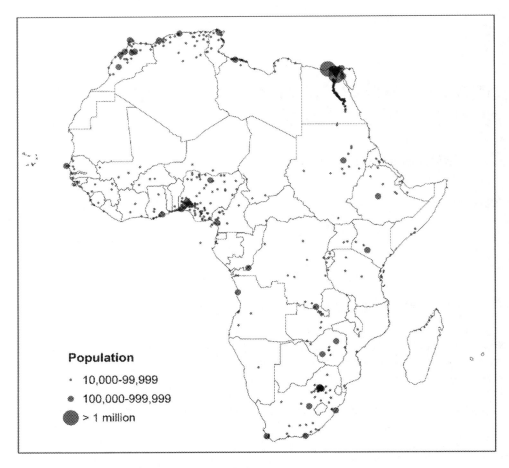

MAP 13.1 African cities by size range, 1950.
Source: Derived from OECD/SWAC (2020), drawn by Stefan de Jong. Madagascar is excluded.

Figure 13.1 counts the number of cities and their corresponding share of the total population in 1950–2015. It reveals that by 1950 only 11% resided in 302 urban agglomerations. However, in 1990, the number of urban centers in sub-Saharan Africa had risen more than six-fold to 1,955, housing almost a third of Africa's population. By 2015, 39% (i.e., ~400 million) of Africans resided in urban centers spread across 5,779 urban agglomerations. Thus, between 1950 and 2015, the percentage of Africa's urban population nearly quadrupled, while the number of cities increased 19 times, reflecting both exceptional migration inflows and the natural growth of former villages transforming into towns. This makes Africa the region with the lowest levels of urbanization worldwide, but with the highest rates of urban growth. At those rates, by 2035, every second African will live in urban centers (United Nations 2018), which is bound to significantly impact the economic landscapes of urban hinterlands as urban demand for building material, food, and energy will soar (Parnell and Pieterse 2014, 1).

One key feature of Africa's urban revolution is the rapid rise in the number of large cities with populations ≥300,000 (Table 13.1). While in 1950, on average 19% of Africa's

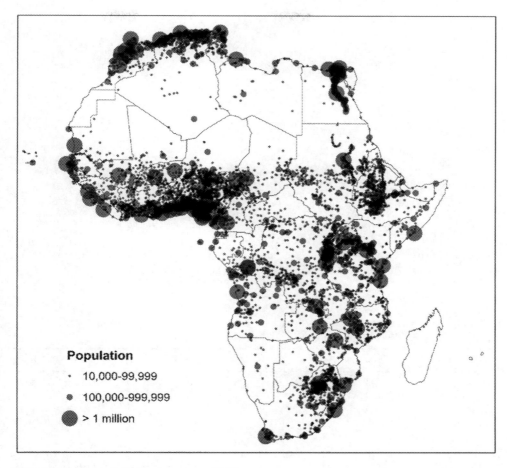

MAP 13.2 African cities by size range, 2015.
Source: Derived from OECD/SWAC (2020), drawn by Stefan de Jong. Madagascar is excluded.

urban population lived in those cities,[4] by 2020 they housed more than half of Africa's urban dwellers. Table 13.1 shows that prior to 1960 there were no African settlements with populations larger than 1 million. In 1950 there were seven African cities with more than 300,000 residents, of which four were located in South Africa. By 2020, this number had grown to 187 cities, with Lagos, Kinshasa, and Luanda leading in population size. However, Africa did not only witness the emergence of mega-cities (≥1 million) from zero in 1950 to 55 in 2020, but it also saw substantial expansion of cities with populations below 1 million, which make up almost 70% of the population living in cities ≥300,000. This suggests that over time urbanization and urban migration has also become more diversified.

Drawing on demographic data, this chapter examines the *shifting patterns* and *key drivers* of rural-urban migration in East and West Africa since 1950 – from mostly temporary and male to increasingly permanent and gender-equal in nature. East and West Africa make an intriguing comparative regional case study. Historically, more densely populated West Africa also had much deeper urban roots and hence urban migration than East Africa. West Africa's early urban advantage then persisted into the present day, despite the colonial

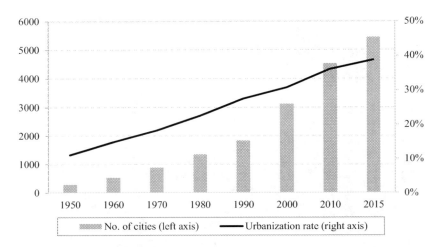

FIGURE 13.1 Urban agglomerations (≥10,000) and urbanization in sub-Saharan Africa, 1950–2015.
Sources: OECD/SWAC (2020) for cities; World Bank (2020) for urbanization rates.

TABLE 13.1 Number of major urban settlements (>300,000) by size in sub-Saharan Africa, 1950–2020

City sizes	1950	1960	1970	1980	1990	2000	2010	2020
300,000–500,000	4	5	12	25	30	34	47	71
500,000–1,000,000	3	6	10	14	25	28	46	61
1,000,000–5,000,000	–	1	4	10	18	30	34	51
5,000,000–10,000,000	–	–	–	–	–	–	2	2
>10,000,000	–	–	–	–	–	–	1	2
Total	**7**	**12**	**26**	**49**	**73**	**92**	**130**	**187**
% of total urban population	19	21	32	41	46	48	49	52

Source: United Nations (2018).

era decisively accelerating rural-urban migration in both regions. Moreover, West African cities retained a powerful female presence in terms of residence and market trading during the colonial era, contrary to the male-dominated migrant cities of East Africa. Contrary to Southern Africa, where urban migration was closely linked to manufacturing industries and mineral discoveries, in East and West Africa those factors played a less obvious role in rural-urban migration processes.

The chapter is organized as follows. Section 2 traces shifting patterns and drivers of urban growth in East and West Africa. Section 3 summarizes some of the opportunity gaps that motivate rural-urban mobility. Section 4 reviews the empirical literature and distills some key insights on shifting individual profiles of urban migrants with regard to gender, education, and age profiles. Section 5 unpacks the paradox that rapid African city growth appears barely affected by urban poverty, slum formation, and overall economic performance. Section 6 concludes.

2 Urban growth in East and West Africa

Although rapid urban growth in Africa is a 20th-century phenomenon and much of present-day urban development originated in the colonial era, urbanism has been an important social feature of Africa's pre-colonial history (Coquery-Vidrovitch 1991; Anderson and Rathbone 2000, 1). Urban centers, and associated urban migration, have deeper roots in historically more densely populated West Africa than in East Africa.[5] Early cities in the West African savanna emerged from trans-Saharan trade and as places of Islamic scholarship as early as 300–1600.[6] In the West African forest belt the towns of Ife, Benin City, and Old Oyo represented commercial and political centers. The Sahelian towns of Katsina, Zaria, and Kano became important commercial hubs of Islamic influence from the 10th century onward (Hance 1970, 212). In contrast to West Africa's urban focus in non-coastal areas, in East Africa most towns located along the Arab-Swahili coast as centers of Indian Ocean trade, including the port cities of Mombasa, Bagamoyo, Zanzibar, Lindi, and Mogadishu. Even earlier exceptions include Meroë, along the Nile in present-day Sudan, and Aksum, situated on present-day Ethiopia's highland plateau. However, by the 19th century, there were no urban civilizations in Eastern Africa to match West Africa's scale (Anderson and Rathbone 2000, 5). In 1850, 10 of the 11 African cities ≥40,000 in 1850 were West African (Chandler 1987).

Figures 13.1 and 13.3 reveal that those regional differences in pre-colonial urbanization persisted into the late colonial era and up to the present day. In 1950, West Africa harbored 9.3% of its population in 147 cities, making up half of total African cities with a population exceeding 10,000 of which two-thirds concentrated in Nigeria alone, home to half of West Africa's population. Yet, Figure 13.2 shows parallel urbanization trends between the West African average and Nigeria, suggesting that Nigeria was not driving the region's urban development alone. In contrast, East Africa was half as urbanized with 31 cities home to 4.9% of its population.[7] No large differences in urbanization levels are observed between

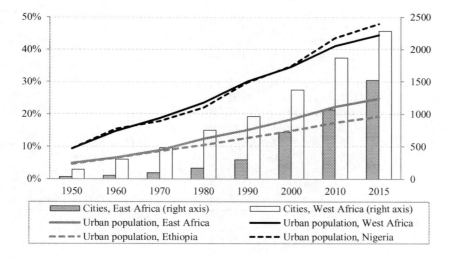

FIGURE 13.2 Urbanization rates and number of urban centers in East and West Africa, 1950–2015.
Sources: OECD/SWAC (2020); United Nations (2018, 2019).

East Africa and Ethiopia, home to about a third of East Africans and with historically deeper urban roots. Despite rapid urbanization in both regions, by 2015 West Africa continued to be almost twice as urbanized (44%) as East Africa. The convergence in the number of cities (≥10,000), despite persistent urbanization differences, suggests that West African cities on average tend to be larger.

How then did the colonial era affect African urbanization patterns? Did pre-colonial cities attract fewer migrants and thus grow slower after 1950 than cities founded during the colonial era due to specific locational advantages, such as external trade? To explore urban continuity, Table 13.2 ranks the 20 major urban agglomerations in East and West Africa since the late colonial era. In both 1950 and 2015, West African cities made up about three in four of the largest cities. The Nigerian city bias is clearly visible; in particular, in 1950 eight of top 20 cities are Nigerian. Cities can be either broadly classified into cities with pre-colonial roots or created during colonialism (both indicated for 1950 in Table 13.2). Colonizers often selected pre-existing urban structures often located in accessible trading areas, such as ports, as their African capitals but also founded entirely new ones (Thomas 1965; Coquery-Vidrovitch 1991).

In 1950, about half of the largest urban agglomerations were pre-colonial interior commercial hubs and political centers, often located at junctions of ancient trade routes (Table 13.2). For example, Kano, a Sahelian capital city which became a major cloth manufacturing

TABLE 13.2 The largest 20 urban agglomerations by population (million) in East and West Africa

Rank	1950		1970		1990		2015	
1	Ibadan[a]	0.44	Lagos	1.49	Lagos	4.87	Lagos[b]	11.85
2	Addis Ababa[a]	0.36	Addis Ababa	0.80	Khartoum	2.17	Nairobi[b]	5.88
3	Lagos[b]	0.29	Ibadan	0.77	Abidjan	2.11	Dar es Salaam[b]	5.33
4	Khartoum	0.23	Khartoum	0.66	Addis Ababa	1.80	Khartoum[b]	5.26
5	Dakar[b]	0.23	Accra	0.62	Ibadan	1.62	Abidjan[b]	4.72
6	Accra[b]	0.16	Abidjan	0.58	Dakar	1.59	Accra[b]	4.45
7	Nairobi[b]	0.14	Dakar	0.56	Nairobi	1.38	Kano[a]	3.89
8	Ogbomosho	0.13	Nairobi	0.53	Kano	1.31	Kampala[b]	3.79
9	Kano[a]	0.12	Kano	0.39	Dar es Salaam	1.23	Addis Ababa[a]	3.71
10	Oshogbo[a]	0.12	Conakry	0.36	Accra	1.19	Ibadan[a]	3.09
11	Ife[a]	0.11	Dar es Salaam	0.35	Conakry	0.90	Dakar[b]	3.07
12	Asmara[b]	0.10	Kumasi	0.35	Kampala	0.86	Kumasi[a]	2.80
13	Iwo[a]	0.10	Kampala	0.34	Kaduna	0.79	Bamako[b]	2.78
14	Mombasa[a]	0.09	Mombasa	0.25	Bamako	0.75	Ouagadougou[b]	2.30
15	Kumasi[a]	0.09	Onitsha	0.25	Benin City	0.73	Oyo[a]	2.27
16	Bamako[a b]	0.08	Ilorin	0.25	Kumasi	0.68	Kigali[b]	2.20
17	Abeokuta[a]	0.08	Port Harcourt	0.24	Mogadishu	0.67	Conakry[b]	2.19
18	Dar es Salaam[b]	0.08	Mogadishu	0.23	Onitsha	0.62	Hawassa	2.18
19	Freetown[b]	0.07	Asmara	0.22	Port Harcourt	0.58	Abuja	2.00
20	Onitsha[a]	0.07	Kaduna	0.21	Ouagadougou	0.58	Port Harcourt	1.85

Source: OECD/SWAC (2020).
Notes:
a   Pre-colonial commercial or major political center.
b   Colonial capital cities in 1950.
  Kenyan (Embu, Kisii, Kisumu), Nigerian (Onitsha), and Ugandan (Mbale) county or province populations have been classified by OECD/SWAC (2020) as urban agglomerations, and thus have been dropped.

center; Ibadan, grown as refugee settlement during the Yoruba wars; Kumasi, the capital of the Ashanti kingdom; Bamako, a major market town along the Niger River and center for Islamic scholarship; Mombasa, center of Indian Ocean trade; and Addis Ababa founded by Emperor Menelik in 1886. The other group of cities were colonial capitals mostly on the coast, to facilitate global market access (i.e., Lagos, Accra, Dakar, Dar es Salaam, Freetown), and in the hinterland, Nairobi, founded by the British as a colonial railway depot in 1899, and Asmara, initially a village that grew quickly after Italian occupation in 1889. By 1970, the two West African port cities of Conakry and Abidjan, initially created by French colonists, as well as British Kampala adjoining the Buganda kingdom's court, entered the top 20. All those (colonial) capitals became connected to the railway, developed into the main economic hubs of their colonies, and continued growing post-independence (Jedwab, Kerby, and Moradi 2017). Contrarily, pre-colonial towns that were "bypassed" by colonial transportation and administration investments lost their former position. For example, some important pre-colonial urban centers, such as Bagamoyo in Tanzania, Cape Coast in Ghana, Saint-Louis in Senegal, and Porto Novo in Benin experienced a reversal of fortune under colonialism, with Dar es Salaam, Accra, Dakar, and Cotonou, respectively, emerging as colonial capitals (Coquery-Vidrovitch 1991). Harboring the seats of government, the largest commercial markets, and chief manufacturing centers, capital cities attracted the bulk of rural-urban migration (Storeygard 2016). For example, Greater Accra, Abidjan, and Freetown captured 88%, 56%, and 41% of the total net migration to all urban areas, respectively (Little 1973, 8; Zachariah and Condé 1981, 96), while 82% of Kenyan rural-urban migration targeted Nairobi and Mombasa in 1969 (Rempel 1981, 46–7).

By 2015, Table 13.2 reveals that 12 colonial capitals were among the top 20 cities, suggesting that settlements selected or founded as colonial capital cities appear to have attracted relatively more migrants and consequently grown faster over colonial and post-colonial eras. Indeed, between 1950 and 2015, colonial capital cities' populations in East and West Africa (excluding non-colonized Ethiopia and Liberia) had on average grown about three times as rapidly as non-capital cities (with ≥10,000 inhabitants) in 1950. The colonial era thus to some extent redefined patterns of urban development, and hence the direction of urban migration.

What stimulated Africa's rapid expansion of urban populations? There are three sources of urban growth: (i) cities' own *natural increase*, which is the excess of births over deaths in an urban area, (ii) *rural-urban migration*, and (iii) *densification in rural areas,* resulting in the reclassification from rural to urban.

For 11 countries for which data was available in 1960–70, Figure 13.3 disaggregates their urban growth into annual natural increase and annual residual migration.[8] It shows that in the decade following independence, urban areas expanded in particular due to rural-urban migration, accounting for 55% of urban growth on average. In Côte d'Ivoire, Tanzania, Kenya, and Liberia, where urban growth was above 6%, net migration constituted on average even 63% of urban growth. Dar es Salaam alone grew annually at 6.8% over the period 1948–71 (Sabot 1979, 46), of which an impressive 78% was due to net migration. Abidjan grew at an even faster rate of 9.3% during 1965–70 fueled by a massive domestic rural and foreign migrant influx (Joshi, Lubell, and Mouly 1975). Only 29% of Abidjan's population was born there. In 1965, 95% of Nairobi's inhabitants had arrived less than ten years ago (Coquery-Vidrovitch 1997, 79). In 1957, 66% of Kampala's enumerated labor force originated from outside Kampala's surrounding province of Buganda (Elkan 1960, 33).

Similarly, 60% of Lagos' inhabitants were born outside the capital in 1950, respectively, about half from the surrounding Yoruba Western Region (Abiodun 1974). Farrel (2018) estimated that the urban natural increase already contributed to 56% of Nigerian urban growth in the 1960s, while rural-urban migration and rural-urban reclassification made up the remaining 23% and 21%, respectively. According to the 1970 Ghana census, 43% and 46% of the population of Kumasi and Greater Accra, respectively, were born there. Overall, both lower urban migrant shares on both the city and the country level in West Africa suggest that they experienced earlier migration, comprising larger settled (i.e., non-migratory) populations, than the comparatively more recent urban and colonial capital city-based growth in East Africa and the Côte d'Ivoire.

Figure 13.4 decomposes annual urban growth into natural increase and residual migration for ten selected African counties in 2000–10. It shows that compared to the 1960s (Figure 13.3), the contribution of the natural increase and migration have reversed over time. On average, the natural increase accounted for 60% of urban growth. Similarly, Beauchemin and Bocquier (2004) report that while two-thirds of urban growth in Francophone West Africa was due to migration and urban reclassification in the 1960s, this dropped to one-third during the 1990s. The natural urban increase in Benin, Kenya, Mali, and Rwanda even exceeded the natural rural increase in the 2010s (Fox 2017). In West and Central Africa, the contribution of natural growth to urbanization was also markedly superior to migration reclassification since the 1980s, while in East and South Africa urban natural growth exceeded migration classification growth only by the 2000s (Menashe-Oren and Bocquier 2021). This shift from migration (and reclassification) as a main source of urban growth toward cities expanding primarily by their own natural increase can be explained by (i) lower infant and child mortality in cities than in rural areas (Günther and Harttgen 2012);

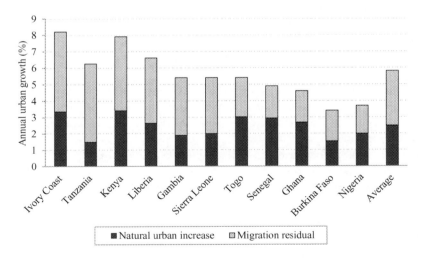

FIGURE 13.3 Natural increase and residual migration in urban growth, c. 1960–70.
Sources: Côte d'Ivoire, Liberia, The Gambia, Sierra Leone, Togo, Senegal, and Burkina Faso (Zachariah and Condé 1981, 82) based on varying periods in 1960–75. Tanzania is the weighted average of its seven largest towns, 1948–71 (Sabot 1979, 46). Kenya (1970s) and Ghana (1960s) from Chen, Valente, and Zlotnik (1998, 80). Nigeria's residual migration includes both migration and reclassification (Farrell 2018). Averages are not weighted by population.

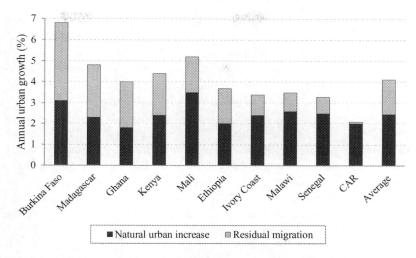

FIGURE 13.4 Natural increase and residual migration in urban growth, 2000–10 average. *Source*: Adapted from Jedwab, Christiaensen, and Gindelsky (2017), Web-Appendix Table 3. CAR experienced counter-urbanization. Average is not weighted by population.

(ii) relatively high urban birth rates, underpinned by a stalled urban fertility transition (Menashe-Oren and Bocquier 2021), changing age structures associated with in-migration of young people, and the relatively minor urban representation of the elderly (see Figures 13.8 and 13.9); (iii) the shift from predominantly male labor cities to the increasing presence of young women in cities, reflected in narrowing urban sex ratios over the second half of the 20th century (see Figure 13.5); (iv) superior urban socio-economic dynamics and access to healthcare (Potts 2009; Fox 2017).

3 Rural-urban opportunity gaps

Why do some people migrate to towns, while others stay behind? Rural-urban migration is by and large a response to economic incentives. Some move with the entire household; others send a household member. According to the classic migration model of Harris and Todaro (1970), better economic opportunities, both formal and informal, at urban destinations act as incentives for rural-urban migration. They model that rational individuals in rural areas base their urban migration decision on a careful cost-benefit analysis, comparing expected returns of migration (urban wages) to their rural agricultural income. In the case of superior urban real wages, the income maximization objective is fulfilled and rural people may decide to migrate to the city. Moreover, if expected urban income premiums are sufficiently high, rural-urban migrants may endure a period of employment search (Mazumdar 1987). De Haas (2017) presents empirical evidence that until the 1950s cotton and coffee cultivation in rural Uganda was more lucrative than urban unskilled wages, and thus provided few incentives for farmers to exchange agricultural with urban unskilled work.[9] Frankema and van Waijenburg (2012) suggest a similar mechanism for Ghana, observing that laborers on cocoa farms earned comparable real wages as their urban counterparts. Consequently, laborers directed their migration destination toward cocoa plantations during the beginnings of Ghana's cocoa revolution (Hill 1963). This highlights that people in rural sending regions have been conscious of *opportunity gaps* between the countryside and town.

Economic incentives remain key to most migration decisions. Indeed, 88% of rural–urban migrants in Ghana stated that they were induced by "jobs, money and consumer goods" in 1963 (Caldwell 1969, 89). Still, there are various kinds of opportunity differentials that have attracted young people to African urban areas, including the prospect of men earning cash to pay bride price, as well as achieving a degree of social status unreachable by junior members of rural traditional systems (Little 1973, 18). Young people may also be motivated to move to the city to further their education or to find a suitable marriage partner, far away from traditional elders' control over marriage choices. Likewise, cities can offer women an escape from an unwanted marriage or divorce, free of the pressures of rural customs (Coquery-Vidrovitch 1997, 74–5).

Often, however, urban migration is not an individual decision but taken jointly within rural households with a clear family welfare-maximizing strategy (Bigsten 1996). Urban migrants, for example, can support their rural family through remittances, which raise consumption and investment (e.g., farm inputs, school fees) at home. Costs and benefits of rural-urban migration, however, materialize at different speeds. The loss of farm productivity and social networks incurred by migration and the costs of moving as well as higher urban living costs are felt immediately, while benefits only accrue after urban arrival, finding work, and earning sufficiently to remit back home. Such serious investments suggest that some rural households cannot afford urban migration or are able to send only one household member. The transaction costs of urban-rural remittances have reduced substantially with the uptake of mobile phone technology and mobile money in the 21st century, making the transfer of purchasing power from urban-dwelling relatives to rural recipients more feasible (Jack and Suri 2014; Munyegera and Matsumoto 2016).

Uneven opportunity structures may be caused by the lack of economic opportunities in rural areas, triggered, for example, by high volatility in agricultural commodity export prices that affect rural incomes. Moreover, rapid rural population growth paired with environmental degradation intensifies pressure upon the land, which sets in motion rural outmigration. Africa is the region most vulnerable to the impacts of climate change. Weather anomalies, such as irregular rainfall patterns and temperature increases, negatively impact African rain-fed agriculture on which rural livelihoods depend. Climate change can thus accelerate rural-urban migration, as a risk diversification strategy in response to increased volatility in rural incomes (Bryceson and Jamal 1997). Indeed, shortages in rainfall have been linked to increased urbanization (Barrios, Bertinelli, and Strobl 2006; Mueller et al. 2020), in particular in regions in which cities are likely to be manufacturing centers providing escapes to adverse precipitation shocks. However, only 25% of cities can be classified as "production cities" (Henderson, Storeygard, and Deichmann 2017). Instead, African countries heavily dependent on natural resource exports (oil and minerals) tended to generate "consumption cities" where a large share of the workforce specializes in informal/non-tradable services (Gollin, Jedwab and Vollrath 2016).

4 Who is the rural-urban migrant?

Rural-urban migration is a complex choice, influenced by various individual motives and household decision-making processes.[10] Migrants are thus expected to distinguish themselves from their rural population of origin in certain characteristics. At what age did people leave their village and move to towns? Were women equally as likely to migrate as men? And was it the desperate poor or the aspiring educated who sought their luck in cities? This section explores the changing profiles of urban migrants with regard to gender, age structures, and education over the second half of the 20th century.

4.1 The feminization of rural-urban migration

Urban sex ratios provide a useful departure point for tracing sex selectivity in rural-urban migration. They measure the number of males for every female in the urban population. A ratio of 100 means that the urban population comprises equal numbers of both sexes. A ratio greater than 100 indicates a greater presence of men than women. A city's sex ratio can be affected by (i) sex-selective rural-urban migration and (ii) the urban natural increase. Whereas the natural urban increase generally levels urban populations toward parity (100), sex-selective rural-urban migration distorts the sex ratio. Therefore, the greater the rural-urban migration's contribution to urban growth, the more meaningful do sex ratios become as measures of sex-selective urban migration. Figure 13.5 presents sex ratios for a selection of seven major cities in East and West Africa, identified from Table 13.2, over the 1948–2015 period.[11] It conveys three messages.

First, by the late colonial era urban sex ratios were strongly male-biased, consistent with (circular) male urban migration systems (Elkan 1967). Colonial governments, (mission) schools, and hospitals, as well as commercial firms employed mostly men, which rural migration strategies anticipated. Rural men were more likely to leave their family members in search of urban employment. If successful, they remitted any spare money to their rural families. Wives and children that remained on the family farm guaranteed continuity of land rights, family's subsistence, and a source of income from cultivation, which would otherwise have been abandoned in the case of wives joining their husbands (Coquery-Vidrovitch

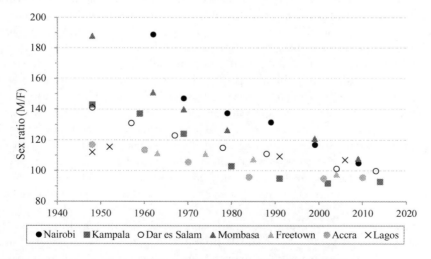

FIGURE 13.5 Sex ratios in East and West Africa's major cities, 1948–2015.
Sources: Various census returns. Nairobi's sex ratio was 352 in 1948, which is not shown due to capping of sex ratios at 200. Sex ratio of 100 = equality.

1997, 74). Those urban-rural ties provided insurance and diversify economic risks in the event of the husband's inability to find urban employment. This practice of *circular migration* thus represented a common strategy for maintaining two bases in order to optimize livelihoods and mitigate risks of permanent settlement in economically precarious cities. Typically, after a period of urban work of a couple of months or years, husbands returned for an extended stay to their rural family, ideally to help during the agricultural peak season before moving back to the city again (Gugler and Ludwar-Ene 1995). During the early and mid-colonial era, characterized by low wages and labor shortages, this was a viable strategy. According to Little (1973, 18–9), there was even an incentive for village elders and parents to prevent their daughters from migrating to cities because they worried that once women left the farm, their migrating men would never return or send remittances.

Second, Figure 13.5 documents the transition from male-selective urban migration toward parity. By the 1990s, sex ratios were close to par in all major cities, reflecting the rise in the proportion of women in urban areas over the second half of the 20th century. The movement of families replacing male migration also indicates the transition from temporary to more permanent employment opportunities. Moreover, rural families' circular migration strategy lost its financial viability once urban unemployment increased. Rural–urban migrants could simply not afford months of job search, and therefore men held on to their urban jobs. More permanent settlement in cities was a response to higher urban wages after the mid-20th century, which allowed men to sustain their family in the urban setting. Moreover, the (colonial) government intending to stabilize the urban labor force increasingly invested into housing and schooling, which encouraged men to permanently settle in town with their families. Bienefeld and Sabot (1971) described this transition in Nairobi as follows: "The urban labor force is now stable and most migrants appear to be committed to wage employment for the remainder of their working lives." As a result, men either kept their rural visits shorter or were joined by their wives and children in the city, causing sex ratios to decline from the 1960s onward. This surge in feminization of urban residence was famously phrased by Gugler (1989): "Women stay on the farm no more," in which he ascribed four factors that weakened the economic rationale for women and children to stay behind in the countryside: (i) increased urban wages allowed men to bring their family to town; (ii) improved urban employment opportunities for women; (iii) lower market prices from cash crops due to adverse pricing policies of marketing boards which lowered rural incomes; and (iv) comparatively higher-quality education and healthcare in urban areas.

The gradual decline in African cities' sex ratios was a precondition for natural increase becoming the key driver of urban growth. Yet, little of this increase in female urban migration initially appeared to be directed toward jobs. Formal urban labor opportunities for women remained modest. Rather, women tended to join their husbands' urban move. For example, during the early 1970s, 49% of women who arrived to Kampala were accompanying or following their husband – 31% came alone (Obbo 1980, 71). In Tanzania, 73% of female rural-urban migrants in 1971 stated that they arrived to live with their husband or relatives, while only 9% indicated to have moved to find work (Sabot 1979, 91). In sharp contrast, 70% of male rural-urban migrants stated that they had migrated to seek employment. Similarly, only 7% of female migrants to Benin City in Nigeria came for employment-related reasons in 1980 (Okojie 1984). In Accra, only 9% of women worked for a wage in 1960. Likewise, 7% of the enumerated labor force of Dakar was female in 1955 of which half were petty traders (Haut Commisariat 1955).

From the 1950s onward formal urban occupations, in nursing, midwifery, teaching, secretarial work, as well as light manufacturing, became increasingly available to women, primarily for the well-educated classes (Coquery-Vidrovitch 1997, 75; Meier zu Selhausen 2014; Meier zu Selhausen and Weisdorf 2016, 2021). Also, in Kenya and Tanzania domestic service, an occupation predominantly held by men, became increasingly feminized from the late 1950s onward (Stichter 1977; Bujra 2000). Over the second half of the 20th century, gender gaps in educational attainment declined (Baten et al. 2021) and female urban labor force participation gradually increased. Urban earning opportunities outside the village economy provided young women a chance of economic independence denied to them previously. Cities' transition toward balanced sex ratios also reflects both rural areas' growing social acceptance of women coming to cities on their own (Lattof et al. 2018) and some degree of emancipation from the control of rural elders over their marriage decisions (Gugler and Ludwar-Ene 1995).

Third, clear differences in the sex composition between East and West African urban centers can be observed in Figure 13.5. Until the 1990s, the proportion of men among East Africa's urban population was significantly higher than in West Africa's major cities, where sex ratios had equalized earlier. While the sex ratios in Freetown, Accra, and Lagos never exceeded a ratio of 120, all four East African cities consistently ranged higher. In particular, the comparatively more recently founded cities of Nairobi and Kampala showed clearly more distorted sex ratios. The sex ratio of Nairobi, which was founded only in 1899 as a depot on the Uganda Railway, stood in fact at 800 in 1931 and 352 in 1948, which created significant demand for female sex work and associated female migration into Nairobi (Davies 1993). Still, in 1969, women made up hardly one-third of Nairobi's or Mombasa's adult population. How come there were considerably more women in West Africa's coastal cities? Were West African migrant women more independent movers?

Unskilled real wages in colonial East Africa's major cities were close to subsistence until the 1950s (Frankema and van Waijenburg 2012; de Haas 2017). Colonial wage-setting practices geared wages to the needs of a single male worker (Coquery-Vidrovitch 1997, 74). Consequently, on the basis of subsistence wages male rural-urban migrants in East Africa could not afford their wives abandoning farming and joining them in town. Rural-urban migration was thus mostly male and temporary, in which men saved up and sent some remittances before returning home. Contrarily, urban unskilled real wages in colonial West Africa were on average almost twice as high during the first half of the 20th century (Frankema and van Waijenburg 2012). Rural-urban migration was thus more sex-balanced and permanent. This allowed male urban migrants employed in formal work to send for their families or migrate jointly much earlier than in East Africa. The legislature on minimum wage levels, pressed by trade unions, sharply increased urban real wages in both East and West Africa from the 1950s onward. The improvement in urban purchasing power by formal laborers enabled unskilled labor migrants to increasingly take their families to town, which not only fueled urban growth but also resulted into converging sex ratios between the two regions. Moreover, the opening of skilled wage jobs to Africans in Uganda and Kenya increased migration toward the urban economies (Rempel 1981, 27).

Another important difference that may explain West Africa's lower sex ratios is that West African urban women enjoyed a greater degree of mobility and economic independence.[12] They historically dominated urban market trading (Sudarkasa 1977) – a status largely preserved despite missionary domesticity teachings over the colonial era (Meier zu Selhausen and Weisdorf 2021). Earnings from urban market trading not only secured West African women's economic independence from their husbands (Gugler 1972) but allowed them to contribute to household finances, diversifying risks and maximizing income. In this sense, urban West African centers have historically been more open to female commercial activity, and thus in-migration, than those in East Africa. For example, in 1948 and 1960, 89% and 82% of economically active women in Accra were listed as retail and wholesale traders, respectively (Little 1973, 34). In Abidjan, 70% of adult women worked as sales workers, compared to about 21% of men (Robertson 1984). Many West African female traders were organized in voluntary associations that promoted their economic interests (Little 1973, 49–60).

Whereas trade was at the core of women's survival in urbanized areas of colonial West Africa, East African women participated much less in urban trade during most of the colonial era (Kyomuhendo and McIntosh 2006, 57; Meier zu Selhausen and Weisdorf 2021). For example, in Dar es Salaam 77% of adult women in 1967 were categorized as homemakers and only 1% as sales workers. The exclusion from trading and formal economic opportunities relegated female urban migrants mostly to participate in the informal economy as petty traders, beer brewers, and prostitutes (Davis 2000; White 2009). Single female migrants were also discriminated against. In Kampala, during the 1950s there were laws requiring the repatriation of single women found on the streets who were branded as "prostitutes" (Obbo 1980, 26). In particular, Nairobi's severely distorted male-female ratio during 1950–70 (see Figure 13.5) and scarce colonial supply of housing offered economic opportunity for female sex work (White 1986). Overall, larger gender imbalances in access to urban economic opportunities seemingly prevented many women from migrating in East Africa for most of the colonial era, except for joining their husbands and prostitution (White 2009). Those major differences in the levels of East and West African sex ratios then suggest that natural increase became the primary driver in West African urban growth even earlier, as indicated in Figure 13.3.

The post-independence era, however, saw East African women catching up in urban trade – 41% of Kampala's market venders were female in the 1960s (Temple 1969). In Nairobi, women made up almost half of all major market traders during the late 1980s (Robertson 1997, 26). Although the branding of female urban migrants as prostitutes by rural elders was intended to discourage female migration, its deterrent powers were limited since rural areas provided comparatively fewer economic opportunities (Obbo 1980, 28). Single women were consistently more likely to migrate than married women in both East and West African countries in the late 1980s (Brockerhoff and Eu 1993). Rather than following their husbands, female migrants to Nairobi sought their own or their families' economic advancement since the 1980s (Robertson 1997, 277). Moreover, about 40% of female urban spinsters got married two years after their move (Brockerhoff and Eu 1993), suggesting that the urban marriage market was an important motivation for migration and that women enjoyed increasing autonomy to do so. Those changing conditions then transformed gendered migration patterns over the second half of the 20th century in both East and West Africa.

4.2 Young adult migration

At what age did people leave their villages to seek their urban luck? Age profiles of city populations, in the absence of detailed mid-colonial-era data on age at migration, serve as a departure point. Figure 13.6 presents the age distribution of Lagos' population (>61 years) in 1931. It shows that 15–34-year-old men and women accounted for about 50% of the city's population, while the 45–60-year-old made up merely 8%. Those low shares of the elderly are consistent with the fact that colonial-era cities received large influxes of working-age migrants (often circular or short-term). Since few were entitled to pensions, covered by social security, or owned urban property (Gugler and Ludwar-Ene 1995), a significant proportion of urban migrants did not settle permanently in the city. Instead, they retired in their rural homes with their relatives. Therefore, urban migrants typically maintained land and retained strong ties with their regions of origin, so they could return when their working days were over or they had failed to achieve an urban career (Cooper 1996, 462; Gugler 2002). In 1960, nine out of ten urban migrants in Ghana stated their intention of returning to their place of origin (Caldwell 1969). In Sierra Leone, although urban-rural return migration was a common feature across adults in the early 1970s, its share was largest among those older than 35 (Byerlee, Tommy, and Fatoo 1976). Men older than 45 were more likely to leave towns than migrate into them (Byerlee 1974).

For the late colonial and contemporary eras, more detailed data on individuals' age of migration is available. Figure 13.7 presents the proportion of Kampala migrants by age in 1951 from household surveys conducted by Southall and Gutkind (1957) among dwellers in two suburbs of Kampala. It clearly shows that the majority of adults, both male and female, decided to migrate young. About 50% of urban migrants were aged 16–30 and 75% were aged 16–45. Urban in-migration after age 45 was almost negligible. Also, in Ghana and Nigeria, the highest propensity to migrate occurred around age 15–24 and old-age outmigration flows set in at age 45 (Callaway 1967; Caldwell 1969, 199). Indeed, over 90% of migrants still living in town intended to return to their home village. As a result, the number of returning urban migrants to their rural origins exceeded the number of rural-urban outmigrants. Similarly, in Sierra Leone, 86% of rural-urban adult migrants in 1974 moved at age 15–34 (Byerlee, Tommy, and Fatoo 1976). In Dar es Salaam, age at migration was even more skewed toward younger age cohorts as 82% of those migrating after their 14th birthday arrived to the capital at ages 14–29 (Sabot 1979, 86–7).

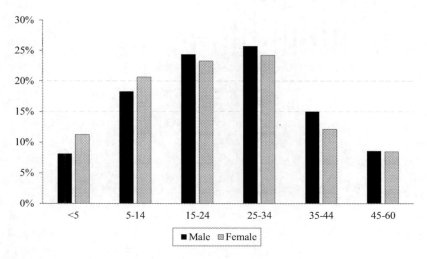

FIGURE 13.6 Age distribution of Lagos' population, 1931.
Source: Census of Nigeria (1932), Vol. IV, Census of Lagos, 35–6.

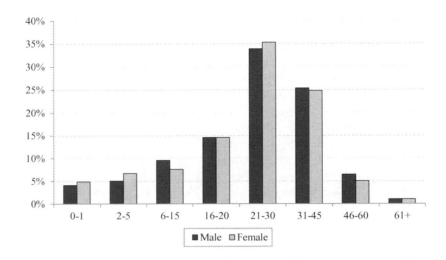

FIGURE 13.7 Age at migration to Kampala, 1951.
Source: Southall and Gutkind (1957, 226–7), based on a survey of 2,026 men and 1,417 women.

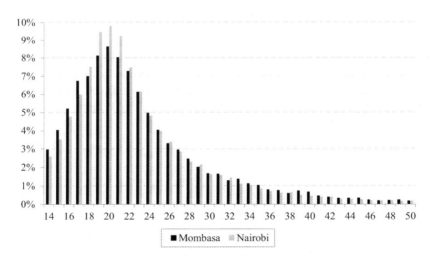

FIGURE 13.8 Age at migration to Mombasa and Nairobi (>14 years), 1999 and 2009.
Source: Kenya census 1999 and 2009, accessed via Minnesota Population Center (2019).

Note: Shows the migrant stock in 1999 and 2009. Excludes migrants who returned to their birth region or elsewhere.

For the more recent period, Figure 13.8 shows adults' (14–50 years) age at migration of those who had previously migrated to Kenya's largest cities of Mombasa and Nairobi in 1999 and 2009. I use the Kenyan 1999 and 2009 census and compute the age at urban in-migration of those who enumerated in Mombasa and Nairobi but were born outside the two city districts, which form the two major urban hubs in Kenya. This stock approach necessarily only captures those who stayed in the city and thus were enumerated there – not those who returned to their rural areas due to unemployment or old age. Also, multiple movements remain undetected. Figure 13.8 shows that rural–urban migration decisions to the main urban centers of Nairobi and Mombasa formed disproportionally during early adulthood. Three in four urban residing migrants enumerated had arrived at age 14–25.

4.3 Human capital on the move

Are urban migrants the most needy, those unable to find a job in rural areas, or those with most aspirations? Education is a useful measure because it indicates parents' investment (capacity) into their offspring's human capital – costs borne in anticipation of enjoying returns in the future. It thus also reflects families' financial situation, as poorer parents are expected to have fewer resources to invest into their children's education because they may not be able to afford associated (opportunity) costs of schooling.

Surveys from the 1960s in rural Ghana reveal that there has been a strong association between individuals' level of education and their propensity to migrate to urban areas (Caldwell 1969, 68). Migrants were significantly more likely to have acquired literacy and knowledge of English – relevant abilities for a productive urban life. Also, in Sierra Leone, in 1974 rural–urban adult migrants had attained on average nearly 2.5 years of education more than rural–rural migrants and non-migrants (Byerlee, Tommy, and Fatoo 1976). While only 1% and 4% of non-migrants and rural–rural migrants, respectively, had attended secondary school, 33% of rural–urban migrants had enrolled in secondary schooling. Also, Nairobi migrants had accumulated on average about three more years of schooling than rural residents in both 1979 and 1989 Kenyan censuses. Indeed, the rural youth in Kenya with higher primary school academic test scores were found more likely to migrate to urban areas in the following ten years (Miguel and Hamory 2009). Also, Tanzanian men who had acquired some secondary education were five times more likely to migrate to cities than those with some primary education (Barnum and Sabot 1977). Similarly, Nigerian rural–urban migrants were three times as likely to have completed secondary school than rural–rural or rural non-migrants in 1993 (Mberu 2005).

Superior accumulation of human capital is still a feature of migrants in Africa today. Figure 13.9 shows the educational attainment gap between rural and urban areas in 2010. It highlights that individuals with more schooling have higher urban migration rates in Kenya, Uganda, Nigeria, and Senegal. Urban migrants were much more likely to have attained some secondary and higher education than rural non-migrants. Overall, education is a critical determinant of urban migration. Since education represents a considerable proportion of parental rural investment, rural–urban migration thus embodies a substantial human capital transfer toward urban areas.

5 Migration into urban poverty?

Rural–urban migration is a common feature of a country's economic development process. Although many developing regions today witness high rates of urbanization at comparatively low levels of industrialization (Gollin, Jedwab, and Vollrath 2016), Africa is urbanizing at lower levels of per capita GDP than any other region. Africa's urban population has grown at the world's fastest rate of about 4.5% annually since 1970, despite lower economic

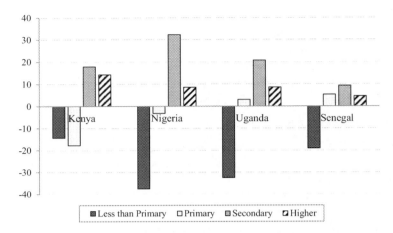

FIGURE 13.9 Educational attainment gap of rural residents and urban migrants, 2010.
Source: Calculated from De Brauw, Mueller, and Lee (2014, 38). Includes individuals ≥ 16 years. It shows the percentage point difference between the share of educational attainment of rural residents and non-migrants. A positive gap means that rural-urban migrants had higher attainment shares than rural non-migrants.

growth (0.6%) and prolonged phases of economic stagnation in the 1970s–90s, which has been coined as "urbanization without growth" (Fay and Opal 2000).[13] Higher urban productivity may thus just reflect the selection of more skilled workers and firms into cities – not cities actually enhancing productivity (Bryan, Glaeser, and Tsivanidis 2020).

The expansion of the public sector since the late colonial era has acted as an important engine of urban African growth (Tacoli 2001, 145). Although the government, the largest urban employer (Simson 2019), could not absorb everyone into formal employment, the demand for services from this sector has consequently given rise to an urban *informal economy*, involving petty trading, transport, crafts, and artisanry (Hart 1973), accounting for about three in four urban jobs (Cobbinah et al. 2015). Compared with other cities in Asia or Latin America, these structural conditions cause African cities to produce fewer goods, mostly for local consumers, rather than for export markets (Lall, Henderson, and Venables 2017, 13), which limits employment growth. In particular, African countries heavily dependent on natural resource exports (oil and minerals) tended to generate "consumption cities" where a large share of the workforce specializes in non-tradable services (Gollin, Jedwab, and Vollrath 2016).

With the increasing influx of urban migrants around independence, unemployment in Africa's major cities began to rise rapidly (Iliffe 1987, 171) to 8% of male adults in Monrovia (1959), 10% of the workforce in Dakar (1955), 18% in Abidjan (1955), and 22% in Lagos (1964). In 1957, only the best-paid 10% of Nairobi's workforce were able to save and invest into their houses, while the lowest 34% depended on rural subsidies and endured a poor diet during the last days of the month (Wallace Forrester 1962, 121, 128). During the early 1960s, the largest category of unemployed in Nairobi were young men, aged 16–25, with some primary education, seeking their first urban job. Also, in Kampala 69% of the unemployed were younger than 25. According to Iliffe (1987, 172), such young migrants often lacked family responsibilities and could sit out long periods until finding a job.

By the 1970s, Africa's major cities "were increasingly coming to be seen as centers of poverty and social deprivation" (Anderson and Rathbone 2000, 8). During the era of the debt crisis and structural adjustment programs the rural-urban income gap in many African countries had reversed in the 1970s and 1980s in favor of farmers (Rakodi 1997). Despite an initial rise in minimum wages after independence, real unskilled urban wages fell dramatically over the 1970s and 1980s in both East and West Africa (Jamal and Weeks 1994), pushing large proportions of wage-earning households into urban poverty. In Kenya, an estimated 30% of urban wage earners were unable to attain the minimum calories needed to sustain a family of five (Jamal and Weeks 1994). In urban Uganda, the minimum monthly wage in the early 1980s could only buy one week of food supply. Equally, in Sierra Leone the urban minimum wage could barely cover the cost of 10 family meals per month in 1987 (Potts 1995). Consequently, urban-rural remittances declined (Bah et al. 2003), eroding the ability of impoverished urban migrants to maintain rural ties.

Rural-urban migration patterns adapted to the inhospitable urban economic conditions, resulting in increasing rates of migration from the urban to the rural sector (Bigsten and Kayizzi-Mugerwa 1992; Potts 1995; Beauchemin 2011). The relative decline in rural-urban migration contributing to city growth increasingly in favor of cities' natural increase (Figure 13.3) then suggests that migration rates have somehow adjusted to declining urban opportunity. In Kenya, urban migrants' linkage status with their rural origins has even sometimes reversed from urban-rural remittance senders to temporary receivers of rural supplements of food and income (Owuor 2007). Also, Beauchemin and Bocquier (2004) have documented the reinvention of migratory circulation and rural-urban links in Francophone West Africa during the economic crisis. Family return migration can also only be split or temporary, with especially the wife and children moving back to the rural home to cultivate family land and attend village school, which relieves the costs of supporting and educating them in the city. Indeed, in Nairobi's slums, women and children were severely under-represented among migrants compared to non-slum areas in 1999 (Archambault, de Laat, and Zulu 2012).

Persistent rapid urban growth in a context of stagnating economic performance and insufficient structural change to absorb rural-urban migrant inflows then resulted in a situation whereby cities grew in tandem with poverty and rising levels of informal settlements. Although migrants arrive to exploit urban areas' greater economic opportunity, initially they often reside in *slums*[14] that facilitate affordable urban access. Figure 13.10 shows that in 1990 about three in four urban dwellers, in both East and West Africa, lived in slums. Despite a reduction in slum incidence over 1990–2014, the majority (56%) of Africa's urban population still lives in slum conditions (UN-Habitat 2016). According to Fox (2014), slums are the most visible manifestation of Africa's urban poverty, inequality, and underinvestment in housing and infrastructure by urban planners.

With rapid urban growth, living conditions in slums appear to have deteriorated. Slum dwellers are confronted with high premiums of living in city proximity. Marx, Stoker, and Suri (2013) calculated that the average monthly housing rent for rural Kenyan households amounted to 1% of household consumption and 10% for urban households, as opposed to nearly one-third of non-food expenditures for the average Kibera slum dweller.[15] Transport costs from long commutes between slums and the wider urban system further eat into budgets.

Although on average children are healthier in Africa's more densely populated areas (van de Poel, O'Donnell, and van Doorslaer 2009; Günther and Harttgen 2012; Fink,

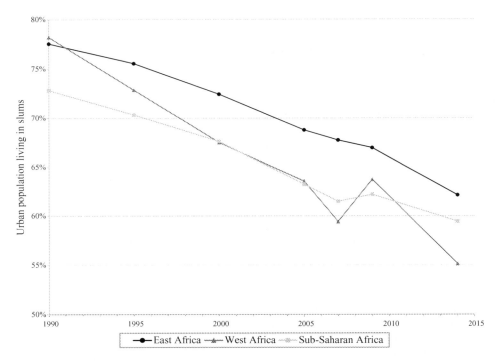

FIGURE 13.10 Slum population as percentage of urban population, 1990–2014.
Sources: Calculated from World Bank (2020), UN-Habitat (2016). Unweighted country averages.

Günther, and Hill 2014), there is increasing evidence that the urban health advantage has diminished in some countries due to poor living conditions in expanding slums (Gould 1998; APHRC 2002; Kimani-Murage et al. 2014). For example, the prevalence of underweight, stunting, and wasting is greater in Freetown's slums than in rural Sierra Leone. Also, in Nairobi's Kibera, Africa's largest slum, incomes have stagnated with duration of residency (Marx, Stoker, and Suri 2013), suggesting that slum living does not necessarily represent a transitory phase in the life cycle of urban migrants.[16] Moreover, the infectious disease burden among slum-dwelling children under three years in Nairobi was considerably higher than in Kenya's non-slum urban or rural areas (APHRC 2002). Children born in slums to women who were pregnant at the time of migration even had a higher risk of dying than those in rural or formal urban settlements (Bocquier et al. 2010). Finally, the urban poor tend to be at greater risk of HIV infection (Magadi 2013, 2017). Altogether, this suggests that urban environments can impose a higher health burden on rural-urban migrants.

So, on the one hand urban slums can help to lift urban migrants out of rural poverty representing affordable and proximate entry points to urban labor markets. On the other hand, urban poverty can confine residents to enduring harsh living and working conditions. What can explain this apparent paradox of city growth and urban migration being barely affected by urban hardship and overall economic performance?

First, poverty rates are on average still consistently higher in rural areas than in cities. Ravallion, Chen, and Sangraula (2007) estimate that Africa's rural poverty rate was more than twice the urban rate in 1993–2002. Second, in densely populated rural areas with scarcity of farmland, firewood, and limited off-farm opportunities, continued population pressure is likely to shrink farm sizes and increase land fragmentation, causing further expansion of youth outmigration to urban areas (Holden and Otsuka 2014; Jayne, Chamberlin, and Headey 2014). Despite unemployment and widespread slum conditions in urban Africa, Tacoli and Mabala (2010) assert that migrants still prefer urban areas to rural areas because of limited rural livelihood options and restrictive rural power relations (e.g., marriage choices). Second, urban areas still provide more income opportunities, social mobility, and higher real wages than rural areas. Although rural-urban income- and unemployment-rate ratios affect the probability of urban migration in Ghana, individuals appear to assign more weight to income differentials than to unemployment differentials (Duplantier et al. 2017). Third, childhood migration to African cities significantly raises primary school completion, school attendance, and literacy rates, suggesting that rural-to-urban migration on average improves the human capital of children (van Maarseveen 2021). Finally, currently urban access to water, sanitation, and electricity is nearly two times higher than in rural areas (World Bank 2020). Also, the supply of and access to health and schooling facilities is generally superior in urban areas, resulting in lower child mortality for rural-urban migrants (Bocquier, Madise, and Zulu 2011).

6 Conclusion

Rural-urban migration and urbanization are (interlinked) key demographic features of Africa's long 20th century. This chapter highlighted five major transitions in African urban growth patterns over the 20th century. First, although, for most of African history, rural-rural migration has been the most important type of migration, by the mid-20th century migrant flows were primarily rural-urban, leading to unprecedented urban growth rates and urbanization levels. Second, Africa's exceptional urban growth, primarily driven by rural-urban migration for most of the 20th century, has shifted toward urban centers nowadays mainly growing out of their own natural population increase. Third, while most urban migrants initially targeted capital or port cities, the expansion in the number of medium-sized cities suggests that urban migration has become less concentrated. Fourth, city growth appeared barely affected by rising urban poverty, slum formation, and overall economic performance. Fifth, while urban migration used to be a male privilege during colonial times, in the second half of the 20th century cities have seen an increase in rural-urban migration of women and children, balancing Africa's urban sex ratios.

Today, West Africa remains almost twice as urbanized as East Africa. This difference mainly seems to be a difference of initial conditions and timing that continued to affect the two regions' urbanization and urban migration patterns over the 20th century. At the beginning of the colonial era, West Africa was already more commercialized and urbanized than East Africa. Consequently, over the 20th century it also had larger cities, experienced higher urbanization rates, and saw an earlier equalization of urban sex ratios, a stabilization of the urban population, a more balanced urban age pyramid, and thus more urban natural growth relative to migration. Also, most West African cities had emerged as "African cities," not established or developed as colonial cities established by white settlers. With the exception of sex-selective migration, urban migrant characteristics appear similar between East and West Africa.

Notes

1 Hereafter Africa.
2 See De Haas and Travieso (Chapter 11, this volume).
3 See Frederick and Van Nederveen Meerkerk (Chapter 12, this volume) on pre-1960 city growth and rural-urban migration in Southern Rhodesia and the Belgian Congo.
4 There were large regional differences. In 1950, 44% in Southern Africa lived in large cities (>300,000) versus 10% in East Africa, 12% in West Africa, and 16% in Central Africa.
5 See Pallaver (Chapter 4, this volume) on pre-colonial roots of East African migration.
6 Examples include Kumbi Saleh (Mauritania), Timbuktu, Djenné, and Gao (Mali).
7 Figures are derived by dividing the aggregate city population for East and West Africa (OECD/SWAC 2020) by their regional population in 1950 (Frankema and Jerven 2014). East Africa excludes Madagascar, Malawi, Mozambique, and Zambia.
8 There is insufficient data to accurately determine the relative contribution of rural reclassification to urban growth. Its contribution, however, is not negligible. Rapid population growth has caused the emergence of entirely new cities. The number of cities with populations ≥10,000 increased from just 292 in 1950 to 5,448 in 2015 (Figures 13.1 and 13.2).
9 Due to comparatively higher living costs in urban Kampala, the many male labor migrants from Ruanda-Urundi preferred to work for rural rather than urban employers (de Haas 2019).
10 Various stakeholders participate in the migration decision of African labor migrants (Byerlee, Tommy, and Fatoo 1976): migrant (32%), rural household head (40%), other rural relatives (16%), town relatives (7%), and spouse (5%).
11 Sex ratios shown represent the entire urban population, not adult sex ratios, which would give higher ratios.
12 This is not to deny that restrictions toward female urban migration existed. In Nigeria the migration patterns of female Hausa Muslims were highly restricted and seen as tantamount to prostitution (Sudarkasa 1977; Pittin 1984).
13 We still observe a positive correlation between African countries' income per capita and urbanization (De Brauw, Mueller, and Lee 2014; Meier zu Selhausen 2018).
14 A slum household is defined as a group of individuals living under the same roof lacking one or more of the following conditions: access to improved water, access to improved sanitation, sufficient living area, and durability of housing (UN-Habitat 2016).
15 Food makes up 61% of average consumption.
16 Study only captures permanent slum dwellers. Only 15% of the Kibera sample exited 2003–07.

References

Abiodun, Josephine Olu. 1974. "Urban Growth and Problems in Metropolitan Lagos." *Urban Studies* 11(3): 341–7.
African Population and Health Research Center (APHRC). 2002. *Population and Health Dynamics in Nairobi Informal Settlements*. Nairobi: African Population and Health Research Center.
Anderson, David, and Richard Rathbone. 2000. *Africa's urban past*. Oxford: James Currey.
Archambault, Caroline S., Joost de Laat, and Eliya Msiyaphazi Zulu. 2012. "Urban Services and Child Migration to the Slums of Nairobi." *World Development* 40(9): 1854–69.
Bah, Mahmoud, Salmana Cisse, Bitrina Diyamett, Gouro Diallo, Fred Lerise, David Okali, Enoch Okpara, Janice Olawoye, and Cecilia Tacoli. 2003. "Changing Rural–Urban Linkages in Mali, Niger and Tanzania." *Environment and Urbanization* 15(1): 13–23.
Barnum, Howard, and Richard H. Sabot. 1977. "Education, Employment Probabilities, and Rural-Urban Migration in Tanzania." *Oxford Bulletin of Economics and Statistics* 39(2): 109–26.
Barrios, Salvador, Luisito Bertinelli, and Eric Strobl. 2006. "Climatic Change and Rural-Urban Migration: The Case of sub-Saharan Africa." *Journal of Urban Economics* 60: 357–71.
Baten, Joerg, Michiel de Haas, Elisabeth Kempter, and Felix Meier zu Selhausen. 2021. "Educational Gender Inequality in Sub-Saharan African: A Long-term Perspective." *Population and Development Review* 47(3): 813–49.

Beauchemin, Cris. 2011. "Rural-Urban Migration in West Africa: Towards a Reversal? Migration Trends and Economic Situation in Burkina Faso and Côte d'Ivoire." *Population, Space and Place* 17(1): 47–72.

Beauchemin, Cris, and Philippe Bocquier. 2004. "Migration and Urbanisation in Francophone West Africa: An Overview of the Recent Empirical Evidence." *Urban Studies* 41(11): 2245–72.

Bienefeld, Manfred A., and Richard H. Sabot. 1971. *NUMEIST*. Ministry of Economic Affairs and Development Planning and Economic Research Bureau, Dar es Salaam.

Bigsten, Arne. 1996. "Circular Migration of Smallholders in Kenya." *Journal of African Economies* 5(1): 1–20.

Bigsten, Arne, and Steve Kayizzi-Mugerwa. 1992. "Adaptation and Distress in the Urban Economy: A Study of Kampala Households." *World Development* 20(10): 1423–41.

Bocquier, Philippe, Donatien Beguy, Eliya M. Zulu, Kanyiva Muindi, Adama Konseiga, and Yayoumé Yé. 2010. "Do Migrant Children Face Greater Health Hazards in Slum Settlements? Evidence from Nairobi, Kenya." *Journal of Urban Health* 88(S2): S266–81.

Bocquier, Philippe, Nyovani J. Madise, and Eliya M. Zulu. 2011. "Is There an Urban Advantage in Child Survival in Sub-Saharan Africa? Evidence from 18 Countries in the 1990s." *Demography* 48: 531–58.

Brockerhoff, Martin, and Hongsook Eu. 1993. "Demographic and Socioeconomic Determinants of Female Rural to Urban Migration in Sub-Saharan Africa." *International Migration Review* 27(3): 557–77.

Bryan, Gharad, Edward Glaeser, and Nick Tsivanidis. 2020. Cities in the Developing World. *Annual Review of Economics* 12: 273–97.

Bryceson, Deborah Fahy, and Vali Jamal. 1997. *Farewell to Farms: De-agrarianisation and Employment in Africa*. Aldershot: Ashgate Publishing.

Bujra, Janet. 2000. *Serving Class: Masculinity and the Feminisation of Domestic Service in Tanzania*. Edinburgh: Edinburgh University Press.

Byerlee, Derek. 1974. "Rural-Urban Migration in Africa: Theory, Policy and Research Implications." *International Migration Review* 8(4): 543–66.

Byerlee, Derek, Joseph Tommy, and Habib Fatoo. 1976. "Rural-Urban Migration in Sierra Leone: Determinants and Policy Implications." *African Rural Economic Paper* 13. Michigan State University.

Caldwell, John. 1969. *African Rural-Urban Migration: The Movement to Ghana's Towns*. Canberra: Australian National University Press.

Callaway, Archibald. 1967. "Educational Expansion and the Rise of Youth Unemployment." In *The City of Ibadan*, edited by P. C. Lloyd, Akin L. Mabogunje, and Bolanle Awe. London: Cambridge University Press.

Chandler, Tertius. 1987. *Four Thousand Years of Urban Growth: An Historical Census*. Lewiston, NY: St. David's University Press.

Chen, Nancy, Paolo Valente, and Hania Zlotnik. 1998. "What Do We Know about Recent Trends in Urbanization." In *Migration, Urbanization, and Development: New Directions and Issues*, edited by Richard Bilsborrow, 59–88. New York: Kluwert Academic Publishers.

Cobbinah, Patrick Brandful, Michael Odei Erdiaw-Kwasie, and Paul Amoateng. 2015. "Africa's Urbanisation: Implications for Sustainable Development." *Cities* 47: 62–72.

Cooper, Frederick. 1996. *Decolonization and African Society: The Labor Question in French and British Africa*. Cambridge: Cambridge University Press.

Coquery-Vidrovitch, Catherine. 1991. "The Process of Urbanization in Africa (From the Origins to the Beginning of Independence." *African Studies Review* 34(1): 1–98.

Coquery-Vidrovitch, Catherine. 1997. *African Women: A Modern History*. Boulder, CO: Westview Press.

Coquery-Vidrovitch, Catherine. 2005. *The History of African Cities South of the Sahara: From the Origins to Colonization*. Princeton, NJ: Markus Wiener.

Davies, C. B. 1993. "Epilogue: Representations of Urban Life in African Women's Literature." In *Women's Lives and Public Policy: The International Experience*, edited by Meredeth Turshen and Briavel Holcomb, 171–82. Westport, CT: Greenwood.

Davis, Paula Jean. 2000. "On the Sexuality of "Town Women" in Kampala." *Africa Today* 47(3): 29–60.

De Brauw, Alan, Valerie Mueller, and Hak Lim Lee. 2014. The Role of Rural-Urban Migration in the Structural Transformation of Sub-Saharan Africa. *World Development* 63: 33–42.

De Haas, Michiel 2017. "Measuring Rural Welfare in Colonial Africa: Did Uganda's Smallholders Thrive?." *Economic History Review* 70(2): 605–31.

De Haas, Michiel. 2019. "Moving beyond Colonial Control? Economic Forces and Shifting Migration from Ruanda-Urundi to Buganda, 1920–60." *Journal of African History* 60(3): 379–406.

Duplantier, Anne, Christopher Ksoll, Kim Lehrer, and William Seitz. 2017. "The Internal Migration Choices of Ghanian Youths." Unpublished manuscript, UNU-WIDER.

Elkan, Walter. 1960. *Migrants and Proletarians: Urban Labour in the Economic Development of Uganda.* London: Oxford University Press.

Elkan, Walter. 1967. "Circular Migration and the Growth of Towns in East Africa." *International Labour Review* 96: 581–89.

Farrell, Kyle. 2018. "An Inquiry into the Nature and Causes of Nigeria's Rapid Urban Transition." *Urban Forum* 29: 277–98.

Fay, Marianne, and Charlotte Opal. 2000. "Urbanization without Growth: A Not-So-Uncommon Phenomenon." *World Bank Policy Research Working Paper* 2412, World Bank.

Fink, Günther, Isabel Günther, and Kenneth Hill. 2014. "Slum Residence and Child Health in Developing Countries." *Demography* 51: 1175–97.

Fox, Sean. 2014. "The Political Economy of Slums: Theory and Evidence from Sub-Saharan Africa." *World Development* 54: 191–203.

Fox, Sean. 2017. "Mortality, Migration, and Rural Transformation in Sub-Saharan Africa's Urban Transition." *Journal of Demographic Economics* 83: 13–30.

Frankema, Ewout, and Marlous van Waijenburg 2012. "Structural Impediments to African Growth? New Evidence from British African Real Wages, 1880–1965." *Journal of Economic History* 72(4): 895–926.

Gollin, Douglas, Remi Jedwab, and Dietrich Vollrath. 2016. "Urbanization with and without Industrialization." *Journal of Economic Growth* 21(1): 35–70.

Gould, William. 1998. "African Mortality and the New "Urban Penalty"." *Health Place* 4(2): 171–81.

Gugler, Josef. 1972. "The Second Sex in Town." *Canadian Journal of African Studies* 6(2): 289–301.

Gugler, Josef. 1989. "Women Stay on the Farm No More: Changing Patterns of Rural-Urban Migration in Sub-Saharan Africa." *Journal of Modern African Studies* 27(2): 347–52.

Gugler, Josef. 2002. "The Son of the Hawk Does Not Remain Abroad: The Urban-Rural Connection in Africa." *African Studies Review* 45(1): 21–41.

Gugler, Josef, and Gudrun Ludwar-Ene. 1995. "Gender and Migration in Africa South of the Sahara." In *The Migration Experience in Africa*, edited by Jonathan Baker, and Tade Akin Aina, 257–68. Uppsala: Nordiska Afrikainstitutet.

Günther, Isabel, and Kenneth Harttgen. 2012. "Deadly Cities? Spatial Inequalities in Mortality in Sub-Saharan Africa." *Population and Development Review* 38(3): 469–86.

Hance, William 1970. *Population, Migration, and Urbanization in Africa.* New York: Colombia University Press.

Harris, John, and Michael Todaro. 1970. "Migration, Unemployment & Development: A Two-Sector Analysis." *American Economic Review* 60(1): 126–42.

Hart, Keith. 1973. "Informal Income Opportunities and Urban Employment in Ghana." *Journal of Modern African Studies* 11(1): 61–89.

Haut Commissariat de l'Afrique Occidentale Francaise. 1955. Resentment démographique de Dakar.

Henderson, J. Vernon, Adam Storeygard, and Uwe Deichmann. 2017. "Has Climate Change Driven Urbanization in Africa?." *Journal of Development Economics* 124: 60–82.

Hill, Polly. 1963. *The Migrant Cocoa-farmers of Southern Ghana: A Study in Rural Capitalism.* Cambridge: Cambridge University Press.

Holden, Stein T., and Keijiro Otsuka. 2014. "The Roles of Land Tenure and Land Markets in the Context of Population Growth and Land Use Intensification in Africa." *Food Policy* 48: 88–97.

Iliffe, John. 1987. *The African Poor: A History.* Cambridge: Cambridge University Press.

Jack, William, and Tavneet Suri. 2014. "Risk Sharing and Transactions Costs: Evidence from Kenya's Mobile Money Revolution." *American Economic Review* 104(1): 183–223.

Jamal, Vali, and John Weeks. 1994. *Africa Misunderstood: Or Whatever Happened to the Rural-Urban Gap?*. Basingstoke: Macmillan.

Jayne, Thomas, Jordan Chamberlin, and Derek Headey. 2014. "Land Pressures, the Evolution of Farming Systems, and Development Strategies in Africa: A Synthesis." *Food Policy* 48: 1–17.

Jedwab, Remi, Luc Christiaensen, and Marina Gindelsky. 2017. "Demography, Urbanization and Development: Rural Push, Urban Pull and... Urban Push?." *Journal of Urban Economics* 98: 6–16.

Jedwab, Remi, Edward Kerby, and Alexander Moradi. 2017. "History, Path Dependence and Development: Evidence from Colonial Railways, Settlers and Cities in Kenya." *The Economic Journal* 127(603): 1467–94.

Joshi, Heather, Harold Lubell, and Jean Mouly. 1975. "Urban Development and Employment in Abidjan." *International Labour Review* 111(4): 289–306.

Kimani-Murage, E. W., J. C. Fotso, T. Egondi, B. Abuya, P. Elungata, A. K. Ziraba, C. W. Kabiru, and N. Madise. 2014. "Trends in Childhood Mortality in Kenya: The Urban Advantage Has Seemingly Been Wiped Out." *Health & Place* 29: 95–103.

Kyomuhendo, Grace Bantebya, and Marjorie Keniston McIntosh. 2006. *Women, Work & Domestic Virtue in Uganda, 1900–2003*. Oxford: James Currey.

Lall, Somik Vinay, J. Vernon Henderson, and Anthony Venables. 2017. *Africa's Cities: Opening Doors to the World*. Washington, DC: World Bank.

Lattof, Samantha, Philomena Nyarko, Ernestina Coast, and Tiziana Leone. 2018. "Contemporary Female Migration in Ghana: Analyses of the 2000 and 2010 Censuses." *Demographic Research* 39(44): 1182–226.

Little, Kenneth. 1973. *African Women in Towns*. Cambridge: Cambridge University Press.

Magadi, Monica. 2013. "The Disproportionate High Risk of HIV Infection among the Urban Poor in sub-Saharan Africa." *AIDS and Behavior* 17(5): 1645–54.

Magadi, Monica. 2017. "Understanding the Urban–Rural Disparity in HIV and Poverty Nexus: The Case of Kenya." *Journal of Public Health* 39(3): 63–72.

Marx, Benjamin, Thomas Stoker, and Tavneet Suri. 2013. "The Economics of Slums in the Developing World." *Journal of Economic Perspectives* 27(4): 187–210.

Mazumdar, Dipak. 1987. "Rural-Urban Migration in Developing Countries." In *Handbook of Regional and Urban Economics*, edited by Edwin S. Mills, 1097–1128. Amsterdam: Elsevier.

Mberu, Blessing. 2005. "Who Moves and Who Stays? Rural Out-Migration in Nigeria." *Journal of Population Research* 22: 141–61.

McKinsey Global Institute. 2011. Urban World: Mapping the Economic Power of Cities. http://www.mckinsey.com/~/media/mckinsey/featured%20insights/Urbanization/Urban%20 world/MGI_urban_world_mapping_economic_power_of_cities_full_report.ashx.

Meier zu Selhausen, Felix. 2014. "Missionaries and Female Empowerment in Colonial Uganda: New Evidence from Protestant Marriage Registers 1880–1945." *Economic History of Developing Regions* 29(1): 74–112.

Meier zu Selhausen, Felix. 2021. "Growing Cities: Urbanization in Africa." In *The History of African Development. An Online Textbook for a New Generation of African Students and Teachers*, edited by Ewout Frankema, Ellen Hillbom, Ushe Kafuakurinani, and Felix Meier zu Selhausen. African Economic History Network. www.aehnetwork.org/textbook/

Meier zu Selhausen, Felix, and Jacob Weisdorf. 2016. "A Colonial Legacy of African Gender Inequality? Evidence from Christian Kampala, 1895–2011." *Economic History Review* 69(1): 229–57.

Meier zu Selhausen, Felix, and Jacob Weisdorf. 2021. "Colonial Influences, Labour Market Outcomes, and Gender Inequality: Evidence from Christian Converts in Urban British Africa." Unpublished manuscript, Wageningen University.

Menashe-Oren, Ashira, and Philippe Bocquier. 2021. "Urbanization Is No Longer Driven by Migration in Low- and Middle-Income Countries (1985–2015)." *Population and Development Review* 47(3): 639–63.

Miguel, Edward, and Joan Hamory. 2009. "Individual Ability and Selection into Migration in Kenya." *Human Development Research Paper* 2009/45, UNDP.

Minnesota Population Center. 2019. Integrated Public Use Microdata Series, International: Version 7.2 [dataset]. Minneapolis, MN: IPUMS.

Mueller, Valerie, Glenn Sheriff, Xiaoya Dou, and Clark Gray. 2020. "Temporary Migration and Climate in Eastern Africa." *World Development* 126: 104704.

Munyegera, Ggombe Kasim, and Tamoya Matsumoto. 2016. "Mobile Money, Remittances, and Household Welfare: Panel Evidence from Rural Uganda." *World Development* 79: 127–37.

Obbo, Christine. 1980. *African Women: Their Struggle for Economic Independence.* London: Zed Press.

OECD/SWAC (2020), *Africapolis* (database), www.africapolis.org (accessed 11 February 2020).

Okojie, Christiana E. 1984. "Female Migrants in the Urban Labour Market: Benin City, Nigeria." *Canadian Journal of African Studies* 18(3): 547–62.

Owuor, Samuel. 2007. "Migrants, Urban Poverty and the Changing Nature of Urban–Rural Linkages in Kenya." *Development Southern Africa* 24(1): 109–22.

Parnell, Susan, and Edgar Pieterse. 2014. *Africa's Urban Revolution.* London: Zed Books.

Pittin, Renée. 1984. "Migration of Women in Nigeria: The Hausa Case." *International Migration Review* 18(4): 1293–314.

Potts, Deborah. 1995. "Shall We Go Home? Increasing Urban Poverty in African Cities and Migration Processes." *The Geographical Journal* 161(39): 245–64.

Potts, Deborah. 2009. "The Slowing of Sub-Saharan Africa's Urbanization: Evidence and Implications for Urban Livelihoods." *Environment & Urbanization* 21(1): 253–9.

Rakodi, Carole. 1997. *The Urban Challenge in Africa: Growth and Management of Its Large Cities.* New York: United Nations University Press.

Ravallion, Martin, Shaohua Chen, and Prem Sangraula. 2007. "New Evidence on the Urbanization of Global Poverty." *Population and Development Review* 33(4): 667–701.

Rempel, Henry. 1981. *Labor Migration into Urban Centers and Urban Unemployment in Kenya.* Laxenburg: International Institute for Applied Systems Analysis.

Robertson, Claire. 1984. "Women in the Urban Economy." In *African Women South of the Sahara*, edited by Margaret Jean Hay and Sharon Stichter, 33–52. London: Longman.

Robertson, Claire. 1997. *Trouble Showed the Way: Women, Men, and Trade in the Nairobi Area, 1890–1990.* Bloomington: Indiana University Press.

Sabot, Richard H. 1979. *Economic Development and Urban Migration: Tanzania 1900–1971.* Oxford: Clarendon Press.

Simson, Rebecca. 2019. "Africa's Clientelist Budget Policies Revisited: Public Expenditure and Employment in Kenya, Tanzania and Uganda, 1960–2010." *Economic History Review* 72(4): 1409–38.

Southall, Aiden, and Peter Gutkind. 1957. *Townsmen in the Making: Kampala and Its Suburbs.* Kampala: East African Institute of Social Research.

Sudarkasa, Niara. 1977. "Women and Migration in Contemporary West Africa." *Signs* 3(1): 178–89.

Stichter, Sharon B. 1977. "Women and the Labor Force in Kenya, 1895–1964." *Discussion Paper* 258, Nairobi: Institute for Development Studies, University of Nairobi.

Storeygard, Adam. 2016. "Farther on Down the Road: Transport Costs, Trade and Urban Growth in Sub-Saharan Africa." *Review of Economic Studies* 83(3): 1263–95.

Tacoli, Cecilia. 2001. "Urbanization and Migration in Sub-Saharan Africa: Changing Patterns and Trends." In *Mobile Africa: Changing Patterns of Movement in Africa and beyond*, edited by Mirjam de Brujn, Rijk van Dijk, and Dick Foeken, 141–52. Leiden: Brill.

Tacoli, Cecilia, and Richard Mabala. 2010. "Exploring Mobility and Migration in the Context of Rural Urban Linkages: Why Gender and Generation Matter." *Environment & Urbanization* 22(2): 389–96.

Temple, Paul. 1969. "The Urban Markets of Greater Kampala." *Tijdschrift voor economische en sociale geografie* 60(6): 346–59.

Thomas, Benjamin. 1965. "The Location and Nature of West African Cities." In *Urbanization and Migration in West Africa*, edited by Hilda Kuper, 23–38. Berkeley and Los Angeles: University of California Press.

Thompson, H. N. G. 1932. *Census of Nigeria Vol IV, Census of Lagos* 1931. Lagos: Government Printer.

United Nations, Department of Economic and Social Affairs, Population Division. 2018. *World Urbanization Prospects: The 2018 Revision*. Online Edition.

United Nations, Department of Economic and Social Affairs, Population Division. 2019. *World Population Prospects 2019*. Online Edition. Rev. 1.

UN-Habitat. 2016a. *World Cities Report 2016, Urbanization and Development: Emerging Futures*. New York: UN-Habitat.

UN-Habitat. 2016b. *Slum Almanac 2015–2016: Tracking Improvements in the Lives of Slum Dwellers*. Nairobi: United Nations Human Settlements Programme.

Van de Poel, Ellen, Owen O'Donnell, and Eddy Van Doorslaer. 2009. "What Explains the Rural/Urban Gap in Infant Mortality: Household or Community Characteristics?." *Demography* 46(4): 827–50.

Van Maarseveen, Raoul. 2021. "The Effect of Urban Migration on Educational Attainment: Evidence from Africa." Unpublished manuscript Uppsala University.

White, Luise. 1986. "Prostitution, Identity, and Class Consciousness in Nairobi during World War II." *Signs* 11(2): 255–73.

White, Luise. 2009. *The Comforts of Home: Prostitution in Colonial Nairobi*. Chicago: University of Chicago Press.

World Bank. 2020. *World Development Indicators*. Washington, DC: World Bank.

Zachariah, Kunniparampil Curien, and Julien Condé. 1981. *Migration in West Africa: Demographic Aspects*. Washington, DC: World Bank.

PART FIVE

Conflict and Mobility in the 20th Century

14

AFRICAN MILITARY MIGRATION IN THE FIRST AND SECOND WORLD WARS

David Killingray

1 Introduction

In an interview some 40 years ago, the elderly Agolley Kusasi spoke of one of the most important events in his youth when he was a peasant farmer in the northeastern reaches of the Gold Coast. He recalled with bitterness one day in 1939: "The chief picked out some men and sent them to Bawku. … The chief told me to go and do something there and I was put in the army."[1] In this abrupt way the 19-year-old Agolley was forced into the path of military migrancy and to a range of new experiences in an alien region of the Gold Coast, and eventually in India and Burma. He returned to his home in the Northern Territories in 1946. His lot was not uncommon for men throughout much of colonial Africa in the first half of the 20th century. In the two world wars the belligerent empires exploited Africa's human resources as military combatants and as non-combatant labor for imperial purposes.[2] Local African elites, subject to the demands of the colonial state, were pressured to provide manpower for wartime military and civilian labor service. The impact on individuals and family life and on the socio-economic well-being of mainly rural communities was profound and far-reaching.

This chapter is concerned with tropical Africa in the first half of the 20th century. First, a brief account is given of the migratory patterns and purposes of African colonial military forces. Second, the major focus is on the two world wars, the strategic policies and purposes of the imperial powers that led to the use and deployment of African colonial armed forces and supporting labor services within and beyond the continent, and the contrasts in the migratory experience of the two global conflicts. Migratory paths for military recruits were long and contorted, taking men from their rural homes to towns, and then, for some, to distant parts of a global empire. The mobilization of tropical Africa's human resources for the war effort, particularly overseas service during the Second World War, was the largest concerted and concentrated movement of Africans out of the continent since the centuries of the slave trade.

DOI: 10.4324/9781003225027-20

2 Colonial armies

Imperial authority in Africa relied on colonial states' ability to maintain law and order. To affect this the colonial powers largely relied on locally enlisted military forces often recruited from the peripheral areas of a colony or from a neighboring colony, commanded by white officers. African armies were effectively mercenary forces, comprising "common man collaborators," migrants who, it was hoped, would prove to be loyal aliens in securing and maintaining the imperial reach and upholding its interests. Most African colonial forces were effectively gendarmerie, uniformed light infantry armed with older rifles and light artillery. Physical fitness and height were basic requirements for recruits and few questions were asked about their status or origin.

Military service was one form of wage labor available to Africans seeking work distant from home. Military recruitment bore close similarities to other movements of African migrant labor on farms and in mines (also see Juif; De Haas and Travieso, Chapters 10 and 11, this volume). Soldiers were fewer in number, but they came from the same areas as many other migrants, for example, in the Gold Coast, drawn south from the northern peripheral areas of the colony, or from neighboring French colonies. Marginal rural societies often became the traditional recruiting grounds for colonial armies across tropical Africa. Methods of recruiting by colonial powers were similar: official pressure on local elites to provide men was often met by sending slaves, troublemakers, and those deemed a burden on society; conscription; soldiers on leave bringing back recruits and thus earning "bringing money"; and the touring recruiting party accompanied by a band (also see Okia, Chapter 8, this volume).

African soldiers used for European imperial purposes outside the continent long preceded the late 19th-century colonial partition of Africa. The Portuguese employed African soldiers in their South and East Asian colonies (Pinto 2008). Slaves in the Caribbean were enlisted into the British West India regiments for service in West Africa, pensioned-off veterans then establishing settlements around Freetown and Bathurst aptly named "Soldier Town." In the Western Sudan, the French established "liberty villages," places for freed slaves and a source of future *tirailleurs* (Klein 1998).[3] From 1832 to 1872, the Dutch recruited soldiers at their West African coastal enclaves for service in the East Indies, some descendants of these black Dutchmen settling in the Netherlands after Indonesian independence (Van Kessel 2005; Van Kessel 2012). In the 1860s the French *Battalion Noire Egyptien* enlisted slaves from the Middle Nile region for war in Mexico (Hill and Hogg 1995; Lamothe 2011). The *Tirailleurs Sénégalais* from 1857 conquered and garrisoned much of the Western Sudanic region for the French and saw active service in Equatorial Africa, Madagascar, and North Africa before the First World War (Echenberg 1991). The Italians developed Eritrea as a military colony producing *ascaris* for use in Libya, the governor complaining to Rome in 1914 that "I have to point out how damaging the consequences were going to be for the colony and that it was inopportune to destroy a colony in order to conquer another" (Negash 1982, Chapter 2; Abede 2017).

Tropical military campaigns required the support of a large labor force to carry supplies of food and munitions. Carriers, or porters, were an essential component of military operations in areas where draft animals died from trypanosomiasis (sleeping sickness). Even in small military operations carriers often outnumbered the forces they supported, for example, the short Asante campaign of 1900 required 30,000 carriers enlisted locally and from Sierra Leone and even from Zanzibar (Armitage and Montanara 1901). Civilians conscripted for ill-paid unpopular migrant labor deserted at every opportunity.

By the late 19th century, European officials identified certain African peoples as having martial qualities. These typecasts were constructs of European minds. Martial identity focused on Muslims, pastoralists, equine societies, and "tribes" deemed to have a military history (Kirk-Greene 1980; Lunn 1999a; Parsons 1999; Marjomaa 2003; Osborne 2014; Stapleton 2019). Essentially, recruiters sought men malleable to military discipline. The "Hausa," an ill-defined linguistic and ethnic group mainly in Northern Nigeria, were labeled martial and recruited by the British, the Germans, and the Belgians for service in the Congo Free State. The French identified Susu and Bambara recruits as the people best for soldiering in West Africa; the Belgians preferred Lingala speakers; the Germans preferred the Yao; the Italians ascribed military prowess to Eritreans; and in East Africa the British regarded the Kakwa from the Southern Sudan and men from the Western Nile region of Uganda as having martial qualities. The Kikuyu and Kamba in what became Kenya Colony were preferred as soldiers for the King's African Rifles. Military recruiters tended to avoid peoples who had a successful history of resistance to European conquest, for example, in the Gold Coast the Asante were viewed as unreliable and disloyal. Across Africa designated recruiting grounds provided soldiers for peacetime service and as primary areas of recruitment during both world wars. In Cape Colony locally recruited soldiers fought frontier campaigns for the British. Following the creation of the Union of South Africa in 1910, the white regime refused to arm Africans, fearing they might pose a threat to white supremacy.

The reasons why men enlisted were similar to those of other migrants, although the number involved in peacetime was much smaller: wages, an alternative to tedious agricultural labor, escape from rule by conservative elders, flight from wife and commitments, and the anonymity of military service which might bring adventure, rewards, and spoils, particularly women (Klein 1998, 81–2). Military employ offered some distinct advantages: regular food; additional pay from overseas service, by promotion and from acquiring new skills; and in some cases relief from certain taxes; and for French *tirailleurs* exemption from native jurisdiction. Peacetime employment was also guaranteed for three or more years, and in wartime for the duration of the war. In the late colonial period, there was compensation for injury and death. Only soldiers serving 25 years or more received a small pension. Colonial armies were more selective in recruiting compared to civil labor. Colonial labor laws were often arbitrarily administered, whereas military discipline, despite its harsh elements, was more clearly defined. Soldiers could and did desert although in wartime mutiny and desertion were punishable by death (Killingray 1982, 234–53; Mann 2006, Chapter 4).

Volunteers for military service had to assess the cost of migration, although this might be borne in part by the army. Military life imposed rigors of new discipline, but it meant a uniform and a possible welfare package. Loyalty was transferred from local African ruler to white officer and/or unit, or so it was hoped. The migrant journey of the soldier was made easier and speedier by an improved colonial transport infrastructure. Information about army life might come from a soldier on leave or from a father who had served his time. Veterans' settlements, created with official encouragement and often near major towns, served as reserves of military-trained men and a source of potential recruits from soldiers' sons. The army, particularly in peacetime, helped soldiers shape a new sense of identity as men apart from others (Killingray 1982, 375–84). As Parsons says, "Africans also manipulated martial identity for their own purposes," the term "Kalenjin" (meaning "I tell you") being invented by soldiers recruited from linguistically related groups during the Second World War in order to counter the weight of the more numerous Luo and Kikuyu (Parsons 1999, 55).

Military migration was overwhelmingly male, although some wives followed their men. Askari villages existed in the German colonies, Moyd (2014, 167) describing those in German East Africa as having an "askari subculture." Some colonial armies had formal barracks, especially for single men, notably the French who deployed colonial troops overseas. Until the 1930s in British West African colonies, military accommodation, or the African "lines," was modeled on a village structure. Soldiers' wives prepared the food, kept home, and raised children. Wives also established and ran trading and business networks, a feature of many barracks across Africa. Prostitutes hung around army lines and soldiers helped spread venereal infection, more rapidly in the Second World War when the incidence of sexually transmitted diseases soared (Vaughan 1992). The military "lines" in peacetime were unofficially regulated by the wife of a senior non-commissioned officer (NCO) who set standards of behavior and conduct for soldiers' wives. When Lettow-Vorbeck's ragged army surrendered in Northern Rhodesia at the end of the Great War, it included over 800 women, one-fifth of the force, "who had stuck to their husbands through all those years of hardships, carrying huge loads, some with children born during the campaign" (*Bulawayo Chronicle*, quoted by Sir Lawrence Wallace in Lucas 1925, 305–6). The changing nature of the military by the late 1930s, and particularly in wartime with the development of a modern army destined for service overseas, changed the gender structure of military life. A soldiers' lot now became similar to many civilian migrants, separated from wives and children and as a result more likely to break marital allegiances.

Migrants leave communities, some for a long time, some never to return. Soldiers were not seasonal migrants, so what were the effects on rural sending areas from regular losses of mainly younger men? What were the causes and consequences of migratory flows on the population of those areas in terms of loss and advantage? Loss of men placed additional labor burdens on women, children, and the elderly. Where hunting, largely a male preserve, helped supplement local income and diet such loss was soon felt. Demographic changes only became evident in the longer term. On the positive side, military service brought money into the sending community as remittances or the accumulated savings of returning soldiers. The presence of the military, with soldiers paid in coin, helped encourage the circulation of a new currency. At the end of the two world wars soldiers' savings inflated bride price, with consequences for other male migrants.

Labor migration raises two questions: how did people view new colonial permeable frontiers, and to what extent did they help foster new ideas of identity (Miles 1994, Chapter 4)? Occasionally, military recruiters ignored modern frontiers and the origin of recruits, especially in times of urgency to enlist men. African soldiers might develop an allegiance to a regiment or to an individual white officer, but essentially many were mercenaries who served for payment. In both world wars, captured enemy soldiers were re-enlisted in the captor's army. These questions will be addressed in the sections on both world wars.

3 The First World War

When war broke out in Europe in August 1914, the colonial powers hoped to exclude the conflict from Africa. A primary reason was to maintain the myth of white prestige, but it was also believed that Africans were mentally and physically disadvantaged for war with European opponents in a temperate zone. Most African colonial military forces were small bodies of a few thousand men, important for maintaining colonial law and order, and in some cases still involved in "savage wars" of pacification to consolidate colonial rule. African colonies were of value to the belligerents for their mineral and agricultural exports and as locations for naval bases and strategic radio stations. Thus, a European war soon became a "total" global war, affecting the whole continent and involving further exploitation of Africa's human resources.

Four campaigns were fought in tropical Africa from 1914 to 1918. In West Africa, the British and French initiated a brief campaign to wrest Togo from the Germans, and an allied operation from 1914 to 1916 to capture Kamerun, resulting in some 10,000 refugees fleeing into neighboring neutral Spanish Guinea. A third campaign, conducted by South African white forces using a 35,000 strong black labor force, took German South West Africa by mid-1915. In German East Africa a long "hit-and-run" guerrilla war was fought, which lasted until after the end of the conflict, with soldiers living off the land, sustained by long lines of carriers, and with combatants and civilians subject to the ravages of disease and acute food shortages. The major theater in East Africa required large numbers of conscripted soldiers and laborers drawn from across tropical Africa (Killingray, 2014) (Map 14.1).

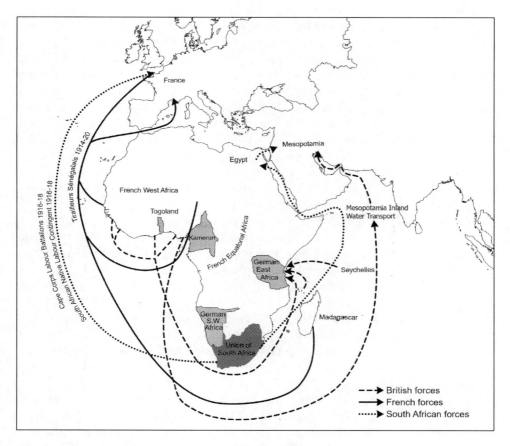

MAP 14.1 African military migration: the First World War.
Source: Author's own, digitized by Stefan de Jong.

France faced a demographic deficit with Germany in the early years of the 20th century; General Mangin successfully argued that soldiers from sub-Saharan colonies should be deployed as garrison troops in North Africa, thus releasing Maghreb soldiers for frontline military service in France. Conscription was introduced into French West Africa in 1912 and two years later the role of *tirailleur sénégalais* had changed from garrison duties to combatants. In total, 140,000 *tirailleurs* served on France's eastern front and in other campaigns. Some 31,000 Africans lost their lives. Colonial troops suffered from the cold of northern French winters, and a policy of moving them south in late Autumn (*hivernage*) was adopted. Service in the metropole exposed *tirailleurs* to a range of new experiences as they viewed the modern world. They were introduced to new diets, some learned to speak and read French, and a few had close relations with European women (Echenberg 1991, Chapter 5; Lunn 1999b, Chapter 6; Mann 2006). European service probably also gave them a dramatic picture of the economic and organizational might of imperial power. Traveling on large ships, seeing industrial towns, and experiencing at first-hand the huge destructive power of modern warfare indicated why imperial powers were imperial. French people who had personal encounters with African soldiers often saw them as ordinary human beings rather than the "savages" portrayed in newspapers and popular literature.

Recruitment campaigns in French West Africa in 1915–17 met with strong resistance and revolt. Colonial or "savage wars" were resumed at a time when the French hoped they were in the past. Although *tirailleurs* could live off the land, such operations ravaged large areas and sent people fleeing to places of greater safety (Saul and Royer 2001). Colonial campaigns also required large numbers of carriers, most being coerced. People living near international borders fled to neighboring jurisdictions to avoid recruiters. In 1975, when Klein and Mbodj were gathering oral evidence on the First World War in southern Saalum, they "did not find a single person who had served [in the military]. Informants old enough to be called up all spent the war years in the Gambia or in hiding" (Klein 1998, 217, 310). The number of people who fled from French recruiters in the Assinie circle of Côte d'Ivoire into the British Gold Coast in 1916–17 was estimated to be 18,000 (Asiwaju 1976, 590), a pattern of resistance to be seen all over tropical Africa.

After the armistice, colonial troops formed part of the French forces occupying the Rhineland. It was an unusual aspect of the African migrant experience: black men, often described by wartime German reports as barbaric savages, now walking the streets of German towns as victors over defeated white people. Predictably, the result in Germany was fierce outrage (Van Galen Last 2015, Chapters 7–9). The French were not being deliberately provocative to German sensitivities but pursuing a practical military policy. France, faced with the destructive effects of a world war fought largely on its own soil, was eager to demobilize French soldiers to aid economic recovery. Colonial troops were to hand and could be more economically deployed in an area that France hoped might soon come to her as part of the future peace settlement.

Many *tirailleurs* were slaves, often sent by their masters, or caught in the French wartime recruiting drives in the western Sudan. Some slaves saw military service as a means of escaping their servile role. The war acted as the great liberator, writes Klein, destroying "slavery among the western Soninke. Veterans refused to accept the authority of masters. Many had learned to read or picked up other useful skills. Many created separate villages" (Klein 1998, 216–7). Slaves unofficially emancipated by war service returned to their home communities and went in search of former families. However, many demobilized *tirailleurs* never returned home, seeking opportunities elsewhere.

Tirailleurs in France were used as uniformed laborers digging trenches, unloading trains and ships, but also in agricultural work and in factories, roles that were deeply resented. From early 1915, the French government and private industries began recruiting civilian labor from the colonies. By 1918, the colonial workforce numbered 185,000 men. The largest number came from Indochina and North Africa, although 4,500 were from Madagascar and a smaller number from West Africa. In January 1916, the *Service de l'Organisation de Travail* began managing workers employed in factories, in mines, and on farms. Africans worked alongside French workers, including women who formed a growing part of the wartime workforce (Stovall 1993). Inevitably, French trade unions opposed measures that they perceived as likely to undercut members' wages.

The British colonial policy was to employ local African military forces within the colony or region of recruitment. With a large Indian army available for imperial purposes, there was no need to expose African troops to overseas campaigns. However, the demands of war led to African troops being recruited for service in distant African colonies. By 1916, the war in East Africa was being fought mainly by African troops, making up a polyethnic migrant army. Although men fought and labored mainly in their own colonial units, the dictates of war meant that they rubbed shoulders together, met socially, exchanged ideas and experiences, and learned from each other. Most soldiers and carriers were non-literate, and their stories were rarely recorded. At the end of the war, some West Africans returned home with a knowledge of Swahili, or another Bantu language. New words were introduced to languages and there was a cultural interchange, particularly from East to West Africa. A small number of West Africans remained in East Africa, marrying, settling down, and finding employment as artisans and truck drivers (*West Africa* 1919, 85; Migeod 1926, 82; White 1966, 186).

The manpower crisis of 1916 changed British official opposition to the use of African military labor outside the continent (Killingray 1979).[4] In mid-1916 it was agreed to supply 1,800 West Africans to work on the *Inland Water Transport Services* in Mesopotamia, and 1,350 lorry drivers to East Africa. The need for more labor at the French Channel ports was met by South Africa in 1915 with a 6,000 strong "Coloured" *Cape Labour Corps*, and then, in early 1916, the formation of the *South African Native Labour Contingent* (SANLC) of 19,000 men (Willan 1978). Stationed in France, the SANLC lived in compounds similar to those imposed on migrant mine labor in Kimberley and on the Rand (also see Juif, Chapter 10, this volume). Segregated by race, under white officers, there were few opportunities for men to meet people outside the compounds. A slight sense of normality and relief came when men went to the reserve camps in Kent and Devon in Southern England. As one recruit from Basutoland observed:

> It was our first experience of living in a society without a colour bar. ... We were aware, when we returned, that we were different from the other people at home. Our behaviour, as we showed the South African, was something more than they expected from a Native, more like what was expected among them of a white man.
>
> (*Jingoes* 1975, 92–3)

The sinking of the "*Mendi*" in the English Channel in February 1917 and the drowning of 615 men of the SANLC stirred black consciousness in South Africa. Thereafter "Mendi

318 David Killingray

TABLE 14.1 Carrier forces in military campaigns, 1914–18

German Africa	384,160
Togoland	2,000
Kamerun	20,000
South West Africa (Namibia)	35,000
German East Africa (Tanzania)	327,160
British Africa	**738,750**
East African Protectorate (Kenya)	190,150
Uganda	186,235
Nyasaland (Malawi)	292,656
Zanzibar	3,542
Northern Rhodesia	56,000
British West Africa	9,391 9
Seychelles	776
Portuguese Africa	**90,014**
Mozambique	90,014

Sources: Killingray and Matthews (1979, 8–11); Killingray (1982, 437, Appendix 6); Hodges (1986, 110–1, Table 3); Grundlingh (1987, chapter 4); Page (2000, 53, Table 2).

Note: The informal recruitment of wartime carriers makes it difficult to give exact overall figures.

Day" became a day of remembrance for Africans who lost their lives in a distant war (Willan 1978) (Table 14.1).

In the tropical African campaigns, carriers or porters were a vital element of military operations. It was hard and harsh labor, and carriers earned less than migrant workers on farms or in mines. Even in peacetime, it was unpopular work and officials resorted to conscription to secure the labor required. In the war years, conscription on a large scale became standard practice. The British and French rounded up 25,000 to 30,000 carriers for the Kamerun campaign. The arbitrary nature of that enlistment was echoed in the words of a British official speaking for carrier "number 1475," seized in Southern Nigeria:

> We came back one night from our yam farm. The chief called us and handed us over to a Government messenger. I did not know where we were going to, but the chief and the messenger said that the white man had sent for us and so we must go. After three days we reached the white man's compound. Plenty of others had arrived from other villages far away. The white man wrote our names in a book, tied a brass number ticket round our neck, and gave each man a blanket and food. Then he told us that we were going to the great war to help the King's soldiers, who were preventing the Germans coming to our country and burning it. We left and marched far into the bush. The Government police led the way, and allowed no man to stop behind.[5]

The long drawn-out East African campaign called for hundreds of thousands of carriers, men, women, and children. Carriers came from wherever they could be had across a large swathe of East and Central Africa. Recruiting policies were ruthless with little regard to the welfare of the societies from which people were seized. The Belgians in Kivu not only took men but requisitioned food for the army; the province faced near famine conditions in

1916 and the population was reduced by flight. In Ruanda, drought and military demands brought famine – the "Rumanura" of 1916 which killed an estimated 50,000 people (Lugan 1976).[6] In excess of 1 million people were enlisted as carriers for military operations in the East Africa campaign. Death rates were high, with more than 100,000 carriers perishing in conditions only belatedly acknowledged by the British as "a scandal."[7] Many carriers who deserted died in their desperate attempts to return home. Demands for carrier labor took migrant labor from farms, docks, and railway work. Nyasaland supplied 200,000 carriers for the war of *thangata*, a Chichewa word which one informant said involved "work which was done without any real benefit" (Page 2000, 6, 53). The small colony already had a sizable number of migrants in other Central Africa colonies, mainly in the mines of Southern Rhodesia. For many men, military carrying offered an immediate local source of wages without an initial long migrant journey, even if their subsequent migrant role involved hard conditions and the prospect of death.

The effects of the war for the peoples of Central and Eastern Africa were disastrous. Communities were destabilized, normal patterns of planting and harvesting disrupted, and crops pillaged by rival armies; social and economic life was undermined by drought, famine, and disease. People fled the coercive reach of military and labor recruiters, and with the removal of men a large burden was placed on women, the elderly, and children. These huge labor demands are thinly documented; people moved all over the place and suffered grievously (Killingray and Matthews 1979; Hodges 1986). Toward the end of the war, the influenza pandemic struck with great ferocity, further undermining already impoverished, fragile communities and weakened indigenous economies. Areas of Central and East Africa appear to have suffered a demographic decline due to the war and the influenza pandemic, with 4%–6% of the population dying (Paice 2007, 392–8). Large carrier centers were established in Nairobi and Dar es Salaam, areas today identified by corruptions of the word carrier corps, respectively, Kariokor and Kariakoo. Another African area of Dar es Salaam was Ilala, named after the hometown in Nyasaland of many of the Yao soldiers who settled there after the war (Leslie 1965, 22). The conflict in East Africa greatly accelerated coerced migrancy, one result being that by the end of the war many Africans were reluctant to migrate to find paid work.

Wars do not merely consist of military campaigns. They have pervasive effects on social and economic life far from scenes of military action. Urban centers grew slowly during the First World War, in South Africa spurred by the withdrawal of white men for the war effort and by increased openings for black unskilled labor driven to the towns by the impoverishment of the reserves. African workers became more stabilized urban dwellers, more outspoken in their demands for wage increases in response to wartime inflation, and less inclined to heed (as often were white employers) the racially restrictive labor legislation of the pre-war years. As white workers were inclined to go on strike, so were African workers in the immediate post-war years of labor militancy in South Africa. Similar labor unrest occurred across tropical Africa in the post-war inflationary years.

What impact did the migratory experience have on the hundreds of thousands of soldiers and carriers exploited during the Great War? In Terence Ranger's (1975, 45) words, "[t]he First World War was the most awe-inspiring, destructive, and capricious demonstration of European "absolute power" that eastern Africa ever experienced." First-hand accounts by Africans are few, probably more in French than in English. Many whose lives had been grievously disrupted by the war, wished to forget it. Sea voyages in large ships was an experience endured by few other African migrants.[8] Some men returned from war with a wider knowledge of the world, with new skills which helped reshape their civilian lives. Soldiers paid in wartime scrip (metal was in short supply) in West Africa helped pave the way for the acceptance of paper currency. Any idea that Africans thought whites superior (and it was mainly Europeans who advanced such views) was disabused by the experience of the turmoil of war and the battlefield. The war destabilized large areas of Africa, the French facing great difficulties in demobilizing large numbers of discontented *tirailleurs* who rampaged in towns and villages in West Africa (Mann 2006, 74–8).

4 The Second World War

In the crisis years of 1939–45, total war gripped Africa more tightly. European imperial states extended their power over colonial economies to mobilize human and material resources as never before. Large armies of Africans were recruited and deployed as combatants and non-combatants in military campaigns fought in Europe, within Africa (including Madagascar), the Levant, and Asia. In addition, hundreds of thousands of Africans across the continent were conscripted for civilian war work. Large numbers of African men also served as merchant seamen. People in increasing numbers moved to the towns and cities of sub-Saharan Africa in response to wartime demands for higher economic output. In the 1940s Africa's people were truly on the move.

The Second World War started in Africa when Italy attacked Abyssinia in 1935. Italy boasted an army of 200,000 African troops supported by tanks, artillery, poisonous gas, and bomber aircraft. These changes to sub-Saharan warfare forced other colonial powers to re-equip their local forces for modern technical warfare. In addition to infantry, new technical branches of the army expanded after 1939–40 manned by literate and numerate recruits, many from urban areas, hitherto rarely enlisted. This opened new opportunities to learn skills, as signalers, radio operators, nursing assistants, and in mechanical and electrical engineering. In the years 1940 to 1947 more than 1 million African soldiers were sent to fight and labor in Europe, Northeast and North Africa, the Levant, and Asia. The French continued to conscript colonial troops, with many thousands being employed in the short war against Germany in 1939–40. Harsh treatment by their German captors exposed some to experiences unknown to civilian migrants. After the French defeat in June 1940, the bulk of de Gaulle's *Free French* forces facing the Vichy regime were African troops in French Equatorial Africa. British policy at the start of the war was to try and confine African troops to African campaigns against other African forces, an ambition maintained until Italy entered the war in mid-1940. African troops, mainly from West and East Africa, were then deployed in the campaign to defeat the Italian army in the Horn of Africa. One debate was how to move large numbers of soldiers from West to East Africa, by road or by sea; the latter means was agreed, and soldiers endured the long sea voyage via South Africa to Mombasa. The success of African troops against the Italian forces convinced London that they might be used elsewhere as garrison and even combatant troops in Asia in the event of a war with Japan (Table 14.2).

British wartime recruitment in East and West Africa was mainly concentrated on the traditional areas from which soldiers customarily came. For example, in the Gold Coast in 1943 some 63% of recruits continued to come from the traditional recruiting areas and 16% from French colonies (Killingray 1982, 298). It was a more concerted program, spurred by

TABLE 14.2 African forces in the Second World War

British Africa	**642,500**
East African colonies	323,000
West African colonies	243,000
Southern and Northern Rhodesia	30,000
High Commission Territories	40,000
Mauritius and the Seychelles	6,500
South Africa	**309,000**
Black and colored (non-combatant)	123,000
White	186,000
French Africa	**200,000**
Italian Africa	**200,000**
Belgian Congo	**40,000**
Total	**1,391,500**

Note: The fluid recruitment and demobilization of African soldiers and labor during the war years means that precise figures for those in military service often vary month by month.

Sources: Killingray (1982, 450, Appendix 13); Grundlingh (1986, Appendix D); Negash (1982, 51 and 55); Saunders and Southey (1998, 193); Echenberg (1991, 62, Table 4.3); Parsons (1999, 71, 72, and 78); Gondola (2002, 98); Thompson (2003, 96–7).

the urgency to secure, train, and equip soldiers for service first in the East African campaign against the Italians, then to secure a labor corps for use in North Africa, men from East Africa for the Madagascar campaign, and then, from 1942 onward, troops mainly from West and East Africa for use in the war in Asia against Japan.

Ill-defined colonial borders often meant little to migrants. To people who lived near international frontiers, and aware that communities had been divided by different imperial jurisdictions, proximity to the border could even work to their advantage. For example, when French labor or military recruiters were in the area, men fled to the bush while occasionally whole villages moved across the border into British territory to escape their grasp. After the creation of the Vichy regime, over 1,000 French colonial soldiers in Côte d'Ivoire crossed into the Gold Coast, most to be absorbed into the *Royal West African Frontier Force*.[9] Africans could exploit new territorial frontiers (often notorious edges of administration and subject to a good deal of crime) to their own advantage in order to resist, thwart, and exploit the colonial state (Map 14.2).

Large numbers of laborers were required to promote the war effort. This included civilian labor and military units, uniformed "pioneers" subject to military discipline. The British drew a large army of pioneers from every colony in their sub-Saharan empire, which was employed in every campaign. Although this was done in a more measured way than the arbitrary actions of the Great War, it nevertheless imposed similar burdens on the societies from which men were recruited. The three British protectorates of Southern Africa, for long a source of seasonal migrant laborers to work in South Africa, became a prime area for military recruiters for the *African Auxiliary Pioneer Corps*. Bechuanaland contributed 10,000 men, with half coming from the Bamangwato Reserve. This was at a time when another 10,000 men from that area were absent as migrant laborers in South Africa. In Kweneng,

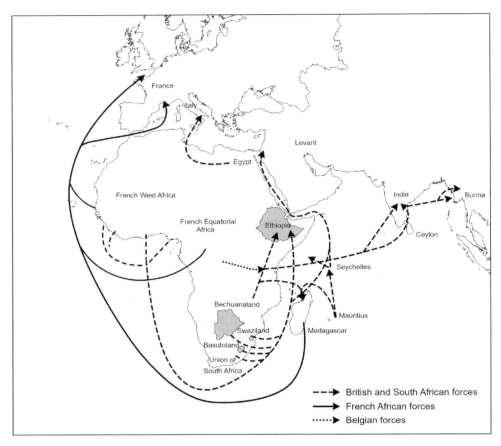

MAP 14.2 African military migration: the Second World War.
Source: Author's own, digitized by Stefan de Jong.

another area of Bechuanaland, by 1945 the area had been stripped of 35% of its male population (Schapera 1947; Kiyaga-Mulindwa 1984; Mokopalgosi III 1986; Jackson 1999). Across Africa military recruitment rivaled other demands for migrant labor. These political issues involved traditional rulers, most of whom supported wartime recruitment, and the colonial authorities. For the latter, military needs competed with civilian demands for migrant labor for South Africa's wartime production. Similar conflicts of interest existed in most tropical colonies. In West and East Africa, areas with a different history of migratory labor to that of Southern Africa, many men were reluctant to enlist and don a uniform as laborers. "Downgrading" soldiers to laboring duties caused "strikes" which could be described as mutinies. Nevertheless, most soldiers enlisted by the British served as laborers in uniform (Killingray 2010, 44).

In the Second World War many colonial forces paid regular remittances to wives and dependents of soldiers, although wartime inflation eroded its real value as many imported consumer goods became increasingly scarce. After the war, returning soldiers brought back to rural societies new ideas about diet (e.g., a taste for bread), and notions of modern technology. Soldiers had been introduced to contraceptives, widely promoted to maintain an army fit for military action. The colonial state often viewed ex-servicemen as useful agents at the local level, possibly as modernizers, conveying ideas of personal and public health, child-care, and new agricultural methods and practices. In contrast to other migrants, soldiers were also seen as useful administrative agents, men schooled in loyalty who would act as chiefs and local officials to buttress the colonial state.

Most men enlisted in the wartime colonial armies were non-literate. Personal written accounts are few, and oral records more numerous but by now a dying asset. The impact of foreign war service on individuals was varied. Many men returned from a war that had severely ruptured their lives and left them with little reward but bitter memories. For others, the migratory journeys of wartime provided a range of new experiences that broadened their view of the world and widened their perceptions and ambitions. They had learned of industrial time, had a disciplined structure of daily life, traveled on large ships on seemingly interminable rolling oceans, and learned to handle a precision-tooled rifle. Some saw large cities with slums and beggars and others religious sites; they encountered faith systems; met other Africans, Egyptians, Indians, and saw the vulnerability of white men. Soldiers learned a bit about foreign women, and many contracted sexually transmitted disease. Army education courses, available for a few soldiers in the immediate post-war years while awaiting demobilization, offered opportunities to learn to read and write and to gain a better knowledge of English or French. For the non-literate, post-demobilization courses sought to introduce veterans to new ideas that might result in increased agricultural production once they returned home. Demobilization for soldiers also differed from the usual migratory cycle; in many instances groups of men were accompanied by a white officer or NCO to their home area at which point their savings would be handed to them as evidence of reward for loyal service (Fursdon 1948). It was not in the political interest of the colonial authorities for ex-servicemen to linger in the towns and to return home having spent their wages and savings. Soldiers should return home with tangible assets (savings) and new skills, a good advertisement for British colonial rule and its new welfare schemes.

Military service, particularly overseas, offered new opportunities but these were always selective. It is probably false to think that Africans reacted in ways markedly different from soldiers from any other ethnic group or country around the world on encountering foreign peoples, new sights, and scenes. Similarities of response outpaced any differences. Some men came home having learned another language, critically observed another culture, had their curiosity excited by seeing a large city. In wartime it is doubtful if an activity which took men to other colonies in the continent, where they might have loose association with other Africans, helped encourage a strong sense of pan-Africanism or solidarity of purpose to challenge colonial rule.

The idea that wartime overseas service exposed soldiers to new political ideas continues to have an appeal. There is minimal evidence, however, that African soldiers sat with Indian activists in the bars of Bombay discussing how empire might be overthrown. In India, official policy and the location of military encampments was designed to segregate African soldiers from civilians, particularly women, in order to protect local communal relations. Visits to towns by selected soldiers did take place but most indications are that they were arranged by officers who acted as guides. In North Africa and the Levant, African pioneers were confined to camps located some distance from towns, a source of perpetual grievance. This is not to suggest that military service did not have political input. Some stimulus came from army education classes run by younger conscripted white officers critical of empire.

324 David Killingray

Demobilization back into economies riven by inflation and post-war shortages challenged the expectations of returning soldiers. French official failure to provide back pay and demobilization premiums to *tirailleurs* former prisoners of war led to a mutiny at Thiaroye, near Dakar, in December 1944. Violent suppression of the unrest by the French resulted in nearly 40 colonial soldiers dead and many severely injured, undermining the country' reputation as a beneficent imperial state (Echenberg 1991, 101–5). Slowness of British demobilization – the last West African soldiers only reached home in early 1947 – fueled grievances, such as the ex-servicemen's demonstration in Accra in 1948, which had a political element.[10] This was rarely incipient nationalism, more likely to be translated into actions that challenged paymasters and traditional rural rulers.

Colonial military service helped shape new loyalties, cemented by fellow soldiers, including those from a different ethnic group. A strong sense of territorial identity was shaped for many men wearing a military uniform which prominently proclaimed on each shoulder that they came from "Nigeria," "Gold Coast," "Kenya," and so on. Regimental and territorial identities were encouraged by overseas service and contact with other alien Africans. Contrary to the experience of most other African migrants, soldiers in wartime traveled overseas and fought age of mass migration Europeans and Asians. If ever Africans had ideas of white superiority, as some whites liked to believe, this would have been severely dented by guarding captured Italian and German soldiers. Negative (or positive) views of colonial rulers were not the sole fruits of soldiers migrating overseas. A handful of ex-servicemen failed to return home, having found a wife, and settled in Europe or Asia. However, for many men, military service was like any other migrant experience. As one former *tirailleur* recorded by Lunn said:

> When [we first] returned to Senegal, I was eager to see my family and to [be with] them. But, then I started [doing my] daily work as I had done before the war. [I was] farming, fishing, and learning the Koran: those were my [only] occupations.
>
> *(Lunn 1999b, 209)*

The war obviously had a profound political impact on colonial Africa. Wars invariably result in great social and economic changes. These were most pronounced in South Africa. The tightening racial restrictions of the 1920s and 1930s that increasingly tried to keep Africans out of towns and in rural reserves as cheap seasonal migrant labor never really worked and came unstuck in the war years. Manufacturing overtook mining as the country's main industrial activity in terms of GDP and employment. The withdrawal of 186,000 white men for military service provided new openings for Africans (Beinart 2001: 129). Black urbanization increased as migrants moved to towns driven by a succession of poor harvests and attracted by the labor demands of the expanding war economy. The African labor force became more stable, with many of the new migrants living in townships or as squatters. The result, as elsewhere in the expanding towns of sub-Saharan Africa, was a rise in workers' militancy and the creation of trade unions set on improving wages and working conditions and also related issues of freedom of movement, housing, education, social welfare, and equality before the law (Stadler 1979; Alexander 2000). This was the potent mix of grievances which accompanied migrant workers, including ex-servicemen, which could be exploited by post-war political parties seeking a nationalist cause.

The *Forced Labour Convention* of 1930 allowed for conscripted labor in dependent colonies in time of war and emergency (also see Okia, Chapter 8, this volume). In 1939–45 this was broadly interpreted and used in many colonies as a smoke-screen to exploit local labor. In white settler colonies labor for military purposes such as building roads and aerodromes competed with the demands of European farmers. In Southern Rhodesia, the *Compulsory Native Labour Act* of June 1940 resulted in wartime conscription, much of it for use on white-owned farms. The official figure was over 33,100 but probably the actual number was more than double that (Killingray 1986; Datta 1988; Vickery 1989). Forced labor was also used to secure sufficient migrant laborers from Northern Nigeria for the tin mines of the Jos plateau. Conscription failed to produce the numbers needed to boost output of this vital war mineral produced by privately owned mining companies. Laborers' accommodation was poor, the climate was unhealthy, foodstuffs were inadequate, mortality rates were high, and many workers absconded. Between September 1942 and February 1944 a total of 100,887 conscripted men were brought to the mines along with 6,200 women to serve as cooks. Bill Freund says that "for labour, the war years were clearly a disaster. … [from which] emerged a new spirit of resistance and militancy" (Freund 1981, 149). Similar patterns of forced labor with conscripted migrant workers were applied across the African colonies, with great severity by both Vichy and Free French authorities (Cooper 1996, Chapter 4; Ash 2015; Brown 2015; Schmidt 2015).

The strategic ports of Africa, Dakar, Freetown, Cape Town, Durban, and Mombasa attracted migrant labor to work on expanded docks, larger numbers of ships, and the building of a wartime infrastructure. The Atlantic supply route, operated with US support even while that country was neutral, required a line of bases from Accra via Kano to Khartum and then down the Nile Valley to Cairo, all built by locally recruited and migrant laborers. The strategic Atlantic port of Freetown is a useful study of migrancy. During the early years of the war the number of people employed in the port and related industries rapidly increased from 10,000 to more than 50,000 by November 1942. Migrants from the neighboring Protectorate followed a path already well trodden by men and women fleeing the declining agricultural output and falling prices of the Depression years. Men found jobs in war-related sectors, while many women worked in the informal economy. In the same period the number of white wartime personnel in Freetown increased from 400 to 7,000 (Howard 2015).

5 Conclusion

Two world wars destabilized colonial Africa, the Great War having a more profound impact on Africans than the conflict of 1939–45. In both conflicts, military service imposed discipline on large numbers of African young men, giving them skills and knowledge vital as future employees of the colonial state as policemen and military reserves. In wartime, many recruits served outside their colony of origin, often overseas, gaining new experiences and a sense of comradeship with other men, and helping to forge an identity with regiment and colony. Compared to most other migrant workers, soldiers had an elite position signified by their uniform. However, men trained to act together in arms could pose a serious threat. Loyalty had its limits!

Unlike civil migrant workers, military recruits faced harsh penalties for default of duty or desertion. Relatively few in number, they were recorded by the colonial state, their apprehension for absence more likely than that for the laborer who fled from farm or mine. On overseas service among people alien in culture and appearance, desertion was more difficult. As migrants, soldiers in wartime could become constant itinerants, moving from one training station to another, to overseas postings, being directed by distant orders and the exigencies of war. Barrack accommodation for soldiers might be similar physically to that provided for migrant labor on the Rand, but only on overseas service were they restrictive compounds. Wartime captivity was endured by a good number of *tirailleurs* in both wars, but only by a few British African troops in the Second World War. Another difference from other migrants is that soldiers on active service, especially when overseas, endured long periods of idleness, an acute concern for military commanders in Asian encampments in 1945–46 as soldiers waited for scarce shipping to return them home. A common and constant longing of many migrants was that very individual desire to return home to family and kin.

Notes

1 Agolley Kusasi, interviewed by the author, Accra, 5 May 1979.
2 The history of wars is not only about conflict but also about impact. Periodization should reflect this, thus for Africa I would suggest for the Great War 1911–26, and for the latter conflict 1935–50.
3 A large part of the Gold Coast Constabulary in the mid-1870s was composed of runaway slaves or slaves formerly bought by the British in Lagos; the National Archives, Kew (TNA). CO96/127/14459, Ussher to Hicks Beach, 12 August 1879, enclosure Molony to Ussher, 7 July 1879.
4 Manpower shortages led to demands that African labor be brought to Britain, proposals strongly resisted by large trade unions. By 1919 Britain's black population had increased, and race "riots" occurred in major port cities; see Jenkinson (2009).
5 Bodleian Library, Oxford. Falk papers. MSS. Afr. s.1808 (6), 'The Carrier's Tale', an account written by an official in an unidentified British newspaper.
6 A worse famine hit Ruanda-Urundi in 1943–44, killing as many as 50,000 people.
7 The National Archives, Kew. CO820/17/22719, 19 May 1934.
8 This is dramatically captured in a novel by the Tigrinyan writer Abba Gäbräyäsus, *The Conscript* (written c. 1927, published 1950), based on his journey on a ship with Eritrean soldiers bound for Libya during the First World War; see Bekele et al. (2018).
9 TNA. WO208/52 and 53, 1940.
10 Killingray, *Fighting for Britain*, chapters 7 and 8, discusses in some detail these questions.

References

Abede, Dechasa, 2017. "Ethiopian and Eritrean Askari in Libya (1911–1932)." *Ethiopian Journal of the Social Sciences and Humanities* 12(2): 29–51.
Alexander, Peter, 2000. *Workers, War and the Origins of Apartheid. Labour and Politics in South Africa 1939–48*. Oxford: James Currey.
Armitage, C. H., and A. F. Montanara. 1901. *Ashanti Campaign 1900*. London: Sands & Co.
Ash, Catherine Borgosian. 2015. "Free to Coerce: Forced Labor During and After the Vichy Years in French West Africa." In *Africa and World War II*, edited by Judith Byfield, Carolyn Brown, Timothy Parsons, and Ahmad Alawad Sikainga, 109–26. New York: Cambridge University Press.
Asiwaju, A. I. 1976. "Migration as Revolt: The Example of the Ivory Coast and the Upper Volta before 1945." *Journal of African History*, 17(4): 577–94.
Beinart, William. 2001. *Twentieth-Century South Africa*. Oxford: Oxford University Press.
Bekele, Shiferaw, Uoldelul Chelati Dirar, Alessandro Volterra, and Massimo Zaccaria. 2018. "Introduction." In *The First World War from Tripoli to Addis Ababa (1911–1924)*, edited by Shiferaw Bekele, Uoldelul Chelati Dirar, Alessandro Volterra, and Massimo Zaccaria. Addis Abeba: Centre Français des Études Éthiopiennes. http://books.openeditor.org/cfee/379, accessed 26 July 2020.

Brown, Carolyn. 2015. "African Labor in the Making of World War II." In *Africa and World War II*, edited by Judith Byfield, Carolyn A. Brown, Timothy Parsons, and Ahmad Alawad Sikainga, 43–67. New York: Cambridge University Press.

Cooper, Frederick. 1996. *Decolonization and African Society. The Labor Question in French and British Africa*. Cambridge: Cambridge University Press.

Datta, Kusum. 1988. "Farm Labour, Agrarian Capital and the State in Colonial Zambia: The African Labour Corps 1942–1952." *Journal of Southern African Studies* 14(3): 371–92.

Echenberg, Myron. 1991. *Colonial Conscripts. The Tirailleurs Sénégalais in French West Africa, 1857–1960*. London: Heinemann.

Freund, Bill. 1981. *Capital and Labour in the Nigerian Tin Mines*. Harlow: Longman.

Fursdon, F. W. E. 1948. "Draft Conductor to Togoland: The West African Goes Home." *Army Quarterly and Defence Journal* 57(1): 101–10.

Gondola, Ch. Didier. 2002. *The History of Congo*. Westport, CN: Greenwood Press.

Grundlingh, Louis. 1986. "The Participation of South African Blacks in the Second World War." D.Litt Diss., Rand Afrikaans University.

Grundlingh, Albert. 1987. *Fighting Their Own War. South African Blacks and the First World War*. Johannesburg: Raven Press.

Hill, Richard, and Peter Hogg. 1995. *A Black Corps d'Elite: An Egyptian Sudanese Conscript Battalion with the French Army in Mexico, 1863–1867, and Its Survivors in Subsequent African History*. East Lansing: Michigan State University Press.

Hodges, Geoffrey. 1986. *Kariakor, The Carrier Corps. The Story of the Military Labour Force in the Conquest of German East Africa, 1914–1918*. New York: Greenwood Press.

Howard, A. M. 2015. "Freetown and World War II: Strategic Militarization, Accommodation, and Resistance." In *Africa and World War II*, edited by Judith Byfield, Carolyn A. Brown, Timothy Parsons, and Ahmad Alawad Sikainga, 183–99. New York: Cambridge University Press.

Jackson, Ashley. 1999. *Botswana 1939–1945. An African Country at War*. Oxford: Clarendon Press.

Jenkinson, Jacqueline. 2009. *Black 1919. Riots, Race and Resistance in Imperial Britain*. Liverpool: Liverpool University Press.

Jingoes, Stimela Jason. 1975. *A Chief is a Chief by the People: The Autobiography of Stimela Jason Jingoes*, recorded and compiled by John and Cassandra Perry. London: Oxford University Press.

Killingray, David. 1979. "The Idea of a British Imperial African Army." *Journal of African History* 20(3): 421–36.

Killingray, David. 1982. "The Colonial Army in the Gold Coast: Official Policy and Local Response, 1890–1947." PhD Diss., University of London.

Killingray, David. 1986. "Labour Mobilisation in British Colonial Africa for the War Effort, 1939–46." In *Africa and the Second World War*, edited by David Killingray and Richard Rathbone, 68–96. Basingstoke: Macmillan.

Killingray, David. 2010. *Fighting for Britain. African Soldiers in the Second World War*. Woodbridge: James Currey.

Killingray, David, 2014. "The War in Africa." In *The Oxford Illustrated History of the First World War*, edited by Hew Strachan, 92–102. Oxford: Oxford University Press.

Killingray, David, and James Matthews. 1979. "Beasts of Burden: British West Africa Carriers in the First World War". *Canadian Journal of African Studies* 13(1–2): 7–23.

Kirk-Greene, Anthony. 1980. "'Damnosa Hereditas": Ethnic Ranking and the Martial Race Imperative in Africa." *Ethnic and Racial Studies* 3(4): 393–414.

Kiyaga-Mulindwa, D. 1984. "Bechuanaland and the Second World War." *Journal of Imperial and Commonwealth History* 12(3): 33–53.

Klein, Martin. 1998. *Slavery and Colonial Rule in French West Africa*. Cambridge: Cambridge University Press.

Lamothe, Ronald. 2011. *Slaves of Fortune: Sudanese Soldiers in the River War 1896–1898*. Woodbridge: James Currey.

Leslie, J. A. K. 1965. *A Survey of Dar es Salaam*. London: Oxford University Press.

Lucas, Charles. 1925. *The Empire at War IV: Africa*. Oxford: The Clarendon Press.

Lugan, Bernard. 1976. "Causes et Effets de la Famine 'Rumanura' au Rwanda, 1916–18." *Canadian Journal of African Studies* 10(2): 347–56.

Lunn, Joe. 1999a. "'Les Races Guerriéres': Racial Preconceptions in the French Military about West African Soldiers in the First World War." *Journal of Contemporary History* 34(4): 517–36.

Lunn, Joe. 1999b. *Memoirs of the Maelstrom. A Sénégalais Oral History of the First World War*. Portsmouth, NH: Heinemann.

Mann, Gregory. 2006. *Native Sons. West African Veterans and France in the Twentieth Century*. Durham, NC: Duke University Press.

Marjomaa, Risto. 2003. "The Martial Spirit: Yao Soldiers in British Service in Nyasaland (Malawi), 1895–1939." *Journal of African History* 44(3): 413–32.

Migeod, F. W. H. 1926. *A View of Sierra Leone*. London: Kegan Paul.

Miles, William. 1994. *Hausaland Divided. Colonialism and Independence in Nigeria and Niger*. Ithaca, NY: Cornell University Press.

Mokopalgosi III, Brian. 1986. "The Impact of the Second World War: The Case of Kweneng in the Then Bechuanaland Protectorate, 1939–1950." In *Africa and the Second World War*, edited by David Killingray and Richard Rathbone, 160–80. Basingstoke: Macmillan.

Moyd, Michelle. 2014. *Violent Intermediaries. African Soldiers, Conquest, and Everyday Colonialism in German East Africa*. Athens: Ohio University Press.

Negash, Tekeste. 1982. *Italian Colonialism in Eritrea, 1882–1941: Policies, Praxis and Impact*. Uppsala: Almqvist & Wiksell International.

Osborne, Myles. 2014. *Ethnicity and Empire in Kenya. Loyalty and Martial Race among the Kamba, c.1800 to the Present*. Cambridge: Cambridge University Press.

Page, Melvin. 2000. *The Chiwaya War. Malawians and the First World War*. Boulder, CO: Westview Press.

Paice, Edward. 2007. *Tip & Run. The Untold Tragedy of the Great War in Africa*. London: Weidenfeld & Nicolson.

Parsons, Timothy. 1999. *The African Rank-and-File. Social Implications of Colonial Military Service in the King's African Rifles, 1902–1964*. Portsmouth, NH: Heinemann.

Pinto, Jeanette. 2008. "The African Native in Indiaspora." In *Uncovering the History of Africans in Asia*, edited by Shihan de Silva Jayasunya and Jean-Pierre Angenot, 139–54. Leiden: Brill.

Ranger, Terence. 1975. *Dance and Society in Eastern Africa 1890–1970. The Beni Ngoma*. London: Heinemann.

Saul, Mahir, and Patrick Royer. 2001. *West African Challenges to Empire: Culture and History in the Volta-Bani Anti-Colonial War*. Athens: University of Ohio Press.

Schapera, Isaac. 1947. *Migrant Labour and Tribal Life*. London: Oxford University Press.

Schmidt, Elizabeth. 2015. "Popular Resistance and Anticolonial Mobilization: The War Effort in French Guinea." In *Africa in World War II*, edited by Judith Byfield, Carolyn Brown, Timothy Parsons, and Ahmad Alawad Sikainga, 441–61. New York: Cambridge University Press.

Stadler, A. W. 1979. "Birds in a Cornfield: Squatter Movements in Johannesburg, 1944–1947." *Journal of Southern African Studies* 6(1): 93–123.

Stapleton, Timothy. 2019. "Martial Identities in Colonial Nigeria (c.1900–1960)." *Journal of African Military History* 3(1): 1–32.

Stovall, Tyler. 1993. "Color-Blind France? Colonial Workers During the First World War." *Race and Class* 35(2): 35–55.

Thompson, Gardner. 2003. *Governing Uganda. British Colonial Rule and Its Legacy*. Kampala: Fountain Press.

Van Galen Last, Dick, with Ralf Futselaar. 2015. *Black Shame. African Soldiers in Europe, 1914–1922*. London: Bloomsbury.

Van Kessel, Ineke. 2005. "West African Soldiers in the Dutch East Indies: From Donkos to Dutchmen." *Transactions of the Historical Society of Ghana* 9: 41–60.

Van Kessel, Ineke. 2012. "Labour Migration from the Gold Coast to the Dutch East Indies: Recruiting African Troops for the Dutch Colonial Army in the Age of Indentured Labour." In *Fractures and Reconnections: Civic Action and the Redefinition of African Political and Economic Spaces: Studies in Honour of Piet J.J. Konings*, edited by Jon Abbink, 61–85. Münster: LIT Verlag.

Vaughan, Megan. 1992. "Syphilis in Colonial East and Central Africa: The Social Construction of an Epidemic." In *Epidemics and Ideas. Essays on the Historical Perception of Pestilence*, edited by Terence O. Ranger and Paul Slack, 290–99. Cambridge: Cambridge University Press.

Vickery, Kenneth. 1989. "The Second World War Revival of Forced Labour in the Rhodesias." *International Journal of African Historical Studies* 22(3): 423–37.

West Africa. 1919. "A Reader of West Africa in East Africa.", 11 January.

White, Stanhope. 1966. *Dan Bana: The Memoirs of a Nigerian Official.* London: Cassell.

Willan, B. P. 1978. "The South African Native Labour Contingent, 1916–1918." *Journal of African History* 19(1): 61–86.

15

FROM INTEGRATION TO REPATRIATION. FLIGHT, DISPLACEMENT, AND EXPULSION IN POST-COLONIAL AFRICA

Ewout Frankema

1 Introduction

The majority of African countries shook off the chains of colonial oppression between 1951 and 1975. The end of colonial rule heralded a contentious era of nation-state building culminating in widespread armed conflict in the closing quarter of the 20th century. As earlier independence struggles in the Americas and Asia had shown, political disorder and violence arose easily in the power vacuums left by retreating imperial forces (Bates, Coatsworth, and Williamson 2007). Colonial rule had bequeathed Africa with more than 50 territorially compartmentalized polities, separated by a web of mostly arbitrary borders, uniting different peoples in a challenge to shape post-colonial societies, while splitting others apart. At the same time, colonial authorities had bolstered ethnic identities, amongst others through the granting of customary land rights, which incentivized local authorities to distinguish insiders from outsiders along ethnic lines and to discourage permanent settlement of ethnic others (Chanock 1991; Peters 2013).

The short breeze of Afro-euphoria that blew across the region in the early 1960s, stirred by visions of pan-African liberty and solidarity, vanished in the wake of mounting political tensions. Conflict broke out over the inheritance of the central institutions of the state, including control over the army, fiscal monopoly, state-owned land, and other economic monopolies. The ideals of democratic negotiation gave way to the praxis of single-party rule, reinstating the autocratic governance cultures of the colonial era (Nugent 2012; Young 2012). According to some scholars, large-scale organized violence was partly also rooted in the unfinished military revolution of the 19th century, which was only temporarily halted by colonial intervention (Reid 2012). In any case, former European metropoles meddled in African conflicts in attempts to preserve their political and economic interests, while Cold War politics guaranteed a steady supply of weapons, military training, ideological support, and financial aid to opposing factions, thus deepening and prolonging intra-African violence during the second half of the 20th Century (Reid 2009, Chapters 20 and 21).

According to Anthony (1991) there were at least three models of colonial state building that set the stage for the type of open violence that generated massive refugee flight. First,

DOI: 10.4324/9781003225027-21

there were forms of "radical separation" between regions in their access to power and resources. The north-south divisions in British-ruled Sudan and French-ruled Chad serve as key examples of such policies of regional inclusion and exclusion, ending up in long civil wars in the post-colonial era. Second, there was the creation of a governing class whose rule was backed up by the imperial power, but was destined to be contested when empire broke down. Key examples are the powers granted to the Tutsi minority in Ruanda-Urundi and the Baganda in Uganda. Third, while all forms of colonial rule were paternalistic in one way or another, there were important differences. The paternalist modes of colonial rule that were practiced in, for instance, Portuguese Africa and the Belgian Congo, focused on preserving so-called "traditional cultures," but stripped these cultures from their authoritarian structures and strongly discouraged social and political emancipation. Consequently, newly independent states came to be ruled by elites who assumed responsibilities of government for which they were ill-prepared.

The wave of violence and disorder that characterized post-colonial Africa constitutes the background for an exploration into the surge of forced migration that shaped a significant part of African mobility patterns from the 1960s unto the early 21st century. My central argument is that, historically, African societies had largely supported the *integration* of "aliens" into systems of domestic slavery to enhance agricultural labor supplies, accumulate wealth, strengthen military capacity, reproduce lineages, and bolster elite status. In colonial times, when slavery was outlawed, forced displacement remained primarily motivated by the desire to concentrate cheap labor in key sites of export production (Okia, Chapter 8, this volume). However, Africa's post-colonial nation-states increasingly turned to the *expulsion* of aliens, to the *deliberate displacement* of enemies within and across national borders, and to the *repatriation* of international refugees. This chapter attributes this shift from integration to repatriation, and the related changes in the attitude of receiving societies, to the long-run demographic transition that has profoundly altered the relative scarcity of rural and urban labor supplies, as well as the juncture in the meaning and legal status of territorial borders and related notions of *national* sovereignty, identity, and citizenship. I further argue that the long shift from absorbing to expelling "outsiders" is likely to continue during the 21st century, but that not all historical forms of *forced migration-cum-integration* have been eliminated. State-building activities of military sects such as Boko Haram or Joseph Kony's Lord's Resistance Army that seek to amass kindred spirits through murder, kidnapping, and brainwashing replicate integrative strategies that had been common in pre-colonial times (Austin, Chapter 2, this volume).

As noted in the introduction, there is no sharp dividing line between "forced" and "free," or "involuntary" and "voluntary" migration (De Haas and Frankema, Chapter 1, this volume). According to the International Organization for Migration (IOM), forced migration contains "an element of coercion [...], including threats to life and livelihood, whether arising from natural or man-made causes" (IOM 2011, 39). The narrow definition I adopt emphasizes three features: forced migration occurs when people experience an *overwhelming pressure* to move due to forces largely *beyond their control* (man-made or otherwise), paired to an *urgency* to leave nearly everything behind at once. This definition separates war refugees, expellees, exiles, as well as raided slaves and forced labor recruits, from migrants who swap the countryside for the city after more extensive deliberations, even though they may feel pressed to do so because of circumstances beyond their control (for a discussion of definitions: Betts 2013; Fiddian-Qasmiyeh et al. 2014).

Under colonial rule, the overwhelming majority of African "subjects" were denied formal citizenship rights (Mamdani 1996). Race, ethnicity, and religion were the principal dimensions of identity, determining people's tax obligations (in-labor, in-kind, or monetary), their access to local indigenous networks of power and land, and possible restrictions on their mobility (e.g., pass laws). In his *Making of the Modern Refugee*, Peter Gatrell (2013, 4–6) points out that refugees turned into a distinct legal category when national borders and citizenship redefined the distinction between "insiders" and "outsiders." Hence, with independence, race, ethnicity, and religion were complemented and partially superseded by notions of national identity that had gained prominence in the struggle against colonial domination. Citizenship rights were underpinned by the issuing of passports and the adoption of immigration acts, quota systems, residence permit systems, and visa entry regulations to control the inflow of foreigners (Peil 1971, 205–7; Adepoju 1995, 166; Flahaux and De Haas 2016). National identity became the basis for large-scale repatriation of refugees and expulsions of immigrants lacking valid residence permits. Exit restrictions targeted at individuals, groups, or even whole societies were adopted by many African countries as well (Lucas 2105, 1473–4). Even though African borders remained porous, they came to function as spatial demarcations between sovereign African nation-states, providing millions of people security after crossing one, while at the same time turning millions into "illegal" residents.

This juncture intertwined with a much more gradual and prolonged but irreversible transition in demographic geographies. In pre-colonial times, the relatively high *labor value* of slaves had been shaped by conditions of (seasonal) labor scarcity and land abundance (Austin 2008). Slaves were raided for export markets, to work on farms, on agricultural estates, and in mines, or to serve in armies, royal courts, or households (Miers and Kopytoff 1977; Lovejoy 2000; Stilwell 2014). To reduce the chance of flight, captives were taken far away from their homeland, crossing various cultural, ethno-linguistic, and political borders. In the colonial era, labor recruits were also forced to work in mines, on landed estates, or at construction sites, often traversing long distances and sometimes working under slave-like conditions (Okia 2012; van Waijenburg 2018; see also Ribeiro da Silva and Alexopoulou, Chapter 9, this volume). In settler colonies such as South Africa, the Rhodesia and Kenya, "native reserves" were established to control the mobility of Africans, involving large-scale displacement and containment, with the aim to commodify labor to fulfill the demand for cheap hands by the settler population (Mosley 1983; Feinstein 2005).

Thus, where forced migration in (pre-)colonial settings had mostly consisted of people being forced *toward* the loci of extraction (or contained for that purpose), the post-colonial era saw more and more people being forcibly *expelled from* territories. Forced displacement without deliberate spatial replacement happened to foreigners as well as resident populations. Demographic expansion shifted the relative proportions of land (and other environmental resources) to labor. The old rationale of relieving local labor shortages by bringing in migrants, by means of force, false propositions, or competitive wages was complemented and partly replaced by a new rationale to expel people in order to preserve resources and job opportunities for locals, original inhabitants, or "sons of the soil" (Boone 2017, 276–7). Large-scale repatriation of refugees as well as voluntary labor migrants started in the 1950s and intensified after independence. Of course, demographic pressures were unevenly distributed and labor demands were sensitive to world market swings, but this long-term transition in relative labor supplies occurred nearly everywhere in Africa. Especially when economic conditions and employment opportunities deteriorated, the colonial legacy of territorial sovereignty and the anti-colonial legacy of national identity helped to juxtapose "citizens" to "illegals." These threats of expulsion applied not only to African labor immigrants, but also to earlier generations of settlers of Asian and European descent, who held valuable assets (land, real estate) that could be stripped for political and economic gain.

The long-term shift from absorption to expulsion that we identify at the macro level of African migration history (De Haas and Frankema, Chapter 1, this volume) closely resonates with Robin Cohen's (2019) three-fold classification of African host society responses to "strangers" – not necessarily forced migrants. Cohen distinguishes between the "swallowing societies" which absorb migrants, the "parallel" or "alternating societies" as the intermediate form referring to oscillating migrant communities in ghettos, and the "vomiting out societies" which expel strangers. A person being kidnapped, traded, and integrated as a slave into a new host society, or a war refugee being repatriated back to his/her home country, falls on the far ends of this spectrum of absorption and expulsion. Intermediate patterns have occurred throughout African history, but they have arguably become more common with the post-colonial refugee crises: many refugees have ended up living in the twilight zone of parallel communities, in refugee camps or ghettos, where they were neither integrated nor repatriated. The adoption of these typologies in the remainder of this chapter is not intended to deny personal experiences of flight and displacement, but rather to highlight a long-term shift in the mental and political systems that have shaped these varied personal experiences.

2 Clusters of conflict and refugee mobility

During the 1940s and 1950s the world's major refugee crises occurred in Europe and Asia, not in Africa. In 1945, in the final stages of the Second World War, more than 10% of the European population, some 40 million people, were displaced. In addition, there were some 13 million ethnic Germans (*Volksdeutsche*) expelled from Eastern European countries and the Soviet Union and another 11 million displaced people working in Germany as forced laborers to support the Nazi war machine, of which about 700,000 people were confined in concentration camps (UNHCR 2000, 13; Orth 2009, 194). In the immediate aftermath of the war, a million people fled from the advancing Soviet army. The Japanese invasion of China and the ensuing Second Sino-Japanese war between 1937 and 1945 resulted in a death toll of 20 to 25 million, and an estimated 30 million displaced (Schoppa 2011). The artificial border that partitioned British India into an Islamic majority state (Pakistan) and a Hindu majority state (India) in 1947 initiated a two-way mass exodus by an estimated 17 million people, and resulted in a death toll of at least 1 million (Khan 2007; Bharadwaj and Ali Mirza 2019, 1). The Korean war of 1950–53 resulted in estimated 4 million military and civilian casualties and several millions of refugees and displaced persons (Cummings 2011, 35). Independence struggles in Indochina (1946–54) and Indonesia (1945–49) also led to mass displacement in response to famine, warfare, and territorial partition (Windrow 1998; Luttikhuis and Moses 2014).

These incomprehensible orders of magnitude had been uncommon in Africa, but in the 1960s the gravity center of humanitarian crises began to shift (Adepoju 1982; Nindi 1986). As shown in Figure 15.1, Africa's share in the registered global refugee population after 1960 hovered around 30% with a peak of 50% in the late 1970s, and was consistently higher than Africa's share in the world population (about 10–18%). The cracks in the bulwarks of

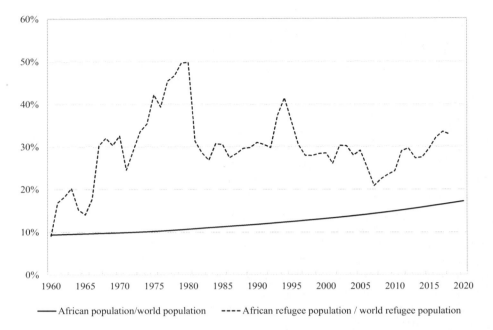

FIGURE 15.1 African refugees as a percentage share of the world total and relative to the African population as a share of the world total, 1960–2020.

Source: Refugee data from UNHCR, Population Statistics Database, accessed 29-03-2020; Population data from United Nations, World Population Prospects 2019, accessed 29-03-2020.

colonial order had become visible in the Algerian War of Independence (1954–62) and the violent repression of the *Mau Mau* rebellion in Kenya (1952–60). The mass exodus of Algerians and evacuation of *pieds-noirs* to France and Corsica following Algerian independence involved close to 1 million people (Eldridge 2016).[1] In the 1960s violence-induced refugee crises also emerged in Portuguese Africa, the Great Lakes area, the southern Congo, the Horn of Africa, Chad, and eastern Nigeria. By 1969, about two-thirds of the *United Nations High Commissioner for Refugees*' (UNHCR's) global program funds were directed to Africa (UNHCR 2000, 37).

Figure 15.2 shows the rise in the number of armed conflicts divided into interstate conflicts, intrastate conflicts, and independence wars.[2] The spread of economic crises in the 1970s, provoked by declining world market prices for primary export commodities, escalating debt positions, and inflationary pressures, further deepened social tensions. Structural adjustment programs prescribed severe austerity policies, which at least temporarily pushed more people into poverty. An increasing number of African countries got pulled into a vicious cycle of economic decline and political instability in the 1980s (Bates 2008, Nugent 2012). During the 1970s to 1990s more than 20 out of 50 African nations witnessed outflows or inflows of refugees exceeding 100,000 persons, while Ethiopia, Sudan, Somalia, the Democratic Republic of Congo (DRC), Uganda, Burundi, and Angola experienced such large flows in both directions.[3]

After 1995 the number of countries trapped in intrastate warfare declined, but this trend was soon reversed by the outbreak of the First and especially the Second Congo War. At its peak the *Great War* of Africa involved 9 countries and some 20 different armed groups,

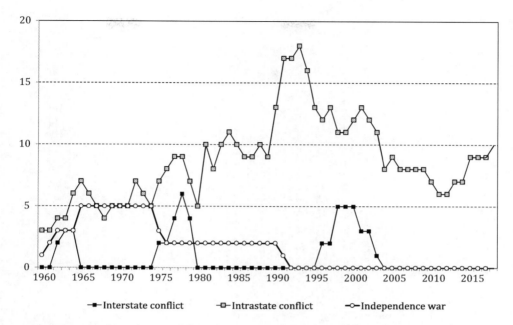

FIGURE 15.2 Number of countries involved in major armed conflicts in Africa, 1960–2018.
Source: Centre for Systemic Peace, Database of Major Episodes of Political Violence, 1946–2018, accessed 29-10-2019.

Note: Episodes of "conflict" are defined by the systematic and sustained use of lethal violence by organized groups that results in at least 500 directly related deaths over the course of the episode.

causing one of the biggest humanitarian crises in post-colonial Africa (Prunier 2009). Most of the war was fought within the DRC and led to an estimated death toll of 3 to 4 million people, often as a result of starvation, disease, and collapse of basic public health facilities. After the signing of a peace agreement in 2002 the intensity of warfare on the continent declined, even though peace was never fully restored in eastern Congo. This trend again reversed in 2012 with the deterioration of political and social relations in the African Sahel that drew an increasing number of countries into new spirals of violence.

Figure 15.3 shows the total number of refugees in Africa and the share of refugees in the total African population. These estimates include all persons with an *officially registered* refugee status in their host country, living in a designated refugee camp, or scattered across villages, towns, and cities in border areas, or further abroad. We are looking here at lower bound estimates since only officially registered refugees end up in the statistics. Comparable data on internally displaced persons (IDPs henceforth) is harder to obtain because of a larger proportion who are unregistered. In many conflicts, the number of IDPs tends to exceed the number of international refugees, especially in larger countries where violence is concentrated in specific areas while other areas remain unaffected.[4]

Figure 15.3 shows that the official number of refugees rose from about half a million in 1965 to 6.5 million at the peak of the Rwandan genocide in 1994, close to 1% of the continental population. Part of the rise in the 1960s has probably to be attributed to improved (international) record keeping, but most of it was caused by the rapid spread of armed

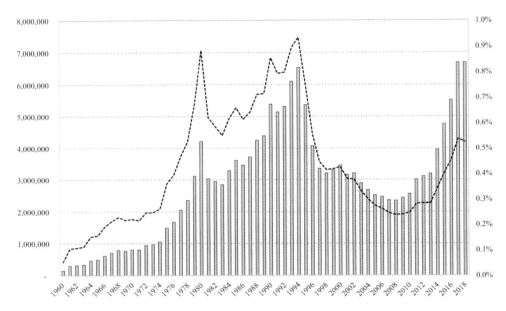

FIGURE 15.3 Total number of refugees in Africa (bars, left-hand Y-axis) and as a % share of Africa's population (line, right-hand Y-axis), 1960–2018.
Source: UNHCR, Population Statistics Database, accessed 29-03-2020.

conflict. The numbers then started to decline to around 3 million in 1998, and further down to 2.3 million in 2008. It appears as if the Great War of Africa (1998–2002) did not raise the number of registered refugees, but it should be kept in mind that the number of refugees caused by the civil wars in Angola, Mozambique, and Liberia were declining at the same time, thus compensating for the compounding effect of Congolese refugees. Moreover, the majority of people fleeing the violence ended up as IDPs within the DRC. After 2008, and especially the renewed outbreak of the Sudanese civil war in 2012, the numbers again rose dramatically.

In combination with Table 15.1, which lists the most disruptive wars in Africa in terms of total refugees and IDPs, Figure 15.4 shows the trends in mass flight from various African conflict hotbeds. Between 1960 and 2010 the Great Lakes area, the Horn of Africa, and Angola constituted the three largest spatial clusters of forced migration. In West Africa the civil wars in Liberia and Sierra Leone stand out. The Sudanese civil war, including the operations in Darfur and the secession of South Sudan and ensuing civil war, has led to a steep spike in the 2010s (also because the new border turned many IDPs into international refugees). At the time of writing, there were about 2 million IDPs in South Sudan and over 2 million South Sudanese refugees in Sudan, Ethiopia, and Uganda.[5] Compared to these eruptions of mass displacement, other parts of Western, Eastern, and Southern Africa have remained (far) more stable.

The clustering of violence-induced mobility is partly caused by historical genealogies of conflict. For instance, the Congo wars were in part provoked by refugees flowing into the DRC after the Rwandan genocide of 1994, and the slumbering threat of raids into Rwanda organized by Hutu extremists (*Interahamwe* militias) who were controlling the refugee camps in the eastern part of the Congo (Clark 2002). To exterminate these militias and to prevent new attacks, the Tutsi-dominated Rwandan army invaded eastern Congo with support from Ugandan and Burundian troops. These forces also supported the rebel groups under the command of Laurent-Desiré Kabila, who ousted Mobutu Sese Seko from power. Whereas the Great War of Africa is impossible to understand without the Rwandan genocide preceding it (Prunier 2009; Nugent 2012, 466–7), the Rwandan genocide of 1994, in turn, is impossible to understand without the way in which the colonial authorities molded ethnic divisions between *Hutu* and *Tutsi* to govern Ruanda-Urundi. This is just one of many examples of historical reproduction of violent conflict which has connected groups of migrants in time through a ramifying cycle of flight and return.

Other factors come into play as well. For instance, in the West African Sahel violence between *Hausa* farmers and *Fulani* herders is flaring up time and again. In this case distributional conflicts concerning scarce economic resources (e.g., land, water), religious dividing lines, fragile environmental conditions, and difficulties to establish a state monopoly on the use of violence are key ingredients of continuous conflict that stretch back to the jihads of the 18th and 19th centuries. In the Lake Chad area, the national borders between Niger, Nigeria, Chad, and Cameroon are used by terrorist groups to escape persecution, to pile up new resources, and to plan new activities (Lovejoy 2016; Oginni, Opoku and Alupo 2018).

Finally, we need to factor in the interference of external powers, including the former metropoles. External interventions do not explain the spatial clustering of conflict as such, but the decisions to intervene (openly or secretly) were often guided by specific economic and geo-political interests, such as the presence of strategic natural resources (e.g., uranium, coltan, oil) or strategic allies who held their bases in a specific region. The assassination of Patrice Lumumba in 1961, the first prime minister of independent Congo, was commissioned by leaders of the Katanga secessionist movement, who were openly backed by the Belgian government (Vanthemsche 2010, 94–8). South Africa's apartheid regime backed RENAMO in Mozambique and UNITA in Angola to oppose the dominance of the Marxist parties of FRELIMO and MPLA, who sought to establish a socialist one-party state (Nugent 2012, 286–95).[6] A very recent example is the meddling of Turkey, Russia, France, Italy, the United Arab Emirates, Egypt, Saudi Arabia, and the US in the Libyan civil war, supporting opposing factions in the struggle for control over the country and its exclusive economic zone in the Mediterranean Sea.[7]

As we can see in Table 15.1, the great majority of refugees moved to a neighbor country, often by foot, or on carts, bicycles, lorries, and buses. Consequently, island states such as Madagascar or Mauritius have comparatively little experience with hosting refugees. Despite being the focus of much media and scholarly attention (Abegunrin and Abidde 2021), the number of African refugees outside Africa has remained low compared to those accommodated by mainland African countries. Refugees who made it to Europe, the US, or a more distant African country (e.g., South Africa) were often part of small-scale refugee resettlement schemes or went into exile as political dissidents. The recent influx of young Eritrean men into Europe, fleeing from excessive state repression, is no exception. Compared to the millions of Eritrean refugees living in neighboring Sudan, Ethiopia, and Djibouti, Eritrean communities in Europe are tiny (Bariagaber 2006; Schmidt, Kimathi and Owiso 2019).

While the statistics shown in Figure 15.4 do no justice to the sheer variety of individual experiences of deprivation, anxiety, hunger, humiliation, structural dependence, and loss of loved ones, they do reveal that for many refugees the migration experience was a prolonged

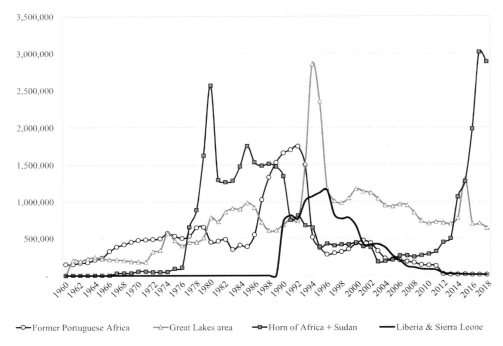

FIGURE 15.4 Number of refugees from major African sending areas, 1960–2018.
Source: UNHCR, Population Statistics Database, accessed 29-03-2020.

one. Fleeing a country is a matter of hours to a few days at most. Yet, returning to one's place of origin often involves years of waiting, false hopes, and shattered illusions. In many cases the full cycle of a major upsurge in refugee migration followed by stepwise repatriation took a decade at the very least, and a considerable share of refugee populations never returned home. Many also lost reason to aspire a return, as they built new livelihoods, forged new social relations, invested in immobile assets, or raised children who internalized the languages and customs of the host society.

3 Colonial borders and post-colonial realities

In pre-colonial times "foreign" territory was hardly a safehouse for people who tried to escape violence. As Gareth Austin (Chapter 2) points out in this book, crossing borders implied the risk of being enslaved by neighboring peoples. This risk was particularly high in the coastal zones of Western Africa during the 18th and 19th century (Whatley 2020). To escape raiding militia, the default option was to move into areas where one could physically hide and organize defenses (e.g., mountains, forests, lakes), rather than flee into no man's land, or cross into alien territory. In fact, living in the proximity of borders could already be dangerous. Islamic law offered protection to Muslims, who would not enslave their fellowmen, but such legal protection did not extend to the non-Muslim populations living at the fringes of the Islamic heartlands in West and East Africa. Religious dividing lines thus put additional pressure on people living in border areas that were within the reach of expanding Jihadist state armies (Lovejoy 2016).

TABLE 15.1 Numbers and shares of internally displaced persons (IDPs) and international refugees (RFGs) in major African wars, 1954-present

	Period	Peak year	IDPs	IDP/POP	Peak year	Refugees	RFG/POP	Main destination(s)
			000s	*%*		*000s*	*%*	
North Africa								
Algeria (independence war)	1954-62	1960	1,200	10.9	1960	260	2.4	Morocco/Tunisia
Former Portuguese Africa								
Angola (independence war)	1961-75	1976	350	4.8	1979	652	8.1	Congo-Kinshasa
Angola (civil war)	1975-2001	2002	4,300	24.5	2001	471	2.8	Congo-Kinshasa
Mozambique (civil war)	1976-92	1990	3,500	27.0	1992	1,445	10.5	Malawi
Great Lakes area								
Rwanda (civil war)	1959-62	1965	…	…	1964	166	5.2	Uganda/Tanzania/Burundi
Rwanda (civil war)	1990-94	1995	1,545	26.5	1994	2,258	38.0	DRC/Tanzania/Burundi
DRC (Second Congo war)	1998-2002	2003	3,200	6.2	2004	462	0.9	Tanzania/Congo Rep.
Uganda (civil war)	1980-86	1983	…	…	1983	315	2.3	Sudan/DRC/Rwanda
Horn of Africa								
Ethiopia/Eritrea (civil war)	1974-91	1984	1,650	4.0	1980	2,568	7.0	Somalia/Sudan
Somalia (civil war)	1980s-	2006	1,300	12.1	2012	1,137	8.9	Kenya
Sudan (civil war)	1983-2011	2011	2,423	5.4	2017	2,440	4.7	Chad/South Sudan
West Africa								
Nigeria (Biafra war)	1967-70	1969	3,500	6.7	1969	41	0.1	Equatorial Guinea
Sierra Leone (civil war)	1991-2002	2000	750	16.4	1999	490	11.0	Guinea
Liberia (First Liberian civil war)	1989-1996	1994	1,100	55.4	1994	798	40.2	Guinea/Côte d'Ivoire

Sources: Estimates of IDPs from Centre for Systemic Peace, *Database of Forcibly Displaced Populations, 1964-2008*, accessed . Data on refugees and main destination(s) from UNHCR Population Statistics http://popstats.unhcr.org/en/time_series; Population data from UN World Population Prospects 2020. IDP and refugee data Algeria from UNHCR (2000, 39-41); Refugee data Nigeria from CSP.

The conquest of African territories by European powers marked the beginning of the "slow death" of slavery in Africa (Miers and Roberts 1988; Lovejoy and Hogendorn 1993). Given the reluctance to disturb relations with local power-brokers and to undermine social order, the first attempts to suppress slavery were directed at raiding and trading, leaving ownership untouched. Yet, colonial occupation itself provided slaves with an opportunity to flee into areas where slavery was legally prohibited. Runaway slaves could appeal at courts against attempts of their masters to bring them back. In several parts of West Africa, such as the French Soudan and the defeated Sokoto Caliphate (mainly present-day Nigeria), the new political and legal realities set a mass exodus in motion involving hundreds of thousands of former slaves leaving their masters and returning to the villages from which they were once taken (Hogendorn and Lovejoy 1988, 395–400; Klein 1998). Many people never reached their homeland, as they got caught in the machineries of colonial state formation projects, ending up in colonial armies, in forced labor schemes, or being subjected to anti-vagrancy laws which restricted their mobility (Stilwell 2014, 192–8).

Colonial borders also played a role in the regulation of voluntary labor migration. Opportunities of wage employment motivated millions of Africans to cross borders to earn cash for tax obligations, to complement household incomes, to accumulate bridewealth or luxury goods, and also to escape forced labor obligations at home (De Haas 2019; De Haas and Travieso, Chapter 11, this volume). In most instances these forms of labor migration to mining or cash-crop areas was deliberately kept circular. Receiving societies controlled "foreign" immigrants through segregated living spaces and temporary labor contracts and by restricting access to land. Sending societies that experienced a drain of labor to adjacent areas often tried to prevent exit by closing borders, but such attempts were only successful when there were alternative propositions. For instance, the copper mines in Northern Rhodesia that opened up in the late 1920s diverted migrants away from the mines in Katanga (southeast of Belgian Congo), which in turn stimulated so-called "labor stabilization" policies to accommodate structural labor shortages (Juif and Frankema 2017; Juif, Chapter 10, this volume). Yet, border controls failed to stop the large recurring flows of labor migration from Ruanda-Urundi into Buganda, and from Côte d'Ivoire and Haute Volta to the Gold Coast's cocoa belt (De Haas and Travieso, Chapter 11, this volume).

At independence, these colonial borders rapidly assumed a new meaning. While the region had consisted of five major, albeit spatially unequal, empires (British, French, Portuguese, Belgian, and Italian) and most borders ran within unified imperial spaces, the region was ultimately carved up into more than 50 sovereign political entities. Hosting "foreigners" who fled from neighboring countries became an increasingly sensitive issue. For example, in the late 1950s, the British Bechuanaland Protectorate developed into a safe haven for political refugees from South Africa's apartheid regime. Nelson Mandela, alias David Motsamayi, used the opportunity to escape persecution using the Bechuanaland corridor, as did many others with him (Parsons 2008). When more and more guerrilla fighters began to use the country as an operating base, the government closed the border for a while, to relieve tensions with South Africa. The border re-opened again when the government of newly independent Botswana (1966) started to support the anti-apartheid movement more actively, using its status as an independent sovereign nation to protect opposition groups, and relying in turn on foreign (British) support to prevent a military invasion from South Africa. Rapid economic growth boosted Botswana's self-confidence and claims to nationhood. Botswana's reputation as a safe haven resulted in a large influx of refugees after the Soweto rising of 1976 (Parsons 2008, 17).

In virtually all of the long-drawn conflicts in post-colonial Africa, the cross-border presence of militarized groups was a complicating factor. The presence of militarized refugees complicated the reception of civil asylum-seekers as they raised the risk of being drawn into an international war. It did not help that new national borders often cut across existing social, economic, cultural, or ethno-linguistic spaces where movement "beyond the frontier" was the norm, not the exception. Many Rwandan refugees who went to Burundi did not cross a clearly distinguishable ethno-linguistic or cultural border. Refugees moving into Uganda were following in the footsteps of previous generations of migrants who had traveled up and down these routes for decades, as circular labor migrants seeking employment on the coffee and cotton plantations of Baganda farmers, or fleeing the *Rwakayihura* famine in 1928–29 and the *Ruzagayura* famine in 1943–44 (Newbury 2005, 258–60; De Haas 2019).

Yet, whereas militarized refugees were mostly men, the lion's share of the refugee flows consisted of women and children. While men stayed to fight, were imprisoned, or got killed, women and children bore the brunt of transposing their livelihoods from a known environment into one of permanent insecurity and heightened competition for resources. Whether they ended up in refugee camps just across the border or settled further away in rural or urban areas by themselves, or with relatives, their social position had to be renegotiated, their lives to be rebuild. Women and children were in a particularly vulnerable position. In their 1980 report, the UNHCR recognized this vulnerability, as well as the change in attitude toward refugees that I will discuss in the next section:

> Hospitality towards the traveller, the exile is a characteristic of African societies, a deeply rooted tradition which has allowed vast numbers of refugees in Africa to rebuild their lives among their former neighbours. Ideal as this solution may appear from a distance, experience has shown that it can hide patterns of severe hardship to both the host and refugee populations. Refugees who may be integrated with relative ease in areas where cultivable land is abundant are liable to find themselves condemned to the bottom of the social ladder in regions where resources are already stretched thin.
>
> *(UNHCR 1980, 17; quoted in Adepoju 1982, 26)*

4 From integration to repatriation

Refugee scholars have argued that policies focusing on integration appear to work better in areas where population densities are low enough to avoid competition over land, where new settlements alleviate local labor shortages and stimulate economic exchange, and where refugee settle among people with a shared ethno-linguistic background or a mutually acknowledged degree of cultural affinity (Porter et al. 2008, 232). Tanzania has long been the poster child of the integrationist ideal. The country has hosted some of the largest refugee populations since the 1970s, with peaks in the 1990s exceeding 600,000 refugees.[8] At the same time, Tanzania is one of the few African countries that has never produced substantial outflows of refugees. The 1966 *Refugee Act* underpinning Tanzania's famous "open door" policy included liberal granting of refugee status to groups, generous allocation of land, and large-scale offers of Tanzanian citizenship through naturalization (Kamanga 2005, 103). Asylum-seekers who entered in tidal waves from many neighboring countries including the DRC, Uganda, Rwanda, Burundi, and Mozambique benefited from this humanitarian approach of refugee crises, for which its architect, Julius Nyerere, received the *Nansen Refugee Award* in 1983.

342 Ewout Frankema

Tanzania's tolerant approach may be attributed to various factors. First, the vast land borders of the country were very difficult to control with the limited means the Tanzanian state had at its disposal. Second, the northwestern border region which experienced the largest refugee inflows from Rwanda and Burundi was a thinly populated area. Nyerere once remarked that "*I know you will get some people who will say, we don't have enough land in Tanzania, but that idea is absurd. The country is empty*" (Kamanga 2005, 103). Third, in the northwestern region there were clear ethno-linguistic connections between the refugees and local residents. Cultural affinity and cohesion among ethnic "cousins" dampened social tensions (Daley 1993; Kamanga 2005; Newbury 2005). Fourth, the socialist state ideology embraced by the Nyerere regime encapsulated visions of pan-African liberation, egalitarianism, and solidarity, which prescribed an open attitude toward "victims" as well as "freedom fighters." Fifth, Rwandan refugees were not posing an explicit security threat to the national government as the militarized Rwandan refugees in the Congo did (Whitaker 2003). Finally, sixth, even though hard to verify, the Tanzanian government, as well as international aid agencies, exploited their handling of the situation to raise publicity and attract external funds (Kamanga 2005, 102; Mogire 2011). The political recognition that the "open door" policy paid off in terms of additional aid and international goodwill may explain why Tanzania sustained this policy well into the 1990s.

The 1998 *Refugee Act*, which replaced the 1966 *Refugee Act*, strengthened the legal basis for the repatriation of refugees. The Tanzanian government began to expel refugees under threat of force, in similar ways as the Kenyan government tried to deport Somali refugees (Mogire 2011). The massive inflow of Rwandan refugees in 1994 compromised limited public resources and increasing competition for land and other natural resources created more tensions. Moreover, the long economic depression, in large part due to the failure of *Ujamaa* policies, had caused severe hardship in the countryside. The shift in migration policy in Tanzania may be seen as a response to several mechanisms that applied more widely to African host societies: persistent rural poverty, growing youth unemployment, and gradual closure of open land frontiers (Felleson 2003). The recent expansion of the *Nduta* and *Mtendeli* camps for Burundi refugees in Kigoma district, whose numbers grew from about 50,000 in May 2015 to over 250,000 by September 2017, has produced major grievances among Tanzanian farmers who had previously used the land for agricultural purposes (Felix Da Costa 2017, 31). Calls for border controls and repatriation were growing louder.

There are also examples where local perceptions of refugee problems differ significantly from the views held by the central government. Angolans who fled to northwest Zambia after the outbreak of the independence war in 1966 were long allowed to self-settle in the border area and lay claim to the land they occupied. Some of the villages in the Mwinilunga district held a majority population of Angolans, or children from Angolan parents. Local inhabitants had grown accustomed to these refugee settlements and did not experience major problems with newcomers. The efforts undertaken by the Zambian government to repatriate Angolan refugees in the late 1990s, in cooperation with the UNHCR, were largely motivated by politicians' desires to be recognized as "problem solvers" and could reckon with little support of locals (Bakewell 2000).

Yet, there were also many cases where local attitudes toward refugees hardened over time. For instance, the Liberian refugees who found shelter in the *Buduburam* camp in Ghana have been exposed to growing distrust and resentment as their expected temporary stay turned into permanent settlement. The camp, located in the Gomoa district some 35 kilometers west of Accra, was established in 1990 with assistance of the UNHCR to accommodate the influx of thousands of Liberian refugees who fled the first Liberian civil war (1989–96). The camp was situated in a poor rural environment. Attempts in the late 1990s to close the camp and repatriate the refugees to Liberia, after the war had ended, had little effect. During the second Liberian civil war (1999–2003) the camp expanded again. As humanitarian aid by the UNHCR was scaled down, camp-dwellers became more self-reliant and in interviews they emphasized their economic independence as a precondition for integration (Dick 2002; Porter et al. 2008). In 2007 the UNHCR joined the Ghanaian government in their call for voluntary repatriation, but the majority of the then approximately 40,000 inhabitants refused to leave. Other examples of refugee camps that have grown into quasi-self-sustaining cities are the *Dadaab* and *Kakuma* camps in northern Kenya. Because of their isolated location these camps developed even stronger features of ghettoization than *Buduburam* (Pérouse de Montclos and Kagwanja 2000; Jansen 2016).

Field interviews have revealed a variety of factors playing a role in refugees' preferences to stay, including their access to social networks and illicit employment opportunities, the depth of war trauma, their personal resources, and access to diaspora networks (Porter et al. 2008; Omata 2013). Among the Liberians in Ghana there were hopes that some camp-dwellers would be selected for resettlement in a third country, especially the US, where a number of refugees had Liberian relatives who supported them financially. Such third-country resettlement schemes also played a role in the Kenyan camps, where people have been observed to claim insecurity and negotiate vulnerability (Jansen 2008). Another oft-mentioned coping mechanism among the *Buduburam* refugees is investment in the education of their children, a mobile asset that can help to secure livelihoods in varying environments (Hardgrove 2019).

Over time, the growing concentration of Liberian refugees relative to the resident population raised the competition over scarce resources such as land, fuelwood, water, and waste disposal. The predominantly urban background of the *Budubaram* refugees led to growing distrust and feelings of alienation expressed by the resident farmer population. The Libero-American youth identity is characterized by "big dressing," lack of reverence for traditional authority (e.g., the elderly), and explicit social codes that were perceived by local Ghanaians as testimonies to violence, robbery, and general disrespect. The connections with relatives in the US and the financial assistance some Liberians received further compounded such perceptions (Porter et al. 2008, 243–5). Research has also shown that large-scale provisions of food and other goods to camp-dwellers incited envy in host communities, where people wonder why public welfare programs would prioritize "strangers" over impoverished, tax-paying citizens (Lawrie and van Damme 2003).

5 The age of mass expulsions

The broad historical shift from integration to repatriation of aliens not only applies to refugees, but also to the millions of "illegal" immigrants, who voluntarily migrated into host countries, to then be expelled under the threat of force. Between the late 1950s and early 2000s, a wave of mass expulsions occurred (Peil 1971; Adepoju 1995). While refugees entered into host countries under threat of violence, labor migrants moved largely on a voluntary basis, attracted by prospects of employment, commerce, forest resources, or land. However, once settled, refugees could count on the legal protection associated with their official refugee status, while the "illegal" immigrant had few alternatives but to go into hiding to prevent deportation.

At the eve of independence, virtually all African states held groups of labor immigrants within their borders, but some countries had been particularly attractive (see also Juif, Chapter 10; De Haas and Travieso, Chapter 11, this volume). Large flows of voluntary labor migration continued unabated in the early post-colonial era, although employment opportunities partly shifted from the cash-crop and mining areas, toward the expanding urban and industrial zones where all sorts of service sector activities (e.g., domestic services, commerce, transportation) relied on the availability of cheap labor. Without a valid residence or labor permit, these immigrants were formally "illegal" residents. In many cases the bureaucratic procedures to obtain a permit were so complicated, and strangled with red tape, that immigrants would not bother to apply, but this began to matter when media or politicians started to frame "illegality" as a social problem.

Table 15.2 presents a selection of some of the largest mass expulsions between 1950 and 2000. This table is by no means exhaustive and the estimates have large margins of error, but they do illustrate the sheer weight that mass expulsions have had in Africa's post-colonial migration history. The table draws on a survey by Sylvie Bredeloup (1995) of about 50 episodes of expulsions between 1954 and 1995 involving the expulsion of West Africans, and the list compiled by Aderanti Adepoju (1995) for all of sub-Saharan Africa. Some of these expulsions involved a few dozen people, but the largest instances, such as the Nigerian expulsion of immigrants from Ghana, Chad, and Niger (amongst others), involved an estimated 1.5 million people at once.

There were differences in the degree of force and the nature of the sanctions deployed to expel such large numbers of people. For example, when in 1955 the *Sierra Leone Selection Trust* (SLST) abandoned its smaller mining concessions, an estimated 200,000 prospectors from French West Africa poured into the country looking for opportunities of artisanal diamond mining. The event is remarkable because of the speed with which the retreat of SLST provoked large-scale migratory inflows from Guinée, the Soudan (Mali), Senegal,

TABLE 15.2 Selection of mass expulsions in Africa, 1950–2000

Country	Year	No. expelled	Main destinations
Sierra Leone	1956	50,000	AOF
Ghana	1969	500,000–1,000,000	Nigeria, Togo, Burkina Faso, Niger
Zambia	1971	150,000	Zimbabwe, Congo, Botswana, Tanzania
Uganda	1972	50,000	India, UK
Nigeria	1983	1,500,000	Ghana, Niger, Chad
Nigeria	1985	700,000	Ghana, Niger
Senegal, Mauritania	1989	360,000	Senegal, Mauritania
South Africa	1992–94	270,000	Mozambique, Zimbabwe, DRC, Nigeria
Gabon	1995	55,000	n.a.
Ethiopia	1998–2000	80,000	Eritrea

Sources: Estimates taken from Bredeloup (1995) and Adepoju (1995). For Uganda the data are from Mutibwa (1992, 67, 93); for Ethiopia from Human Rights Watch, *Human Rights Watch World Report 2001 - Africa Overview*, 7.

and Côte d'Ivoire. In 1956, the colonial government called upon the immigrants to leave the country voluntarily, without announcing sanctions in case of non-compliance. Ultimately, about a quarter of this group returned back home, possibly motivated by the realization that swelling numbers of competing miners made it increasingly unlikely to amass a fortune (Bredeloup 1995, 118). Yet, the great majority stayed in Sierra Leone. In many other cases, however, threat of force was used to deter immigrants and ensure their departure.

Mass expulsions were especially common in the wake of economic depression. The expulsions in Nigeria in 1983 and 1985 occurred right in the middle of one of the countries' most severe economic crises. During the 1970s, when oil prices went through the roof, the rapid accumulation of wealth and related growing consumer expenditures attracted many workers from neighboring West African countries who tried to tap into growing opportunities of urban commerce and to do the "dirty" low-paid jobs that Nigerians no longer wished to take up. Yet, by 1983, Nigerian GDP had shrunk to about 15% to 20% compared to 1980 (World Bank, 2014). The political response was to close the borders and expel foreigners to "preserve" jobs for Nigerian citizens. The government imposed an employment freeze and announced, on 18 January 1983, that all "illegal" residents were given two weeks to leave the country (Adepoju 1995, 168). A similar combination of rising economic nationalism in the context of economic depression had led to the mass expulsion of more than 0.5 million Nigerians, Burkinabé, and Togolese, amongst others, from Ghana in 1969. Ghana's economy had been stagnant for almost a decade in the 1960s, closing a long period of growth with tangible improvements in living standards from the 1900s onward (Frankema and van Waijenburg 2012). The Ghanaian government started to accuse immigrants of draining the Ghanaian economy, blaming part of the long depression on their presence (Adomako-Sarfoh 1974).

Whereas in West Africa immigrants were attracted to Nigeria, Ghana, Côte d'Ivoire, Senegal, as well the diamond fields in Sierra Leone and Guinée, and the oil-rich areas in Cameroon, Gabon, and Equatorial Guinea, the largest economic magnet in sub-Saharan Africa was (and is) South Africa. A series of expulsions in the early 1990s included immigrants from Zimbabwe and the Congo who had migrated back and forth for decades, and Mozambicans who had even moved back and forth for centuries (Harries 2014; Juif, Chapter 10, this volume). Unemployment rates in South Africa had increased to double digit figures in the 1980s as a result of long economic stagnation and international sanctions. According to national opinion surveys the intolerance against the approximate 2 million foreigners residing in South Africa around the turn of the millennium has escalated since 1994 (Crush 2000). The surveys reveal that abuse of migrants and refugees rose dramatically and that the idea of migrant rights was highly unpopular. Meanwhile, labor migrants kept entering in search for work. One of the key objectives of the *Immigration Act* of 2002 was "to ensure that the borders of the Republic do not remain porous and illegal immigration through them may be effectively detected, reduced and deterred."[9] Since then, the capacity of its network of detention centers that are used to detain illegal foreigners has expanded, and the issuing of residence permits has been made contingent on possession of occupational skills and knowledge deemed essential for the South African economy.

Asians and Europeans were expelled too. The best-known example is probably the forced departure of about 50,000 Asians – the majority from (British) India – from Uganda, ordered by Idi Amin in 1972. The expulsion of Asians was a clear example of aggressive identity politics, offering a "golden" opportunity to confiscate assets for redistribution among the political and military supporters of the Amin regime (Mutibwa 1992, 93). The position of Indians as commercial middlemen, many of whom had accumulated more wealth under colonial rule than the great majority of Africans, made them an easy target (Jamal 1976). Also, in "tolerant" Tanzania resentment against Indians surfaced, varying from open forms of discrimination (Indians depicted or referred to as "parasites" or "blood suckers" in government communication), to dispossession of real estate owned by Indians. According to Nyerere, one of the aims of the *Building Acquisition Act* of 1971 was "to prevent the emergence of a class of people who live and thrive by exploiting others" (Brennan 2012, 4). It was widely understood who he was referring to.

A final pattern are the two-way expulsions in the context of border wars and negotiated repatriations. Such a two-way exchange occurred in 1989, when the governments of Senegal and Mauritania agreed to repatriate, with foreign help, about 170,000 Mauritanians living in Senegal for 75,000 Senegalese in the middle of an explosive war (Parker 1991, 160). This border war had started with clashes between Fulani herders and Soninke farmers over grazing rights in parts of the degrading Senegal River basin, but it spiraled out of control when state-controlled military forces began to back up these groups and invade into foreign territory. This conflict illustrates how increasing scarcity of water-rich agricultural land led to an ethnic conflict, which in turn escalated into a full-fledged interstate war. Expulsions during the border war of Ethiopia and Eritrea in 1998–2000 provide another example. The Ethiopian government deported thousands of Eritrean residents as well as Ethiopians with Eritrean roots who were considered a security threat. Arrests were followed by detention, by stripping people of their Ethiopian identity papers and property rights, and finally by transportation to the border. The Eritreans, in turn, were accused of incarcerating and expelling Ethiopians, although evidence of the scale of these retaliations remains contested (Wilson 1999).

6 Gazing into the future

To date, in 2021, Africa still hosts a disproportionally large share of the world's refugee population, a situation that emerged in the 1960s, with clearly visible peaks in the 1970s, the mid-1990s, and, again, in the 2010s. The recent upsurge has to be attributed to the Sudanese crisis. In 2017–18 there were an estimated 6.7 million African refugees, of which about 2.2 million were from South Sudan alone. On a total estimate of 19.4 million cross-border migrants in Africa in 2017, refugees take up about one-third (34.5%).[10] Outside Africa, numbers of refugees have surged in the 2010s as well. In 2019, the UNHCR counted about 26 million refugees, 46 million IDPs, and 4.2 million asylum-seekers worldwide. The crises in Syria (6.6 million), Venezuela (3.6 million), Afghanistan (2.7 million), and Myanmar (1.1 million) have especially contributed to a global resurgence of forced displacement.

For the future, the historical analysis presented in this chapter offers several reasons for pessimism and a few sparks of hope. First, as argued above, there are a considerable number of conflict hotbeds that keep smoldering in times when the fire seems to have extinguished. Fragile states such as Somalia or South Sudan do not stabilize overnight. Large states such as the DRC, Ethiopia, Mali, and Nigeria continue to experience problems with regional destabilization. At the time of writing, a mass exodus occurred from Tigrayans in the northern regions of Ethiopia into Sudan to escape excessive violence, murder, rape, and man-made famine conditions in a renewed attempt by the incumbent Ethiopian government to eliminate the *Tigray People's Liberation Front* as a political force. State repression continues to provoke opposition that is not mediated via democratic participation and freedom of speech, but tends to come in eruptions of (violent) protest and counterreactions. Peace agreements may be signed, but these do not take away the memories, distrust, and resentment that are associated with the hardship experienced by so many Africans. The perpetual cycle of ingrained distrust and outbursts of violence are hard to break.

Second, natural resources including land, fuelwood, and water are becoming scarcer under pressure of continuous population growth and increased consumer demands. The African population has grown from about 220 million in 1950 to 1.3 billion in 2020, and the current population is expected to double to a predicted 2.5 billion in 2050 and may be set to grow to 4 billion in 2100, when its share in the world population approaches 35%–40% (UN 2019). It does not require much imagination to see that these demographic prospects will aggravate competition over natural resources within as well as between states. Resource scarcity and resource competition increase the likelihood of future wars, refugee flows, repatriations, and expulsions.

Third, the economic development trajectories of African countries will continue to diverge and converge, as they have done in various episodes of growth and contraction during the 20th century. When cross-country gaps in income levels grow, the incentives for labor migration rise. However, in times of crisis and rising unemployment rates, this can lead to mass expulsion of "illegal" labor immigrants. Politicians have used the presence of "strangers" to divert attention from their own failure to adequately address economic downturns, or worse, to expropriate assets in favor of their support bases. The drivers of this process of attraction and expulsion are likely to remain in place, spurred by ongoing expansion of new generations of un(der)employed youth.

What then are the sparks of hope? First of all, there are reasons to presume that, just as in the Asian and Latin American decolonization experiences, the culmination of violence and humanitarian crises witnessed in the closing quarter of the 20th century was a one-time phenomenon. The era of the "big men," single-party rule, and Cold War proxy wars has been slowly giving away to a rediscovery of popular voice, multipartyism, and a slow but steady widening of civil society. Even though elections can be manipulated and their outcomes can lead to violence, the record of peaceful transfers of power is expanding (Nugent 2012, Chapter 9).

Second, the power of social media is clearly manifesting itself, even though it is a mixed blessing. Social media supports terrorist groups in their recruitment of new members, contributes to the spread of hateful ideologies, and has also been effective in organizing violence. On the other hand, social media has proven to be a powerful tool to uncover acts of violence and state repression to the rest of the world, to extend popular and international engagement with those suffering from violence, and to organize peaceful resistance and civil action. It can serve as an additional check to the arbitrary use of state power as well as a warning device for crises in the early stage of unfolding: it broadens people's abilities to call for change.

Finally, there is a growing recognition that African countries need to cooperate, which is expressed in the recent establishment of a pan-African free trade zone, i.e., the *African Continental Free Trade Area* (AfCFTA). A free trade area does not mean the lifting of barriers to migration, let alone prevention of forced displacement, but it does force African governments to negotiate a joint approach to labor migration instead of ruling through ad hoc decrees. The negotiation of institutions guiding free trade can set an example to design more fine-grained regulations of labor permits, unrestricted intra-African traveling opportunities, and mutual funds to support the development of the private sector (e.g., via the African Development Bank). If such processes gain sufficient traction, the political stakes to promote stability will rise. Should these forces prevail in the decades to come, then it is possible to imagine a dwindling of forced migration, in an era where international labor migration reaches new heights.

Acknowledgment

I wish to thank Michiel de Haas, Felix Meier zu Selhausen, and Elise van Nederveen Meerkerk and the participants of the preparatory workshops in Wageningen (2018, 2020) and Barcelona (2019) for comments on earlier versions of this manuscript. I also gratefully acknowledge financial support from the Netherlands Organisation for Scientific Research for the project "South-South Divergence: Comparative Histories of Regional Integration in Southeast Asia and Sub-Saharan Africa since 1850" (NWO VICI Grant no. VI.C.201.062).

Notes

1 French repression forced tens of thousands of Algerians to seek refuge in Morocco and Tunisia. The *pieds-noirs,* also called *colons,* were settlers of French or European descent, most of whom were born in Algeria during French rule (1830–1962). The group consisted mainly of Catholics and Sephardic Jews and made up about 10% of the Algerian population in 1960.
2 These categories are often overlapping. For instance, Ethiopia's civil war transformed from an intrastate into an interstate conflict after the international recognition of Eritrean independence in 1993, which was, in turn, the result of an independence war.
3 Based on data from UNHCR *Population Statistics Database* and Centre for Systemic Peace *Forcibly Displaced Populations Database,* accessed 10-10-2020.
4 In recent years the registration of IDPs has improved, partly due to specialized agencies that are established to monitor instances of displacement worldwide. See UNHCR, *Population Statistics Database,* https://www.unhcr.org/data.html.
5 https://www.unhcr.org/south-sudan-emergency.html, accessed 01-07-2020.
6 RENAMO refers to Resistência Nacional Moçambicana; UNITA to União Nacional para a Independência Total de Angola; FRELIMO to Frente de Libertação de Moçambique; and MPLA to Movimento Popular de Libertação de Angola.
7 https://www.trtworld.com/magazine/libyan-war-where-key-international-players-stand-37488 (22-06-2020).
8 Estimate based on UNHCR, *Population Statistics Database,* accessed 29-03-2020.
9 Government Gazette Vol. 443, Cape Town 31 May 2002, No. 23478: Immigration Act, 2002, p. 2.
10 Estimates based on UNHCR, *Population Statistics Database,* accessed 29-03-2020.

References

Abegunrin, Olayiwola, and Sabella Ogbobode Abidde. 2021. *African Migrants and the Refugee Crisis.* Cham: Springer.

Adepoju, Aderanti. 1982. "The Dimension of the Refugee Problem in Africa." *African Affairs* 81(322): 21–35.

———. 1984. "Illegals and Expulsion in Africa: The Nigerian Experience." *The International Migration Review* 18(3): 426–36.

———. 1995. "The Politics of International Migration in Post-Colonial Africa." In *The Cambridge Survey of World Migration,* edited by Robin Cohen, 166–71. Cambridge: Cambridge University Press.

Adomako-Sarfoh, J. 1974. "The Effects of the Expulsion of Migrant Workers on Ghana's Economy with Particular Reference to the Cocoa Industry." In *Modern Migrations in West Africa*, edited by Samir Amin, 138–55. London: Oxford University Press.

Anthony, Constance. 1991. "Africa's Refugee Crisis: State Building in Historical Perspective." *The International Migration Review* 25(3): 574–91.

Austin, Gareth. 2008. "Resources, Techniques, and Strategies South of the Sahara: Revising the Factor Endowments Perspective on African Economic Development History." *Economic History Review* 61(3): 587–624.

Bakewell, Oliver. 2000. "Repatriation and Self-settled Refugees in Zambia: Bringing Solutions to the Wrong Problems." *Journal of Refugee Studies* 13(4): 356–73.

Bariagaber, Assefaw. 2006. *Conflict and the Refugee Experience: Flight, Exile, and Repatriation in the Horn of Africa*. Aldershot: Ashgate.

Bates, Robert. 2008. *When Things Fell Apart. State Failure in Late-Century Africa*. New York: Cambridge University Press.

Bates, Robert, John Coatsworth, and Jeffrey Williamson. 2007. "Lost Decades: Postindependence Performance in Latin America and Africa." *The Journal of Economic History* 67(4): 917–43.

Betts, Alexander. 2013. *Survival Migration. Failed Governance and the Crisis of Displacement*. New York: Cornell University Press.

Bharadwaj, Prashant, and Rinchan Ali Mirza. 2019. "Displacement and Development: Long Term Impacts of Population Transfer in India." *Explorations in Economic History* 73 (early online view).

Boone, Catherine. 2014. *Property and Political Order in Africa: Land Rights and the Structure of Politics*. New York: Cambridge University Press.

———. 2017. "Sons of the Soil Conflict in Africa: Institutional Determinants of Ethnic Conflict Over Land." *World Development* 96: 276–93.

Bredeloup, Sylvie. 1995. Tableau Synoptique: Expulsions des Ressortissants Ouest-Africains au Sein du Continent Africain (1954–1995). *Mondes en Developpement* 23(91): 117–21.

Centre for Systemic Peace. *Forcibly Displaced Populations, 1964–2008 (Database)*. https://www.systemicpeace.org/inscrdata.html

Centre for Systemic Peace. *Major Episodes of Political Violence, 1946–2018 (Database)*. https://www.systemicpeace.org/inscrdata.html

Chanock, Martin. 1991. "Paradigms, Policies and Property: A Review of the Customary Law of Land Tenure." In *Law in Colonial Africa*, edited by Kirstin Mann and Richard Roberts, 61–84. Portsmouth, NH: Heinemann.

Cohen, Robin. 2019. "Strangers and Migrants in the Making of African Societies: A Conceptual and Historical Review." *Fudan Journal of the Humanities and Social Sciences* 12(1): 45–59.

Crush, Jonathan. 2000. "The Dark Side of Democracy: Migration, Xenophobia and Human Rights in South Africa." *International Migration* 38(6): 103–33.

Cummings, Bruce. 2011. *The Korean War: A History*. New York: Modern Library.

Daley, Patricia. 1993. "From Kipande to the Kibali: The Incorporation of Refugees and Labour Migrants in Western Tanzania, 1900–1987." In *Geography and Refugees: Patterns and Processes of Change*, edited by Richard Black and Vaughan Robinson, 17–32. London: Belhaven Press.

De Haas, Michiel. 2019. "Moving Beyond Colonial Control? Economic Forces and Shifting Migration from Ruanda-Urundi to Buganda, 1920–1960." *Journal of African History* 60(3): 379–406.

Dick, Shelly. 2002. "Liberians in Ghana: Living without Humanitarian Assistance." *New Issues in Refugee Research Working Paper* No. 57. UNHCR Evaluation and Policy Analysis Unit.

Eldridge, Claire. 2016. *From Empire to Exile: History and Memory Within the Pied-Noir and Harki Communities, 1962–2012*. Manchester: Manchester University Press.

Feinstein, Charles. 2005. *An Economic History of South Africa. Conquest, Discrimination and Development*. Cambridge: Cambridge University Press.

Felix Da Costa, Diana. 2017. *You May Think He is Not a Human Being." Refugee and Host Community Relations in and around Nduta and Mtendeli Refugee Camps, Western Tanzania*. Danish Refugee Council Tanzania.

Felleson, Måns. 2003. *Prolonged Exile in Relative Isolation: Long-term Consequences of Contrasting Refugee Policies in Tanzania*. PhD Thesis, Uppsala University.

Fiddian-Qasmiyeh, Elena, Gil Loescher, Katy Long, and Nando Sigona. 2014. "Introduction." In *The Oxford Handbook of Refugee and Forced Migration Studies*, edited by Elena Fiddian-Qasmiyeh, Gil Loescher, Katy Long, and Nando Sigona, 1–19. Oxford: Oxford University Press.

Flahaux, Marie-Laurence, and Hein de Haas. 2016. "African Migration: Trends, Patterns, Drivers." *Comparative Migration Studies* 4(1): 1–25.

Frankema, Ewout, and Marlous van Waijenburg. 2012. "Structural Impediments to African Growth? New Evidence from Real Wages in British Africa, 1880–1965." *Journal of Economic History* 72(4): 895–926.

Gatrell, Peter. 2013. *The Making of the Modern Refugee*. Oxford: Oxford University Press.

Hardgrove, Abby. 2009. "Liberian Refugee Families in Ghana: The Implications of Family Demands and Capabilities for Return to Liberia." *Journal of Refugee Studies* 22(4): 483–501.

Harries, Patrick. 2014. "Slavery, Indenture and Migrant Labour: Maritime Immigration from Mozambique to the Cape, c. 1780–1880." *African Studies* 73(3): 323–40.

Hogendorn, Jan, and Paul Lovejoy. 1988. "The Reform of Slavery in Early Colonial Northern Nigeria." In *The End of Slavery in Africa*, edited by Suzanne Miers and Richard Roberts, 391–414. Madison: University of Wisconsin Press.

Human Rights Watch 2001. *Human Rights Watch World Report 2001. Africa Overview*. https://www.hrw.org/legacy/wr2k1/download.html

International Organization for Migration. 2011. *Glossary on International Migration* (2nd edn), edited by R. Perruchoud and J. Redpath-Cross. IOM: Geneva.

Jamal, Vali. 1976. "Asians in Uganda, 1880–1972: Inequality and Expulsion." *Economic History Review* 29(4): 602–16.

Jansen, Bram. 2008. "Between Vulnerability and Assertiveness: Negotiating Resettlement in Kakuma Refugee Camp, Kenya." *African Affairs* 107(429): 569–87.

———. 2016. "'Digging Aid': The Camp as an Option in East and the Horn of Africa." *Journal of Refugee Studies* 29(2): 149–65.

Juif, Dacil, and Ewout Frankema. 2018. "From Coercion to Compensation: Institutional Responses to Labour Scarcity in the Central African Copperbelt." *Journal of Institutional Economics* 14(2): 313–43.

Kamanga, Khoti. 2005. "The (Tanzania) Refugees Act of 1998: Some Legal and Policy Implications." *Journal of Refugee Studies* 18(1): 100–16.

Khan, Yasmin. 2007. *The Great Partition. The Making of India and Pakistan*. New Haven, CT; London: Yale University Press.

Klein, Martin. 1998. *Slavery and Colonial Rule in French West Africa*. Cambridge: Cambridge University Press.

Lawrie, Nicolette, and Wim van Damme. 2003. "The Importance of Refugee-Host Relations: Guinea 1990–2003." *The Lancet* 362(9383): 575.

Lovejoy, Paul. 2000. *Transformations in Slavery: A History of Slavery in Africa* (2nd edn) *African Studies*. Cambridge: Cambridge University Press.

———. 2005. *Slavery, Commerce and Production in the Sokoto Caliphate of West Africa*. Trenton, NJ: Africa World Press.

———. 2016. *Jihād in West Africa during the Age of Revolutions*. Athens: Ohio University

Luttikhuis, Bart, and A. Dirk Moses, eds. 2014. *Colonial Counterinsurgency and Mass Violence: The Dutch Empire in Indonesia*. London: Routledge.

Mamdani, Mahmood. 1996. *Citizen and Subject. Contemporary Africa and the Legacy of Late Colonialism*. Princeton, NJ: Princeton University Press.

Miers, Suzanne, and Igor Kopytoff, eds. 1977. *Slavery in Africa: Historical and Anthropological Perspectives*. Madison: University of Wisconsin Press.

Mogire, Edward. 2011. *Victims as Security Threats: Refugee Impact on Host State Security in Africa*. Aldershot: Ashgate.

Mosley, Paul. 1983. *The Settler Economies: Studies in the Economic History of Kenya and Southern Rhodesia, 1900–1963*. Cambridge: Cambridge University Press.

Mutibwa, Phares. 1992. *Uganda since Independence: A Story of Unfulfilled Hopes*. London: Hurst & Co.

Newbury, David. 2005. "Returning Refugees: Four Historical Patterns of 'Coming Home' to Rwanda." *Comparative Studies in Society and History* 47(2): 252–85.

Nindi, B. C. 1986. "Africa's Refugee Crisis in a Historical Perspective." *Transafrican Journal of History* 15: 96–107.

Nugent, Paul. 2012. *Africa since Independence* (2nd edn). New York: Palgrave Macmillan.

Oginni, Simon, Maxwell Opoku, and Beatrice Alupo. 2018. "Terrorism in the Lake Chad Region: Integration of Refugees and Internally Displaced Persons." *Journal of Borderlands Studies*, early online view, 1–17.

Okia, Opolot. 2012. *Communal Labor in Colonial Kenya. Legitimizing Coercion, 1912–1930*. New York: Palgrave Macmillan.

Omata, Naohiko. 2013. "Repatriation and Integration of Liberian Refugees from Ghana: The Importance of Personal Networks in the Country of Origin." *Journal of Refugee Studies* 26(2): 265–82.

Orth, Karin. 2009. "The Genesis and Structure of the National Socialist Concentration Camps." In *Early Camps, Youth Camps, and Concentration Camps and Subcamps under the SS-Business Administration Main Office (WVHA). Encyclopedia of Camps and Ghettos, 1933–1945*, edited by Geoffrey Megargee, 183–96. Bloomington: Indiana University Press.

Parker, Ron. 1991. "The Senegal-Mauritania Conflict of 1989: A Fragile Equilibrium." *The Journal of Modern African Studies* 29(1): 155–71.

Parsons, Neil. 2008. "The Pipeline: Botswana's Reception of Refugees, 1956–68." *Social Dynamics* 34(1): 17–32.

Peil, Margaret. 1971. "The Expulsion of West African Aliens." *The Journal of Modern African Studies* 9(2): 205–29.

Pérouse de Montclos, Marc-Antoine, and Peter Kagwanja. 2000. "Refugee Camps or Cities? The Socio-Economic Dynamics of the Dadaab and Kakuma Camps in Northern Kenya." *Journal of Refugee Studies* 13(2): 205–22.

Peters, Pauline E. 2013. "Conflicts over Land and Threats to Customary Tenure in Africa." *African Affairs* 112(449): 543–62.

Porter, Gina, Kate Hampshire, Peter Kyei, Michael Adjaloo, George Rapoo, and Kate Kilpatrick. 2008. "Linkages between Livelihood Opportunities and Refugee-Host Relations: Learning from the Experiences of Liberian Camp-Based Refugees in Ghana." *Journal of Refugee Studies* 21(2): 230–52.

Prunier, Gérard. 2009. *From Genocide to Continental War: The 'Congolese' Conflict and the Crisis of Contemporary Africa*. London: Hurst & Co.

Reid, Richard. 2009. *A History of Modern Africa: 1800 to the Present*. Malden MA: Wiley-Blackwell.

———. 2012. *Warfare in African History*. Cambridge: Cambridge University Press.

Schmidt, Johannes, Leah Kimathi, and Michael Owiso, eds. 2019. *Refugees and Forced Migration in the Horn and Eastern Africa*. Cham: Springer.

Schoppa, R. Keith. 2011. *In a Sea of Bitterness. Refugees During the Sino-Japanese War*. Boston, MA: Harvard University Press.

Stilwell, Sean. 2014. *Slavery and Slaving in African History*. New York: Cambridge University Press.

United Nations, Department of Economic and Social Affairs, Population Division. 2019. *World Population Prospects 2019*, Online Edition. Rev. 1. https://population.un.org/wpp/

UNHCR. *Population Statistics Database*. https://www.unhcr.org/data.html

———. 1980. *UNHCR: The Last Ten Years*. Geneva: UNHCR.

———. 2000. *The State of the World's Refugees 2000: Fifty Years of Humanitarian Action*. Geneva: UNHCR.

Vanthemsche, Guy. 2010. *Belgium and the Congo, 1885–1980*. Cambridge: Cambridge University Press.

Whatley, Warren. 2020. *Up the River: International Slave Trades and the Transformations of Slavery in Africa*. African Economic History Network Working Paper No. 51/2020.

Whitaker, Beth. 2003. Refugees and the Spread of Conflict: Contrasting Cases in Central Africa. *Journal of Asian and African Studies* 38(2–3): 211–31.

Wilson, Wendy. 1999. "The Deportation of 'Eritreans' from Ethiopia: Human Rights Violations Tolerated by the International Community." *North Carolina Journal of International Law and Commercial Regulation* 24(2): 451.

Windrow, Martin. 1998. *The French Indochina War, 1946–54*. London: Osprey Pub.

World Bank. 2014. *African Development Indicators 2014*. https://databank.worldbank.org/source/africa-development-indicators

Young, Crawford. 2012. *The Postcolonial State in Africa Fifty Years of Independence, 1960–2010*. Madison: University of Wisconsin Press.

PART SIX

The End of the Age of Intra-African Migration

16

COUNTING AND CATEGORIZING AFRICAN MIGRANTS, 1980–2020

Global, Continental, and National Perspectives

Patrick Manning

1 Introduction

This chapter addresses recent processes of African migration, at the scales of the continent, its regions, and its nations. To symbolize Africa's place in global demographic dynamics, I rely on the figure of 80 million lives that have been added to the population of the Earth each year from 1980 to 2000, the peak era of global population growth. By 2020, the annual increase in African population had reached almost 40% of the annual global increase. Similarly, Africa's annual level of urbanization reached 20 million per year by 2020. Also in the period 2010–14, an average of roughly 8 million international migrants per year crossed boundaries within their home continent or moved to other continents; the African portion of this total averaged 1.4 million migrants.[1] Other types of displacements, resulting from social conflict or environmental disaster, were of roughly similar magnitude. These African and global migration statistics resulted from advances since 1980 in the analysis by national governments and international organizations: they improved their breadth of coverage, their conceptualization of migration processes, and the precision of their estimates.

At the *continental* level, the chapter begins by comparing African rates of overseas migration from the 19th century to the present. The focus then turns to comparisons of Africa and other continents, 1980–2020. The data show how expanding African population and migration shifted patterns for Africa and the world. The analysis then reviews the changing conceptualization of types of migration. Based on this framework, continental-level migrations are summarized for urbanization, international economic migration (both flows and stocks), refugee flows, and environmental migration.

At the *regional* level, the various types of migration are explored for five standard regions of Africa (as defined by the United Nations (UN)), beginning with a summary of population by region, 1980–2020. The problems and advances in documentation are then explored for each category of migration. Based on these methods, quantitative details on the various types of migration show such results as the rapid rate of urbanization, the predominance of migration within Africa (but also the rise of a global African diaspora), and the regional variations in refugee flows and environmental migration.

DOI: 10.4324/9781003225027-23

356 Patrick Manning

The chapter then turns to the *national* level, highlighting the varied experience of six African nations on the issues of international migration, refugee populations, and migrant remittances. Newly available statistics on remittances by migrants to their home country pose important questions on African flows of wealth. Nigeria and South Africa, Africa's national powerhouses, have complex migratory histories. Burkina Faso continues to rely on migration of laborers to nearby countries, while Egypt's numerous migrants go overwhelmingly to the Arabian peninsula. Uganda and the Democratic Republic of Congo (DRC), nations of inherent wealth, have been restricted in growth by recurring refugee movements. In sum, these national studies confirm the growing importance of African migration and African population at a world scale.

2 Continental comparisons: populations and migrations

Over the past two centuries, the levels and directions of African migration have fluctuated greatly. From 1750 to 1850, an average of 100,000 African captives per year were delivered overseas (to the north, east, and west) from tropical Africa, which had a population of 100 million in 1800. This translates to a rate of 1.0 migrants per thousand population per year.[2] From 1900 to 1960, African overseas migration fell to near zero (with exceptions in war years, see Killingray, Chapter 14, this volume).[3] After the end of the global slave trade, most African migrants remained within the continent: most numerous were the migrants from Eastern Africa and Western Africa, who remained principally in their home region. With post-war decolonization, a global African diaspora gradually expanded: in the five-year period from 2010 to 2014, African overseas migration reached a new peak of about 700,000 migrants per year. With a continental population of 1.3 billion in 2015, this translates to a rate of 0.5 intercontinental migrants per thousand per year.[4] Thus, overseas outmigration *rates* were considerably higher during the peak of the historical slave trades than they are today. However, today's *total number* of overseas African migrants is much larger, as Africa's continental population has grown ten-fold. Further, since life expectancy in Africa in 1800 was just over 20 years rather than today's 60 years, the effective loss of population through overseas migration was even higher for 19th-century Africa than this comparison suggests (McKeown 2008; Manning 2014a; see also Bales 2004).

From 1980 to 2020, world population increased by 75% (Table 16.1). In that time, the African proportion of world population rose from 11% to 17%. To put this in perspective, African population was less than that of Europe in 1980 but had come close to double the population of Europe by 2020. Phrased differently, Africa's population had grown by 2020 to 30% of the population of Asia. Further, the landmass figures in the final column of Table 16.1 allow calculation of continental population *density* over time, indicating that Africa's population *density* had risen by 2020 to 45% that of Asia.[5]

The annual change in population size is shown by continent in Table 16.2.[6] The *World* category shows that global population has been increasing at just over 80 million persons per year since 1980. This is a valuable measuring rod for comparing the various categories of migration. For instance, between 1980–84 and 2015–19, Africa's share in global population growth rose from 16% to almost 40% of the global total. Further, the numerical growth of African population continues to rise, while absolute growth has been diminishing in other continents.

In addition to growth in total population, three great patterns in migration brought changes to African life after 1980. Rapid urbanization turned the African urban landscape

Counting and Categorizing African Migrants **357**

TABLE 16.1 Population by continent, 1980–2020, in millions, with continental landmass

	Population					Landmass in million km²
	1980	*1990*	*2000*	*2010*	*2020*	
Africa	480	635	818	1,049	1,353	30
Asia	2,642	3,221	3,730	4,194	4,623	45
Europe	694	722	727	737	743	10
Latin America	364	446	526	598	664	18
Northern America	254	280	313	343	369	24
Oceania	23	27	31	37	42	9
World total	4,458	5,330	6,145	6,958	7,795	150

Source: United Nations (2018); landmass from www.britannica.com.

TABLE 16.2 World population: average annual change by continent, within five-year periods, in millions of persons

	1980–84	*1990–94*	*2000–04*	*2010–14*	*2015–19*
Africa	15	18	22	29	32
Asia	55	54	47	45	41
Europe	1	1	0	0	0
Latin America and the Caribbean	8	8	7	7	6
Northern America	2	2	3	3	3
Oceania	0	0	0	0	0
World total	*81*	*84*	*79*	*85*	*83*

Source: United Nations (2018); Manning (2021a).

Note: For each five-year period, the average annual population change is the mean population for the period multiplied by the average annual population growth rate for the period (Manning 2021a).

from small capital cities and widely separated port towns into a continental network of massive urban centers linked by moderate- and small-sized cities (also see Meier zu Selhausen, Chapter 13, this volume). Intra-African international migration grew at a pace slower than total African population, while the global African diaspora, though smaller, grew at a faster pace than the total African population.

To express these general statements in specific numbers: Africa's total population rose from 480 million inhabitants in 1980 to 1,350 million in 2020, growing over those 40 years by an average 2.6% per year. Africa's urban population grew, at an average 3.9% per year, from 129 million in 1980 to 588 million in 2020; the continent had become 43% urban by 2020. Intra-African migration led to stocks of migrant population, within Africa, rising from 13 million in 1990 to 21 million in 2020. Overseas stocks of African migrants rose from 7 million in 1980 to 19 million in 2020. More than half of the continent's overseas migrants came from Northern Africa, but the increase took place in other African regions as well. The stocks of African refugee populations rose with fluctuations from 3 million in 1980 to 6 million in 2020. Over a short period of time, the annual flows of environmental migrants more than doubled from 2009 to 2019, from 1.1 to 2.6 million migrants.[7]

2.1 Conceptualizing migration: cross-community migration and its categories

Each of the categories of African migration fits within the common migratory characteristics of the general theory of "cross-community migration." In each case, individual migrants, especially young adults, move from a home community to another community in which the language and customs are different (Manning 2020, 7–14, 222–9; De Haas and Frankema, Chapter 1, this volume). Migrants in a land of destination, whatever their circumstances, must learn new ways of speaking and acting. They also convey ideas, learn ideas, and create ideas in exchange with those they meet. The migratory passage may be dangerous, relations may vary from cordial to hostile, and migrants may be dominant or subordinate. At the end of the trail, however, these exchanges can contribute substantially to human learning, bringing the essential benefit of cross-community migration in all its varieties.

Africa's five main varieties of cross-community migration consist of rural-urban migration, international economic migration, migration in response to conflict which occurs across (refugees) as well as within national borders (internally displaced persons, IDPs hereafter), and environmental migration. These forms of migration have been documented by a changing set of international organizations and African national governments. Population censuses were extended within Africa especially by the UN Population Division (founded 1946); the same office took major responsibility for documenting rural-urban migration in Africa. The International Organization for Migration (IOM, founded 1951) focused on international economic migration: it gradually extended its scope to Africa, in cooperation with the World Bank (founded 1944).

2.2 Migration to cities

For two centuries, urbanization has been the principal form of migration worldwide. Since 1800, urban populations grew especially in Europe, then in the Americas. By 2020, worldwide urban population was 2.5 times larger than in it had been in 1980 (Table 16.3). African urban populations in the same period had risen by a factor of 4.5, almost twice the global rate of change.[8] As of 2020, European, American, and Oceanic nations remained stable at 75% or 80% urban; Asian and African cities averaged 50% of national population but continued growing. African urban populations exceeded those of Europe and Latin America in 2020; they were nearly double the urban populations of Northern America.

TABLE 16.3 World urban population in millions, by continent

	1980	1990	2000	2010	2020
Africa	129	200	286	409	588
Asia	717	1,040	1,400	1,877	2,361
Europe	469	505	517	538	557
Latin America and the Caribbean	235	315	397	470	539
Northern America	188	211	247	277	305
Oceania	16	19	21	25	29
World total	*1,754*	*2,290*	*2,868*	*3,595*	*4,379*

Source: United Nations (2018).

Counting and Categorizing African Migrants **359**

TABLE 16.4 World urban population: average annual change by continent, within five-year periods, in millions of persons

	1980–84	1990–94	2000–04	2010–14	2015–19
Africa	7	9	11	17	20
Asia	31	36	47	49	49
Europe	4	2	2	2	2
Latin America and the Caribbean	8	8	7	7	7
Northern America	2	3	3	3	3
Oceania	0	0	0	0	0
World total	*52*	*58*	*70*	*78*	*80*

Source: United Nations (2018); Manning (2021b).

Note: For each five-year period, the average annual population change is the mean population for the period multiplied by the average annual population growth rate for the period (Manning 2021b).

Urban population can also be presented in terms of its annual change (Table 16.4). By 2010–14, the world's annual rise in urban population had reached 78 million – that is, the combination of migrants to cities and births to those already living in cities gave a total (less mortality) that was virtually equal to the annual global population increase (Table 16.2). For Africa, the annual increase in urban population rose from 7 million in 1980–84 to 20 million in 2015–19.[9]

2.3 International migration

International migration refers especially to people who cross a national border to seek immediate employment, seek training that will lead to employment, or accompany family members who are workers.[10] The two basic measures of international migration are the *migrant stock* of the foreign-born in each nation at a given moment and the *migrant flow*, the number of international migrants crossing a border within a given time period. When figures on migrant flows are available, they are usually most appropriate for analysis.

A review of international migrant stocks for 2015 reveals four main global patterns in international migration and the place of African migration in those patterns.[11] In 2015 the total stock of persons, worldwide, living outside their homeland was reported as 244 million, or 3.3% of world population (including refugees).[12] The *main* phenomenon in the origin of migrant stocks was migration from one country to another within the same continent. Asia, Europe, Africa, and Latin America, in that order, had large numbers of migrants who stayed on their home continent, totaling a migrant stock of 132 million in 2015 (including 16 million Africans). The *second* phenomenon was south-north migration, from Latin America, Asia, and Africa to Northern America and Europe. These migrants added up to a stock of 73 million in 2015 (including 9 million Africans in Europe and 2 million in Northern America).[13] The *third* phenomenon was migration from Europe to Northern America and Asia, for a total of 14 million migrants in 2015. The *fourth* phenomenon was migration from Africa to Asia: these migrants totaled a stock of 4 million in 2015, mostly from Northern Africa to West Asia.[14]

360 Patrick Manning

2.4 Refugees and IDPs

Post-colonial social conflicts generated large flows of African refugees. The *United Nations High Commission for Refugees* (UNHCR, founded in 1950, with periodic revisions to its charter) has the responsibility for the care of persons who, in response to social conflict, have crossed national boundaries.[15] Definitions are complex: refugees overlap on one side with international economic migrants (crossing borders) and on the other side with IDPs (displaced by conflict). On the first point, refugees and economic migrants may be accounted separately or together – there are reasons for each approach. On the second point, the distinctions among types of "involuntary migrants" are yet to be fully clarified. IDPs are currently defined as "conflict migrants" within national boundaries, yet they overlap with "disaster migrants" or environmental migrants. The Internal Displacement Monitoring Centre (IDMC, founded 2008) began to work in parallel with UNHCR and IOM, to focus on IDPs and especially on defining and accounting for environmental migrants.[16] As environmental disaster expands, the need for classifying and documenting it rises, and the problem deepens of combining it with IDPs who are escaping social conflict. Finally, the World Bank has documented remittances to and from African nations in growing detail since 1980. While there remain unresolved debates and uncollected data, these organizations have achieved an impressive advance in the conceptualization and documentation of African migration, as shown in the regional summaries in the remainder of this section.

For African refugees, Frankema's contribution to this volume (Chapter 15) shows the continental rise in refugees, 1960–95, followed by a decline until roughly 2005 and an increase thereafter. He notes that African refugees, small in number before 1980, ranged between 20% and 40% of the rising global total in the years since 1980. The dramatic increase in reported stocks of refugees reflected both an increase in the number of refugees, as national-level conflicts increased in intensity up to 1995, and an increase in the thoroughness of reporting. On the other hand, the decline in the reported number of refugees to a low point in 2005 indicates that the repatriation of refugees could be successful on a large scale.

Since 1970, Africans have been a large portion of refugee populations worldwide: that is, the largest refugee flows have come from Middle and Northeastern Africa and from the adjoining regions of Southwestern Asia and South Asia. IDPs are observed by the UNHCR but are cared for by national authorities. IDPs are the equivalent of border-crossing refugees who remain in their home country – Sudan Republic has been an example of a country with large numbers of IDPs in addition to the refugees who have fled the country. More commonly, while refugee populations may experience years of difficult exile, many of them are able to achieve resettlement in their home region. Under some circumstances, therefore, refugees might return to their homeland more rapidly than international migrants or might be settled in other countries. For this reason, the totals can be assembled only at an approximate level.

2.5 Environmental migrants

There is a need for careful assessment for the nature and level of environmental crises in Africa, both in the past and at present.[17] African experiences of severe drought in the middle and late 20th century suggest that the long-term cost of environmental crisis in Africa may have been underestimated.[18] On the one hand, the lack of systematic focus on past

TABLE 16.5 Estimated conflict and disaster migrants in Africa. Stocks, in thousands

Year	Conflict	Disaster
2009	2,166	1,121
2010	1,225	1,707
2011	2,418	603
2012	2,350	2,047
2013	3,736	1,599
2014	4,864	658
2015	2,415	1,151
2016	2,785	1,078
2017	5,504	2,559
2018	7,531	2,617

Source: IDMC, *Annual Report*, 2015–18.

environmental migration means that past experiences of such migration may have been a larger portion of migration overall than has been recognized.

On the other hand, the current acceleration of environmental degradation suggests that, for the future, environmental migration will be the second-largest stream of African migration, after urbanization. Because environmental migrants usually experience a safe evacuation and receive support from neighbors, they are better able to resettle than refugees. Yet the effects of global warming mean that environmental migrants will likely grow in number, and their growing numbers may lead to social conflict. As movements for environmental and climate reform gained strength, the specific needs and the numbers of environmental migrants gained more recognition. For the period 2008–18, the IDMC figures for environmental migrants in Africa average just under 1.5 million migrants per year, fluctuating and growing as shown in Table 16.5. In this view, Africa is unusual in that its high level of conflict displacements has exceeded environmental displacements. As is argued in IDMC reports, environmental displacements are taking place all over the world, rather than being regionally focused as are the social conflicts generating refugees.[19]

3 African population and migration, by region

In the period from 1980 to 2020, African populations grew at high rates: 2.1% per year for Northern Africa and Southern Africa and from 2.7% to 3.0% per year in Western, Eastern, and Middle Africa. The results of these high growth rates, compounded, yielded the growing decennial regional populations that are shown in Table 16.6. As a result, populations of Western, Eastern, and Middle Africa grew by a factor of 3 from 1980 to 2020, while the populations of Northern and Southern Africa grew by a factor of 2.2. This section explores five categories of migration for these regions: rural-urban migration, international migration within Africa, international migration overseas, refugee movements across national borders, and IDPs including environmental migrants.

When did Africa's rapid population growth begin? Sub-Saharan Africa had a long history of high mortality and slow growth from early modern times into the 20th century. But by

362 Patrick Manning

TABLE 16.6 African total population by region, in millions

Region	1980	1990	2000	2010	2020
Eastern Africa	148	199	261	347	457
Middle Africa	54	71	96	131	179
Northern Africa	108	141	172	204	246
Southern Africa	30	38	48	56	68
Western Africa	137	181	236	306	403
African total	*480*	*634*	*818*	*1,049*	*1,352*

Source: United Nations (2018).

1950 Africa had shifted, more rapidly than any other continent, to declining mortality and persistent high growth.[20] Northern African growth exceeded that of sub-Saharan Africa before 1950 but was slower thereafter; the cities of Northern and Southern Africa grew before those of sub-Saharan Africa and continue to benefit from greater public investment (Tabutin and Schoumacher 2005). Under colonial rule, overseas migration from sub-Saharan Africa was almost at a halt.

Migration patterns changed in the era of rapid population growth. Intra-African migration of free persons expanded in the early 20th century, especially in sub-Saharan Africa. The war years brought a great decline in Africa's commercial and industrial activity, though also an expansion in military migration. Intra-African migration recovered from the 1950s, with the main destination shifting from rural to urban (De Haas and Travieso; Meier zu Selhausen, Killingray, Chapters 11, 13, and 14, this volume). Numbers of refugees and IDPs were low throughout Africa before 1950 but grew with decolonization, especially in Middle and Northeastern Africa.

3.1 Problems and advances in documenting migration

The work of tabulating and estimating African population involves the collection of primary data, analyzing and integrating data to reveal broad patterns, and publication. Over the years, incremental improvements are beginning to add up. Collecting statistics worldwide according to common rubrics has developed only slowly: studies of international migration began with labor migration to wealthy countries, but then expanded. When complete censuses were not available, data were collected by surveys. For these reasons, as well as the intermittent frequency and often poor quality of migration data provided by national statistical offices, international migration is difficult to measure despite its importance.[21]

In a recent and important development, the level of *bilateral* analysis of African migratory has increased. This approach, developed much earlier for some data but only recently applied to African migrants and remittances, systematically traces inflows and outflows of migrants or funds among each pair of nations for each year. It requires that the data be comprehensive and recorded under uniform standards. A major recent application of this method was the 2019 dataset of bilateral stocks of international migration published by the UN Population Division.[22] While previous bilateral stock datasets had been published, this one was at a new level of rigor. One price of this rigor is that it included an effort to be comprehensive by including all refugee stocks in the analysis.[23] In another project of great importance, the team of Guy Abel developed derived estimates of five-year bilateral migrant

Counting and Categorizing African Migrants **363**

flows from migrant stock data.[24] The resulting migrant flows, shown in Table 16.12, may be compared with Tables 16.9 and 16.10, to show how stocks compare to flows of migrants. In a third such advance, the World Bank began collecting worldwide data on national-level remittances, but only succeeded in producing bilateral national remittance estimates beginning 2010.[25] Even these, as is shown in Tables 16.13–16.16, do not yet account for the many types and scales of remittances.

In addition to the search for better data, issues in demographic theory influence the understanding of African migration. For instance, there have been efforts to determine whether rapid African urban growth is to be attributed to high fertility in urban zones or to expanding migration from rural areas (Keyfitz and Philipov 1981; Jedwab, Christiaensen, and Gindelsky 2017; Meier zu Selhausen, Chapter 13, this volume). Recent interpretations have emphasized the primacy of internal urban growth. In my view, global comparisons make clear that the remarkable growth of Asian and especially African cities stems primarily from rural population growth and persistent migration to urban centers. Arguments that urban populations are responsible for all their own growth do recognize that adult migrants to cities originate from rural areas. But by classifying children of recent rural migrants as urban, they understate the role of rural population dynamics in urban and indeed national growth. An appropriate comparison of cities in different world regions would help to clarify this issue.

3.2 African urban agglomerations

By 2020, African urban populations – those in centers of over 20,000 persons – reached the point where most areas of the continent had become 50% urban. The exception was Eastern Africa, where urbanization was just reaching 30% in 2020 (Table 16.8). The cities of Northern and Southern Africa, each with substantial urban populations of European ancestry, had relatively high levels of public investment, as in public utilities and paved roads.

Cities of Western, Middle, and Eastern Africa, while they grew at even faster rates, had to rely on small-scale, private investment to build urban facilities. As examples of this regional difference, South Africa's urban rail system began in the 1890s, while Cairo's electric rail system opened in 1987. But Lagos, a city of 15 million, did not open its urban rail system until after 2020, a timing shared by other tropical African cities. Tables 16.7 and 16.8 present data that are consistent with average rates of growth in urban population of 2.7% per year in Northern and Southern Africa, and rates from 4.5% to 4.7% per year in Western, Eastern, and Middle Africa.

TABLE 16.7 African urban population by region, in millions

Region	1980	1990	2000	2010	2020
Eastern Africa	21	36	55	85	133
Middle Africa	15	24	38	59	91
Northern Africa	44	65	83	103	129
Southern Africa	15	21	28	35	44
Western Africa	33	54	81	127	192
African total	*129*	*200*	*286*	*409*	*588*

Source: United Nations (2018).

364 Patrick Manning

TABLE 16.8 Urban population as a percentage of total population, by African region, 1980–2020

Region	1980	1990	2000	2010	2020
Eastern Africa	14	18	21	25	29
Middle Africa	28	34	40	45	51
Northern Africa	41	46	48	51	52
Southern Africa	50	55	58	63	65
Western Africa	24	30	34	42	48
African total	*27*	*32*	*35*	*39*	*44*

Source: United Nations (2018).

3.3 Stocks and flows of international migration

Table 16.9 displays the number of foreign-born persons in Africa by the region of their birth. These large stocks of migrants were built up from much smaller flows of migrants each year. Eastern Africa and Western Africa persisted as the source of at least 75% of international migrant stocks within Africa. National-level details confirm that international migrants within Africa remained principally in the region of their birth.[26]

For migrants moving from one part of Africa to another, a total of 21 million migrants were living as "foreign-born" in African countries in 2015. Of that total, 18 million were born in Africa, 1 million were born in Asia, 1 million were born in Europe, and birthplaces are not recorded for another 2 million foreign-born persons in African countries. Flahaux and De Haas (2016, 9–11) constructed valuable maps comparing African rates of international outmigration to Africa and to overseas regions, 1960–2000, demonstrating that migrants moved primarily to African destinations. They also added an analysis of "visa restrictiveness," 1973–2013, showing that African nations overwhelmingly required visas for travel to African nations, though visa restrictions declined somewhat in Western Africa with the formation of Economic Community of West African States (ECOWAS) in the 1980s and in South Africa with democracy in the 1990s. Most African nations required visas for migrants from OECD countries, with the exception of Northern African nations and South Africa after 1994 (Flahaux and De Haas 2016, 18–21).

Table 16.10 shows the number of African-born migrants living outside of Africa, identified by their African region of birth. The stock of these overseas migrants rose from 7 million in 1980 to 19 million in 2020. For the year 2015, of the 17 million persons of African birth who lived outside the continent, roughly 9 million lived in Europe, 4 million lived in Asia, 2 million lived in Northern America, and 0.5 million lived in Oceania (mostly Australia).[27]

TABLE 16.9 International migrant stocks in Africa by region of African origin, in thousands

Region of origin	1990	1995	2000	2005	2010	2015	2019
Eastern Africa	6,723	6,491	4,636	4,290	4,886	6,609	8,532
Middle Africa	1,492	1,361	1,864	1,978	2,177	2,857	3,123
Northern Africa	560	720	790	1,004	857	1,426	1,515
Southern Africa	336	286	306	375	529	715	793
Western Africa	4,318	5,319	5,155	5,677	6,046	6,863	7,245
African total	*13,431*	*14,179*	*12,753*	*13,326*	*14,497*	*18,471*	*21,210*

Source: United Nations (2019).

TABLE 16.10 International migrant stocks overseas by region of African origin, in thousands

Region of origin	1990	1995	2000	2005	2010	2015	2019
Eastern Africa	1,061	1,243	1,444	1,913	2,555	3,520	4,002
Middle Africa	429	496	574	733	826	958	1,028
Northern Africa	4,726	5,132	5,651	7,001	8,398	9,639	10,342
Southern Africa	448	317	426	529	673	694	763
Western Africa	733	972	1,231	1,705	2,167	2,547	2,857
African total	*7,398*	*8,162*	*9,328*	*11,883*	*14,621*	*17,360*	*18,995*

Source: United Nations (2019).

Of these members of the global African diaspora, a clear majority moved from Northern Africa to work and settle in Europe and West Asia. Northern Africans were 63% of all overseas African migrants in 1990; that figure declined steadily to 54% in 2019.[28] Eastern Africa was the next highest region in overseas migrants, from 15% to 20% of the total. A growing number of Eastern African migrants settled in Asia, though at times these migrants have returned to Eastern Africa in large numbers. For Southern Africa the number of outmigrants has been small, except that relatively large numbers of white South Africans left to settle in Europe and Australia.[29]

Comparison of Tables 16.9 and 16.10 shows that African international migrants settling elsewhere in Africa exceeded the number settling overseas except for Northern Africa, where the overwhelming majority of outmigrants left Africa. In all other cases, overseas outmigration has grown at a higher rate than outmigration to Africa. This pattern of relative growth in overseas outmigration, if continued, will in time lead to overseas migration of Africans exceeding continental migration.

3.4 Refugees and IDPs

Unsettled political conditions in Central Africa and especially Northeastern Africa created recurring crowds of refugees after 1960; this portion of Africa is adjacent to Southwest and South Asia, which have similarly experienced large numbers of refugees.[30] The greatest African refugee crisis of the 1990s was the 1994 Rwandan genocide, in which a half million were slaughtered at once, resulting in waves of refugees moving back and forth to Uganda, Tanzania, Burundi, and the DRC for several years. Aftereffects of the Rwandan genocide lasted for at least a decade but, by 2005, refugee populations had declined to a low point. Table 16.11 provides the UNHCR summary for that year: it shows echoes of civil wars in the Great Lakes, Ethiopia, Sierra Leone, Liberia, and Angola.

The second great refugee crisis engulfed South Sudan: after its 2011 independence from Sudan Republic, civil war broke out in 2013 and continued until a peace agreement was reached in 2018. The UNHCR reported roughly 2 million refugees in surrounding nations and 2 million more IDPs, who were only slowly repatriated. As of 2018, the African stock of refugees had doubled from 2005, especially because of the crisis in South Sudan and the preceding crises in Darfur and elsewhere within Sudan Republic. Reports were of 1.5 million refugees in Central Africa and the Lakes, 4.3 million in Eastern Africa, 0.2 million in Southern Africa, and 0.3 million in Western Africa.[31]

366 Patrick Manning

TABLE 16.11 Stocks of migrant groups by African region, 2005, in thousands

Region	Refugees	Returned refugees	Asylum-seekers	Internally displaced
Central Africa – Great Lakes	1,087	119	99	12
East Africa and Horn	1,336	31	90	1,242
North Africa	101	13		
South Central Africa	228	54	31	
Southern Africa	1			
West Africa	409	78	55	279
African total	*3,162*	*295*	*265*	*1,533*

Source: UNHCR (2005, Table 2).

3.5 Environmental migrants

As noted earlier, the term "environmental migrants" is now used widely, replacing a term that treated these displaced persons as refugees. While the UN and national governments attempted to provide relief to the victims of earthquakes, floods, fires, tsunamis, and droughts, such assistance was ad hoc, so that neither administration nor record-keeping was formalized. In the 1990s, the UNHCR gave increasing attention to those displaced by various types of natural disaster. Migrants fleeing natural disaster were initially placed in the category of IDPs, since they remained mostly within national borders. They were later placed in the separate category now known as "environmental migrants."

Reports of the IDMC, 2008–18, identified over 500 African cases of environment displacement by nation, year, and number of persons affected, though without further details. Of the 30 cases that asserted displacement of over 100,000 persons, 11 were in Northeastern Africa (in Sudan, South Sudan, Ethiopia, Somalia, and Kenya); 6 were in Southeast Africa (in Mozambique, Madagascar, and Malawi); 8 were in the Lake Chad basin (Nigeria, Niger, and Chad); and 3 were in Middle Africa (Angola and the DRC).[32] Sadly, it appears that the African regions undergoing the most serious environmental crisis are closely related to the regions where refugees have also been most numerous. It seems clear that environmental migration, now understood to have characteristics that make it distinct from other types of migration, needs to be accounted for more systematically in the documentation of African migration.

4 National-level examples of international migration and remittances

Africa's more than 50 nations, cataloged by the UN into five regions, resist easy summary. However, since the contemporary world is organized into nations, this overview of recent African migration must address aspects of the national experience. I have chosen to focus on the connections among African nations, as seen through the levels of international migration, international remittances, and per-capita remittances. I have chosen one nation from each of the continent's five regions plus a second for the most populous region, Western Africa. The selected nations are Burkina Faso, Nigeria, the DRC, South Africa, Uganda, and Egypt.[33] In addition to their regional distribution, these nations reveal different patterns of interconnection.

4.1 International migration

The bilateral international flows of migrants for these nations, 1980–2014, are shown in Table 16.12 (Abel 2018). These migrant-flow data represent a major advance in the quality of estimates of international migration for these nations. For the whole period from 1980 to 2019, Table 16.12 makes clear the variance in migratory patterns: migration within Africa exceeded overseas migration for Burkina Faso, the DRC, and Uganda, while Egypt's overseas migration greatly exceeded its African migration. For Nigeria and South Africa, African and overseas migration were roughly equal, though with fluctuations for each country. Inmigration to Africa from overseas was tiny in almost every case – the exception was South Africa, with remarkably large numbers of overseas immigration, especially 2005–09. Nevertheless, it is likely that future estimates of bilateral flows will replace those in Table 16.12. For instance, while the underlying data on migrant stocks reported by Egypt and South Africa are the most complete and detailed of the six nations, those of other nations, especially the DRC, had gaps and inconsistencies. Updating of such datasets is a common practice.

The levels of African continental and overseas migration, while growing along with African population, are still relatively small on a global scale. For these six nations, the highest level of migration to Africa was an average of 2 per thousand (2 %oo) of national population each year for Burkina Faso; the highest level of overseas migration was an average 1 %oo per year for Egypt. For the six nations as a group, these ratios were 0.2 %oo for intra-African migration (below the rate of 0.5 %oo for the continent as a whole) and 0.5 %oo for overseas (same as the continental rate), respectively.

TABLE 16.12 Average annual flow of migrants, in thousands, by nation

	Burkina Faso				Nigeria				DRC			
	To Africa	From Africa	To overseas	From overseas	To Africa	From Africa	To overseas	From overseas	To Africa	From Africa	To overseas	From overseas
1990–94	53.0	21.6	0.4	1.7	19.5	7.9	8.8	0.3	13.5	248.4	0.0	5.1
1995–99	43.8	17.5	1.3	0.0	6.9	20.1	33.5	0.0	190.7	2.8	13.9	0.0
2000–04	44.7	24.1	4.4	–	16.1	17.4	34.5	0.0	51.3	11.8	8.5	0.0
2005–09	43.6	21.2	2.5	0.0	27.8	21.7	53.5	0.1	21.4	17.1	4.5	0.2
2010–14	34.5	12.1	2.6	–	22.4	31.3	69.1	0.0	31.7	17.3	6.4	1.6

	South Africa				Uganda				Egypt			
	To Africa	From Africa	To overseas	From overseas	To Africa	From Africa	To overseas	From overseas	To Africa	From Africa	To overseas	From overseas
1990–94	2.0	102.3	0.0	60.4	17.2	13.7	0.0	27.2	12.4	0.4	80.7	1.8
1995–99	1.9	55.7	26.1	3.8	19.1	17.7	9.0	0.9	1.7	1.6	42.9	1.8
2000–04	1.3	117.3	16.0	97.3	12.6	13.5	2.1	0.4	1.7	2.1	32.0	18.4
2005–09	1.8	137.3	25.8	143.3	36.9	17.4	8.1	0.7	0.8	1.3	59.8	3.6
2010–14	5.3	112.8	26.8	39.3	40.8	24.2	13.5	0.0	1.0	6.7	78.8	29.8

Source: Abel (2018).

Notes: Total flows of men and women, based on demographic and migrant stock data published by the UN in 2015, except for South Africa 2000–09, which is based on migration data from 2010 and demographic data from 2013. For further information and data caveats, see discussion in Abel (2018).

368 Patrick Manning

Inmigration from Africa was largest for South Africa, a pattern that clearly reflects the transition from apartheid to a democratic regime. After 2000 and especially after 2010, new economic opportunities in South Africa brought increasing inmigration, especially from neighboring nations. As shown in Table 16.12, South African inmigration was well over 100,000 per year after 2000. For Burkina Faso and Nigeria, inmigration averaged roughly 20,000 per year, while inmigration averaged closer to 15,000 per year for the DRC and Uganda. Refugee flows are clearly visible in the statistics. Annual flows of 248,000 migrants migrated to the DRC in 1990–94 (the era of the Rwandan genocide), followed by annual flows of 190,000 migrants leaving the DRC in 1995–99.

The case of Egypt reveals the general disconnection of Northern African nations from migratory interaction with other African nations – even with each other. The large numbers of Egyptian overseas emigrants – nearly 80,000 per year in 2010–14 – went predominantly to West Asia, especially to Saudi Arabia, though significant numbers also went to European and Northern American destinations. From Algeria and Morocco, the largest numbers of emigrants went to France and elsewhere in Europe. Other nations of large-scale overseas migration were Nigeria and South Africa. Nigeria's overseas emigration rose from 9,000 per year in 1990–94 to 69,000 per year in 2010–14, with most going to Europe and then to Northern America; these doubtless included many professionals. Table 16.12 shows that outmigration from South Africa averaged 24,000 per year, 1995–2014. The study of Cronjé (2006) indicates that this was principally the departure of white South Africans, who moved to Europe in numbers of 9,000 to 15,000 a year, to Australia in numbers from 2,000 to 10,000 per year, and in smaller numbers to Northern America. At a smaller but nonetheless significant scale, overseas emigration from both the DRC and Uganda fluctuated from 2,000 to 14,000 in each of the years from 1995 to 2014.

4.2 Remittance flows

For the same six countries, I turn now to the issue of remittances – incoming and outgoing, to Africa and overseas.[34] Since 1980, the levels of African remittance flows in all directions have increased; further, the thoroughness of recording remittances has also increased. Only within the past decade have the recorded levels of remittance flow become dependable for most countries. Table 16.13 combines two types of data to give a composite picture of the expansion of remittance flows for these six nations since 1980. It shows decennial estimates from 1980 to 2009 followed by three annual estimates since 2010. The main message of Table 16.13 is that international flow of remittances has expanded substantially in all African countries, though with sharply different national patterns. In almost every case, incoming remittances exceeded outgoing flows; only for South Africa were the two flows roughly balanced. Nigeria had the largest inflows, followed closely by Egypt and South Africa, while other nations were far behind.

Table 16.14 shows more complete annual levels of incoming and outgoing remittances for 2010, 2014, and 2018, distinguishing flows within Africa from those to and from overseas regions.[35] As the table confirms, flows of remittances for Burkina Faso and the DRC were limited almost entirely to Africa; Uganda's overseas remittances were near to its African remittances; and Egypt remains focused on earning overseas remittances. Egypt and Nigeria have received the largest remittances in Africa, but Burkina Faso, with its modest population, receives remittances that are almost as large on a per-capita basis.

Counting and Categorizing African Migrants 369

TABLE 16.13 Annual remittances in millions of US dollars by nation, 1980–2018.

Years	Burkina Faso		Nigeria		DRC	
(average)	To	From	To	From	To	From
1980–89	145	47	11	271		
1990–99	58	33	802	13		
2000–09	68	76	9,426	36	10	21
2010	139	279	39,815	310		
2014	120	293	20,872	521	23	62
2018	43	383	24,356	1,411	1,821	126
Years	South Africa		Uganda		Egypt	
(average)	To	From	To	From	To	From
1980–89	63	983			3,133	3
1990–99	161	755	23	23	4,041	154
2000–09	563	897	433	294	4,880	104
2010	1,120	676	769	234	12,453	194
2014	914	2,244	1,029	150	19,571	372
2018	928	413	1,231	573	25,516	464

Source: World Bank (2016) [1980 – 2009]; Table 16.14 [2010–2018].

Note: Empty cells indicate that no data are available.

TABLE 16.14 Annual remittances in millions of US dollars by nation, 2010–2018.

	Burkina Faso				Nigeria				DRC			
	From		To		From		To		From		To	
	Africa	Overseas	Africa	Overseas	Africa	Overseas	Africa	Overseas	Africa	Overseas	Africa	Overseas
2010	115	24	277	2	4,609	15,208	230	80				
2014	116	4	293		6,423	14,449	511	10	13	10	62	
2018	418	18	383		7,349	17,007	1,404	7	1,145	678	126	
	South Africa				Uganda				Egypt			
	From		To		From		To		From		To	
	Africa	Overseas	Africa	Overseas	Africa	Overseas	Africa	Overseas	Africa	Overseas	Africa	Overseas
2010	263	857	666	10	454	314	234		1,160	11,293	25	169
2014	98	815	975	1,269	512	517	119	31	300	19,271	36	336
2018	136	792	2.365	2,105	769	462	526	47	453	25,063	41	423

Source: World Bank, "Bilateral Remittance Matrix," reports for 2010–18.

Note: The columns in Table 16.14 correspond to the columns in Table 16.13, though the data and labels are more detailed in the latter. Thus, for the case of Egypt, the "To" column in Table 16.13 corresponds to the two columns under the "From Africa/Overseas" label.

4.3 Remittances per migrant

Tables 16.15 and 16.16 provide initial estimates of remittances per migrant for each of the six nations during the decade of the 2010s. Remittances per migrant, shown in columns 2 and 4, are calculated as average remittances, 2010–18 (from Table 16.14), divided by the stock of migrant remitters (from columns 1 and 3). As a reminder: remittances move in a direction opposite to the migrants sending the funds. Migrant stock – the number of persons in any nation from each other nation at a given moment – is taken as the best available estimate of migrants sending remittances home. This figure, however, yields a high estimate of the number of migrant workers able to send remittances, because it includes non-working children and retirees. The chief alternative figure, the flow of migrants in any single year, will give far too low an estimate, since migrants are away for indeterminate times, commonly spending several years away at work before returning home. Two further factors complicate the effort to calculate a ratio of remittances per migrant. First, there are cases where high estimates of remittance per migrant clearly reflected financial transactions, unrelated to wage work by migrant laborers. At the other extreme, for refugees counted among migrants, their remittances were tiny at best, as they were rarely able to get regular employment. Tables 16.15 and 16.16 thus reflect preliminary but instructive estimates of remittances per African migrant.

In Table 16.15, for migrants and their remittances within Africa, the estimated annual remittance of $146 for 1.5 million migrants, sent home to Burkina Faso, seems surprisingly low. At the opposite extreme, the per-migrant remittances to Egypt, Nigeria, and Uganda (column 2) are surprisingly high. Meanwhile, the figures in column 4 give relatively consistent indications of out-remittances from all six nations (though, as noted, these are low estimates).

Table 16.16 shows overseas remittances, with most payments incoming to Africa (column 2) but some funds leaving Africa (column 4). Comparison of column 2 in Tables 16.15 and 16.16 – the incoming per-migrant remittances to the six nations from Africa and overseas – yields both expected and unexpected results. For Burkina Faso, the DRC, and Nigeria, the per-migrant remittances received from overseas were two or three times higher than remittances from Africa. This may be called an expected result in that wage levels are generally lower for Africa than for overseas. But for the other three countries – Egypt, South Africa, and Uganda – the per-migrant remittances received from overseas were smaller than remittances from Africa.

4.4 The range of national-level migration patterns

The six nations discussed in this section were chosen more for the differences among them than for their similarities. They provide examples of variance within Africa but do not provide a representative set of cases. Further, the discussion has focused primarily on international migration and on remittances from Africa and overseas, rather than on other aspects of migration. We do gain a sense of typical levels of the annual flow of international migration among African countries. Thus, it appears that nations sending large numbers of international migrants to Africa were led by Burkina Faso, followed by Uganda, the DRC, and Nigeria. Nations receiving substantial flows of entering international migrants from Africa were led by South Africa, with Nigeria, Burkina Faso, and others far behind. Only

Counting and Categorizing African Migrants **371**

TABLE 16.15 African migration stocks and average remittances, 2010–18

Nation	Outmigration to Africa		Inmigration from Africa	
	(1) Stock of outmigrants, in thousands	*(2)* Annual flow of in-remittances per African outmigrant, USD	*(3)* Stock of in-migrants, in thousands	*(4)* Annual flow of out-remittances per overseas in-migrant, USD
Burkina Faso	1,482	$146	653	$487
DRC	1,225	$473	716	$131
Egypt	51	$12,415	91	$375
Nigeria	521	$11,764	1,031	$694
South Africa	89	$1,865	1,969	$347
Uganda	586	$12,415	1,014	$296

Source: Migrant stocks from international migration reports; remittances from Table 14.

TABLE 16.16 Overseas migration stocks and average remittances, 2010–18

Nation	Outmigration to overseas		Inmigration from overseas	
	(1) Stock of outmigrants, in thousands	*(2)* Annual flow of in-remittances per African outmigrant, USD	*(3)* Stock of in-migrants, in thousands	*(4)* Annual flow of out-remittances per overseas in-migrant, USD
Burkina Faso	29	535		
DRC	271	1,266	282	1,096
Egypt	3,064	6,051		
Nigeria	706	22,018	600	12
South Africa	686	1,197	9	3,578
Uganda	137	3,142		

Source: Migrant stocks from International migration reports; remittances from Table 16.14.

South Africa had more in-migrants than outmigrants; for the other five nations studied, outmigrants were the largest proportion, especially for Egypt.

Data on remittances, despite their limitations, reveal some clear patterns. For all six countries, incoming and outgoing remittances rose steadily from 1980 to 2020. For overseas flows, in-remittances to Africa were always higher than out-remittances from Africa, except for South Africa. For Burkina Faso, the DRC, and Uganda after 2010, in-remittances from African countries were greater than from overseas. In contrast, for Nigeria, South Africa, and Egypt, overseas in-remittances were larger than those from Africa. While these national-level conclusions are still preliminary, they show that statistical comparison of African nations can now go beyond population totals and foreign trade to give details on international migration and remittances.

5 Conclusion

The purpose of this chapter has been to set African migration comprehensively in global, African regional, and comparative national contexts. The recurring figure of 80 million more humans each year provides a standard for describing Africa's growing prominence in the world population. For instance, the African portion of that total growth rose from 15 million per year in 1980 to 32 million per year in 2020. African urban population growth worldwide reached 20 million per year by 2020. Annual global international migration was at a flow of 8 million migrants in 2010–14.[36] The African portion of this figure, including both African and overseas migration, was roughly 1.4 million; the overseas portion of African migration flows has caught up with and seems poised to exceed continental migration in the coming decade. Numbers for involuntary migration worldwide, while not yet precise, equal or exceed international migration. In Middle and Eastern Africa, refugees outnumber environmental migrants; in most of the rest of the world, environmental migrants are more numerous. For each dimension of migration, the African experience must now be seen as significant at a global level.

The two outstanding factors in Africa' population and migration since 1980 are the growth in national populations at rates well over 2% per year and the urban growth at nearly 4% per year. Africa already has some 50 cities with over 1 million in population – more than for Europe, Latin America, or Northern America. The third key factor is the great variation in African national migration patterns – in international migration, for various categories of refugees, and environmental migrants. Nor can the continent be summarized through one or two iconic cases: Nigeria and South Africa are the great powers of Africa, yet between them they hold only 20% of the continent's population and just over 30% of its GDP. African migratory analysis, nation by nation, will remain an essential element of the continent's social statistics. As research continues, one may hope for national-level statistics that provide a comprehensive picture of African migratory change at the national level.

Regional patterns are already emerging. Migration data give the impression that ECOWAS, the West African economic union, has made progress in integrating the national economies of Western Africa through migratory exchange. South Africa, historically strong as a regional economy, yet with a long and difficult apartheid era, appears to be making a transition into somewhat more open relations with nations throughout the continent. Eastern, Northern, and Middle Africa each appear to have faced substantial weaknesses as seen through migration patterns. The nations of Eastern Africa might be expected to be developing economic, cultural, and migratory ties within the region, but in these data only the migratory flows are evident. In Northern Africa, with its relatively high levels of health and income, reliance on overseas migration and remittances is at a high level. In sum, all three of Africa's key demographic factors – population growth, urbanization, and the complexity of migration – make Africa different from the rest of the world in population and migration. Yet precisely because African nations are becoming so populous, the varying national experiences must be followed closely.

Acknowledgment

The author greatly appreciates editors Michiel de Haas and Ewout Frankema for their thorough and insightful commentary on earlier versions of this chapter.

Notes

1 Flow data from Abel (2018), based on UN migrant stocks data.
2 Manning (2014a). For an archival collection on African population, overseas and continental enslavement, 1650–1950, see Patrick Manning, compiler, *African Population and Migration Dataverse*, https://dataverse.harvard.edu/dataverse/WH_AfricanPopMigration.
3 During the "age of mass migration" (1840 to 1940) European outmigration averaged 500,000 emigrants per year. With a population of 400 million (including Russia), this implies a rate of 0.8 migrants per 1,000 population per year (McKeown 2008, 55–6).
4 Flow data from Abel (2018), based on UN migrant stocks data.
5 For further details on regional population density in Africa, see Manning (2014b, 67–73).
6 For each five-year period, the average annual population change is the mean population for the period multiplied by the average annual population growth rate for the period.
7 International Displacement Monitoring Centre (IDMC), *Global Report on International Displacement, 2020,* 16.
8 Compare Table 16.3 to Table 16.1 to find the levels of urbanization by continent.
9 For discussion of African urbanization since 1950, see Meier zu Selhausen (Chapter 13, this volume).
10 This category is diverse in that it involves those seeking work at the level of basic skills (perhaps for temporary or seasonal work) but also for long-term settlement; the same category includes long-term settlement by skilled professionals and short-term visits by consultants.
11 These results come from tracing migrant stocks from continent to continent (as cited in IOM reports) and ranking them from the largest to the smallest.
12 This proportion is roughly double that of the earlier peak of international migration in the era from 1910 to 1930, as reported in McKeown (2008, 55–6). For the DEMIG databases, which have launched comparisons on international migration flows to the 19th century, see Vezzoli, Villares-Varela, and de Haas (2014).
13 This continental overview of international migration reinforces the conclusions of Flahaux and De Haas (2016, 2), who contradicted widespread but undocumented notions that African migration was a "South–north 'exodus' driven by poverty and income gaps," through their demonstration that migration to African nations exceeded overseas migration. See also Abel and Sander (2014).
14 Beyond these four main migratory phenomena were numerous other groups of foreign-born with less than 3 million in each continental pairing: to Oceania and from Oceania; from Northern America; and to Africa.
15 Compare, for instance, the categories of migration reported in the UNHCR *Global Trends* reports for 1990 and 2010; also see Frankema (Chapter 15, this volume). An administratively separate category of refugees is that of the Palestinian refugees ejected from their homes as Israel formed in 1948, who receive care from a separate UN organization, the United Nations Relief and Works Agency (UNRWA). In this and some other cases, refugee status has lasted even for generations.
16 Internal Displacement Monitoring Centre, *Annual Report, 2008,* 7. The IDMC has offices in Geneva but is supported especially by Norwegian funding. See Brown (2008); IOM (2016); Borderon et al. (2019).
17 De Haas and Frankema classify environmental crises as an episodic, proximate driver rather than a macro-historical driver of migration (De Haas and Frankema, Chapter 1, this volume). In contrast to the fluctuations of the past, however, there is substantial evidence that the world is now undergoing a historic expansion in environmental crises.
18 On the West African drought of the 1960s and its antecedents, see Lovejoy and Baier (1975). On more recent patterns, see Bassett and Turner (2007).
19 Combining reports of the IDMC, UNHCR, and IOM for 2015, the worldwide flows of economic migrants, international conflict refugees, and domestic conflict refugees were roughly equal – about 8 million migrants per year in each category. For 2016–18, the IDMC has estimated global domestic conflict refugees at roughly 10 million per year and domestic migrants from disasters (environmental) at roughly 20 million per year. IDMC, *Annual Report*, 2015–18; UNHCR, *Global Trends*, 2015; IOM, *Migration Portal Data*, 2015.
20 The exact pace of this transformation has yet to be established empirically. For contrasting views on the rapidity of the change in mortality and net population growth in Africa, especially 1900–50, see Manning (2010); Frankema and Jerven (2014).

374 Patrick Manning

21 African governments contributed to this documentation, although it was difficult to expand their professional staff under the World Bank-imposed structural adjustment programs, especially 1980–2000.
22 United Nations, Population Division. *International Migrant Stock Documentation.* 2019.
23 This version may be followed by later versions in which economic migrants and refugees are distinguished systematically within the overall dataset.
24 The program uses log-linear analysis to estimate "the minimum number of migrant transitions required to match the changes in stock data, controlling for births and deaths in each country over the period" (Abel 2018, 825).
25 World Bank, "Bilateral Remittance Matrix," 2010–17.
26 For newly available data on migrant flows for six African nations over the same years, see Table 16.12. They are calculated based on the bilateral method of Abel (2018).
27 IOM, World Migration Report, 2015.
28 On 1990–2005 migration from the Maghreb to Europe and from Egypt to Saudi Arabia, the Gulf states, and Europe, see Tabutin and Schoumacher (2005, 574–83).
29 On post-1994 migration of South African whites to the UK and especially Australia, see Cronjé (2006).
30 For maps showing that the incidence of refugee departure and IDPs has been centered in Central and Northeastern Africa and in West Asia, with illustrations from 2006 and 2018, see UNHCR, *Global Trends* (2006), 7, 12; and UNHCR, *Global Trends* (2018), 10.
31 UNHCR, *Global Trends*, 2018.
32 IDMC, Annual Reports, 2015–18.
33 For reference, their 2020 populations in millions were Burkina Faso (18), Nigeria (206), the DRC (103), South Africa (60), Uganda (46), and Egypt (101).
34 For an overview of African remittances that accompanied the expansion of World Bank analysis of this topic, see Mohapatra and Ratha (2011).
35 The reports of the World Bank's "Bilateral Remittance Matrix," from which these data are taken, provide matrices without detailed comments on fluctuations in the size of annual figures. Questions about fluctuations in reported levels of remittances must be addressed in separate research.
36 Including refugees. Abel (2014, 2018).

References

Abel, Guy. 2018. "Estimates of Global Bilateral Migration Flows by Gender between 1960 and 2015." *International Migration Review* 52(3): 809–52.

Abel Guy, and Nikola Sander. 2014. "Quantifying Global International Migration Flows." *Science* 343(6178): 1520–22.

Bales, Kevin. 2004. *Disposable People: New Slavery in the Global Economy* (2nd edn). Berkeley: University of California Press.

Bassett, Thomas, and Matthew Turner. 2007. "Sudden Shift or Migratory Drift? Fulbe Herd Movements to the Sudano-Guinean Region of West Africa." *Human Ecology* 35(1): 33–49.

Borderon, Marion, Endale Kebede, Patrick Sakdapolrak, Raya Muttarak, Endale Kebede, Raffaella Pogogna, and Eva Sporer. 2019. "Migration Influenced by Environmental Change in Africa: A Systematic Review of Empirical Evidence," *Demographic Research* 41: 491–544.

Brown, Oli. 2008. "Migration and Climate Change." *IOM Migration Research Series* 31. Geneva: IOM.

Cronjé, Frans. 2006. "Million Whites Leave SA – study |Fin 24," *news24.com*.

Flahaux, Marie-Laurence, and Hein De Haas. 2016. "African Migration: Trends, Patterns, Drivers." *Comparative Migration Studies* 4: 1–25.

Frankema, Ewout, and Morten Jerven. 2014. "Writing History Backwards or Sideways: Towards a Consensus on African Population, 1850–2010." *Economic History Review* 67(4): 907–31.

Internal Displacement Monitoring Centre (IDMC). *Annual Report*, 2014–19. www.internal-displacement.org

Internal Displacement Monitoring Centre (IDMC). 2020. *Global Internal Displacement Database (GIDD)*. www.internal-displacement.org/database/displacement-data

Internal Displacement Monitoring Centre (IDMC). *Global Report on Internal Displacement, 2020*.

International Organization for Migration (IOM). *Displacement Tracking Matrix*, dtm.iom.int

IOM. *Migration Data Portal*. https://gmdac.iom.int/migration-data-portal

IOM. *World Migration Report*, 2004–20. https://www.iom.int/wmr/

IOM. 2016. "Data on environmental migration: How much do we know?" *Global Migration Data Analysis Centre Data Briefings* 2.

Jedwab, Remi, Luc Christiaensen, and Marina Gindelsky. 2017. "Demography, Urbanization and Development: Rural Push, Urban Pull, and … Urban Push?" *Journal of Urban Economics* 98: 6–16.

Keyfitz, Nathan, and Dimiter Philipov. 1981. "Migration and Natural Increase in the Growth of Cities." *Geographical Analysis* 13(4): 287–99.

Lovejoy, Paul, and Stephen Baier. 1975 "The Desert-Side Economy of the Central Sudan." *International Journal of African Historical Studies* 8(4): 551–81.

Manning, Patrick. 1990. *Slavery and African Life: Occidental, Oriental, and African Slave Trades*. Cambridge: Cambridge University Press.

Manning, Patrick. 2010. "African Population: Projections, 1851–1961." In *The Demographics of Empire: The Colonial Order and the Creation of Knowledge*, edited by Karl Ittmann, Dennis Cordell, and Gregory Maddox, 245–75. Athens: Ohio University Press.

Manning, Patrick. 2014a. "African Population, 1650–2000: Comparisons an Implications of New Estimates." *Africa's Development in Historical Perspective*, edited by Emmauel Akyeampong, Robert Bates, Nathan Nunn, and James Robinson, 131–50. New York: Cambridge University Press.

Manning, Patrick. 2014b. "Africa's Place in Globalization: Africa, Eurasia, and their Borderlands." *Journal of Globalization Studies* 5(1): 65–81.

Manning, Patrick, with Tiffany Trimmer. 2020. *Migration in World History* (3rd edn). New York: Routledge.

Manning, Patrick. 2021a. "World Annual Population Growth, 1980–2020." https://doi.org/10.7910/DVN/V3BR6W

Manning, Patrick. 2021b. "World Annual Urban Growth, 1980–2020." https://doi.org/10.7910/DVN/IH1Q1I

McKeown, Adam. 2008. *Melancholy Order Asian Migration and the Globalization of Borders*. New York: Columbia University Press.

Mohapatra, Sanket, and Dilip Ratha. 2011. "Migrant Remittances in Africa: An Overview." *Remittance Markets in Africa*, edited by Sanket Mohapatra and Dilip Ratha, 3–70. Washington, DC: World Bank.

Tabutin, Dominique, and Bruno Schoumacher. 2005. "The Demography of the Arab World and the Middle East from the 1950s to the 2000s: A Survey of Changes and a Statistical Assessment." *Population* 60(5/6): 505–615.

United Nations, Department of Social and Economic Affairs, Population Division. 2018. *World Urbanization Prospects. The 2018 Revision*. Online Edition, Files 3 and 5.

United Nations, Department of Social and Economic Affairs, Population Division. 2019. *International Migrant Stock Documentation*. https://www.un.org/en/development/desa/population/migration/data/estimates2/docs/MigrationStockDocumentation_2019.pdf

United Nations High Commission for Refugees. 2005. *Global Refugee Trends* (Geneva: 9 June 2006). https://www.unhcr.org/4486ceb12.pdf

Vezzoli, Simona, María Villares-Varela, and Hein de Haas. 2014. *Uncovering International Migration Flow Data Insights from the DEMIG Databases*. International Migration Institute (IMI) Working Paper 88 (DEMIG project paper 17).

World Bank. 2016. *Migration and Remittances Factbook 2016* (3rd edn). Washington, DC: World Bank.

World Bank. Migration and Remittances Data, "Bilateral Remittance Matrix," reports for 2010–18.

Epilogue

17
MIGRATION AND DEVELOPMENT
Lessons from Africa's Long-Run Experience

Michiel de Haas and Ewout Frankema

1 Introduction

Our study of two centuries of shifting patterns of African migration generates four pertinent lessons on how development affects patterns of migration. Although this book has looked into a broader spectrum of migration forms, we focus our discussion here on long-term shifts in voluntary *international* migration. We broadly define the term "development" as a long-term, non-linear, and layered process of welfare growth, involving rising per capita income levels, the spread of mass education, increasing longevity, and demographic growth. The insights of our study speak to two influential theoretical notions on the migration-development nexus, which we will introduce in Section 2. In Section 3 we discuss the four lessons, while also addressing the question of what drove the post-1960 shift in African migration to extra-continental destinations, a shift that marked the end of the "Age of Intra-African Migration" (c. 1850–1960) (see De Haas and Frankema, Chapter 1, this volume).

2 Theories of migration and development

Theories on the impact of development on migration (or mobility, more broadly defined) are grounded in the observation that many societies, at different points in time, have undergone a so-called "migration transition," also dubbed a "mobility transition" or an "emigration life cycle." The main idea is that, with welfare development, emigration rates tend to rise up to a particular threshold level, after which they begin to decline (Zelinsky 1971; Clemens 2014; Williamson 2015). This threshold level is difficult to define in absolute terms, as migration transitions unfold in wider international and historical contexts that shape the uneven opportunity structures that provoke migratory responses, as well as the spatial and legal barriers that limit the international mobility of people in varying ways. The key point is that, *all other things being equal,* development induces increasing emigration rates first, and declining emigration rates at a later stage.[1]

DOI: 10.4324/9781003225027-25

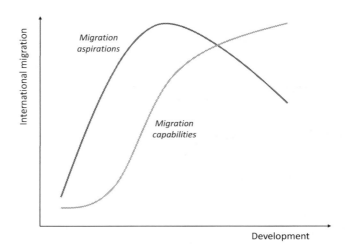

FIGURE 17.1 The relationship between development and migration aspirations and capabilities. *Source*: De Haas (2010, 2014).

The most common explanation among migration scholars for the upward part of the migration curve is that rising income levels lead to growing aspirations to seek opportunities that cannot (yet) be realized at home elsewhere. Meanwhile, with development the capabilities to turn such migration aspirations into practice also increase. As shown in Figure 17.1, only at later stages of development, presumably yet to be reached by almost all African countries, migration aspirations decline as opportunities in home societies improve (Carling and Schewel 2018; Hein de Haas 2019). The idea that migration rates increase from low initial levels with development resonates with older, highly influential strands of literature in African history which argued that large-scale African migration emerged from the *disruptions* caused by colonization and economic modernization (see for a summary and critique Manchuelle 1997, 4–8; see also De Haas and Frankema, Chapter 1, this volume). Whereas Figure 17.1 is primarily used in migration studies to explain migratory change in settings without colonialism, the underlying assumption is strikingly similar: powerful forces of change disrupt a stable "traditional" and "undeveloped" social order in which mobility had been constrained.

A second explanation of the inverted migration U-curve, proposed by economists, sees rising migration as the outcome of a race between a growing and increasingly educated workforce versus economic opportunities in sending regions. When the former gets ahead of the latter, as was the case in Europe during the "Age of Mass Migration" (c. 1850–1940) and, arguably, in sub-Saharan Africa today, emigration rates increase (Hatton and Williamson 2003; Clemens 2014, 2020; Dao et al. 2018). Processes of development have coincided with a demographic transition in every society across the globe, albeit at a varying pace and level of intensity. Rapid population growth raises the demand for jobs and puts pressure on limited natural resources (e.g., land, water, forests). Whenever increasing labor supplies cannot be locally absorbed, young generations are stimulated to move to areas with open land frontiers or tighter labor markets. Rising educational attainment compounds this effect, as it stimulates educated workers to capitalize on their knowledge and skills elsewhere. This informs the prediction that African population growth (Hatton and Williamson 2003) and "overeducation" – i.e., high skill accumulation relative to local employment opportunities (Frankema and van Waijenburg 2019) – increase African emigration rates.

3 Lessons from Africa's long-run experience

Based on the historical analysis of shifting patterns of African mobility presented in this volume, we put the two theoretical mechanisms driving a presumed "migration transition" to the test, and propose four lessons to enrich theories on migration and development.

3.1 Poverty and mobility in (pre-)colonial Africa

The first notion we call into question is the idea that a certain level of development is required for people to overcome mobility constraints and that migration aspirations take time to gestate. An assessment of this notion requires a long-term perspective to reveal migratory patterns before (or in the early phases of) sustained expansion of mass education and population. While long-run migration transitions have been studied for other world regions (Hatton and Williamson 1998; Clemens 2020), work on migration and development in Africa has typically taken the 1960s or 1970s as a starting point (Hatton and Williamson 2003; 2005, 247–64; Lucas 2015; European Commission, Joint Research Centre 2018). This is too short. While a lack of accessible, reliable, and consistent serial data has hitherto complicated analyses with longer timeframes, there is no evidence for claims that before 1960 African migration aspirations were limited, that historical opportunity gaps in Africa were simply too small to warrant large-scale mobility (Hatton and Williamson 2005, 252), or that historical (i.e., colonial-era) migration was more of a political (force and flight) rather than economic nature (Herbst 1990, 186).

This book has provided ample evidence that African migration rates in the 19th and 20th centuries were substantial, and that even in the poorest parts of Africa, migration occurred on a substantial scale.[2] Large flows of emigrants in colonial Africa originated from the least developed regions such as present-day Burkina Faso, Malawi, Mozambique, Niger, and Rwanda.[3] Can these migration flows be simply ascribed to brutal colonial force? To be sure, such flows were partially enforced by colonial policies (Okia; Ribeiro da Silva and Alexopoulou, Chapters 8 and 9, this volume). However, direct colonial efforts to push people onto the migratory labor market were often ineffective, as African migrants proved to have substantial agency to choose their destinations and employers and used mobility to move beyond colonial control (Michiel de Haas 2019; De Haas and Travieso, Chapter 11, this volume). Moreover, the role of state intervention as a driver of mobility in the colonial era appears less decisive when we place it in the context of much larger forced mobility triggered by intense slavery and state formation in the 19th century, as well as the mass expulsions and refugee flows engendered by post-colonial conflict (Austin; Keeton and Schirmer; Frankema, Chapters 2, 6, and 15, this volume).

It is highly problematic to simply set aside colonial-era mobility as an outcome of coercive colonial structures (for such a tendency, see, for example, De Haas, Castles, and Miller 2020). We need to view migrants in the (pre-)colonial era as agents responding to economic incentives, as much as their counterparts today. Indeed, voluntary forms of labor migration from rural areas emerged long before the colonial era (Manchuelle 1997). Already in the 19th century, preceding colonial rule, labor demand on African-owned farms and plantations producing commercial crops such as groundnuts, palm oil, and cocoa resulted in a *widening* of *opportunity gaps* between rural areas. Africans responded with alacrity to such gaps, which resulted in expanding migrant flows. De Haas and Travieso (Chapter 11, Figure 3, this volume) estimate that in the interwar period, migrants were able to augment their incomes by a factor of 2 to 4 by moving over large distances to zones of cash-crop production. For the same period, Frederick and Van Nederveen Meerkerk (Chapter 12, Figure 2, this volume) estimate that unskilled day laborers in the major cities of the Belgian Congo earned triple the wages of their rural counterparts. Ribeiro da Silva and Alexopoulou (Chapter 9, this volume) estimate income gaps between Mozambique and the South African Witwatersrand to have been in the order of 4 to 6.

Summing up, new opportunity gaps that emerged in pre-colonial and grew rapidly during colonial times triggered rising voluntary migration within Africa. Even in poor regions, migrants responded to such opportunities in large numbers, apparently not hindered by a lack of capabilities and aspirations. In fact, many migrants needed very little but their feet to cover impressive distances, year in year out.

3.2 Migration and development in post-colonial Africa

Has migration risen with development since 1960? Figure 17.2 shows continental decadal migration rates and annual GDP per capita. Despite long-term income growth which

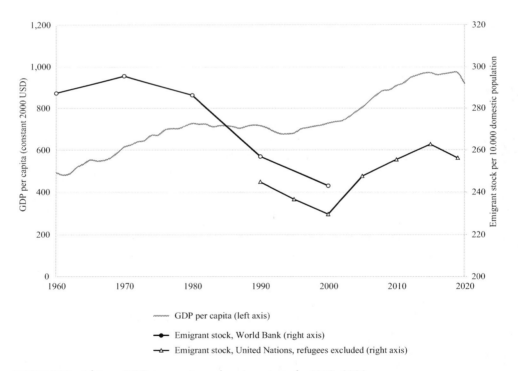

FIGURE 17.2 African GDP per capita and emigrant stock, 1960–2020.

Sources: GDP and population data from the World Bank (https://databank.worldbank.org/source/world-development-indicators). Emigrant stock from the World Bank (https://databank.worldbank.org/source/global-bilateral-migration) and the UN (https://www.un.org/en/development/desa/population/migration/data/ estimates2/estimates19.asp). Refugee stock from the UNHCR (https://www.unhcr.org/data.html). Accessed 15-09-2021.

Notes: Emigrant stock includes all Africans residing outside their country of birth, either within or outside of the continent.

coincided with booming population (from 283 million in 1960 to 1.34 billion in 2020) and massive expansion of school attainment (from 1.3 to 6.7 years of education on average for Africa's full working-age population between 1950 and 2015), the recorded African emigrant stock (including both intra- and extra-continental destinations) as a share of Africa's total population *declined* between 1960 and 2019 (also see Table 1, De Haas and Frankema Chapter 1, this volume).[4] This goes against the notion that migration rates increase with development. In the shorter run, we do observe some correlation between migration and development. As average per capita incomes rose between 1960 and 1980, the total migrant stock also expanded to reach its highest recorded level (in 1970). As GDP per capita plateaued between 1980 and 2000, the estimated stock of African migrants declined, suggesting a "reverse migration transition." As African growth bounced back during the 2000s and early 2010s, the migrant stock began to expand again as well.

Of course, a continental approach is coarse and hides substantial underlying variation (see Manning, Chapter 16, this volume, also Adepoju 2022). Examination of the drivers of bilateral (country-to-country) migration stocks between 1960 and 2000 (Lucas 2015, 1490–500) and 1960 and 2015 (European Commission, Joint Research Centre 2018, 21–2), using a multi-variate "gravity model" approach, reveals that large income differentials between sending and receiving regions as well as low GDP per capita in sending regions are positively correlated with African migration. Thus, more fine-grained country-level evidence further calls into question the idea that rising incomes spur migration and suggests instead, as we have argued above for earlier times, that the size of opportunity gaps matters most. Some sub-national and individual-level evidence does point to higher emigration rates in more developed regions *within* African countries, and among individuals with higher-than-average socio-economic status, but these findings are correlational, and await more rigorous causal analysis (European Commission, Joint Research Centre 2018, 21; UNDP 2019).

Why did migration not unequivocally expand with development in post-colonial Africa? Our main explanation is that many of the opportunity gaps that had emerged in Africa in the early 20th century began to narrow during the second half of the century. We propose that this narrowing reflected a progressing spatial integration of labor markets; the diffusion of public goods (roads, medical services, and fresh water); an expanding supply of skilled as well as unskilled workers due to better education and population growth; and worsening terms of trade for export commodities. Substantial rural-urban income gaps tended to persist somewhat longer, typically as a result of government intervention which sought to suppress earnings in rural areas to sustain labor circularity (as in Southern Rhodesia, see Frederick and Van Nederveen Meerkerk, Chapter 12, Figure 4, this volume) or due to wage increases of a privileged minority of formal wage workers (as in Uganda, see De Haas 2017). Yet, real urban incomes began to decline in many parts of Africa during the 1970s and 1980s as well, after colonial restrictions to urban settlement had been removed and urban growth accelerated (Meier zu Selhausen, Chapter 13, this volume). In the meantime, international immigrants became increasingly less welcome, as reflected by mass expulsions of "illegal" workers in numerous African countries (Frankema, Chapter 15, Table 2, this volume).

In sum, welfare development across the long 20th century did not coincide with a long-term rise, but rather with a long-term decline in *overall migration rates*, which we should understand in the context of narrowing opportunity gaps. Such gaps are always a vector of conditions in sending *as well as receiving* regions. Hence, the first-order question for Africa is

384 Michiel de Haas and Ewout Frankema

not how development has spurred the magnitude of migration, but rather how it has affected shifts in *origins and destinations* over the course of time, and more in particular the resurgence of extra-continental migration since the 1960s.

3.3 Resurging migration out of Africa

Rates of slave-related migration within Africa probably peaked between 1850 and 1910, of cash-crop migration between 1920 and 1960, of urban migration between 1950 and 1990, and of forced migration of refugees and internally displaced persons (IDPs) between 1970 and 2000. In this long-term landscape of shifting patterns of migration, the shift toward destinations outside Africa has most profoundly shaped public perceptions of African migration. Extra-continental migration has been picking up since the 1960s and was initially dominated by North Africans, but African emigration originating from south of the Sahara has undergone a significant and sustained rise as well. Western Europe became the most important destination by far, followed by the Gulf countries and North America (Lucas 2015, 1448–52). Overall, the share of African (sub-Saharan African) migrants residing out of the continent has grown from 28% (5%) to 47% (31%) between 1960 and 2019 (De Haas and Frankema, Chapter 1, Figure 2, this volume). What caused this broad, albeit partial, shift in migration destinations?

Although it would be unfair to suggest that this question has been entirely overlooked in the migration literature (e.g., Lucas 2015, 1493), the long-run perspective of this book allows us to see more clearly how the shift to extra-continental destinations is connected to historical migration shifts *within* Africa. Understanding this connection is important to correct some widespread misperceptions. For example, in their seminal work on two centuries of global migration, Hatton and Williamson (2005, 247–64) rhetorically ask "where are all the Africans?", to argue that poverty in sending societies and restrictive migration policies and the lack of migrant networks in receiving societies have long hampered extra-continental migration of Africans. Concerning intra-African migration they posit that "many African countries have neighbors who are at similar levels of development. Thus, the incentives for cross-border migration have not been large enough in most of Africa to induce any secular migrant floods" (Hatton and Williamson 2005, 252). This conclusion, based on data starting in 1977, might be broadly correct since then (as we argue above), but it is certainly at odds with the migration patterns we have observed in the 19th and earlier 20th century. Indeed, even though their moves were largely restricted to the continent itself, Africans were never absent from the international migration scene.

Without attempting to be exhaustive, we highlight three explanations for the partial shift from intra- to extra-continental destinations. Development in the sending regions has only limited bearing on these explanations, which rather find their origin in the macro-historical drivers that we have discussed in the introduction of this volume (De Haas and Frankema, Chapter 1, this volume).

First, as already indicated, the gains of intra-African migration have declined substantially since the majority of African countries became independent in the 1960s. While most African countries are richer today than they were in 1960, spatial opportunity structures *within* and *between* countries have converged. The gains that migrants were able to reap from rural-rural migration or urban migration in the first half of the 20th century were similar to those of Europeans moving to the New World, or Indians and Chinese converging upon

Southeast Asia during the "Age of Mass Migration" (Hatton and Williamson 1998; 2005, 136–37). With some major exceptions (migrant destinations Côte d'Ivoire and South Africa being the most important), opportunity gaps of such a magnitude had largely disappeared by the third quarter of the 20th century, and have not reappeared since.

In cases where spatial opportunity gaps continued to exist, receiving communities increasingly saw immigrants as competitors for land and jobs, in numerous cases even expelling them in large numbers (Frankema, Chapter 15, this volume). The most telling example is South Africa which, with an income level far exceeding that of neighboring countries such as Lesotho, Malawi, Mozambique, and Zimbabwe, continues to attract scores of migrants from the wider region (over 1.5 million individuals born in these five countries were estimated to reside in South Africa in 2019, according to United Nations (UN) migration data). However, international migrants in South Africa have met with rising intolerance, especially after 1994 (Crush 2000). Contrary to older generations, the young aspiring labor migrants have met expanding restrictions and their status has become increasingly precarious, with violence, detention and deportation as ever-present threats. Thus, those with aspirations to improve their lot and that of their families are more often inclined to attempt a move out of the continent.

Second, after recovery from the Second World War, Western European countries embarked upon a "golden age" of industrial catch-up growth (Eichengreen 2007). Shortages of unskilled labor emerged during the 1960s and 1970s. "Guest workers" from Southern Europe were the first to fill these gaps, but international agreements on temporary labor migration were also signed with countries in North Africa. This period of moderate openness was smothered by the economic recession of the 1980s, but by that time chain migration and family reunion sustained these flows. More recently, new forms of African migration to Europe have emerged, again in a context of tightening labor markets. Southern European countries such as Italy and Spain developed new demand for temporary workers engaged in (informal) occupations with inferior status, harsh labor conditions, and low pay. For example, an increasing number of labor migrants originating from rural areas in West Africa (e.g., Senegal, Mali, Niger) are employed as seasonal workers in agriculture, with or without legal work permits (Hoggart and Mendoza 1999). Europe's demographic decline, aging, and widespread reluctance to engage in certain occupations among its native populations gave the demand for cheap foreign labor a more structural character (De Haas 2008). Meanwhile, in the resource-rich but sparsely populated economies of the Gulf region, demand for migrant workers from Asia as well as Africa, operating under strictly temporary and highly controlled conditions, has also expanded substantially.

Third, access to destinations outside the continent has increased enormously. Initially, linguistic, political, and economic ties with former colonizers were decisive, especially in the case of former French and Portuguese colonies. Migrants from former colonies formed "bridgehead communities" in Europe. In France, for example, there were only 2,000 registered black African workers in the early 1950s (a large majority of whom originated from Senegal and Mali), a number that grew to 660,000 by the mid-1990s, still predominantly from the same regions (Manchuelle 1997, 2). Even in 2019, France still accounted for over half of all African migrants from former French colonies residing in non-African states (3.4 out of 6.8 million, according to UN data). In recent decades, however, increasing shares of African migrants have moved to destinations other than the former colonizers. This is driven by falling transportation and transaction costs due to the diffusion of cheap motorized travel over land and sea and the growth of professional albeit often criminalized networks of migrant recruiters in sending regions, smugglers and other facilitators along the routes, and connectors on the receiving end. On the migrants' end, the rapid surge in mobile and digital information and communication technology from the 1990s onward has made it much easier to gather information, to remain in touch with "home," and to organize multiple attempts to cross fortified borders in the hope that one time will be successful.

Intercontinental African migration has distinctively different faces. For those migrating through *regular* (i.e., legally recognized) channels, the journey itself became shorter and easier to plan with airlines maintaining regular connections. At the same time, formal international cash transfers have become much easier for labor migrants seeking to support their families back home with regular remittances. Education levels have risen massively across Africa since independence, which means that an increasing share of Africa's young generations is both motivated and qualified to migrate to rich countries to study or take up jobs. Indeed, on the country level, more advanced education has been found to correlate with "intercontinental migration [of Africans] but not shorter movements within Africa" (Lucas 2015, 1496). Meanwhile, the appalling conditions under which many *irregular* migrants cross the Sahara and Mediterranean are well known. Notably, this type of migration experience is hardly novel: in the early 20th century it was not uncommon for migrants to walk for weeks to arrive at their destination within Africa, often under pitiful circumstances (Okia; Juif; De Haas and Travieso, Chapters, 9, 10, and 11, this volume). What has changed is primarily that migrants today are able to reach even harder-to-reach destinations, and to bridge even larger cross-community barriers with a comparable level of risk and distress.

In sum, the resurgence of migration out of Africa should be viewed in connection to the narrowing of historically sizable opportunity gaps *within* Africa. In addition, macro-historical drivers in the form of demographic growth, technological change, and processes of decolonization have created conditions for chain migration. But there has also been a countervailing force: changing beliefs regarding the contribution of African immigrants to "development" in Western European societies, which have resulted in severely tightened entry conditions.

3.4 Shifting reception of labor immigrants

Despite the presence of strong forces that make migration out of the African continent more feasible and attractive, contemporary patterns of migration have emerged in a context of newly erected barriers, in particular more restrictive migration regimes and border controls, within as well as outside Africa.[5] The large share of Africans with aspirations to migrate (Carling and Schewel 2018) suggests that without these barriers extra-continental migration would certainly have involved far greater numbers – a key reason why such barriers are erected in the first place. But there is also a different logic to migrant barriers, which applies to both African destinations in the past and non-African destinations today: a strong demand for cheap labor, which benefits from migrants' precarity and marginalization. This results in situations, past and present, where migrants' ability to own property is limited and their legal status is either poorly defined or highly restricted. Moreover, host societies within and beyond Africa have used repatriation as an instrument to limit migrant numbers and to diminish their status.

The mounting barriers to African mobility are important to consider in a global historical perspective. Since the mid-20th century, African population growth began to accelerate, resulting in unprecedented population levels and densities that are expected to peak in the late 21st century. From a comparative perspective, Africa's demographic transition is not just late, but also sharper than in all other world regions and it is turning a long historical equilibrium of low population densities and scarce labor supplies upside down (Austin 2008). Africans' opportunities to migrate and settle in overseas areas are nowhere near substantial enough to absorb a meaningful share of this growing working-age population (Frankema and van Waijenburg 2019). This stands in sharp contrast to the surge in trans-Atlantic migration of Europeans who (typically unlike their non-white counterparts) were welcomed to settle the "open" land frontiers of the US, Canada, Australia, and New Zealand and to a lesser extent the southern cones of Africa and Latin America since 1850. Such migration, made possible by the dramatic fall in the cost of trans-oceanic transport served as a "population valve," offering an escape to millions of socially, religiously, or economically marginalized groups in Europe (Hatton and Williamson 1998). The millions of Chinese and Indians who moved into thinly populated and labor-scarce parts of Southeast Asia (c. 1850–1940) equally sought to escape dismal living conditions in sending regions (McKeown 2010). However, unlike the millions of Europeans, Indians, and Chinese who engaged in overseas migration during the Age of Mass Migration, and who in their respective contexts were often supported and facilitated instead of restricted, there are no present-day equivalent "population valves" that can cushion the effects of rising pressure on environmental resources, public services, and overwhelmed urban job markets in Africa. Neither are there large open land frontiers waiting for Africans to be settled. Indeed, the historical timing of development matters greatly for how migration transitions can play out.

As old windows close, new ones may be opened. The aging of European and Chinese populations will inevitably lead to greater labor shortages in both regions in the decades ahead. Whether shifting ratios of economically active to non-active populations will lead to a willingness to accommodate very large numbers of African migrant workers remains to be seen. A future scenario in which African labor migrants will be invited to come over cannot be written off and present-day anti-immigrant sentiments should not be taken as a given. As a historical perspective demonstrates, gradual, yet deeply transformative, long-run processes of economic, demographic, and political change tend to reconfigure opportunity structures, and how "development" in destination societies can lead to resisting as well as inviting attitudes to newcomers.

Acknowledgment

Ewout Frankema gratefully acknowledges financial support from the Netherlands Organisation for Scientific Research for the project "South-South Divergence: Comparative Histories of Regional Integration in Southeast Asia and Sub-Saharan Africa since 1850" (NWO VICI Grant no. VI.C.201.062).

Notes

1 For a recent application to mobility transition theory to Ethiopia, see Schewel and Asmamaw 2021)
2 Also, in Asia large numbers of extremely poor Chinese and Indians migrated into underpopulated parts of Southeast Asia to work on colonial plantations, in mines, or in port cities. See McKeown (2004) and (2010).
3 Although no historical national income estimates exist yet for these countries, their poverty is clearly indicated by extremely low unskilled wage rates. For studies on African real wages see

Frankema and van Waijenburg (2012); on Rwanda see Michiel de Haas (2019). See also De Haas and Travieso (Chapter 11, this volume).

4 Population from the UN (https://population.un.org/wpp/Download/Standard/Population/). Education from the educational attainment dataset of Barro and Lee (2013) (http://www.barrolee.com/). Accessed 04/01/2022.

5 Herbst (1990). Also see Frankema (Chapter 14, this volume).

References

Adepoju, Aderanti. 2022. "International Migration and Development in Sub-Saharan Africa." in *The Routledge Handbook of African Demography*, edited by Edited By Clifford O. Odimegwu and Yemi Adewoyin, 573-88. London: Routledge.

Barro, Robert, and Jong-Wha Lee. 2013. "A New Data Set of Educational Attainment in the World, 1950-2010. "*Journal of Development Economics* 104: 184–198.

Carling, Jørgen, and Kerilyn Schewel. 2018. "Revisiting Aspiration and Ability in International Migration." *Journal of Ethnic and Migration Studies* 44(6): 945–63.

Clemens, Michael. 2014. "Does Development Reduce Migration?" In *International Handbook on Migration and Economic Development*, edited by Robert Lucas, 152–85. Cheltenham: Edward Elgar Publishing.

Clemens, Michael. 2020. "The Emigration Life Cycle: How Development Shapes Emigration from Poor Countries." Center for Global Development, Working Paper 540.

Crush, Jonathan. 2000. "The Dark Side of Democracy: Migration, Xenophobia and Human Rights in South Africa." *International Migration* 38(6): 103–33.

Dao, Thu Hien, Frédéric Docquier, Chris Parsons, and Giovanni Peri. 2018. "Migration and Development: Dissecting the Anatomy of the Mobility Transition." *Journal of Development Economics* 132: 88–101.

De Haas, Hein. 2008. "The Myth of Invasion: The Inconvenient Realities of African Migration to Europe." *Third World Quarterly* 29(7): 1305–22.

De Haas, Hein. 2010. "Migration and Development: A Theoretical Perspective." *International Migration Review* 44(1): 227–64.

De Haas, Hein. 2014. "Migration Theory. Quo Vadis?" International Migration Institute Working Paper 100 (DEMIG Project Paper 24).

De Haas, Hein. 2019. "Paradoxes of Migration and Development." International Migration Institute Working Paper 1957 (MADE Project Paper 9).

De Haas, Hein, Stephen Castles, and Mark Miller. 2020. "Migrations Shaping African History." Companion Website to *The Age of Migration: International Population Movements in the Modern World*, edited by Hein De Haas, Stephen Castles, and Mark Miller. London: Red Globe Press. Accessed 23 June, 2021. http://www.age-of-migration.com/additional-case-studies.

De Haas, Michiel. 2017. "Measuring Rural Welfare in Colonial Africa: Did Uganda's Smallholders Thrive?". *Economic History Review* 70(2): 605–631.

De Haas, Michiel. 2019. "Moving Beyond Colonial Control? Economic Forces and Shifting Migration from Ruanda-Urundi to Buganda, 1920–60." *Journal of African History* 60(3): 379–406.

Eichengreen, Barry. 2007. *The European Economy since 1945*. Princeton, NY: Princeton University Press.

European Commission, Joint Research Centre. 2018. *Many More to Come? Migration from and within Africa*. Publications Office of the European Union, Luxembourg.

Frankema, Ewout, and Marlous van Waijenburg. 2019. "The Great Convergence. Skill Accumulation and Mass Education in Africa and Asia, 1870–2010." CEPR Discussion Paper 14150

Frankema, Ewout, and Marlous Van Waijenburg. 2012. "Structural Impediments to African Growth? New Evidence from Real Wages in British Africa, 1880–1965." *Journal of Economic History* 72(4): 895–926.

Hatton, Tim, and Jeffrey Williamson. 1998. *The Age of Mass Migration: Causes and Economic Impact*. Oxford: Oxford University Press.

Hatton, Tim, and Jeffrey Williamson. 2003. "Demographic and Economic Pressure on Emigration Out of Africa." *Scandinavian Journal of Economics* 105(3): 465–86.

Hatton, Tim, and Jeffrey Williamson. 2005. *Global Migration and the World Economy: Two Centuries of Policy and Performance*. Cambridge, MA: MIT Press.

Herbst, Jeffrey. 1990. "Migration, the Politics of Protest, and State Consolidation in Africa." *African Affairs* 89(355): 183–203.

Hoggart, Keith, and Cristóbal Mendoza. 1999. "African Immigrant Workers in Spanish Agriculture." *Sociologia Ruralis* 39(4): 538–62.

Lucas, Robert E.B. 2015. "African Migration." In *Handbook of the Economics of International Migration, Volume 1B*, edited by Barry Chiswick, and Paul Miller, 1445–596. Elsevier.

Manchuelle, François. 1997. *Willing Migrants: Soninke Labor Diasporas, 1848–1960*. Athens: Ohio University Press.

McKeown, Adam. 2004. "Global Migration, 1846–1940." *Journal of World History* 15(2): 155–89.

McKeown, Adam. 2010. "Chinese Emigration in Global Context, 1850–1940." *Journal of Global History* 5(1): 95–124.

Schewel, Kerilyn, and Legass Bahir Asmamaw. 2021. "Migration and Development in Ethiopia: Exploring the Mechanisms Behind an Emerging Mobility Transition." *Migration Studies*, forthcoming.

UNDP (2019). *Scaling Fences: Voices of Irregular African Migrants to Europe*. https://www.africa.undp.org/content/rba/en/home/library/reports/ScalingFences.html

Williamson, Jeffrey. 2015. "World Migration in Historical Perspective: Four Big Issues." In *Handbook of the Economics of International Migration, Vol. 1*, edited by Barry R Chiswick and Paul W Miller, 89–101. Amsterdam: Elsevier.

Zelinsky, Wilbur. 1971. "The Hypothesis of the Mobility Transition." *Geographical Review* 61(2): 219–49.

INDEX

Note: **Bold** page numbers refer to tables; *italic* page numbers refer to figures and page numbers followed by "n" denote endnotes.

Abidjan 20, **286**, 287, 294, 298
abolition *see* forced labor; slavery; slave trades
absorption (of migrants) *see* integration
Abyssinia *see* Ethiopia
Accra 20, 47, 170, **286**, 287, 288, *291*, 292, 293, 294, 324, 325
age of intra-African migration *see* intra-African migration
age of mass migration 4–7, 14, 251n, 373n, 380, 384–85, 387
agency (of people) 9, 12–13, 20, 179, 203, 208, 215, 244, 266, 268, 381
agriculture 39, 126, 231–55, 259; consequences of emigration 203, 214–15, 290–93, 314; forced cultivation 191, 259, 270; innovation 8, 40, 114–15, 126, 136, 231, 244, 248, 271, 272, 323; intensive agriculture 39, 40, 97, 104–7, 126, 239; plantations 17, 19, 46, 47, 65, 75–81, 84, 86–89, 124, 158, 165, 167, 171, 180, 181, 191, 193, 235, 240, 259, 270, 381, 387n; *see also* cash crops; seasonality
Algeria: conflict 334; migration from 72, **339**, 348n, 368; migration in **339**; migration to 11, *60*, 72n; slavery in 57, 59, *61*, 63, 70, 72; soldiers from 23
America 82, Afro-American settlers from 18, 343; decolonization 330, 347; investment from 206; migration from 183; migration in 26n, 359; migration to 3, 4, 6, 22, 135, 368, 384, 387; population growth *357*, 358–59; slavery in 64, 68, 77, 78, 180; urbanization in 281, 358; U.S. Civil War 17, 57, 69
Amin, Samir 8–9, 157

Angola: commercial agriculture in 180, 181–82, 191; conflict in 336, 337; diamond mining in 181; migration from 26n, 178, 180, 182, 183, *184*, 188, *190*, *191*, **192**, 195, 196n, **200–2**, 211, **212–13**, 216, **216**, 217, 223, 261, 334, 336, **339**, 342, 366; migration in 180, **181**, 182, 187, **192**, 195, 196n; migration to 145, 183, *185*, 193; soldiers from 186; transportation 183
anthropology 8, 40, 95, 115, 118, 128n, 178, 270, 272
apartheid 149, 214, 224, 225, 337, 340, 368, 372
archaeology 100, 115, 119, 128n
armed forces *see* soldiers
Asante: control over 40–41, 169; migration from 49; migration in 46; migration to 22, 43–44, 49, 236, 247, 312; slavery in 44–45, 46, 47, 170, 236; trade 49; *see also* Ghana
Asia: decolonization 330; expulsion of Asians 345; migration from 4, 6, 18, 244, 333, 359, 360, 364, 374n; migration in 4, 26n, 333, 359, 360, 374n, 385, 387; migration to 5, 23, 26n, 312, 320, 321, 324, 326, 359, 364, 365, 368; population growth 356, **357–58**; urbanization 281, 298, 347, 358, 363; *see also* China; India
aspirations (of migrants) *see* migration concepts

Bagamoyo 76, 83, 84, 85, 89, 285, 287
Bamako 242, **286**, 287
Bechuanaland *see* Botswana
Belgium: colonialism in Africa, 19, 215, 248, 266–68, 270, 271, 273, 313, 318–19; franc 218, 243, *262*; investment in Africa 206, 276; postcolonial interference in Africa 337

392 Index

belief system *see* ideology

Benin: migration from 22, 38, 180; urbanization 288

Benin City 285, **286**, 292

Boers 16, 144, 145, 146, 147, 204–5, 207, 208; *see also* Voortrekkers

borders 6, 10–11, 23, 48, 71, 75, 136, 141–42, 144–46, 182–83, 195, 203, 232, 276, 316, 321, 330–32, 338–46, 360, 363, 368, 388; *see also* frontiers

Botswana: annexation 208; independence 340; migration from 207, 211, **212–13**, 321–22; migration to 196n, 340, 344

bride price *see* bridewealth

bridewealth 83, 97–98, 106, 121, 159, 167, 208, 214, 218, 243, 290, 314, 340; *see also* marriage

Britain: abolition and suppression of slave trades 4, 16, 17, 38, 47, 57, 66, 67, 70, 78, 80, 89, 235; annexations in Africa 38, 45, 108, 136, 141, 144, 145, 165, 169, 205, 208, 265, 315; colonialism in Africa 19, 24, 80, 86, 87, 90, 141, 142–43, 147, 157, 159, 160–61, 162–63, 170, 172, 204, 211, 218, 259, 266, 268, 271, 313, 317–19, 320, 321, 324, 331; empire 312, 333; investment in Africa 206; migration from 88, 142, 145–46, 148; migration to 26n, 326n; postcolonial interference in Africa 340; pound sterling 218; trade 46

British India *see* India

British South Africa Company (BSAC) 146, 206, 216, 259, 266, 269

Buganda: commercial agriculture in 161–64, 234, 244–45, 249; control over 44, 51; migration from 22, 82, 85; migration in 76, *246*; migration to 76, 85, 86, 161–64, 234, 239, 245, *246*, 247–49, 340–41; rainfall seasonality in *242*; slavery in 17–18, 81–82, 236, 237, 251n; soldiers from 85; urbanization in 76, 85, 287, 288; *see also* Uganda

Bulawayo 256, 257, 258, **259**, **261**, 267

Burkina Faso: living standards in 238, *244*, 251n; migration from 7, 170, 232, 240, 244, 340, 356, **367**, 381; migration to **344**, 345, **367**; rainfall seasonality in 242; remittances to 368–71; urbanization in *288*, *289*

Burma *see* Myanmar

Burundi: commercial agriculture in 240, 248; control over 241, 331, 337; famine in 326; forced labor in 248; living standards in 238, 239, 243; migration from 163, 164, 215, 219, 234, 240, 241, 245, 247, 260, 302n, 334, 340, 341, 342; migration to 334, **339**, 341, 365; rainfall seasonality in 242; soldiers from 337

Cabo Verde: commercial agriculture in 180; living standards in 192; migration from 180, **182**, 183, *184*, 186, 188, **190**, 191–92, **192**, 193, **200–2**; migration in **181**; migration to 178, 180, *191*; slavery in 180, 186

Cairo 59, 63, *70*, 145, 325, 363

Cameroon: commercial agriculture in 235; conflict 315, 337; migration to 345; slavery in 51; soldiers from **318**

capabilities (of migrants) *see* migration concepts

Cape Colony 11, 19, 122, 126, 135–40, 141, 142, 143, *144*, 145, 146, 147, 148, 151n, 204, 208, 209, 313, 317; *see also* South Africa

Cape Town 136, 137, 138, 139, 143, 148, 151n, 325

Cape Verde *see* Cabo Verde

Caravan trade 22, 48, 58–59, 61–64, *62*, 68, 72, 76, *79*, 81, 82–85, 89, 101, 102, 103, 104, 106, 117, 235, 236; *see also* porterage; trade

cash crops *see* cocoa, coffee, cotton, groundnuts, palm oil, rubber

cash-crop migration 7, 8, 16–21, 231–55, 381–82

cattle *see* livestock

Central Africa: migration from 17, 180, *207*, **364–65**; migration in 365, **366**; mines 206; population growth 361, **362**; urban growth 288, **302n**, **363–64**

Chad: commercial agriculture in French Equatorial Africa 234; trade 47, 62, 71; conflict in 331, 334, 337, 366; control over 68–69; migration from 60–61, 68, 71; migration to 339, **344**

children: of Cape settlers 135, 137, 140, 143, 151n; child labor 161, 164, 165, 167, 169, 170–71, 173, 205, 314, 318, 319; child soldiers 24; and conflict 121; education of 219, 290, 292, 297, 301, 343; health 288, 299, 300; as migrants 8, 13, 113, 147, 188, 190, 210, 221, 222, 245, 261, 263, 272, 290, 292, 294–97, 299, 301, 314, 341, 363; of slaves 45, 64, 78, 82

China: conflict 333; migration from 4–5, 18, 26n, 159, 210, 224, 251, 384–85, 387; migration to 387; trade 120

Christianity 18, 22, 85, 136, 141; *see also* religion

circular migration *see* sojourning

cities *see* urbanization

climate: adaptation to 58, 128; climate change as a driver of migration 15, 61, 95, 96–97, 106, 107, 119, 192, 290, 360–61; drought 15, 96–97, 99–100, 107, 114, 207–8; spatial variation 104, 107, 113, 114, 215, 237, *242; see also* environment

cocoa 8, 47, 48, 50, 169–71, 187, 193, 231, 232–33, *234*, 235, 236, 240, 241, 243–45, 247, 248, 249–50, 289–90, 340, 381

coffee 88, 103, 161, 167, 179, 231, *234*, 237, 240, 247, 248, 249, 270, 289, 341

colonization *see* frontier colonization

color bar 211, 214, 221, 317; *see also* racism
commercial agriculture *see* cash crops
commercial transition 16–18, 21, 37–38, 47–49, 169, 235–37; *see also* cash crops; slave trades; slavery; trade
concentration camps 147, 333
concessionary companies 179, 181, 187, 196n, 206, 217, 234, 259, 260, 267, 270, 344
conflict: Cold War 330, 347; decolonization wars 23, 149, 185, 334, **339**, 342; as a driver of migration 5, 11, 12, 13, 15, 24, 26n, 42, 46, 49, 57, 61, 68–69, 311–29, 333, 335–38, **339**, 341, 346, 358, 360, **361**, 365–66, 373n; European colonial invasion 18, 85, 142, 147, 208; First World War 5, 23, 314–20; over land 23, 249; postcolonial wars 23, 122, 330, 331, 334–37, **339**, 343, 348n, 346, 381; precolonial wars 37, 100, 105, 122, 126, 142, 287; Second World War 5, 23, 219, 267, 268, 311, 320–25, 333, 362; suppression of 108; U.S. Civil War 17, 57, 69; *see also* Hawk-Dove model; military forces
Congo, Belgian *see* Congo, Democratic Republic of
Congo, Democratic Republic of (DRC): commercial agriculture in 159, 234, 270–71; conflict in 313, 334, 335, 336, 337, 342; industrialization in 256–57, 258, 268, 277n; labor stabilization 215–19, 224, 225n, 226n, 256, 261–62, 269; land alienation 270, 271, 276; living standards in 262–65, 275, 276, 382; migration from 25, 76, 85, 86, 180, 334, **339**, 345, 356, **367**, 368; migration in 193, 215–19, 258–62, 270, 336; migration to 182, 183, **192**, 215–19, 334, 336, **339**, 342, 344, 356, **367**, 368; mining in 180, 203, 204, 206, *220*, 240, 260; population growth in **266**; remittances to 369–71; slavery in 79; soldiers **321**; urbanization in 256–57, 272
Congo Free State *see* Congo, Democratic Republic of
Congo-Brazzaville 150, 158
Congo-Kinshasa *see* Congo, Democratic Republic of
contextual drivers of migration 7, 10, 13, 15, 241
contract labor: Chinese 224; deception 193; desertion 168, 170, 185, 187, 215, **218**, 313; duration of contract 88, 188, 209, 211, 214, 216, 219, 222, 223, 225, 241, 277n; forced 166, 180, 190, 196n; negotiation 50, 87; regulation 160, 183, 187, 188, 190, 194, 215, 216, 218; repatriation upon completion 20, 187, 190, 194, 211, 216, 222, 260, 277n; sector of employment 87, 187, 269, 270
copper: discovery 146, 206, 260; items made of 102, 106; migration to mines 182, 204, **217**, 340; mining 65, 116, 157, 203, 206, 219,

220; price *220*, 221, 224; smelting 65; *see also* Copperbelt; Katanga; Union Minière du Haut Katanga
Copperbelt (in Zambia): labor 204, *220*, **222**; migration to *217*, 222; mining 206; urbanization in 219–23, 224
Côte d'Ivoire: commercial agriculture in *234*, 240, 243, 245, 249; migration from 244, 316, 321, 340, 344–45; migration to 233, 240, 244, 245, 248, 249, **339**, 385; rainfall seasonality in 242; settlers in 248; state formation in 42, 43; urbanization in 287, *288*, *289*; wages in 238, 240, *244*, 251n
cotton: famine (of 1861–65) 17, 57, 58, 64, 69; forced cultivation 191, **192**, 234, 240, 270; peasant cultivation 86, 90n, 161, 163, 231, 234, 235, 237, 240, 248, 289; plantations 17, 88, 235, 341; prices 249; use of slaves in production of 57, 64, 65, 69, 235, 236; *see also* textiles
cotton cloth *see* textiles
cotton fabric *see* textiles
cross-community migration 12, 13, 16, 26n, 76, 105, 112, 115, 117, 136, 143, 149, 358

Dahomey *see* Benin
Dakar 20, **286**, 287, 292, 298, 324
Dar es Salaam 89, **286**, 287, 294, 295, 319
Delagoa Bay *see* Maputo Bay
desertion *see* contract labor, flight
detribalization 8, 222, 225, 271
development: definition 379; as a driver of migration 9, 379–80, 382–84; underdevelopment 8–9, 231, 251n
diamonds: discovery 145, 203, 204; migration to mines 146, 147, 181, 204, **207**, 210, 225n, 345; mining 204–6, 208–10, 225n, 344
diaspora: within Africa 7, 9, 21–22, 37, 48–49, 86; global African 6, 7, 22, 24–25, 355, 356, 357, 365
discourse *see* ideology
displacement *see* expulsion, flight, forced migration, internally displaced person, refugees, slave trades
Domar-Nieboer thesis *see* population
drought *see* climate

Eastern Africa: migration from 17, **56**, 60, 63, 77–82, 115, 124, **364–65**; migration in 15, 16, 17, 19, 21, 75–92, 95–111, 161–69, *233*, 234, 237, 317, 318–19, 321; migration to 182; urbanization 84–86, 281–307, 363–64
ecology *see* environment
economics 8, 39, 47
Egypt: commercial agriculture in 17, 57, 69; migration from 356, **367**, 368; migration to 57, 59–60, 63, 65–66, 67, 68, 72, **367**; remittances to 368–71; slavery in 57, 58, *61*, 64; soldiers from 312

394 Index

emancipation *see* slavery

England *see* Britain

enslaved people *see* slavery

environment: as a driver of migration 13, 15, 96, **192**, 235, 237, 239–41, 250, 290, 355, 360–61, 366; *see also* climate

Equatorial Guinea 235, 315, **339**, 345

Eritrea: conflict in **339**, **344**, 348n; migration from 72, 337, **339**; migration to **344**, 346; soldiers from 312, 313, 326n

Ethiopia: conflict in 3, 320, **339**, **344**, 346, 348; migration from 11, 25, 57, 60, 63, 64, 67, 72, 334, **339**, **344**, 346; migration in 336; migration to 334, 337; trade 95, *98*, 102; urbanization in 285, 286, 287, *289*

ethnicity: and conflict 23, 337; identification 96–97, 108, 115, 118, 245, 272, 313, 324, 330, 332, 342; and labor 88; migrant origins 14, 21, 81, 165, 207, 236, 317; and trade 21–22, 37, 48–49

Europe: abolition of slave trades 71, 159, 340; colonialism in Africa 8–9, 19, 159–60, 193, 203, 231–32; conflict in 314–25, 333; exploration in Africa 59, 71, 121; industrialization 6, 50, 385; migration from 4, 6, 11, 136, 137–38, 178, **185**, 364, 373n, 380, 384, 387; migration in 359; migration to 3, 5, 6, 23, 26n, 58, 71, 72, 337, 345, 348n, 359, 365, 368, 384, 385; population 356, **357**; post-colonialism in Africa 330; trade 45, 61, 82, 101, 231, 243; urbanization 358, **359;** *see also* European settlers

European settlers 8–9, 12, 19, 76, 86–88, 90, 108, 127, 135–53, 158–61, 165–69, 183, 221, 231, 235, 244–45, 248, 258, 259, 265–69, 271–77, 301, 325, 332, 348n; *see also* agriculture; invasion

export commodities *see* cash crops; minerals

expulsion 11, 13, 14, 18, 22–24, 250, 331, 332–33, 342, 343–46, 347, 385

extra-continental migration *see* intercontinental migration

faith *see* religion

famine 11, 24, 46, 83, 107, 117, 121, 124, 160, 192, 318–19, 326n, 333, 341, 346

farmer *see* agriculture

flight: from colonial demands 8, 18, 19, 41, 136, 158–59, 164, 169, 170, 171, 172, 180, 187, 196n, 225n, 232, 234, 240, 316, 319, 321, 340; from famine 124, 192; from violence 16, 23, 24, 43, 48, 123, 125, 142, 143, 333–38; *see also* forced migration; recruitment; refugees; slave trades

forced labor: abolition of 15, 86, 243, 248, 368; colonial-era demise of 18–20, 159–60; forms of forced labor under colonial rule 157–77, 192, 270, 325, 332; in Nazi Germany 333; as a push

factor for migration 164, 180, 240, 340; *see also* flight; forced migration; recruitment; slavery

Forced Labour Convention (1930) 160, 164, 168, 171, 172, 173, 325

forced migration: definition 13, 331; shifts in the nature of 332–33; *see also* expulsion; flight; refugees; slave trades; slavery

forest zones: animal diseases in 40; commercial agriculture in 231, 233–34, 235, 244, 249; migration to 233–34, 236, 237, 240, 244, 245, 247, 248; slavery in 44, 45; states in 43; trade 47; urbanization in 285

France: abolition and suppression of slave trades 4, 17, 38, 63, 159, 312; colonialism in Africa 38, 63, 70, 158, 159, 160, 164, 170, 172, 173n, 234, 240–41, 248, 268, 312, 313, 314, 315, 316, 318, 320, 324, 325, 348n; conflict in 314–25; franc *238*, 243; migration from 135, 136, 137; migration to 22, 316–17, 317, 334, 368, 385; postcolonial interference in Africa 248, 337

free migration, definition of 13, 331

freetown **286**, 287, *291*, 293, 300, 312, 325

French West Africa: forced labor 160, 164, 169, 172, 173, 240, 248, 316; migration from 170, 240, 248; migration in 240, 248; migration to 344; slavery 45–46

frontier colonization 5, 11, 12, 15–16, 37, 39, 40, 41–44, 46, 49, 105, 114, 136–43, 151n, **181**, 204, 249, 250, 256, 259, 287, 313, 314, 321, 341, 342, 380, 387

Fulani *see* Fulbe

Fulbe 12, 15, 16, 42–43, 337, 346

Gabon: migration from 344; migration to 345

Gambia: commercial agriculture in 46, 50, 231, 232, 234, 236, 247, 249; control over 38, 180; living standards in 238, 241; migration from 48; migration to 47–48, 48, 232, 237, 240, 241, 245, 246, *247*, 248, 316; rainfall seasonality in 242; urban growth in 288

gender: composition of migrant flows 8, 11, 21, 48, 79, 83, 88, 148, 210, 221, 245, 261, 283, 299, 302, 314, 341; division of labor 48, 107, 148, 161, 164, 167, 170, 171–72, 205, 224, 291–94, 317, 319, 325; and slavery 17, 46, 65–66, 78, 82, 85, 86, 170–71; and urbanization 261–62, 273, 289, 291–94; women's protest 148, 169

German East Africa *see* Tanzania

German South West Africa *see* Namibia

Germany: colonialism in Africa 24, 80, 87, 88, 108, 313, 315, 320; conflict in 268, 333; migration to 316

Ghana: commercial agriculture in 8, 48, 171, 232–33, *234*, 236, 245, 249; control over 38; forced labor in 169–72; gold mining in 44, 46; infrastructure in 171; migration from 25,

26n, 38, 250, 311, 343, **344**, 345; migration in 48, 232–33, 237, 240, **246**, 251n, 290, 295, 297; migration to 49, 233–34, 237, 240, 245, **246**, 316, 320, 340, 342–43, **344**; nationalism 324; rainfall seasonality in 241–42; slavery in 48, 236; soldiers from 26n, 311, 312, 326; state formation in 40, 43; trade 163; urbanization in **288**, **289**; wages in 238, 243, *244*, 248, 289, 301; *see also* Asante

gold: as currency 194; discovery 145, 203, 205; items made of 116; mining 44, 46, 65, 147, 169, 170, 182, 194, 203, *207*, 210, 211, 214, 223, 236, 258–59; *see also* Rand

Gold Coast *see* Ghana

Great Britain *see* Britain

Great Depression 148, 211, 215, 218, 219, 221, 262, 263, 268, 270, 272, 325

Great Trek *see* Voortrekkers

groundnuts 38, 46, 48, 50, 231, 232, 233, *234*, 236, 237, 245, 250, 381

Guinea 61, 248, **339**

Guinea-Bissau: commercial agriculture in 46, 191; migration from 180, 182, 188, *190*; migration in 180, **181**, **192**; migration to 182, 183; soldiers from 186

Gulf region *see* Middle East

Harare 146, 247, 258, 259, **261**, 265, 267, 275

Harries, Patrick 7, 9, 112, 117, 128n

Hausa: conflict 337; slave raiding among 62, 63; soldiers 313; trading diaspora 21, 47–49; *see also* Sokoto Caliphate

Haute Volta *see* Burkina Faso

Hawk-Dove model 120–21, *127*, 133–34

health: as a driver of migration 15, 21, 114, 137, 192, 289, 292; facilities 209, 218, 225, 260, 272, 281, 335; of migrants 8, 209, 215, 217, **218**, 226n, 244, 301, 323, 325; mortality transition 373n; sexually transmitted disease 314, 323; of slaves 64; in slums 300

historiography 7–10, 26n, 138

home-community migration 11, 12, 136, 148

Horn of Africa: conflict 320; refugees *334*, 336, **339**, 360, 362, 365

identity *see* ethnicity; gender; nationalism; racism

ideology: and black labor circularity 214, 224, 225; discourses on forced labor 157, 159–60, 173; as a driver of migration 6, 15, 50, 204; and labor stabilization 204; and segregation 272, 273; socialist 342; and violence 24, 347

immobility (theory) 12–13, 41–42

imprisonment 61, 88, 160, 164, 168, 172, 209, 215, 324, 341

indentured labor 4, 18, 87, 251n

independent (post-colonial) Africa: commercial agriculture in 244; decolonization 149, 330,

339, 342; economic fortunes 224, 299, 382–84; economic policies 249; expulsions in 343–46; migration in and from 18, 24–25, 223–24, 330–52, 367–68, 382–87; nationalization in 206; refugee crisis 333–38, 360; remittances to 368–71; state formation in 332, 338–41; trends in scholarship on migration 8–10; urbanization in 287, 281–307

India: conflict in 333; migration from 4–5, 6, 18, 26n, 78, 87, 137, 149, 166, **182**, 183, 188, 251n, 384, 387; migration to 78, *81*, 311, 323, 344, 345–46; soldiers from 317; *see also* South Asia

Indian Ocean: slavery and slave trade 3, 77–78, 124, 137; trade 115–16, 119; urbanization on the coast 285, 287

indirect rule 169, 188

industrialization 6, 50, 147, 148, 149, 232, 256–58, 262, 264, 266, 267, 256–80, 297, 385; *see also* mining

infrastructure: and city formation 81, 84, 287; construction and forced labor 19, 87, 158–59, 162, 164, 167–72, 180, 191, 270; construction and migration 86, 87, 89, 145, 157, 164, 174, 180; and state capacity 40; and trade potential 22, 40, 206, 208, 234, 237, 248; used by migrants 5, 20, 22, 183, 248, 313, 320, 385–86, 387; *see also* porterage

integration (of migrants) 22–24, 64, 96–97, 105, 108, 125, 127, 232, 237, 331, 333, 341–43

intercontinental migration 3–6, 24–25, 356, 367–68; growth since 1960 6, 24–25, 384–86; remittances 368–71; during the world wars 311–29; *see also* slave trades

internally displaced person (IDP) 335–36, **339**, 346, 348n, 360, 365, **366**, 384

International Labour Organization (ILO) 8, 160

International Organization for Migration (IOM) 331, 358

intra-African migration: age of 3–7; shifting patterns 14–24, 379–80, 382–84

invaders (as a type of migrants) 12, 16, 18, 24, 112, 113, 136, 143; *see also* European settlers

iron 83, 99, 101, 106, 114, 115, 116, 117, 120, 267

Islam 18, 42, 48, 49, 57, 64, 68, 81, 86, 285, 287, 302n, 313, 333, 338; *see also* Jihad

Italy: colonialism in Africa 63, 287, 312, 313, 320, 321; migration to 385; postcolonial interference in Africa 337

itinerants (as a type of migrants) 12, 21, 48, 143, 149, 326

ivory: items made of 118; trade 75, 76, 82–84, 85, 89, 95–96, 99, 100–4, 106, 123, 161

Ivory Coast *see* Côte d'Ivoire

Japan 320, 321, 333

Jihad 16, 17, 23, 37, 38, 40, 42, 43, 46, 47, 57, 68–69, 337; *see also* Islam

396 Index

Kamerun *see* Cameroon
Kano 47, 49, 62, 71, 236, 237, 285, 286, 325
Katanga: labor 204, 215–19, *220*, 221, **222**, 257, 263; migration to 182, 183, **192**, **216**, *217*, 218, 260; mining 206, 224, 225n; secessionist movement 337; wages *263; see also* Congo; copper
Kenya: bicycle imports **163**; colonial policies in 86–89, 108, 165–69; commercial agriculture in 11, 86–89, 235, 239; conflict in 334; education in *298*; forced labor in 165–69; intensive agriculture in *98*, 106; living standards in 300; migration from 79, 83, 342; migration in 87, 88, 99, 105, 160, 165, 287, *296*, 297, 299, 332; migration to 167, **339**, 343; nationalism in 324; pastoralism in 95, 96, **98**, 99–104; soldiers from 313, **318**; urban growth *288, 289*
Khartoum 286, 325
Khoesan 122, 136, 137, 138, 139, 141, 142, 151n
Kikuyu 88, 102, 105, 313
Kimberley *see* diamonds
Kinshasa 258, 260, 261, 262, 263, 264, 268, 283
Kopytoff, Igor 11, 16, 37, 39–44, 49–50, 51n, 277n
Kwazulu-Natal 114, 123, 124, 129n, 144, 208

labor contract *see* contract labor
labor reserve 8–9, 170, 178, **182**, 195, 224, 231, 240
labor scarcity 6, 14, 17, 19, 23, 39, 41, 44, 50, 158, 161, 193, 219, 221, 235, 237, 239, 331, 32, 387; *see also* Nieboer-Domar thesis
labor stabilization *see* stabilization of labor
Lagos 38, 47, 242, 283, **286**, 288, *291, 295*, 298, 363
land abundance 17, 23, 40, 41, 44, 50, 113, 125, 129n, 158, 235, 236, 237, 239, 241, 332, 341; *see also* Nieboer-Domar thesis
land alienation 19, 90, 108, 136, 137, 148–49, 158, 165, 208, 239, 258, 266, 269–71, 276
land frontier *see* frontier colonization
land reform 11, 149–50
land scarcity 11, 14, 119, 126, 239, 249–50, 270, 290, 301, 332, 347, 380
League of Nations 160, 215
legitimate commerce *see* commercial transition
Leopoldville *see* Kinshasa
Lesotho 142, 211, **212–13**, 385
Levant *see* Middle East
Liberia: conflict in 336; migration from 170, *334*, **339**, 342–43; urbanization in *288*
Libya: conflict in 312, 337; migration to 57, 59, *60*, 66–68, 70, 72, 312; slavery in 57, 58, *61*
Limpopo River 117, 118, 124, 125, 136, 145–47, 150
livestock disease 15, 40, 83, 96, 106, 107, 114, 137, 207–8, 312; *see also* pastoralism

living standards *see* health; wages
Lourenço Marques *see* Maputo
Lovejoy, Paul 18, 45, 47, 50n, 51n, **56**, 79

Maasai 12, 97, 99, 100, 101, 102, 103, 105–7, 108
macro-historical drivers (of migration) *see* migration concepts
Madagascar: conflict in 312, 321; migration from 78, 137, 317; migration to 337; soldiers from 317; urban growth in 289
Malawi: commercial agriculture in 235; conflict in 318; control over 146; migration from 182, 204, 211, **212**, 214, **216**, 223, 258–59, 267, 269–70, 273, 319, 381, 385; migration to **182**, 339; urban growth in 289
Mali: commercial agriculture in 240; living standards in 238; migration from 47–48, 61, 240, 244, 340, 344–45, 385; migration in 158; rainfall seasonality in 242; urban growth in 288, *289*
Manchuelle, François 7, 9
Manning, Patrick 11, 105, 112, 136, 137, 143, 148, 149, 151n
Mapungubwe 113, 117, 118–21; equilibrium 113, 118–21, 127, 134
Maputo 180, **181**, *186, 190*
Maputo Bay 115, 117, 122, 123, 124, 126, 129n, 142, 208
marriage 11, 41, 49, 64, 82, 97, 98, 105, 106, 121, 135, 138, 140, 165, 218, 221, **222**, 243, 245, 264–65, 272, 273, 275, 290, 293, 294, 301, 317; *see also* bridewealth
Mascarenes *see* Mauritius
Mauritania: migration from **344**, 346; migration to 64–65, **344**, 346
Mauritius: migration from 137; migration to 78, *81*, 124, 337; slavery in 17; soldiers from 321
Mfecane 113, 142–43; equilibrium 113, *122*, 125–27, 134
Mfengu 142, 143, 225n
Middle Africa *see* Central Africa
Middle East: conflict in 317, 320, 323; migration from 6, 18; migration to 6, 78, 317, 359, 374n, 384, 385; slavery in 65, 66
migrant journeys: routes 14, *62, 72, 79, 103, 145, 207, 217, 233, 315, 322*, 341; travel 20, 48, 63, 90, 117, 146, 147, 150, 162, 163, 167, 168, 170, 172, 206–7, 208, 211, 231, 237, 248, 316, 385–86; *see also* caravan trade; infrastructure; porterage
migrant selectivity *see* cross-community migration; skill selectivity and migration
migration definitions: agency of migrants 12–13; aspirations 10, 12–13, 15, 20, 24–25, 243, 297, 380, 381, 382, 386; capabilities 12–13, 15, 25, 248, *380*, 382; flow 13–14; forced migration 13, 331; macro-historical drivers 7, 10, 14–16, 373,

384, 386; migrant 10–12; pattern 14; system 14; typology 11–12, 136; voluntary migration 13; *see also* migration theory; modern migration; traditional migration

migration rates 5–6, 10, 21, 356, 379–84

migration theory: colonial 8; demographic 9; dependency theory 8–9, 157; dual-sector model 239; Marxist 8; modernization theory 8–9; push-pull 12; transition theory 379–89; shifts in theory 7–10, 379–80; underdevelopment 8–9, 231–32, 251; *see also* development; migration concepts; Nieboer-Domar thesis

military forces: 23, 24, 26n, 42–43, 66, 78, 85, 125, 137, 185, **186**, 311–29, 337, 341; *see also* conflict

military migration *see* conflict; military forces

mining *see* copper; diamonds; gold

missionaries *see* religion

modern migration 7–10, 13, 16, 19–20, 96; *see also* traditional migration

Mombasa 76, 87, 89, 101, 163, 285, **286**, 287, *291*, 293, *296*, 320, 325

monetization, as an effect of migration 191, 192, 194, 211, 240, 314

Morocco: control over 58, 71; migration from 368; migration to 57, 59–60, 63, 66–68, 70, 72, **339**, 348n; slavery in 57, 64–65, 70; soldiers in 66

mortality *see* health

Mozambique: commercial agriculture in 180, 191, 234; conflict in 336, 337, **339**; living standards 382, 385; migration from 26, 78, 83, 124, 125, 137, 178, **182**, 183, *184*, 188, *190*, **192**, 194, **200–2**, 203, 207–8, 210, 211, **212–13**, 258–59, 270, 273, **339**, 381; migration in 180, **181**, **192**, **339**; migration to 150, **181**, 183, *186*, 191, **192**, 194, **344**; soldiers in 186, 318

Myanmar 311, 346

Nairobi **286**, 287, *291*, 292, 293, 294, *296*, 297, 298, 299, 300, 319

Namibia: genocide 24; migration to 144; soldiers 315, 318

nationalism 150, 324, 331–33, 345

native reserve 8, 87–88, 108, 165, 167, 214, 258, 265, 269, 273, 277n, 278n, 319, 324, 332

Ndebele 113, 124, 125, 143, 259, 265, 266

Nieboer-Domar thesis 37, 39–41, 44—47, 129n

Niger: control over 337; living standards in 238; migration from 381, 385

Nigeria: commercial agriculture in 39, 46, 47, 50, 233, *234*, 236, 237, 244, 247, 249, 250; conflict in 334, **339**, 346; control over 38, 43, 68; land scarcity in 239, 241, 249; living standards in 238, 248; migration from 25, 60, 170, 233, **339**, 344, 345, **367**; migration in 233, 237, 242, 244,

247, 302n, 325, **339**, **344**; migration to 170, 345, **367**; nationalism in 324; rainfall seasonality in 241, *242*; remittances to 368–71; slavery 18, 47, 50, 68, 236; soldiers from 313, 318; taxation in 240; trade in 48; transportation in 237; urbanization in 285, 286, *288*, 295, 297, *298; see also* Hausa; Sokoto Caliphate; Yoruba

Northeastern Africa *see* Horn of Africa

Northern Africa: migration from 5, 24, 357, 359, **364–65**, 368, 384, 385; migration to 17, 56–74, 312, 316, 320, 321, 323, 364, 366; population growth 361, **362**; soldiers from 317; urban growth **363–64**

Northern Rhodesia *see* Zambia

Nyamwezi 19, 21, 76, 77, 81, 82, 83, 84, 85, 88, 89, 102

Nyasaland *see* Malawi

Orange Free State 122, 143, 144, 147, 204–5

palm oil 38, 46, 47, 170, 231, 233, 236, 270, 381

pastoralism 8, 11–12, 16, 19, 39, 95–111, 114, 115, 136, 138, 139, 151n, 313

Pedi 113, 118, 120, 121, 125, 207, 208, 210

population: decline 96, 99, 108, 142, 319, 385; demographic consequences of migration 7, 20, 26n, 105, 136, 242, 245–46; demography 9; density 19, 23, 38, 39, 42, 47, 114, 119, 126, 136, 204, 341, 386–87; dynamics as a driver of migration 10, 14, 23, 24, 249, 331, 332; dynamics in pastoral societies 95–96, 99; growth 3, 5–6, 16, 22, 85, 249, **266**, 290, 332, **335**, 347, 355, 356–57, *357*, **358–59**, 361–62, 371, 379, 380, 383, 386–87; and state formation 40–41

porterage 19, 21, 22, 48, 57, 59, 75, 76, 77, 83–84, 85, 87, 89, 117, 161, 162, 167, 168, 170, 171, 312, 315–19; *see also* caravan trade; transportation

Portugal: colonialism in Africa 19, 26, 146, 158, 159, 178–202, 211, 217, 223, 225n, 234, 268, 312, 331; migration from 145, 178; migration to 385; slave trade 43, 124

post-colonial Africa *see* independent Africa

poverty 19, 108, 139, 140, 147, 188, 192, 208, 214, 231, 239–41, 250, 264–65, 281, 284, 297–301, 319, 334, 342, 343, 373n, 381–82, 384, 387n

racism 141, 149, 196n, 210, 211, 214, 224, 225, 272, 275, 317, 319, 324, 326n, 332, 346; *see also* apartheid; color bar

Rand *see* Witwatersrand

recruitment: catchment area 87, 188, 193, 204, 209, 210–16, 250, 260, 269–70, 273, 312–14, 320; forced recruitment 19, 158, 161, 163, 166, 167, 170, 259, 316, 318, 325, 331, 332; policies 88, 158, 171, 178–202, 203–28, 312, 317;

398 Index

recruiters 13, 209–10, 386; role of chiefs 158, 214; *see also* contract labor; military forces

refugees: camps 11, 333, 335, 336, 341, 342–43; climate refugees 15, 360–61, 366; colonial 315, 340, 362; definition of 13, 331, 333, 373n; global review of 333, 373n; pre-colonial 113, 142, 287; post-colonial 11, 24, 71–72, 332, 333–38, **339**, 341, 346, 356, 360–61, 365–66, 384; repatriation of 331, 332, 341–43; scholarship on 9, 10, 26n; *see also* expulsion; flight; forced migration; slave trade

religion: and conflict 85, 337; consequences of migration 18, 85, 86, 136; as a driver of migration 136, 141, 142, 145, 150, 387; as identity marker 332; of migrants 14, 21–22, 37, 48–49; missionaries 18, 22, 85, 89, 121, 145–46, 161, 162, 166, 218, 219, 291, 293; *see also* Christianity; Islam; Jihad

remittances 9, 12, 26n, 194, 290, 292, 293, 299, 314, 322, 356, 360, 362, 363, 368–71

Rhodes, Cecil 146, 205, 209

Ruanda-Urundi *see* Burundi; Rwanda

rubber 47, 158, 159, 215, 236, 267

Rwanda: commercial agriculture in 240, 248; control over 107, 215, 241, 331, 337; famine in 319, 326; forced labor in 248; living standards in 239, 243; migration from 162, 163, 164, 215, 219, 234, 240, 241, 245, 247, 248, 260, 302n, 335, 336, **339**, 340, 341, 342, 365, 368, 381; migration to **339;** pastoralism in 102; urban growth in 288

Sahara Desert *see* trans-Saharan migration

Sahel 15, 38, 232, 241, 285, 286, 335, 337

Salisbury *see* Harare

salt 47, 61, 65, 83, 99, 101, 115, 117

São Tomé and Príncipe: commercial agriculture in 159, 179, 186–87; living standards in 194; migration from *191*, **202**; migration to 178, 179, 180, 182, *184*, 186, 188, *189*, *190*, 191–93, 195, **200–1**

savanna: commercial agriculture in 237, 248; economic activity in 99; migration from 7, 43, 60, 232, 233, 237, 239, 242, 243; migration in 233, 241; state formation in 17, 38, 43; urban growth 285

seasonality 39, 47, 48, 58, 83, 87, 88, 97, 108, 138, 159, 167, 180, 193, 209, 232, 233, 237, 241–45, 248, 250, 292, 321, 324, 332, 385

Senegal: commercial agriculture in 46, 50, 231, 232, 234, 236, 247, 249; control over 38, 180; education in 298; living standards in 238, 241; migration from 48, 344, 346, 385; migration in 47–48, 232, 240, 241, 297; migration to 47–48, 232, 240, 241, 248, 324, **344**, 345, 346; soldiers from 312, 316; urban growth in 288, 289

Senegambia *see* Gambia; Senegal

settlers (as a type of migrants) 12, 112, 136, 137, 138, 143, 245–50; *see also* European settlers; stabilization of labor

sex *see* gender

Sierra Leone: conflict in 336; control over 38; living standards in 299, 300, **339**; migration from 170, 312, 334, **344**; migration in 295, 297, **339**; migration to 344–45; soldiers from 312; urban growth in 288

skill selectivity and migration 21–22, 83, 167, 178, 179, **182**, 183, **185**, 293, 297, *298*, 345, 373n, 380

skilled labor 20–21, 167, **182**, 183, *185*, 187, 214, 219, 225, 274, 313, 320

slave trades and their abolition: Atlantic 3–4, 17, 38, 40, 46, 48, 49, **56**, 57, 67, 68, 77, 180, 235, 236; Indian Ocean 3, **56**, 77–82, 89; Intercontinental 3–5, 16, 17, 26n, 76, 124, 356; Red Sea 3, **56**; Trans-Saharan 3, 38, 56–74; *see also* forced migration

slavery: abolition 4, 18–19, 57–58; in Eastern Africa 77–82, 87; emancipation 18, 58, 64, 70, 139, 140, 141, 232, 236–37, 248, 316–17; expansion 16–18, 47, 50, 381; as migration 12; nature of African 44–46; in Northern Africa 56–74; in Southern Africa 123, *138*, 139–40; in Western Africa 37–55, 235–37, 248; *see also* forced labor; Nieboer-Domar thesis

sociology 8, 10, 178

sojourning 11, 12, 14, 18, 20, 21, 22, 75, 76, 82–84, 87, 88, 89, 149, 158, 178, 181, 182–83, 195, 203–4, 208, 211, 214, 221, 224, 225, 232, 233, 242, 245–50, 256–63, 268, 271, 275, 276, 283, 291, 292, 293, 295, 299, 340, 341, 342, 373n, 383, 385; *see also* seasonality

Sokoto 12, 17, 37, 38, 43, 44–47, 60, 62, 68, 69, 239, 241, 242, 243, 340

soldiers *see* military forces

Somalia: migration from 72, 334, **339**; migration to 334, **339**, 342; trade 95, 101, 102, 103–4

Soninke 7, 9, 22, 241, 243, 316, 346

Sotho 120, 124, 125, 128n, 207, 208; *see also* Lesotho

Soudan, The *see* Mali

South Africa: living standard in 139, 140, 147, 149, 208–9, 210, 211, 214, 215, 223, 382, 385; migration from 149–50, 340, **344**, 365, 367, **367**, 368, 374n; migration in 20, 19, 112–34, 135–53, 206–15, 223, 332; migration to 88, 89, 159, 180, 182, 194, 196n, 197n, 206–15, 216, 223, 233, 321, 345, **367**, 268; mining in 203, 204–6; remittances to 368–71; soldiers from 315, 317, **321**; urbanization in 283

South Asia *see* India

South Sudan: migration from 346, 365; migration in 365

Index 399

Southern Africa: migration from 84, **364–65**; migration in 11, 20, 21, 112–34, 135–53, 203–28, 284, 321, **364–65**, 366; migration to 7, 9, 128n, 179; population growth in 361, **362**; urbanization in 302, **363–64**

Southern Rhodesia *see* Zimbabwe

stabilization of labor 21, 164, 203–4, 211, 214, 218, 219, 223, 224, 225, 257, 258, 260, 261, 262, 265, 269, 271–75, 277n, 292, 301, 319, 340

sub-Sahara Africa: migration from *5*, 16, **25**, 56, 384; *see also* Central Africa; Eastern Africa; Southern Africa; Western Africa

Sudan: control over 57, 66, 68, 336; migration from 57, 60, 63, 64, 67, 69, 70, 72, **339**, 360; migration in 360; migration to **339**, 346

sugar 78, 124, 180, 181, 208, 235

Swahili 21, 81, 85, 86, 104, 317

Tabora 76, 81, 82, 83, 85, 86, 89, 90n

Tanganyika *see* Tanzania

Tanzania: colonial policies in 108, 163; control over 84, 108, 315; intensive agriculture in 106; migration from 167, **212–13**, 223; migration in 84; migration to 97, 99, 339, 341–42, **344**, 346, 365; pastoralism in 95, 101, 102, 106; slavery in 76, 81, 87; soldiers from 314, **318**; urban growth in 288, 292, 293, 297; *see also* Zanzibar

taxation 21, 65, 141, 161–62, 164, 167, 169, 193, 194, 195, 251n, 269, 332, 343; as a driver of migration 8, 87, 145, 158, 161–62, 165, 191, 208, 240–41, 269, 270, 313, 340; labor taxes 158, 162, 164–65, 168–69, 171–72, 240, 249, 269; of trade 22, 40, 249; paid by migrants 211, 214, 216; protest and evasion 24, 166, 188; *see also* flight

temporary migration *see* sojourning

textiles: manufacturing 47, 48, 118, 148, 243, 268, 286; trade 47, 61, 62, 82, 83, 86, 95, 101, 103, 104, 116, 118, 159, 167, 243, 251n, 267

Togo: control over 315; migration to 344; soldiers from 318; urban growth in *288*

trade *see* caravan trade; cash crops; commercial transition; mining; slave trade

traditional migration 7–10, 11, 13, 15–16, 19–20, 96, 259, 380; *see also* modern migration

transportation *see* infrastructure

trans-Saharan migration 6, 13, 14, 17, 22, 38, 46, 56–74, 386

Tswana 118, 121, 122, 123, 125, 128n, 207; *see also* Botswana

Tunisia: migration to 57, 59, 72, 339, 348n; slavery in 63, 70

Uganda: commercial agriculture in 86, 157, 160, 161–64, 289; conflict in 331; forced labor in 161–64; living standards in 163, *234*, 299,

383; migration from 86, 167, 250, 334, 341, **344**, 345, **367**; migration in 161–64, 239, *298*, 339; migration to 161–64, 334, 336, 365, **367**; pastoralism in 96, 99, 102, 107; remittances to 368–70; soldiers from 313, *318*, 337; transportation 87, 234; *see also* Buganda

Ujiji 76, 81, 85, 86, 90n

unemployment 13, 196n, 215, 222, 223, 224–25, 262, 263, 264, 275, 276, 277n, 292, 297, 298, 301, 342, 345, 347

Union Minière du Haut Katanga (UMHK) 204, 206, 215–19, 260; *see also* Congo; copper; Katanga

United Nations High Commissioner for Refugees (UNHCR) 24, 334, 341, 342, 343, 346, 358, 360, 365, 366

United Nations 5, 26n, 281, 335, 366, 373n, 385

Unyamwezi *see* Nyamwezi

Upper Volta *see* Burkina Faso

urbanization: living standards 149, 222, 238, 272–73, 262–65, 270, 271, 274–75, 281, 289–90, 297–301, 383; migration from cities 224, 299, 320, 343; migration to cities 20–21, 26n, 72n, 76, 84–86, 89, 136, 147–80, **181**, 218, 245, 249, 256–80, 281–307, 319, 324, 325, 344, 358–59, 362, 384; natural growth in cities 288–89; scholarship on 9–10; urban growth 75, 76, *79*, 84–86, 117, 118, 122, 181, 219–23, 224–25, 256–57, 281–89, 319, 355, 356–57, **358–59**, 363–64, 372; urban population composition 257, 259, 261–62, 271–75, 289, 290–97; urban slavery 64, 65, 66; *see also* stabilization of labor

violence *see* conflict

Voortrekkers 16, 126, 135, 136, 141–47, 151n; *see also* Boers

wages: payment 190, 194, 216, 218, 222, 225, 241, 277n; wage gaps as a driver of migration 12, 14, 20, 86, 162, 164, 166, 167, 188–89, **192**, 193–94, 208, 209, 225n, 237–38, 239, 243, *244*, 248, 251n, 262–65, 269, 270, 274–75, 276, 289, 292, 293, 299, 301, 313, 340, 381–82, 383; wage labor markets and policies 18, 19, 44, 76, 77, 84, 87, 157–77, 187, 188, 206, 210, 211, 214, 219, 223, 236, 239, 248, 260, 265, 268, 269, 270, 275, 276, 278, 319, 370; *see also* contract labor; recruitment; taxation

war *see* conflict

Western Africa: migration from 38, 57, 67–68, 78, 317, **364–65**; migration in 7, 14, 15, 16, 17, 19, 20, 21, 23, 37–55, 169, 170, 235–37, 242–43, 248, **339**, 340, 344, 345, 356, **364**, **366**, 372; migration to 18, 312, 317, 324; population growth in **362**; urbanization 21, 281–307, **363–64**

Western Sahara 65, 72

400 Index

whole-community migration (as a type of migration) 11–12, 15
Witwatersrand 145, 147, 182–83, 190, **192**, 194, 203, 204, 205, *207*, 210, 214, 211, 225n, 226n, 317, 326, 382; *see also* gold; South Africa
Witwatersrand Native Labour Association (WNLA) 179, 211, 214, 223
women *see* gender
World Bank 358, 360, 363, 374n

Xhosa 138, 142

Yao 81, 83, 313, 319
Yoruba 22, 48, 236, 244, 247, 287, 288
youth *see* children

Zambia: conflict in 314; migration from 86, 184, **201**, **212–13**, **216**, *217*, 218, 223, 258, **259**, 260, 269–70, **344**; migration in 204, 221–23; migration to 196n, 221–23, 340, 342; mining in 204, 206, 220, 221, 224; soldiers from 318, 321; urbanization in 219, 224; *see also* Copperbelt
Zanzibar: commercial agriculture in 75, 76, 78, 79, 86; migration to 75, 76, 79, 80, 81, 82, 86, 88; soldiers from 312, **318**; urbanization in 285; *see also* Tanzania
Zimbabwe: commercial agriculture in 11, 158, 160, 235; conflict in 124; control over 119, 124, 146, 178, 256, 257, 265; industrialization in 256–57, 267, 277n; living standards in 264–65, 269–70, 272–75, 276; migration from 150, 182, *184*, **212–13**, 214, 385; migration in 256, 257, 258–59, **259**, 272–75; migration to 125, 180, 182, 183, 194, 221, **259**, 267, 277n, 319, 344; mining in 160, 319; population growth in 266; soldiers from 325; urbanization in 225n, 256, **257**, **261**, 267, 273–75
Zulu 113, 124, 129n, 142, 143, 144, 207, 225

Printed in the United States
by Baker & Taylor Publisher Services